RESPONDING TO LITERATURE

World Literature

Senior Consultants

ARTHUR N. APPLEBEE
State University of New York at Albany

JUDITH A. LANGER
State University of New York at Albany

Authors

MARY HYNES-BERRY

BASIA C. MILLER

 **McDougal, Littell & Company**
Evanston, Illinois
New York • Dallas • Sacramento • Columbia, SC

ISBN 0-8123-7083-X (softcover)
ISBN 0-8123-7074-0 (hardbound)

Copyright © 1992 by McDougal, Littell & Company
Box 1667, Evanston, Illinois 60204

01 02 03 -DCI- 10 9 8 7 6

Acknowledgments

Aunt Lute Books "The Youngest Doll" by Rosario Ferré from *Reclaiming Medusa: Short Stories by Contemporary Puerto Rican Women*, edited and translated by Diana Vélez. Copyright © 1988 by Diana Vélez. Reprinted by permission of Aunt Lute Books.

Bantam Books Excerpt from *The Aeneid of Virgil, A Verse Translation* by Allen Mandelbaum. Copyright © 1971 by Allen Mandelbaum. Used by permission of Bantam Books, a division of Bantam, Doubleday, Dell Publishing Group, Inc.

Bibliotheca Islamica, Inc. "The Happy Man" from *God's World* by Naguib Mahfouz, translated by Akef Abadir and Roger Allen. Copyright © 1973, 1988 by Akef Abadir and Roger Allen. Reprinted by permission of the publisher, Bibliotheca Islamica, Box 14474, Minneapolis, MN 55414.

Robert Bly "Ode to My Socks" by Pablo Neruda from *Neruda and Vallejo: Selected Poems*, Beacon Press, Boston, 1976, edited and translated by Robert Bly. Copyright © 1975 by Robert Bly. Reprinted by permission of Robert Bly.

Judith H. Ciardi Cantos I, III and V of *The Inferno* by Dante Alighieri, a verse rendering for the modern reader by John Ciardi. Copyright 1954, © 1982 by John Ciardi. Reprinted by permission of Judith H. Ciardi.

Joan Daves "Time" by Gabriela Mistral from *Selected Poems of Gabriela Mistral*, translated and edited by Doris Dana. Copyright © 1961, 1964, 1970, 1971 by Doris Dana. Reprinted by permission of Joan Daves.

Doubleday Excerpt from *The Iliad* by Homer, translated by Robert Fitzgerald. Translation copyright © 1974 by Robert Fitzgerald. Excerpt from *When Heaven and Earth Changed Places* by Le Ly Hayslip. Copyright © 1989 by Le Ly Hayslip and Charles Jay Wurts. Reprinted by permission of Bantam, Doubleday, Dell Publishing Group, Inc.

Farrar, Straus and Giroux, Inc. Excerpts from *Earthly Paradise* by Colette. Copyright © 1966 by Farrar, Straus and Giroux, Inc. "What I Have Been Doing Lately" from *At the Bottom of the River* by Jamaica Kincaid. Copyright © 1978, 1979, 1981, 1982, 1983 by Jamaica Kincaid. "When in Early Summer" from *The Seeker and Other Poems* by Nelly Sachs. Translation copyright © 1970 by Farrar, Straus and Giroux, Inc. Reprinted by permission of Farrar, Straus and Giroux, Inc.

Foreign Languages Press, Beijing Excerpt from *From Emperor to Citizen: The Autobiography of Aisin-Gioro P'u Yi*. Copyright © 1964, 1965 by Foreign Languages Press. Copyright © 1987 by Oxford University Press. Reprinted by permission of Foreign Languages Press.

Grove Press, Inc. "The Form of the Sword" from *Ficciones* by Jorge Luis Borges, translated by Anthony Kerrigan. Copyright © 1962 by Grove Press, Inc. Spanish translation copyright © 1956 by Emece Editores, Buenos Aires. "Rhinoceros" from *The Colonel's Photograph* by Eugène Ionesco, translated by Jean Stewart. Copyright © 1967 by Faber and Faber, Limited. Reprinted by permission of Grove Weidenfeld.

Harcourt Brace Jovanovich, Inc., and Wylie, Aitken & Stone "Santa's Children" from *Marcovaldo or The Seasons in the City* by Italo Calvino, translated by William Weaver. Copyright

(continued on page 769)

SENIOR CONSULTANTS

The senior consultants guided all conceptual development for the *Responding to Literature* series. They participated actively in shaping tables of contents and prototype materials for all major components and features, and they reviewed completed units to ensure consistency with current research and the philosophy of the series.

Arthur N. Applebee, Professor of Education, State University of New York at Albany; Director, Center for the Learning and Teaching of Literature

Judith A. Langer, Professor of Education, State University of New York at Albany; Co-Director, Center for the Learning and Teaching of Literature

AUTHORS

The authors of this text wrote lessons for the literary selections.

Mary Hynes-Berry, Writer and Educator, Chicago, Illinois

Basia C. Miller, Tutor on the Faculty at St. John's College, Santa Fe, New Mexico

ACADEMIC CONSULTANTS

The academic consultants worked with the senior consultants to establish the theoretical framework for the series and the pedagogical design of the lessons. The consultants reviewed prototype lessons for the student book and Teacher's Guide and read selected units to ensure philosophical consistency.

Susan Hynds, Director of English Education, Syracuse University, Syracuse, New York

James Marshall, Associate Professor of English and Education, University of Iowa, Iowa City

Robert E. Probst, Professor of English Education, Georgia State University, Atlanta

William Sweigart, Assistant Professor of English, Indiana University Southeast, New Albany; formerly, Research Associate, Center for the Study of Writing, University of California at Berkeley

LITERARY AND LINGUISTICS CONSULTANTS

The literary consultants commented on the table of contents for this text and suggested reorganizations, additions, and deletions. The linguistics consultant provided pronunciations of names and terms from foreign languages and conceptualized the essay on translation.

Carlos J. Cumpián, Editor and Researcher, Hispanic Literature, Chicago, Illinois

James M. Lindholm, Linguist and Language Teacher, formerly Assistant Professor of Tamil and Linguistics, University of Chicago

Edris Makward, Professor, African Studies Program, University of Wisconsin, Madison

Carrie E. Reed, Pre-doctoral Teaching Associate I in Chinese, Department of Asian Language and Literature, University of Washington, Seattle

CONSULTANT-REVIEWERS

The consultant-reviewers responded to the table of contents, evaluated the lesson design, and reviewed selections for the purpose of assessing effectiveness and appropriateness for students and teachers.

Michael F. Bernauer, Language Arts Instructor, Forest Lake Senior High School, Forest Lake, Minnesota

Clifton Browning, Department Head, English, Jefferson Davis High School, Montgomery, Alabama

Bonnie M. Davis, Staff Development Teacher, Mehlville School District, St. Louis, Missouri

Harriet C. Fether, Language Arts Chairperson, Miami Senior High School, Miami, Florida

Sister Sheila Holly, S.S.J., Teacher/ Chairperson, Department of English, Saint Maria Goretti High School, Philadelphia, Pennsylvania

Roy J. Horton, English Department Chairperson, Taft High School, Chicago, Illinois

Sandra Lewis, Language Arts Coordinator, High School Zone, Boston Public Schools, Boston, Massachusetts

Olivia M. Pass, Teacher, Lafayette High School, Lafayette, Louisiana

Nancy Schultz Potter, Teacher, Shorecrest High School, Seattle, Washington

Patricia J. Smith, Chairperson, English Department, Decatur High School, Federal Way, Washington

Sandra Sullivan, Teacher/ English Department Chairman, Garden Grove High School, Garden Grove, California

STUDENT ADVISORS

The student advisors reviewed literary selections to assess their appeal for high school students.

Chelsea Arthur, Raissa Bailey, Carmen Delgado, Jenny Lee, Michelle McCarthy, Stephen Mufuka, Scott Turnbull

---

Design: Design 5

Tests and Vocabulary Worksheets: Sense and Nonsense

Teacher's Guide Lessons: Brown Publishing Network

Contents

Unit 1 COMMON BELIEFS: TEACHING THROUGH LITERATURE   22

Unit 2 COURAGE AND CONVICTION:
THE HERO IN LITERATURE   124

Unit 3 HEARTS AND MINDS:
LITERATURE OF SELF-EXPRESSION 262

Unit **5**   THE CRITICAL EYE: LITERATURE OF INSIGHT   **464**

Unit 6 CREATIVE DIVERSIONS: LITERATURE TO ENTERTAIN 652

"A knowledge of different literatures is the best way to free one's self from the tyranny of any of them."

JOSÉ MARTÍ

Jacqueline Reading, 1957, PABLO PICASSO.

Dear Student,

As a reader and as a thinker, you are unique. Your process of reading literature reflects your individuality, the particular way in which you view the world. As you read, you make predictions about what intrigues you. You question statements that are confusing to you. You understand what you read in your own way, a way that comes as much from your own experiences, ideas, and feelings as from the words of the writer or translator.

As you read, you continually rethink meaning, arriving at a concept, or vision, that is uniquely your own. *Responding to Literature* gives you the tools to develop this vision.

Responding to Literature eases you into the reading process by

- giving you enough background to understand a work from the first line or paragraph
- previewing words that are essential to understanding
- focusing on issues from your own experience that are important in the literary work you are about to read

Responding to Literature supports your reading process by

- defining essential words as you come to them
- pronouncing and explaining unfamiliar names and terms
- giving you extra help for difficult pieces

Responding to Literature extends your reading process by

- guiding you to rethink your understanding of the work
- suggesting interesting issues to discuss and write about
- challenging you to make new connections between literary works and between your own experiences and the world around you

As you use this World Literature book, you will be exposed to literary works from a great variety of cultures. You will read the words of writers who view the world from perspectives quite different from your own, yet who write for many of the same reasons that you write. You will discover—maybe for the first time—that you have much in common with people from distant times and places. Through your study of world literature, you will expand your horizons, gradually becoming more aware of the richness of human experience and more open to new experiences in your own life.

The Authors and Editors

Literary Map of the World

This map shows the geographical locations represented in this World Literature book. Below the map and on the next page are listed countries and regions, keyed to the numbers on the map, and the authors and works associated with these locations.

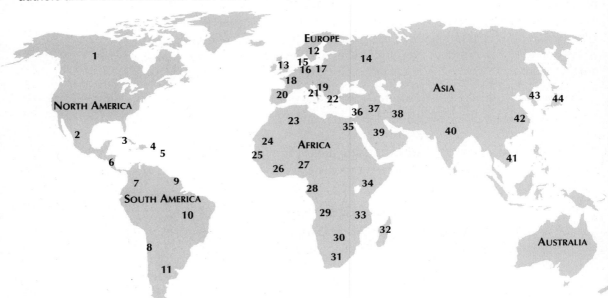

NORTH AMERICA

1 CANADA
Folk Tale

2 MEXICO
Sor Juana Inés de la Cruz
Rosario Castellanos
Juan Rulfo
Octavio Paz

3 CUBA
José Martí

4 PUERTO RICO
Rosario Ferré

5 ANTIGUA
Jamaica Kincaid

6 CENTRAL AMERICA
Quiché Maya

SOUTH AMERICA

7 COLOMBIA
Gabriel García Márquez

8 CHILE
Gabriela Mistral
Pablo Neruda

9 FRENCH GUIANA
Léon Damas

10 BRAZIL
Carolina Maria de Jesus
Rachel de Queiroz

11 ARGENTINA
Jorge Luis Borges
Julio Cortázar
Luisa Valenzuela

EUROPE

12 SWEDEN
Selma Lagerlöf

13 UNITED KINGDOM
William Shakespeare
William Wordsworth

14 RUSSIA / SOVIET UNION
Alexander Pushkin
Leo Tolstoy

15 DENMARK
Isak Dinesen

16 GERMANY
Heinrich Heine
Nelly Sachs
Christa Reinig

EUROPE (continued)

17 POLAND
Czeslaw Milosz
Stanislaw Łem

18 FRANCE
Marie de France
Montesquieu
Molière
Élisabeth Vigée Lebrun
Honoré de Balzac
Guy de Maupassant
Charles Baudelaire
Colette
Eugène Ionesco

19 YUGOSLAVIA
Ivo Andrić

20 SPAIN
Rosalía de Castro

21 ITALY
Virgil
Ovid
Tacitus
Dante Alighieri
Petrarch
Giovanni Boccaccio
Italo Calvino

22 GREECE
Sappho
Homer
Sophocles
Plato
Odysseus Elytis

AFRICA

23 ALGERIA
Albert Camus

24 WEST AFRICA
Gassire's Lute

25 SENEGAL
Léopold Sédar Senghor
Nafissatou Diallo

26 SIERRA LEONE
Abioseh Nicol

27 NIGERIA
Yoruba

28 EQUATORIAL AFRICA
Fang

29 ANGOLA
Oscar Ribas

30 BOTSWANA
Bessie Head

31 SOUTH AFRICA
Nadine Gordimer
Mark Mathabane

32 MADAGASCAR
Jean-Joseph Rabéarivelo

33 MALAWI
Ngoni

34 KENYA
Jomo Kenyatta

35 EGYPT
The Book of the Dead
Naguib Mahfouz

ASIA

36 ISRAEL
Old Testament
New Testament
Aharon Megged
Dahlia Ravikovitch

37 IRAQ
The Epic of Gilgamesh

38 IRAN
One Thousand and One
  Arabian Nights
Omar Khayyám

39 SAUDI ARABIA
The Koran

40 INDIA
The Rig Veda
The Ramayana
Buddhist Scripture
Rabindranath Tagore
Ruth Prawer Jhabvala
Anita Desai

41 VIETNAM
Đặng Trăn Côn
Phan Huy Ích
Le Ly Hayslip

42 CHINA
Folk Tale
T'ao Ch'ien
Li Po
Aisin-Gioro P'u Yi
Ru Zhijuan

43 KOREA
Sŏ Kiwŏn

44 JAPAN
Folk Tale
Matsuo Bashō
Kobayashi Issa
Takarai Kikaku
Yosa Buson
Yukio Mishima

These writers now reside in the United States:
   Rosario Ferré (Puerto Rico)   Mark Mathabane (South Africa)
   Le Ly Hayslip (Vietnam)   Czeslaw Milosz (Poland)
   Jamaica Kincaid (Antigua)

The following writers also have emigrated from
one country to another:
   Albert Camus (Algeria/France)
   Bessie Head (South Africa/Botswana)
   Eugène Ionesco (Romania/France)
   Ruth Prawer Jhabvala (Germany/India)
   Aharon Megged (Poland/Israel)
   Nelly Sachs (Germany/Sweden)

The Translator at Work

Literature written in distant times and places enables you to enter new worlds of experience and to respond to voices speaking in different languages and from different world views. Before you can take the first step, though, the works must be written in a language you can read. That is the work of the translator. Translators do more than just present the words of one language in another. They also open the doors to other cultures and in doing so make it possible for you to reach beyond the parameters of your own experiences and your own familiar English-language home.

Translators do not practice an exact science. If they did, each work of literature would have one definitive translation. In fact, a work may have several effective translations, none perfect, each arguably good and each perhaps superior to the others in some way. All of them, however, share the same goal: to communicate the ideas, feelings, and overall effect of the author's original work as faithfully as possible. When you read a story or poem or essay that was written in a language other than English, the printed words are the words of the translator, but the thoughts expressed are for the most part those of the author.

The Challenges of Translation

A translator at work is always concerned with two basic aspects of language:

- the actual words on the page
- the meaning, or message, being communicated

Words. When focusing on the words themselves, the translator studies ways to preserve features of the original language, such as the sounds of the words, their rhyme patterns, the rhythms created by combinations of words, parallel constructions, and the order in which the words appear. Language features differ markedly even among languages that have much in common. For example:

French: Je t'aime

English: I you love

Language features pose particular challenges for translators of poetry, for sound is integral to the sense of any poem.

Meaning. When focusing on meaning, the translator struggles to convey the cultural concepts and layers of associations that surround the words. These concepts and associations can differ quite dramatically from one culture to the next. For example, in Western literature images of dark clouds suggest foreboding and despair. In East Indian literature the connotations are exactly the opposite. Images of dark clouds signify hope and renewal, feelings connected with the coming of the life-giving monsoon rains.

Related to both words and meaning is the issue of *nonequivalence:* that is, a word in one language may not have an exact equivalent in another language. For example, English has the word *brother* but no single word that means "elder brother" or "younger brother." On the other hand, many languages have separate words for elder brother and younger brother but no one word meaning just "brother."

The Art of Translation

The following examples illustrate the painstaking process of translating two lines of poetry written about 1500 years ago in Tamil, a language spoken in southern India. The examples show how several translators dealt with the two basic aspects of language and trace the compromises these translators made as they tried to remain true to the intent of the author.

■ The following is the poem as it is written in Tamil. The boxed area highlights the repetition in the lines.

முக நக நட்பது நட்பு அன்று; நெஞ்சத்து
அக நக நட்பது நட்பு.

■ In the example below the Tamil words are transcribed as they might sound to an American listener. The next line shows the English translation of each individual word in the lines.

Tamil:	முக	நக	நட்	ப து	நட்பு	அன் று	நெஞ் சத்து
Transcription:	moo' hə	nə' hə	nət'	pə thoo	nət' poo	ən' droo	nen' jət too
English:	face	smiling	love	- ing	love	is_not	heart's

Tamil:	அக	நக	நட்	ப து	நட்பு	
Transcription:	ə' hə	nə' hə	nət'	pə thoo	nət' poo	
English:	interior	smiling	love	- ing	love	

◄ **Notice that the string of English words does not make sense, even though each Tamil word has been translated into English. Notice too the repeated sounds and rhythm in the transcription lines.**

■ Here, the words have been reordered and adjusted to fit English syntax.

Loving, the face smiling, is not love; loving,
the heart's interior smiling, [is] love.

◀ **Notice that the English lines still don't sound very natural or make much sense.**

■ The following versions of the poem show how four translators transformed the lines into a message that makes sense to readers of English.

H. A. POPLEY
True friendship is not merely that of the smiling face;
It is the friendship of the inner joy of the heart.

        The Sacred Kural

◀ **Notice how this translator uses *friendship*, which is part of the concept of the Tamil word translated as *love*. The word *friendship* is repeated, echoing the repetition in the Tamil lines.**

REV. G. U. POPE
Not the face's smile of welcome shows the friend sincere,
But the heart's rejoicing gladness when the friend is near.

        The Sacred Kural of Tiruvalluva-Nayanar

◀ **This late nineteenth-century translator was willing to introduce words and ideas not in the original in order to achieve end rhyme, which is characteristic of English poetry.**

C. RAJAGOPALACHARI
The face may wear a smile at the sight of one, but he alone is
a friend whose sight brings about an internal joy which
bathes the whole soul in a smile.

        Kural: The Great Book of Tiru-Valluvar

◀ **This native Tamil speaker introduced the word *soul* to better capture the rich cultural associations of the Tamil word meaning "interior." Like the preceding translator, he has sacrificed the structure and sound pattern of the original.**

J. LINDHOLM
Love is not the loving of a smiling face;
Love is the loving of a smiling inner heart.

Love is not the loving of a smiling face;
Love is the loving of a smiling heart's inner being.

Love is not the loving in the smile of a face;
Love is the loving in the inner smile of the heart.

Love is not the loving when the face smiles;
Love is the loving when the inner self smiles in the heart.

◀ **Notice the common elements in these four contemporary versions by the same translator. These variations attempt to re-create the patterns of repetition and to capture the brevity of the Tamil original.**

 As you enjoy the literary works in this book, keep somewhere in the back of your mind a thought of appreciation for the efforts of the translators, for they have opened for you the doors to the literary and cultural riches of the world.

Accompanying the following poem is a transcription of the spoken comments made by a student, Diane Hajicek, while reading "The Story of Pyramus and Thisbe" for the first time. Her comments will give you a glimpse into the mind of a reader actively engaged in the process of reading. After each of Diane's comments is a label identifying her reading strategy: questioning, predicting, or making meaning. Questioning involves trying to figure out something confusing such as a word, a sentence, or an entire passage, even when the text doesn't provide much of a clue. Predicting means using what is known to predict what might happen. Making meaning includes an array of mental acts, such as interpreting, recalling, or noticing details. To get the most benefit from Diane's response, first read the poem. Question, predict, and make meaning as you read. Then read Diane's response and compare it to your own.

The Story of Pyramus and Thisbe
from The Metamorphoses

Writer:

OVID

Student Reader:

DIANE HAJICEK

"Pyramus and Thisbe: both the best-looking
Of young people in the East were next-door
Neighbors; they lived within a high-walled, brick-built
City made (so it was said) by Queen Semiramis.
Proximity was the first reason why
They came to know each other; as time passed
Love flourished, and if their parents had
Not come between them, then they would have shared
A happy wedding bed. And yet no parent
10 Can check the heat of love, therefore, the lovers
Burned with mutual flames. Nor friend nor servant
Spoke for them; their speech was in the gesture
Of a nod, a smile; the more they banked the flames
The more they smouldered with a deeper heat.
5 There was a fissure in the wall between

"The first sentence is interesting. 'Best-looking' suggests there was some kind of standard for judging people's appearance."
(making meaning)

"This sounds like Romeo and Juliet."
(making meaning)

"This ['Nor friend nor servant / Spoke for them'] *is confusing."*
(questioning)

Their homes, a small, thin crevice that no one
Had seen. What eyes are sharper than the eyes
Of love? The lovers found the slit and made it
The hidden mouthpiece of their voices where

20 Love's subtle words in sweetest whispers came
And charmed the ear. And as they took their places,
Thisbe on one side, Pyramus on his,
Both waited, listening for the other's breath.
'O cold and bitter wall,' they said, 'why stand

25 Between two lovers at your side? Let limbs
And bodies join; at least open your gate
To take our kisses. Yet we do not show
Ingratitude, nor shall we, nor forget
The way through which our words met lovers' ears.'

30 Divided as they were, each futile day
Was spent in whispers, closing with 'Good night.'
Both pressed their lips against the silent wall.
Next day when dawn outshone the lamps of night
And Sun had dried the dew on frost-white grasses,

35 The lovers took their places at the wall
And in soft cries complained of heartless fate.
But as they talked they came to a decision:
Under the quiet darkness of the night
To glide from eyes that watched them out of doors,

40 To leave the town behind them; to prevent
The chance of being led astray they chose
The site of Ninus' tomb to meet each other,
There in the shadow of a famous tree,
The white tall mulberry that waved its branches

45 Not far from a bright flashing stream of water;
The plot delighted them, but from that moment
The day seemed all too long; the quick Sun lagged,
Then dove into the sea where Night came up.

"No sooner dark than Thisbe, veiled, unseen,
50 Slipped out of doors, a shade among the shadows,
Ran to the tomb, and took her place beneath
The appointed tree. For love had given her
Audacity. But look! A lioness!
And through the moonlit distance Thisbe saw her

55 With bloody lamb-fed jaws came up the road
And headed toward well waters for a drink
Where through the moonlit distance Thisbe saw her.
The Babylonian girl, trembling yet swift,
Turned to the recess of a darkening cave,

"I get the feeling that they feel a lot of pressure from people."
(making meaning)

"It's good to know which is the male and which is the female. I couldn't tell before."
(making meaning)
"This speech doesn't sound natural to me." (making meaning)

"I liked this a lot. They kissed the wall—the closest they can get to each other. Sometimes, there are emotional barriers where even if you can touch someone you're still not close."
(making meaning)

"It doesn't seem to me that running away solves any problems." (making meaning)

"Here's 'white' again."
(making meaning)

"That's neat the way night pops up like out of a toaster."
(making meaning)

"I like that. ['For love had given her / Audacity.']" (making meaning)

And as she ran dropped her white cloak behind her.
Meanwhile the beast had had her fill of drinking
And as she wandered back between the trees
She stepped across the cloak that Thisbe wore,
Now empty of its mistress, worried it
Between her teeth and left it stained with blood.
A moment later Pyramus arrived
Who saw the footprints of the beast in dust;
Then turned death-pale, but when he found the torn
Blood-tinted cloak, he said, 'One night shall be
The killing of two lovers. She whom I love
Deserves the longer life; on me all guilt
Should fall, for it was I who sent her out
Through deepest night into this evil place
Where I arrived too late. May all the lions
Who breed beneath this rocky cliff come at me,
Tear at my body and eat its guilt away—
But only cowards merely ask for death.'
At which he gathered up his Thisbe's cloak
And walked within the shadow of the tree,
There where he kissed the cloak and covered it
With tears. 'Now drink my blood,' he said aloud
And thrust the sword he wore into his side
Then in death's frenzy quickly drew it out,
Torn from warm flesh, and straightway fell
Backward to earth. And as a split lead joint
Shoots hissing sprays of water into air,
So his blood streamed above him to the tree,
Staining white fruit to darkest red, coloring
Tree's roots and growing fruit with purple dye.

"Then Thisbe came from shelter, fearful, shaken,
Thinking perhaps her lover had misplaced her,
Looked for him with her eyes, her soul, her heart,
Trembling to tell him dangers she escaped.
And though she knew the landmarks, the tall tree,
She wondered at the color of its fruit,
Doubting if it was the same tree she saw,
And while she wavered, glanced where something moved,
Arms, legs it had, stirring on blood-soaked ground,
Then she stepped back; her face had turned as pale
As the green boxwood leaf, her body tremulous
As fair lake waters rippling in the wind.
But when she saw that it was he, her lover,

"Everything is white."
(making meaning)

"I wonder if somehow they're going to break up. Maybe the lioness represents her or their love."
(predicting)

"The line 'only cowards merely ask for death' seems noble in a fake way to me."
(making meaning)

"I thought for a second the lioness had gotten her, but it's the lamb's blood on her cloak."
(questioning)

"Oh, my gosh! I can't believe he stabs himself! He's very rash."
(making meaning)

"This is intense. Their royalty and loyalty to their families won't let them be together."
(making meaning)

"The supernatural occurs here: it seems like the fruit changed color. I can't tell until I reread if the fruit was white and changed color or if the author just hadn't told us that it was purple."
(questioning)

"I like the word [wavered]. *You can tell that she's trying to make a decision."*
(making meaning)

"'Green' seems very full of life. Other color images have been bleak."
(making meaning)

She tore her hair and clasped her arms with grief,
Then fondled him, tears poured in wounds and blood.
105 And as she kissed his death-cold lips she cried,
'Pyramus, what misfortune takes you from me?
And O, Pyramus, speak to answer me.
It is your darling Thisbe calling you.
Listen, my dear, raise up your lazy head.'
110 At Thisbe's name, Pyramus raised an eyelid,
Weighted with death; her face seen in a vision,
And then his eyes had closed forever more.

"When she discovered her own cloak, the empty
Ivory sheath that held his sword, she said,
115 'By your own hand even your love has killed you,
Unlucky boy. Like yours my hand has courage,
My heart, love for the last act. I have the strength
To share your death and some shall say I was
The unhappy cause, the partner of your fate;
120 Only Lord Death had power to take you from me,
Yet even he cannot divorce us now.
O twice unhappy parents, his as mine,
Come, take our prayers, nor think the worse of us
Whom true love and death's hour have made one
125 And we shall sleep in the same bed, our tomb.
And you, O tree whose branches weave their shadows
Dark over the pitiful body of one lover
Shall soon bear shade for two; O fateful tree
Be the memorial of our twin deaths,
130 And your dark fruit the color of our mourning.'
Then Thisbe placed sword's point beneath her breast
The blade still warm with blood from her love's heart,
And leaned upon it till she sank to earth.
Her prayers had reached the gods, had moved both parents:
135 The ripe fruit of the tree turned deep rose color;
And they who loved sleep in a single urn."

"This ['death-cold lips'] *reminds me of* The Unquiet Grave. *It's a medieval ballad. One of the lovers is sitting on a dead lover's grave and wants to kiss her."*
(making meaning)

"I wonder who's speaking, who's telling this story."
(questioning)

"I don't always think that dying shows strength. In fact I never think that suicide shows strength."
(making meaning)

"That's really cold ['in the same bed, our tomb'].*"*
(making meaning)

"'Dark fruit' makes me think of an Aesop fable—why a fruit is a certain color."
(making meaning)

"This ['The blade still warm with blood from her love's heart'] *is really melodramatic!"*
(making meaning)

"It's too bad that it takes death to bring parents to understanding."
(making meaning)

After reading and commenting on "The Story of Pyramus and Thisbe," Diane was asked to express her overall impressions of the poem. She responded as follows:

"This poem reminds me so much of Romeo and Juliet *that it's difficult not to think of that play while reading—which obviously colors my impression of the whole poem. I think it's interesting that the author takes emotion—strong emotion like love that's being prevented—and treats it like a fable. I feel like I'm watching a scene happen behind a pane of glass. I can't touch the characters and get into the story even though I can feel the emotions in it. It seems like they [Pyramus and Thisbe] are doomed from the beginning. Their relationship is molded, and no one is flexible enough to change the way things are going. The kids don't even try to talk to their parents. It's interesting to think about how parents and children get along. The parents once experienced what the children are experiencing, but instead of communicating and trying to understand, they pretend they never felt that way. Pyramus and Thisbe never do anything to help their parents understand the way they feel."*

Responding in Writing

As you study the literature in this book, you will write *about* the literature and *from* the literature. Through writing, you will discover ideas about yourself, about the world, and about what you read. Much of your writing will be shared with your classmates who, together with you and your teacher, form a community of readers and writers. Some pieces you write will be shared with the broader community outside the classroom. Other writing will be personal writing for you alone.

On the following pages you will find practical information that you can apply in many different writing situations. You can refer to this information any time you need help in expressing your ideas.

The Reader's Journal

One place to record your responses to literature is in a reader's journal, which might also be called a reading log, literature journal, response journal, or reader's notebook. Whatever you call it, a journal can serve as a rich source of writing ideas and as a place to record notes as you prepare for writing assignments.

A journal may be a simple notebook, a place to jot down ideas without attention to form or completeness. Another kind of journal is a more formal log, designed to make writing an integral part of the reading process.

Here are some tips for keeping a journal:

GUIDE:

*Keeping
a Journal*

- Set aside the first part of your journal as the place to write as you read. Use a two-column format. In the first column, record words, passages, and lines that trigger ideas. Identify each quotation with a line number or with page and paragraph numbers. In the second column, note your responses to these ideas.

- Leave space after each set of reading notes for the journal writing suggested in the lesson and for the notes needed for the writing assignments.

- Reserve a part of your journal for observations, quotations, and imaginative writing that is not connected directly with a literary selection.

- Label each entry with a title and date.

➤ **ACTIVITY 1:** *Using a Journal*

Reread "The Story of Pyramus and Thisbe." Take notes about each character's actions and personal qualities. Save these notes to use as you work through this writing handbook.

The Writing Process

Writing is a process unique to each writer and to each writing situation. However, certain activities need to take place during most writing experiences. These activities include the following:

- **Exploring ideas:** reflecting on what you know, what you need to know, and how you might approach the assignment
- **Gathering material:** remembering, imagining, reading, observing, interviewing, surveying, experimenting, discussing, notetaking
- **Discovering connections:** exploring the way ideas fit together, encouraging new ideas to surface, elaborating and pushing ideas to their limits
- **Eliminating barriers to communication:** rethinking content, reshaping structure, refining mechanics and usage

In many books about writing, each of these activities is assigned to a specific stage of the writing process: prewriting, drafting and discovery, revision (and editing), or publishing and presenting. Research and the experience of writers, however, have shown that the activities can take place at any point in the process.

The Writer as Decision-Maker

During the writing process, writers make a series of decisions that direct and redirect their writing. These decisions concern the key issues of purpose, audience, subject, point of view, and form. The following list of questions can guide you in thinking about these issues as you plan your writing, as you get your ideas down on paper, and as you revise your work.

GUIDE:

Making Key Decisions

Purpose

Is a purpose stated or implied in the assignment?

What are my personal goals?

What do I really want to accomplish in this piece: express my ideas or feelings? inform? entertain? analyze? persuade?

How do I want my audience to respond? What do I want them to think? to feel?

Audience

Am I writing for an imagined audience?

Who will read my writing?

What do my readers already know?

What might they need to know?

What might they find interesting? entertaining? informative?

Subject

What exactly am I writing about: my own thoughts and feelings? a work of literature? information from outside sources?

What information must I pull together or research?

Will I need to fill in details from my imagination?

How detailed must I be for my audience?

Point of View

In whose voice am I writing: my own? that of a character in a story? an imagined person?

What does the narrator, or "voice," know? think? feel?

Form

Is a form named in the assignment?

What is the most effective organization to accomplish my purpose?

What should the final product look like?

Do I need a model of the form? If so, where can I find one?

☞ **ACTIVITY 2:** *Making Decisions*

The following assignment is an example of the kinds of writing assignments in this book. This particular assignment is based on "The Story of Pyramus and Thisbe."

Assignment: *Put yourself in the role of a director planning a series of short classics for public television. Create a **casting call** in which you describe the kind of actor and actress desired for the roles of Pyramus and Thisbe and specify the particular challenges of the role.*

Assume that you've been given this assignment. Begin planning your writing by exploring further the ideas about Pyramus and Thisbe that you noted in Activity 1 or by drafting some preliminary paragraphs. Think about purpose, audience, subject, point of view, and form only as much as seems comfortable for you at this time. Save any writing that you do.

The Writer as Problem-Solver

Although every writer's process is personal, many writers experience the same kinds of difficulties. The questions they ask tend to resemble these:

1. Where do I start? Where do I get ideas? What do I do with them?

2. Who can help me? When should I ask for help?

3. How do I know when I've written enough? How do I find out what's wrong with my writing? How do I fix it?

The strategies given here provide some concrete ways to help you deal with these common problems.

Strategies: *Tree Diagrams*

When you need to explore further the ideas in your reader's journal, to generate new ideas, or to discover connections among ideas, you might want to try creating a tree diagram. A tree diagram shows a central idea (a trunk) and related ideas (branches and leaves). The sample diagram shows the central idea "Pyramus" surrounded by words and phrases that describe his qualities: those that can be inferred from the poem and those that were imagined by the student.

GRAPHIC:

Tree Diagram

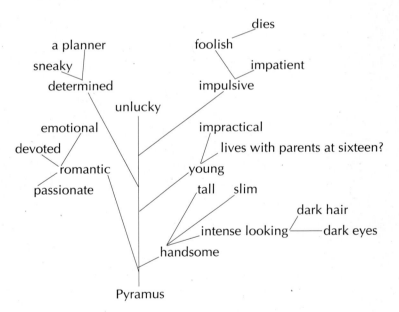

☞ ACTIVITY 3: *Creating a Tree Diagram*

Create a tree diagram describing Thisbe. Use the ideas in your journal or the paragraphs you drafted in Activity 2 as a starting point, and fill in real and imagined details. Save your diagram.

STRATEGIES: *Outlines, Charts, and Venn Diagrams*

Outlines, charts, and Venn diagrams can help you to discover connections as well as to pinpoint where you need to gather more material. Outlines are especially useful for expository essays and other writing in which you explain information or present the results of your research. The first example reviews standard outline form, which is often required for research papers. The second example shows a more informal approach, which can be adapted for just about any assignment.

GRAPHIC:

Standard and Informal Outlines

Title

Statement of Purpose:
I. (Main Point)
  A. (First subpoint)
  B. (Second subpoint)
    1.
    2. (Details and subdetails)
    3.
      a.
      b.

Pyramus

Romantic
— passionate
— devoted
— emotional

Handsome
— tall
— slim
— intense looking
    dark eyes
    dark hair

The next two types of graphics are also useful for organizing ideas. The opinion/conclusion chart—or some variation of that chart—works well for persuasive writing and for writing that presents generalizations about multiple works. A Venn diagram is a good way to identify similarities and differences in preparation for comparing and contrasting two or more subjects.

GRAPHIC:

Opinion / Conclusion Chart

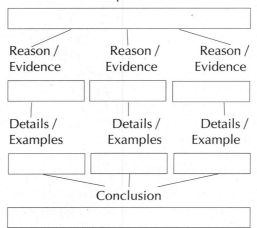

GRAPHIC:

Venn Diagram

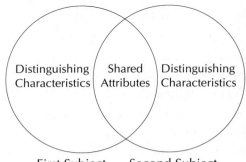

Distinguishing Characteristics | Shared Attributes | Distinguishing Characteristics

First Subject   Second Subject

☞ ACTIVITY 4: *Using Graphics for Writing*

1. Put yourself once again into the role of a film director. Outline the plot of "The Story of Pyramus and Thisbe" in preparation for describing the roles of the main characters for the actors and actresses interested in the parts.

2. Using information from the sample tree diagram on page 15 and from the tree diagram you created in Activity 3, present your opinion of Pyramus and Thisbe for someone totally unfamiliar with their story. Incorporate into your writing process the opinion/conclusion chart, the Venn diagram, or both. Save your writing.

STRATEGIES: *Peers as Partners*

As an active participant in a community of readers and writers, you can work collaboratively at any point in the writing process. You can co-develop a writing plan with a partner, bounce ideas off a friend, ask a classmate to be a peer editor or peer responder, or in some cases co-author a piece. Involving peers in your problem-solving process can help you in exploring and clarifying ideas, in seeing a subject from a different perspective, in identifying and eliminating problems in communication, and in assessing potential impact on your reading audience.

A key question to ask yourself before involving a partner in your writing process is: How much feedback do I really want? If the answer is "a lot," you might try this technique. Read your writing aloud to a classmate, pausing after each paragraph or passage to ask: What are you feeling? What are you thinking about? What questions do you have? Another approach is to give a peer reader a copy of your writing with pauses marked. At each pause, the reader records what is going on in his or her mind either next to the writing or on a separate sheet of paper.

Another technique for getting detailed feedback is to give a classmate the piece of writing along with a list of thought-provoking questions like the following.

- What aspects of the writing are most memorable?
- What message do you think I am trying to get across? Summarize it.
- What do you want to know more about? What parts need to be pared down?
- Did the beginning work for you? Did the ending?
- Did you have any trouble following my ideas?
- What questions were answered for you? What questions still linger in your mind?

STRATEGIES: *Self-Evaluation*

Sometimes a first draft of a piece of writing needs little revision. Other times you may have to write several drafts, perhaps going back to rethink your basic premises. When trying to figure out what's wrong with a piece of writing that just isn't working, you can start with a quick check like the following.

- The main point I am trying to make is _____ .
- I want my reader to respond to my writing by thinking or feeling that _____ .
- In looking back over the piece, I like _____ . I don't like _____ .
- I have accomplished my personal goals by _____ . I still need to _____ .

At this point you'll also want to read your writing aloud, listening for ideas that are unclear or unnecessary, ideas that don't connect logically, abrupt transitions from one idea to the next, a dull or choppy style, and words that don't sound quite right or aren't right for your audience.

To evaluate your expository and persuasive essays, you might try writing two sentences about the entire essay and then two sentences about each paragraph or section. The first sentence in each pair should describe content: what the essay, paragraph, or section *says*. The second sentence should focus on what the essay, paragraph, or section *does*. When you analyze the sentences, you'll be able to tell whether you've covered the main points and whether the structure of your essay works. You can use this technique for eliciting peer response as well as for evaluating your own writing.

STRATEGIES: *The Final Edit*

No one knows all the rules of grammar, spelling, capitalization, punctuation, and usage and all the synonyms and meanings for every word in the English language. What anyone can learn, however, is where to go for this kind of information. Here are some ideas:

- **To check spelling:** dictionary, spelling dictionary, computer spellchecker
- **To check punctuation, capitalization, grammar, and usage:** composition and grammar textbook such as *The Writer's Craft*
- **To check word meanings and synonyms:** dictionary, thesaurus
- **To check facts:** encyclopedia, world atlas, and other reference books in your school or public library
- **To check bibliographic style:** composition and grammar textbook, style manual

One point to check carefully when writing about literature is the accuracy of your quotations and of spellings of names and titles. The literature itself and the index of titles and authors are your sources for this information.

☞ **ACTIVITY 5:** *Completing an Assignment*

Finish the assignment that asks you to write a **casting call** for the roles of *Pyramus and Thisbe (Activity 2). Refer back to the writing you did for Activity 3 and Activity 4.*

STRATEGIES: *The Evaluation Task*

Each kind of writing has certain unique characteristics. For example, creative writing is judged on whether it sparks the reader's imagination. Persuasive writing is considered effective if it influences a reader's opinions. However, an evaluator can assess the strengths and weaknesses of most writing using general guidelines in three key areas: (1) content, (2) form, and (3) grammar, usage, and mechanics.

The following is a description of a well-developed piece of writing, which you might use when you are acting as a peer evaluator and when judging whether your own work is ready for a final evaluation or in need of further revision.

GUIDE:

*Evaluating
Content*

The content of a well-developed piece of writing . . .

Is clearly focused throughout the piece

Maintains a consistent tone and point of view

Uses precise verbs, nouns, and modifiers and incorporates descriptive and figurative language as appropriate

Elaborates on the ideas with supporting details, examples, and summaries, as appropriate

Presents well-founded opinions and accurate information, as appropriate

Demonstrates a clear sense of purpose

Demonstrates a clear sense of audience through choice of language and details

GUIDE:

Evaluating Form

The form of a well-developed piece of writing . . .

Maintains clear relationships among ideas through effective transitions

Demonstrates an awareness of correct and effective paragraphing

Includes sentences with a variety of structures

GUIDE:

Evaluating Grammar, Usage, and Mechanics

The final draft of a well-developed piece of writing . . .

Demonstrates understanding and application of editing and proofreading skills

Contains few if any minor errors in grammar and usage

Contains few if any minor errors in spelling, capitalization, and punctuation

The Writer as Learner

One way to learn from a writing experience is through an objective evaluation of your final product by a teacher or a peer reader. Another way is to evaluate the process itself, using questions like the following to focus on various aspects of the writing and learning experience.

GUIDE:

Learning from the Writing Process

- Am I pleased with my final product?
- Did I become involved in my topic?
- Did I learn something from writing about it?
- Which aspects of the writing were easiest? Which were most difficult?
- What aspect of writing is becoming easier?
- What was the biggest problem I encountered? How did I solve the problem? How might I avoid the problem next time?
- When I compare this piece of writing with others in my working folder or portfolio, can I see changes in my writing style? in my writing skill?
- Have I seen anything in the writing done by my peers or by professional writers that I would like to try myself?

ACTIVITY 6: *Evaluating Process and Product*

Evaluate the assignment that you completed for Activity 4, assignment 2, or for Activity 5. First evaluate your own writing. Assess strengths and weaknesses. Then, ask a classmate to do the same, and compare the results. Finally, think through the process itself, using Guide: Learning from the Writing Process.

The Writer as Communicator

When the time comes to share your writing, you have many choices. A few of these choices are listed below.

OPTIONS:

Publishing and Presenting

- Trade papers with the classmate who helped you refine your ideas.
- Trade papers with a classmate unfamiliar with your work.
- Read your writing to a small group of classmates or to the class.
- Ask a classmate to read your writing aloud.
- Read your writing to younger children or to adults in your family or community.
- Discuss the ideas explored in your writing and your conclusions.
- Choose appropriate ideas to share in a discussion and save others for future use.
- Present a dramatic reading with sound effects.
- Tape-record a reading of the piece.
- Stage your work as simple Readers Theater or as a more elaborate performance.
- Publish a booklet of your own writing or of writing by many contributors.
- Display your writing in the classroom or in the school library.
- Submit your writing to the school newspaper or literary magazine.
- Mail your writing to a magazine or newspaper with a wider circulation.
- Add your writing to your notebook or portfolio for later sharing.

Whatever option you choose, share your work in the spirit of learning and of growing in the skill and confidence needed to be an effective writer.

ACTIVITY 7: *Publishing and Presenting*

Brainstorm with your class about ways to share your writing about "The Story of Pyramus and Thisbe." Choose one way or several ways, plan how to share, and then implement your plan.

Woodcut, LYND WARD.
From *God's Man* by Lynd Ward. Courtesy of May McNeer Ward.

Common Beliefs:
Teaching Through Literature

*"World literature is ... a kind of
collective body and a common spirit,
a living unity of the heart which reflects
the growing spiritual unity of mankind."*

ALEXANDER SOLZHENITSYN

Recognizing Spiritual Connections

Almost all groups of people have literature that is considered sacred—that is used in rituals of worship, initiation, celebration, and mourning. Such literature may be preserved in holy books, in the memories of designated "word-keepers," or in the oral language of all members of the community. Passed down from one generation to the next, hymns, chants, prayers, myths, and other forms of sacred literature express the core beliefs of a group of people. Sacred literature can be seen as answering such basic questions as Who created us? How should we live? How should we view death? and Why are things as they are? Such literature reflects the fundamental order that people see in the universe. Through it, people recognize the spiritual connections between humans and gods, between any one individual and all of humanity, and between past and present and future.

PRAISE POEMS

As human beings consider the miracle of their own existence and the beauty and power of the world around them, they are often moved to praise a divine force. Hymns and chants praising gods are common to most cultures; the latest American gospel recordings have their equivalents in ancient Egyptian papyruses. Although the impulse to extol a deity is universal, conceptions of the divine are varied. A group may worship one supreme god, a pantheon of gods governing different realms, innumerable animating spirits, or natural elements such as the earth or the rain. The praise poems in this unit, drawn from three different cultures, reveal the unique perception of divinity held by each culture. These works also express a range of attitudes toward gods, including awe at their creative and destructive powers, gratitude for their favor, fear of their wrath, and submission to their will.

SPIRITUAL LESSONS

Another purpose of sacred literature besides serving to glorify gods is to communicate profound insights about life. Sermons can impart such wisdom, but so can songs, poems, stories, proverbs, and other forms. One section of this unit contains selections from the scriptures and oral tradition of the Buddhist, Jewish, Christian, Islamic, and traditional East African religions. There is a remarkable consistency in the spiritual lessons that these works teach: Death comes to all human beings without exception; Wealth is not the highest good; Be kind and generous to one another.

MYTHIC ACCOUNTS

Myths, yet another form of sacred literature, provide explanations of how the world came to be, why it is as it is, and how it might end. There are striking similarities among the world's myths. Every culture has an account of how humans were created; this unit contains an example from an ancient Mayan civilization. Also widespread are myths that speak of disasters befalling the human race; examples of such myths also appear in the unit. Like praise poems, myths show the relationship of people to their gods. Myths also reflect the entire way of life in a culture, from diet to burial practices to overriding values. Myth making is a basic impulse of human beings, one of many impulses that unite us as a species.

Literary Vocabulary

INTRODUCED IN THIS SECTION

Imagery. Imagery refers to words and phrases that re-create sensory experiences for a reader. Though the majority of images are visual, some may appeal to the sense of smell, hearing, taste, or touch or to any combination of senses. In "The Story of Pyramus and Thisbe" on page 7, the visual image "when dawn outshone the lamps of night" re-creates the moment when the morning sun fills the sky. "And Sun had dried the dew on frost-white grasses" appeals to two senses—touch and sight—in representing the effect of sunlight on the frost-covered grass.

Myth. A myth is a traditional story, once widely believed to be true, that attempts to explain why the world is the way it is or why things in nature happen as they do. For example, one Greek myth explains how Prometheus brought fire to humans by dipping his torch into the sun.

Mandala from *The Mandala Coloring Book* by Janet Izard & Michael Izard. © 1973 by Ducks Books. Used by permission of Doubleday, a division of Bantam Doubleday Dell Publishing Company.

Adoration of the Disk
from The Book of the Dead   EGYPT

To Indra
from The Rig Veda   INDIA

Homages to Orisha
YORUBA   NIGERIA

*A*pproaching the Poems

"Adoration of the Disk" dates from 2000 B.C., when the Egyptian pharoah Akhnaten (äkh nä′ tən) established devotion to Ra, the god of the sun. The poem is from The Book of the Dead, a collection of prayers, hymns, and spells important to Egyptian burial rites. "To Indra" is taken from The Rig Veda (rig vä′ də), a collection of ten books of Hindu hymns composed about 1500 B.C. in India. "Homages to Orisha" (ō′ rē shä) are traditional poems of the Yoruba (yō′ rōō bə) people, who live in southwestern Nigeria and parts of Benin and Togo in Africa. These poems honor two Orisha, or spirits: Ogun (ō′ gōōn), the god worshipped by hunters, warriors, and blacksmiths; and Shango (shôn′ gō), the thunder god.

*B*uilding Vocabulary

These essential words are defined alongside the poems.

suppliant (sup′ lē ənt): Stirrer to action of the poor and lowly, of priest, of **suppliant** who sings his praises (page 29, line 11)

succor (suk′ ər): They invoke to give them **succor** (page 29, line 17)

covenant (kuv′ ə nənt): One does not break **covenant** with Ogun. (page 30, line 10)

*C*onnecting Writing and Reading

Think of your school song, the national anthem, religious hymns, and any other poems that praise someone or something. In your journal identify the subjects praised and the qualities admired. As you read the following three praise poems, compare the qualities admired in each to the qualities you noted in your journal.

Adoration of the Disk

Thy dawn, O Ra, opens the new horizon,
And every realm that you hast made to live
Is conquered by thy love, as joyous Day
Follows thy footsteps in delightful peace.

5   And when thou settest, all the world is bleak;
Houses are tombs where blind men lie in death;
Only the lion and the serpent move
Through the black oven of the sightless night.

Dawn in the East again! the lands awake,
10   And men leap from their slumber with a song;
They bathe their bodies, clothe them with
    fresh garments,
And lift their hands in happy adoration.

The cattle roam again across the fields;
Birds flutter in the marsh, and lift their wings
15   Also in adoration, and the flocks
Run with delight through all the pleasant meadows.

Both north and south along the dazzling river
Ships raise their sails and take their course before thee;
And in the ocean, all the deep-sea fish
20   Swim to the surface to drink in thy light.

For thou art all that lives, the seed of men,
The son within his mother's womb who knows
The comfort of thy presence near, the babe
To whom thou givest words and growing wisdom;

25   The chick within the egg, whose breath is thine,
Who runneth from its shell, chirping its joy,
And dancing on its small, unsteady legs
To greet the splendor of the rising sun.

Thy heart created all, this teeming earth,
30   Its people, herds, creatures that go afoot,
Creatures that fly in air, both land and sea,
Thou didst create them all within thy heart.

Men and their fates are thine, in all their stations,
Their many languages, their many colors,
35 All thine, and we who from the midst of peoples,
Thou madest different, Master of the Choice.

And lo, I find thee also in my heart,
I, <u>Khu en Aten</u>,[1] find thee and adore.
O thou, whose dawn is life, whose setting, death,
40 In the great dawn, then lift up me, thy son.

1. Khu en Aten (khōō en ä′ tən).

To Indra

[handwritten marginalia: repetition—emphasis, importance, remember; consistent rhythm]

He who, just born, chief god of lofty spirit by power and
    might became the gods' protector,
Before whose breath through greatness of his valor the two
    worlds trembled, he, O men, is Indra.

[handwritten: alliteration   signals ending stanza]

[handwritten: bard compliments subsistence; purpose—conflict, struggle]

He who <u>fixed fast and firm</u> the earth that staggered, and
    set at rest the agitated mountains,
Who measured out the air's wide middle region and gave
    the heaven support, he, men, is Indra.

5 Who slew the dragon, freed the seven rivers, and <u>drove the
    kine</u>[1] forth from the cave of Vala,[2]
Begat the fire between two stones, the spoiler in warrior's
    battle, he, O men, is Indra.

1. kine (kīn): cattle.
2. Vala (vu′ lə): a demon.

By whom this universe was made to tremble, who chased
    away the humbled brood of demons,
Who, like a gambler gathering his winnings, seized the
    foe's riches, he, O men, is Indra.

Of whom, the terrible, they ask, Where is he? or verily
    they say of him, He is not.
10 He sweeps away, like birds, the foe's possessions. Have
    faith in him, for he, O men, is Indra.

Stirrer to action of the poor and lowly, of priest, of
    suppliant[3] who sings his praises;
Who, fair-faced, favors him who presses soma[4] with stones
    made ready, he, O men, is Indra.

He under whose supreme control are horses, all chariots,
    and the villages, and cattle;
He who gave being to the sun and morning, who leads the
    waters, he, O men, is Indra.

15 To whom two armies cry in close encounter, both enemies
    the stronger and the weaker;
Whom two invoke upon one chariot mounted, each for
    himself, he, O ye men, is Indra.

Without whose help our people never conquer; whom,
    battling, they invoke to give them succor;[5]
He of whom all this world is but the copy, who shakes
    things moveless, he, O men, is Indra.

He who hath smitten, ere they knew their danger, with his
    hurled weapon many grievous sinners;
20 Who pardons not his boldness who provokes him, who
    slays the Dasyu,[6] he, O men, is Indra.

He who discovered in the fortieth autumn Sambara[7] as he
    dwelt among the mountains;
Who slew the dragon putting forth his vigor, the demon
    lying there, he, men, is Indra.

Who with seven guiding reins, the bull, the mighty, set
    free the seven great floods to flow at pleasure;
Who, thunder-armed, rent Rauhina[8] in pieces when
    scaling heaven, he, O ye men, is Indra.

3. suppliant (sup′ lē ənt): one who begs or pleads earnestly.

4. soma (sō′ mə): an East Indian vine that was used to make an intoxicating beverage of ancient India; the beverage, used in sacred rites, that was made from this vine.

I need his support to conquer

5. succor (suk′ ər): help, relief from trouble.

to strike down

6. Dasyu (dus′ yōō): an aboriginal people in India who opposed the invasion of the Aryans c. 1500 B.C.

allusion "sinners"

7. Sambara (shum′ bə rə): Sanskrit word for a demon.

8. Rauhina (rou′ hin ə): a demon of drought.

25 Even the heaven and earth bow down before him, before
    his very breath the mountains tremble.
Known as the soma-drinker, armed with thunder, who
    wields the bolt, he, O ye men, is Indra.

Who aids with favor him who pours the soma and him
    who brews it, sacrificer, singer,
Whom prayer exalts, and pouring forth of soma, and this
    our gift, he, O ye men, is Indra.

Thou verily art fierce and true who sendest strength to the
    man who brews and pours libation.
30 So may we evermore, thy friends, O Indra, speak loudly to
    the synod[9] with our heroes.

9. synod (sin' əd): a council, especially a religious council.

Homages to Orisha

To Ogun

god of hunters, warriors, & blacksmiths

physical description

The day Ogun came down from his hill
He was clothed in fire
And wore a garment of blood;
Then he borrowed palm fronds from palm trees;
5 Attired in fresh palm fronds, he entered Ire[1]
And was immediately proclaimed king.
Owner of two machetes:
    with one he prepares the farm
    with the other he clears the road.
10 One does not break covenant[2] with Ogun.

more powerful than human beings

) 2 opposite uses

foreboding

1. Ire (ē' r̠ā).

2. covenant (kuv' ə nənt): agreement made between two parties.

To Shango

[handwritten: thunder god]

He dances savagely in the courtyard of the impertinent   *[handwritten: no respect, rude to authority]*
He sets fire to the house of the man who lies
Owner of the destroying ax,
He sounds his maracas[1] like iron handbells.

[handwritten: physical description]

5   With eyes white as bitter kola
Cheeks puffed out with kola nuts
The masquerade who emits fire from his mouth
The god who frightens cats.
Elegant and leisurely husband of the kola-seller;
10   If someone is brazen-faced to you — *[handwritten: seek vengence on individual's behalf]*
Shango will teach him a lesson;
With eyes white as bitter kola
Shango, fierce lord!

1. maracas (mə rä′ kəs):
percussion instruments made
of dried gourds that contain
dried seeds or pebbles.

Thinking About the Poems

A PERSONAL RESPONSE

*sharing
impressions*

1. How did you respond to the gods who are the subjects of these praise poems? Jot down your impressions in your journal.

*constructing
interpretations*

2. Why did you think each of these gods is praised by his or her people?
   Think about
   • the qualities admired in each god
   • the behavior punished by Ogun and Shango
   • the reasons why the subjects you identified in your journal are praised

3. Which of the gods has the greatest appeal for you personally? Support your answer with references to the praise poems.

A CREATIVE RESPONSE

4. How might the effect of the praise poem "Adoration of the Disk" be different if the speaker had described the destructive power of the sun?

5. Compare Ra, Indra, Ogun, or Shango to another supreme being, such as that of the Judeo-Christian tradition. Support your comparison with examples of specific similarities and differences.

6. Passages from The Book of the Dead sometimes were inscribed on Egyptian tombs or written on scrolls placed within the tombs. The Egyptians believed that the passages would guide souls on their journey to the other world. What features of "Adoration of the Disk" might have made it especially suitable as a guide in the afterlife? Cite lines from the poem in explaining your ideas.

Analyzing the Writer's Craft

IMAGERY

Think about the vivid pictures of Ogun and Shango provided in "Homages to Orisha."

Building a Literary Vocabulary. Imagery refers to words and phrases that re-create sensory experiences for a reader. Though the majority of images are visual, some may appeal to the sense of smell, hearing, taste, or touch or to any combination of senses. For example, in "Homages to Orisha" the images "clothed in fire" and "a garment of blood" appeal primarily to the sense of sight but also appeal to the sense of touch. The images suggest the terror Ogun inspired before he put on palm fronds.

Application: Identifying Images. Get together with a classmate. One of you should make a chart listing several images from "Adoration of the Disk," and the other should make a chart listing several images from "To Indra." Next to each image, identify the sense or senses appealed to, as shown in the following example:

"Adoration of the Disk"

Image	Sensory Appeal
"Birds flutter in the marsh"	sight, hearing

After you and your partner have completed your charts, analyze how the contrast between Ra and Indra is reflected in the imagery of the two poems.

Connecting Reading and Writing

1. Write a **praise poem** that you might present on a solemn occasion. For example, you might write about the qualities you admire in a religious or national leader or even a sports hero.

Option: Write a **eulogy** in prose about someone you admire and present it to your class.

2. Select one of the gods—Ra, Indra, Ogun, or Shango—to be featured on the cover of a national news magazine. Write a **letter from the editor** to the readers of the magazine to justify your selection.

Option: Defend your selection in a **memo** to the editorial board of the magazine.

3. Write an **encyclopedia entry** that explains the importance of The Book of the Dead.

Option: In **notes** for a research paper, explore the connection between The Book of the Dead and the ancient Egyptian concept of the afterlife.

4. Research information about the Orisha, the gods and spirits of the Yoruba. Write a **report** for your classmates presenting the information that you have uncovered.

Option: Create a **chart** that will accompany an article on the Yoruba. Include the names of the gods and spirits and their qualities or functions.

The Mustard Seed
from Buddhist Scripture

from Ecclesiastes
from The Old Testament

To the Earth
NGONI   MALAWI

Approaching the Selections

The following selections represent three different religious traditions. "The Mustard Seed" is a story dating from twenty-five hundred years ago. It expresses the Buddhist (bood′ ist) idea of *anicca* (ə nich′ ə), the concept that life is impermanent. Ecclesiastes is one of the books of the Old Testament, the Holy Scriptures that are sacred to Judaism. "To the Earth" is a song of the Ngoni (ŋgō′ nē) people, who live in Malawi in southeastern Africa. The song is sung at marriages and other gatherings.

Connecting Writing and Reading

If a young child asked you about death and why living things have to die, how would you answer? In your journal write something you might tell the child. As you read these selections, drawn from the literatures of three widely varying cultures, notice how each passage deals with the reality of life and death.

The Mustard Seed

ONCE GOTAMI, AN Indian woman, came to the Buddha crying, "O Exalted One, my only son has died. I went to everyone and asked, 'Is there no medicine to bring my son back to life?' And they replied, 'There is no medicine; but go to the Exalted One, he may be able to help you.' Can you, O Exalted One, give me medicine to bring my only son back to life?"

Looking at her compassionately, the Buddha replied, "You did well Gotami, in coming here for medicine. Go, and bring me for medicine some tiny grains of mustard seed from every house where no one—neither parent, child, relative, nor servant—has died."

Gotami, delighted in her heart, went away to fetch as many tiny grains of mustard seed as she could find. From one house to the other, she moved frantically all day long, as each time she was told, "Alas! Gotami, great is the count of the dead in this house."

Overcome with exhaustion, she finally went to the burning-ground outside the city with her dead son in her arms. "My dear little boy," said she, "I thought you alone had been overtaken by this thing which men call *death*. But now I see that you are not the only one, for *this is a law common to all mankind*." And so saying, she cast the little corpse into the fire.

Then she sang:

No village law, no law of market town,
No law of a single house is *this* [death].
Of all the world, and all the worlds of gods,
This only is law: *All things are anicca*. ✳

When she returned to the Buddha, she was greeted by him. "Gotami, did you get the tiny grains of mustard seed for medicine?"

"Done, O Exalted One, is the business of the mustard seed! Only give me refuge."

[handwritten annotations: dramatic irony / purpose — self revelation (epiphany) / perspective changed]

[handwritten annotation: ✳ impermanent life does not last forever]

ALL THINGS COME alike to all: there is one event to the righteous, and to the wicked, to the good and to the clean, and to the unclean; to him that sacrificeth, and to him that sacrificeth not: as is the good, so is the sinner, and he that sweareth, as he that feareth an oath. This is an evil among all things that are done under the sun, that there is one event unto all: yea also the heart of the sons of men is full of evil, and madness is in their heart while they live, and after that they go to the dead.

For to him that is joined to all the living there is hope: for a living dog is better than a dead lion. For the living know that they shall die: but the dead know not any thing, neither have they any more a reward, for the memory of them is forgotten. Also their love, and their hatred, and their envy, is now perished; neither have they any more a portion for ever in any thing that is done under the sun.

Go thy way, eat thy bread with joy, and drink thy wine with a merry heart; for God now accepteth thy works. Let thy garments be always white; and let thy head lack no ointment. Live joyfully with the wife, whom thou lovest, all the days of the life of thy vanity, which he hath given thee under the sun, all the days of thy vanity: for that is thy portion in this life, and in thy labor which thou takest under the sun. Whatsoever thy hand findeth to do, do it with thy might: for there is no work, nor device, nor knowledge, nor wisdom, in the grave, whither thou goest.

I returned, and saw under the sun, that the race is not to the swift, nor the battle to the strong, neither yet bread to the wise, nor yet riches to men of understanding, nor yet favor to men of skill; but time and chance happeneth to them all. For man also knoweth not his time: as the fishes that are taken in an evil net, and as the birds that are caught in the snare, so are the sons of men snared in an evil time, when it falleth suddenly upon them.

[handwritten annotations:]

warning: temptation

death is universal, but do not forget about living life to the fullest

#1 never know when dead is coming, be prepared

status - dog & lion
better to live a hard life, than an easy dead life now ended

To the Earth

verse [handwritten]

The earth does not get fat
 It makes an end of those who wear the head plumes   _high status_ [handwritten]
The earth does not get fat
 It makes an end of those who act swiftly as heroes
5 Shall we die on earth?   _rhetorical question, frustration_ [handwritten]

Listen, O earth; we shall mourn because of you
Listen, shall we all die on the earth?   _disbelief_ [handwritten]

The earth does not get fat
 It makes an end of the chiefs
10 Shall we all die on the earth?
The earth does not get fat
 It makes an end of the women-chiefs   _*male dominated society_ [handwritten]
 Shall we die on the earth?

Listen, O earth; we shall mourn because of you
15 _Listen, shall we all die on the earth?_

The earth does not get fat
 It makes an end of the nobles
 Shall we die on the earth?
The earth does not get fat
20 It makes an end of the royal women
 Shall we die on the earth?

Listen, O earth; we shall mourn because of you
Listen, shall we all die on the earth?

The earth does not get fat
25 It makes an end of the common people
 Shall we die on earth?
The earth does not get fat
 It makes an end of all the animals   _low status_ [handwritten]
 Shall we die on earth?

30 Listen, you who are asleep
 Who are left tightly closed in the land
Shall we all sink into the earth?   _metaphor_ [handwritten]
Listen, O earth, the sun is setting tightly
We shall all enter into the earth. → _acceptance_ [handwritten]

repetition — litany (prayer) [handwritten, left margin]

death comes to all, nondiscriminatory [handwritten, bottom]

Thinking About the Selections

A PERSONAL RESPONSE

sharing impressions

1. How did you react to these thoughts about death? Describe your reactions in your journal.

constructing interpretations

2. What do the three selections say to you about life and death? Explain the messages in your own words.

Think about
- the line "The earth does not get fat" from "To the Earth"
- this saying from Ecclesiastes: "A living dog is better than a dead lion"
- what Gotami learns from the Buddha in "The Mustard Seed"
- what you wrote in your journal

3. Which of the three selections do you think presents the message most effectively? Support your opinion.

A CREATIVE RESPONSE

4. How might the effect of the selections vary according to the age of the reader?

A CRITICAL RESPONSE

5. Consider the techniques employed in the three selections. How do they affect the impact of the message?

Think about
- the list of examples in Ecclesiastes
- the single, developed example in "The Mustard Seed"
- the repetition or parallelism in "To the Earth"

6. Filmmaker Woody Allen once complained that the worst part about death is the hours. Author George Santayana wrote that "there is no cure for birth and death save to enjoy the interval." What other contemporary statements or sayings can you identify that express attitudes or beliefs about death? Compare these to the message about death conveyed in the three selections.

The Beatitudes
from The New Testament

The Night
from The Koran

Approaching the Selections

Profound lessons about living can be found in the writings of all religions. An important purpose of these lessons is to identify the qualities that distinguish good from evil.

For Christians, The Beatitudes specify these qualities. According to Christian belief, The Beatitudes are Jesus' own pronouncements about spiritual wealth. They are listed in Matthew's gospel, the first book of the New Testament, written probably between A.D. 42 and 70.

For Muslims, "The Night" sets forth the qualities of goodness. According to Muslim belief, "The Night" expresses the teachings of God given to Mohammed by the angel Gabriel. "The Night" is found in The Koran, which dates back approximately to A.D. 652.

Connecting Writing and Reading

Think of the friend or family member you care most about. Then think of the person you dislike the most. In your journal list the qualities of each person. As you read, assess what qualities in people are valued and rewarded and what qualities are not.

Liked Person	Disliked Person

The Beatitudes — *perfect blessedness or happiness* [handwritten]

Blessed are the poor in spirit: for theirs is the kingdom of
  heaven.
Blessed are they that mourn: for they shall be comforted.
Blessed are the meek: for they shall inherit the earth.
Blessed are they which do hunger and thirst after
  righteousness: for they shall be filled. *doing what is morally right* [handwritten]
5 Blessed are the merciful: for they shall obtain mercy.
Blessed are the pure in heart: for they shall see God.
Blessed are the peacemakers: for they shall be called the
  children of God.
Blessed are they which are persecuted for righteousness'
  sake: for theirs is the kingdom of heaven.
Blessed are ye, when men shall revile you, and persecute
  you, and shall say all manner of evil against you falsely
  for my sake.
10 Rejoice, and be exceeding glad: for great is your reward in
  heaven.

[handwritten margin notes: repetition emphasis; positive tone; x punishment; alliteration rhythm; detailed guide; action-result; reassurance; delayed gratification; subtext]

The Night

In the Name of Allah,[1] *the Compassionate, the Merciful*
By the night, when she lets fall her darkness, and by the
  radiant day! By Him that created the male and the
  female, your endeavors have different ends! *personification* [handwritten]
For him that gives in charity and guards himself against
  evil and believes in goodness, We shall smooth the path
  of salvation; but for him that neither gives nor takes and
  disbelieves in goodness, We shall smooth the path of
  affliction. When he breathes his last, his riches will not
  avail him. *negative streames* [handwritten]
It is for Us to give guidance. Ours is the life of this world,
  Ours the life to come. I warn you, then, of the blazing
  fire, in which none shall burn save the hardened sinner,
  who denies the truth and gives no heed. But the good
  man who purifies himself by almsgiving shall keep away
  from it: and so shall he that does good works for the sake
  of the Most High only, not in recompense for a favor. *one of the pillars* [handwritten]
  Such men shall be content.

1. **Allah** (al′ ə): the Muslim name for God.

Thinking About the Selections

A PERSONAL RESPONSE

sharing impressions

1. What feelings did the spiritual lessons inspire in you? Record your impressions in your journal.

constructing interpretations

2. Provide several examples of conduct that you think demonstrate the ideas put forth in The Beatitudes and "The Night."

Think about
- the qualities valued and rewarded in each selection
- the positive qualities you listed in your journal
- other examples from your own experience

3. If you had to select only one beatitude or one idea presented in "The Night" as a guide for living, which one would you select, and why?

A CREATIVE RESPONSE

4. How might the impact of The Beatitudes be different if Jesus also had mentioned evil qualities, introducing each with the words "Unhappy are"?

A CRITICAL RESPONSE

5. How difficult do you think it is to live today according to the lessons taught by The Beatitudes and "The Night"? Cite passages from the two works in explaining your opinion.

6. Alice Walker's novel *The Temple of My Familiar* includes a chapter titled the "Gospel According to Shug," in which one character provides this personal beatitude: "Helped are those who live in quietness, knowing neither brand name nor fad; they shall live every day as if in eternity, and each moment shall be as full as it is long." What connection do you see between this beatitude and the teachings of Jesus and Mohammed?

from The Popol Vuh

QUICHÉ MAYA   CENTRAL AMERICA

from The Epic of Gilgamesh

BABYLONIA

*A*pproaching the Myths

These two selections are myths. The first selection is a creation myth recorded in The Popol Vuh (pô′ pôl vooh), a sacred book of the Quiché Mayan (kē chā′ mä′ yən) people of Guatemala. The excerpt you will read starts with an account of the world at the beginning of time. In the second paragraph, "it" refers to the world itself. The second selection, a flood myth, is from _The Epic of Gilgamesh_, a Babylonian text that is regarded as the oldest known work of literature. In one episode, the hero-king Gilgamesh, grieving at the death of his best friend, seeks to learn the secret of eternal life from Utnapishtim (oot nə pish′ tim), the only mortal who ultimately escaped death. Utnapishtim is the narrator of the excerpt you will read. In it he tells Gilgamesh how he survived a great flood sent by the gods.

*B*uilding Vocabulary

These essential words are footnoted within the selections.

fruition (froo ish′ ən): It did not come to **fruition**. (page 45)

invoked (in vōkt′): How else can we be **invoked** and remembered? (page 45)

recompense (rek′ əm pens′): Our **recompense** is in words. (page 45)

stupor (stoo′ pər): A **stupor** of despair went up to heaven. (page 51)

libation (lī bā′ shən): I made a sacrifice and poured out a **libation**. (page 53)

*C*onnecting Writing and Reading

What stories have you read in literature that deal with the relationship between gods and humans? For example, some of the Greek myths might come to mind. Jot down notes that describe the myths you remember. As you read the following selections from two ancient texts, notice how they depict the relationship between gods and humans.

from The Popol Vuh

THIS IS THE account, here it is:

> Now it still ripples, now it still murmurs, ripples, it still sighs, still hums, and it is empty under the sky.

Here follow the first words, the first eloquence: _repetition_

There is not yet one person, one animal, bird, fish, crab, tree, rock, hollow, canyon, meadow, forest. Only the sky alone is there; the face of the earth is not clear. Only the sea alone is pooled under all the sky; there is nothing whatever gathered together. It is at rest; not a single thing stirs. It is held back, kept at rest under the sky.

Whatever there is that might be is simply not there: only the pooled water, only the calm sea, only it alone is pooled.

Whatever might be is simply not there: only murmurs, ripples, in the dark, in the night. Only the Maker, Modeler alone, Sovereign Plumed Serpent, the Bearers, Begetters are in the water, a glittering light. They are there, they are enclosed in quetzal[1] feathers, in blue-green.

Thus the name, "Plumed Serpent." They are great knowers, great thinkers in their very being.

And of course there is the sky, and there is also the Heart of Sky. This is the name of the god, as it is spoken.

And then came his word, he came here to the Sovereign Plumed Serpent, here in the blackness, in the early dawn. He spoke with the Sovereign Plumed Serpent, and they talked, then they thought, then they worried. They agreed with each other, they joined their words, their thoughts. Then it was clear, then they reached accord in the light, and then humanity was clear, when they conceived the growth, the generation of trees, of bushes, and the growth of life, of humankind, in the blackness, in the early dawn, all because of the Heart of Sky, named Hurricane. Thunderbolt Hurricane comes first, the second is Newborn Thunderbolt, and the third is Raw Thunderbolt. _three gods in one_

So there were three of them, as Heart of Sky, who came to the Sovereign Plumed Serpent, when the dawn of life was conceived:

"How should it be sown, how should it dawn? Who is to be the provider, nurturer?"

"Let it be this way, think about it: this water should be removed, emptied out for the formation of the earth's own plate and platform, then comes the sowing, the dawning of the sky-earth. But there will be no high days and no bright praise for our work, our design, until the rise of the human work, the human design," they said.

And then the earth arose because of them, it was simply their word that brought it forth. For the forming of the earth they said "Earth." It arose suddenly, just like a cloud, like a mist, now forming, unfolding. Then the mountains were separated from the water, all at once the great mountains came forth. By their genius alone, by their cutting edge alone they carried out the conception of the mountain plain, whose face grew instant groves of cypress and pine.

---

1. **quetzal** (ket säl′): a large, beautiful Central American bird worshiped by both the Aztecs and the Mayans.

And the Plumed Serpent was pleased with this:

"It was good that you came, Heart of Sky, Hurricane, and Newborn Thunderbolt, Raw Thunderbolt. Our work, our design will turn out well," they said.

And the earth was formed first, the mountain plain. The channels of water were separated; their branches wound their ways among the mountains. The waters were divided when the great mountains appeared.

Such was the formation of the earth when it was brought forth by the Heart of Sky, Heart of Earth, as they are called, since they were the first to think of it. The sky was set apart, and the earth was set apart in the midst of the waters.

Such was their plan when they thought, when they worried about the completion of their work.

Now they planned the animals of the mountains, all the guardians of the forests, creatures of the mountains: the deer, birds, pumas, jaguars, serpents, rattlesnakes, yellowbites, guardians of the bushes.

A Bearer, Begetter speaks:

"Why this pointless humming? Why should there merely be rustling beneath the trees and bushes?"

"Indeed—they had better have guardians," the others replied. As soon as they thought it and said it, deer and birds came forth.

And then they gave out homes to the deer and birds:

"You, the deer: sleep along the rivers, in the canyons. Be here in the meadows, in the thickets, in the forests, multiply yourselves. You will stand and walk on all fours," they were told.

So then they established the nests of the birds, small and great:

"You, precious birds: your nests, your houses are in the trees, in the bushes. Multiply there, scatter there, in the branches of trees, the branches of bushes," the deer and birds were told.

When this deed had been done, all of them had received a place to sleep and a place to stay. So it is that the nests of the animals are on the earth, given by the Bearer, Begetter. Now the arrangement of the deer and birds was complete.

And then the deer and birds were told by the Maker, Modeler, Bearer, Begetter:

"Talk, speak out. Don't moan, don't cry out. Please talk, each to each, within each kind, within each group," they were told—the deer, birds, puma, jaguar, serpent.

"Name now our names, praise us. We are your mother, we are your father. Speak now:

'Hurricane,
Newborn Thunderbolt, Raw Thunderbolt,
Heart of Sky, Heart of Earth,
Maker, Modeler,
Bearer, Begetter,'

speak, pray to us, keep our days," they were told. But it didn't turn out that they spoke like people: they just squawked, they just chattered, they just howled. It wasn't apparent what language they spoke; each one gave a different cry. When the Maker, Modeler heard this:

"It hasn't turned out well, they haven't spoken," they said among themselves. "It hasn't turned out that our names have been named. Since we are their mason and sculptor, this will not do," the Bearers and Begetters said among themselves. So they told them:

"You will simply have to be transformed. Since it hasn't turned out well and you haven't spoken, we have changed our word:

"What you feed on, what you eat, the places where you sleep, the places where you stay, whatever is yours will remain in the canyons, the forests. Although it turned out that our days were not kept, nor did you pray to us, there may yet be strength in the keeper of days, the giver of praise whom we have yet to make. Just accept your service, just let your flesh be eaten.

"So be it, this must be your service," they were told when they were instructed—the animals, small and great, on the face of the earth.

And then they wanted to test their timing again, they wanted to experiment again, and they wanted to prepare for the keeping of days again. They had not heard their speech among the animals; it did not come to fruition[2] and it was not complete.

And so their flesh was brought low: they served, they were eaten, they were killed—the animals on the face of the earth.

Again there comes an experiment with the human work, the human design, by the Maker, Modeler, Bearer, Begetter:

"It must simply be tried again. The time for the planting and dawning is nearing. For this we must make a provider and nurturer. How else can we be invoked[3] and remembered on the face of the earth? We have already made our first try at our work and design, but it turned out that they didn't keep our days, nor did they glorify us.

"So now let's try to make a giver of praise, giver of respect, provider, nurturer," they said.

So then comes the building and working with earth and mud. They made a body, but it didn't look good to them. It was just separating, just crumbling, just loosening, just softening, just disintegrating, and just dissolving. Its head wouldn't turn, either. Its face was just lopsided, its face was just twisted. It couldn't look around. It talked at first, but senselessly. It was quickly dissolving in the water.

"It won't last," the mason and sculptor said then. "It seems to be dwindling away, so let it just dwindle. It can't walk and it can't multiply, so let it be merely a thought," they said.

So then they dismantled, again they brought down their work and design. Again they talked:

"What is there for us to make that would turn out well, that would succeed in keeping our days and praying to us?" they said. Then they planned again:

"We'll just tell Xpiyacoc, Xmucane, Hunahpu Possum, Hunahpu Coyote,[4] to try a counting of days, a counting of lots,"[5] the mason and sculptor said to themselves. Then they invoked Xpiyacoc, Xmucane.

Then comes the naming of those who are the midmost seers: the "Grandmother of Day, Grandmother of Light," as the Maker, Modeler called them. These are names of Xpiyacoc and Xmucane.

When Hurricane had spoken with the Sovereign Plumed Serpent, they invoked the daykeepers, diviners, the midmost seers:

"There is yet to find, yet to discover how we are to model a person, construct a person again, a provider, nurturer, so that we are called upon and we are recognized: our recompense[6] is in words.

---

2. fruition (fr$\overline{oo}$ ish′ ən): a state of bearing fruit, of having results.
3. invoked (in vōkt′): named in a sacred prayer, especially in order to summon forth.
4. Xpiyacoc, Xmucane, Hunahpu Possum, Hunahpu Coyote (shpē yä′ kôk, shmoo kä′ ne, hoo nuh′ poo): divine figures, acording to Quiché Mayan belief. Xpiyacoc and Xmucane are older than all other gods and are thus addressed as grandparents.
5. lots: pebbles, chips of woods, seeds, dice, etc., used to determine a question by chance.
6. recompense (rek′ əm pens′): repayment.

Midwife, matchmaker,
our grandmother, our grandfather,
Xpiyacoc, Xmucane,
let there be planting, let there be the
    dawning
of our invocation, our sustenance,
    our recognition
by the human work, the human design,
the human figure, the human mass.

So be it, fulfill your names:

Hunahpu Possum, Hunahpu Coyote,
Bearer twice over, Begetter twice over,
Great Peccary,[7] Great Tapir,[8]
lapidary, jeweler,
sawyer, carpenter,
Maker of the Blue-Green Plate,
Maker of the Blue-Green Bowl,
incense maker, master craftsman,
Grandmother of Day, Grandmother
    of Light.

You have been called upon because of our work, our design. Run your hands over the kernels of corn, over the seeds of the coral tree, just get it done, just let it come out whether we should carve and gouge a mouth, a face in wood," they told the daykeepers.

And then comes the borrowing, the counting of days; the hand is moved over the corn kernels, over the coral seeds, the days, the lots.

Then they spoke to them, one of them a grandmother, the other a grandfather.

This is the grandfather, this is the master of the coral seeds: Xpiyacoc is his name.

And this is the grandmother, the daykeeper, diviner who stands behind others: Xmucane is her name.

And they said, as they set out the days:

"Just let it be found, just let it be discovered,
say it, our ear is listening,
may you talk, may you speak,

just find the wood for the carving and
    sculpting
by the builder, sculptor.
Is this to be the provider, the nurturer
when it comes to the planting, the
    dawning?
You corn kernels, you coral seeds,
you days, you lots:
may you succeed, may you be accurate,"

they said to the corn kernels, coral seeds, days, lots. "Have shame, you up there, Heart of Sky: attempt no deception before the mouth and face of Sovereign Plumed Serpent," they said. Then they spoke straight to the point:

"It is well that there be your manikins, woodcarvings, talking, speaking, there on the face of the earth."

"So be it," they replied. The moment they spoke it was done: the manikins, woodcarvings, human in looks and human in speech.

This was the peopling of the face of the earth:

They came into being, they multiplied, they had daughters, they had sons, these manikins, woodcarvings. But there was nothing in their hearts and nothing in their minds, no memory of their mason and builder. They just went and walked wherever they wanted. Now they did not remember the Heart of Sky.

And so they fell, just an experiment and just a cutout for humankind. They were talking at first but their faces were dry. They were not yet developed in the legs and arms. They had no blood, no lymph. They had no sweat, no fat. Their complexions were dry, their faces were crusty. They flailed their legs and arms, their bodies were deformed.

---

7. peccary (pek′ ə rē): piglike mammal of North and South America.

8. tapir (tā′ pər): another hoglike mammal of tropical America.

And so they accomplished nothing before the Maker, Modeler who gave them birth, gave them heart. They became the first numerous people here on the face of the earth.

Again there comes a humiliation, destruction, and demolition. The manikins, woodcarvings were killed when the Heart of Sky devised a flood for them. A great flood was made; it came down on the heads of the manikins, woodcarvings.

The man's body was carved from the wood of the coral tree by the Maker, Modeler. And as for the woman, the Maker, Modeler needed the pith of reeds for the woman's body. They were not competent, nor did they speak before the builder and sculptor who made them and brought them forth, and so they were killed, done in by a flood:

There came a rain of resin from the sky.

There came the one named Gouger of Faces: he gouged out their eyeballs.

There came Sudden Bloodletter: he snapped off their heads.

There came Crunching Jaguar: he ate their flesh.

There came Tearing Jaguar: he tore them open.

They were pounded down to the bones and tendons, smashed and pulverized even to the bones. Their faces were smashed because they were incompetent before their mother and their father, the Heart of Sky, named Hurricane. The earth was blackened because of this; the black rainstorm began, rain all day and rain all night. Into their houses came the animals, small and great. Their faces were crushed by things of wood and stone. Everything spoke: their water jars, their tortilla griddles, their plates, their cooking pots, their dogs, their grinding stones, each and every thing crushed their faces. Their dogs and turkeys told them:

"You caused us pain, you ate us, but now it is *you* whom *we* shall eat." And this is the grinding stone:

"We were undone because of you.

Every day, every day,
in the dark, in the dawn, forever,
r-r-rip, r-r-rip,
r-r-rub, r-r-rub,
right in our faces, because of you.

This was the service we gave you at first, when you were still people, but today you will learn of our power. We shall pound and we shall grind your flesh," their grinding stones told them.

And this is what their dogs said, when they spoke in their turn:

"Why is it you can't seem to give us our food? We just watch and you just keep us down, and you throw us around. You keep a stick ready when you eat, just so you can hit us. We don't talk, so we've received nothing from you. How could you not have known? You *did* know that we were wasting away there, behind you.

"So, this very day you will taste the teeth in our mouths. We shall eat you," their dogs told them, and their faces were crushed.

And then their tortilla griddles and cooking pots spoke to them in turn:

"Pain! That's all you've done for us. Our mouths are sooty, our faces are sooty. By setting us on the fire all the time, you burn us. Since *we* felt no pain, *you* try it. We shall burn you," all their cooking pots said, crushing their faces.

The stones, their hearthstones were shooting out, coming right out of the fire, going for their heads, causing them pain. Now they run for it, helter-skelter.

They want to climb up on the houses, but they fall as the houses collapse.

They want to climb the trees; they're thrown off by the trees.

They want to get inside caves, but the caves slam shut in their faces.

Such was the scattering of the human work, the human design. The people were ground down, overthrown. The mouths and faces of all of them were destroyed and crushed. And it used to be said that the monkeys in the forests today are a sign of this. They were left as a sign because wood alone was used for their flesh by the builder and sculptor.

So this is why monkeys look like people: they are a sign of a previous human work, human design—mere manikins, mere wood-carvings.

And here is the beginning of the conception of humans, and of the search for the ingredients of the human body. So they spoke, the Bearer, Begetter, the Makers, Modelers named Sovereign Plumed Serpent:

"The dawn has approached, preparations have been made, and morning has come for the provider, nurturer, born in the light, begotten in the light. Morning has come for humankind, for the people of the face of the earth," they said. It all came together as they went on thinking in the darkness, in the night, as they searched and they sifted, they thought and they wondered.

And here their thoughts came out in clear light. They sought and discovered what was needed for human flesh. It was only a short while before the sun, moon, and stars were to appear above the Makers and Modelers. Broken Place, Bitter Water Place is the name: the yellow corn, white corn came from there.

And these are the names of the animals who brought the food: fox, coyote, parrot, crow. There were four animals who brought the news of the ears of yellow corn and white corn. They were coming from over there at Broken Place, they showed the way to the break.

And this was when they found the staple foods.

And these were the ingredients for the flesh of the human work, the human design, and the water was for the blood. It became human blood, and corn was also used by the Bearer, Begetter.

And so they were happy over the provisions of the good mountain, filled with sweet things, thick with yellow corn, white corn, and thick with pataxte and cacao, countless zapotes, anonas, jocotes, nances, matasanos,[9] sweets —the rich foods filling up the citadel named Broken Place, Bitter Water Place. All the edible fruits were there: small staples, great staples, small plants, great plants. The way was shown by the animals.

And then the yellow corn and the white corn were ground, and Xmucane did the grinding nine times. Corn was used, along with the water she rinsed her hands with, for the creation of grease; it became human fat when it was worked by the Bearer, Begetter, Sovereign Plumed Serpent, as they are called.

After that, they put it into words:

the making, the modeling of our first
   mother-father,
with yellow corn, white corn alone for the
   flesh,
food alone for the human legs and arms,
for our first fathers, the four human works.

It was staples alone that made up their flesh.

These are the names of the first people who were made and modeled.
This is the first person: Jaguar Quitze.[10]
And now the second: Jaguar Night.
And now the third: Mahucutah.[11]
And the fourth: True Jaguar.

---

9. **pataxte and cacao . . . zapotes, anonas, jocotes, nances, matasanos:** tropical fruits and seeds.
10. **Quitze** (kē chä′).
11. **Mahucutah** (mu hoo koo′ tuh).

And these are the names of our first mother-fathers. They were simply made and modeled, it is said; they had no mother and no father. We have named the men by themselves. No woman gave birth to them, nor were they begotten by the builder, sculptor, Bearer, Begetter. By sacrifice alone, by genius alone they were made, they were modeled by the Maker, Modeler, Bearer, Begetter, Sovereign Plumed Serpent. And when they came to fruition, they came out human:

They talked and they made words.
They looked and they listened.
They walked, they worked.

They were good people, handsome, with looks of the male kind. Thoughts came into existence and they gazed; their vision came all at once. Perfectly they saw, perfectly they knew everything under the sky, whenever they looked. The moment they turned around and looked around in the sky, on the earth, everything was seen without any obstruction. They didn't have to walk around before they could see what was under the sky; they just stayed where they were.

As they looked, their knowledge became intense. Their sight passed through trees, through rocks, through lakes, through seas, through mountains, through plains. Jaguar Quitze, Jaguar Night, Mahucutah, and True Jaguar were truly gifted people.

And then they were asked by the builder and mason:

"What do you know about your being? Don't you look, don't you listen? Isn't your speech good, and your walk? So you must look, to see out under the sky. Don't you see the mountain plain clearly? So try it," they were told.

And then they saw everything under the sky perfectly. After that, they thanked the Maker, Modeler:

"Truly now,
double thanks, triple thanks

that we've been formed, we've been given
our mouths, our faces,
we speak, we listen,
we wonder, we move,
our knowledge is good, we've understood
what is far and near,
and we've seen what is great and small
under the sky, on the earth,
Thanks to you we've been formed,
we've come to be made and modeled,
our grandmother, our grandfather."

They said when they gave thanks for having been made and modeled. They understood everything perfectly, they sighted the four sides, the four corners in the sky, on the earth, and this didn't sound good to the builder and sculptor:

"What our works and designs have said is no good:
'We have understood everything, great and small,' they say." And so the Bearer, Begetter took back their knowledge.

"What should we do with them now? Their vision should at least reach nearby, they should see at least a small part of the face of the earth, but what they're saying isn't good. Aren't they merely 'works' and 'designs' in their very names? Yet they'll become as great as gods, unless they procreate, proliferate at the sowing, the dawning, unless they increase."

"Let it be this way: now we'll take them apart just a little, that's what we need. What we've found out isn't good. Their deeds would become equal to ours, just because their knowledge reaches so far. They see everything," so said

Guide for Interpretation

Think about the gods' predicament in having created perfect human beings. As you read the rest of the selection and discover their solution, consider what this conclusion to the myth of creation reveals about the Quiché Mayans' view of themselves, their gods, and the world.

gods need to be needed,
humans no longer need
gods

from The Popol Vuh 49

the Heart of Sky, Hurricane,
Newborn Thunderbolt, Raw Thunderbolt,
Sovereign Plumed Serpent,
Bearer, Begetter,
Xpiyacoc, Xmucane,
Maker, Modeler,

as they are called. And when they changed the nature of their works, their designs, it was enough that the eyes be marred by the Heart of Sky. They were blinded as the face of a mirror is breathed upon. Their eyes were weakened. Now it was only when they looked nearby that things were clear.

And such was the loss of the means of understanding, along with the means of knowing everything, by the four humans. The root was implanted.

And such was the making, modeling of our first grandfather, our father, by the Heart of Sky, Heart of Earth.

from The Epic of Gilgamesh

YOU KNOW THE city Shurrupak,[1] it stands on the banks of Euphrates? That city grew old and the gods that were in it were old. There was Anu,[2] Lord of the firmament, their father, and warrior Enlil[3] their counselor, Ninurta[4] the helper, and Ennugi[5] watcher over canals; and with them also was Ea.[6] In those days the world teemed, the people multiplied, the world bellowed like a wild bull, and the great god was aroused by the clamor. Enlil heard the clamor and he said to the gods in council, 'The uproar of mankind is intolerable and sleep is no longer possible by reason of the babel.'[7] So the gods agreed to exterminate mankind. Enlil did this, but Ea because of his oath warned me in a dream. He whispered their words to my house of reeds, 'Reed-house, reed-house! Wall, O wall, hearken reed-house, wall reflect; O man of Shurrupak, son of Ubara-Tutu; tear down your house and build a boat, abandon possessions and look for life, despise worldly goods and save your soul alive. Tear down your house, I say, and build a boat. These are the measurements of the barque as you shall build her: let her beam equal her length, let her deck be roofed like the vault that covers the abyss; then take up into the boat the seed of all living creatures.'

"When I had understood I said to my lord, 'Behold, what you have commanded I will honor and perform, but how shall I answer the people, the city, the elders?' Then Ea opened his mouth and said to me, his servant, 'Tell them this: I have learnt that Enlil is wrathful against me, I dare no longer walk in his land nor live in his city; I will go down to the Gulf[8] to dwell with Ea my lord. But on you he will

---

1. **Shurrupak** (shoo′ roo puk).
2. **Anu** (u′ noo): god of the sky.
3. **Enlil** (ên′ lil): god of the atmosphere.
4. **Ninurta** (ni noor′ tə).
5. **Ennugi** (en′ oog i).
6. **Ea** (e′ ə): god of water.
7. **babel** (bā′ bəl): a confusion of sounds.
8. **Gulf:** the great depths of water where Ea was supposed to dwell.

rain down abundance, rare fish and shy wild-fowl, a rich harvest-tide. In the evening the rider of the storm will bring you wheat in torrents.'

"In the first light of dawn all my household gathered round me, the children brought pitch and the men whatever was necessary. On the fifth day I laid the keel and the ribs, then I made fast the planking. The ground-space was one acre; each side of the deck measured one hundred and twenty cubits,[9] making a square. I built six decks below, seven in all; I divided them into nine sections with bulkheads between. I drove in wedges where needed, saw to the punt-holes, and laid in supplies. The carriers brought oil in baskets; I poured pitch into the furnace and asphalt and oil; more oil was consumed in caulking, and more again the master of the boat took into his stores. I slaughtered bullocks for the people and every day I killed sheep. I gave the shipwrights wine to drink as though it were river water, raw wine and red wine and oil and white wine. There was feasting then as there is at the time of the New Year's festival; I myself anointed my head. On the seventh day the boat was complete.

"Then was the launching full of difficulty; there was shifting of ballast above and below till two-thirds was submerged. I loaded into her all that I had of gold and of living things, my family, my kin, the beasts of the field both wild and tame, and all the craftsmen. I sent them on board, for the time that Shamash had ordained[10] was already fulfilled when he said, 'In the evening, when the rider of the storm sends down the destroying rain, enter the boat and batten her down.' The time was fulfilled, the evening came, the rider of the storm sent down the rain. I looked out at the weather and it was terrible, so I too boarded the boat and battened her down. All was now complete, the battening and the caulking; so I handed the tiller to Puzur-Amurri[11] the steersman, with the navigation and the care of the whole boat.

"With the first light of dawn a black cloud came from the horizon; it thundered within where Adad, Lord of the storm, was riding. In front over hill and plain Shullat and Hanish, heralds of the storm, led on. Then the gods of the abyss rose up; Nergal pulled out the dams of the nether waters, Ninurta the warlord threw down the dykes, and the seven judges of hell, the Annunaki, raised their torches, lighting the land with their livid flame. A stupor[12] of despair went up to heaven when the god of the storm turned daylight to darkness, when he smashed the land like a cup. One whole day the tempest raged, gathering fury as it went. It poured over the people like the tides of battle; a man could not see his brother nor the people to be seen from heaven. Even the gods were terrified at the flood; they fled to the highest heaven, the firmament of Anu; they crouched against the walls, cowering like curs.

"Then Ishtar[13] the sweet-voiced Queen of Heaven cried out like a woman in travail: 'Alas, the days of old are turned to dust because I commanded evil; why did I command this evil in the council of all the gods? I commanded wars to destroy the people, but are they not my people, for I brought them forth? Now like the spawn of fish they

> **Guide for Interpretation**
>
> Think back to the gods' use of a flood in The Popol Vuh. Consider the similarities and differences between these two examples of destruction by flood.

---

9. **one hundred and twenty cubits** (kyoo′ bits): between 179 and 207 feet.
10. **ordained** (ôr dānd′): established by declaration or decree.
11. **Puzur-Amurri** (poo′ zoor u′ moo ri).
12. **stupor** (stoo′ pər): a state of emotional numbness or loss of feeling.
13. **Ishtar** (ish′ tär): goddess of love, fertility, maternity, and war.

Gilgamesh Under Attack by Wild Animals, 8th Century B.C. Western Iranian artist.
Werner Forman Archive, London.

float in the ocean.' The great gods of heaven and of hell wept; they covered their mouths.

"For six days and six nights the winds blew, torrent and tempest and flood overwhelmed the world, and tempest and flood raged together like warring hosts. When the seventh day dawned the storm from the south subsided, the sea grew calm, the flood was stilled. I looked at the face of the world and there was silence; all mankind was turned to clay. The surface of the sea stretched as flat as a rooftop; I opened a hatch and the light fell on my face. Then I bowed low, I sat down and I wept; the tears streamed down my face, for on every side was the waste of water. I looked for land in vain, but fourteen leagues distant there appeared a mountain, and there the boat grounded. On the mountain of Nisir the boat held fast; she held fast and did not budge. One day she held, and a second day on the mountain of Nisir she held fast and did not budge. A third day and fourth day she held fast on the mountain and did not budge; a fifth day and a sixth day she held fast on the mountain. When the seventh day dawned I loosed a dove and let her go. She flew away, but finding no resting place she returned. Then I loosed a swallow and she flew away, but finding no resting place she returned. I loosed a raven, she saw that the waters had retreated, she ate, she flew around, she cawed, and she did not come back. Then I threw everything open to the four winds; I made a sacrifice and poured out a libation[14] on the mountain top. Seven and again seven cauldrons I set up on their stands; I heaped up wood and cane and cedar and myrtle. When the gods smelled the sweet savor, they gathered like flies over the sacrifice. Then, at last, Ishtar also came; she lifted her necklace with the jewels of heaven that once Anu had made to please her. 'O you gods here present, by the lapis lazuli[15] round my neck I shall remember these days as I remember the jewels of my throat; these last days I shall not forget. Let all the gods gather round the sacrifice, except

Enlil. He shall not approach this offering, for without reflection he brought the flood; he consigned my people to destruction.'

"When Enlil had come, when he saw the boat, he was wrathful and swelled with anger at the gods, the host of heaven. 'Has any of these mortals escaped? Not one was to have survived the destruction.' Then the god of the wells and canals Ninurta opened his mouth and said to the warrior Enlil, 'Who is there of the gods that can devise without Ea? It is Ea alone who knows all things.' Then Ea opened his mouth and spoke to warrior Enlil, 'Wisest of gods, hero Enlil, how could you so senselessly bring down the flood?

Lay upon the sinner his sin,
Lay upon the transgressor his transgression,
Punish him a little when he breaks loose,
Do not drive him too hard or he perishes;
Would that a lion had ravaged mankind
Rather than the flood,
Would that a wolf had ravaged mankind
Rather than the flood,
Would that famine had wasted the world
Rather than the flood,
Would that pestilence had wasted mankind
Rather than the flood.

It was not I that revealed the secret of the gods; the wise man learned it in a dream. Now take your counsel what shall be done with him.'

"Then Enlil went up into the boat, he took me by the hand and my wife and made us enter the boat and kneel down on either side, he standing between us. He touched our foreheads to bless us saying, 'In time past Utnapishtim was a mortal man; henceforth he and his wife shall live in the distance at the mouth of the rivers.' Thus it was that the gods took me and placed me here to live in the distance, at the mouth of the rivers."

---

14. **libation** (lī bā′ shən): a drink poured onto the ground in honor of the gods.

15. **lapis lazuli** (lap′ is laz′ yoo lī): a semiprecious stone of rich azure blue.

Thinking About the Myths

A PERSONAL RESPONSE

sharing impressions

1. What do you think of the accounts of creation and other cosmic events presented in these two myths? Write your reaction to these accounts in your journal.

constructing interpretations

2. How would you describe the Mayan gods in The Popol Vuh and the Babylonian gods in the Gilgamesh epic?

Think about
- their powers and realms of responsibility
- how closely they fit your image of a divine being
- their relationship with humans
- the similarities and differences between the Mayan and Babylonian gods

3. Characterize the human beings and their relationship to the gods in each selection. Cite examples to support your views.

4. Which flood seems more terrible to you, the one in The Popol Vuh or the one in *The Epic of Gilgamesh*? Tell why.

Think about
- the reasons the gods have for sending each flood
- the language used to describe each flood
- the aftermath of each flood

A CREATIVE RESPONSE

5. How might the Mayan or Babylonian gods respond to contemporary human beings? Explain why you think so.

A CRITICAL RESPONSE

6. Based on what you have learned from these selections, what do you find most interesting about the ancient Mayan and Babylonian cultures?

Think about
- valued personal qualities and social behavior
- each culture's view of the world and of its gods

7. Point out parallels that you recognize between these stories and others you may be familiar with, such as the Biblical account of creation, the story of Noah and the ark, or the Greek myth of Deucalion and Pyrrha.

8. Attempting to account for the large number of flood myths from around the world, author Penelope Farmer writes, "I would ascribe these myths . . . to that basic and clearly universal human longing—manifested less dramatically when a man changes jobs or his house—to get rid of an unsatisfying past and start all over again." Do you accept Farmer's idea, or does some other possible explanation for the large number of flood myths come to mind? Support your opinion.

Analyzing the Writer's Craft

MYTHS

What distinguishes these myths from other traditional stories, such as folk tales and fairy tales? Think about some specific differences.

Building a Literary Vocabulary. Unlike other types of traditional stories, a myth is a story, once widely believed to be true, that attempts to explain why the world is the way it is or why things in nature happen as they do. Usually myths interpret events as resulting from the actions of supernatural beings. For example, The Popol Vuh answers the basic question How was the earth created? by explaining that the gods of the sea and sky caused land to appear simply by saying, "Earth." Myths can be viewed as essentially religious, presenting the cosmic view of a cultural group.

Application: Analyzing Myths. Identify at least five natural phenomena besides floods that are explained by these two myths. Write these explanations in the form of questions and answers.

Connecting Reading and Writing

1. Write a **proposal** to a publishing company explaining why you think that either The Popol Vuh or the Gilgamesh epic should be published in an illustrated edition. Refer to sections of the myth that lend themselves to vivid illustration.

Option: In **notes** to a book editor, write illustration suggestions for either work. Indicate the content and placement of each illustration.

2. In a **feature article** for a humor magazine, write a myth-like explanation of some aspect of the modern world. For example, you might explain why cars break down or why seniors treat sophomores as they do.

Option: Present your modern explanation in the form of a **script** for a skit.

3. According to Joseph Campbell, myths have four functions: to instill a sense of awe at the mystery of the universe, to explain the workings of the natural world, to support and validate certain social customs, and to guide people through the trials of living. In a brief **introduction** to either The Popol Vuh or the Gilgamesh epic, explain how the work performs one of the functions described by Campbell.

Option: In a **letter** to your teacher, justify your choice of one of the myths as the topic for a research paper.

4. Based on what you have learned from these two myths and from the other selections in **Recognizing Spiritual Connections**, write a **sermon** about the various ways that people have viewed divinity.

Option: Create a **dialogue** to be read in class depicting the relationship between one of the gods you have read about and a human being.

The End of the World

FANG EQUATORIAL AFRICA

Approaching the Myth

Just as people want to know how the world began, so too are they concerned with how it may end. You may have heard warnings about Judgment Day, nuclear annihilation, destruction of the ozone layer, or some other cause of global doom. Here is a prediction of the Fang people, who come from the thickly-forested land of Gabon in equatorial Africa. Think about the story in connection with other myths you have read, considering the qualities attributed to deities in each culture.

THE TRIBE LISTENS silently. Only one man speaks.

"In the beginning sun and moon were man and wife. The moon bore the sun many children and they were called the stars. This family did not eat food of the kind we eat; it nourished itself on fire, and so the whole family shone and gave light to us on earth. In the beginning sun and moon were man and wife. The stars were their children.

"And then one day there came to the village a young man so handsome that the moon's heart was instantly enflamed by love. She gave him a token and said, 'Wait for me at the bend in the road and I will fly away with you forever.'

" 'Where is she?' the sun asked his children the stars when he noticed the moon's absence. They did not know. 'Where is she I ask you?' But now he shone so angrily the stars ran away from him. 'You must have helped her flee,' he said and began to hunt them down. Every time he caught a star he devoured it, and that star shone no more. But the rest were too scattered and numerous for him to catch and eat them all.

"And so each day still the sun chases moon and stars across the sky. Sometimes he eats another of the stars; the moon, good mother that she is, tries to protect her children, warning them of the sun's rising and taking them with her to her hiding place.

"This chase will last a long time. But it must come to an end some day. And that day will be brought about by us, us men. It is for us to uphold the rule of good on earth. If we do not, then evil will reign instead. And on the day that evil reigns the sun will capture his wife at last, but this time he will not devour her. The sun will lock the moon in a deep ditch at the center of the earth and he will never let her rise again. As for the stars, her children: their father, the sun, will soon catch and eat them, every one."

"And what will be our fate?" asks the tribe.

The speaker sighs. "Who knows? Who knows? I do not know, my brothers."

Offering
Worldly Wisdom

Among all the forms of human expression, the tale is surely one of the oldest. From the beginning of human culture, the telling of tales has served as a way to get through an evening, to keep out the darkness or the rain, to remember harder times or better ones, to refresh the spirit, to distract the mind, to educate the young. Throughout centuries of storytelling, the tale has been a way to examine and give form to human experience—a way to offer worldly wisdom to every new generation. To be sure, other literary forms are old and valuable. Poetry expresses the subtleties of human emotions or recounts the glories of epic achievement. Myths and hymns of praise survey lofty ideals, probe deeper spiritual concerns. The tale, though, is perhaps best able to display everyday human behavior and its consequences. It thus illuminates the very texture of life.

FOLK TALES WITH A MORAL

In every human culture, the narrative art has been used both to entertain and to convey cherished values. For example, a folk tale that delights listeners or readers might also warn of the dangers of greed or ingratitude. The heroine of a fairy tale might embody the most highly regarded virtues of a society. A good tale, then, is more than an amusement; it is also a demonstration of the art of living.

As you read the tales that follow, watch for cause and effect in the actions of characters. Be ready to identify and evaluate human qualities, such as pride, loyalty, and distrust. Observe that the unfolding of a plot can sometimes demonstrate a principle of moral conduct.

IN THE FOLK TRADITION

The typical folk tale is a product of oral tradition. That is, it has been passed down by word of mouth among a people, perhaps for hundreds of years, and has no single author. Some tales, however, are the creation of individual writers who have used this literary form to convey important lessons about society or individual human conduct. As you read the folk tales that follow, think about the wisdom they may have to offer. Note their unique ability to imitate life and transmit human values.

Whether spun from the folk imagination of many generations or wrought by a gifted writer, tales are part of the legacy of any culture. They embody the accumulated wisdom of civilization and are among its most precious artifacts.

*L*iterary Vocabulary

INTRODUCED IN THIS SECTION

Plot. Plot refers to the actions and events in a literary work. In the plot of "The Mustard Seed," Gotami asks Buddha for a medicine that will bring her son back to life. Buddha instructs her to collect mustard seeds from every house in which no one has died. Gotami finds that no house has been untouched by death.

Suspense. Suspense is the excitement or tension that readers feel as they become involved in the plot and eager to know the outcome. In the excerpt from The Popol Vuh, a certain degree of suspense arises as the reader becomes curious about each attempt to create the world.

Folk Tale. A folk tale is a story that is handed down, usually by word of mouth, from generation to generation. Folk tales reflect the unique characteristics of a region, such as how the inhabitants live and what their values are. One type of folk tale is the fairy tale, a children's story in which magic plays a central role.

Motif. A motif is an element that recurs in a literary work or in a group of literary works. Some of the same motifs can be found in tales from a variety of cultures. The motif of the fairy godmother, for example, appears in the familiar Italian tale "Pinocchio" as well as in many other tales from around the world.

Allegory. A narrative in which characters and actions stand for or illustrate abstract ideas is called an allegory. Through the relationship between characters and their actions, the writer of an allegory is able to teach a lesson about human conduct or experience. For example, the writer of an allegory might create characters that stand for good and evil, thus expressing a specific idea about human nature.

Characterization. Characterization refers to the techniques that a writer uses to develop characters. Describing physical appearance is one way to communicate something about a character. A character's nature may be revealed through his or her own speech, thoughts, feelings, or actions, as well as through the speech, feelings, thoughts, or actions of other characters. In addition, direct comments made by the narrator can often provide insight into the character's nature and previous experience. In "Ogun," one of the "Homages to Orisha," physical description and description of actions allow the reader to perceive Ogun as a mighty warrior-god who is to be feared.

Point of View. Point of view is the narrative method used in a literary work. In the first-person point of view, the narrator is a character in the selection who describes the action in his or her own words. In the third-person point of view, the story is told by a narrator who is outside the action of the story. "The End of the World" and the excerpt from The Popol Vuh employ a third-person narrator. If a story is told from an omniscient, or all-knowing, third-person point of view, the narrator sees into the minds of more than one character.

The Lady Who Was a Beggar

Approaching the Tale

This story was first written down in the seventeenth century, but the events narrated take place in twelfth-century China, the time of the Sung Dynasty. During this period, China had a complex, highly stratified social system governed by a network of scholar-officials.

The work combines prose with verse, using a form that first appeared at the end of the tenth century. The Chinese considered prose fiction a lesser form of expression than poetry. Prose was thought to have merit only if it offered moral guidance. Because of this negative view of prose, many writers who had their prose published, including the author of "The Lady Who Was a Beggar," did so anonymously.

As you encounter the Chinese names in this story, be aware that the family name is listed first; thus, Chin Lao-ta (jin lou tä) belongs to the Chin family, and Mo Chi (mō jē) to the Mo family. Certain other names, Jade Slave and Scabby, are probably translations of Chinese nicknames.

Building Vocabulary

These essential words are footnoted within the story.

aspirations (as′ pə rā′ shəns): Being a man of social **aspirations**, he decided to relinquish this post. (page 61)

auspicious (ô spish′ əs): They selected an **auspicious** day, and the Chin family even provided clothes for Mo Chi to wear at the wedding. (page 62)

contravene (kän′ trə vēn′): She did not like to **contravene** his wishes. (page 64)

predestined (prē des′ tind): A marriage is **predestined**: no objection can prevail. (page 69)

Connecting Writing and Reading

If you wanted to improve your social position in your school, how would you go about it? In your journal, list several actions that you might take. After considering these actions, note the possible effects of the actions on how you feel about yourself and on how others regard you. As you read this story, think about the view of social position it presents.

*I*T IS TOLD that in the Shao-hsing[1] reign period of the Sung dynasty (1131–1163), although Lin-an had been made the capital city and was a wealthy and populous district, still the great number of beggars had not diminished. Among them was one who acted as their head. He was called the "tramp-major" and looked after all the beggars. Whenever they managed to beg something, the tramp-major would demand a fee for the day. Then when it was raining or snow lay on the ground, and there was nowhere to go to beg, the tramp-major would boil up a drop of thin gruel and feed the whole beggar band. Their tattered robes and jackets were also in his care. The result was that the whole crowd of the beggars were careful to obey him, with bated breath like a lot of slaves, and none of them dared offend him.

The tramp-major was thus provided with a regular income, and as a rule he would lend out sums of money among the beggars and extort a tidy interest. In this way, if he neither gambled nor went carousing, he could build up a going concern out of it. He depended on this for his livelihood, and never for a moment thought of changing his profession. There was only one drawback: a tramp-major did not have a very good name. Though he acquired land by his efforts, and his family had prospered for generations, still he was a boss of the beggars and not to be compared with ordinary respectable people. No one would salute him with respect if he showed himself out-of-doors, and so the only thing for him to do was to shut his doors and play the great man in his own home.

And yet, distinguishing the worthy from the base, we count among the latter only actors, yamen-runners,[2] and soldiers: we certainly do not include beggars. For what is wrong with beggars is not that they are covered in sores, but simply that they have no money. There have been men like the minister Wu Tzu-hsü,[3] of Ch'un-ch'iu[4] times, who as a fugitive from oppression played his pipes and begged his food in the marketplace of Wu; or Cheng Yüan-ho of T'ang times, who sang the beggar's song of "Lien-hua lo" but later rose to wealth and eminence and covered his bed with brocade. These were great men, though beggars: clearly, we may hold beggars in contempt, but we should not compare them with the actors, the runners, and soldiery.

Let us digress no longer, but tell now how in the city of Hangchow there was once a tramp-major by the name of Chin Lao-ta. In the course of seven generations, his ancestors had developed the profession into a perfect family business so that Chin Lao-ta ate well and dressed well, lived in a fine house and cultivated good land. His barns were well stocked with grain and his purse with money; he made loans and kept servants; if not quite the wealthiest, he was certainly one of the rich. Being a man of social aspirations,[5] he decided to relinquish this post of tramp-major into the hands of a relative, "Scabby" Chin, while he himself took his ease with what he had and mingled no more with the beggar band. But unfortunately, the neighbors were used to speaking of "the tramp-major's family," and the name persisted in spite of his efforts.

Chin Lao-ta was over fifty. He had lost his wife and had no son, but only a daughter whose name was Jade Slave. Jade Slave was beautiful, as we are told by a verse about her:

---

1. **Shao-hsing** (shou Hiŋ).
2. **yamen-runners** (yäm' ən run' ərz): people who run errands for a Chinese government official or department.
3. **Wu Tzu-hsü** (wo͞o dzə Hü).
4. **Ch'un-ch'iu** (cho͞on chyo͞o).
5. **aspirations** (as' pə rā' shəns): ambitions.

Pure to compare with jade,
Gracious to shame the flowers,
Given the adornments of the court
Here would be another Chang Li-hua.[6]

Chin Lao-ta prized his daughter as a jewel and taught her from an early age to read and write. By the age of fifteen, she was adept in prose and verse, composing as fast as her hand could write. She was equally proficient in the womanly crafts and in performing on the harp or flute: everything she did proclaimed her skill. Her beauty and talent inspired Chin Lao-ta to seek a husband for her among the scholar class. But the fact was that among families of name and rank it would be difficult to find anyone anxious to marry the girl—no one wanted a tramp-major's daughter. On the other hand, Lao-ta had no desire to cultivate a liaison with humble and unaspiring tradespeople. Thus, while her father hovered between high and low, the girl reached the age of seventeen without betrothal.

And then one day an old man of the neighborhood came along with news of a student by the name of Mo Chi who lived below the T'ai-ping Bridge. This was an able youth of nineteen, full of learning, who remained unmarried only because he was an orphan and had no money. But he had graduated recently and was hoping to marry some girl in whose family he could find a home.

"This youth would be just right for your daughter," said the neighbor. "Why not take him as your son-in-law?"

"Then do me the favor of acting as go-between," said Chin Lao-ta; and off went the old man on his errand, straight to the T'ai-ping Bridge.

There he sought out the graduate Mo Chi, to whom he said, "There is one thing I am obliged to tell you: the ancestors of Chin Lao-ta followed the profession of tramp-major. But this was long ago: and think, what a fine girl

she is, this daughter of his—and what's more, what a prosperous and flourishing family! If it is not against the young gentleman's wishes, I will take it upon myself to arrange the whole thing at once."

Before giving his reply, Mo Chi turned the matter over in his mind: "I am not very well off for food and clothes right now, and I am certainly not in a position to take a wife in the usual way. Why not make the best of it and marry into this family? It would be killing two birds with one stone; and I needn't take any notice of ridicule." Turning to the old man, he said, "Uncle, what you propose seems an admirable plan. But I am too poor to buy the usual presents. What do you suggest?"

"Provided only that you accept this match," replied the old man, "you will not even be called on to supply so much as the paper for the exchange of horoscopes. You may leave everything to me." With this he returned to report to Chin Lao-ta. They selected an auspicious[7] day, and the Chin family even provided clothes for Mo Chi to wear at the wedding.

When Mo Chi had entered the family and the ceremony was over, he found that Jade Slave's beauty and talents exceeded his wildest hopes. And this perfect wife was his without the outlay of a single copper! He had food and clothes in abundance, and indeed everything he could wish. Even the ridicule he had feared from his friends was withheld, for all were willing to make allowances for Mo Chi's penniless condition.

When their marriage had lasted a month, Chin Lao-ta prepared a generous banquet at which his son-in-law could feast his graduate friends and thus enhance the dignity of the house. The drinking went on for a week: but what was not foreseen was the offense which

---

6. Chang Li-hua (jäŋ lē hwä).

7. auspicious (ô spish′ əs): favoring or tending to encourage success; lucky.

all this gave to the kinsman Scabby Chin. Nor was Scabby without justification.

"You're a tramp-major just as much as I am," said he in his heart; "the only thing is that you've been one a few generations longer and have got some money in your pocket. But if it comes to ancestors, aren't yours the very same as mine? When my niece Jade Slave gets married, I expect to be invited to drink a toast—here's a load of guests drinking for a week on end to celebrate the first month, but not so much as a one-inch by three-inch invitation card do I receive. What is this son-in-law of yours—he's a graduate, I know, but is he a President of a Board or a Prime Minister as well? Aren't I the girl's own uncle and entitled to a stool at your party? Very well," he concluded, "if they're so ready to ignore my existence, I'll go and stir them up a bit and see how that pleases them."

Thereupon he called together fifty or sixty of his beggars and took the lot of them along to Chin Lao-ta's house. What a sight—

Hats bursting into flower, shirts tied up in knots,
A rag of old matting or a strip of worn rug, a bamboo stick and a rough chipped bowl.
Shouting "Father!" shouting "Mother!" shouting "Benefactor!" what a commotion before the gate!
Writhing snakes, yapping dogs, chattering apes and monkeys, what sly cunning they all display!
Beating clappers, singing "Yang Hua," the clamor deafens the ear;
Clattering tiles, faces white with chalk, the sight offends the eye.
A troop of rowdies banded together, not Chung K'uei himself could contain them.

When Chin Lao-ta heard the noise they made, he opened the gate to look out, whereupon the whole crowd of beggars, with Scabby

at their head, surged inside and threw the house into commotion. Scabby himself hurried to a seat, snatched the choicest of the meats and wines and began to stuff himself, calling meanwhile for the happy couple to come and make their obeisances before their uncle.

So terrified were the assembled graduates that they gave up at once and fled the scene, Mo Chi joining in their retreat. Chin Lao-ta was at his wits' end and pleaded repeatedly, "My son-in-law is the host today; this is no affair of mine. Come another day when I will buy in some wine specially for you, and we will have a chat together." He distributed money among the beggar band and brought out two jars of fine wine and some live chickens and geese, inviting the beggars to have a banquet of their own over at Scabby's house; but it was late at night before they ceased their rioting and took their leave, and Jade Slave wept in her room from shame and rage.

That night Mo Chi stayed at the house of a friend, returning only when morning came. At the sight of his son-in-law, Chin Lao-ta felt keenly the disgrace of what had happened, and his face filled with shame. Naturally enough, Mo Chi on his part was strongly displeased; but no one was anxious to say a word. Truly,

When a mute tastes the bitterness of cork-tree wood
He must swallow his disgust with his medicine. ·

Let us rather tell how Jade Slave, conscious of her family's disrepute and anxious that her husband should make his own name for himself, exhorted him to labor at his books. She grudged neither the cost of the works, classical and recent, which she bought for his use, nor the expense of engaging tutors for learned discussion with him. She provided funds also for the entertaining that would widen her husband's circle of acquaintances. As a result, Mo

Chi's learning and reputation made daily advances.

He gained his master's degree at the age of twenty-two, and ultimately his doctorate, and at last the day came when he left the great reception for successful candidates and, black hat, doctor's robes and all, rode back to his father-in-law's house. But as he entered his own ward of the city, a crowd of urchins pressed about him, pointing and calling—"Look at the tramp-major's son-in-law! He's an official now!"

From his elevated position Mo Chi heard them, but it was beneath his dignity to do anything about it. He simply had to put up with it; but his correct observance of etiquette on greeting his father-in-law concealed a burning indignation. "I always knew that I should attain these honors," he said to himself, "yet I feared that no noble or distinguished family would take me in as a son-in-law, and so I married the daughter of a tramp-major. Without question, it is a lifelong stain. My sons and daughters will still have a tramp-major for their grandfather, and I shall be passed from one man to the next as a laughing stock! But the thing is done now. What is more, my wife is wise and virtuous; it would be impossible for me to divorce her on any of the seven counts. Marry in haste, repent at leisure—it's a true saying after all!"

His mind seethed with such thoughts, and he was miserable all day long. Jade Slave often questioned him, but received no reply and remained in ignorance of the cause of his displeasure. But what an absurd figure, this Mo Chi! Conscious only of his present eminence, he has forgotten the days of his poverty. His wife's assistance in money and effort are one with the snows of yesteryear, so crooked are the workings of his mind.

Before long, Mo Chi presented himself for appointment and received the post of Census Officer at Wu-wei-chün.[8] His father-in-law provided wine to feast his departure, and this time awe of the new official deterred the beggar band from breaking up the party.

It so happened that the whole journey from Hangchow to Wu-wei-chün was by water, and Mo Chi took his wife with him, boarded a junk and proceeded to his post. After several days their voyage brought them to the eddies and whirlpools below the Colored Stone Cliff, and they tied up to the northern bank. That night the moon shone bright as day. Mo Chi, unable to sleep, rose and dressed and sat in the prow enjoying the moonlight. There was no one about; and as he sat there brooding on his relationship with a tramp-major, an evil notion came into his head. The only way for him to be rid of lifelong disgrace was for his wife to die and a new one to take her place. A plan formed in his mind. He entered the cabin and inveigled Jade Slave into getting up to see the moon in its glory.

Jade Slave was already asleep, but Mo Chi repeatedly urged her to get up, and she did not like to contravene[9] his wishes. She put on her gown and crossed over to the doorway, where she raised her head to look at the moon. Standing thus, she was taken unawares by Mo Chi, who dragged her out on to the prow and pushed her into the river.

Softly he then woke the boatmen and ordered them to get underway at once—extra speed would be handsomely rewarded. The boatmen, puzzled but ignorant, seized pole and flourished oar. Mo Chi waited until the junk had covered three good miles before he moored again and told them that his wife had fallen in the river while gazing at the moon and that no effort would have availed to save her. With this, he rewarded the boatmen with three ounces of silver to buy wine. The boatmen caught his meaning, but none dared open

---

8. **Wu-wei-chün** (wōō wā jün).
9. **contravene** (kän′ trə vēn′): act in opposition to.

his mouth. The silly maidservants who had accompanied Jade Slave on board accepted that their mistress had really fallen in the river. They wept for a little while and then left off, and we will say no more of them. There is a verse in evidence of all this:

The name of tramp-major pleases him ill;
Hardened by pride he casts off his mate.
The ties of Heaven are not easily broken;
All he gains is an evil name.

But don't you agree that "there is such a thing as coincidence"? It so happened that the newly appointed Transport Commissioner for Western Huai, Hsü Te-hou,[10] was also on his way to his post; and his junk moored across from the Colored Stone Cliff just when Mo Chi's boat had disappeared from view. It was the very spot where Mo Chi had pushed his wife into the water. Hsü Te-hou and his lady had opened their window to enjoy the moonlight and had not yet retired but were taking their ease over a cup of wine. Suddenly they became aware of someone sobbing on the river bank. It was a woman, from the sound, and her distress could not be ignored.

At once Hsü ordered his boatmen to investigate. It proved indeed to be a woman, alone, sitting on the bank. Hsü made them summon her aboard and questioned her about herself. The woman was none other than Jade Slave, Madam Chin, the wife of the Census Officer at Wu-wei-chün. What had happened was that when she found herself in the water, her wits all but left her, and she gave herself up for dead. But suddenly she felt something in the river which held up her feet while the waves washed her close to the bank. Jade Slave struggled ashore; but when she opened her eyes, there was only the empty expanse of the river and no sign of the Census Officer's junk. It was then that she realized what had happened: "My husband, grown rich, has forgotten his

days of hardship. It was his deliberate plan to drown his true wife to pave the way for a more advantageous marriage. And now, though I have my life, where am I to turn for support?"

Bitter reflections of this kind brought forth piteous weeping, and, confronted by Hsü's questioning, she could hold nothing back but told the whole story from beginning to end. When she had finished, she wept without ceasing. Hsü and his wife in their turn were moved to tears, and Hsü Te-hou tried to comfort her: "You must not grieve so; but if you will agree to become my adopted daughter, we will see what provision can be made."

Hsü had his wife produce a complete change of clothing for the girl and settle her down to rest in the stern cabin. He told his servants to treat her with the respect due to his daughter and prohibited the boatmen from disclosing anything of the affair. Before long he reached his place of office in Western Huai. Now it so happened that among the places under his jurisdiction was Wu-wei-chün. He was therefore the superior officer of Mo Chi, who duly appeared with his fellows to greet the new Commissioner. Observing the Census Officer, Hsü sighed that so promising a youth should be capable of so callous an action.

Hsü Te-hou allowed several months to pass, and then he addressed the following words to his staff: "I have a daughter of marriageable age, and possessing both talent and beauty. I am seeking a man fit to be her husband, whom I could take into my family. Does any of you know of such a man?"

All his staff had heard of Mo Chi's bereavement early in life, and all hastened to commend his outstanding ability and to profess his suitability as a son-in-law for the Commissioner. Hsü agreed: "I myself have had this man in mind for some time. But one who has graduated at such a youthful age must cherish

---

10. Hsü Te-hou (Hü də hō).

high ambitions: I am not at all sure that he would be prepared to enter my family."

"He is of humble origin," the others replied. "It would be the happiest of fates for him to secure your interest, to 'cling as the creeper to the tree of jade'—there can be no doubt of his willingness."

"Since you consider it practicable," said Hsü, "I should like you to approach the Census Officer. But to discover how he reacts, say that this plan is of your own making: it might hinder matters if you disclose my interest."

They accepted the commission and made their approach to Mo Chi, requesting that they should act as go-betweens. Now to rise in society was precisely Mo Chi's intention; moreover, a matrimonial alliance with one's superior officer was not a thing to be had for the asking. Delighted, he replied, "I must rely entirely on you to accomplish this; nor shall I be slow in the material expression of my gratitude."

"You may leave it to us," they said; and thereupon they reported back to Hsü.

But Hsü demurred: "The Census Officer may be willing to marry her," said he, "but the fact is that my wife and I have doted on our daughter and have brought her up to expect the tenderest consideration. It is for this reason that we wish her to remain in her own home after marriage. But I suspect that the Census Officer, in the impatience of youth, might prove insufficiently tolerant; and if the slightest discord should arise, it would be most painful to my wife and myself. He must be prepared to be patient in all things before I can accept him into my family."

They bore these words to Mo Chi, who accepted every condition.

The Census Officer's present circumstances were very different from those of his student days. He signified acceptance of the betrothal by sending fine silks and gold ornaments on the most ample scale. An auspicious date was selected, and Mo Chi itched in his very bones as he awaited the day when he should become the son-in-law of the Transport Commissioner.

But let us rather tell how Hsü Te-hou gave his wife instructions to prepare Jade Slave for her marriage. "Your stepfather," Mrs. Hsü said to her, "moved by pity for you in your widowhood, wishes to invite a young man who has gained his doctorate to become your husband and enter our family. You must not refuse him."

But Jade Slave replied, "Though of humble family, I am aware of the rules of conduct. When Mo Chi became my husband, I vowed to remain faithful to him all my life. However cruel and lawless he may have been, however shamefully he may have rejected the companion of his poverty, I shall fulfil my obligations. On no account will I forsake the true virtue of womanhood by remarrying."

With these words her tears fell like rain. Mrs. Hsü, convinced of her sincerity, decided to tell her the truth, and said, "The young graduate of whom my husband spoke is none other than Mo Chi himself. Appalled by his mean action and anxious to see you reunited with him, my husband passed you off as his own daughter and told the members of his staff that he was seeking a son-in-law who would enter our family. He made them approach Mo Chi, who was delighted by the proposal. He is to come to us this very night; but when he enters your room, this is what you must do to get your own back. . . ."

As she disclosed her plan, Jade Slave dried her tears. She remade her face and changed her costume and made preparations for the coming ceremony.

With evening there duly appeared the Census Officer, Mo Chi, all complete with mandarin's hat[11] and girdle:[12] he was dressed in red brocade and had gold ornaments in his

---

11. mandarin's hat: hat with a distinctive button indicating that its wearer is a high government official.

12. girdle (gŭrd′ ′l): a wide belt for carrying things.

cap. Under him was a fine steed with decorated saddle and before him marched two bands of drummers and musicians. His colleagues were there in force to see him married, and the whole procession was cheered the length of the route. Indeed,

> To the roll and clang of music the white
>   steed advances,
> But what a curious person, this fine
>   upstanding groom:
> Delighted with his change of families, beg-
>   gar for man of rank,
> For memories of the Colored Stone Cliff
>   his glad heart has no room.

That night the official residence of the Transport Commissioner was festooned with flowers and carpeted, and to the playing of pipe and drum all awaited the arrival of the bridegroom. As the Census Officer rode up to the gate and dismounted, Hsü Te-hou came out to receive him, and then the accompanying junior officers took their leave. Mo Chi walked straight through to the private apartments, where the bride was brought out to him, veiled in red and supported by a maidservant on either side. From beyond the threshold the master of ceremonies took them through the ritual. The happy pair made obeisances to heaven and earth and to the parents of the bride; and when the ceremonial observances were over, they were escorted into the nuptial chamber for the wedding feast. By this time Mo Chi was in a state of indescribable bliss, his soul somewhere above the clouds. Head erect, triumphant, he entered the nuptial chamber.

But no sooner had he passed the doorway than from positions of concealment on either side there suddenly emerged seven or eight young maids and old nannies, each one armed with a light or heavy bamboo. Mercilessly they

began to beat him. Off came his silk hat; blows fell like rain on his shoulders; he yelled perpetually, but, try as he might, he could not get out of the way.

Under the beating the Census Officer collapsed, to lie in a terrified heap on the floor, calling on his parents-in-law to save him. Then he heard, from within the room itself, a gentle command issued in the softest of voices: "Beat him no more, our hardhearted young gentleman, but bring him before me."

At last the beating stopped, and the maids and nannies, tugging at his ears and dragging at his arms like the six senses tormenting Amida Buddha in the parable, hauled him, his feet barely touching the ground, before the presence of the bride. "What is the nature of my offense?" the Census Officer was mumbling; but when he opened his eyes, there above him, correct and upright in the brilliance of the candlelight, was seated the bride—who was none other than his former wife, Jade Slave, Madam Chin.

Now Mo Chi's mind reeled, and he bawled, "It's a ghost! It's a ghost!" All began to laugh, until Hsü Te-hou came in from outside and addressed him: "Do not be alarmed, my boy: this is no ghost, but my adopted daughter, who came to me below the Colored Stone Cliff."

Mo Chi's heart ceased its pounding. He fell to his knees and folded his hands in supplication. "I, Mo Chi, confess my crime," he said. "I only beg your forgiveness."

"This is no affair of mine," replied Hsü, "unless my daughter has something to say. . . ."

Jade Slave spat in Mo Chi's face and cursed him: "Cruel wretch! Did you never think of the words of Sung Hung? 'Do not exclude from your mind the friends of your poverty, nor from your house the wife of your youth.' It was empty-handed that you first came into my family and thanks to our money that you were able to study and enter society, to make your name and enjoy your present good fortune. For my part, I looked forward to the day when I should share in your glory. But you—forgetful of the favors you had received, oblivious of our early love, you repaid good with evil and threw me into the river to drown. Heaven took pity on me and sent me a savior, whose adopted daughter I became. But if I had ended my days on the riverbed and you had taken a new wife—how could your heart have been so callous? And now, how can I so demean myself as to rejoin you?"

Her speech ended in tears and loud wails, and "Cruel, cruel!" she continued to cry. Mo Chi's whole face expressed his shame. He could find no words but pleaded for forgiveness by kowtowing[13] before her. Hsü Te-hou, satisfied with her demonstration of anger, raised Mo Chi to his feet and admonished Jade Slave in the following words: "Calm your anger, my child. Your husband has now repented his crime, and we may be sure that he will never again treat you ill. Although in fact your marriage took place some years ago, so far as my family is concerned, you are newlywed; in all things, therefore, show consideration to me, and let an end be made here and now to recriminations." Turning to Mo Chi, he said, "My son, your crime is upon your own head; lay no blame on others. Tonight I ask you only to show tolerance. I will send your mother-in-law to make peace between you."

He left the room, and shortly his wife came in to them. Much mediation was required from her before the two were finally brought into accord.

On the following day Hsü Te-hou gave a banquet for his new son-in-law, during which he returned all the betrothal gifts, the fine silks and gold ornaments, saying to Mo Chi, "One bride may not receive two sets of presents. You took such things as these to the Chin family on the previous occasion; I cannot accept them all over again now." Mo Chi lowered his head and said nothing, and Hsü went on: "I believe it was your dislike of the lowly status of your father-in-law which put an end to your love and almost to your marriage. What do you think now of my own position? I am only afraid that the rank I hold may still be too low for your aspirations."

Mo Chi's face flushed crimson, and he was obliged to retire a few steps and acknowledge his errors. There is a verse to bear witness:

Full of fond hopes of bettering himself by marriage,
Amazed to discover his bride to be his wife;
A beating, a cursing, an overwhelming shame:
Was it really worth it for a change of in-laws?

From this time on, Mo Chi and Jade Slave lived together twice as amicably as before. Hsü Te-hou and his wife treated Jade Slave as their own daughter and Mo Chi as their proper son-in-law, and Jade Slave behaved towards them exactly as though they were her own parents. Even the heart of Mo Chi was touched, so that he received Chin Lao-ta, the tramp-major, into his official residence and cared for him to the end of his days. And when in the fullness of time Hsü Te-hou and his wife died, Jade Slave, Madam Chin, wore the heaviest mourning of coarse linen for each of them in recompense for their kindness to her; and generations of descendants of Mo and of Hsü regarded each other as cousins and never failed in friendship. A verse concludes:

---

13. kowtowing (kou′ tou′ iŋ): kneeling and touching the forehead to the ground as a sign of respect.

Sung Hung remained faithful and was
     praised for his virtue;
Huang Yun divorced his wife and was
     reviled for lack of feeling.

Observe the case of Mo Chi, remarrying
     his wife:
A marriage is <u>predestined</u>:[14] no objection
     can prevail.

_____

14. predestined (prē des' tind): determined in
advance by fate or divinity.

Thinking About the Tale

A PERSONAL RESPONSE

*sharing
impressions*

1. What is your impression of Mo Chi? Write your reaction in
your journal.

*constructing
interpretations*

2. Consider the extremes to which Mo Chi goes to improve his social
position. Do you think his punishment is sufficient?

3. What might account for Mo Chi's initial meanness and final repentance?

4. Contrast Jade Slave with Mo Chi.
   Think about
   • your answers to questions 2 and 3
   • Jade Slave's attitude toward Mo Chi's deeds
   • her punishment of Mo Chi

5. What values are promoted in this moral tale?
   Think about
   • actions that are praised or rewarded
   • actions that are condemned or punished

A CREATIVE RESPONSE

6. How might the story have turned out if Jade Slave had refused to show
anger toward Mo Chi?

7. Tell whether you find Jade Slave and Mo Chi believable as characters. Cite examples of their actions to support your opinion.

8. What do the scattered verses contribute to the story?
   Think about
   • the subjects of the verses
   • the placement of the verses
   • how they make you feel

9. What relevance does this story have to contemporary life in the United States?
   Think about
   • what you wrote earlier about achieving social position
   • how traditional Chinese values compare with current American values
   • whether Mo Chi is a universal character or a figure unique to one culture

 nalyzing the Writer's Craft

PLOT AND SUSPENSE

The chain of events in this story is complicated, involving thwarted hopes, secret schemes, and surprising coincidences. How did you feel as the action unfolded? Were you impatient to learn what would happen next?

Building a Literary Vocabulary. Plot refers to the actions and events in a story. Suspense is the excitement or tension that readers feel as they become involved in a story and eager to know the outcome. Questions arise in the minds of readers as suspense builds, questions such as "How will Mo Chi handle the disgrace of being married to a beggar's daughter?"

Application: Relating Suspense to Plot Events. If you were reading this story aloud to children, where would you stop reading to make them beg for more? Choose the three places in the story that you think are the most suspenseful. Write down phrases to identify these points in the story. Also jot down questions your listeners might have in their minds at these points. Later, compare your choices with your classmates' choices.

Connecting Reading and Writing

1. Think about your response to question 9, which asked about the relevance of this story to contemporary life in the United States. In a group of three or four, adapt this story to a modern American setting. What profession in our culture is as dishonorable as that of "tramp-major"? What position would an ambitious man like Mo Chi aspire to? Write your story as a **synopsis** of a television miniseries.

Option: Write a detailed description of the cast of characters as it would appear on the first page of a **dramatic script** for the miniseries.

2. Imagine that a primary-grade teacher has asked you to read this story to his or her class. Would you want the children to subscribe wholeheartedly to the values that the story promotes? Write a **memo** to the teacher, outlining what you consider to be the positive and negative values presented in the story.

Option: Create a **checklist** of positive and negative values in the story that you can refer to in a discussion with the teacher.

3. What do you learn about twelfth-century Chinese culture from reading this story? What aspects of this culture are not touched upon? Research more information about the society depicted in the story. Then prepare **lecture notes** for a class to be taught on the subject.

Option: Use the researched information to write **captions** for an imaginary set of photographs depicting life in twelfth-century China.

4. In a **character sketch**, describe an ambitious person who reminds you of Mo Chi. Make specific comparisons between this person's actions and those of Mo Chi.

Option: Make the comparisons in two or more **quatrains,** four-line poems modeled on the ones that appear in the story.

The Tale of the Anklet

from One Thousand and One Arabian Nights

PERSIA

Benizara and Kakezara

JAPAN

The Indian Cinderella

CANADA

*A*pproaching the Tales

The story of Cinderella may be the world's best-known folk tale. No one knows how old it is, but a Chinese version dates from the ninth century A.D. One folklore study has identifed nine hundred versions of the story from the cultures of Europe, Africa, and Asia. The specific details vary from place to place, but the basic plot remains the same: a young, mistreated girl is rewarded in the end. In this lesson you will read versions of this story from three different parts of the world: Persia, Japan, and Canada.

*C*onnecting Writing and Reading

Imagine that you have been asked to write a television script retelling the story of Cinderella. In your journal make notes of the most important events of the story. Include what you believe are Cinderella's most important virtues and indicate the rewards she receives because of them. As you read and take notes on the three versions of the Cinderella tale that follow, think about the rewards for virtue described in these tales.

The Tale of the Anklet

from One Thousand and One Arabian Nights

I F A READER were to search through the Stories of Three, he might find there Delilah who was the youngest of three sisters. Perhaps I should say stepsisters, for their father had two daughters before his first wife died. Then he married, in his old age, the beautiful mother of Delilah, and his third daughter grew up with her mother's beauty of face and soul. But when the old man and his young wife died, the three sisters lived together as happily as two scorpions and a mouse.

Delilah's two sisters were jealous of her face, which was as lovely as the tamarind[1] flower, of her hair, whose waves gleamed like the night sea under a moon, of her hands, as long and delicate as fronded leaves, and of her little feet, as small and delicate as a baby fawn's. She tried to ease their jealousy by dressing in very plain and modest clothes, but it became their sport and pastime to make her as unhappy as she was beautiful.

They set her to work in a dark corner of the house, and Delilah sat and spun the fluff of wool and the floss of cotton, and looked at the wall until she knew every brick, stone, dent, crack, and cockroach as well as her morning prayers. From what she earned, the sisters allowed her to keep the few pennies she needed to buy food.

But one day, instead of buying her usual sesame bun she came home with a little vase instead, and put some wildflowers in it, and put it in front of her while she worked. Her sisters laughed and jeered at her for buying such an ugly little vase, but Delilah placidly went on spinning, while they went out to the bazaar to spend all the rest of the money she had earned.

"And what is so magic about you, little vase?" she said as the door closed behind them. "The old man who sold you to me said that you were magic. Was I foolish to believe him just because of the length and whiteness of his beard?"

"No," said the vase. "Ask for any luxury and I will bring it to you."

So Delilah lifted the flowers out of the vase and asked for a little something to eat (since she had gone without food to buy the vase). Immediately, a fountain of dates, apricots, sweetmeats, grapes, almond cakes, and all manner of good things poured out of the neck of the vase and arranged themselves in front of her.

Delilah's happiness was lovely to see. But only the little vase saw it.

Whenever her sisters went out, Delilah would ask the little vase to brighten her weary day, and the vase would fabricate gorgeous clothes, delicious tidbits, enthralling books or the music of enchanting instruments. It was particularly adept at making jewelry—bracelets and necklaces more beautiful than Delilah knew how to request. Her happiness was as lovely as the jewels. But only the little vase saw it.

For fear of making her sisters more jealous, Delilah would change back into her cheap, drab clothes before they returned to the house, and hide or give away the little vase's produce.

One day, however, the joy she took in her ordinary work and her extraordinary vase seemed too large for the little house, and she

---

1. **tamarind** (tam′ ə rind): a tree with bright, red-striped, yellow flowers.

decided to chance a small adventure. Asking the vase for a costume more fabulous than any before, she dressed herself in more finery than the sun does at sunset and pattered on her little feet all the way to the royal palace. No one barred the way to a lady as splendid and bejewelled as she was, and she found her way to the very heart of the King's harem. Women as lissom as waving grass and as fair as shocks of wheat decorated every chair and cushion, but they all clapped their hands and drew sharp breaths at the sight of Delilah. Her clothes set off her natural beauty as a clear, navy sky sets off the crescent moon.

"Are you to be the Prince's wife?" they asked. "Emissaries have been scouring the realm for a beauty befitting the Prince's nobility and wealth, his breeding and good taste. Surely you are the answer to their prayers!"

Delilah only laughed to herself that they could be so mistaken. At their heartfelt description of the young Prince, she asked if she might be allowed to glimpse the Royal Heir. So they took her to a lattice window that overlooked a courtyard, and below her she saw a group of young men playing football. Delilah thought to herself, "The Royal Prince might be as highborn as an eagle of the mountaintops, but I would dance from here to China across the sharp bed of the sea for a kiss from the young man in wine-colored velvet."

"Which is the Prince?" she asked.

"Why, he's the tallest of the young men—the one dressed in wine-colored velvet."

Just then, beyond the courtyard and beyond the palace wall, Delilah glimpsed the two towering hairstyles of her stepsisters as they rolled home from the bazaar, crushing every caterpillar and beetle under their impressively monumental feet.

Empty of all thoughts but the thought of getting home before them, Delilah fled down the palace stairs and across the courtyard to the nearest gate in the palace wall. The Prince was dimly aware of a jag of color of the kind the eye sees if shut very tightly. He turned to see what lady of the palace would leave it in full flight with evening already approaching, but Delilah had already gone.

She leaped the shallow trough dug in the courtyard for the horses to drink from: she leaped it like a gazelle. But the anklet of diamonds she wore round her ankle slipped over her tiny foot and dropped into the water. Her feet were as quick as they were small, and she reached the house before her sisters and changed out of her clothes before they clattered in at the door. It did not show, but her throat was still damp with the running and her heart was still sore for the young man in wine-colored velvet.

The following day there was a commotion at the palace when the sun reached its height, for the palace horses would not drink from the trough. A flashing in the water made them shy away, flaring their nostrils. When the Royal Ostler removed the diamond anklet from the trough, the Prince was standing close by with his horse.

"Look at the size of it!" said the Prince, holding it up on the tips of three fingers.

"Look at the cut of the diamonds," said the ostler, as the rainbow-colored light spilled on the ground in all directions.

"Look at the quality of the silverwork," said the King when his son showed it to him.

"Yes, but look at the *size* of it," repeated the Prince. "If any mortal woman has a foot so delicate that it will pass through that anklet, I could die for love of her!"

"What would that achieve?" said the King, who had forgotten about such things as love. "Tell your mother if you want to marry the owner of the anklet. I have forgotten about such things."

"Mother, I want to marry the girl who wore this anklet," said the Prince to the Queen.

"Allah finds baffling ways of pairing a man and a woman," said the Queen. "I suppose the smallness of a woman's foot is as good a reason as any. I shall order a search of the city. Can we assume that the anklet will fit no one but the lady to whom it belongs?"

"Could there be two women with such delicate ankles?" asked the Prince by way of reply.

House by house, the Queen's emissaries carried out their search for the owner of the anklet. What washing of feet took place among the women of marriageable age! What shrinking of feet in bowls of cold water! But no one could fit the anklet over her feet until the emissaries came to the house of Delilah and her sisters.

"She never goes out," said one stepsister, pushing Delilah into a corner and pulling up her own skirts.

"She has no jewelry at all," said the other, sitting down on Delilah's lap to try on the diamond anklet. But the emissary looked sidelong at the four gigantic feet held out toward him and lifted only the folds of material covering Delilah's feet.

"The Prince's bride," he said simply, before even slipping the anklet over her foot.

As Delilah prepared for the wedding, her happiness was almost a pain inside her. In secret she requested a wedding dress—in crimson and gold—from the magic vase and put it on, but she could feel the jealousy of her two sisters beating against her like blackbird-wings. She knew their jealousy was hurting them more sharply than her happiness and was very sorry that they could not be as happy as she. So she told them the secret of the magic vase and wished them much joy of it, for she said she had magic enough in the Prince's love.

The sisters huddled together over the vase, asking it for this and that, all raucous with laughter when their wishes came true. But when Delilah went to show the neighbors her wedding dress, the one said to the other, "Watch me, sister, and see if I can't put a stop to this selfish girl's wickedness and all the vile happiness that is clogging up the house like leaves clogging a drain . . ."

When Delilah came back from showing off her wedding dress, her sisters offered to dress her hair for the wedding. They braided it with gold and scattered it with pearls—all given them by the magic of the little vase.

"Now, a pin here and a second here and another to fasten your plait, my beautiful little sister, and your head will be so exquisite that the Prince will forget he fell in love with your feet."

But as the last pin sank into her glossy hair, the hair became wool-white and feathered into the herls and quills of a young dove. The jealous sisters had asked the magic vase for three enchanted pins which would transform any living creature into a bird.

The stepsisters sent word that the bride-to-be had so hated the thought of the Prince that she had fled the country rather than be married to him; and they turned the dove off the windowsill and pelted it with dry rice when it fluttered back toward the house.

The Prince's disappointment felt almost like a sickness inside him. He refused to eat or leave his room, and he would hear no mention of alternative brides, though the King and Queen promised to send emissaries on their hands and knees to measure all the feet in the kingdom. His only comfort came from the visits of a crested dove at his window. The little wool-white bird crooned so gently and sorrowfully that the Prince felt befriended and set out food for the bird.

She would not touch it. Soon she seemed so weak that the Prince picked her up in the palm of his hand and stroked her head and neck. The crest seemed spiny to the touch, and when the Prince lifted her head feathers it seemed that three pins were sticking deep into her delicate skull. Pulling them out, his hand thought it would break from his arm, for he found himself supporting the weight of a full-grown woman in crimson and gold wedding raiment. She might have weighed more but for the incredible slimness of her ankles and the smallness of her feet.

Delilah told the Prince her story, and the wedding took place before dark, to the great astonishment of the King and Queen and the emissaries who were already searching the land on their hands and knees. When the noise of the festivities—the clamor of cymbals, the blowing of reed pipes, and the clatter of drums—wreathed down into the city, and the people began dancing, and benches were laid in the streets to celebrate the marriage of nobility to loveliness, then the two sisters of Delilah feared for their lives. They asked the magic vase to rescue them from the Royal Guards and the Palace Police.

"Hide us somewhere where no one can see us," they begged, little realizing that the guards were already at the window with the Prince's orders to fetch them to him in chains.

The magic vase opened its neck and swallowed up the two sisters with a satisfied gulp. And the Palace Guards carried the little vase—at arm's length—to the Prince and his royal bride.

"Shall I order the vase to give up your sisters so that they can be beaten soundly and turned into jackdaws?" asked the Prince.

"No," said Delilah. "Place the vase on the highest shelf in the palace, and if someone should discover its secret in years to come, that person can decide what to do with two big-footed girls and enough envy to fill a barn."

Benizara and Kakezara

LONG AGO IN a certain place there were two sisters. One was named Benizara, "Crimson Dish," and the other Kakezara, "Broken Dish." Benizara was a former wife's child, while Kakezara was the stepmother's child. Benizara was a very honest and gentle girl, but her stepmother was very cruel to her.

One day she sent the two girls out to gather chestnuts. She gave Benizara a bag with a hole in the bottom, but she gave Kakezara a good one. "You must not come back until you have each filled your bag," she said.

The two set off for the mountains and began to pick up chestnuts. Before long Kakezara's bag was full, and she returned home, leaving Benizara alone. Benizara was an honest girl, and so she worked as hard as she could picking up chestnuts until it began to get dark. It got darker and darker, and she thought she heard a rustling sound, *gasa gasa*, as though a wolf were coming toward her. She suddenly realized how dangerous it was and ran off without even looking where she was going. In the meantime it had become very dark, and she was completely lost. She was filled with despair, but she knew that it would do no good to cry; so she kept on walking, thinking that perhaps she might find a house. Suddenly just ahead she saw a light. She went to where it was and found an old woman alone spinning thread. Benizara explained that she had gone to gather chestnuts but that it was late and she couldn't return home; then she asked if she might please stay overnight there.

The old woman said: "I would like to let you stay here, but both my sons are *oni*.[1] They will soon be coming home and would eat up anyone they found here. Instead, I will tell you how to find your way home." And she carefully explained which road to take. Then she filled her bag with chestnuts and gave her a little box and a handful of rice. "Take the chestnuts to your mother. This little box is a magic box; if there is ever anything that you need, just say what you would like, then tap on the box three times and what you want will appear. Now if you meet my *oni* sons on your way home, chew some of the rice and spread it around your mouth; then lie down and pretend that you are dead."

Benizara thanked her for everything and started for home on the road she had been told to take. After a while she heard the sound of a flute coming toward her. She chewed some of the rice and spread it around her mouth, then lay down by the side of the road and pretended that she was dead. Soon a red *oni* and a blue *oni* came along. "Hey, older brother, I smell human beings," said one and went over to the side of the road to look. "It's no good, older brother, she's already rotten. Her mouth is full of worms," he said. And they went on down the road blowing their flutes.

Benizara listened to the sound of the flutes growing fainter and fainter in the distance; then she continued on down the road that she had been told to take.

Soon morning came. At home her stepmother was thinking to herself that during the night the wolves would have surely eaten Benizara, when just then the girl arrived home. Far from being dead, she had a whole bag full of chestnuts; so the stepmother had nothing to scold her about.

---

1. oni (ō′ nē): ogres or demons.

One day some time after this a play was to be given in the village. The stepmother took Kakezara and went to see it, giving Benizara a great deal of work which had to be done before they returned home. Benizara was working as hard as she could, when some of her friends came and asked her to go with them to see the play. Benizara said that her stepmother had given her so much work to do that she could not go, but her friends said, "We will help you and then you can go," and so, all working together, they soon finished a whole day's work.

Her friends were all wearing beautiful kimonos, but Benizara had nothing but rags to wear. She wondered what she should do; then she thought about the little box she had received from the old woman in the mountains. She took it out and said that she would like to have a kimono. She was given a beautiful kimono. She put it on and went to see the play. When she got there, Kakezara was begging her mother for some candies and Benizara threw her some. When she did this, a nobleman who had come to see the performance of the play saw what happened.

The next day the nobleman's colorful procession came to the village. The lord's palanquin[2] stopped in front of Benizara's house. Kakezara's mother was overjoyed and dressed Kakezara in her very best to meet him. The lord got out of the palanquin and said, "There should be two girls here; bring out the other one too."

The stepmother had put Benizara in the bathtub to hide her, but there was nothing she could do but obey the lord's command, and so she brought her out. In comparison to Kakezara, Benizara looked very shabby, but the lord said, "Which one of these two came to see the performance of the play yesterday?"

"It was this one, Kakezara."

"No, it wasn't that one," said the lord, but the mother kept insisting that it was. Finally it was decided to ask each of them to compose a song. The lord took a plate and put it on a tray; then he piled some salt in the plate and stuck a pine needle in it. He commanded that they each compose a poem, using that as a subject.

In a loud voice Kakezara sang,

> Put a plate on a tray,
> Put some salt on the plate,
> Stick a pine needle in the salt;
> It'll soon fall over.

Then she hit the lord on the head and ran off. Next Benizara sang,

> A tray and plate, oh!
> A mountain rises from the plate,
> On it, snow has fallen.
> Rooted deep into the snow,
> A lonely pine tree grows.

When he heard this song, the lord praised it very highly. Preparations were soon made, and Benizara was put into a beautiful palanquin; then she rode off to the lord's palace.

Kakezara's mother watched in silence; then she put Kakezara in a huge empty basket, saying, "Now, Kakezara, you too may go to the lord's palace." She dragged her along, but she did it so violently that Kakezara tumbled over the edge of a deep ditch and fell to her death.

---

2. **palanquin** (pal′ ən kēn′): an enclosed carriage, carried on the shoulders of several people.

The Indian Cinderella

ON THE SHORES of a wide bay on the Atlantic coast, there dwelt in old times a great Indian warrior. It was said that he had been one of Glooskap's best helpers and friends, and that he had done for him many wonderful deeds. But that, no man knows. He had, however, a very wonderful and strange power; he could make himself invisible; he could thus mingle unseen with his enemies and listen to their plots. He was known among the people as Strong Wind, the Invisible. He dwelt with his sister in a tent near the sea, and his sister helped him greatly in his work. Many maidens would have been glad to marry him, and he was much sought after because of his mighty deeds; and it was known that Strong Wind would marry the first maiden who could see him as he came home at night. Many made the trial, but it was a long time before one succeeded.

Strong Wind used a clever trick to test the truthfulness of all who sought to win him. Each evening as the day went down, his sister walked on the beach with any girl who wished to make the trial. His sister could always see him, but no one else could see him. And as he came home from work in the twilight, his sister as she saw him drawing near would ask the girl who sought him, "Do you see him?" And each girl would falsely answer, "Yes." And his sister would ask, "With what does he draw his sled?" And each girl would answer, "With the hide of a moose," or "With a pole," or "With a great cord." And then his sister would know that they all had lied, for their answers were mere guesses. And many tried and lied and failed, for Strong Wind would not marry any who were untruthful.

There lived in a village a great chief who had three daughters. Their mother had long been dead. One of these was much younger than the others. She was very beautiful and gentle and well-beloved by all, and for that reason her older sisters were very jealous of her charms and treated her very cruelly. They clothed her in rags that she might be ugly; and they cut off her long black hair; and they burned her face with coals from the fire that she might be scarred and disfigured. And they lied to their father, telling him that she had done these things herself. But the young girl was patient and kept her gentle heart and went gladly about her work.

Like other girls, the chief's two eldest daughters tried to win Strong Wind. One evening, as the day went down, they walked on the shore with Strong Wind's sister and waited for his coming. Soon he came home from his day's work, drawing his sled. And his sister asked as usual, "Do you see him?" And each one, lying, answered, "Yes." And she asked, "Of what is his shoulder strap made?" and each, guessing, said, "Of rawhide." Then they entered the tent where they hoped to see Strong Wind eating his supper; and when he took off his coat and his moccasins they could see them, but more than these they saw nothing. And Strong Wind knew that they had lied, and he kept himself from their sight, and they went home dismayed.

One day the chief's youngest daughter with her rags and her burnt face resolved to seek Strong Wind. She patched her clothes with bits of birch bark from the trees, and put on the few little ornaments she possessed, and went forth to try to see the Invisible One as all the other girls of the village had done before. And her sisters laughed at her and called her "fool"; and as she passed along the road all the people laughed at her because of her tattered frock and her burnt face, but silently she went her way.

Strong Wind's sister received the little girl kindly, and at twilight she took her to the beach. Soon Strong Wind came home drawing his sled. And his sister asked, "Do you see him?" And the girl answered, "No," and his sister wondered greatly because she spoke the truth. And again she asked, "Do you see him now?" And the girl answered, "Yes, and he is very wonderful." And she asked, "With what does he draw his sled?" And the girl answered, "With the Rainbow," and she was much afraid. And she asked further, "Of what is his bowstring?" And the girl answered, "His bowstring is the Milky Way."

Then Strong Wind's sister knew that because the girl had spoken the truth at first her brother had made himself visible to her. And she said, "Truly, you have seen him." And she took her home and bathed her, and all the scars disappeared from her face and body; and her hair grew long and black again like the raven's wing; and she gave her fine clothes to wear and many rich ornaments. Then she bade her take the wife's seat in the tent. Soon Strong Wind entered and sat beside her and called her his bride. The very next day she became his wife, and ever afterwards she helped him to do great deeds. The girl's two elder sisters were very cross and they wondered greatly at what had taken place. But Strong Wind, who knew of their cruelty, resolved to punish them. Using his great power, he changed them both into aspen trees and rooted them in the earth. And since that day the leaves of the aspen have always trembled, and they shiver in fear at the approach of Strong Wind; it matters not how softly he comes, for they are still mindful of his great power and anger because of their lies and their cruelty to their sister long ago.

*Milky Way,
the Southern Cross.*
Yerkes Observatory,
University of Chicago.

Thinking About the Tales

A PERSONAL RESPONSE

sharing impressions

1. What are your feelings about the three Cinderella characters? Use your journal to explain.

constructing interpretations

2. Think about the three tales you have read and the Cinderella tale you described in your journal. What similarities and differences do you find in the four versions?
Think about
- the rewards for virtue
- the outcome of each tale
- the moral conveyed in each tale

3. In which of the three tales is the fate of the evil sisters or stepsisters the most satisfying to you? Explain.

A CREATIVE RESPONSE

4. What do you think might have happened to any one of the three Cinderella characters if she had not been discovered and rescued?

A CRITICAL RESPONSE

5. The Japanese and Canadian versions of this story seem to follow closely the original oral folktales told by ancient storytellers. "The Tale of the Anklet," however, is apparently an adaptation, written by someone who reshaped the original tale to create a more complex and polished story. What aspects of the Persian tale indicate that it has been reworked?
Think about
- any differences in style, such as word choice, sentence length, or figurative language
- any passages that sound as if a writer might have elaborated on the basic story

6. Why do you think the Cinderella story has such a universal appeal for children and adults around the world?
Think about
- how the reader feels about Cinderella as events unfold
- the rewards for virtue
- the hopes or aspirations typical of most people

7. In an article titled "America's Cinderella," Jane Yolen concludes that the American Cinderella character is more helpless and sentimentalized than she was in earlier versions. Consider any stories you may be familiar with from books, movies, TV, or real life that remind you of the Cinderella tale. Do these tend to support or contradict Yolen's thesis?

Analyzing the Writer's Craft

MOTIFS IN FOLK TALES

Have you noticed that the basic Cinderella tale shares certain characteristics with totally different types of tales?

Building a Literary Vocabulary. People who study folklore have identified various elements, or motifs, that tend to recur in folk tales and especially in fairy tales, a type of folk tale in which magic plays a central role. A motif might be any aspect of a tale, such as a certain type of character or particular events in the plot. For example, the fairy godmother figure who appears in some versions of "Cinderella" also shows up in "Sleeping Beauty."

Application: Identifying Motifs. Working with a partner, look in any of these Cinderella tales for motifs that also appear in other familiar fairy tales. As a starting point, you might consider tales such as "Snow White," "Sleeping Beauty," "The Princess and the Pea," and "Rumplestiltskin."

Connecting Reading and Writing

1. Take **notes** for an oral report to be delivered to your classmates in which you compare and contrast the values of the cultures represented in the three tales.

Option: Using one of the comparison and contrast graphics suggested in **Responding in Writing,** prepare a **textbook diagram** that depicts the similarities and differences in the values associated with each culture.

2. Choose a modern setting and write your version of the Cinderella tale in the form of a **soap opera.**

Option: Write a **parody** of the Cinderella story for a humor magazine.

3. Create a series of **diary entries** written by Cinderella's wicked stepmother. Have her explain her feelings and give her reasons for the way she treats the Cinderella character.

Option: Record the wicked stepmother's explanation in a **social worker's report.** Include comments by the social worker.

4. "Lowly hero marries princess" is another recognized folk motif. In a scene from a **play,** construct what might happen when a male Cinderella character must pass some kind of test in order to be worthy of a princess.

Option: Present this scene as a **comic strip.**

from The Persian Letters

MONTESQUIEU 1689–1755 FRANCE

A biography of Montesquieu appears on page 748.

Approaching the Selection

Baron de Montesquieu (mōn tes kyö′) was a French political philosopher whose ideas about government influenced many national constitutions, including the Constitution of the United States. *The Persian Letters* is one of his early works, published in 1721 during the reign of Louis XV. Because political ideas could not be discussed freely under the monarchy, Montesquieu conveyed his views indirectly in this book. His main characters are imaginary Persian travelers who journey through France, commenting on French customs. The four letters that make up this selection are written by Usbek (ōoz′ bek), a Persian lord, in reply to Mirza (mir′ zə), a friend writing from Persia. Mirza has asked Usbek to explain what he means by asserting that people are virtuous and that justice is innate. Usbek says that he will not set forth abstract arguments but will instead tell a story.

Building Vocabulary

These essential words are footnoted within the selection.

virtue (vur′ chōo): For there were in this country two remarkable men, who were humane, just, and lovers of **virtue**. (page 85)

cupidity (kyōo pid′ ə tē): **Cupidity** was alien to this happy land, and . . . he who presented the gift always believed himself the favored one. (page 86)

ardor (är′ dər): In their hearts burned a previously unknown **ardor**. (page 87)

exacting (eg zak′ tiŋ), **morality** (mō ral′ i tē): You prefer to submit yourselves to a prince and to obey his laws, which would be less **exacting** than your own **morality**. (page 88)

Connecting Writing and Reading

Imagine how the student body of your school would behave if there were no principal, administrators, or counselors and the students themselves had to run the school. Would the school and the student body still be able to function? In your journal, jot down your ideas about what would happen and then state your view about the need for figures of authority. As you read, think about what the events in this story suggest about the need for a figure of authority.

from The Persian Letters

I N ARABIA THERE once lived a small tribe called the Troglodytes,[2] descendants of those ancient Troglodytes who, if we can believe the historians, more resembled beasts than men. But the people of whom I speak were not that deformed; they were not shaggy like bears, nor did they hiss, and they had two eyes. However, they were so brutal and ferocious that there was no principle of equity or justice among them.

They had a king of foreign origin who, hoping to correct the brutality of their nature, treated them harshly; but they conspired against him, killed him, and exterminated the entire royal family.

Having struck the blow, they assembled to choose a government, and after much dissent they elected magistrates. No sooner had they been elected, however, than they became intolerable, and they too were massacred.

Freed from this new yoke, the people now consulted only their own savage nature. All of them agreed that they would no longer obey anyone at all; each was to attend only to his personal interests, and to consider none other.

This unanimous resolution was extremely pleasing to all. Each said: "Why should I kill myself working for people who don't matter to me? I will think only of myself. I will be happy; what is it to me if the others are happy or not? I will satisfy all my needs, and after that, I won't care if the other Troglodytes are miserable."

When the month for sowing came, each said: "I will cultivate only as much of my fields as is needed to furnish me with grain for my sustenance; a greater quantity would be use-less, and I am not going to trouble myself for nothing."

The land of this little realm was not all alike; some was high and arid, and in the lowlands some was watered by many streams. The first year was very dry, so that land in the high places was completely unproductive, while that which could be irrigated was very fertile. Thus the mountain people almost all perished of hunger, because their merciless neighbors refused to share their harvest.

The next year was very wet, and the high places were extraordinarily productive, while the lowlands were flooded. Again, half of the people cried famine, but they found the others to be as heartless as they themselves had been.

One of the chief men had a very beautiful wife; his neighbor fell in love with her and carried her off. This occasioned a great quarrel, and after many insults and blows they agreed to abide by the decision of a Troglodyte who had had some distinction under the earlier republic. They went to him and asked that he hear their arguments. "What is it to me," the man said, "whether this woman is yours, or yours? I have my field to cultivate; I am not going to waste my time in settling your differences and doing your business while I neglect my own. I ask you to leave me alone and not bother me any longer with your quarrels." Thereupon he left them, and went to work his land. The ravisher, who was the stronger man,

---

1. **Ispahan** (is' pə hän): also spelled **Isfahan** (is' fə hän); city in Iran; former capital of Persia.
2. **Troglodytes** (träg' lō dīts'): savage cave dwellers of ancient legend, said to have lived in the area of the Red Sea.

swore to die rather than return the woman; and the other, wounded by his neighbor's injustice and the hardness of the judge, was returning home in despair, when he saw in his path a young and pretty woman returning from the well. No longer having a wife, he was attracted to her, and the more so when he discovered that she was the wife of the man he had hoped to employ as a judge, and who had been so insensitive to his misery. He seized her, and carried her off to his house.

Another man possessed a very fertile field, which he cultivated with great care. Two of his neighbors banded together, chased him from his house, and occupied his fields. Between them they made a compact to defend each other from anyone who in turn might seek to overthrow them, and, indeed, they managed to stay there for several months. But one man, tired of sharing what he could have for himself, killed the other and became sole master of the field. His rule did not last long: two other Troglodytes attacked him, and, too weak to defend himself, he was slaughtered.

Yet another Troglodyte, almost naked, saw some wool for sale and asked its price. The merchant said to himself, "At market price I could expect from this wool only enough money to buy two measures of grain; but I will sell it for four times that, so I can get eight measures." The other needed the wool, and paid the price. "I am pleased at this," said the merchant; "now I can buy some grain." "What was that?" the buyer replied. "You need grain? I have some to sell, but the price may astonish you; you know grain is extremely expensive now, for famine reigns everywhere. But give me back my money, and I will give you one measure—but not one bit more, even if you were dying of hunger."

Meanwhile a dreadful disease was ravaging the country. A skillful physician came from a nearby country, and dispensed medicine so effectively that all those in his care were cured.

When the disease had died out, he went to those he had treated and requested his fee. But he met with refusals everywhere, and returned to his own country, worn out by the rigors of a long journey. Shortly afterward, he learned that the same disease had sprung up again and was afflicting the ungrateful land even more than before. This time they did not wait for him to come to them but came to him themselves. "Begone," he told them. "Unjust men, your souls contain a poison more fatal than that which you want cured. You do not deserve a place on the earth, because you have no humanity, no sense of the rules of justice. I believe I would offend the gods who are punishing you, if I opposed their just anger."

Erzeroum,[3] *the 3rd of the moon of Gemmadi II, 1711*

from Letter XII—Usbek to the same, at Ispahan

You have seen, my dear Mirza, how the Troglodytes perished by their wickedness and became victims of their own injustice. Only two families in the entire nation escaped its ruin. For there were in this country two remarkable men, who were humane, just, and lovers of <u>virtue</u>.[4] As much united by their upright hearts as by the corruption all about them, they regarded the general desolation with a pity that became a new bond between them. They labored together for their mutual benefit; their only differences were those that spring from sweet and tender friendship; and in a remote part of the country, apart from compatriots unworthy of their presence, they led a happy and tranquil life. The earth, culti-

---

3. Erzeroum (ar′ zə rōōm): also spelled **Erzurum**; city in northeast Turkey.
4. virtue (vʉr′ chōō): general moral excellence; right action and thinking.

vated by such virtuous hands, seemed to fructify spontaneously.

They loved their wives, and were beloved by them. Their entire attention was directed to educating their children in the ways of virtue; the miseries of their fellow countrymen were constantly represented to them and held up as the sorriest of examples. Above all, they were taught that individual interest is always bound to the common interest, that to try to separate them was to invite ruin, that virtue is not something costly to achieve or painful to exercise, and that justice for others is a blessing for ourselves.

They soon had the consolation of virtuous fathers, seeing their children develop in their image. The young race grew before their eyes and increased through happy marriages; the community grew, but the bond of union remained, and virtue, far from dispersing in the crowd, was instead strengthened by new examples.

Who could describe the happiness of these Troglodytes? So just a people could not fail to gain the gods' favor. From the moment they first learned of the gods, they learned also to fear them, and religion softened manners that nature had left hard.

They instituted feasts in honor of the gods. Boys and young girls adorned with flowers paid them homage with dancing and the harmonies of rustic music; festival banquets followed at once, joyful yet frugal. In such assemblies untutored nature spoke. There young people learned to exchange their hearts, and blushing virgins were surprised into confessions soon to be ratified by their fathers; there tender mothers delighted to predict sweet and faithful unions to come.

When they prayed in the temple for favor from the gods, it was not their own wealth and abundance they sought—for such wishes were unworthy of these happy Troglodytes, who knew only how to request good for their fellows. They went to the altars only to seek health for their parents, unity among their brethren, love from their wives, and affection and obedience from their children. Girls came to submit the tender sacrifice of their hearts, asking no other blessing than the power to make a Troglodyte happy.

In the evening, when the flocks had left the meadows and the weary oxen returned with the plow, they gathered together at a modest supper, where they sang of the wickedness and the miseries of the early Troglodytes, of the revival of virtue in the new people, and of their happiness. They celebrated the grandeur of the gods, their unfailing aid to men who implore it, and their inevitable vengeance on those who do not fear them. They next described the delights of a simple rural life, and the joys of an existence graced with innocence. Then they gave themselves up to a sleep which care and grief never disturbed.

Nature supplied their desires as well as their needs. Cupidity[5] was alien to this happy land, and when they gave presents to each other, he who presented the gift always believed himself the favored one. All the Troglodytes considered themselves members of a single family; their flocks always mingled, and the only trouble they spared themselves was that of separating them.

Erzeroum, the 6th of the moon of Gemmadi II, 1711

from Letter XIII—Usbek to the same

I cannot tell you enough of the Troglodytes' virtue. One of them once said, "Tomorrow my father is to work his field; but I will get up two hours earlier, and when he goes to his work, he will find it all done."

---

5. cupidity (kyo͞o pid′ ə tē): greed for wealth and material possessions.

Another said to himself: "It seems to me that my sister has taken a liking to a young Troglodyte related to us. I must speak to my father and convince him to arrange a marriage."

Another was told that thieves had carried off his herd. "I am very sorry," he said, "because in it there was a white heifer I intended to sacrifice to the gods."

One man was overheard telling another, "I must go to the temple to give thanks to the gods, for my brother, whom my father and I love so dearly, has recovered his health."

And again, "The field bordering my father's is always exposed to the heat of the sun; I must plant some trees in it, so those who work there may have some place in the shade to rest occasionally."

One day, in a group of Troglodytes, an old man mentioned a youth whom he suspected of committing a crime and reproached him for it. "We don't believe him guilty," the young Troglodytes said, "but if he is, may he be the last member of his family to die!"

Another Troglodyte was informed that strangers had sacked his house and carried off everything in it. "If they had not been wicked men," he answered, "I would wish that the gods grant them a longer use of my things than I had of them myself."

All this prosperity was not unenvied; neighboring tribes banded together and decided, on some pretext, to carry off their herds. As soon as they learned of this decision, the Troglodytes sent ambassadors, who spoke as follows:

"What have the Troglodytes done to you? Have they carried off your women, stolen your animals, or ravished your lands? No, for we are just and fear the gods. What, then, do you ask of us? Do you want wool to make clothing? Do you want milk from our herds, or the fruits of our lands? Lay down your arms, come to us, and we will give you all that. But we swear by all that is most sacred, that if you enter our country as enemies, we will consider you wicked people and treat you like wild beasts."

These words were scornfully rejected, and the barbaric tribes came armed into the land of the Troglodytes, whom they believed were defended only by their innocence.

They were, however, quite able to defend themselves. They had put their wives and children within their defenses. It was the wickedness of their enemies which horrified them, not their great numbers. In their hearts burned a previously unknown ardor.[6] One wished to die for his father, another for his wife and children; this one for his brothers, that one for his friends; all for the Troglodyte nation. The place of each dying man was at once taken by another, who had not only the common cause to defend but a particular death to avenge.

Such was the struggle between injustice and virtue. The wretched tribes, whose only object was plunder, were not ashamed to flee; thus, though unaffected by the Troglodytes' virtue, they were forced to succumb to it.

Erzeroum, the 9th of the moon of Gemmadi II, 1711

from Letter XIV—Usbek to the same

As the Troglodyte nation grew larger every day, the people felt it appropriate that they choose a king. They agreed that the crown must go to the most just, and their thoughts turned toward a man respected both for his age and his virtue. He, however, had refused to attend the meeting and, stricken with grief, had shut himself into his house.

Deputies were sent to inform him that he had been chosen. "God forbid," he said, "that I should so wrong the Troglodytes as to make them believe that no one among them was

---

6. **ardor** (är′ dər): very warm feeling; great enthusiasm.

more just than I. You offer me the crown, and if you absolutely insist, I must of course accept it; but rest assured that I will die of grief to see the Troglodytes, free since my birth, submit now to a master." With these words he burst into tears. "O miserable day!" he exclaimed. "Why have I lived so long?" Then his voice became severe. "I see very well what is happening, Troglodytes. Your virtue is beginning to burden you. In your present leaderless state you must be virtuous in spite of yourselves, for if you were not you could not exist, and you would fall into your ancestors' misery. But this yoke seems too hard; you prefer to submit yourselves to a prince and to obey his laws, which would be less <u>exacting</u>[7] than your own <u>morality</u>.[8] You know that under such laws you will be able to indulge your ambition, acquire riches, and languish in mean pleasures; you know that, so long as you avoid actual crime, you will not need virtue." He stopped for a moment; his tears flowed faster than ever. "And what do you suppose I could do? How could I command anything of a Troglodyte? Would you have an act deemed virtuous because I required it, when it would have been done anyway, by natural instinct? O Troglodytes, I am at the end of my life; the blood grows colder in my veins. I will soon rejoin your revered ancestors; why do you ask me to afflict them, and oblige me to tell them that I have left you under a yoke other than that of virtue?"

Erzeroum, the 10th of the moon of Gemmadi II, 1711

---

7. exacting (eg zak′ tiŋ): strict and severely demanding.
8. morality (mō ral′ i tē): principles of right and wrong in conduct; ethics.

Thinking About the Selection

A PERSONAL RESPONSE

sharing impressions

1. Will the success of the second group of Troglodytes continue? Write your comments in your journal.

constructing interpretations

2. Usbek relates this story to show that humans "were born to be virtuous and that justice is a quality as innate in them as existence." How does the story prove these ideas in your view?

Think about
- the differences between the two groups of Troglodytes
- the behavior presented as natural for humans
- the reason the chosen Troglodyte is so unhappy at the thought of being crowned king

3. Compare your prereading ideas about the need for a figure of authority with those expressed by Montesquieu. How has your opinion been influenced by this reading? Explain.

A CREATIVE RESPONSE

4. If someone from the second group of Troglodytes were able to view contemporary American society, what opinion would this person have of life in the United States?

A CRITICAL RESPONSE

5. Evaluate and discuss whether this piece is successful as a story.

Think about
- the writer's development of character, setting, and plot
- the theme of the story
- the use of the letter format
- whether you would recommend it to a friend

6. English political philosopher Thomas Hobbes, who wrote several decades before Montesquieu, believed that humans were innately selfish and uncooperative. He thought it was necessary for people to submit to the authority of an all-powerful monarch in order to escape violent anarchy. What response to the ideas of Hobbes do you find in the Troglodyte story? Explain your answer.

Analyzing the Writer's Craft

ALLEGORY

Recall why Usbek tells this story to Mirza—not to entertain him but to explain certain ideas to him. How does the story achieve this purpose?

Building a Literary Vocabulary. The Troglodyte story is a famous allegory, a narrative in which characters and actions stand for or illustrate abstract ideas. Through the relationship between characters and their actions, the writer of an allegorical tale is able to teach a lesson about human conduct or experience. Montesquieu uses the Troglodytes to stand for humanity. As the Troglodytes progress from the primitive state described in the first letter to a more civilized state, Montesquieu is able to illustrate certain truths about the innate qualities of human beings.

Application: Interpreting Allegory. With a partner, decide what each of the following elements of the story stands for and what it helps illustrate about human life and society.

- the king and the magistrates
- the plague that kills off the first group of Troglodytes
- the evolution of the second group of Troglodytes
- the thieves who invade the second group of Troglodytes
- the Troglodytes' victory
- the Troglodytes' offering to make the older Troglodyte king

Discuss your conclusions with other pairs of students in the class.

Connecting Reading and Writing

1. Read about the seventeenth-century English civil war, including Montesquieu's discussion of the war in *The Spirit of Laws.* In a **book review** of *The Persian Letters,* compare the events in England with those in the story of the Troglodytes.

Option: Create a **chart** that compares events during the English civil war with the Troglodyte story.

2. The later Troglodytes believed that "individual interest is always bound to the common interest, that to try to separate them was to invite ruin, that virtue is not something costly to achieve or painful to exercise, and that justice for others is a blessing for ourselves." Drawing on your own experiences,

respond to any one of these assertions in a **letter** to Montesquieu.

Option: Imagine that these ideas are being debated in your civics or English class. Prepare **notes** that will support your position in the debate and will rebut the opposition.

3. Create a **travel brochure** to lure people to your own ideal world, which incorporates features of Montesquieu's world.

Option: Give your ideal world a name, and compose a brief **encyclopedia article** about this imaginary society.

The Silver Mine

SELMA LAGERLÖF   1858–1940   SWEDEN

A biography of Lagerlöf appears on page 745.

Approaching the Story

Any good story has a theme, or message, but sometimes a writer seems to go farther, using the story to convey an important moral lesson. Such a story is often called a parable. "The Silver Mine" is that kind of story, written by a Swedish winner of the Nobel Prize. It takes place in a remote Swedish village in the late eighteenth century, when Gustaf III (goos' täf) was King.

Building Vocabulary

These essential words are footnoted within the story.

apprehended (ap' rē hend' id): The King **apprehended** that a more satisfactory response was not to be had immediately. (page 93)

arbitrary (är' bə trer' ē): "He's a bit **arbitrary**," said the man. . . ." [He] wants to be the only one to counsel and rule in this parish." (page 93)

renounced (ri nounsd'); **allurements** (ə loor' mənts): "Or how would you advise that I get such a man to show me the mountain—a man who has **renounced** his sweetheart and all the **allurements** of life?" (page 99)

taciturn (tas' ə tʉrn'): Without stood the group of people as quiet and **taciturn** as they were when he went in. (page 99)

Connecting Writing and Reading

If great wealth were to come to you suddenly and unexpectedly, how do you think it would affect your life? Would it change where you live, your family life, who your friends are, where you go to school, what you do in your free time, your overall attitude toward other people? In your journal create a two-column chart. In the first column record ways in which your life would definitely change. In the second, record ways in which you feel your life would not change. Next to each item in the first column, write a **P** if you think the change is positive; write an **N** if you think the change is negative. In this story you will read about how different people respond to a sudden increase in wealth.

The Silver Mine

KING GUSTAF III was traveling through Dalecarlia. He was pressed for time, and all the way he wanted to drive like lightning. Although they drove with such speed that the horses were extended like stretched rubber bands and the coach cleared the turns on two wheels, the King poked his head out of the window and shouted to the postilion, "Why don't you go ahead? Do you think you are driving over eggs?"

Since they had to drive over poor country roads at such a mad pace, it would have been almost a miracle had the harness and wagon held together! And they didn't, either; for at the foot of a steep hill the pole broke—and there the King sat! The courtiers sprang from the coach and scolded the driver, but this did not lessen the damage done. There was no possibility of continuing the journey until the coach was mended.

When the courtiers looked around to try to find something with which the King could amuse himself while he waited, they noticed a church spire looming high above the trees in a grove a short distance ahead. They intimated to the King that he might step into one of the coaches in which the attendants were riding and drive up to the church. It was a Sunday, and the King might attend services to pass the time until the royal coach was ready.

The King accepted the proposal and drove toward the church. He had been traveling for hours through dark forest regions, but here it looked more cheerful, with fairly large meadows and villages, and with the Dal River gliding on light and pretty, between thick rows of alder bushes.

But the King had ill luck to this extent: the bell ringer took up the recessional chant just as the King was stepping from the coach on the church knoll and the people were coming out from the service. But when they came walking past him, the King remained standing, with one foot in the wagon and the other on the footstep. He did not move from the spot—only stared at them. They were the finest lot of folk he had ever seen. All the men were above the average height, with intelligent and earnest faces, and the women were dignified and stately, with an air of Sabbath peace about them.

The whole of the preceding day the King had talked only of the desolate tracts he was passing through, and had said to his courtiers again and again, "Now I am certainly driving through the very poorest part of my kingdom!" But now, when he saw the people, garbed in the picturesque dress of this section of the country, he forgot to think of their poverty; instead his heart warmed, and he remarked to himself, "The King of Sweden is not so badly off as his enemies think. So long as my subjects look like this, I shall probably be able to defend both my faith and my country."

He commanded the courtiers to make known to the people that the stranger who was standing among them was their King and that they should gather around him, so he could talk to them.

And then the King made a speech to the people. He spoke from the high steps outside the vestry, and the narrow step upon which he stood is there even today.

The King gave an account of the sad plight in which the kingdom was placed. He said that the Swedes were threatened with war by both Russians and Danes. Under ordinary circumstances it would not be such a serious matter, but now the army was filled with traitors, and he did not dare depend upon it. Therefore there was no other course for him to take than to go himself into the country settlements and ask his subjects if they would be loyal to their King and help him with men and money, so he could save the Fatherland.

The peasants stood quietly while the King was speaking, and when he had finished they gave no sign either of approval or disapproval.

The King himself thought that he had spoken well. The tears had sprung to his eyes several times while he was speaking. But when the peasants stood there all the while, troubled and undecided, and could not make up their minds to answer him, the King frowned and looked displeased.

The peasants understood that it was becoming monotonous for the King to wait, and finally one of them stepped out from the crowd.

"Now, you must know, King Gustaf, that we were not expecting a royal visit in the parish today," said the peasant, "and therefore we are not prepared to answer you at once. I advise you to go into the vestry and speak with our pastor, while we discuss among ourselves this matter which you have laid before us."

The King apprehended[1] that a more satisfactory response was not to be had immediately, so he felt that it would be best for him to follow the peasant's advice.

When he came into the vestry, he found no one there but a man who looked like a peasant. He was tall and rugged, with big hands, toughened by labor, and he wore neither cassock nor collar, but leather breeches and a long white homespun coat, like all the other men.

He rose and bowed to the King when the latter entered.

"I thought I should find the parson in here," said the King.

The man grew somewhat red in the face. He thought it annoying to mention the fact that he was the parson of this parish, when he saw that the King had mistaken him for a peasant. "Yes," said he, "the parson is usually on hand in here."

The King dropped into a large armchair which stood in the vestry at that time and which stands there today, looking exactly like itself, with this difference: the congregation has had a gilded crown attached to the back of it.

"Have you a good parson in this parish?" asked the King, who wanted to appear interested in the welfare of the peasants.

When the King questioned him in this manner, the parson felt that he couldn't possibly tell who he was. "It's better to let him go on believing that I'm only a peasant," thought he, and replied that the parson was good enough. He preached a pure and clear gospel and tried to live as he taught.

The King thought that this was a good commendation but he had a sharp ear and marked a certain doubt in the tone. "You sound as if you were not quite satisfied with the parson," said the King.

"He's a bit arbitrary,"[2] said the man, thinking that if the King should find out later who he was, he would not think that the parson had been standing here and blowing his own horn. Therefore he wished to come out with a little faultfinding also. "There are some, no doubt, who say the parson wants to be the only one to counsel and rule in this parish," he continued.

"Then, at all events, he has led and managed in the best possible way," said the King. He didn't like it that the peasant complained of one who was placed above him. "To me it appears as though good habits and old-time simplicity were the rule here."

---

1. apprehended (ap′ rē hend′ id): understood.
2. arbitrary (ar′ bə trer′ ē): given to making decisions without consultation.

"The people are good enough," said the curate, "but then they live in poverty and isolation. Human beings here would certainly be no better than others if this world's temptations came closer to them."

"But there's no fear of anything of the sort happening," said the King, with a shrug.

He said nothing further, but began thrumming on the table with his fingers. He thought he had exchanged a sufficient number of gracious words with this peasant and wondered when the others would be ready with their answer.

"These peasants are not very eager to help their King," thought he. "If I only had my coach, I would drive away from them and their palaver!"

The pastor sat there troubled, debating with himself as to how he should decide an important matter which he must settle. He was beginning to feel happy because he had not told the King who he was. Now he felt that he could speak with him about matters which otherwise he could not have placed before him.

After a while the parson broke the silence and asked the King if it was an actual fact that enemies were upon them and that the kingdom was in danger.

The King thought this man ought to have sense enough not to trouble him further. He simply glared at him and said nothing.

"I ask because I was standing in here and could not hear very well," said the parson. "But if this is really the case, I want to say to you that the pastor of this congregation might perhaps be able to procure for the King as much money as he will need."

"I thought that you said just now that everyone here was poor," said the King, thinking that the man did not know what he was talking about.

"Yes, that's true," replied the rector, "and the parson has no more than any of the others.

But if the King would condescend to listen to me for a moment, I will explain how the pastor happens to have the power to help him."

"You may speak," said the King. "You seem to find it easier to get the words past your lips than your friends and neighbors out there, who never will be ready with what they have to tell me."

"It is not so easy to reply to the King! I'm afraid that, in the end, it will be the parson who must undertake this on behalf of the others."

The King crossed his legs, folded his arms, and let his head sink down on his breast. "You may begin now," he said, in the tone of one already asleep.

"Once upon a time there were five men from this parish who were out on a moose hunt," began the clergyman. "One of them was the parson of whom we are speaking. Two of the others were soldiers, named Olaf and Eric Svärd; the fourth man was the innkeeper in this settlement, and the fifth was a peasant named Israel Per Persson."[3]

"Don't go to the trouble of mentioning so many names," muttered the King, letting his head droop to one side.

"Those men were good hunters," continued the parson, "who usually had luck with them, but that day they had wandered long and far without getting anything. Finally they gave up the hunt altogether and sat down on the ground to talk. They said there was not a spot in the whole forest fit for cultivation; all of it was only mountain and swampland. 'Our Lord has not done right by us in giving us such a poor land to live in,' said one. 'In other localities people can get riches for themselves in abundance, but here, with all our toil and drudgery we can scarcely get our daily bread.'"

The pastor paused a moment, as if uncertain that the King heard him, but the latter moved

---

3. **Israel Per Persson** (is′ ru el par par′ sôn).

his little finger to show that he was awake.

"Just as the hunters were discussing this matter, the parson saw something that glittered at the base of the mountain, where he had kicked away a moss tuft. 'This is a queer mountain,' he thought, as he kicked off another moss tuft. He picked up a sliver of stone that came with the moss and which shone exactly like the other. 'It can't be possible that this stuff is lead,' said he.

"Then the others sprang up and scraped away the turf with the butt ends of their rifles. When they did this, they saw plainly that a broad vein of ore followed the mountain.

" 'What do you think this might be?' asked the parson.

"The men chipped off bits of stone and bit into them. 'It must be lead, or zinc at least,' said they.

"'And the whole mountain is full of it,' added the innkeeper."

When the parson had got thus far in his narrative, the King's head was seen to straighten up a little and one eye opened. "Do you know if any of these persons knew anything about ore and minerals?" he asked.

"They did not," replied the parson.

Then the King's head sank and both eyes closed.

"The clergyman and his companions were very happy," continued the speaker, without letting himself be disturbed by the King's indifference; "they fancied that now they had found that which would give them and their descendants wealth. 'I'll never have to do any more work,' said one. 'Now I can afford to do nothing at all the whole week through, and on Sundays I shall drive to church in a golden chariot!' They were otherwise sensible men, but the great find had gone to their heads, and they talked like children. Still they had enough presence of mind to put back the moss tufts and conceal the vein of ore. Then they carefully noted the place where it was, and

went home. Before they parted company, they agreed that the parson should travel to Falun[4] and ask the mining expert what kind of ore this was. He was to return as soon as possible, and until then they promised one another on oath not to reveal to a single soul where the ore was to be found."

The King's head was raised again a trifle, but he did not interrupt the speaker with a word. It appeared as though he was beginning to believe that the man actually had something of importance he wished to say to him, since he didn't allow himself to be disturbed by his indifference.

"Then the parson departed with a few samples of ore in his pocket. He was just as happy in the thought of becoming rich as the others were. He was thinking of rebuilding the parsonage, which at present was no better than a peasant's cottage, and then he would marry a dean's daughter whom he liked. He had thought that he might have to wait for her many years. He was poor and obscure and knew that it would be a long while before he should get any post that would enable him to marry.

"The parson drove over to Falun in two days, and there he had to wait another whole day because the mining expert was away. Finally he ran across him and showed him the bits of ore. The mining expert took them in his hand. He looked at them first, then at the parson. The parson related how he had found them in a mountain at home in his parish, and wondered if it might not be lead.

" 'No, it's not lead,' said the mining expert.

" 'Perhaps it is zinc, then?' asked the parson.

" 'Nor is it zinc,' said the mineralogist.

"The parson thought that all the hope within him sank. He had not been so depressed in many a long day.

---

4. **Falun** (fô′ lo͞on).

" 'Have you many stones like these in your parish?' asked the mineralogist.

" 'We have a whole mountainful,' said the parson.

"Then the mineralogist came up closer, slapped the parson on the shoulder, and said, 'Let us see that you make such good use of this that it will prove a blessing both to yourselves and to the country, for this is silver.'

" 'Indeed?' said the parson, feeling his way. 'So it is silver!'

"The mineralogist began telling him how he should go to work to get legal rights to the mine and gave him many valuable suggestions; but the parson stood there dazed and did not listen to what the mineralogist was saying. He was thinking how wonderful it was that at home in his poor parish stood a whole mountain of silver ore, waiting for him."

The King raised his head so suddenly that the parson stopped short in his narrative. "It turned out, of course, that when he got home and began working the mine, he saw that the mineralogist had only been fooling him," said the King.

"Oh, no, the mineralogist had not fooled him," said the parson.

"You may continue," said the King as he settled himself more comfortably in the chair to listen.

"When the parson was at home again and was driving through the parish," continued the clergyman, "he thought that first of all he should inform his partners of the value of their find. And as he drove alongside the innkeeper Sten Stensson's place, he intended to drive up to the house to tell him they had found silver. But when he stopped outside the gate, he noticed that a broad path of evergreen was strewn all the way up to the doorstep.

" 'Who has died in this place?' asked the parson of a boy who stood leaning against the fence.

" 'The innkeeper himself,' answered the boy. Then he let the clergyman know that the innkeeper had drunk himself full every day for a week. 'Oh, so much brandy, so much brandy, has been drunk here!'

" 'How can that be?' asked the parson. 'The innkeeper used never to drink himself full.'

" 'Oh,' said the boy, 'he drank because he said he had found a mine. He was very rich. He should never have to do anything now but drink, he said. Last night he drove off, full as he was, and the wagon turned over and he was killed.'

"When the parson heard this, he drove homeward, distressed over what he had heard. He had come back so happy, rejoicing because he could tell the great news.

"When the parson had driven a few paces, he saw Israel Per Persson walking along. He looked about as usual, and the parson thought it was well that fortune had not gone to his head too. Him he would cheer at once with the news that he was a rich man.

" 'Good day!' said Per Person. 'Do you come from Falun now?'

" 'I do,' said the parson. 'And now I must tell you that it has turned out even better than we had imagined. The mineralogist said it was silver ore that we had found.'

"That instant Per Persson looked as though the ground had opened under him. 'What are you saying, what are you saying? Is it silver?'

" 'Yes,' answered the parson. 'We'll all be rich men now, all of us, and can live like gentlemen.'

" 'Oh, is it silver?' said Per Persson once again, looking more and more mournful.

" 'Why, of course it is silver,' replied the parson. 'You mustn't think that I want to deceive you. You mustn't be afraid to be happy.'

" 'Happy!' said Per Persson. 'Should I be happy? I believed it was only glitter that we had found, so I thought it would be better to take the certain for the uncertain; I have sold my share in the mine to Olaf Svärd for a hundred dollars.'

"He was desperate, and when the parson drove away from him, he stood on the highway and wept.

"When the clergyman got back to his home, he sent a servant to Olaf Svärd and his brother to tell them that it was silver they had found. He thought that he had had quite enough of driving around and spreading the good news.

"But in the evening, when the parson sat alone, his joy asserted itself again. He went out in the darkness and stood on a hillock upon which he contemplated building the new parsonage. It should be imposing, of course, as fine as a bishop's palace. He stood there long that night; nor did he content himself with rebuilding the parsonage! It occurred to him that, since there were such riches to be found in the parish, throngs of people would pour in, and finally a whole city would be built around the mine. And then he would have to erect a new church in place of the old one. Toward this object a large portion of his wealth would probably go. And he was not content with this, either, but fancied that, when his church was ready, the King and many bishops would come to the dedication. Then the King would be pleased with the church, but he would remark that there was no place where a king might put up, and then he would have to erect a castle in the new city."

Just then one of the King's courtiers opened the door of the vestry and announced that the big royal coach was mended.

At the first moment the King was ready to withdraw, but on second thought he changed his mind. "You may tell your story to the end," he said to the parson. "But you can hurry it a bit. We know all about how the man thought and dreamed. We want to know how he acted."

"But while the parson was still lost in his dreams," continued the clergyman, "word came to him that Israel Per Persson had made away with himself. He had not been able to bear the disappointment of having sold his share in the mine. He had thought, no doubt, that he could not endure to go about every day seeing another enjoying the wealth that might have been his."

The King straightened up a little. He kept both eyes open. "Upon my word," he said, "if I had been that parson, I should have had enough of the mine!"

"The King is a rich man," said the parson. "He has quite enough, at all events. It is not the same thing with a poor curate who possesses nothing. The unhappy wretch thought instead, when he saw that God's blessing was not with his enterprise, 'I will dream no more of bringing glory and profit to myself with these riches, but I can't let the silver lie buried in the earth! I must take it out, for the benefit of the poor and needy. I will work the mine, to put the whole parish on its feet.'

"So one day the parson went out to see Olaf Svärd, to ask him and his brother what should be done immediately with the silver mountain. When he came in the vicinity of the barracks he met a cart surrounded by armed peasants, and in the cart sat a man with his hands tied behind him and a rope around his ankles.

"When the parson passed by, the cart stopped and he had time to regard the prisoner, whose head was tied up so it was not easy to see who he was. But the parson thought he recognized Olaf Svärd. He heard the prisoner beg those who guarded him to let him speak a few words with the parson.

"The parson drew nearer, and the prisoner turned toward him. 'You will soon be the only one who knows where the silver mine is,' said Olaf.

"'What are you saying, Olaf?' asked the parson.

"'Well, you see, parson, since we have learned that it was a silver mine we had found, my brother and I could no longer be as good friends as before. We were continually quarreling. Last night we got into a controversy over which one of us five it was who first discovered the mine. It ended in strife between us, and we came to blows. I have killed my brother and he has left me with a souvenir across the forehead to remember him by. I must hang now, and then you will be the only one who knows about the mine; therefore I wish to ask something of you.'

" 'Speak out!' said the parson. 'I'll do what I can for you.'

" 'You know that I am leaving several little children behind me,' began the soldier, but the parson interrupted him.

" 'As regards this, you can rest easy. That which comes to your share in the mine they shall have, exactly as if you yourself were living.'

" 'No,' said Olaf Svard, 'it was another thing I wanted to ask of you. Don't let them have any portion of that which comes from the mine!'

"The parson staggered back a step. He stood there dumb and could not answer.

" 'If you do not promise me this, I cannot die in peace,' said the prisoner.

" 'Yes,' said the parson slowly and painfully. 'I promise you what you ask of me.'

"Thereupon the murderer was taken away, and the parson stood on the highway thinking how he should keep the promise he had given him. On the way home he thought of the wealth which he had been so happy over. What if it really were true that the people in this community could not stand riches? Already four were ruined who hitherto had been dignified and excellent men. He seemed to see the whole community before him, and he pictured to himself how this silver mine would destroy one after another. Was it befitting that he, who had been appointed to watch over these poor human beings' souls, should let loose upon them that which would

be their destruction?"

All of a sudden the King sat bolt upright in his chair. "I declare!" said he, "you'll make me understand that a parson in this isolated settlement must be every inch a man."

"Nor was what had already happened enough," continued the parson, "for as soon as the news about the mine spread among the parishioners, they stopped working and went about in idleness, waiting for the time when great riches should pour in on them. All the ne'er-do-wells there were in this section streamed in, and drunkenness and fighting were what the parson heard talked of continually. A lot of people did nothing but tramp around in the forest searching for the mine, and the parson marked that as soon as he left the house people followed him stealthily to find out if he wasn't going to the silver mountain and to steal the secret from him.

"When matters were come to this pass, the parson called the peasants together to vote. To start with, he reminded them of all the misfortunes which the discovery of the mountain had brought upon them, and he asked them if they were going to let themselves be ruined or if they would save themselves. Then he told them that they must not expect him, who was their spiritual adviser, to help in their destruction. Now he had decided not to reveal to anyone where the silver mine was, and never would he himself take riches from it. And then he asked the peasants how they would have it henceforth. If they wished to continue their search for the mine and wait upon riches, then he would go so far away that no word of their misery could reach him; but if they would give up thinking about the silver mine and be as heretofore, he would remain with them. 'Whichever way you may choose,' said the parson, 'remember this, that from me no one shall ever know anything about the silver mountain.' "

"Well," said the King, "how did they decide?"

"They did as their pastor wished," said the parson. "They understood that he meant well by them when he wanted to remain poor for their sakes. And they commissioned him to go to the forest and conceal the vein of ore with evergreen and stone, so that no one would be able to find it—neither they themselves nor their posterity."

"And ever since the parson has been living here just as poor as the rest?"

"Yes," answered the curate, "he has lived here just as poor as the rest."

"He has married, of course, and built a new parsonage?" said the King.

"No, he couldn't afford to marry, and he lives in the old cabin."

"It's a pretty story that you have told me," said the King. After a few seconds he resumed, "Was it of the silver mountain that you were thinking when you said that the parson here would be able to procure for me as much money as I need?"

"Yes," said the other.

"But I can't put the thumbscrews on him," said the King. "Or how would you advise that I get such a man to show me the mountain—a man who has renounced[5] his sweetheart and all the allurements[6] of life?"

"Oh, that's a different matter," said the parson. "But if it's the Fatherland that is in need of the fortune, he will probably give in."

"Will you answer for that?" asked the King.

"Yes, that I will answer for," said the clergyman.

"Doesn't he care, then, what becomes of his parishioners?"

"That can rest in God's hands."

The King rose from his chair and walked over to the window. He stood for a moment and looked upon the group of people outside. The longer he looked, the clearer his large eyes shone; and his figure seemed to grow. "You may greet the pastor of this congregation and say that for Sweden's King there is no sight more beautiful than to see a people such as this!"

Then the King turned from the window and looked at the clergyman. He began to smile. "Is it true that the pastor of this parish is so poor that he removes his black clothes as soon as the service is over and dresses himself like a peasant?" asked the King.

"Yes, so poor is he," said the curate, and a crimson flush leaped into his rough-hewn face.

The King went back to the window. One could see that he was in his best mood. All that was noble and great within him had been quickened into life. "You must let that mine lie in peace," said the King. "Inasmuch as you have labored and starved a lifetime to make this people such as you would have it, you may keep it as it is."

"But if the kingdom is in danger?" said the parson.

"The kingdom is better served with men than with money," remarked the King. When he had said this, he bade the clergyman farewell and went out from the vestry.

Without stood the group of people, as quiet and taciturn[7] as they were when he went in. As the King came down the steps, a peasant stepped up to him.

"Have you had a talk with our pastor?" said the peasant.

"Yes," said the King. "I have."

"Then of course you have our answer?" said the peasant. "We asked you to go in and talk with our parson, that he might give you an answer from us."

"I have the answer," said the King.

---

5. renounced (ri nounsd′): gave up.

6. allurements (ə loor′ mənts): things that tempt strongly.

7. taciturn (tas′ ə turn′): not liking to talk.

Thinking About the Story

A PERSONAL RESPONSE

sharing impressions

1. How did you react to the parson's decision? Take a minute to describe this reaction in your journal.

constructing interpretations

2. In your view is the parson right to keep the location of the mine a secret?
   Think about
   • what happened shortly after the mine was discovered
   • the poverty of the people
   • the effects of his decision upon them
   • the effects upon his own life

3. Why do you think the King decides to let the mine "lie in peace"?

A CREATIVE RESPONSE

4. If the parson and the community had gone ahead and mined the silver, what might the outcome have been?

A CRITICAL RESPONSE

5. Do you agree with the lesson conveyed by the story?
   Think about
   • news items you might have read about people who have experienced a sudden increase in wealth
   • how important money is in our culture
   • what you wrote in your prereading chart

6. Compare the role of the parson in "The Silver Mine" to the ideas about authority presented in the excerpt from *The Persian Letters*.
   Think about
   • how the first group of Troglodytes responds to authority
   • the absence of an authority figure in the second group of Troglodytes
   • whether the parson's decision making works for his community

Analyzing the Writer's Craft

CHARACTERIZATION

Think about the two main characters in this story. What pieces of information presented by the writer contribute to your impression of them?

Building a Literary Vocabulary. Characterization refers to the techniques that a writer uses to develop characters. Describing physical appearance is one way to communicate something about a character. A character's nature may be revealed through his or her own speech, thoughts, feelings, or actions, as well as through the speech, thoughts, feelings, or actions of other characters. In addition, direct comments made by the narrator can often provide insight into the character's nature and previous experience. In "The Silver Mine," for example, the King's impatient nature is suggested by his own actions and also by the actions of his attendants. The King's self-importance is shown by his thoughts and actions as he listens to the parson's story. Near the end of the story, an important aspect of the King is shown by the decision he makes. Further information about the King comes by way of the narrator's interpretive comment "All that was noble and great within him had been quickened into life."

Application: Analyzing Characterization. Make a detailed study of how the author develops the character of the parson. Working with two or three classmates, find one or two examples of each of the following means of characterization: physical description; the character's speech, thoughts, feelings, or actions; the speech, thoughts, feelings, or actions of other characters; and the direct comments of the narrator. For each example, decide which quality of the parson's is being brought out. Discuss which methods of characterization are most important in giving a clear picture of the parson's character. Share your conclusions with other members of your class.

Connecting Reading and Writing

1. Write a human-interest **story** for a community newspaper describing how sudden wealth has affected a person or family. Model some of the facts of this story after "The Silver Mine," but change the outcome or the message if you like.

Option: Based on the same situation, write a modern **parable** for a short story collection.

2. The parson tells the King that the people are better off because they live in "poverty and isolation." Do you agree with this view? Write a newspaper **editorial** setting forth your position.

Option: Write a **sermon** that deals with the effects of poverty and isolation on people today.

3. Read Mark Twain's short story "The Man That Corrupted Hadleyburg." Write a **report** for your class in which you summarize the story and compare it with "The Silver Mine" in terms of the temptations faced by characters, the characters' responses, and the way characters feel at the end.

Option: Prepare a **chart** that indicates the similarities and differences between the two stories.

Mussoco

OSCAR RIBAS   1909–1961   ANGOLA

A biography of Ribas appears on page 751.

*A*pproaching the Story

Angola, a country on the southwestern coast of Africa, was the birthplace of Oscar Ribas, who became the most important writer of Portuguese Africa. Ribas's father was Portuguese, and his mother came from the Kimbundu people, the main inhabitants of the region. Ribas devoted eighteen years to researching the religion and culture of this people. He wrote "Mussoco" in Portuguese. The story takes place in Luanda, the capital of Angola, where hundreds of thousands of poor people live. In this story the author presents the voices of the main characters as well as those of several unidentified members of the community.

*B*uilding Vocabulary

These essential words are footnoted within the story.

premonition (prem' ə nish' ən): The **premonition** of death was already spreading. (page 105)

pretext (prē' tekst): Should she go in or not? And under what **pretext?** (page 106)

irremediable (ir' ri mē' dē ə bəl): To call up **irremediable** evil, Donana went to Ambriz. (page 106)

inexorable (in eks' ə rə bəl): The vengeful curse took its **inexorable** course. (page 109)

*C*onnecting Writing and Reading

Imagine that a grocery store clerk mistakenly gives you a five-dollar bill instead of a one-dollar bill for change. Do you point out the error? What if you found a hundred-dollar bill lying on a locker room floor? Would you return the money? Jot down your responses in your journal and keep them in mind as you read about money—lost and found—and about the choice someone else makes.

*I*N THE MORNING, as soon as she was inside the house, Mussoco triumphantly announced:

"Hey, Auntie, I'm in luck! I've found lots of money!"—and she showed her a small parcel.

"Shh, don't shout, someone might hear you outside! Let's go into the room," advised her aunt, who, sitting on a small stool, was calmly cleaning her teeth with a piece of coal and some salt.

Grandmother, who was sweeping the yard, also with a coal and salt in her mouth, hurried up to them when she overheard what they were talking about.

"What? What's this?" she asked curiously.

"I've had bad luck . . . I was caught . . . in a snare . . . for partridges! . . ."

A dove could be heard cooing in the next hut.

Finally, the doors were closed; the three women sat down on the iron bedstead and, with beating hearts, nervously counted and recounted the money. Two hundred and ten escudos![1] That's something! The Lord is generous, he does not forget his sinners!

"Now keep your trap shut. You haven't seen anything, you hear? With this kind of money, daughter, you could buy a house and have a good life," advised the grandmother.

"No, Grannie! What do I want a house for? We'll buy nice fabrics and expensive jewelry . . . and a hand-turned sewing machine, if there's enough money . . ."

"Of course, you can buy something for yourself . . . But our hovel's a hovel, there's no other word for it . . . Don't be a fool!" objected her aunt.

"A house! Nice clothes, yes! Can't I even handle my own money, then?"

Her head was spinning; she got up quickly and took a few quick paces round the room in order to shake off at least some of the feeling of joy that had overwhelmed her.

Two emotions were warring within her—self-respect and fear.

Smiling, the grandmother clapped her hands and then snapped her fingers:

"You see! Money makes people lose their heads!"

"Dance, daughter, dance; your patron saints have been kind to you . . . ," added her aunt jokingly.

A little time passed and one of the women neighbors began wailing all over the district:

"Who's found 210 escudos? Whoever's found them ought to give them back, because I've lost them. Come on! Who's found the money? People, you work too, you know what a hard life it is for the poor, so don't hide my money from me! I've lost 210 escudos. Who's found them? For God's sake, let me have them back! If someone has a heart of stone, then his grave shall be of stone. Listen, folks, I appeal to you all!"

On hearing her neighbor's wails, Mussoco decided to return the money to its rightful owner. Two emotions were warring within her—self-respect and fear. It was one thing when you didn't know who the money belonged to, but now . . . knowing whose it was! No! And a neighbor too!

"Listen, Auntie. I'm going to give the money back to Donana. D'you hear what she's saying? If someone has a heart of stone, that person shall have a stone grave!" continued the girl agitatedly.

Auntie replied cunningly with an impassive face:

"What d'you mean return it? You didn't steal the money, did you? You found it on the street. That means it's yours. What are you scared of, then?"

"Don't turn down your own happiness! Finding isn't stealing. If somebody finds some-

---

1. **two hundred and ten escudos** (es kōō' dōs): about $460.

thing, it's been found, there's nothing bad can come of that. Don't be a fool!" said the old woman in support of the aunt.

At the sight of the wretched Donana, her clothes in disarray, proclaiming her grief to the world at large, all the people felt sorry for her. So much money! Poor woman! But who had picked it up? No, they hadn't found anything. They weren't bloodsuckers. But how could anyone resist such a plea? Keep that money when the owner was in such distress over it? How cold-hearted could you get? No one could be guilty of such a crime; everybody knew how hard life was.

"Donana, where did you lose your money?" asked the passersby as they gathered round her.

The unhappy woman repeated, as if by clockwork:

"I don't know, my dears. This morning, as usual, I left for Quanza to pay for the tobacco and find some work. I got as far as Alta station . . . and . . . horrors! My God! I suddenly realized the money was gone! I went home as fast as I could and looked over every inch of the road. When I got home, I turned everything upside down like crazy. I hunted through the trunks, the drawers, the clothes. Not a sign anywhere! I felt in all the nooks and crannies. Even in the mattress. But I still couldn't find it." She groaned. "All that work, all that hunger and fear in the forest, and all I went through in the market for those choosy customers—and what for? To lose everything I worked so hard to earn! Oi!" and she wrung her hands in despair. "I've already shouted it all over Ingombota.[2] I've shouted it in Bungo, too. I've shouted it in Maianga.[3] I've shouted it out at the fish and meat market as well. I'm done in! I've screamed my head off everywhere! Oi-oi-oi! I'm worn out! But nobody's turned up with the money—no one!"

"Ai-ai-ai! Who picked up the money, and why hasn't it been returned! Listen to the woman weeping, she's in agony, and they can't even give back what isn't theirs! Well, well! What mean folks there are in this world! Taking something that doesn't belong to them!"

"Yours, yours, yours, but it'll turn against you!" recited a little gray bird with a white breast, lightly hopping from branch to branch in a mulberry tree.

The days dragged on in wearisome tension. All the poor of Luanda, as if personally hit by the disaster, sympathized deeply with Donana in her grief. After all, how could the inhabitants, who were all in equally dire straits,[4] react calmly to such unheard-of meanness? They all knew how hard it was to earn money, they tasted the bitter bread of work, they slept badly at night, and so they were not indifferent to someone else's misfortune. No, a thousand times no! They would never do such a thing; the poor always help the poor! Washing or cooking in the houses of the masters, haggling in the streets or busy in their own hovels, they had never found life easy. At work they had to listen to the insults and abuse of their masters, obey their whims, deprive themselves of everything to satisfy them. And in their own homes, they had more than their share of worry and suffering. And God alone knew how many times they had to work themselves to the bone in order to earn some money and fill their bellies just once!

A warning that had traveled round the whole city was again heard in every spot. Not as an anguished complaint this time, but as an evil, fuming threat:

"I've prayed. I've screamed about the money I've lost, but nobody's answered. Listen, listen carefully and don't say afterwards that I'm a witch: I'm going to have spells cast. You hear me? I'm going to have spells cast! So don't

---

2. **Ingombota** (iŋ gõm bô′ tə).
3. **Maianga** (mī än′ gə).
4. **dire straits** (dīr strāts): very serious difficulties.

complain about it afterwards . . . Whoever took that money is going to die. Whoever washes that corpse shall die. Whoever cuts its hair shall die. Whoever dresses it shall die. Whoever goes to bury it shall die. And whoever says, 'Woe is me!' shall also die!"

"Get away with you!" muttered the women in fright, although they understood deep down inside what was behind this hysterical outburst.

Others, in the grip of the same superstition, added with a bitter sneer:

"It's going to go badly for whoever took someone else's money."

Mothers, some with small children slung behind them with a strip of cloth, promised themselves to check the children's hidey-holes carefully. Sometimes, as is known, children could find money (why not?) and spend it on all kinds of sweets and toys.

"A child is kindred to a lunatic," babbled one old crone, thereby strengthening the mothers in their decision.

Chiming in the evening air that was lit by the glittering rays of the evening sun, the bells of Carmo church solemnly announced that an infant had been admitted to the holy faith. A little urchin, indifferent to the woman who was spreading such horror around, chanted something of his own to the music of the bells.

In the meantime, the premonition[5] of death was already spreading round and sowing the horror of disaster everywhere. Lord, who had found that money? Begone, evil! Begone, evil! Where are you, heart of stone? Why don't you own up?

More terrified than anybody, Mussoco was no longer able to contain her growing sense of panic, in spite of her family's reassurances. Her neighbor's curses, which had disturbed their hut many times before, rang insistently in her ears: "All you people who work, who know the sufferings of the poor, don't hide what I'm looking for!" A decline of spirits gradually took over from the initial exultation. The fine fabrics, the beautiful and expensive jewelry, the pleasures—all had fallen into a bottomless pit. She again spoke to her aunt and grandmother about returning the money. But both of them said: "No, no; don't be a fool." And again, as before, they talked her out of it. But now, under the stress of those curses, she ought to give up the money she had found, whether they liked the idea or not.

"Auntie!" she began meaningfully, "Have you heard what Donana's been saying?"

"Of course. Let her go and cast as many spells as she wants. Let her!"

"All that talk about spells . . . Well, she isn't joking! . . ." said Mussoco uneasily.

But the old woman, unwilling to lose their unexpected wealth and irritated by the girl's stubborn petty-mindedness, declared:

"You see! You too, now! Is the money burning your hands? Ignore that nonsense. It's all to put the wind up folks. I wasn't born yesterday, you know!"

"But Grandma . . ."

"Take no notice! And don't be such a nuisance! All that fear over nothing! If we'd stolen the money, then you could expect trouble. But you only picked it up in the street . . ."

"It's all just her talk! She's lying, she doesn't mean to do anything! So she'll go and have spells cast, only where? Don't give up the money, your luck's in! A fine one you are!" she added, smacking her lips. "If she found that money, d'you think she'd hand it back?" added her aunt heatedly, lifting up her left eyelid with her index finger.

Morally crushed again, Mussoco weakly gave in to her former reasoning. Poor girl! Inwardly, this behavior tormented her, consumed her with fire. Cursed be the moment when she had found that money! Just so that

---

5. premonition (prem' ə nish' ən): a feeling, in advance of the event, that something is going to happen.

she could be tormented like this? Was the money burning her hands? her grandmother had asked. Yes, it was burning all right, only not her hands, but her heart; it was burning her whole life up all the time. "I'm going to have spells cast! D'you hear? I'm going to have spells cast!" Oh, how that voice was torturing her! Oh, these cruel relatives, these cruel friends! The proverb was right: "Honey outside, ice within!"

"I've wept, I've screamed about the money I lost, but nobody's answered. Listen, listen carefully and don't say afterwards that I'm a witch: I'm going to have spells cast! D'you hear! I'm going to have spells cast! So don't complain about it afterwards . . . Whoever washes that corpse shall die. Whoever trims its nails shall die. Whoever dresses it shall die. Whoever goes to bury it shall die! Whoever says, 'Woe is me!' shall also die." So Donana went about, hurling curses everywhere.

That evening, perhaps because of what she had been through during the day, Mussoco felt a decision forming within her: she would return the money to its owner. Elated, she went out. Why tell her aunt and her grandmother first? No, they would only interfere.

Hiding the money in her clothes, she walked with uncertain steps through the dusk that was filled with the sound of people talking and the chirping of the cicadas. Her neighbor's hut was quite near, but, as if in obedience to some unconscious impulse, her legs took her in the opposite direction. Calming down and panicking by turns, she argued with herself: Give her the money now? Yes, but how are you going to explain what happened? Won't you be ashamed to hand it over after so many days have gone by?

While lost in thought, she suddenly realized with astonishment that she was standing at the door of Donana's hut. Should she go in or not? And under what pretext?[6] Yes, what pretext, indeed? Could she bring herself to do

this? No, she certainly could not!

It was not her family but her timidity that got the better of her this time. She was ashamed, deeply ashamed! That damned money was destroying her peace of mind.

And so Donana appealed and threatened. But with no result. In spite of everything, the money had not been found. There was only one thing left now—vengeance to the death! Should she meekly tolerate her loss so that some coldhearted stranger should enjoy what she had achieved at the cost of such labor and self-sacrifice? No, it must never happen! Whoever it might be, that person must have heard her prayers. Yes, must have heard; for her cries had attracted attention everywhere. Everybody had noticed. For eight days on end, her voice had rung out over all the districts in the city, even among the whining of the beggars and the shrieks of the insane. She had sworn to have spells cast, and now she was going to do just that. Pity? For whom? Had the person who found her money taken pity on her in her grief? To the heart of stone, a grave of stone!

To call up irremediable[7] evil, Donana went to Ambriz. In those parts, as rumor had it, she would find the best witchdoctors. With the help of the *jimbambi*,[8] they would quickly dispatch the culprit to the other world. Yes, and in no time at all.

"I have come to talk to the elders and their ancestors. I want you to bring down the evil spirits on whoever found the money I lost. Use your powers so that the elders and their ancestors will act quickly," said Donana to one of the witchdoctors.

She went into the witchdoctor's cage that was stood about with idols and all the para-

---

6. **pretext** (prē′ tekst): an excuse.
7. **irremediable** (ir′ ri mē′ dē ə bəl): not capable of being corrected or remedied.
8. *jimbambi* (zhim bäm′ bi): evil spirits.

phernalia of witchcraft, knelt down, struck the ground with the flat of her hands and through her tears uttered oaths and appeals for revenge.

"To you, Honji and Vunji, Muene-Congo[9] and the Lord, Lord Almighty, I appeal for justice. For eight days I have wept, cried out everywhere about the money I lost, but no one has answered at all. Those who could see merely looked at me, those who could hear merely listened. O elders and your forefathers, if whoever found my money is far away and did not hear my appeals, let nothing bad happen to him; but if he heard and did not answer, I want you to rip him apart as with a knife, the way they cut up meat into pieces at the market. Let that person die who found the money and anyone who helps in spending it. And let that person die who washes the corpse, who trims its nails, who cuts its hair, who dresses it, or who says, 'Woe is me.' May all die—all, all, all, because all heard me and no one opened his heart!"

Drawing sound out of a dusty goat's horn, the witchdoctor sent that curse out into space—first to the east, then to the west, and then repeated it before blowing on the horn.

"And now beware of the dead! Mind where you go, and don't say 'Woe is me!' Remember your words—the *jimbambi* are no laughing matter," the witchdoctor warned Donana.

At last! What joy! Soon, soon, when the rains come, the curse will begin to act. And the villain will never make fun of her; will the heart of stone fall into a stone grave? Is she a witch? No. How could they call her so? Didn't she warn everyone of her intentions? And who had confessed? No one. No, she had not acted like a witch: a witch doesn't warn you but brings death out of envy. But she was not consumed by envy. The gods could see that she had not brought death on anyone; it had been sought. It had been sought by the culprit who had ignored her pleas. Now let that person reap the fruits.

Mussoco had been feeling ill for several days. In spite of treatment at home, the sickness did not pass off: she had a constant temperature, fever and stomach cramps, and she kept spitting blood.

"Perhaps we ought to fetch the witchdoctor," suggested her grandmother quietly during the night's vigil; she was already worried about Donana's curse.

The aunt yawned uneasily and nodded her head in agreement. She had been troubled by vague gnawings of conscience ever since the day when the confounded illness had begun. Although she was in sympathy with the grandmother, she did not want to admit her feelings: some sort of shame, cowardice, a morbid inadequacy spoke in her, making her wait for the tragic denouement. Yes, tragic, for she had already recognized the workings of the curse.

The local healer appeared next morning. But nothing, absolutely nothing could dispel the illness. According to *mumzamba*, the supernatural prophecy, if the accursed witchcraft entered a house, it would surely empty it in a very short space of time. And all because of money, money found in the street and hidden from the owner.

"Lord, I'm so young to die! And all because of the money I never even used," sighed Mussoco as she faded slowly away.

That night, a thunderstorm raged. The aunt and the grandmother, faced with the ghastly truth, loudly gave voice to their repentance:

"Lord, Mussoco! What wrong have we done

> *Guide for Interpretation*
>
> Consider the extent of the curse, which includes whoever found Donana's money and any person remotely connected with her loss. In one sense, the curse simply reveals the depth of Donana's rage. In a larger sense, the curse seems central to the message of the story. As you continue your reading, think about what the curse might symbolize.

---

9. **Muene-Congo** (mwe′ ne kõŋ′ gô).

to you to make you leave us like this? Oi-oi-oi, our poor little girl! Who will we have left now?"

Their agitated neighbor hurried in on hearing the noise.

"Izabel, Sule! What's happened? What's the matter?" asked the bewildered Donana, not suspecting the truth.

"We don't know how it happened ourselves, dear neighbor! Our little girl's been sick for eight days . . . and she's gone!" they said, pointing to the dead girl who was lying on the bed with a fixed expression of despair on her face.

Another eight days passed, and again the whole district was thrown into a turmoil.

"Have you heard? Donana is dead!"

"Dead?"

"It's the truth! And they say there was a red cock on her drain!"

"A red cock? That's a devil!"

"True, that's a devil. Of course, it's all because of witchcraft . . . What else would make the rain fall when the evening mist was descending?"

"Yes, she went to Ambriz because of that money . . ."

"She went to have spells cast . . . She wanted the *jimbambi* to find the culprit . . ."

"There you are! She wanted to bewitch someone and she came under the spell herself . . ."

"But what rain it was!"

"The *jimbambi* are like that . . . They only come with the rain or the wind: they're not like other spells . . ."

"Well, well. A devil on the drain. Yesterday it was banging away. I even trembled, brother!"

"When you hear a noise like that, it's beating its wings. In the forest, if he and she sit down and you don't make way for them, hey presto, you're done for, Mama mia! They look like a cock and a hen, but they run like partridges."

"I know, I know. They sometimes even lose a few scales—that's their feathers . . ."

"Yesterday they saw the devil on the drain of the dead woman's hut. I don't know whether it was him or her . . ."

"That was a real disaster! But why cast spells like that? All she did in the end was bewitch herself . . ."

"That's what comes of witchcraft . . . If she had gone to church and prayed to St. Antony, then whoever took the money would have been found . . . And the owner wouldn't have died . . ."

"It's fate, really . . ."

A few days later:

"Have you heard? Izabel's died!"

"There you are! The niece died the other day, and the aunt dies today. What a catastrophe!"

"Yes, it never rains but it pours!"

"The funny thing is that the people who were at the funerals of Mussoco and Donana were taken so ill that they passed away."

"God forgive me, but I've already heard it was Mussoco who picked up the money."

"Really?"

"I don't know, but they gossip such a lot round here. Anyway, other sinners like ourselves are saying she was the one who found the money. Poor thing, she wanted to give it back to the owner, but her aunt and grandmother talked her out of it."

"Oh Lord! Those old women too! Why use other folks' money?"

"They were friends . . ."

"To hell with it! What sort of friends were they? Friendship outside and emptiness within?"

"Our old men were right: 'We know the face but we don't know the heart.' But I'm sorry for the poor girl, dying so young. She was such a nice person. And the aunt, now . . ."

"The lord forgive me, she's no longer with

us. But why make her out to have been kind-hearted? Our mothers are also saying a thing or two! They were so stubborn, the aunt and the grandmother, that the poor child died, and Donana too."

"As for Donana, I've had enough of her. She didn't know how to cast spells. Why did she drag in other folks who had nothing to do with that money? Whoever washes the corpse shall die. Whoever goes to the funeral shall die. Whoever says 'Woe is me!' To hell with it all!"

Guide for Interpretation

The curse would suggest that the community is somehow involved in the misdeed. Think about the role of the community as you continue reading this story.

"More's already been done than she wanted. But anger means something too. A person weeps and shouts and nothing happens. It wasn't easy for her either. Let's drop all this. We'd have done the same!"

But death continued on its way.

"Have you heard the bad news? They're dying in the street now!"

"Impossible! Who's the unlucky one?"

"Didn't you know? Katarina!"

"Ai-ai-ai! Poor woman! Where?"

"In Cabino, near the railway. The poor thing was on the way to see the healer."

"Fancy that! We're still walking about, but we're already dying."

"That's the truth, my dear. The flesh is still alive, but the soul is already dead."

So it went on, with fever, stomach cramps, and the spitting of blood—the locals died one after another and the black terror crept deeper and deeper into their souls. As was said in the curse, when they went to the funeral, they paid with their lives for defying the taboo. Frightened friends, in spite of their natural solidarity, tried not to show up on such occasions. Even the parents, when struck by misfortune, did not carry out their sacred duty of tending the sick.

To climax it all, a new and terrible item of news started doing the rounds: to shake off the curse, Mussoco's family, already much thinned down, were scattering that accursed money about in the streets! How dangerous for the children! Even though they'd been warned, how would they be able to resist such a temptation? And if the whole sum . . . But no, they were scattering it about piecemeal, an escudo here, an escudo there. What a diabolical temptation! Damned money! Many innocent people had already died because of it; the Lord alone knew how many more were going to.

"Mind you don't pick up any money off the street! D'you hear? It's bewitched! Look how people are dying!" mothers warned their children.

But death continued to lay people low. The vengeful curse took its inexorable[10] course: "Whoever washes the corpse shall die! Whoever trims its nails shall die! Whoever cuts its hair shall die! Whoever dresses it shall die! Whoever goes to bury it shall die. Whoever says: 'Woe is me!' shall also die." Salvation? Where was it to be sought? Before that abyss, the healer admitted that he was powerless to help—the curse was such a terrible one. Falling from the clouds, it entered the flesh of those who ignored the warnings, and it secretly compelled them to obey the dread command: "Die!"

"It's an epidemic," declared the doctors.

But you can't fool the people, and along with the healers, the people protested:

"Rubbish. What epidemic? It's the bad *jim-bambi*!"

"The whites! What do they know anyway?" say the blacks contemptuously.

"True! Witchcraft doesn't get at them! . . ."

---

10. inexorable (in eks′ ə rə bəl): not to be stopped by any means.

"It's like that accident at Xamavo Market . . ."

"True! They say the roof fell in because of a high wind . . ."

"A high wind? It fell in because of the *jim-bambi* . . ."

And those deaths, like the tragic year of 1921, for which various explanations were found, are still fresh in the memories of Luanda's inhabitants, not in terms of scientific conclusions, but in terms of the dogmas of their beliefs.

*T*hinking *About the Story*

A PERSONAL RESPONSE

sharing impressions

1. How do you feel about what happens in this story? Record your impressions in your journal.

constructing interpretations

2. In your opinion, who is to blame for what happens?
   Think about
   - Mussoco's choice not to return the money
   - her relationship with her aunt and grandmother
   - Donana's curse
   - the community's involvement

3. Who do you think suffers more—Donana, who lost the money, or Mussoco, who finds it?
   Think about
   - what the money represents for Donana
   - Donana's public pleas
   - Mussoco's inner struggles

4. How might the story have been different if Mussoco's aunt and grandmother had encouraged her to return the money?

A CRITICAL RESPONSE ———————————————————————————

5. What message or messages does the story seem to offer?
   Think about
   • the character traits depicted, such as timidity and greed
   • the issue of vengeance
   • the relationship depicted between the individual and the community
   • what the curse might symbolize

6. Do you think that the events in this story could have happened in another time and place? Support your opinion with evidence from the story.

7. Compare the message or messages of this story with those found in other selections in Offering Worldly Wisdom.
   Think about
   • the characters and the choices they make
   • the conflicts depicted

*A*nalyzing the Writer's Craft

POINT OF VIEW ——————————————————————————

Consider what you learn about the thoughts and feelings not only of Mussoco but also of the other characters in the story.

Building a Literary Vocabulary. Point of view refers to the narrative method used in a short story, novel, or nonfiction selection. "Mussoco" is written from the third-person omniscient point of view. The narrator is all-knowing about the thoughts and feelings of the characters. By using this point of view, the writer can reveal the emotional responses of all the characters and can comment at will on the events taking place.

Application: Understanding Point of View. Make a chart consisting of five columns and label them "Mussoco," "Grandmother," "Aunt," "Donana," and "Others in the community." Go back through the story and look for sentences that tell you the thoughts and feelings of the different characters. Under each label jot down three sentences and the page numbers on which they appear. After you have completed your chart, get together with one or more classmates and discuss what Ribas gains by telling the story from the third-person omniscient point of view rather than from that of any one character.

Connecting Reading and Writing

1. Guided by the details about Mussoco in the story, write her **obituary** for the local newspaper.

Option: Based on your understanding of Mussoco's character, write her a **letter** of advice about how to deal with her aunt and her grandmother.

2. Think about the Kimbundu saying "The flesh is still alive, but the soul is already dead." In an **expository essay,** show your classmates the connection between the saying and the plot of the story.

Option: Restate the proverb in your own words. Then combine it with other proverbs you know to create a **montage** of sayings for display in your classroom.

3. Create a literary magazine feature that retells the **story** from Donana's point of view.

Option: Create an **interview** with Donana for a human-interest magazine. Have her justify her decisions.

4. Write **notes** for a class presentation comparing the community in "Mussoco" and that in "The Silver Mine."

Option: Write a **dialogue** in which Mussoco's aunt and one of the early Troglodytes from Montesquieu's *The Persian Letters* discuss self-interest in their communities.

How Much Land Does a Man Need?

LEO TOLSTOY   1828–1910   RUSSIA

A biography of Tolstoy appears on page 753.

Approaching the Story

Count Leo Tolstoy was a Russian writer whose novels *War and Peace* (1869) and *Anna Karenina* (1877) rank among the masterpieces of world literature. After completing these novels, Tolstoy experienced a spiritual crisis that changed him greatly. Though an aristocrat by birth, he began to dress like a peasant, to labor in the fields, and to work in soupkitchens and barns. More and more strongly, he came to believe that literature must teach morality and must be easily understood by the common people. In the story you are about to read, both goals are achieved.

I

AN ELDER SISTER came to visit her younger sister in the country. The elder was married to a tradesman in town, the younger to a peasant in the village. As the sisters sat over their tea talking, the elder began to boast of the advantages of town life: saying how comfortably they lived there, how well they dressed, what fine clothes her children wore, what good things they ate and drank, and how she went to the theater, promenades, and entertainments.

The younger sister was piqued, and in turn disparaged the life of a tradesman, and stood up for that of a peasant.

"I would not change my way of life for yours," said she. "We may live roughly, but at least we are free from anxiety. You live in better style than we do, but though you often earn more than you need, you are very likely to lose all you have. You know the proverb, 'Loss and gain are brothers twain.' It often happens that people who are wealthy one day are begging their bread the next. Our way is safer. Though a peasant's life is not a fat one, it is a long one. We shall never grow rich, but we shall always have enough to eat."

The elder sister said sneeringly:

"Enough? Yes, if you like to share with the pigs and the calves! What do you know of elegance or manners! However much your good man may slave, you will die as you are living—on a dung heap—and your children the same."

"Well, what of that?" replied the younger. "Of course our work is rough and coarse. But, on the other hand, it is sure, and we need not bow to anyone. But you, in your towns, are surrounded by temptations; today all may be right, but tomorrow the Evil One may tempt your husband with cards, wine, or women, and all will go to ruin. Don't such things happen often enough?"

Pakhom,[1] the master of the house, was lying on the top of the stove and he listened to the women's chatter.

"It is perfectly true," thought he. "Busy as we are from childhood tilling mother earth, we peasants have no time to let any nonsense settle in our heads. Our only trouble is that we haven't land enough. If I had plenty of land, I shouldn't fear the Devil himself!"

The women finished their tea, chatted a while about dress, and then cleared away the tea things and lay down to sleep.

But the Devil had been sitting behind the stove, and had heard all that was said. He was pleased that the peasant's wife had led her husband into boasting, and that he had said that if he had plenty of land he would not fear the Devil himself.

"All right," thought the Devil. "We will have a tussle. I'll give you land enough; and by means of that land I will get you into my power."

II

Close to the village there lived a lady, a small landowner who had an estate of about three hundred acres. She had always lived on good terms with the peasants until she engaged as her steward an old soldier, who took to burdening the people with fines. However careful Pakhom tried to be, it happened again and again that now a horse of his got among the lady's oats, now a cow strayed into her garden, now his calves found their way into her meadows—and he always had to pay a fine.

Pakhom paid up, but grumbled, and going home in a temper, was rough with his family. All through that summer, Pakhom had much trouble because of this steward, and he was

even glad when winter came and the cattle had to be stabled. Though he grudged the fodder when they could no longer graze on the pasture land, at least he was free from anxiety about them.

In the winter the news got about that the lady was going to sell her land and that the keeper of the inn on the high road was bargaining for it. When the peasants heard this they were very much alarmed.

"Well," thought they, "if the innkeeper gets the land, he will worry us with fines worse than the lady's steward. We all depend on that estate."

So the peasants went on behalf of their commune,[2] and asked the lady not to sell the land to the innkeeper, offering her a better price for it themselves. The lady agreed to let them have it. Then the peasants tried to arrange for the commune to buy the whole estate, so that it might be held by them all in common. They met twice to discuss it, but could not settle the matter; the Evil One sowed discord among them and they could not agree. So they decided to buy the land individually, each according to his means; and the lady agreed to this plan as she had to the other.

Presently Pakhom heard that a neighbor of his was buying fifty acres, and that the lady had consented to accept one-half in cash and to wait a year for the other half. Pakhom felt envious.

"Look at that," thought he, "the land is all being sold, and I shall get none of it." So he spoke to his wife.

"Other people are buying," said he, "and we must also buy twenty acres or so. Life is becoming impossible. That steward is simply crushing us with his fines."

---

1. Pakhom (pu khôm′).

2. commune (käm′ yo͞on′): a form of social organization common in prerevolutionary Russia in which work and resources were shared within a community.

So they put their heads together and considered how they could manage to buy it. They had one hundred rubles laid by. They sold a colt and one-half of their bees, hired out one of their sons as a laborer and took his wages in advance, borrowed the rest from a brother-in-law, and so scraped together half the purchase money.

Having done this, Pakhom chose out a farm of forty acres, some of it wooded, and went to the lady to bargain for it. They came to an agreement, and he shook hands with her upon it and paid her a deposit in advance. Then they went to town and signed the deeds; he paying half the price down, and undertaking to pay the remainder within two years.

So now Pakhom had land of his own. He borrowed seed, and sowed it on the land he had bought. The harvest was a good one, and within a year he had managed to pay off his debts both to the lady and to his brother-in-law. So he became a landowner, ploughing and sowing his own land, making hay on his own land, cutting his own trees, and feeding his cattle on his own pasture. When he went out to plough his fields, or to look at his growing corn, or at his grass meadows, his heart would fill with joy. The grass that grew and the flowers that bloomed there seemed to him unlike any that grew elsewhere. Formerly, when he had passed by that land, it had appeared the same as any other land, but now it seemed quite different.

III

So Pakhom was well-contented, and everything would have been right if the neighboring peasants would only not have trespassed on his cornfields and meadows. He appealed to them most civilly, but they still went on: now the communal herdsmen would let the village cows stray into his meadows, then horses from the night pasture would get among his corn. Pakhom turned them out again and again, and forgave their owners, and for a long time he

forbore to prosecute anyone. But at last he lost patience and complained to the district court. He knew it was the peasants' want of land, and no evil intent on their part, that caused the trouble, but he thought:

"I cannot go on overlooking it or they will destroy all I have. They must be taught a lesson."

So he had them up, gave them one lesson, and then another, and two or three of the peasants were fined. After a time Pakhom's neighbors began to bear him a grudge for this, and would now and then let their cattle on to his land on purpose. One peasant even got into Pakhom's wood at night and cut down five young lime trees for their bark. Pakhom passing through the wood one day noticed something white. He came nearer and saw the stripped trunks lying on the ground, and close by stood the stumps where the trees had been. Pakhom was furious.

"If he had only cut one here and there it would have been bad enough," thought Pakhom, "but the rascal has actually cut down a whole clump. If I could only find out who did this, I would pay him out."

He racked his brains as to who it could be. Finally he decided: "It must be Simon—no one else could have done it." So he went to Simon's homestead to have a look round, but he found nothing, and only had an angry scene. However, he now felt more certain than ever that Simon had done it, and he lodged a complaint. Simon was summoned. The case was tried, and retried, and at the end of it all Simon was acquitted, there being no evidence against him. Pakhom felt still more aggrieved, and let his anger loose upon the elder and the judges.

"You let thieves grease your palms," said he. "If you were honest folk yourselves you would not let a thief go free."

So Pakhom quarrelled with the judges and with his neighbors. Threats to burn his building began to be uttered. So though Pakhom had more land, his place in the commune was much worse than before.

About this time a rumor got about that many people were moving to new parts.

"There's no need for me to leave my land," thought Pakhom. "But some of the others might leave our village and then there would be more room for us. I would take over their land myself and make my estate a bit bigger. I could then live more at ease. As it is, I am still too cramped to be comfortable."

One day Pakhom was sitting at home when a peasant, passing through the village, happened to call in. He was allowed to stay the night, and supper was given him. Pakhom had a talk with this peasant and asked him where he came from. The stranger answered that he came from beyond the Volga,[3] where he had been working. One word led to another, and the man went on to say that many people were settling in those parts. He told how some people from his village had settled there. They had joined the commune, and had had twenty-five acres per man granted them. The land was so good, he said, that the rye sown on it grew as high as a horse, and so thick that five cuts of a sickle made a sheaf. One peasant, he said, had brought nothing with him but his bare hands, and now he had six horses and two cows of his own.

Pakhom's heart kindled with desire. He thought:

"Why should I suffer in this narrow hole, if one can live so well elsewhere? I will sell my land and my homestead here, and with the money I will start afresh over there and get everything new. In this crowded place one is always having trouble. But I must first go and find out all about it myself."

Toward summer he got ready and started. He went down the Volga on a steamer to Samara,[4] then walked another three hundred miles on foot, and at last reached the place. It was just as the stranger had said. The peasants had plenty of land: every man had twenty-five acres of communal land given him for his use, and anyone who had money could buy, besides, at two shillings an acre as much good freehold land as he wanted.

Having found out all he wished to know, Pakhom returned home as autumn came on, and began selling off his belongings. He sold his land at a profit, sold his homestead and all his cattle, and withdrew from membership of the commune. He only waited till the spring, and then started with his family for the new settlement.

IV

As soon as Pakhom and his family reached their new abode, he applied for admission into the commune of a large village. He stood treat[5] to the elders and obtained the necessary documents. Five shares of communal land were given him for his own and his sons' use: that is to say—125 acres (not all together, but in different fields) besides the use of the communal pasture. Pakhom put up the buildings he needed, and bought cattle. Of the communal land alone he had three times as much as at his former home, and the land was good corn land. He was ten times better off than he had been. He had plenty of arable[6] land and pasturage, and could keep as many head of cattle as he liked.

At first, in the bustle of building and settling down, Pakhom was pleased with it all, but when he got used to it he began to think that even here he had not enough land. The first year, he sowed wheat on his share of the

---

3. **Volga** (väl′ gə): river in Russia that flows into the Caspian Sea.

4. **Samara** (sə mär′ ə): old name for a town in southeast Russia, in the Volga valley.

5. **stood treat:** discussed forms of accommodation or settlement.

6. **arable** (ar′ ə bəl): fit for plowing and planting.

communal land and had a good crop. He wanted to go on sowing wheat, but had not enough communal land for the purpose, and what he had already used was not available; for in those parts wheat is only sown on virgin soil or on fallow[7] land. It is sown for one or two years, and then the land lies fallow till it is again overgrown with prairie grass. There were many who wanted such land and there was not enough for all; so that people quarrelled about it. Those who were better off wanted it for growing wheat, and those who were poor wanted it to let to dealers, so that they might raise money to pay their taxes. Pakhom wanted to sow more wheat, so he rented land from a dealer for a year. He sowed much wheat and had a fine crop, but the land was too far from the village—the wheat had to be carted more than ten miles. After a time Pakhom noticed that some peasant-dealers were living on separate farms and were growing wealthy; and he thought:

"If I were to buy some freehold land and have a homestead on it, it would be a different thing altogether. Then it would all be nice and compact."

The question of buying freehold land recurred to him again and again.

He went on in the same way for three years, renting land and sowing wheat. The seasons turned out well and the crops were good, so that he began to lay money by. He might have gone on living contentedly, but he grew tired of having to rent other people's land every year, and having to scramble for it. Wherever there was good land to be had, the peasants would rush for it and it was taken up at once, so that unless you were sharp about it you got none. It happened in the third year that he and a dealer together rented a piece of pasture land from some peasants; and they had already ploughed it up, when there was some dispute and the peasants went to law about it, and things fell out so that the labor was all lost.

"If it were my own land," thought Pakhom, "I should be independent, and there would not be all this unpleasantness."

So Pakhom began looking out for land which he could buy; and he came across a peasant who had bought thirteen hundred acres, but having got into difficulties was willing to sell again cheap. Pakhom bargained and haggled with him, and at last they settled the price at fifteen hundred rubles, part in cash and part to be paid later. They had all but clinched the matter when a passing dealer happened to stop at Pakhom's one day to get a feed for his horses. He drank tea with Pakhom and they had a talk. The dealer said that he was just returning from the land of the Bashkirs,[8] far away, where he had bought thirteen thousand acres of land, all for one thousand rubles. Pakhom questioned him further, and the tradesman said:

"All one need do is to make friends with the chiefs. I gave away about one hundred rubles worth of silk robes and carpets, besides a case of tea, and I gave wine to those who would drink it; and I got the land for less than a penny an acre." And he showed Pakhom the title deeds, saying:

"The land lies near a river, and the whole prairie is virgin soil."

Pakhom plied him with questions, and the tradesman said:

"There is more land there than you could cover if you walked a year, and it all belongs to the Bashkirs. They are as simple as sheep, and land can be got almost for nothing."

"There now," thought Pakhom, "with my one thousand rubles, why should I get only thirteen hundred acres, and saddle myself with a debt besides? If I take it out there, I can get more than ten times as much for the money."

---

7. **fallow** (fal′ ō): allowed to remain unplanted in order to be refreshed.

8. **Bashkirs** (bȧsh kērz])

V

Pakhom inquired how to get to the place, and as soon as the tradesman had left him, he prepared to go there himself. He left his wife to look after the homestead, and started on his journey taking his man with him. They stopped at a town on their way and bought a case of tea, some wine, and other presents, as the tradesman had advised. On and on they went until they had gone more than three hundred miles, and on the seventh day they came to a place where the Bashkirs had pitched their tents. It was all just as the tradesman had said. The people lived on the steppes, by a river, in felt-covered tents. They neither tilled the ground, nor ate bread. Their cattle and horses grazed in herds on the steppe. The colts were tethered behind the tents, and the mares were driven to them twice a day. The mares were milked, and from the milk kumiss[9] was made. It was the women who prepared kumiss, and they also made cheese. As far as the men were concerned, drinking kumiss and tea, eating mutton, and playing on their pipes, was all they cared about. They were all stout and merry, and all the summer long they never thought of doing any work. They were quite ignorant, and knew no Russian, but were good-natured enough.

As soon as they saw Pakhom, they came out of their tents and gathered round their visitor. An interpreter was found, and Pakhom told them he had come about some land. The Bashkirs seemed very glad; they took Pakhom and led him into one of the best tents, where they made him sit on some down cushions placed on a carpet, while they sat round him. They gave him some tea and kumiss, and had a sheep killed, and gave him mutton to eat. Pakhom took presents out of his cart and distributed them among the Bashkirs, and divided the tea amongst them. The Bashkirs were delighted. They talked a great deal among themselves, and then told the interpreter to translate.

"They wish to tell you," said the interpreter, "that they like you, and that it is our custom to do all we can to please a guest and to repay him for his gifts. You have given us presents, now tell us which of the things we possess please you best, that we may present them to you."

"What pleases me best here," answered Pakhom, "is your land. Our land is crowded and the soil is exhausted; but you have plenty of land and it is good land. I never saw the like of it."

The interpreter translated. The Bashkirs talked among themselves for a while. Pakhom could not understand what they were saying, but saw that they were much amused and that they shouted and laughed. Then they were silent and looked at Pakhom while the interpreter said:

"They wish me to tell you that in return for your presents they will gladly give you as much land as you want. You have only to point it out with your hand and it is yours."

The Bashkirs talked again for a while and began to dispute. Pakhom asked what they were disputing about, and the interpreter told him that some of them thought they ought to ask their chief about the land and not act in his absence, while others thought there was no need to wait for his return.

VI

While the Bashkirs were disputing, a man in a large fox-fur cap appeared on the scene. They all became silent and rose to their feet. The interpreter said, "This is our chief himself."

Pakhom immediately fetched the best dressing gown and five pounds of tea, and offered these to the chief. The chief accepted them, and seated himself in the place of honor. The Bashkirs at once began telling him something.

---

9. kumiss (ko͞o′ mis): an intoxicating beverage made in Russia from mare's or camel's milk.

The chief listened for a while, then made a sign with his head for them to be silent, and addressing himself to Pakhom, said in Russian:

"Well, let it be so. Choose whatever piece of land you like; we have plenty of it."

"How can I take as much as I like?" thought Pakhom. "I must get a deed to make it secure, or else they may say, 'It is yours,' and afterwards may take it away again."

"Thank you for your kind words," he said aloud. "You have much land, and I only want a little. But I should like to be sure which bit is mine. Could it not be measured and made over to me? Life and death are in God's hands. You good people give it to me, but your children might wish to take it away again."

"You are quite right," said the chief. "We will make it over to you."

"I heard that a dealer had been here," continued Pakhom, "and that you gave him a little land, too, and signed title deeds to that effect. I should like to have it done in the same way."

The chief understood.

"Yes," replied he, "that can be done quite easily. We have a scribe, and we will go to town with you and have the deed properly sealed."

"And what will be the price?" asked Pakhom.

"Our price is always the same: one thousand rubles a day."

Pakhom did not understand.

"A day? What measure is that? How many acres would that be?"

"We do not know how to reckon it out," said the chief. "We sell it by the day. As much as you can go round on your feet in a day is yours, and the price is one thousand rubles a day."

Pakhom was surprised.

"But in a day you can get round a large tract of land," he said.

The chief laughed.

"It will all be yours!" said he. "But there is one condition: If you don't return on the same day to the spot whence you started, your money is lost."

"But how am I to mark the way that I have gone?"

"Why, we shall go to any spot you like, and stay there. You must start from that spot and make your round, taking a spade with you. Wherever you think necessary, make a mark. At every turning, dig a hole and pile up the turf; then afterwards we will go round with a plough from hole to hole. You may make as large a circuit as you please, but before the sun sets you must return to the place you started from. All the land you cover will be yours."

Pakhom was delighted. It was decided to start early next morning. They talked a while, and after drinking some more kumiss and eating some more mutton, they had tea again, and then the night came on. They gave Pakhom a feather bed to sleep on, and the Bashkirs dispersed for the night, promising to assemble the next morning at daybreak and ride out before sunrise to the appointed spot.

VII

Pakhom lay on the feather bed, but could not sleep. He kept thinking about the land.

"What a large tract I will mark off!" thought he. "I can easily do thirty-five miles in a day. The days are long now, and within a circuit of thiry-five miles what a lot of land there will be! I will sell the poorer land, or let it to peasants, but I'll pick out the best and farm it. I will buy two ox teams, and hire two more laborers. About a hundred and fifty acres shall be plough land, and I will pasture cattle on the rest."

Pakhom lay awake all night, and dozed off only just before dawn. Hardly were his eyes closed when he had a dream. He thought he was lying in that same tent and heard somebody chuckling outside. He wondered who it could be, and rose and went out, and he saw the Bashkir chief sitting in front of the tent holding his sides and rolling about with laughter. Going nearer to the chief, Pakhom asked: "What are you laughing at?" But he saw that it was no longer the chief, but the dealer who had recently stopped at his house and had told him about the land. Just as Pakhom was going to ask, "Have you been here long?" he saw that it was not the dealer, but the peasant who had come up from the Volga, long ago, to Pakhom's old home. Then he saw that it was not the peasant either, but the Devil himself with hoofs and horns, sitting there and chuckling, and before him lay a man barefoot, prostrate[10] on the ground, with only trousers and a shirt on. And Pakhom dreamt that he looked more attentively to see what sort of man it was that was lying there, and he saw that the man was dead, and that it was himself! He awoke horror-struck.

"What things one does dream," thought he.

Looking round he saw through the open door that the dawn was breaking.

"It's time to wake them up," thought he. "We ought to be starting."

He got up, roused his man (who was sleeping in his cart), bade him harness; and went to call the Bashkirs.

"It's time to go to the steppe to measure the land," he said.

The Bashkirs rose and assembled, and the chief came too. Then they began drinking kumiss again, and offered Pakhom some tea, but he would not wait.

"If we are to go, let us go. It is high time," said he.

VIII

The Bashkirs got ready and they all started: some mounted on horses, and some in carts. Pakhom drove in his own small cart with his servant and took a spade with him. When they reached the steppe, the morning red was beginning to kindle. They ascended a hillock (called by the Bashkirs a *shikhan*) and dismounting from their carts and their horses, gathered in one spot. The chief came up to Pakhom and stretching out his arm toward the plain:

"See," said he, "all this, as far as your eye can reach, is ours. You may have any part of it you like."

Pakhom's eyes glistened: it was all virgin soil, as flat as the palm of your hand, as black as the seed of a poppy, and in the hollows different kinds of grasses grew breast high.

The chief took off his fox-fur cap, placed it on the ground and said:

"This will be the mark. Start from here, and return here again. All the land you go round shall be yours."

Pakhom took out his money and put it on the cap. Then he took off his outer coat, remaining in his sleeveless undercoat. He unfastened his girdle and tied it tight below his stomach, put a little bag of bread into the breast of his coat, and tying a flask of water to his girdle, he drew up the tops of his boots, took the spade from his man, and stood ready to start. He considered for some moments which way he better go—it was tempting everywhere.

"No matter," he concluded, "I will go toward the rising sun."

He turned his face to the east, stretched himself, and waited for the sun to appear above the rim.

"I must lose no time," he thought, "and it is easier walking while it is still cool."

The sun's rays had hardly flashed above the horizon, before Pakhom, carrying the spade over his shoulder, went down into the steppe.

Pakhom started walking neither slowly nor quickly. After having gone a thousand yards he stopped, dug a hole, and placed pieces of turf one on another to make it more visible. Then

---

10. prostrate (präs′ trāt): lying flat, in submission or from physical exhaustion.

he went on; and now that he had walked off his stiffness he quickened his pace. After a while he dug another hole.

Pakhom looked back. The hillock could be distinctly seen in the sunlight, with the people on it, and the glittering tires of the cartwheels. At a rough guess Pakhom concluded that he had walked three miles. It was growing warmer; he took off his undercoat, flung it across his shoulder, and went on again. It had grown quite warm now; he looked at the sun, it was time to think of breakfast.

"The first shift is done, but there are four in a day, and it is too soon yet to turn. But I will just take off my boots," said he to himself.

He sat down, took off his boots, stuck them into his girdle, and went on. It was easy walking now.

"I will go on for another three miles," thought he, "and then turn to the left. This spot is so fine, that it would be a pity to lose it. The further one goes, the better the land seems."

He went straight on for a while, and when he looked round, the hillock was scarcely visible and the people on it looked like black ants, and he could just see something glistening there in the sun.

"Ah," thought Pakhom, "I have gone far enough in this direction, it is time to turn. Besides I am in a regular sweat, and very thirsty."

He stopped, dug a large hole, and heaped up pieces of turf. Next he untied his flask, had a drink, and then turned sharply to the left. He went on and on; the grass was high, and it was very hot.

Pakhom began to grow tired: he looked at the sun and saw that it was noon.

"Well," he thought, "I must have a rest."

He sat down, and ate some bread and drank some water; but he did not lie down, thinking that if he did he might fall asleep. After sitting a little while, he went on again. At first he walked easily: the food had strengthened him; but it had become terribly hot and he felt sleepy. Still he went on, thinking: "An hour to suffer, a lifetime to live."

He went a long way in this direction also, and was about to turn to the left again, when he perceived a damp hollow: "It would be a pity to leave that out," he thought. "Flax[11] would do well there." So he went on past the hollow, and dug a hole on the other side of it before he turned the corner. Pakhom looked toward the hillock. The heat made the air hazy: it seemed to be quivering, and through the haze the people on the hillock could scarcely be seen.

"Ah!" thought Pakhom, "I have made the sides too long; I must make this one shorter." And he went along the third side, stepping faster. He looked at the sun: it was nearly halfway to the horizon, and he had not yet done two miles of the third side of the square. He was still ten miles from the goal.

"No," he thought, "though it will make my land lop-sided, I must hurry back in a straight line now. I might go too far, and as it is I have a great deal of land."

So Pakhom hurriedly dug a hole, and turned straight toward the hillock.

IX

Pakhom went straight toward the hillock, but he now walked with difficulty. He was done up with the heat, his bare feet were cut and bruised, and his legs began to fail. He longed to rest, but it was impossible if he meant to get back before sunset. The sun waits for no man, and it was sinking lower and lower.

"Oh dear," he thought, "if only I have not blundered trying for too much! What if I am too late?"

He looked toward the hillock and at the sun. He was still far from his goal, and the

---

11. flax (flaks): a plant used to make fabric, oil, and a variety of other things.

sun was already near the rim.

Pakhom walked on and on; it was very hard walking but he went quicker and quicker. He pressed on, but was still far from the place. He began running, threw away his coat, his boots, his flask, and his cap, and kept only the spade which he used as a support.

"What shall I do?" he thought again, "I have grasped too much and ruined the whole affair. I can't get there before the sun sets."

And this fear made him still more breathless. Pakhom went on running; his soaking shirt and trousers stuck to him and his mouth was parched. His breast was working like a blacksmith's bellows, his heart was beating like a hammer, and his legs were giving way as if they did not belong to him. Pakhom was seized with terror lest he should die of the strain.

Though afraid of death, he could not stop. "After having run all that way they will call me a fool if I stop now," thought he. And he ran on and on, and drew near and heard the Bashkirs yelling and shouting to him, and their cries inflamed his heart still more. He gathered his last strength and ran on.

The sun was close to the rim, and cloaked in mist looked large, and red as blood. Now, yes, now, it was about to set! The sun was quite low, but he was also quite near his aim. Pakhom could already see the people on the hillock waving their arms to hurry him up. He could see the fox-fur cap on the ground and the money on it, and the chief sitting on the ground holding his sides. And Pakhom remembered his dream.

"There is plenty of land," thought he, "but will God let me live on it? I have lost my life, I have lost my life! I shall never reach that spot!"

Pakhom looked at the sun, which had reached the earth: one side of it had already disappeared. With all his remaining strength he rushed on, bending his body forward so that his legs could hardly follow fast enough to keep him from falling. Just as he reached the hillock it suddenly grew dark. He looked up—the sun had already set! He gave a cry: "All my labor has been in vain," thought he, and was about to stop, but he heard the Bashkirs still shouting, and remembered that though to him, from below, the sun seemed to have set, they on the hillock could still see it. He took a long breath and ran up the hillock. It was still light there. He reached the top and saw the cap. Before it sat the chief laughing and holding his sides. Again Pakhom remembered his dream, and he uttered a cry: his legs gave way beneath him, he fell forward and reached the cap with his hands.

"Ah, that's a fine fellow!" exclaimed the chief. "He has gained much land!"

Pakhom's servant came running up and tried to raise him, but he saw that blood was flowing from his mouth. Pakhom was dead!

The Bashkirs clicked their tongues to show their pity.

His servant picked up the spade and dug a grave long enough for Pakhom to lie in, and buried him in it. Six feet from his head to his heels was all he needed.

Reviewing Concepts

LITERATURE AND ITS MESSAGE: LEARNING ABOUT LIFE

*making
connections*

All the selections in this unit teach something about what it means to be human. One way to review the selections is to classify them according to the messages taught. The message of a selection might concern the nature of the individual, the relationship between individuals, or the connection between the individual and a higher power. In "The Mustard Seed," for example, the individual must learn that death is inevitable. *The Persian Letters* carries two messages: that the individual is capable of being virtuous and that cooperation within the community benefits the individual.

Review in your mind the selections you have read in this unit and the messages they impart. Then, on a sheet of paper, create a chart like the one following, writing the message of each selection in the appropriate column. You may find that certain selections have more than one message.

Selections	The individual	Relationship between individuals	Connection between individual and higher power
"To Indra"			1. Indra is almighty. 2. Indra should be praised.
"The Mustard Seed"	Death comes to all.		
The Persian Letters	Humans are capable of being virtuous.	Cooperation within the community benefits each individual.	

*describing
connections*

After you have completed the chart, prepare an **oral presentation** that reveals which of the three categories seems best represented across cultures, and discuss why this might be so. Also identify which categories, if any, are represented by only a small number of works.

Guardian Figure, Kamakura period,
Japanese artist.
The Art Institute of Chicago.

Courage and Conviction:

The Hero in Literature

*"A hero in one age
will be a hero in another."*

CHARLOTTE LENNOX

Celebrating
the Cultural Hero

In literature, the word *hero* has come to mean simply the main character of a work. In the early literature of most cultures, however, the hero is this and much more; he is a figure who ranks somewhere between ordinary human beings and the gods. The role of the hero is to provide a noble image that will inspire and guide the actions of mortals.

This kind of cultural hero is not the construct of an individual artist working in creative isolation from the rest of society. In the early epics, the hero's life and actions grew out of legend and myth, tales told around campfires or sung to the sound of a lute. The epics reflected the values of their cultures—what the people and poets believed the gods wanted from them.

The ancient hero is almost always a physically courageous male, in part because these cultures were usually male-dominated warrior societies.* Beyond that, if the culture valued cleverness, the hero is clever. If the culture valued spirituality, the hero displays great spiritual resources and abilities.

Most heroes, however grand and courageous, are not invincible. They struggle, as do ordinary people, to overcome their weaknesses and to resolve the conflicts that are thrust upon them. They also fall victim to emotions that lead them into error. In certain cases, the hero takes on legendary status because of his flaws. Despite these limitations, the hero's story is always one of glory, both for him and for the culture he represents.

*Later in the unit, in the section titled **Presenting the Individual as Hero,** several selections consider heroic females.

Literary Vocabulary

Epic. An epic is a long narrative poem on a serious subject presented in an elevated or formal style. An epic traces the adventures of a hero of high status whose actions consist of courageous, even superhuman, deeds. Such deeds represent the ideals and values of a group of people such as a nation or race. The plot of an epic usually involves a long and dangerous journey complicated by supernatural events and beings. The setting is large in scale and ranges over many locales. For example, *The Epic of Gilgamesh* is the story of a powerful hero-king from Babylonia who is part god and part human. The epic describes his long search for immortality—an odyssey that proves Gilgamesh's courage and ability as a warrior. An excerpt from this great epic is found in Unit 1.

Simile. A simile is a figure of speech that makes a comparison between two things that are actually unlike yet have something in common. Similes express the comparison by using the word *like* or *as*. In the poem "To Indra," from The Rig Veda, the following simile compares Indra to a gambler: "Who, like a gambler gathering his winnings, seized the foe's riches, he, O men, is Indra."

Metaphor. Like a simile, a metaphor is a figure of speech that makes a comparison between two things that are actually unlike yet have something in common. A metaphor, however, does not use the word *like* or *as*. In "Adoration of the Disk," from The Book of the Dead, "Houses are tombs where blind men lie in death" is a metaphor that compares houses to tombs. The metaphor conveys the effect of the setting sun on the human world.

REVIEWED IN THIS SECTION

Imagery

from The Ramayana

Translated and adapted by R. K. Narayan

Approaching the Epic

The Ramayana (rä mä′ yə nə) is one of two ancient epics from India, the other being _The Mahabharata_ (mə hä′ bä′ rə tə). _The Ramayana_ was composed by the poet Valmiki between 500 and 200 B.C. In its original form the epic was fifty thousand lines of Sanskrit verse; over the centuries it was translated into many different Indian languages. The selection you will read, by the twentieth-century Indian writer R. K. Narayan, is an English translation and adaptation of a Tamil version written by Kamban in the eleventh century.

The Ramayana pervades the culture of India and is appreciated as entertainment, literature, and religious scripture. According to Narayan, "Everyone of whatever age, outlook, education, or station in life knows the essential part of the epic and adores the main figures in it." For Hindu people in particular, the main character of _The Ramayana_ serves as a model for the devotion and duty desired of Hindu men.

Like epics from other cultures and time periods, _The Ramayana_ celebrates the heroic achievements of both human and divine beings. The epic relates the story of Rama (rä′ mə), a prince who is the seventh incarnation of the god Vishnu (vish′ nōō). The poem describes Rama's royal birth, his instruction by the sage Viswamithra (vis wə mi′ trə), and his feat of bending the bow of Shiva (shi′ və) at a tournament, thus winning the hand of Sita (sē′ tä), the daughter of King Janaka (jä′ nə kə). In a dispute over the throne, Rama's father exiles him. For fourteen years he lives in the forest along with his wife, Sita, and his half-brother Lakshmana (luksh′ mə nə).

At the point in the epic where this excerpt begins, Sita has been kidnapped by Ravana (rä′ və nə), the ten-headed, twenty-armed demon-king of the island of Lanka (luŋ′ kə). Hanuman (hu′ nōō män), a flying monkey in Rama's army, has located Sita and helped build a bridge to Lanka so that all of Rama's forces, including Lakshmana and the monkey captain Sugreeva (sōō grē′ və), can cross over and rescue her. Ravana prepares to defend his land, expecting help from his brother Kumbakarna (kōōm bə kur′ nə) and his son Indrajit (in′ drə jēt).

Building Vocabulary

These essential words are footnoted within the epic.

imprecations (im′ pri kā′ shənz): The air was filled with the cries of fighters, their challenges, cheers, and **imprecations**. (page 130)

ramparts (ram′ pärts′): Ravana was surprised to hear again the cheers of the enemy hordes outside the **ramparts**. (page 131)

invincibility (in vin′ sə bil′ ə tē): "Why should you despair? You have Brahma's gift of **invincibility**." (page 132)

incarnation (in kär nā′ shən): Another conch, called "Panchajanya," which belonged to Mahavishnu (Rama's original form before his present **incarnation**), sounded of its own accord in answer. (page 134)

impervious (im pur′ vē əs): Ravana was so insensible to pain and **impervious** to attack. (page 135)

incantations (in kan tā′ shənz): He was an adept in the use of various asthras which could be made dynamic with special **incantations**. (page 135)

parrying (par′ ē iŋ): The fight became one of attack with supernatural powers, and **parrying** of such an attack. (page 135)

formidable (fôr′ mə də bəl): The mortal whom he had so contemptuously thought of destroying . . . was proving **formidable**. (page 135)

esoteric (es′ ə ter′ ik): While he was breathing out that incantation, an **esoteric** syllable in perfect timing, the trident collapsed. (page 136)

primordial (prī môr′ dē əl): "Perhaps this man is the **primordial** being, the cause behind the whole universe." (page 136)

dross (drôs): Rama's arrows had burnt off the layers of **dross**, the anger, conceit, . . . and egotism which had encrusted his real self. (page 137)

Connecting Writing and Reading

Think about someone who is considered a cultural hero. He or she might be a sports figure, a spiritual or political leader, a military hero, or some other individual admired by large numbers of people. In your journal create a tree diagram similar to the one in **Responding in Writing**, page 17. Write the name of the person. On the "branches and leaves," jot down the qualities that make him or her heroic.

As you read, consider whether the same heroic qualities are displayed by the hero in this epic battle.

from The Ramayana
The Siege of Lanka

RAVANA DEPLOYED THE pick of his divisions to guard the approaches to the capital and appointed his trusted generals and kinsmen in special charge of key places. Gradually, however, his world began to shrink. As the fight developed he lost his associates one by one. No one who went out returned.

He tried some devious measures in desperation. He sent spies in the garb of Rama's monkey army across to deflect and corrupt some of Rama's staunchest supporters, such as Sugreeva, on whom rested the entire burden of this war. He employed sorcerers to disturb the mind of Sita, hoping that if she yielded, Rama would ultimately lose heart. He ordered a sorcerer to create a decapitated head resembling Rama's and placed it before Sita as evidence of Rama's defeat. Sita, although shaken at first, very soon recovered her composure and remained unaffected by the spectacle.

At length a messenger from Rama arrived, saying, "Rama bids me warn you that your doom is at hand. Even now it is not too late for you to restore Sita and beg Rama's forgiveness. You have troubled the world too long. You are not fit to continue as King. At our camp, your brother, Vibishana,[1] has already been crowned the King of this land, and the world knows all people will be happy under him."

Ravana ordered the messenger to be killed instantly. But it was more easily said than done, the messenger being Angada,[2] the son of mighty Vali.[3] When two rakshasas[4] came to seize him, he tucked one of them under each arm, rose into the sky, and flung the rakshasas down. In addition, he kicked and broke off the tower of Ravana's palace, and left. Ravana viewed the broken tower with dismay.

Rama awaited the return of Angada, and, on hearing his report, decided that there was no further cause to hope for a change of heart in Ravana and immediately ordered the assault on Lanka.

As the fury of the battle grew, both sides lost sight of the distinction between night and day. The air was filled with the cries of fighters, their challenges, cheers, and imprecations;[5] buildings and trees were torn up and, as one of his spies reported to Ravana, the monkeys were like a sea overrunning Lanka. The end did not seem to be in sight.

At one stage of the battle, Rama and Lakshmana were attacked by Indrajit, and the serpent darts employed by him made them swoon on the battlefield. Indrajit went back to his father to proclaim that it was all over with Rama and Lakshmana and soon, without a leader, the monkeys would be annihilated.

Ravana rejoiced to hear it and cried, "Did not I say so? All you fools believed that I should surrender." He added, "Go and tell Sita that Rama and his brother are no more. Take her high up in Pushpak Vimana,[6] my chariot, and show her their bodies on the battlefield." His words were obeyed instantly. Sita, happy to have a chance to glimpse a long-lost face, accepted the chance, went high up, and saw

---

1. **Vibishana** (vi bē′ shə nə).
2. **Angada** (uŋ′ gə də).
3. **Vali** (vä′ lē): king of the monkeys.
4. **rakshasas** (räk′ shə səz): demons.
5. **imprecations** (im′ pri kā′ shənz): curses.
6. **Pushpak Vimana** (p̄oosh′ puk vi mä′ nə).

her husband lying dead in the field below. She broke down. "How I wish I had been left alone and not brought up to see this spectacle. Ah, me . . . Help me to put an end to my life."

Trijata,[7] one of Ravana's women, whispered to her, "Don't lose heart, they are not dead," and she explained why they were in a faint.

In due course, the effect of the serpent darts was neutralized when Garuda,[8] the mighty eagle, the born enemy of all serpents, appeared on the scene; the venomous darts enveloping Rama and Lakshmana scattered at the approach of Garuda and the brothers were on their feet again.

From his palace retreat Ravana was surprised to hear again the cheers of the enemy hordes outside the ramparts;[9] the siege was on again. Ravana still had about him his commander in chief, his son Indrajit, and five or six others on whom he felt he could rely at the last instance. He sent them one by one. He felt shattered when news came of the death of his commander in chief.

"No time to sit back. I will myself go and destroy this Rama and his horde of monkeys," he said and got into his chariot and entered the field.

At this encounter Lakshmana fell down in a faint, and Hanuman hoisted Rama on his shoulders and charged in the direction of Ravana. The main combatants were face to face for the first time. At the end of this engagement Ravana was sorely wounded, his crown was shattered, and his chariot was broken. Helplessly, barehanded, he stood before Rama, and Rama said, "You may go now and come back tomorrow with fresh weapons." For the first time in his existence of many thousand years, Ravana faced the humiliation of accepting a concession, and he returned crestfallen to his palace.

He ordered that his brother Kumbakarna, famous for his deep sleep, should be awakened. He could depend upon him, and only on him,

now. It was a mighty task to wake up Kumbakarna. A small army had to be engaged. They sounded trumpets and drums at his ears and were ready with enormous quantities of food and drink for him, for when Kumbakarna awoke from sleep, his hunger was phenomenal and he made a meal of whomever he could grab at his bedside. They cudgelled, belabored, pushed, pulled, and shook him, with the help of elephants; at last he opened his eyes and swept his arms about and crushed quite a number among those who had stirred him up. When he had eaten and drunk, he was approached by Ravana's chief minister and told, "My lord, the battle is going badly for us."

"Which battle?" he asked, not yet fully awake.

And they had to refresh his memory. "Your brother has fought and has been worsted; our enemies are breaking in, our fort walls are crumbling. . . ."

Kumbakarna was roused. "Why did not anyone tell me all this before? Well, it is not too late; I will deal with that Rama. His end is come." Thus saying, he strode into Ravana's chamber and said, "Don't worry about anything anymore. I will take care of everything."

Ravana spoke with anxiety and defeat in his voice. Kumbakarna, who had never seen him in this state, said, "You have gone on without heeding anyone's words and brought yourself to this pass. You should have fought Rama and acquired Sita. You were led away by mere lust and never cared for anyone's words. . . . Hm . . . This is no time to speak of dead events. I will not forsake you as others have done. I'll bring Rama's head on a platter."

Kumbakarna's entry into the battle created havoc. He destroyed and swallowed hundreds

foreboding

7. **Trijata** (tri′ jə tə).

8. **Garuda** (gu′ roo də).

9. **ramparts** (ram′ pärts′): embankments of earth encircling a castle or fort, for defense against attack.

and thousands of the monkey warriors and came very near finishing off the great Sugreeva himself. Rama himself had to take a hand at destroying this demon; he sent the sharpest of his arrows, which cut Kumbakarna limb from limb; but he fought fiercely with only inches of his body remaining intact. Finally Rama severed his head with an arrow. That was the end of Kumbakarna.

When he heard of it, Ravana lamented, "My right hand is cut off."

One of his sons reminded him, "Why should you despair? You have Brahma's[10] gift of invincibility.[11] You should not grieve." Indrajit told him, "What have you to fear when I am alive?"

Indrajit had the power to remain invisible and fight, and accounted for much destruction in the invader's camp. He also created a figure resembling Sita, carried her in his chariot, took her before Rama's army and killed her within their sight.

This completely demoralized the monkeys, who suspended their fight, crying, "Why should we fight when our goddess Sita is thus gone?" They were in a rout until Vibishana came to their rescue and rallied them again.

Indrajit fell by Lakshmana's hand in the end. When he heard of his son's death, Ravana shed bitter tears and swore, "This is the time to kill that woman Sita, the cause of all this misery."

A few encouraged this idea, but one of his councillors advised, "Don't defeat your own purpose and integrity by killing a woman. Let your anger scorch Rama and his brother. Gather all your armies and go and vanquish Rama and Lakshmana, you know you can, and then take Sita. Put on your blessed armor and go forth."

---

10. Brahma (bruh' mə): the creator of the universe. (See footnote for Mahavishnu, page 134.)

11. invincibility (in vin' sə bil' ə tē): quality of being unbeatable.

Rama and Ravana in Battle

Every moment, news came to Ravana of fresh disasters in his camp. One by one, most of his commanders were lost. No one who went forth with battle cries was heard of again. Cries and shouts and the wailings of the widows of warriors came over the chants and songs of triumph that his courtiers arranged to keep up at a loud pitch in his assembly hall. Ravana became restless and abruptly left the hall and went up on a tower, from which he could obtain a full view of the city. He surveyed the scene below but could not stand it. One who had spent a lifetime in destruction, now found the gory spectacle intolerable.

Groans and wailings reached his ears with deadly clarity; and he noticed how the monkey hordes revelled in their bloody handiwork. This was too much for him. He felt a terrific rage rising within him, mixed with some admiration for Rama's valor. He told himself, "The time has come for me to act by myself again."

He hurried down the steps of the tower, returned to his chamber, and prepared himself for the battle. He had a ritual bath and performed special prayers to gain the benediction of Shiva; donned his battle dress, matchless armor, armlets, and crowns. He had on a protective armor for every inch of his body. He girt his swordbelt and attached to his body his accoutrements for protection and decoration.

When he emerged from his chamber, his heroic appearance was breathtaking. He summoned his chariot, which could be drawn by horses or move on its own if the horses were hurt or killed. People stood aside when he came out of the palace and entered his chariot. "This is my resolve," he said to himself: "Either that woman Sita, or my wife Mandodari,[12] will soon have cause to cry and roll in the dust in grief. Surely, before this day is done, one of them will be a widow."

The gods in heaven noticed Ravana's determined move and felt that Rama would need all the support they could muster. They requested Indra to send down his special chariot for Rama's use. When the chariot appeared at his camp, Rama was deeply impressed with the magnitude and brilliance of the vehicle. "How has this come to be here?" he asked.

"Sir," the charioteer answered, "my name is Matali.[13] I have the honor of being the charioteer of Indra. Brahma, the four-faced god and the creator of the Universe, and Shiva, whose power has emboldened Ravana now to challenge you, have commanded me to bring it here for your use. It can fly swifter than air over all obstacles, over any mountain, sea, or sky, and will help you to emerge victorious in this battle."

Rama reflected aloud, "It may be that the rakshasas have created this illusion for me. It may be a trap. I don't know how to view it." Whereupon Matali spoke convincingly to dispel the doubt in Rama's mind. Rama, still hesitant, though partially convinced, looked at Hanuman and Lakshmana and asked, "What do you think of it?" Both answered, "We feel no doubt that this chariot is Indra's; it is not an illusory creation."

Rama fastened his sword, slung two quivers full of rare arrows over his shoulders, and climbed into the chariot.

The beat of war drums, the challenging cries of soldiers, the trumpets, and the rolling chariots speeding along to confront each other, created a deafening mixture of noise. While Ravana had instructed his charioteer to speed ahead, Rama very gently ordered his chariot driver, "Ravana is in a rage; let him perform all the antics he desires and exhaust himself. Until then be calm; we don't have to hurry forward. Move slowly and calmly, and you must strictly follow my instructions; I will tell you when to drive faster."

Ravana's assistant and one of his staunchest supporters, Mahodara[14]—the giant among giants in his physical appearance—begged Ravana, "Let me not be a mere spectator when you confront Rama. Let me have the honor of grappling with him. Permit me to attack Rama."

"Rama is my sole concern," Ravana replied. "If you wish to engage yourself in a fight, you may fight his brother Lakshmana."

Noticing Mahodara's purpose, Rama steered his chariot across his path in order to prevent Mahodara from reaching Lakshmana. Whereupon Mahodara ordered his chariot driver, "Now dash straight ahead, directly into Rama's chariot."

The charioteer, more practical minded, advised him, "I would not go near Rama. Let us keep away." But Mahodara, obstinate and intoxicated with war fever, made straight for Rama. He wanted to have the honor of a direct encounter with Rama himself in spite of Ravana's advice; and for this honor he paid a heavy price, as it was a moment's work for Rama to destroy him, and leave him lifeless and shapeless on the field. Noticing this, Ravana's anger mounted further. He com-

---

12. **Mandodari** (mun dō′ də rē).
13. **Matali** (mä′ tə lē).
14. **Mahodara** (mu hō′ də rə).

manded his driver, "You will not slacken now. Go." Many ominous signs were seen now— his bowstrings suddenly snapped; the mountains shook; thunders rumbled in the skies; tears flowed from the horses' eyes; elephants with decorated foreheads moved along dejectedly. Ravana, noticing them, hesitated only for a second, saying, "I don't care. This mere mortal Rama is of no account, and these omens do not concern me at all." Meanwhile, Rama paused for a moment to consider his next step; and suddenly turned toward the armies supporting Ravana, which stretched away to the horizon, and destroyed them. He felt that this might be one way of saving Ravana. With his armies gone, it was possible that Ravana might have a change of heart. But it had only the effect of spurring Ravana on; he plunged forward and kept coming nearer Rama and his own doom.

Rama's army cleared and made way for Ravana's chariot, unable to stand the force of his approach. Ravana blew his conch[15] and its shrill challenge reverberated through space. Following it another conch, called "Panchajanya,"[16] which belonged to Mahavishnu[17] (Rama's original form before his present incarnation[18]), sounded of its own accord in answer to the challenge, agitating the universe with its vibrations. And then Matali picked up another conch, which was Indra's, and blew it. This was the signal indicating the commencement of the actual battle. Presently Ravana sent a shower of arrows on Rama; and Rama's followers, unable to bear the sight of his body being studded with arrows, averted their heads. Then the chariot horses of Ravana and Rama glared at each other in hostility, and the flags topping the chariots—Ravana's ensign of the Veena[19] and Rama's with the whole universe on it—clashed, and one heard the stringing and twanging of bowstrings on both sides, overpowering in volume all other sound. Then followed a shower of arrows from Rama's own bow. Ravana stood gazing at the chariot sent by Indra and swore, "These gods, instead of supporting me, have gone to the support of this petty human being. I will teach them a lesson. He is not fit to be killed with my arrows but I shall seize him and his chariot together and fling them into high heaven and dash them to destruction." Despite his oath, he still strung his bow and sent a shower of arrows at Rama, raining in thousands, but they were all invariably shattered and neutralized by the arrows from Rama's bow, which met arrow for arrow. Ultimately Ravana, instead of using one bow, used ten with his twenty arms, multiplying his attack tenfold; but Rama stood unhurt.

Ravana suddenly realized that he should change his tactics and ordered his charioteer to fly the chariot up in the skies. From there he attacked and destroyed a great many of the monkey army supporting Rama. Rama ordered Matali, "Go up in the air. Our young soldiers are being attacked from the sky. Follow Ravana, and don't slacken."

There followed an aerial pursuit at dizzying speed across the dome of the sky and rim of the earth. Ravana's arrows came down like rain; he was bent upon destroying everything in the world. But Rama's arrows diverted, broke, or neutralized Ravana's. Terror-stricken, the gods watched this pursuit. Presently Ravana's arrows struck Rama's horses and pierced the heart of Matali himself. The charioteer fell. Rama paused for a while in grief,

15. **conch** (känch): a large, spiral shell, used as a trumpet.
16. **Panchajanja** (pän chə jun' yə).
17. **Mahavishnu** (mu hä vish' noo): the Supreme God, who divides himself into a trinity named Brahma, Vishnu, and Shiva.
18. **incarnation** (in' kär nā' shən): the bodily form taken on by a spirit.
19. **Veena** (vē' nä): a stringed musical instrument.

undecided as to his next step. Then he recovered and resumed his offensive. At that moment the divine eagle Garuda was seen perched on Rama's flag post, and the gods who were watching felt that this could be an auspicious sign.

After circling the globe several times, the duelling chariots returned, and the fight continued over Lanka. It was impossible to be very clear about the location of the battleground as the fight occurred here, there, and everywhere. Rama's arrows pierced Ravana's armor and made him wince. Ravana was so insensible to pain and impervious[20] to attack that for him to wince was a good sign, and the gods hoped that this was a turn for the better. But at this moment, Ravana suddenly changed his tactics. Instead of merely shooting his arrows, which were powerful in themselves, he also invoked several supernatural forces to create strange effects: He was an adept in the use of various asthras[21] which could be made dynamic with special incantations.[22] At this point, the fight became one of attack with supernatural powers, and parrying[23] of such an attack with other supernatural powers.

Ravana realized that the mere aiming of shafts with ten or twenty of his arms would be of no avail because the mortal whom he had so contemptuously thought of destroying with a slight effort was proving formidable,[24] and his arrows were beginning to pierce and cause pain. Among the asthras sent by Ravana was one called "Danda," a special gift from Shiva, capable of pursuing and pulverizing its target. When it came flaming along, the gods were struck with fear. But Rama's arrow neutralized it.

Now Ravana said to himself, "These are all petty weapons. I should really get down to proper business." And he invoked the one called "Maya"—a weapon which created illusions and confused the enemy.

With proper incantations and worship, he sent off this weapon and it created an illusion of reviving all the armies and their leaders—Kumbakarna and Indrajit and the others—and bringing them back to the battlefield. Presently Rama found all those who, he thought, were no more, coming on with battle cries and surrounding him. Every man in the enemy's army was again up in arms. They seemed to fall on Rama with victorious cries. This was very confusing and Rama asked Matali, whom he had by now revived, "What is happening now? How are all these coming back? They were dead." Matali explained, "In your original identity you are the creator of illusions in this universe. Please know that Ravana has created phantoms to confuse you. If you make up your mind, you can dispel them immediately." Matali's explanation was a great help. Rama at once invoked a weapon called "Gnana"[25]—which means "wisdom" or "perception." This was a very rare weapon, and he sent it forth. And all the terrifying armies who seemed to have come on in such a great mass suddenly evaporated into thin air.

Ravana then shot an asthra called "Thama," whose nature was to create total darkness in all the worlds. The arrows came with heads exposing frightening eyes and fangs, and fiery tongues. End to end the earth was enveloped in total darkness and the whole of creation was paralyzed. This asthra also created a deluge of rain on one side, a rain of stones on the other, a hailstorm showering

---

20. impervious (im pʉr′ vē əs): not capable of being penetrated; not affected by.
21. asthras (us′ trəz): missiles, arrows, or other weapons powered by supernatural forces.
22. incantations (in kan tā′ shənz): chants intended to bring forth supernatural powers.
23. parrying (par′ ē iŋ): warding off or turning aside.
24. formidable (fôr′ mə də bəl): causing fear or dread; hard to handle or overcome.
25. Gnana (nyä′ nə).

down intermittently, and a tornado sweeping the earth. Ravana was sure that this would arrest Rama's enterprise. But Rama was able to meet it with what was named "Shivasthra."[26] He understood the nature of the phenomenon and the cause of it and chose the appropriate asthra for counteracting it.

Ravana now shot off what he considered his deadliest weapon—a trident[27] endowed with extraordinary destructive power, once gifted to Ravana by the gods. When it started on its journey there was real panic all round. It came on flaming toward Rama, its speed or course unaffected by the arrows he flung at it.

When Rama noticed his arrows falling down ineffectively while the trident sailed toward him, for a moment he lost heart. When it came quite near, he uttered a certain mantra[28] from the depth of his being and while he was breathing out that incantation, an esoteric[29] syllable in perfect timing, the trident collapsed. Ravana, who had been so certain of vanquishing Rama with his trident, was astonished to see it fall down within an inch of him, and for a minute wondered if his adversary might not after all be a divine being although he looked like a mortal. Ravana thought to himself, "This is, perhaps, the highest God. Who could he be? Not Shiva, for Shiva is my supporter; he could not be Brahma, who is four faced; could not be Vishnu, because of my immunity from the weapons of the whole trinity. Perhaps this man is the primordial[30] being, the cause behind the whole universe. But whoever he may be, I will not stop my fight until I defeat and crush him or at least take him prisoner."

With this resolve, Ravana next sent a weapon which issued forth monstrous serpents vomiting fire and venom, with enormous fangs and red eyes. They came darting in from all directions.

Rama now selected an asthra called "Garuda" (which meant "eagle"). Very soon

thousands of eagles were aloft, and they picked off the serpents with their claws and beaks and destroyed them. Seeing this also fail, Ravana's anger was roused to a mad pitch and he blindly emptied a quiverful of arrows in Rama's direction. Rama's arrows met them halfway and turned them round so that they went back and their sharp points embedded themselves in Ravana's own chest.

Ravana was weakening in spirit. He realized that he was at the end of his resources. All his learning and equipment in weaponry were of no avail and he had practically come to the end of his special gifts of destruction. While he was going down thus, Rama's own spirit was soaring up. The combatants were now near enough to grapple with each other and Rama realized that this was the best moment to cut off Ravana's heads. He sent a crescent-shaped arrow which sliced off one of Ravana's heads and flung it far into the sea, and this process continued; but every time a head was cut off, Ravana had the benediction of having another one grown in its place. Rama's crescent-shaped weapon was continuously busy as Ravana's heads kept cropping up. Rama lopped off his arms but they grew again and every lopped-off arm hit Matali and the chariot and tried to cause destruction by itself, and the tongue in a new head wagged, uttered challenges, and cursed Rama. On the cast-off heads of Ravana devils and minor demons, who had all along been in terror of Ravana and had obeyed and pleased him, executed a dance of death and feasted on the flesh.

---

26. **Shivasthra** (sʰiv us′ trə).
27. **trident** (trīd′ 'nt): a spear with three prongs.
28. **mantra** (mun′ trə): a word, sound, or phrase used to call up special power.
29. **esoteric** (es′ ə ter′ ik): understood by only a chosen few.
30. **primordial** (prī môr′ dē əl): existing at or from the beginning.

Ravana was now desperate. Rama's arrows embedded themselves in a hundred places on his body and weakened him. Presently he collapsed in a faint on the floor of his chariot. Noticing his state, his charioteer pulled back and drew the chariot aside. Matali whispered to Rama, "This is the time to finish off that demon. He is in a faint. Go on. Go on."

But Rama put away his bow and said, "It is not fair warfare to attack a man who is in a faint. I will wait. Let him recover," and waited.

When Ravana revived, he was angry with his charioteer for withdrawing, and took out his sword, crying, "You have disgraced me. Those who look on will think I have retreated." But his charioteer explained how Rama suspended the fight and forbore to attack when he was in a faint. Somehow, Ravana appreciated his explanation and patted his back and resumed his attacks. Having exhausted his special weapons, in desperation Ravana began to throw on Rama all sorts of things such as staves, cast-iron balls, heavy rocks, and oddments he could lay hands on. None of them touched Rama, but glanced off and fell ineffectually. Rama went on shooting his arrows. There seemed to be no end of this struggle in sight.

Now Rama had to pause to consider what final measure he should take to bring this campaign to an end. After much thought, he decided to use "Brahmasthra,"[31] a weapon specially designed by the Creator Brahma on a former occasion, when he had to provide one for Shiva to destroy Tripura,[32] the old monster who assumed the forms of flying mountains and settled down on habitations and cities, seeking to destroy the world. The Brahmasthra was a special gift to be used only when all other means had failed. Now Rama, with prayers and worship, invoked its fullest power and sent it in Ravana's direction, aiming at his heart rather than his head, Ravana being vulnerable at heart. While he had prayed for indestructibility of his several heads and arms, he had forgotten to strengthen his heart, where the Brahmasthra entered and ended his career.

Rama watched him fall headlong from his chariot face down onto the earth, and that was the end of the great campaign. Now one noticed Ravana's face aglow with a new quality. Rama's arrows had burnt off the layers of dross,[33] the anger, conceit, cruelty, lust, and egotism which had encrusted his real self, and now his personality came through in its pristine form—of one who was devout and capable of tremendous attainments. His constant meditation on Rama, although as an adversary, now seemed to bear fruit, as his face shone with serenity and peace. Rama noticed it from his chariot above and commanded Matali, "Set me down on the ground." When the chariot descended and came to rest on its wheels, Rama got down and commanded Matali, "I am grateful for your services to me. You may now take the chariot back to Indra."

Surrounded by his brother Lakshmana and Hanuman and all his other war chiefs, Rama approached Ravana's body, and stood gazing on it. He noted his crowns and jewelry scattered piecemeal on the ground. The decorations and the extraordinary workmanship of the armor on his chest were blood-covered. Rama sighed as if to say, "What might he not have achieved but for the evil stirring within him!"

At this moment, as they readjusted Ravana's bloodstained body, Rama noticed to his great shock a scar on Ravana's back and said with a smile, "Perhaps this is not an episode of glory for me as I seem to have killed an enemy who was turning his back and retreating. Perhaps I was wrong in shooting the Brahmasthra into him." He looked so

---

31. **Brahmasthra** (bruh mus′ trə).
32. **Tripura** (tri poor′ ə).
33. **dross** (drôs): waste matter; worthless material.

concerned at this supposed lapse on his part that Vibishana, Ravana's brother, came forward to explain. "What you have achieved is unique. I say so although it meant the death of my brother."

"But I have attacked a man who had turned his back," Rama said. "See that scar."

Vibishana explained, "It is an old scar. In ancient days, when he paraded his strength around the globe, once he tried to attack the divine elephants that guard the four directions.

When he tried to catch them, he was gored in the back by one of the tuskers and that is the scar you see now; it is not a fresh one though fresh blood is flowing on it."

Rama accepted the explanation. "Honor him and cherish his memory so that his spirit may go to heaven, where he has his place. And now I will leave you to attend to his funeral arrangements, befitting his grandeur."

Thinking About the Epic

A PERSONAL RESPONSE

sharing impressions

1. What is your reaction to the battle between Rama and Ravana? Note your response in your journal.

constructing interpretations

2. Ravana, with his ten heads and twenty arms, would seem to have an advantage over Rama. Why do you think Rama is able to defeat him?

Think about
- the temperaments of the two foes
- the aid each gets from his supporters
- the nature of the weapons each uses

3. Give your reaction to the heroic code that Rama lives by.
> **Think about**
> - the message he sends to Ravana that it is not too late to return Sita and beg forgiveness
> - the chance Rama gives Ravana to renew his weapons
> - the might Rama shows as a warrior
> - what Rama tells Ravana's brother after Ravana has been killed

4. Do you consider Ravana heroic?
> **Think about**
> - the heroic qualities you identified in your journal
> - differences and similarities between Ravana and Rama
> - the description of Ravana as he falls from the chariot
> - Rama's final instructions to Ravana's brother Vibishana

A CREATIVE RESPONSE

5. How would your reaction to the selection be different if Ravana had won?

A CRITICAL RESPONSE

6. R. K. Narayan, the translator of this selection, calls *The Ramayana* "a book of perennial philosophy" whose symbolism is relevant to daily life. In what ways might this story apply to meeting challenges in your life?
> **Think about**
> - Rama's and Ravana's attitudes toward each other
> - the outcome of their confrontation
> - your feelings about Rama and Ravana

7. Compare Rama's heroic qualities with those of the cultural hero you identified in your journal. With your classmates, evaluate whether the same qualities are considered heroic across cultures.

8. *The Ramayana* was originally composed in verse, and there have been many verse translations. Compare the following verse description of Kumbakarna's death with the corresponding passage in Narayan's prose translation (page 132). Which version do you think is more effective?

Deadly arrows keen and flaming from the
    hero's weapon broke,
Kumbha-karna faint and bleeding felt his
    death at every stroke,

Last, an arrow pierced his armor, from his
    shoulders smote his head,
Kumbha-karna, lifeless, headless, rolled
    upon the gory bed,

Hurled unto the heaving ocean
    Kumbha-karna's body fell,
And as shaken by a tempest, mighty was
    the ocean's swell!

          —*Translated by Romesh C. Dutt*

Analyzing the Writer's Craft

EPIC

Consider the plot and setting of this story, which goes beyond the realm of ordinary life.

Building a Literary Vocabulary. An epic is a long narrative poem on a serious subject presented in an elevated or formal style. An epic traces the adventures of a hero of high status whose actions consist of courageous, even superhuman, deeds. Such deeds represent the ideals and values of a nation. The plot of an epic usually involves a long and dangerous journey complicated by supernatural events and beings; the epic hero shows superhuman qualities as he accomplishes great deeds. The setting is large in scale and ranges over many locales. An epic addresses universal concerns, such as good and evil, life and death, and sin and redemption.

Application: Recognizing Characteristics of an Epic. In a small group, discuss how this excerpt from *The Ramayana* shows the characteristics of an epic. Also consider whether contemporary American culture has produced a work that approaches epic status.

Connecting Reading and Writing

1. Write a **radio newscast** that recounts the battle between Rama and Ravana as it is unfolding.

Option: Compose a **narrative poem** that describes an episode of the battle for presentation in front of the class.

2. In an **essay** for your teacher, compare this story to a contemporary work that depicts a battle between good and evil. You might choose a popular film, such as one of the *Star Wars* or *Superman* movies, or a television police drama.

Option: Show your comparison in a **chart** you create for a classroom display.

3. Imagine that a Hollywood producer is trying to decide whether to do a film version of *The Ramayana*. In a **memo** to the producer, evaluate the appeal of such a film to a contemporary audience.

Option: Comment on the contemporary appeal of *The Ramayana* in **ad copy** for a new paperback edition of the epic.

4. Prepare **director's notes** for a film version of this excerpt from *The Ramayana*. Include a list of actors and actresses whom you would cast in the various roles. Also indicate the location of the filming and any places in the excerpt requiring special effects.

Option: Prepare several brief **character sketches** that will help the actors and actresses understand the character they are going to play in a film version of *The Ramayana*.

from The Iliad

HOMER   8TH CENTURY B.C.   ANCIENT GREECE

Translated by Robert Fitzgerald

Approaching the Epic

The Iliad is the oldest surviving Greek poem, believed to have been composed by Homer in the eighth century B.C. _The Iliad_ describes events from the ten-year war waged between Greece and the city of Troy, or Ilium, in Asia Minor. Archaeologists who have excavated the ruins of Troy generally believe that the war was fought in the mid-thirteenth century B.C. In composing _The Iliad_, Homer made use of the many accounts and legends about the Trojan War that had been passed down orally for five centuries.

Both _The Iliad_ and _The Odyssey_, Homer's other epic of the Trojan War, convey the essence of ancient Greek culture, reflecting the richness of its history, mythology, and storytelling heritage. Ancient Greeks viewed _The Iliad_ as a work that revealed all-important truths about human beings and their place in the universe. Children of ancient Greece were often required to memorize portions of _The Iliad_ and to model their behavior according to the heroic code set forth by Homer.

Hardly anything is known about Homer. Legend has it that he was blind; however, some scholars believe that this idea may have arisen due to a recurring paradoxical figure in Greek lore—that of the wise, all-knowing individual who is physically blind yet possesses inner vision.

Like the accounts and legends Homer used as sources, Homer's epics were first told orally. It is believed that they were composed in verse form partly because the rhyme and rhythm make them easier to memorize.

In _The Iliad_, Homer employed a two-level plot. On one level, humans battle each other on earth. On the other level, the gods and goddesses use their influence on the humans to stage their own form of war. For example, Athena, goddess of war and practical wisdom, sides with the Greeks; Aphrodite, goddess of love and beauty, sides with the Trojans.

According to Homer's poem, the war begins when Agamemnon (ag′ ə mem′ nän′), king of Mycenae, leads an army of Greeks to bring back Helen from Troy. Helen, the most beautiful of women and the wife of Agamemnon's brother, had fallen in love with Paris, son of King Priam, and had run off with him to Troy. While the Greeks besiege Troy, a quarrel breaks out between Agamemnon and his greatest warrior, Achilles. As a result, the angry Achilles decides to remain in his tent and let the fighting go on without him.

In the excerpt from *The Iliad* that you are about to read, Thetis (thē' tis), a goddess of the sea, has come to visit her son Achilles. Achilles grieves for his best friend, Patroclus (pə trō' kləs), who has been killed by the Trojan champion, Hector.

Building Vocabulary

These essential words are defined alongside the epic.

rancor, envenoms (raŋ' kər; en ven' əmz): "Let strife and **rancor** / perish from the lives of gods and men, / with anger that **envenoms** even the wise." (page 146, lines 46–48)

arbiters (är' bət ərz): "We'll summon gods here as our witnesses, / . . . **arbiters** of a pact." (page 147, lines 79–80)

bane (bān): "War for the Trojans would be eased / if you were blotted out, **bane** that you are." (page 148, lines 119–120)

exulted (eg zult' id): He fell / aside into the dust. And Prince Achilles / now **exulted**. (page 150, lines 168–170)

defiled (dē fīld'): Zeus gave him to his enemies / to be **defiled** in his own fatherland. (page 152, lines 256–257)

surfeit (sur' fit): "I / might have had **surfeit** and relief of tears." (page 153, lines 281–282)

felicity (fə lis' i tē): "Shining gifts / at the gods' hands he had from birth: **felicity**, / . . . a bride immortal at his mortal side." (page 155, lines 357–360)

suppliant (sup' lē ənt): "**Suppliant** though you are, / I may not spare you." (page 156, lines 395–396)

Connecting Writing and Reading

Imagine that someone in your school has just insulted or deliberately injured a close friend of yours. Would loyalty to your friend make you decide to get involved? Or would your response depend on the circumstances? Write your ideas about how you would react in your journal. As you read this excerpt from *The Iliad*, think about whether loyalty to a friend means the same thing to Achilles as it does to you.

from Book 18:
The Immortal Shield

Achilles [handwritten]

Bending near Thetis [handwritten]

her groaning son, the gentle goddess wailed
and took his head between her hands in pity,
saying softly:

"Child, why are you weeping?
5   What great sorrow came to you? Speak out,
do not conceal it. Zeus
did all you asked: Achaean[1] troops,
for want of you, were all forced back again
upon the ship sterns, taking heavy losses
10   none of them could wish."

The great runner

groaned and answered:

"Mother, yes, the master
of high Olympus[2] brought it all about,
but how have I benefited? My greatest friend
is gone: Patroclus, comrade in arms, whom I
15   held dear above all others—dear as myself—
now gone, lost; Hector cut him down, despoiled him
of my own arms, massive and fine, a wonder
in all men's eyes. The gods gave them to Peleus[3]
that day they put you in a mortal's bed—
20   how I wish the immortals of the sea
had been your only consorts! How I wish
Peleus had taken a mortal queen! Sorrow
immeasurable is in store for you as well,
when your own child is lost: never again
25   on his homecoming day will you embrace him!
I must reject this life, my heart tells me,
reject the world of men,
if Hector does not feel my battering spear
tear the life out of him, making him pay
30   in his own blood for the slaughter of Patroclus!"

Letting a tear fall, Thetis said:

1. **Achaean** (ə kē′ ən):
another name referring
to the Greeks.

♦ **Lines 6–7:** Achilles had asked
his mother, Thetis, to persuade
Zeus to turn the tide of the
battle so that the Greeks
would see how much they
needed Achilles.

♦ **Line 10:** The reference to
Achilles as "the great runner"
is an example of an epithet, a
brief phrase that points out
traits associated with a
particular person or thing.
Look for other epithets in
The Iliad.

2. **Olympus** (ō lim′ pəs):
mountain in Greece; in Greek
mythology, the home of the
gods and goddesses.

♦ **Lines 16 –17:** Patroclus wore
Achilles' armor to frighten the
Trojans. "Despoiled him of
my own arms" refers to
Hector's robbing Patroclus
of Achilles' armor.

3. **Peleus** (pē′ lē əs):
Achilles' father, a human.

Harpist, 1974, HANS ERNI. From *The Iliad,*
translated by Robert Fitzgerald,
Doubleday & Co./Random House.

"You'll be

foreboding [handwritten annotation]

swift to meet your end, child, as you say:
your doom comes close on the heels of Hector's own."

Achilles the great runner ground his teeth
35   and said:
                              "May it come quickly. As things were,
I could not help my friend in his extremity.
Far from his home he died; he needed me
to shield him or to parry the death stroke.
For me there's no return to my own country.
40   Not the slightest gleam of hope did I
afford Patroclus or the other men
whom Hector overpowered. Here I sat,
my weight a useless burden to the earth,
and I am one who has no peer in war
45   among Achaean captains—

     though in council [handwritten annotation]
     Homeric simile [handwritten annotation]

there are wiser. Ai! let strife and rancor[4]
perish from the lives of gods and men,
with anger that envenoms[5] even the wise
and is far sweeter than slow-dripping honey,
50   clouding the hearts of men like smoke: just so
the marshal of the army, Agamemnon,
moved me to anger. But we'll let that go,
though I'm still sore at heart; it is all past,
and I have quelled my passion as I must.

55   Now I must go to look for the destroyer
of my great friend. I shall confront the dark
drear spirit of death at any hour Zeus
and the other gods may wish to make an end.
Not even Heracles escaped that terror
60   though cherished by the Lord Zeus. Destiny
and Hera's bitter anger mastered him.
Likewise with me, if destiny like his
awaits me, I shall rest when I have fallen!
Now, though, may I win my perfect glory
65   and make some wife of Troy break down,
or some deep-breasted Dardan[6] woman sob
and wipe tears from her soft cheeks. They'll know then
how long they had been spared the deaths of men,
while I abstained from war!
70   Do not attempt to keep me from the fight,
though you love me; you cannot make me listen."

4. **rancor** (raŋ′ kər): long-lasting and bitter hate or ill will.

5. **envenoms** (en ven′ əmz): makes poisonous; fills with hate.

◆ **Lines 51–52:** Agamemnon kidnapped the daughter of Achilles' priest. Achilles was forced to trade a captive woman for her return. As a result, Achilles in anger refused to fight with Agamemnon against the Trojans.

◆ **Lines 59–61:** Hera (hir′ ə), the wife of Zeus and an immortal, tried to harm his children born to mortal women. Hera devised the Twelve Labors of Heracles (her′ ə klēz), a child of Zeus. These labors indirectly led to the death of Heracles.

◆ **Lines 62–63:** Note how Achilles' loyalty to Patroclus affects his attitude toward his own life.

6. **Dardan** (där′ dən): another word for Trojan.

Achilles seeks to avenge Patroclus by slaughtering Trojans. Apollo, the god who protects Troy, opens the gates of Troy so that the Trojans can rush to safety inside the walls of the city. Only Hector is left outside. Achilles chases him around the walls of Troy three times. Finally Athena appears to Hector disguised as Hector's brother, Deïphobos (dē if′ ə bəs), and persuades him to fight Achilles.

from Book 22:
Desolation Before Troy

And when at last the two men faced each other,
Hector was the first to speak. He said:

"I will no longer fear you as before,
son of Peleus, though I ran from you
round Priam's town three times and could not face you.
Now my soul would have me stand and fight,
whether I kill you or am killed. So come,
we'll summon gods here as our witnesses,
none higher, arbiters⁷ of a pact: I swear
that, terrible as you are,

7. arbiters (är′ bət ərz): those selected to judge a dispute.

I'll not insult your corpse should Zeus allow me
victory in the end, your life as prize.
Once I have your gear, I'll give your body
85   back to Achaeans. Grant me, too, this grace."

But swift Achilles frowned at him and said:

"Hector, I'll have no talk of pacts with you,
forever unforgiven as you are.
As between men and lions there are none,
90   no concord between wolves and sheep, but all
hold one another hateful through and through,
so there can be no courtesy between us,
no sworn truce, till one of us is down
and glutting with his blood the war god Ares.[8]
95   Summon up what skills you have. By god,
you'd better be a spearman and a fighter!
Now there is no way out. Pallas Athena
will have the upper hand of you. The weapon
belongs to me. You'll pay the reckoning
100   in full for all the pain my men have borne,
who met death by your spear."

                                He twirled and cast
his shaft with its long shadow. Splendid Hector,
keeping his eye upon the point, eluded it
by ducking at the instant of the cast,
105   so shaft and bronze shank passed him overhead
and punched into the earth. But unperceived
by Hector, Pallas Athena plucked it out
and gave it back to Achilles. Hector said:

"A clean miss. Godlike as you are,
110   you have not yet known doom for me from Zeus.
You thought you had, by heaven. Then you turned
into a word-thrower, hoping to make me lose
my fighting heart and head in fear of you.
You cannot plant your spear between my shoulders
115   while I am running. If you have the gift,
just put it through my chest as I come forward.
Now it's for you to dodge my own. Would god
you'd give the whole shaft lodging in your body!
War for the Trojans would be eased
120   if you were blotted out, bane[9] that you are."

◆ **Lines 84–85:** The Greeks and
Trojans generally returned the
bodies of the slain.

8. Ares (ā′ rēz).

◆ **Lines 97–98:** Hera and
Athena, daughter of Zeus, lost
a beauty contest to Aphrodite,
goddess of love and beauty.
The contest was judged by
Paris of Troy. In vengeance,
Hera sent Athena to protect
the Greeks, namely Achilles,
to ensure the Trojans' defeat.

9. bane (bān): cause of
distress, death, or ruin.

With this he twirled his long spearshaft and cast it,
hitting his enemy mid-shield, but off
and away the spear rebounded. Furious
that he had lost it, made his throw for nothing,
125 Hector stood bemused. He had no other.
Then he gave a great shout to Deïphobos
to ask for a long spear. But there was no one
near him, not a soul. Now in his heart
the Trojan realized the truth and said:
130 "This is the end. The gods are calling deathward.
I had thought
a good soldier, Deïphobos, was with me.
He is inside the walls. Athena tricked me.
Death is near, and black, not at a distance,
135 not to be evaded. Long ago
this hour must have been to Zeus' liking
and to the liking of his archer son.
They have been well disposed before, but now
the appointed time's upon me. Still, I would not
140 die without delivering a stroke,
or die ingloriously, but in some action
memorable to men in days to come."

With this he drew the whetted blade that hung
upon his left flank, ponderous and long,
145 collecting all his might the way an eagle
narrows himself to dive through shady cloud
and strike a lamb or cowering hare: so Hector
lanced ahead and swung his whetted blade.
Achilles with wild fury in his heart
150 pulled in upon his chest his beautiful shield—
his helmet with four burnished metal ridges
nodding above it, and the golden crest
Hephaestus locked there tossing in the wind.
Conspicuous as the evening star that comes,
155 amid the first in heaven, at fall of night,
and stands most lovely in the west, so shone
in sunlight the fine-pointed spear
Achilles poised in his right hand, with deadly
aim at Hector, at the skin where most
160 it lay exposed. But nearly all was covered
by the bronze gear he took from slain Patroclus,
showing only, where his collarbones
divided neck and shoulders, the bare throat
where the destruction of life is quickest.

◆ **Lines 134–142:** As you read these lines, think about Hector's heroic code.
◆ **Line 137:** Zeus' archer son is Apollo. "Archer son" is another example of an epithet.

◆ **Line 153:** Hephaestus (hē fes′ təs), the ironsmith god, had made the new armor for Achilles.

◆ **Lines 160–161:** Hector wears the original armor of Achilles, which he took from the slain body of Patroclus.

from The Iliad 149

165 Here, then, as the Trojan charged, Achilles
drove his point straight through the tender neck,
but did not cut the windpipe, leaving Hector
able to speak and to respond. He fell
aside into the dust. And Prince Achilles
170 now exulted:[10] *bragging, taunting*

"Hector, had you thought
that you could kill Patroclus and be safe?
Nothing to dread from me; I was not there.
All childishness. Though distant then, Patroclus'
comrade in arms was greater far than he—
175 and it is I who had been left behind
that day beside the deep-sea ships who now
have made your knees give way. The dogs and kites[11]
will rip your body. His will lie in honor
when the Achaeans give him funeral."

180 Hector, barely whispering, replied:
"I beg you by your soul and by your parents,
do not let the dogs feed on me
in your encampment by the ships. Accept
the bronze and gold my father will provide *foreshadowing*
185 as gifts, my father and her ladyship
my mother. Let them have my body back,
so that our men and women may accord me
decency of fire when I am dead."

Achilles the great runner scowled and said:

190 "Beg me no beggary by soul or parents,
whining dog! Would god my passion drove me
to slaughter you and eat you raw, you've caused
such agony to me! No man exists
who could defend you from the carrion pack—[12]
195 not if they spread for me ten times your ransom,
twenty times, and promise more as well;
aye, not if Priam, son of Dardanus,[13]
tells them to buy you for your weight in gold!
You'll have no bed of death, nor will you be
200 laid out and mourned by her who gave you birth.
Dogs and birds will have you, every scrap."

Then at the point of death Lord Hector said:

---

10. exulted (eg zult′ id): felt great joy, especially in one's own triumph.

11. kites: birds with long, pointed wings and, usually, forked tails.

◆ **Line 178:** "His" refers to Patroclus' body.

◆ **Lines 185–186:** Hector's father is Priam, King of Troy, and his mother is Hecuba.
◆ **Line 188:** Burning the bodies of the dead was customary. Truces were often arranged for this purpose.
◆ **Lines 190–201:** Characterize Achilles at this moment.

12. carrion pack (kar′ ē ən): group of animals, such as vultures and jackals, that feed on dead flesh.
13. Dardanus (där′ də nəs).

"I see you now for what you are. No chance
to win you over. Iron in your breast
205 your heart is. Think a bit, though: this may be
a thing the gods in anger hold against you
on that day when Paris and Apollo
destroy you at the Gates, great as you are."

Even as he spoke, the end came, and death hid him;
210 spirit from body fluttered to undergloom,
bewailing fate that made him leave his youth
and manhood in the world. And as he died
Achilles spoke again. He said:

"Die, make an end. I shall accept my own
215 whenever Zeus and the other gods desire."

At this he pulled his spearhead from the body,
laying it aside, and stripped
the bloodstained shield and cuirass[14] from his shoulders.
Other Achaeans hastened round to see
220 Hector's fine body and his comely face,
and no one came who did not stab the body.
Glancing at one another they would say:

"Now Hector has turned vulnerable, softer
than when he put the torches to the ships!"

225 And he who said this would inflict a wound.
When the great master of pursuit, Achilles,
had the body stripped, he stood among them,
saying swiftly:

                   "Friends, my lords and captains
of Argives,[15] now that the gods at last have let me
230 bring to earth this man who wrought
havoc among us—more than all the rest—
come, we'll offer battle around the city,
to learn the intentions of the Trojans now.
Will they give up their strong point at this loss?
235 Can they fight on, though Hector's dead?

                                    But wait:
why do I ponder, why take up these questions?
Down by the ships Patroclus' body lies
unwept, unburied. I shall not forget him

♦ **Lines 205–208:** According
to legend, it had been
prophesied that Achilles
would be killed if he killed
a son of Apollo. Hector's
brother Paris and Apollo
later kill Achilles with an
arrow after he has killed
Tenes, Apollo's son, in
battle.

14. cuirass (kwi ras'):
breastplate.

15. Argives (är' gīvz):
another name for the Greeks.

While I can keep my feet among the living.
240 If in the dead world they forget the dead,
I say there, too, I shall remember him,
my friend. Men of Achaea, lift a song!
Down to the ships we go, and take this body,
our glory. We have beaten Hector down,
245 to whom as to a god the Trojans prayed."

Indeed, he had in mind for Hector's body
outrage and shame. Behind both feet he pierced
the tendons, heel to ankle. Rawhide cords
he drew through both and lashed them to his chariot,
250 letting the man's head trail. Stepping aboard,
bearing the great trophy of the arms,
he shook the reins, and whipped the team ahead
into a willing run. A dust cloud rose
above the furrowing body; the dark tresses
255 flowed behind, and the head so princely once
lay back in dust. Zeus gave him to his enemies
to be defiled[16] in his own fatherland.
So his whole head was blackened. Looking down,
his mother tore her braids, threw off her veil,
260 and wailed, heartbroken to behold her son.
Piteously his father groaned, and round him
lamentation spread throughout the town,
most like the clamor to be heard if Ilium's[17]
towers, top to bottom, seethed in flames.
265 They barely stayed the old man, mad with grief,
from passing through the gates. Then in the mire
he rolled, and begged them all, each man by name:

"Relent, friends. It is hard; but let me go
out of the city to the Achaean ships.
270 I'll make my plea to that demonic heart.
He may feel shame before his peers, or pity
my old age. His father, too, is old.
Peleus, who brought him up to be a scourge
to Trojans, cruel to all, but most to me,
275 so many of my sons in flower of youth
he cut away. And, though I grieve, I cannot
mourn them all as much as I do one,
for whom my grief will take me to the grave—
and that is Hector. Why could he not have died
280 where I might hold him? In our weeping, then,

◆ **Line 240:** The "dead world" is the house of Hades, or the underworld, where the Greeks believed the dead reside.

16. defiled (dē fīld'): violated; made ceremonially unclean.

17. Ilium (il' ē əm): another name for Troy.

◆ **Lines 268–270:** Consider Priam's decision to approach Achilles. Analyze what this reveals about his sense of honor and loyalty.

his mother, now so destitute, and I
might have had <u>surfeit</u>[18] and relief of tears."

18. surfeit (sur' fit): an
excessive amount.

*Achilles and his forces return to their camp and carry out the
burial rites for Patroclus. Achilles drags Hector's body behind
his chariot three times around Patroclus' grave. Afterwards,
the gods heal the body perfectly, and Zeus asks Thetis to tell
Achilles to return the body to the Trojans. Priam sets out for
the Greek camp, accompanied only by an old servant, to ask
Achilles to return the body. He is not aware that Mercury helps
him by putting the sentries to sleep and opening the gates.
Mercury leads Priam to Achilles' tent and then vanishes.*

from Book 24:
A Grace Given in Sorrow

Priam, ⟩ *submission*

the great king of Troy, passed by the others,
285   knelt down, took in his arms Achilles' knees,
and kissed the hands of wrath that killed his sons.
When, taken with mad Folly in his own land,
a man does murder and in exile finds

refuge in some rich house, then all who see him
290 stand in awe.
So these men stood.
Achilles
gazed in wonder at the splendid king,
and his companions marveled too, all silent,
with glances to and fro. Now Priam prayed
295 to the man before him:

"Remember your own father,
Achilles, in your godlike youth: his years
like mine are many, and he stands upon
the fearful doorstep of old age. He, too,
is hard pressed, it may be, by those around him,
300 there being no one able to defend him
from bane of war and ruin. Ah, but he
may nonetheless hear news of you alive,
and so with glad heart hope through all his days
for sight of his dear son, come back from Troy,
305 while I have deathly fortune.

Noble sons
I fathered here, but scarce one man is left me.
Fifty I had when the Achaeans came,
nineteen out of a single belly, others
born of attendant women. Most are gone.
310 Raging Ares cut their knees from under them.
And he who stood alone among them all,
their champion, and Troy's, ten days ago
you killed him, fighting for his land, my prince,
Hector.
It is for him that I have come
315 among these ships, to beg him back from you,
and I bring ransom without stint.

Achilles,
be reverent toward the great gods! And take
pity on me, remember your own father.
Think me more pitiful by far, since I
320 have brought myself to do what no man else
has done before—to lift to my lips the hand
of one who killed my son."

Now in Achilles
the evocation of his father stirred

new longing, and an ache of grief. He lifted
325 the old man's hand and gently put him by.
Then both were overborne as they remembered:
the old king huddled at Achilles' feet
wept, and wept for Hector, killer of men,
while great Achilles wept for his own father
330 as for Patroclus once again; and sobbing
filled the room.

But when Achilles' heart
had known the luxury of tears, and pain
within his breast and bones had passed away,
he stood then, raised the old king up, in pity
335 for his gray head and graybeard cheek, and spoke
in a warm rush of words:

"Ah, sad and old!
Trouble and pain you've borne, and bear, aplenty.
Only a great will could have brought you here
among the Achaean ships, and here alone
340 before the eyes of one who stripped your sons,
your many sons, in battle. Iron must be
the heart within you. Come, then, and sit down.
We'll probe our wounds no more but let them rest,
though grief lies heavy on us. Tears heal nothing,
345 drying so stiff and cold. This is the way
the gods ordained the destiny of men,
to bear such burdens in our lives, while they
feel no affliction. At the door of Zeus
are those two urns of good and evil gifts
350 that he may choose for us; and one for whom
the lightning's joyous king dips in both urns
will have by turns bad luck and good. But one
to whom he sends all evil—that man goes
contemptible by the will of Zeus; ravenous
355 hunger drives him over the wondrous earth,
unresting, without honor from gods or men.
Mixed fortune came to Peleus. Shining gifts
at the gods' hands he had from birth: felicity,[19]
wealth overflowing, rule of the Myrmidons,[20]
360 a bride immortal at his mortal side.
But then Zeus gave afflictions too—no family
of powerful sons grew up for him at home,
but one child, of all seasons and of none.
Can I stand by him in his age? Far from my country

Lines 336–346: Compare your impression of Achilles in Book 22, lines 87–94, with your impression now.

19. felicity (fə lis′ i tē): happiness; good fortune.
20. Myrmidons (mʉr′ mə dänz): the people of Thessaly, Achilles' home.

Line 363: "Of all seasons and of none" suggests that Achilles realizes that his death will be untimely.

365 I sit at Troy to grieve you and your children.
You, too, sir, in time past were fortunate,
we hear men say. From Macar's isle of Lesbos[21]
northward, and south of Phrygia[22] and the Straits,
no one had wealth like yours, or sons like yours.
370 Then gods out of the sky sent you this bitterness:
the years of siege, the battles and losses.
Endure it, then. And do not mourn forever
for your dead son. There is no remedy.
You will not make him stand again. Rather
375 await some new misfortune to be suffered."
The old king in his majesty replied:

"Never give me a chair, my lord, while Hector
lies in your camp uncared for. Yield him to me
now. Allow me sight of him. Accept
380 the many gifts I bring. May they reward you,
and may you see your home again.
You spared my life at once and let me live."

Achilles, the great runner, frowned and eyed him
under his brows:

                         "Do not vex me, sir," he said.
385 "I have intended, in my own good time,
to yield up Hector to you. She who bore me,
the daughter of the Ancient of the sea,
has come with word to me from Zeus. I know
in your case, too—though you say nothing, Priam—
390 that some god guided you to the shipways here.
No strong man in his best days could make entry
into this camp. How could he pass the guard,
or force our gateway?

                         Therefore, *let me be*.
Sting my sore heart again, and even here,
395 under my own roof, suppliant[23] though you are,
I may not spare you, sir, but trample on
the express command of Zeus!"
                         When he heard this,
the old man feared him and obeyed with silence.
Now like a lion at one bound Achilles
400 left the room. Close at his back the officers
Automedon and Álkimos[24] went out—
comrades in arms whom he esteemed the most

21. **Lesbos** (lez' bōs).
22. **Phrygia** (frij' ē ə).

♦ **Lines 372–375:** Consider Achilles' advice to Priam and how it fits or does not fit your own image of a hero.

♦ **Line 387:** The epithet "Ancient of the sea" refers to Pontus, father of sea goddess Thetis.

23. **suppliant** (sup' lē ənt): one who begs or pleads earnestly.

24. **Automedon and Álkimos** (ô tō' me dän; äl' kim əs).

after the dead Patroclus. They unharnessed
mules and horses, led the old king's crier
405 to a low bench and sat him down.
Then from the polished wagon
they took the piled-up price of Hector's body.
One khiton[25] and two capes they left aside
as dress and shrouding for the homeward journey.
410 Then, calling to the women slaves, Achilles
ordered the body bathed and rubbed with oil—
but lifted, too, and placed apart, where Priam
could not see his son—for seeing Hector
he might in his great pain give way to rage,
415 and fury then might rise up in Achilles
to slay the old king, flouting Zeus' word.
So after bathing and anointing Hector
they drew the shirt and beautiful shrouding over him.
Then with his own hands lifting him, Achilles
420 laid him upon a couch, and with his two
companions aiding, placed him in the wagon.
Now a bitter groan burst from Achilles,
who stood and prayed to his own dead friend:

                                         "Patroclus,
do not be angry with me, if somehow
425 even in the world of Death you learn of this—
that I released Prince Hector to his father.
The gifts he gave were not unworthy. Aye,
and you shall have your share, this time as well."
The Prince Achilles turned back to his quarters.
430 He took again the splendid chair that stood
against the farther wall, then looked at Priam
and made his declaration:

                                  "As you wished, sir,
the body of your son is now set free.
He lies in state. At the first sight of Dawn
435 you shall take charge of him yourself and see him.
Now let us think of supper. We are told
that even Niobe in her extremity
took thought for bread—though all her brood had
    perished,
her six young girls and six tall sons. Apollo,
440 making his silver longbow whip and sing,
shot the lads down, and Artemis with raining

25. khiton (kī′ tən): a Greek
garment.

*does not want
Priam to see
until after*

◆ **Lines 436–455:** Niobe (nī′ ə
bē) claimed to be superior to
the goddess Leto (lē′ tō)
because she had more
children than Leto. Leto's son
and daughter, Apollo and
Artemis, then killed all of
Niobe's children. Niobe
turned to stone after nine
days of grieving.

arrows killed the daughters—all this after
Niobe had compared herself with Leto,
the smooth-cheeked goddess.
                              She has borne two children,
445 Niobe said, How many have I borne!
But soon those two destroyed the twelve.
                                        Besides,
nine days the dead lay stark, no one could bury them,
for Zeus had turned all folk of theirs to stone.
The gods made graves for them on the tenth day,
450 and then at last, being weak and spent with weeping,
Niobe thought of food. Among the rocks
of Sipylus'[26] lonely mountainside, where nymphs
who race Acheloüs[27] river go to rest,
she, too, long turned to stone, somewhere broods on
455 the gall immortal gods gave her to drink.

Like her we'll think of supper, noble sir. → *homeric simile*
Weep for your son again when you have borne him
back to Troy; there he'll be mourned indeed."

*Priam and Achilles agree to an eleven-day truce. During that
time, the Trojans will mourn Hector's body before burial.*

26. **Sipylus** (si′ pil əs).
27. **Acheloüs** (äk ə lō′ əs):
the largest river in ancient
Greece; also, the god of the
river.

Thinking About the Epic

A PERSONAL RESPONSE

sharing impressions

1. What is your impression of Achilles? Jot down your thoughts and feelings in your journal.

constructing interpretations

2. How would you describe the relationship between Achilles and Priam?
Think about
- Achilles' killing of Hector
- the dialogue between the two men
- why Achilles gives Hector's body to Priam

3. To what extent do Achilles and Hector match your idea of a hero?
Think about
- the kind of warrior each man is
- Achilles' loyalty to his friend
- Hector's sense of loyalty
- Hector's speech that begins "This is the end. . . ." (page 149, line 130)
- Achilles' treatment of Hector's body
- Achilles' response to Priam

A CREATIVE RESPONSE

4. How would your impression of Achilles change if he had refused to give Hector's body to Priam?

A CRITICAL RESPONSE

5. Which conflict presents the greater challenge for Achilles: his external conflict or his internal conflict?
Think about
- the definition of conflict as a struggle between opposing forces
- the fight to the death with Hector
- the decision whether to return Hector's body to Priam

6. Compare the fight between Achilles and Hector with that between Rama and Ravana in *The Ramayana*.
Think about
- the role the gods play in each fight
- the weapons used by each warrior
- the methods used by Rama and Achilles to kill their foes

7. *The Iliad* has inspired countless readers for more than twenty-five hundred years. One such reader was Sir John Denham, a seventeenth-century English poet, who wrote the following lines:

> I can no more believe old Homer blind
> Than those who say the Sun hath never
>   shined;
> The age wherein he lived was dark,
>   but he
> Could not want sight who taught the
>   world to see.

What did Homer teach you about human feelings and behavior? Support your ideas with evidence from the text.

 ## *Analyzing the Writer's Craft*

SIMILE AND METAPHOR

When Hector is about to die, he says to Achilles, "Iron in your breast / your heart is." What do his words suggest about Achilles?

Building a Literary Vocabulary. Similes and metaphors are figures of speech that make comparisons between two things that are actually unlike yet have something in common. Similes express the comparison by using the word *like* or *as*, whereas metaphors do not. Hector's metaphor suggests that Achilles is utterly unyielding and without human feelings.

Application: Interpreting Simile and Metaphor. With a partner, go back through the poem and look for examples of similes and metaphors. (Note that in this translation, some similes are introduced by the words *so* and *likewise*.) Then make a chart with two columns. In one column write the similes and metaphors that you find. In the second column write what each comparison suggests. Use your chart to prepare an oral presentation on Homer's use of figurative language in *The Iliad*.

1. The goddess Thetis knew that her son Achilles was fated to choose between a short and noble life or a long life without glory. Record an **interview** with Thetis in which she comments on Achilles' decision to kill Hector.

Option: Write a **letter** from Thetis to Peleus explaining their son's decision.

2. Important to *The Iliad* is the idea of fate, or destiny. Write an **introduction** for the general reader in which you explain how Achilles, Hector, and Priam view fate. Use evidence from the excerpt in your explanation.

Option: Write a **eulogy** for Hector that explains his death in terms of fate.

3. Imagine that a modern-day Achilles has moved to your neighborhood. Write a **diary entry** in which you describe the kind of person he is, his work in school, and his friends.

Option: Create a **comic strip** depicting Achilles' first day at school.

4. Think of a job that requires a certain amount of heroism. Design a **job application** and fill it out for Achilles so that it reflects his heroic qualities.

Option: Write a **letter of recommendation** to Achilles' potential employer that explains why he is uniquely suited for this job.

5. In a **report** for your class, present what archaeologists have discovered and hypothesized about the real Troy.

Option: Present your information in a **chart** for display in the classroom.

from The Aeneid

VIRGIL   70–19 B.C.   ANCIENT ROME

A biography of Virgil appears on page 753.

*A*pproaching the Epic

Around 30 B.C., the Roman poet Virgil was asked to write a patriotic poem celebrating the city of Rome, through its history and its ideals. The result, *The Aeneid*, is perhaps the greatest national epic in Western literature.

Writing in the Latin language, Virgil based his twelve-book poem on themes, characters, and techniques in Homer's *The Iliad* and *The Odyssey*. Virgil's main character is the Trojan hero Aeneas, who is the son of the mortal Anchises (an ki′ sēz) and the goddess Venus, and the cousin of another Trojan hero warrior, Hector. (See *The Iliad*, page 142.) Aeneas escapes the burning city of Troy and, aided by the gods, sets off in search of another home. After many adventures he settles in Italy to found the city that will later become the Roman state. Along the way he must sacrifice personal goals in order to fulfill his historic destiny.

Virgil presents the origins of the Roman Empire as part of a divine plan. His message is that Rome has the mission of bringing peace and justice to the world. Aeneas symbolizes the ideal Roman, one whose devotion to duty is more important than his personal pleasures.

The Aeneid begins shortly after the end of the Trojan War. Aeneas and his followers set sail for Italy. Near Sicily a storm separates Aeneas from his companions, and he lands on the African coast. There he is welcomed by Dido, the beautiful queen of Carthage. Strongly attracted to Aeneas, she gives a banquet for him and asks to hear about his adventures. He begins telling her the story of the fall of Troy—how the Greeks, with their gift of a wooden horse, gained entrance to the city and brought about its flaming destruction. In the excerpt that follows, Aeneas tells Dido what happened to Priam, the king of Troy, after the fall of the city.

*B*uilding Vocabulary

These essential words are defined alongside the epic.

degenerate (dē jen′ ər it): "Let him know / my sorry doings, how **degenerate** / is Neoptolemus." (page 165, lines 56–58)

effigy (ef′ i jē): "There before me rose the **effigy** / of my dear father." (page 165, lines 75–76)

plundered (plun′ dərd): "Before me rose Crëusa,. . . / my **plundered** home, the fate of small Iülus." (page 165, lines 77–79)

conflagrations (kän flə grā′ shənz): "Bright **conflagrations** give me light as I / wander." (page 166, lines 87–88)

goads: "He himself **goads** on the gods / against the Dardan weapons." (page 167, lines 156 –157)

sack: "I have lived beyond one fall and **sack** / of Troy." (page 168, lines 188–189)

stratagem (strat′ ə jəm): "What other **stratagem** or chance is left?" (page 168, line 207)

omen (ō′ mən): "But even then there comes / a sudden **omen**." (page 169, lines 242–243)

fanatic (fə nat′ ik): "Is there any use / in giving way to such **fanatic** sorrow?" (page 173, lines 367–368)

Connecting Writing and Reading

Imagine that you are not far from home when your house and family are threatened by an overwhelming disaster, such as a flood or a tornado. Think about your options, such as praying, finding your loved ones, fleeing, or staying to help strangers. At a time like this, what do you think you would do? Write your thoughts in your journal. As you read this episode of *The Aeneid*, compare your response to danger with that of Aeneas, who is faced with a wartime calamity.

"Perhaps you now will ask the end of Priam.
When he has seen his beaten city ruined—
the wrenching of the gates, the enemy
among his sanctuaries—then in vain
5   the old man throws his armor, long unused,
across his shoulders, tottering with age;
and he girds on his useless sword; about
to die, he hurries toward the crowd of Greeks.

"Beneath the naked round of heaven, at
10   the center of the palace, stood a giant
shrine; at its side an ancient laurel leaned
across the altar stone, and it embraced
the household gods within its shadow. Here,
around that useless altar, Hecuba
15   together with her daughters—just like doves
when driven headlong by a dark storm—huddled;
and they held fast the statues of the gods.
But when she saw her Priam putting on
the armor he had worn when he was young,
20   she cried: 'Poor husband, what wild thought drives you
to wear these weapons now? Where would you rush?
This is no time for such defense and help,
not even were my Hector here himself.
Come near and pray: this altar shall yet save
25   us all, or you shall die together with us.'
When this was said she took the old man to her
and drew him down upon the sacred seat.

"But then Polites,[1] one of Priam's sons
who had escaped from Pyrrhus'[2] slaughter, down
30   long porticoes, past enemies and arrows,
races, wounded, across the empty courts.
But after him, and hot to thrust, is Pyrrhus;
now, even now he clutches, closing in;
he presses with his shaft until at last
35   Polites falls before his parents' eyes,
within their presence; he pours out his life
in streams of blood. Though in the fist of death,
at this, Priam does not spare voice or wrath:

Line 1: Recall Priam's reaction to the death of his son Hector in *The Iliad.* As you continue to read, consider Priam's actions in light of all that has happened to him.

Line 13: "Household gods" refers to patron spirits of the home, represented by statues and other sacred objects kept in a special place.

Line 14: You may recall from *The Iliad* that Hecuba is Priam's wife and Hector's mother.

Lines 13–16: Many effective images in this poem arise from similes and metaphors. An example is the comparison of Hecuba and her daughters to doves driven before a storm. Think about the details that make this image a powerful one.

Line 23: Hector was killed by the Greek hero Achilles.

1. **Polites** (pə li′ tēz).
2. **Pyrrhus** (pir′ əs).

'If there is any goodness in the heavens
40 to oversee such acts, for this offense
and outrage may you find your fitting thanks
and proper payment from the gods, for you
have made me see the murder of my son,
defiled a father's face with death. Achilles—
45 you lie to call him father—never dealt
with Priam so—and I, his enemy;
for he had shame before the claims and trust
that are a suppliant's. He handed back
for burial the bloodless corpse of Hector
50 and sent me off in safety to my kingdom.'
The old man spoke; his feeble spear flew off—
harmless; the hoarse bronze beat it back at once;
it dangled, useless now, from the shield's boss.[3]
And Pyrrhus: 'Carry off these tidings; go
55 and bring this message to my father, son
of Peleus; and remember, let him know
my sorry doings, how degenerate[4]
is Neoptolemus.[5] Now die.' This said,
he dragged him to the very altar stone,
60 with Priam shuddering and slipping in
the blood that streamed from his own son. And Pyrrhus
with his left hand clutched tight the hair of Priam;
his right hand drew his glistening blade, and then
he buried it hilt-high in the king's side.
65 This was the end of Priam's destinies,
the close that fell to him by fate: to see
his Troy in flames and Pergamus[6] laid low—
who once was proud king over many nations
and lands of Asia. Now he lies along
70 the shore, a giant trunk, his head torn from
his shoulders, as a corpse without a name.

"This was the first time savage horror took me.
I was astounded; as I saw the king
gasping his life away beneath a ruthless
75 wound, there before me rose the effigy[7]
of my dear father, just as old as Priam;
before me rose Creüsa,[8] left alone,
my plundered[9] home, the fate of small Iülus.[10]
I look behind and scan the troops around me;
80 all of my men, worn out, have quit the battle,
have cast their bodies down along the ground
or fallen helplessly into the flames.

◆ **Lines 35–58:** Here Priam's son, Polites, is killed by Achilles' son, Pyrrhus. Priam declares that Achilles, who had returned the body of Hector to Priam (as told in *The Iliad*), would never have acted so cruelly and dishonorably as his son is acting now. Pyrrhus replies that Priam can die and carry a message to the dead Achilles, letting him know how "degenerate" his son has become.

3. **boss:** a decorative knob.

4. **degenerate** (dē jen′ ər it): having sunk below a former condition; morally corrupt.

5. **Neoptolemus** (nē ôp tô′ lə məs): another name for Pyrrhus.

6. **Pergamus** (pʉr′ gə məs): name of the citadel of Troy.

◆ **Lines 68–71:** Contrast the description of Priam as "a corpse without a name" and "proud king over many nations."

◆ **Lines 72–75:** As you read, speculate about why Priam's death has such a profound effect on Aeneas.

7. **effigy** (ef′ i jē): a likeness or image.

8. **Creüsa** (krē yo͞o′ sə): wife of Aeneas.

9. **plundered** (plun′ dərd): robbed by force.

10. **Iülus** (yo͞o′ ləs): the small son of Aeneas.

from The Aeneid 165

"And now that I am left alone, I see
the daughter of Tyndareos clinging
85 to Vesta's[11] thresholds, crouching silently
within a secret corner of the shrine;
bright conflagrations[12] give me light as I
wander and let my eyes read everything.
For she, in terror of the Trojans—set
90 against her for the fall of Pergamus—
and of the Danaans'[13] vengeance and the anger
of her abandoned husband; she, the common
Fury of Troy and of her homeland, she
had hid herself; she crouched, a hated thing,
95 beside the altars. In my mind a fire
is burning; anger spurs me to avenge
my falling land, to exact the debt of crime.
'Is she to have it so: to leave unharmed,
see Sparta[14] and her home Mycenae,[15] go —
100 a victor queen in triumph—to look on
her house and husband, parents, children, trailing
a train of Trojan girls and Phrygian[16] slaves?
Shall Troy have been destroyed by fire, Priam
been beaten by the blade, the Dardan[17] shore
105 so often soaked with blood, to this end? No.
For though there is no memorable name
in punishing a woman and no gain
of honor in such victory, yet I
shall have my praise for blotting out a thing
110 of evil, for my punishing of one
who merits penalties; and it will be
a joy to fill my soul with vengeful fire,
to satisfy the ashes of my people.'

"And carried off by my mad mind, I was
115 still blurting out these words when, with such brightness
as I had never seen, my gracious mother
stood there before me; and across the night
she gleamed with pure light, unmistaken goddess,
as lovely and as tall as she appears
120 whenever she is seen by heaven's beings.
And while she caught and held my right hand fast,
she spoke these words to me with her rose lips:
'My son, what bitterness has kindled this
fanatic anger? Why this madness? What
125 of all your care for me—where has it gone?
Should you not first seek out your father, worn

[margin note: wants to kill Helen]

◆ **Lines 79–113:** Aeneas, witnessing these events, might have entered the battle, but his men are not able to join him. However, he does see a way of revenging himself upon Helen, "daughter of Tyndareos" (tin dä' rē əs), whom he holds responsible for what is taking place. (See Approaching the Epic for *The Iliad*, page 142.)

11. Vesta (ves' tə): a Roman goddess of the hearth.

12. conflagrations (kän' flə grā' shənz): big, destructive fires.

13. Danaans (də nā' ənz): another name for the Greeks.

14. Sparta: the place of Helen's birth.

15. Mycenae (mī sē' nē): the city where Helen lived with her husband, Menelaus, before she was taken to Troy.

16. Phrygian (frij' ē ən): referring to Phrygia, a region from which slaves were often taken.

17. Dardan (där' dən): another word for Trojan.

[margin note: Venus stops Aeneas, distract from real anger & remind of his family duties]

◆ **Line 116:** "My gracious mother" refers to Venus, or Aphrodite.

with years, Anchises, where you left him; see
if your own wife, Creüsa, and the boy
Ascanius[18] are still alive? The Argive

130   lines ring them all about; and if my care
had not prevented such an end, by now
flames would have swept them off, the hostile sword
have drunk their blood. And those to blame are not
the hated face of the Laconian[19] woman,

135   the daughter of Tyndareos, or Paris:
It is the gods' relentlessness, the gods',
that overturns these riches, tumbles Troy
from its high pinnacle. Look now—for I
shall tear away each cloud that cloaks your eyes

140   and clogs your human seeing, darkening
all things with its damp fog: you must not fear
the orders of your mother; do not doubt,
but carry out what she commands. For here,
where you see huge blocks ripped apart and stones

145   torn free from stones and smoke that joins with dust
in surges, Neptune[20] shakes the walls, his giant
trident is tearing Troy from its foundations;
and here the first to hold the Scaean gates[21]
is fiercest Juno;[22] girt with iron, she

150   calls furiously to the fleet for more
Greek troops. Now turn and look: Tritonian Pallas[23]
is planted there; upon the tallest towers
she glares with her storm cloud and her grim Gorgon.[24]
And he who furnishes the Greeks with force

155   that favors and with spirit is the Father
himself, for he himself goads[25] on the gods
against the Dardan weapons. Son, be quick
to flee, have done with fighting. I shall never
desert your side until I set you safe

160   upon your father's threshold.' So she spoke,
then hid herself within the night's thick shadows.
Ferocious forms appear—the fearful powers
of gods that are the enemies of Troy.

"At this, indeed, I saw all Ilium[26]

165   sink down into the fires; Neptune's Troy
is overturned; even as when the woodsmen
along a mountaintop are rivals in
their striving to bring down an ancient ash,
hacked at with many blows of iron and ax;

170   it always threatens falling, nodding with

18. Ascanius (as kā′ nē əs): another name for Iülus.

19. Laconian (lə kō′ nē ən): from the region where Sparta is located.

◆ **Lines 134–157:** The "hated face" is a reference to the legendary beauty of Helen, whom everyone blames for the disastrous war. Notice that Venus does not blame Helen, the "Laconian woman," or Paris, who carried her off. Blame for the fall of Troy, Venus says, lies elsewhere. Meanwhile, she has been protecting Aeneas' family from harm during these tragic events.

20. Neptune: Roman name for the god of the sea, known to the Greeks as Poseidon.

21. Scaean (skē′ ən) **gates:** a main entrance to Troy.

22. Juno: the wife of the supreme god, Jupiter (the Greek Zeus), known to the Greeks as Hera; she is bitterly hostile to Troy.

23. Tritonian Pallas: a name for the goddess Minerva (the Greek Athena), who is friendly to the Greek cause.

24. Gorgon (gôr′ gən): a creature so terrible that those who see her are turned to stone. Minerva had the face of the Gorgon on her shield.

◆ **Line 155:** "The father" refers to Jupiter, the Greek Zeus.

25. goads: drives or urges on.

26. Ilium (il′ ē əm): another name for Troy.

◆ **Line 165:** Neptune (Poseidon) had helped to build Troy, although he is now hostile to it.

from The Aeneid   **167**

its trembling leaves and tossing crest until,
slowly, slowly, the wounds have won; it gives
one last great groan, then wrenches from the ridges
and crashes into ruin. I go down
175 and, guided by a god, move on among
the foes and fires; weapons turn aside,
the flames retire where I make my way.

"But now, when I had reached my father's threshold,
Anchises' ancient house, our home—and I
180 longed so to carry him to the high mountains
and sought him first—he will not let his life
be drawn out after Troy has fallen, he
will not endure exile; 'You whose lifeblood
is fresh, whose force is still intact and tough,
185 you hurry your escape; if heaven's lords
had wanted longer life for me, they would
have saved my home. It is enough—and more—
that I have lived beyond one fall and sack[27]
of Troy. Call out your farewell to my body
190 as it is now, thus laid out, thus; and then
be gone. I shall find death by my own hand;
the enemy will pity me and seek
my spoils. The loss of burial is easy.
For hated by the gods and useless, I
195 have lingered out my years too long already,
since that time when the father of the High Ones
and king of men let fly his thunderbolt
against me with the winds, touched me with lightning.'

"These were the words he used. He did not move.
200 We stood in tears—my wife, Creüsa, and
Ascanius and all the household—begging
my father not to bring down everything
along with him and make our fate more heavy.
He will not have it. What he wants is set;
205 he will not leave his place. Again I take
to arms and, miserable, long for death.
What other stratagem[28] or chance is left?
And then I ask: 'My father, had you thought
I could go off and leave you here? Could such
210 unholiness fall from a father's lips?
For if it please the High Ones that no thing
be left of this great city, if your purpose
must still persist, if you want so to add

♦ **Lines 166–173:** Note how Troy is compared to an ash tree and the destruction of the city to the felling of the tree. This comparison is an example of an epic simile, a type of simile often used by Homer and Virgil, in which a comparison is extended and elaborately worked through, creating a strong and lasting image.

27. sack: the robbing or looting of a captured city.

♦ **Lines 196–198:** Jupiter is "the father of the High Ones," who punished Anchises by striking him with a lightning bolt for being the lover of the goddess Venus. The thunderbolt lamed him.

28. stratagem (strat′ ə jəm): a scheme for deceiving an enemy.

yourself and yours to Ilium's destruction—
215 why then, the door to death is open: Pyrrhus—
who massacres the son before his father's
eyes, and then kills the father at the altars—
still hot from Priam's blood, will soon be here.
And was it, then, for this, my gracious mother,
220 that you have saved me from the blade, the fire—
that I might see the enemy within
the heart of home, my son Ascanius,
my father and Creüsa at their side,
all butchered in each other's blood? My men,
225 bring arms; the last light calls upon the beaten.
Let be, and let me at the Greeks again,
to make my way back to new battles. Never
shall we all die this day without revenge.'

"At that I girded on my sword again
230 and fixed it firm, passing my left hand through
my shield strap as I hurried from the house,
but suddenly Creüsa held me fast
beside the threshold; clinging to my feet,
she lifted young Iülus to his father:
235 'If you go off to die, then take us, too,
to face all things with you, but if your past
still lets you put your hope in arms, which now
you have put on, then first protect this house.
To whom is young Iülus left, to whom
240 your father and myself, once called your wife?'

"So did Creüsa cry; her wailing filled
my father's house. But even then there comes
a sudden omen[29]—wonderful to tell:
between the hands, before the faces of
245 his grieving parents, over Iülus' head
there leaps a lithe flame tip that seems to shed
a radiance; the tongue of fire flickers,
harmless, and plays about his soft hair, grazes
his temples. Shuddering in our alarm,
250 we rush to shake the flames out of his hair
and quench the holy fire with water. But
Anchises raised his glad eyes to the stars
and lifted heavenward his voice and hands:
'O Jupiter, all-able one, if you
255 are moved by any prayers, look on us.
I only ask you this: if by our goodness

Line 228: Consider the heroic code displayed by Aeneas thus far. As you read, note whether or not revenge plays a role in the decisions Aeneas makes.

29. omen (ō' mən): a thing or happening that is supposed to foretell a future event.

Lines 242–267: Anchises' refusal to leave home threatens the possible escape of the family, and Aeneas has buckled on his arms again, ready to do battle. Then startling signs and omens suddenly begin to appear: a flame, thunder, a shooting star. According to a belief of the Greeks, when thunder is heard on the left, it meant that the gods had something important to impart. At this point the very air seems charged with the clash of titanic forces, both earthly and heavenly.

we merit it, then, Father, grant to us
your help and let your sign confirm these omens.'

"No sooner had the old man spoken so
260   than sudden thunder crashed upon the left,
and through the shadows ran a shooting star,
its trail a torch of flooding light. It glides
above the highest housetops as we watch,
until the brightness that has marked its course
265   is buried in the woods of Ida:[30] far

and wide the long wake of that furrow shines,
and sulfur smokes upon the land. At last,
won over by this sign, my father rises,
to greet the gods, to adore the sacred star:
270   'Now my delay is done; I follow; where
you lead, I am. Gods of my homeland, save
my household, save my grandson. Yours, this omen;
and Troy is in your keeping. Yes, I yield.
My son, I go with you as your companion.'

275   "These were his words. But now the fire roars
across the walls; the tide of flame flows nearer.
'Come then, dear father, mount upon my neck;
I'll bear you on my shoulders. That is not
too much for me. Whatever waits for us,
280   we both shall share one danger, one salvation.
Let young Iülus come with me, and let
my wife Creüsa follow at a distance.

And servants, listen well to what I say:
along the way, just past the city walls,
285   in an abandoned spot there is a mound,
an ancient shrine of Ceres;[31] and nearby
an ancient cypress stands, one that our fathers'
devotion kept alive for many years.

From different directions, we shall meet
290   at this one point. My father, you will carry
the holy vessels and our homeland's gods.
Filthy with war, just come from slaughter, I
must never touch these sacred things until
I bathe myself within a running stream.'

295   "This said, I spread a tawny lion skin
across my bent neck, over my broad shoulders,
and then take up Anchises; small Iülus
now clutches my right hand; his steps uneven,

Statue of Diadoumenos, 440 B.C. Roman copy of a Greek original.
The Metropolitan Museum of Art, New York; Fletcher Fund.

he is following his father; and my wife
300 moves on behind. We journey through dark places;
and I, who just before could not be stirred
by any weapons cast at me or by
the crowds of Greeks in charging columns, now
am terrified by all the breezes, startled
305 by every sound, in fear for son and father.

"And now, as I approached the gates and thought
I had found the way of my escape, the sudden
and frequent tramp of feet was at my ears;
and peering through the shades, Anchises cries:
310 'My son, take flight; my son, they are upon us.
I see their gleaming shields, the flashing bronze.'
At this alarm I panicked: some unfriendly
god's power ripped away my tangled mind.
For while I take a trackless path, deserting
315 the customary roads, fate tears from me
my wife Creüsa in my misery.
I cannot say if she had halted or
had wandered off the road or slumped down, weary.
My eyes have never had her back again.
320 I did not look behind for her, astray,
or think of her before we reached the mound
and ancient, sacred shrine of Ceres; here
at last, when all were gathered, she alone
was missing—gone from husband, son, companions.

325 "What men, what gods did I in madness not
accuse? Did I see anything more cruel
within the fallen city? I commit
Ascanius, Anchises, and the gods
of Troy to my companions, hiding them
330 inside a winding valley. I myself
again seek out the city, girding on
my gleaming arms. I want to meet all risks
again, return through all of Troy, again
give back my life to danger. First I seek
335 the city walls, the gateway's shadowed thresholds
through which I had come before. And I retrace
my footsteps; through the night I make them out.
My spirit is held by horror everywhere;
even the very silence terrifies.
340 Then I move homeward—if by chance, by chance,
she may have made her way there. But the Danaans

◆ **Lines 338–339:** Think about the conflicts Aeneas faces at this point.

had flooded in and held the house. At once
the hungry conflagration rolls before
the wind, high as the highest rooftop; flames
345 are towering overhead, the boiling tide
is raging to the heavens. I go on;
again I see the house of Priam and
the fortress. Down the empty porticoes,
in Juno's sanctuary, I can see
350 both Phoenix[32] and the fierce Ulysses,[33] chosen
as guardians, at watch over the booty.
And here, from every quarter, heaped together,
are Trojan treasures torn from burning altars—
the tables of the gods, and plundered garments,
355 and bowls of solid gold; and Trojan boys
and trembling women stand in a long line.

"And more, I even dared to cast my cries
across the shadows; in my sorrow, I—
again, again, in vain—called for Creüsa;
360 my shouting filled the streets. But as I rushed
and raged among the houses endlessly,
before my eyes there stood the effigy
and grieving shade[34] of my Creüsa, image
far larger than the real. I was dismayed;
365 my hair stood stiff, my voice held fast within
my jaws. She spoke; her words undid my cares:

"'O my sweet husband, is there any use
in giving way to such fanatic[35] sorrow?
For this could never come to pass without
370 the gods' decree; and you are not to carry
Creüsa as your comrade, since the king
of high Olympus[36] does not grant you that.
Along your way lie long exile, vast plains
of sea that you must plow; but you will reach
375 Hesperia,[37] where Lydian Tiber[38] flows,
a tranquil stream, through farmers' fruitful fields.
There days of gladness lie in wait for you:
a kingdom and a royal bride. Enough
of tears for loved Creüsa. I am not
380 to see the haughty homes of Myrmidons
or of Dolopians,[39] or be a slave
to Grecian matrons—I, a Dardan woman
and wife of Venus' son. It is the gods'
great Mother who keeps me upon these shores.

32. Phoenix (fē' niks): an elderly Greek counselor, tutor of Achilles.

33. Ulysses (yoo lis' ēz'): in Greek, Odysseus (ō dis' ē əs), a leader of the Greek forces in the Trojan War. The legend of his later wanderings is the subject of Homer's *The Odyssey*.

34. shade: a ghost or specter.

35. fanatic (fə nat' ik): unreasonably extreme.

36. Olympus: the dwelling place of the gods.

♦ **Lines 373–378:** Creüsa, from her vantage point of the next world, can give Aeneas further glimpses into his destiny.

37. Hesperia (hes pir' ē ə): another name for Italy.

38. Lydian Tiber: the river on which Rome is located.

39. Myrmidons (mur' mə dänz) . . . **Dolopians** (də lō' pē ənz): peoples of Thessaly, the home of Achilles.

♦ **Lines 383–384:** "The gods'/ great Mother" refers to Cybele, a mother-goddess worshipped at Troy.

from The Aeneid **173**

385   And now farewell, and love the son we share.'

"When she was done with words—I weeping and
wanting to say so many things—she left
and vanished in transparent air. Three times
I tried to throw my arms around her neck;
390   three times the Shade I grasped in vain escaped
my hands—like fleet winds, most like a winged dream.

"And so at last, when night has passed, I go
again to my companions. Here I find,
to my surprise, new comrades come together,
395   vast numbers, men and women, joined for exile,
a crowd of sorrow. Come from every side,
with courage and with riches, they are ready
for any lands across the seas where I
may lead them. Now the star of morning rose
400   above high Ida's ridges, guiding the day.
The Danaans held the gates' blockaded thresholds.
There was no hope of help. Then I gave way
and, lifting up my father, made for the mountains."

As Aeneas tells Dido the story of his wanderings, the two fall in
love. The goddess Juno, for political reasons, encourages their
affair. Aeneas stays with Dido in Carthage until the god
Mercury, sent by Jupiter, sharply reminds him that his goal is
Rome. Aeneas then abandons Dido, who commits suicide. He
sails on and eventually reaches Italy, where after further battles
and adventures he marries a princess and founds the city that is
to become Rome.

Thinking About the Epic

A PERSONAL RESPONSE

sharing impressions

1. After reading this selection, what are your impressions of Aeneas? Write your impressions in your journal.

constructing interpretations

2. Do you think that Aeneas practices good judgment throughout this episode?
Think about
- whether he should have fought Pyrrhus after witnessing Priam's death
- whether he could have done something to prevent Creüsa's death
- his decision to carry his father on his back and lead his son through fallen Troy

3. In your opinion, what are Aeneas' heroic qualities and what are his flaws?
Think about
- his response to danger
- his relationships with others
- what he accomplishes

4. Think back to your prereading notes about what you would do if faced with a catastrophe. How does your response to danger compare with Aeneas'?

A CREATIVE RESPONSE

5. How would events have turned out if the gods had stayed out of the action?

A CRITICAL RESPONSE

6. Rama, Achilles, and Aeneas are all heroes with qualities idealized by their cultures. Decide which of the three seems most heroic according to today's standards. Cite examples from the three epics to support your conclusion.

7. Reread the description of Priam's fallen body (lines 69–71). Then read the following translations of the same description.

> On the distant shore
> The vast trunk headless lies without a name.
> —Robert Fitzgerald

> On the bleak shore now lies the abandoned king,
> A headless carcase, and a nameless thing!
> —John Dryden

Which of the three translations do you like the best, and why?

Analyzing the Writer's Craft

IMAGERY

Reread the opening eight lines of the selection, which describe King Priam as he witnesses his city's downfall. What details in this description create a picture of Priam?

Building a Literary Vocabulary. Imagery refers to words and phrases that re-create sensory experiences for a reader. Images are usually visual, but they can appeal to any of the senses. Images make it easier for a reader to imagine or identify with the action. In line 6, for example, the phrase "tottering with age" conveys a clear, sharp picture of Priam in the reader's imagination.

Application: Interpreting Imagery. Imagine that this excerpt from *The Aeneid* is to be part of a TV miniseries, and you are planning a 30-second preview of the episode. With two or three classmates, identify at least ten visual and sound images that you might use. Prepare a storyboard, a series of sketches with captions, outlining the action of the preview. Be ready to identify for the class the lines in the epic that inspired your choice of images.

Connecting Reading and Writing

1. Prepare a **diary entry** written by Aeneas following his escape from Troy in which he comments on the role of destiny in his experiences.

Option: Write an **interview** with Aeneas for a news magazine in which he explains the role of destiny.

2. Imagine that the hero you identified in question 6 has been nominated as the best candidate for election to your school's student council. Create a **campaign poster** for the hero.

Option: Write a **political speech** that praises the hero-candidate you identified.

3. What do you think might have happened to Creüsa after she was separated from her family during the flight from the city? Imagine that Virgil has decided to let Creüsa's ghost tell more of her story to Aeneas. Write a **poem** modeled after the style of *The Aeneid* that could be inserted in the poem to extend Creüsa's story. Try to include an epic simile.

Option: Write a **prose monologue** that could be added as an epilogue to the poem to extend Creüsa's story.

4. Use information provided in this lesson, in *The Iliad* lesson, and in research sources to create a **family tree** of the Trojan nobility to be displayed in your class. Make sure to point out the relationships between mortals and immortals, including the one between Aeneas and his immortal mother, Venus.

Option: Create a **cast of characters** for this excerpt of *The Aeneid* that could be used as a study sheet by fellow classmates. Include a phrase or two for each character that describes his or her relationship to others.

Gassire's Lute

WEST AFRICA

*A*pproaching the Epic

Gassire's Lute is an example of oral literature from the Sudan region in West Africa. The poem is one of the few surviving pieces of an earlier epic, *The Dausi* (dä′ ᴏᴏ sē), most of which has been lost to time. The epic retold the legends of the Soninke (sō niŋ′ kə) people and was sung or chanted by bards. *Gassire's Lute*, which was the opening section of *The Dausi*, tells how a hero of the Soninke became their first bard.

Four times
   Wagadu[1] rose.
   A great city, gleaming in the light of day.
Four times
5   Wagadu fell.
   And disappeared from human sight.
     Once through vanity.
     Once through dishonesty.
     Once through greed.
10   Once through discord.[2]
Four times
   Wagadu changed her name.
     First she was called Dierra,[3]
      then Agada,[4]
15   then Gana,[5]
      then Silla.[6]
Four times
   Wagadu turned about,
     facing first to the north,
20   then to the west,
      then to the east,
      then to the south.

1. Wagadu (wä gä dᴏᴏ′): a Soninke word meaning "place of herds." From earliest times the Soninke gave this name to whatever area they considered their homeland.

2. discord (dis′ kôrd): quarreling and lack of harmony.

3. Dierra (je′ rə): the first Wagadu, ruled by the Fasa dynasty.

4. Agada (ä′ gä də): the second Wagadu.

5. Gana (gä′ nə): the third Wagadu, probably the great Soninke kingdom of the fourth to the thirteenth centuries, located between the Senegal and Niger rivers.

6. Silla (sil′ ə): the fourth Wagadu, a small city-state on the Niger. It is now a town in Soninkeland.

From *Gassire's Lute* retold by Alta Jablow and illustrated by Leo and Diane Dillon.
© 1971 Leo and Diane Dillon, New York.

Four gates
    have always led into Wagadu.
25   Thus men have always seen them.
        One to the north.
        One to the west.
        One to the east, and
        one to the south.
30 From these directions
Comes the strength of Wagadu.
Her power, which endures
Whether she be built of stone,
        of wood, or
35   of earth.
Or whether she lives only as a shadow
In the memory and hopes of her children.
For in truth, Wagadu is not of stone,
        not of wood,
40   nor of earth.
Wagadu is the strength
Which lives in the hearts of men.
Sometimes she becomes known
      when men's eyes see her,
45   and their ears hear
    the clash of swords and the clang of shields.
Sometimes lost to view,
      when wearied and oppressed
      by the strife of men,
50   she sleeps.
For the first time
      Sleep came to Wagadu through vanity.
      The second time through dishonesty.
      The third time through greed.
55   The fourth time through discord.
Should Wagadu ever rise again,
      She will live with such power
    in the minds of men
      that she can never again be lost.
60 She will endure with such strength
      that vanity,
     dishonesty,
      greed,
      discord,
65   can never again harm her.

Hoooh!
    Dierra, Agada, Gana, Silla!
Hoooh!
    Fasa![7]

7. **Fasa** (fä′ sə): the ruling class of Dierra.

70 Each time Wagadu was destroyed
    through the faults of men,
She reappeared with a greater splendor.
Vanity brought the song of the bards.
Dishonesty brought a shower of gold and precious stones.
75 Greed brought the art of writing to the women of Wagadu.
The fifth Wagadu will arise from discord
    to endure as the rain of the South,
        as the rocks of the Sahara.
Every man then will bear Wagadu in his heart.
80 Every woman will have Wagadu in her sons.
Hoooh!
    Dierra, Agada, Gana, Silla!
Hoooh!
    Fasa!
85 First, facing north,
    and called Dierra,
    ruled by Nganamba Fasa,[8]
    Wagadu was lost through vanity.
Strong were the Fasa,
90   and brave.
Day after day they fought
    against the Burdama[9]
    and the Boroma[10] slaves.
There was no end to the fighting.
95 And out of the fighting
    the strength of the Fasa grew.
All Nganamba's men were heroes.
All the women lovely,
    and proud of their men.
100 But the Fasa were growing old.
All who had not fallen
    in single combat with the Burdama
    were growing old.
Nganamba was very old.
105 Gassire, his son,
    himself with eight sons,
    each son with sons.

8. **Nganamba Fasa** (ŋu′ num bə fä′ sə): the last Soninke king of the Fasa dynasty.

9. **Burdama** (bʊr dä′ mə): the Soninke name for a certain tribe of the Sahara Desert.
10. **Boroma** (bô′ rỗ mə): a people subject to the Soninke.

Nganamba ruled over them,
    and over all the Fasa,
110   and over the doglike Boroma.
Because of him,
    because he grew so old,
Wagadu was lost.
The Boroma crept away,
115   fleeing from the old Fasa's rule.
Again they became slaves to the Burdama.
And with the Burdama swords,
    together they conquered Wagadu,
     called Dierra.
120 Had Nganamba died sooner,
    would Wagadu have fallen for the first time?
Hoooh!
    Dierra, Agada, Gana, Silla!
Hoooh!
125   Fasa!

Nganamba did not die.
A jackal gnawed at Gassire's heart.
Each day Gassire asked his heart:
    "When will Nganamba die?
130   When will Gassire be king?"
Each day Gassire longed for the death of his father
    as a lover watches for the evening star to rise.
By day, when Gassire fought as a hero
    against the Burdama.
135 When he drove the treacherous Boroma before him
with the leather girth of his saddle.
Then he thought only of the fighting,
    of his sword,
    of his shield,
140   of his horse.
With the evening he rode into the city,
And sat in the circle of men and his sons.
Gassire heard the heroes praise his deeds,
But his heart was not with them.
145 His heart was full of misery and longing,
Longing for the shield of his father.
    The shield which he might carry
    only when his father was dead.

Longing for the sword of his father.
150   The sword which he might draw
        only when he was king.
Each day Gassire's rage and longing grew.
Sleep passed him by.
Gassire lay, and a jackal gnawed at his heart.
155 Gassire lay, and anguish climbed into his throat.
One night he could no longer rest.
He sprang from his bed,
        leaving his house.
To the wise man, Kiekorro,[11] went Gassire.
160 "Kiekorro!
        When will my father die?
        When shall I carry his shield and sword?"
"Ah, Gassire!
        Nganamba will die soon enough.
165   But you will never carry his sword and shield.
        Sword and shield will others inherit.
        You will carry a lute.[12]
        And your lute shall cause the loss of Wagadu!
Ah, Gassire!"
170 "Kiekorro!
        You are not as wise as I thought.
        How can Wagadu be lost?
        Her heroes triumph daily.
        Your vision is false,
175   And you are a fool.
Kiekorro!"
Then the wise old man spoke again:
"Ah, Gassire!
        You may not believe what I say now.
180   But your fate will lead you
to the guinea hens in the fields.
        You will hear and understand
what they say.
        They will tell of your fate
185   and the fate of Wagadu."
Hoooh!
        Dierra, Agada, Gana, Silla!
Hoooh!
        Fasa!

190 Gassire was angry.
Again he went into battle with the Burdama.

11. Kiekorro (kye′ kô̑ r̂ô̑).

12. lute: an early stringed instrument related to the guitar.

He called to the heroes:
    "Stay here.
    Today I fight alone."
195 He rode forth to battle.
    Gassire hurled his spear.
    Gassire charged the Burdama.
    Gassire swung his sword.
    He struck down Burdama on the right.
200   He struck them down on the left.
Gassire's sword was as a sickle mowing the grain.
The Burdama were stricken with terror.
They cried:
    "That is no Fasa.
205   That is no mere hero.
That is a Damo!"[13]
The Burdama turned their horses.
The Burdama threw down their spears.
Each of them threw down his two spears,
210   and they fled.
Gassire called his men.
Gassire said:
    "Gather up the spears."
They sang as they gathered the spears:
215   "The Fasa are all heroes.
    Gassire has always been the greatest of the Fasa.
    Gassire has always done great deeds.
    But today Gassire was greater than Gassire!"
The heroes rode behind Gassire into the city.
220 They sang:
    "Never before has Wagadu taken
    so many spears as today."
In the city Gassire was honored.
But when the men gathered,
225 Gassire did not join them.
Gassire wandered into the fields.
He heard the guinea hens.
Gassire drew close to them.
A guinea hen sat upon a bush and sang:
230   "Hear the Dausi!
    Hear my deeds!"
The guinea hen sang of its battle with the snake.
The guinea hen sang:
    "All creatures must die, be buried, and vanish.

13. Damo (dä′ mȏ): probably a supernatural being or force.

235   Kings and heroes die, are buried, and vanish.
        I, too, shall die, shall be buried, and vanish.
        But the Dausi,
            the song of my battles,
            shall not die.
240   It shall be sung again and again.
        It shall outlive all kings and heroes.
        Hoooh! that I might do such deeds!
        Hoooh! that I might sing the Dausi!
        Wagadu will be lost,
245   But the Dausi shall endure and live!"
Hoooh!
        Dierra, Agada, Gana, Silla!
Hoooh!
        Fasa!

250   Gassire went again to the old wise man.
    "Kiekorro!
        I was in the fields.
        I understood the guinea hens.
        The guinea hen boasted that the song of its deeds
255   would outlive Wagadu.
        The guinea hen sang the Dausi.
        Tell me,
            Are there men who know the Dausi?
            And can the Dausi last beyond life and death?"
260   The wise man said:
        "Gassire, you are rushing to meet your fate.
        No one can stop you.
        And since you will not be a king,
            you shall be a bard.
265   Ah, Gassire!
        When the kings of the Fasa lived by the sea,
            they were also great heroes then.
    They fought against men who carried lutes,
        men who sang the Dausi.
270   The Dausi of the enemy often struck terror
        into the hearts of the Fasa,
        who were themselves heroes.
    But the Fasa never sang the Dausi,
    because they were of the first rank,
275   the Horro.[14]
    The Dausi could be sung

14. Horro (hô′ rô̂): the class of nobles among the Soninke.

only by those of the second rank,
    the Diaru.[15]
The Diaru fought
280   not so much as warriors,
      to win the battle of the day,
but as drinkers,
    to relish the fame of the evening.
But you, Gassire,
285   now that you will no longer be
      the second of the first,
    now shall you be
      the first of the second.
    And Wagadu will be lost because of it."
290 And Gassire answered:
    "Then let Wagadu be lost!"
Hoooh!
    Dierra, Agada, Gana, Silla!
Hoooh!
295   Fasa!

Gassire sought out a smith.[16]
He said:
    "Make me a lute."
And the smith said:
300   "I will make you a lute.
    But it will not sing."
Gassire said:
    "Smith, you do your work.
    The rest is my affair."
305 The smith made the lute.
He brought the lute to Gassire.
Gassire seized the lute.
He struck upon it.
The lute did not sound.
310 Gassire said:
    "What is this?
    The lute does not sing."
And the smith replied:
    "I told you it would not.
315   I have done my work.
    The rest is your affair."
Gassire asked:
    "What must I do then?"

15. Diaru (jä′ roo): the Soninke word for "bard."

16. smith: a skilled worker in metal, wood, or other materials. Smiths also were regarded by the Soninke people as magicians. The lute made by the smith for Gassire thus has magical properties.

The smith spoke:
320   "The lute is but a piece of wood.
    Without a heart it cannot sing.
    You must give it a heart.
    Carry the wood on your back when you go to battle.
    The wood must ring with the strokes of your sword.
325   The wood must absorb the blood of your blood,
       the breath of your breath.
    Your pain must be its pain.
    Your fame its fame.
    The lute cannot then be just the wood of a tree.
330   It must blend with you and your people.
    Therefore it must live not only with you,
       but with your sons.
    Then the singing that comes from your heart
       will echo in the ear of your son
335   and live on in your people.
    And your son's lifeblood, oozing from his heart,
       will live on in this piece of wood.
    Only then will it sound.
    But Wagadu will be lost because of it."
340 Gassire said:
    "Then let Wagadu be lost!"
Hoooh!
    Dierra, Agada, Gana, Silla!
Hoooh!
345   Fasa!

Gassire called his eight sons.
    "My sons, today we go to battle.
    But the strokes of our swords shall echo
       not only through the Sahel,[17]
350   but shall ring for the ages.
    You and I, my sons, will live on.
    We shall outlive all other heroes.
    We shall live on in the Dausi.
    My eldest son, today we two,
355   You and I, will be first in the combat."
Gassire placed the lute over his shoulder.
And together with his eldest son went first into the field.
They charged the Burdama.
Gassire and his eldest son fought as the first.
360 They left the other heroes far behind them.

17. Sahel (su hāl'): a belt of grassland along the southern edge of the Sahara.

Gassire fought not like a human being,
      but like a Damo.
His eldest son fought not like a human being,
      but like a Damo.
365 In the thick of the fighting
Gassire was hard pressed by eight Burdama.
His son came swiftly to his side
and struck four of them down.
Then one of the Burdama thrust a spear through his heart.
370 Gassire's eldest son fell dead from his horse.
In his rage, Gassire gave a great shout.
And the Burdama fled.
Gassire dismounted and lifted the body of his son
upon his back.
375 Then he mounted and turned,
      and rode slowly back to the other heroes.
The heart's blood of his eldest son dropped,
      dropped onto the lute.
Thus Gassire, at the head of his heroes,
380   rode into Dierra.
Hoooh!
      Dierra, Agada, Gana, Silla!
Hoooh!
      Fasa!

385 Gassire's eldest son was buried as a hero.
And all Dierra mourned.
That night Gassire took his lute
and struck against the wood.
Still the lute did not sing.
390 Gassire's anger mounted.
He called his sons and said:
      "Tomorrow we ride again to combat."
For seven days Gassire rode with the heroes to battle.
And every day he took one of his sons with him
395 to be the first in the fighting.
And on every one of these days
      Gassire carried the body of one of his sons
      over his shoulder and over the lute
      as they rode back into the city.
400 Thus, at the end of every day
      the blood of one of his sons

dropped onto the lute.
After the seven days of fighting
there was great mourning in Dierra.
405 All the heroes and all the women
wore their mourning clothes of red and white.
All the women wailed.
All the men were angry.
Before the eighth day of the fighting
410 all the heroes of Dierra gathered
and they spoke to Gassire:
"Gassire, this must come to an end.
We fight willingly, but only as we must.
In your rage, you go on fighting
415 without need, and without end.
Now go forth from Dierra!
Take those who would join you.
Take your slaves and your cattle.
As for us, we desire more of life than fame.
420 And while we should not like to live fameless,
we have no wish to die for fame alone."
And the old wise man said:
"Ah, Gassire!
Thus will Wagadu be lost today for the first time
425 because of your vanity."
Hoooh!
Dierra, Agada, Gana, Silla!
Hoooh!
Fasa!

430 Then rode Gassire out into the desert.
And with him rode his last, his youngest, son.
And his wives, his friends, his slaves, and his cattle.
They rode through the Sahel.
The heroes who had fought beside Gassire
435 rode with him
through the gates of the city.
Then many turned back.
But some followed Gassire and his son
into the Sahara.
440 They traveled far.
Day and night they rode.
They came into the wilderness.
And there in the loneliness, they rested.

All slept: all the heroes, the women, the slaves.
445 Gassire's youngest son slept.
But Gassire himself did not sleep.
Gassire sat alone by the fire, listening.
Then close beside him, Gassire heard a voice.
The lute was sounding!
450 It rang as though it came from within himself.
Gassire listened and trembled,
    as the lute sang the Dausi.

When the lute had sung the Dausi
        for the first time,
455 King Nganamba died in the city, Dierra.
When the lute had sung the Dausi
        for the first time,
Gassire's rage melted; Gassire wept.
When the lute had sung the Dausi
460   for the first time,
Wagadu was lost
        for the first time.
Hoooh!
    Dierra, Agada, Gana, Silla!
465 Hoooh!
    Fasa!

Four times
    Wagadu rose.
    A great city, gleaming in the light of day.
470 Four times
    Wagadu fell.
    And disappeared from human sight.
        Once through vanity.
        Once through dishonesty.
475   Once through greed.
        Once through discord.
Four times
    Wagadu changed her name.
        First she was called Dierra,
480   then Agada,
            then Gana,
            then Silla.
Four times
    Wagadu turned about,

485   facing first to the north,
       then to the west,
       then to the east,
       then to the south.
Four gates
490   have always led into Wagadu.
     Thus men have always seen them.
       One to the north.
       One to the west.
       One to the east, and
495   one to the south.
From these directions
Comes the strength of Wagadu.
Her power, which endures
Whether she be built of stone,
500   of wood, or
       of earth.
Or whether she lives only as a shadow
In the memory and hopes of her children.
For in truth, Wagadu is not of stone,
505   not of wood,
       nor of earth.
Wagadu is the strength
Which lives in the hearts of men.
Sometimes she becomes known
510   when men's eyes see her,
     and their ears hear
     the clash of swords and the clang of shields.
Sometimes lost to view,
     when wearied and oppressed
515   by the strife of men,
     she sleeps.
For the first time
     Sleep came to Wagadu through vanity.
     The second time through dishonesty.
520   The third time through greed.
     The fourth time through discord.
Should Wagadu ever rise again,
     She will live with such power
in the minds of men
525   that she can never again be lost.
She will endure with such strength

that vanity,
  dishonesty,
    greed,
530   discord,
can never again harm her.
Hoooh!
  Dierra, Agada, Gana, Silla!
Hoooh!
535   Fasa!
Each time Wagadu was destroyed
  through the faults of men,
She reappeared with a greater splendor.
Vanity brought the song of the bards.
540 Dishonesty brought a shower of gold and precious stones.
Greed brought the art of writing to the women of Wagadu.
The fifth Wagadu will arise from discord
  to endure as the rain of the South,
    as the rocks of the Sahara.
545 Every man then will bear Wagadu in his heart.
Every woman will have Wagadu in her sons.
Hoooh!
  Dierra, Agada, Gana, Silla!
Hoooh!
550   Fasa!

Presenting
the Individual as Hero

The hero of ancient epic poetry was a little lower than the gods, the embodiment of all that the culture believed was best. As the centuries passed, a different kind of hero began to emerge—one who did not necessarily command the attention and admiration of an entire culture. Writers began to focus on the plight of the individual whose actions and decisions reflect personal courage.

This new hero might be a philosopher searching for wisdom, a religious person fighting for his or her beliefs, a soldier crusading for a cause, or a person coping with devastating loss. The conflict faced is not on an epic scale but instead involves a moral dilemma presented in the course of living. Basic questions arise: What is right? How ought we to behave? Who has the power to decide an individual's fate? How can we live a better life?

The very fact that the individual hero grapples with such issues separates him or her from the traditional epic hero, who served the gods and the culture faithfully. Instead, the individual hero is often in conflict with established authority, for his or her actions challenge accepted beliefs. The hero makes decisions that may even result in death. Nevertheless, the hero survives as a model for generations of readers.

Literary Vocabulary

INTRODUCED IN THIS SECTION

Argumentation. Argumentation is speech or writing intended to convince an audience that a proposition is true or false. The structure of argumentation begins typically with the statement of an idea or opinion, followed by logical supporting evidence.

Symbol. A symbol is a person, place, object, or activity that stands for something beyond itself. Literary symbols take on meaning within the context of a literary work. For example, in "The Silver Mine" in Unit 1, the mine could be considered a symbol of greed. Its power over those who approach it is devastating; those who resist its temptation are rewarded with a good life.

Dramatic Irony. Irony is a contrast between what is expected and what actually exists or happens. Dramatic irony is one type of irony. It occurs when the reader or viewer is aware of information of which the character is unaware. In Shakespeare's famous play *Romeo and Juliet,* Romeo discovers Juliet's body and assumes that she is dead. The reader's or viewer's knowledge that Juliet is not dead creates dramatic irony.

Figurative Language. Figurative language is language that communicates ideas beyond the literal meanings of the words. The words in a figurative expression are not literally true; rather, they create impressions in the reader's mind. Two of the most common forms of figurative language are **simile** and **metaphor,** which are introduced in Unit 1. Another form of figurative language, **personification,** is a figure of speech in which human qualities are attributed to an object, animal, or idea. In the Fang myth titled "The End of the World," the sun and moon are personified as husband and wife who bear the stars as their children. Other examples of personification include brief phrases that create an image or feeling. In *The Persian Letters,* for example, Montesquieu attributes the human quality of speech to nature in the phrase "untutored nature spoke."

REVIEWED IN THIS SECTION

Simile

Metaphor

from The Apology

PLATO   c. 427–347 B.C.   ANCIENT GREECE

A biography of Plato appears on page 749.

Approaching the Selection

In *The Apology* Plato presents Socrates, one of the most admired figures in the history of Western civilization. As a teacher and philosopher in ancient Greece, he devoted his life to seeking truth and goodness and to encouraging others to do the same. Socrates taught in the streets and in the marketplace, using questions to probe for the truth. However, his honesty and intelligence made him many enemies among prominent Athenians, who accused him of corrupting the youth and of showing disrespect for religious traditions. As a result he was brought to trial, found guilty, and given poison hemlock to drink. In *The Apology*, Plato describes Socrates' defense at his trial and records his final words spoken both to those who condemned him to death and to those who voted for his acquittal.

Building Vocabulary

These essential words are footnoted within the selection.

disparage (di spar′ ij): You are going to earn . . . the blame from those who wish to **disparage** our city. (page 195)

effrontery (e frunt′ ər ē): It is not a lack of arguments that has caused my condemnation, but a lack of **effrontery**. (page 195)

iniquity (i nik′ wi tē): My accusers, who are clever and quick, have been overtaken by the faster—by **iniquity**. (page 195)

vengeance (ven′ jəns): As soon as I am dead, **vengeance** shall fall upon you. (page 195)

Connecting Writing and Reading

Have you ever been tempted to lie about why you didn't do your homework? to take money from your parents? to skip school or work? to cheat on a test? to go out with a friend's boyfriend or girlfriend? In your journal, describe either a time when you didn't yield to one of these (or similar) temptations because of your conscience or a time when you did yield to temptation because you ignored your conscience. As you read, compare your experience with the way that Socrates responds to the voice of his conscience.

**W**ELL, gentlemen, for the sake of a very small gain in time you are going to earn the reputation—and the blame from those who wish to disparage[1] our city—of having put Socrates to death, "that wise man"—because they will say I am wise even if I am not, these people who want to find fault with you. If you had waited just a little while, you would have had your way in the course of nature. You can see that I am well on in life and near to death. I am saying this not to all of you but to those who voted for my execution, and I have something else to say to them as well.

No doubt you think, gentlemen, that I have been condemned for lack of the arguments which I could have used if I had thought it right to leave nothing unsaid or undone to secure my acquittal. But that is very far from the truth. It is not a lack of arguments that has caused my condemnation, but a lack of effrontery[2] and impudence, and the fact that I have refused to address you in the way which would give you most pleasure. You would have liked to hear me weep and wail, doing and saying all sorts of things which I regard as unworthy of myself, but which you are used to hearing from other people. But I did not think then that I ought to stoop to servility because I was in danger, and I do not regret now the way in which I pleaded my case. I would much rather die as the result of this defense than live as the result of the other sort. In a court of law, just as in warfare, neither I nor any other ought to use his wits to escape death by any means. In battle it is often obvious that you could escape being killed by giving up your arms and throwing yourself upon the mercy of your pursuers, and in every kind of danger there are plenty of devices for avoiding death if you are unscrupulous enough to stick at nothing. But I suggest, gentlemen, that the difficulty is not so much to escape death; the real difficulty is to escape from doing wrong, which is far more fleet of foot. In this present instance I, the slow old man, have been overtaken by the slower of the two, but my accusers, who are clever and quick, have been overtaken by the faster—by iniquity.[3] When I leave this court I shall go away condemned by you to death, but they will go away convicted by truth herself of depravity and wickedness. And they accept their sentence even as I accept mine. No doubt it was bound to be so, and I think that the result is fair enough.

Having said so much, I feel moved to prophesy to you who have given your vote against me, for I am now at that point where the gift of prophecy comes most readily to men—at the point of death. I tell you, my executioners, that as soon as I am dead, vengeance[4] shall fall upon you with a punishment far more painful than your killing of me. You have brought about my death in the belief that through it you will be delivered from submitting your conduct to criticism, but I say that the result will be just the opposite. You will have more critics, whom up till now I have restrained without your knowing it, and being younger they will be harsher to you and will cause you more annoyance. If you expect to stop denunciation of your wrong way of life by putting people to death, there is something amiss with your reasoning. This way of escape is neither possible nor creditable. The best and easiest way is not to stop the mouths of others, but to make yourselves as good men as you can. This is my last message to you who voted for my condemnation.

---

1. **disparage** (di spar′ ij): speak lightly of; belittle.
2. **effrontery** (e frunt′ ər ē): unshamed boldness.
3. **iniquity** (i nik′ wi tē): lack of righteousness or justice; wickedness.
4. **vengeance** (ven′ jəns): the return of an injury for an injury; revenge.

As for you who voted for my acquittal, I should very much like to say a few words to reconcile you to the result, while the officials are busy and I am not yet on my way to the place where I must die. I ask you, gentlemen, to spare me these few moments. There is no reason why we should not exchange fancies while the law permits. I look upon you as my friends, and I want you to understand the right way of regarding my present position.

Gentlemen of the jury—for *you* deserve to be so called—I have had a remarkable experience. In the past the prophetic voice to which I have become accustomed has always been my constant companion, opposing me even in quite trivial things if I was going to take the wrong course. Now something has happened to me, as you can see, which might be thought and is commonly considered to be a supreme calamity; yet neither when I left home this morning, nor when I was taking my place here in the court, nor at any point in any part of my speech did the divine sign oppose me. In other discussions it has often checked me in the middle of a sentence, but this time it has never opposed me in any part of this business in anything that I have said or done. What do I suppose to be the explanation? I will tell you. I suspect that this thing that has happened to me is a blessing, and we are quite mistaken in supposing death to be an evil. I have good grounds for thinking this, because my accustomed sign could not have failed to oppose me if what I was doing had not been sure to bring some good result.

We should reflect that there is much reason to hope for a good result on other grounds as

well. Death is one of two things. Either it is annihilation, and the dead have no consciousness of anything, or, as we are told, it is really a change—a migration of the soul from this place to another. Now if there is no consciousness but only a dreamless sleep, death must be a marvelous gain. I suppose that if anyone were told to pick out the night on which he slept so soundly as not even to dream, and then to compare it with all the other nights and days of his life, and then were told to say, after due consideration, how many better and happier days and nights than this he had spent in the course of his life—well, I think that the Great King himself, to say nothing of any private person, would find these days and nights easy to count in comparison with the rest. If death is like this, then, I call it gain, because the whole of time, if you look at it in this way, can be regarded as no more than one single night. If on the other hand death is a removal from here to some other place, and if what we are told is true, that all the dead are there, what greater blessing could there be than this, gentlemen? If on arrival in the other world, beyond the reach of our so-called justice, one will find there the true judges who are said to preside in those courts, Minos and Rhadamanthus and Aeacus and Triptolemus[5] and all those other half-divinities who were upright in their earthly life, would that be an unrewarding journey? Put it in this way. How much would one of you give to meet Orpheus and Musaeus, Hesiod and Homer?[6] I am willing to die ten times over if this account is true. It would be a specially interesting experience for me to join them

---

5. **Minos** (mī′ näs′) **and Rhadamanthus** (rad ə man′ thəs) **and Aeacus** (ē′ ə kəs) **and Triptolemus** (trip′ tô′ lə məs): four figures in Greek mythology who became judges in the afterlife.

6. **Orpheus** (ôr′ fē əs) **and Musaeus** (myo͞o zē′ əs), **Hesiod** (hē′ si əd) **and Homer:** poets and religious teachers.

there, to meet Palamedes[7] and Ajax, the son of Telamon,[8] and any other heroes of the old days who met their death through an unfair trial, and to compare my fortunes with theirs—it would be rather amusing, I think. And above all I should like to spend my time there, as here, in examining and searching people's minds, to find out who is really wise among them, and who only thinks that he is. What would one not give, gentlemen, to be able to question the leader of that great host against Troy, or Odysseus, or Sisyphus,[9] or the thousands of other men and women whom one could mention, to talk and mix and argue with whom would be unimaginable happiness? At any rate I presume that they do not put one to death there for such conduct, because apart from the other happiness in which their world surpasses ours, they are now immortal for the rest of time, if what we are told is true.

You too, gentlemen of the jury, must look forward to death with confidence, and fix your minds on this one belief, which is certain—that nothing can harm a good man either in life or after death, and his fortunes are not a matter of indifference to the gods. This present experience of mine has not come about mechanically. I am quite clear that the time had come when it was better for me to die and be released from my distractions. That is why my sign never turned me back. For my own part I bear no grudge at all against those who condemned me and accused me, although it was not with this kind intention that they did so, but because they thought that they were hurting me; and that is culpable of them. However, I ask them to grant me one favor. When my sons grow up, gentlemen, if you think that they are putting money or anything else before goodness, take your revenge by plaguing them as I plagued you; and if they fancy themselves for no reason, you must scold them just as I scolded you, for neglecting the important things and thinking that they are good for something when they are good for nothing. If you do this, I shall have had justice at your hands, both I myself and my children.

Now it is time that we were going, I to die and you to live, but which of us has the happier prospect is unknown to anyone but God.

---

7. **Palamedes** (pal ə mē′ dēz): a Greek leader at Troy wrongly accused of treason and executed.
8. **Ajax, the son of Telamon** (tel′ ə män): Greek warrior who committed suicide after Achilles' armor was awarded to the Greek warrior **Odysseus** (ō dis′ ē əs) instead of to him.
9. **Sisyphus** (sis′ ə fəs): a greedy king of Corinth doomed in Hades to roll a heavy stone uphill, only to have it always roll down again.

Thinking About the Selection

A PERSONAL RESPONSE

sharing
impressions

1. In general, what are your feelings about Socrates as a person? Take a moment to jot down your impressions in your journal.

constructing
interpretations

2. What do you think Socrates values most in life? Explain.
   Think about
   • what he refuses to do
   • what he says about the voice of his conscience
   • the favor he asks at the end of the selection

3. Speculate about the impact of Socrates' death.
   Think about
   • what his accusers might do after his death
   • what his followers might do
   • the possible effect of his death on his family
   • other deaths you have known about and the impact they have had

A CREATIVE RESPONSE

4. What attitude do you think Socrates would have had toward his accusers if he had been pardoned?

A CRITICAL RESPONSE

5. Do you consider Socrates a hero? Why or why not?
   Think about
   • the qualities he possesses
   • how his actions and motivations compare with those of other heroes, such as Achilles and Aeneas

6. How might Socrates' principles be applied to life in twentieth-century America?
   Think about
   • what you wrote in your journal about temptation and conscience
   • local or national issues about which Socrates might have an opinion

Analyzing the Writer's Craft

ARGUMENTATION

Think of how you felt about Socrates at the end of the selection. Had you decided at that point whether he was right or wrong in any of his views or actions? What did he say that caused you to form an opinion?

Building a Literary Vocabulary. Argumentation is speech or writing intended to convince an audience that a proposition is true or false. For example, at the beginning of this selection, Socrates claims that the reason he has been condemned is not because his arguments are insufficient. To support this proposition, he reasons that his very innocence is what has caused him to be found guilty, because he refused to compromise his principles by pretending to be guilty and pleading for mercy.

Application: Analyzing an Argument. Working with a small group of classmates, identify a position that Socrates takes on a particular issue in this selection. Analyze the reasoning that he employs to support his proposition. Another group of students should try to find weaknesses in the same argument. Then debate the two viewpoints. The rest of the class can then vote to select the winning group in the debate.

Connecting Reading and Writing

1. Based on all or part of the material in this excerpt, write a brief **dramatic scene** that can be acted in front of the class. The cast should include Socrates, his friends, and his accusers. Make up any additional dialogue that you wish. Include stage directions suggesting the behavior and responses of the characters.

Option: Use the same material to write a brief **short story** that might be published in a high school literary magazine.

2. Write a **petition** urging Socrates' release and circulate it among your classmates. Include at the top of the petition a list of supporting reasons.

Option: Write a newspaper **editorial** calling for the pardon of Socrates.

3. "The unexamined life is not worth living" is one of the most famous statements made by Socrates

in *The Apology*. What did Socrates mean by this statement? Write a **speech** to be delivered before the class in which you explain and defend this idea.

Option: Write a **fable** that illustrates the truth of this saying.

4. Research the lives of leaders such as Mahatma Gandhi, Martin Luther King, Jr., and Nelson Mandela, who, like Socrates, got into trouble with the authorities and paid some kind of penalty. Create a **description** of an award that might be given to these people for the courage and conviction they displayed.

Option: Based on the information you found in your research, write an **article** that might appear as a feature in a textbook on history, philosophy, or political science.

Seraphim, come

SOR JUANA INÉS DE LA CRUZ 1648?–1695 MEXICO

A biography of Sor Juana appears on page 741.

Approaching the Poem

The following poem by Sor Juana Inés de la Cruz (sôr hwä′ nä ē nes′ de lä krōos) celebrates the martyrdom of St. Catherine of Alexandria. According to legend, Catherine angered the Roman emperor Maximus (c. A.D. 305) through her attempts to convert both him and the empress to Christianity. After Catherine's successful conversion of the empress, Maximus ordered Catherine tortured on a spiked wheel, which mysteriously collapsed at her touch. He then had her beheaded.

In this poem, Catherine is portrayed as a rose. The seraphim mentioned in line 1 are the highest order of angels surrounding the throne of God.

Building Vocabulary

These essential words are defined alongside the poem.

fructified (fruk′ tə fīd): be **fructified** / by its own sweet moisture (page 201, lines 8–9)

complement (käm′ plə mənt): Far too long the world has known / that virtue attracts sin as **complement**. (page 201, lines 22–23)

rancor (raŋ′ kər): **Rancor**, ever a coward, / is afraid of a simple death. (page 201, lines 28–29)

Connecting Writing and Reading

In your journal jot down words and phrases that come to mind when you think of a rose. As you read the poem that follows, compare the qualities suggested by your words and phrases with the qualities of a rose described by the speaker.

Saint's Day of Catherine of Alexandria,
Oaxaca, 1691, from the Fifth Villancico

Refrain
Seraphim, come,
come here and ponder
a Rose that, when cut,
lives all the longer.
5   So far from wilting,
it will be revived
when cruelly tortured,
be <u>fructified</u>[1]
by its own sweet moisture:
10   And thus to cut it
renews the wonder.
Gardeners, come,
come here and ponder
a Rose that, when cut,
15   lives all the longer.

Verses
     Against one frail Rose
a thousand storm winds plot.
Sheer envy is its lot,
though one brief span is all the life it knows.
20   Men envy the Rose its beauty,
its wiseness they resent.
Far too long the world has known
that virtue attracts sin as <u>complement</u>.[2]
     Thus they guarantee
25   that the slash of whirling knives
from one breath will draw a thousand,
give one heart thorns to pierce a thousand lives.
     <u>Rancor</u>,[3] ever a coward,
is afraid of a simple death:
30   to snuff out a single life,
it finds a thousand ways to stifle breath.
     But wily, witless evil
is blind and cannot see
that the wicked torturer's wheel
35   is destined for the chariot of victory.
     Thus, the whirling instrument,
considerate in its blades,

1. fructified (fruk′ tə fīd):
made to bear fruit.

2. complement (käm′ plə
mənt): either of two parts that
complete each other.

3. rancor (raŋ′ kər): long-
lasting and bitter hate or ill
will.

makes its every revolution
one more song in glorious Catherine's praise.
40   The Rose can hardly find it new
to feel the piercing barbs,
since every rose since time began
has made the prickly thorns its regal guards.

Thinking About the Poem

A PERSONAL RESPONSE

sharing impressions

1. What feelings about St. Catherine do you have after reading this poem? Describe them in your journal.

constructing interpretations

2. What is the speaker's attitude toward Catherine and toward her torturers? Cite the lines and phrases that you think reveal each attitude most clearly.

3. Which qualities attributed to the rose in the poem were those you expected, and which were surprising?

Think about
- the qualities of a rose suggested in the poem
- the words and phrases you wrote in your journal

A CREATIVE RESPONSE

4. How would your reading of the poem be different if there were no refrain?

A CRITICAL RESPONSE

5. Explain the following paradox, or apparent contradiction, as it relates to Catherine's life and as it might relate to other situations: "a Rose that, when cut, / lives all the longer."

6. Who strikes you as more admirable, St. Catherine, as depicted in this poem, or Socrates, as depicted in *The Apology?* Cite details from each work to support your opinion.

Analyzing the Writer's Craft

SYMBOL

Think about why Sor Juana uses details about a rose to suggest the wonder of Catherine.

Building a Literary Vocabulary. A symbol is a person, place, object, or activity that stands for something beyond itself. Literary symbols take on meaning within the context of a literary work. Throughout the poem, Sor Juana uses the symbol of a rose to convey the wonder, beauty, and mystery of Catherine.

Application: Interpreting a Symbol. Working with a partner, make a chart like the sample here. In one column list the qualities of a rose mentioned or suggested in the poem. In the second column list the corresponding characteristics relating to Catherine.

A rose	Catherine
cut thorns beauty	executed spikes of wheel virtue

After you have completed the chart, prepare an oral report that explains your findings and that evaluates the effectiveness of the symbol.

Antigone

SOPHOCLES   496–406 B.C.   ANCIENT GREECE

Translated by Dudley Fitts and Robert Fitzgerald
A biography of Sophocles appears on page 752.

*A*pproaching the Play

Sophocles (säf′ ə klēz′) was one of the great dramatists of ancient Greece, and *Antigone* (an tig′ ə nē′) is one of his greatest plays. As the play begins, Antigone and her sister Ismene (is mē′ nē) recall their dead father Oedipus, the doomed king of Thebes, who unknowingly killed his father and then married his mother. Upon discovering the truth, Oedipus blinded himself and went into exile, where he was cared for until his death by his two daughters. When his sons Eteocles (ē tē′ ə klēz) and Polyneices (päl′ i nī′ sēz′) grew up, they killed each other in combat. Their uncle Creon (krē′ on), who then became king, planned to honor one corpse and insult the other. *[handwritten: → brother in law & uncle of Oedipus]*

*B*uilding Vocabulary

These essential words are defined alongside the play.

repulse (ri puls′): *Dawn of the day after the* **repulse** *of the Argive army from the assault on Thebes.* (page 205)

anarchists (an′ ər kists′): *Stiff-necked* **anarchists**, *putting their heads together, / Scheming against me in alleys.* (page 214, lines 125–126)

sententiously (sen ten′ shəs lē): *And they have bribed my own guard to do this thing. / (***sententiously***) Money!* (page 214, lines 127–128)

diviners (də vīn′ ərz): *We shall soon see, and no need of* **diviners**. (page 223, line 4)

perverse (pər vʉrs′): *If you were not my father, / I'd say you were* **perverse**. (page 227, lines 124–125)

lamentation (lam′ ən tā′ shən): *Neither love nor* **lamentation;** *no song, but silence.* (page 231, line 52)

*C*onnecting Writing and Reading

Think about a family member or friend whom you care about deeply. What are some ways in which you show your love for that person? Jot down your ideas in your journal. As you read *Antigone*, compare your ways of showing love with the ways that each of the main characters shows the depth of his or her love.

Greek theater tragic mask. Historical Pictures Service, Chicago.

CHARACTERS

Antigone (an tig′ ə nē′) ⎫
Ismene (is mē′ nē) ⎭ daughters of Oedipus, former King of Thebes
Creon (krē′ on), king of Thebes, uncle of Antigone and Ismene
Haemon (hē′ mən), Creon's son, engaged to Antigone
Eurydice (yōō rid′ ə sē′), wife of Creon
Teiresias (tī rē′ sē əs), a blind prophet
Chorus, made up of about fifteen elders of Thebes
Choragos (kō rā′ gəs), leader of the Chorus
A Boy, who leads Teiresias
A Sentry
Guards
Servants
A Messenger

Scene: *Before the palace of Creon, king of Thebes. A central double door, and two doors at the side. A platform extends the length of the stage, and from this platform three steps lead down into the orchestra, or chorus-ground.*

Time: *Dawn of the day after the repulse[1] of the Argive army from the assault on Thebes.*

1. **repulse** (ri puls′): the act of turning away or beating back.

PROLOGUE

(Antigone *and* Ismene *enter from the central door of the palace.*)

Antigone. Ismene, dear sister,
You would think that we had already suffered enough
For the curse on Oedipus:
I cannot imagine any grief
5 That you and I have not gone through. And now—
Have they told you of the new decree of our King
    Creon?

Ismene. I have heard nothing: I know
That two sisters lost two brothers, a double death
In a single hour; and I know that the Argive army
10 Fled in the night; but beyond this, nothing.

Antigone. I thought so. And that is why I wanted you
To come out here with me. There is something we
    must do.

Ismene. Why do you speak so strangely?

Antigone. Listen, Ismene:
15 Creon buried our brother Eteocles
With military honors, gave him a soldier's funeral,
And it was right that he should; but Polyneices,
Who fought as bravely and died as miserably—
They say that Creon has sworn
20 No one shall bury him, no one mourn for him,
But his body must lie in the fields, a sweet treasure
For carrion birds to find as they search for food.
That is what they say, and our good Creon is coming
    here
To announce it publicly; and the penalty—
25 Stoning to death in the public square!
                                        There it is,
And now you can prove what you are:
A true sister, or a traitor to your family.

Ismene. Antigone, you are mad! What could I
    possibly do?

Antigone. You must decide whether you will help me
    or not.

30 **Ismene.** I do not understand you. Help you in what?

Lines 9–10: The Argives, long-standing enemies of Thebes, sided with Polyneices against Eteocles in the struggle for the throne of Thebes.

Lines 19–23: As you read the next lines, think about what they reveal about the depth of Antigone's love for her brother.

Lines 28–35: Notice the contrast between Antigone and Ismene suggested in the conversation between the two.

Antigone. Ismene, I am going to bury him. Will you
come?

Ismene. Bury him! You have just said the new law
forbids it.

Antigone. He is my brother. And he is your brother,
too.

Ismene. But think of the danger! Think what Creon
will do!

35 **Antigone.** Creon is not strong enough to stand in my
way.

Ismene. Ah sister!
Oedipus died, everyone hating him
For what his own search brought to light, his eyes
Ripped out by his own hand; and Jocasta died,
40 His mother and wife at once: she twisted the cords
That strangled her life; and our two brothers died,
Each killed by the other's sword. And we are left:
But oh, Antigone,
Think how much more terrible than these
45 Our own death would be if we should go against
Creon
And do what he has forbidden! We are only women.
We cannot fight with men, Antigone!
The law is strong, we must give in to the law
In this thing, and in worse. I beg the dead
50 To forgive me, but I am helpless: I must yield
To those in authority. And I think it is dangerous
business
To be always meddling.

Antigone.   If that is what you think,
I should not want you, even if you asked to come.
You have made your choice, you can be what you
want to be.
55 But I will bury him; and if I must die,
I say that this crime is holy: I shall lie down
With him in death, and I shall be as dear
To him as he to me.
It is the dead,
Not the living, who make the longest demands:
60 We die forever . . .
You may do as you like,

◆ **Lines 39–41:** Jocasta (jō kas′ tə), the mother of Antigone and Ismene, hanged herself when she realized the truth about her relationship with Oedipus.

Since apparently the laws of the gods mean nothing
    to you.

Ismene. They mean a great deal to me; but I have no
    strength
To break laws that were made for the public good.

Antigone. That must be your excuse, I suppose. But as
    for me,
65   I will bury the brother I love.

Ismene.   Antigone,
I am so afraid for you!

Antigone.   You need not be:
You have yourself to consider, after all.

Ismene. But no one must hear of this, you must tell no
    one!
I will keep it a secret, I promise!

Antigone.   Oh tell it! Tell everyone!
70   Think how they'll hate you when it all comes out
If they learn that you knew about it all the time!

Ismene. So fiery! You should be cold with fear.

Antigone. Perhaps. But I am doing only what I must.

Ismene. But can you do it? I say that you cannot.

75   **Antigone.** Very well: when my strength gives out, I
    shall do no more.

Ismene. Impossible things should not be tried at all.

Antigone. Go away, Ismene:
I shall be hating you soon, and the dead will, too,
For your words are hateful. Leave me my foolish plan:
80   I am not afraid of the danger; if it means death,
It will not be the worst of deaths—death without
    honor.

Ismene. Go then, if you feel that you must.
You are unwise.
But a loyal friend indeed to those who love you.

(*Exit into the palace. Antigone goes off, left. Enter the*
Chorus *and* Choragos.)

PARADOS

85 **Chorus.** Now the long blade of the sun, lying
Level east to west, touches with glory
Thebes of the Seven Gates. Open, unlidded
Eye of golden day! O marching light
Across the eddy and rush of Dirce's stream,[2]
90 Striking the white shields of the enemy
Thrown headlong backward from the blaze of
    morning!

Choragos. Polyneices their commander
Roused them with windy phrases,
He the wild eagle screaming
95 Insults above our land,
His wings their shields of snow,
His crest their marshaled helms.

Chorus. Against our seven gates in a yawning ring
The famished spears came onward in the night;
100 But before his jaws were sated with our blood,
Or pine fire took the garland of our towers,
He was thrown back; and as he turned, great
    Thebes—
No tender victim for his noisy power—
Rose like a dragon behind him, shouting war.

105 **Choragos.** For God hates utterly
The bray of bragging tongues;
And when he beheld their smiling,
Their swagger of golden helms,
The frown of his thunder blasted
110 Their first man from our walls.

Chorus. We heard his shout of triumph high in the air
Turn to a scream; far out in a flaming arc
He fell with his windy torch, and the earth struck
    him.
And others storming in fury no less than his
115 Found shock of death in the dusty joy of battle.

Choragos. Seven captains at seven gates
Yielded their clanging arms to the god
That bends the battle line and breaks it.
These two only, brothers in blood,
120 Face to face in matchless rage,

♦ **Line 85:** The Parados is the first song of the Chorus, who represent the leading citizens of Thebes. According to many critics, the chorus, used in many Greek tragedies, is an ideal spectator of the events of a play. As you read the songs of the chorus, ask yourself what effect they have on your interpretation of what happens in the play.

2. Dirce's (dur′ sēz) **stream:** the stream flowing past Thebes, named after a murdered queen who was thrown into it.

♦ **Lines 98–99:** Thebes had seven gates, which the Argives attacked all at once.

♦ **Lines 105–110:** Zeus (zoos), the king of the gods, threw a thunderbolt, which killed the first Argive attacker. As you read this play, look for evidence of the kind of conduct approved or hated by the gods.

♦ **Lines 116–118:** When the seven captains were killed, their armor was stripped and offered as a sacrifice to Ares (ā′ rēz), the god of war.

Mirroring each the other's death.
Clashed in long combat.

Chorus. But now in the beautiful morning of victory
Let Thebes of the many chariots sing for joy!
125   With hearts for dancing we'll take leave of war:
Our temples shall be sweet with hymns of praise,
And the long night shall echo with our chorus.

SCENE 1

Choragos. But now at last our new king is coming:
Creon of Thebes, Menoeceus'[1] son.
In this auspicious dawn of his reign
What are the new complexities
5   That shifting fate has woven for him?
What is his counsel? Why has he summoned
The old men to hear him?

(*Enter* Creon *from the palace, center. He addresses the*
Chorus *from the top step.*)

Creon. Gentlemen: I have the honor to inform you
that our ship of state, which recent storms have
10   threatened to destroy, has come safely to harbor at
last, guided by the merciful wisdom of heaven. I have
summoned you here this morning because I know that
I can depend upon you: your devotion to King Laïus[2]
was absolute; you never hesitated in your duty to our
15   late ruler Oedipus; and when Oedipus died, your
loyalty was transferred to his children. Unfortunately,
as you know, his two sons, the princes Eteocles and
Polyneices, have killed each other in battle, and I, as
the next in blood, have succeeded to the full power of
· 20   the throne.
I am aware, of course, that no ruler can expect
complete loyalty from his subjects until he has been
tested in office. Nevertheless, I say to you at the very
outset that I have nothing but contempt for the kind
25   of governor who is afraid, for whatever reason, to
follow the course that he knows is best for the state;
and as for the man who sets private friendship above
the public welfare—I have no use for him, either. I
call God to witness that if I saw my country headed
30   for ruin, I should not be afraid to speak out plainly;

1. **Menoeceus** (mə nē′ sōōs).

♦ **Lines 2–7:** The Greeks
believed that human destiny
was controlled by three
sisters, the Fates: Clotho
(klō′ thō), who spun the
thread of human life;
Lachesis (lak′ ə sis), who
determined its length; and
Atropos (at′ rō päs), who cut
the thread.

2. **Laïus** (lā′ yəs): the father
of Oedipus.

♦ **Lines 21–55:** Think of how
you feel about Creon as he
states his principles of
government; consider
whether he is justified in
dishonoring Polyneices by
this treatment of his corpse.

and I need hardly remind you that I would never have any dealings with an enemy of the people. No one values friendship more highly than I; but we must remember that friends made at the risk of wrecking
35 our ship are not real friends at all.

These are my principles, at any rate, and that is why I have made the following decisions concerning the sons of Oedipus: Eteocles, who died as a man should die, fighting for his country, is to be buried
40 with full military honors, with all the ceremony that is usual when the greatest heroes die; but his brother Polyneices, who broke his exile to come back with fire and sword against his native city and the shrines of his fathers' gods, whose one idea was to spill the
45 blood of his blood and sell his own people into slavery—Polyneices, I say, is to have no burial: no man is to touch him or say the least prayer for him; he shall lie on the plain, unburied; and the birds and the scavenging dogs can do with him whatever they like.
50 This is my command, and you can see the wisdom behind it. As long as I am king, no traitor is going to be honored with the loyal man. But whoever shows by word and deed that he is on the side of the state—he shall have my respect while he is living and my
55 reverence when he is dead.

Choragos. If that is your will, Creon, son of Menoeceus,
You have the right to enforce it: we are yours.

Creon. That is my will. Take care that you do your part.

Choragos. We are old men: let the younger ones carry it out.

60 **Creon.** I do not mean that: the sentries have been appointed.

Choragos. Then what is it that you would have us do?

Creon. You will give no support to whoever breaks this law.

Choragos. Only a crazy man is in love with death!

Creon. And death it is; yet money talks, and the wisest

65 Have sometimes been known to count a few coins
   too many.

(*Enter* Sentry *from left.*)

Sentry. I'll not say that I'm out of breath from
running, King, because every time I stopped to think
about what I have to tell you, I felt like going back.
And all the time a voice kept saying, "You fool, don't
70 you know you're walking straight into trouble?"; and
then another voice: "Yes, but if you let somebody else
get the news to Creon first, it will be even worse than
that for you!" But good sense won out, at least I hope
it was good sense, and here I am with a story that
75 makes no sense at all; but I'll tell it anyhow, because,
as they say, what's going to happen's going to happen,
and—

Creon. Come to the point. What have you to say?

Sentry. I did not do it. I did not see who did it. You
80 must not punish me for what someone else has done.

Creon. A comprehensive defense! More effective,
perhaps,
If I knew its purpose. Come: what is it?

Sentry. A dreadful thing . . . I don't know how to put
it—

Creon. Out with it!

Sentry.   Well, then:
85 The dead man—
                    Polyneices—

(*Pause. The* Sentry *is overcome, fumbles for words. Creon
waits impassively.*)

                              out there—
                                   someone—
New dust on the slimy flesh!

(*Pause. No sign from* Creon.)

Someone has given it burial that way, and
Gone . . .

(*Long pause. Creon finally speaks with deadly control.*)

Creon. And the man who dared do this?

Sentry.   I swear I

90   Do not know! You must believe me.

                                                Listen:

The ground was dry, not a sign of digging, no,
Not a wheeltrack in the dust, no trace of anyone.
It was when they relieved us this morning: and one of
        them,
The corporal, pointed to it.

                                    There it was.

95   The strangest—

                Look:

The body, just mounded over with light dust: you see?
Not buried really, but as if they'd covered it
Just enough for the ghost's peace. And no sign
Of dogs or any wild animal that had been there.

100   And then what a scene there was! Every man of us
Accusing the other: we all proved the other man did
        it.
We all had proof that we could not have done it.
We were ready to take hot iron in our hands,
Walk through fire, swear by all gods.

105   *It was not I!*
        —I do not know who it was, but it was not I!

(Creon's *rage has been mounting steadily, but the* Sentry *is
        too intent upon his story to notice it.*)

And then, when this came to nothing, someone said
A thing that silenced us and made us stare
Down at the ground: you had to be told the news,

110   And one of us had to do it! We threw the dice,
And the bad luck fell to me. So here I am,
No happier to be here than you are to have me:
Nobody likes the man who brings bad news.

Choragos. I have been wondering, King: can it be
        that the gods have done this?

115   **Creon** (*furiously*). Stop!
        Must you doddering wrecks
        Go out of your heads entirely? "The gods!"
        Intolerable!
        The gods favor this corpse? Why? How had he served
                them?

120   Tried to loot their temples, burn their images,

◆ **Lines 89–98:** Consider
Creon's assumption that a
man must be guilty of the
crime. Notice that the burial
of Polyneices is symbolic and
ritualistic rather than actual.

◆ **Lines 115–123:** Notice how
quickly Creon rejects a
reasonable question posed
by the Choragos. Creon is
convinced that he knows
how the gods think.

Yes, and the whole state, and its laws with it!
Is it your senile opinion that the gods love to honor
    bad men?
A pious thought!—
              No, from the very beginning
There have been those who have whispered together,

125   Stiff-necked anarchists,[3] putting their heads together,
Scheming against me in alleys. These are the men,
And they have bribed my own guard to do this thing.
(*sententiously*)[4] Money!
There's nothing in the world so demoralizing as
    money.

130   Down go your cities,
Homes gone, men gone, honest hearts corrupted,
Crookedness of all kinds, and all for money!
              (*to* Sentry) But you—!
I swear by God and by the throne of God,
The man who has done this thing shall pay for it!

135   Find that man, bring him here to me, or your death
Will be the least of your problems: I'll string you up
Alive, and there will be certain ways to make you
Discover your employer before you die;
And the process may teach you a lesson you seem to
    have missed:

140   The dearest profit is sometimes all too dear:
That depends on the source. Do you understand me?
A fortune won is often misfortune.

Sentry. King, may I speak?

Creon.   Your very voice distresses me.

Sentry. Are you sure that it is my voice, and not your
    conscience?

145 **Creon.** By God, he wants to analyze me now!

Sentry. It is not what I say, but what has been done,
    that hurts you.

Creon. You talk too much.

Sentry.   Maybe; but I've done nothing.

Creon. Sold your soul for some silver: that's all you've
    done.

Sentry. How dreadful it is when the right judge judges
    wrong!

3. anarchists (an′ ər kists′):
persons favoring the
overthrow of government.

4. sententiously (sen ten′
shəs lē): speaking in a way
that is especially trite or
moralistic.

150 **Creon.** Your figures of speech
  May entertain you now; but unless you bring me the
    man,
  You will get little profit from them in the end.

  (*Exit* Creon *into the palace.*)

Sentry. "Bring me the man"—!
  I'd like nothing better than bringing him the man!
155 But bring him or not, you have seen the last of me
    here.
  At any rate, I am safe!

  (*Exit* Sentry.)

ODE 1

Chorus. Numberless are the world's wonders, but
    none
  More wonderful than man; the storm-gray sea
  Yields to his prows, the huge crests bear him high;
160 Earth, holy and inexhaustible, is graven
  With shining furrows where his plows have gone
  Year after year, the timeless labor of stallions.

  The light-boned birds and beasts that cling to cover,
  The lithe fish lighting their reaches of dim water,
165 All are taken, tamed in the net of his mind;
  The lion on the hill, the wild horse windy-maned,
  Resign to him; and his blunt yoke has broken
  The sultry shoulders of the mountain bull.

  Words also, and thought as rapid as air,
170 He fashions to his good use; statecraft is his,
  And his the skill that deflects the arrows of snow,
  The spears of winter rain: from every wind
  He has made himself secure—from all but one:
  In the late wind of death he cannot stand.

175 O clear intelligence, force beyond all measure!
  O fate of man, working both good and evil!
  When the laws are kept, how proudly his city stands!
  When the laws are broken, what of his city then?
  Never may the anarchic man find rest at my hearth,
180 Never be it said that my thoughts are his thoughts.

◆ **Lines 157–180:** An ode is a song chanted by the Chorus. Think about what this ode conveys about human greatness and tragic limitation.

SCENE 2

(*Reenter* Sentry, *leading* Antigone.)

Choragos. What does this mean? Surely this captive woman
    Is the princess, Antigone. Why should she be taken?

Sentry. Here is the one who did it! We caught her
    In the very act of burying him.—Where is Creon?

5   **Choragos.** Just coming from the house.

                          (*Enter* Creon, *center.*)

Creon.   What has happened?
    Why have you come back so soon?

Sentry (*expansively*).   O King,
    A man should never be too sure of anything:
    I would have sworn
    That you'd not see me here again: your anger
10   Frightened me so, and the things you threatened me
       with;
    But how could I tell then
    That I'd be able to solve the case so soon?

    No dice throwing this time: I was only too glad to
       come!

    Here is this woman. She is the guilty one:
15   We found her trying to bury him.
    Take her, then; question her; judge her as you will.
    I am through with the whole thing now, and glad of
       it.

Creon. But this is Antigone! Why have you brought
    her here?

Sentry. She was burying him, I tell you!

Creon (*severely*).   Is this the truth?

20   **Sentry.** I saw her with my own eyes. Can I say more?

Creon. The details: Come, tell me quickly!

Sentry.   It was like this:
    After those terrible threats of yours, King,
    We went back and brushed the dust away from the
    body.

◆ **Lines 7–13:** Note the change in attitude on the part of the sentry, and consider how his line "A man should never be too sure of anything" might apply to Creon.

The flesh was soft by now, and stinking,
25 So we sat on a hill to windward and kept guard.
No napping this time! We kept each other awake.
But nothing happened until the white round sun
Whirled in the center of the round sky over us:
Then, suddenly,
30 A storm of dust roared up from the earth, and the sky
Went out, the plain vanished with all its trees
In the stinging dark. We closed our eyes and endured
    it.
The whirlwind lasted a long time, but it passed;
And then we looked, and there was Antigone!
35 I have seen
A mother bird come back to a stripped nest, heard
Her crying bitterly a broken note or two
For the young ones stolen. Just so, when this girl
Found the bare corpse, and all her love's work wasted,
40 She wept, and cried on heaven to damn the hands
That had done this thing.
                          And then she brought more dust
And sprinkled wine three times for her brother's
    ghost.

♦ **Lines 36–45:** Think about how the sentry's speech creates sympathy for Antigone before Creon confronts her.

From the 1960 movie *Antigone,* starring Irene Papas.
Culver Pictures, New York.

We ran and took her at once. She was not afraid,
Not even when we charged her with what she had
   done.
45 She denied nothing.
                    And this was a comfort to me,
And some uneasiness: for it is a good thing
To escape from death, but it is no great pleasure
To bring death to a friend.
                    Yet I always say
There is nothing so comfortable as your own safe
   skin!

50 **Creon** (*slowly, dangerously*). And you, Antigone,
   You with your head hanging—do you confess this
      thing?

Antigone. I do. I deny nothing.

Creon (*to* Sentry).   You may go. (*Exit* Sentry.)
   (*to* Antigone) Tell me, tell me briefly:
   Had you heard my proclamation touching this matter?

55 **Antigone.** It was public. Could I help hearing it?

Creon. And yet you dared defy the law.

Antigone.   I dared.
   It was not God's proclamation. That final justice
   That rules the world below makes no such laws.

   Your edict, King, was strong,
60 But all your strength is weakness itself against
   The immortal unrecorded laws of God.
   They are not merely now: they were, and shall be,
   Operative forever, beyond man utterly.

   I knew I must die, even without your decree:
65 I am only mortal. And if I must die
   Now, before it is my time to die,
   Surely this is no hardship: can anyone
   Living, as I live, with evil all about me,
   Think death less than a friend? This death of mine
70 Is of no importance; but if I had left my brother
   Lying in death unburied, I should have suffered.
   Now I do not.
               You smile at me. Ah Creon,
   Think me a fool, if you like; but it may well be
   That a fool convicts me of folly.

◆ **Lines 64–71:** Consider what
these lines suggest about
Antigone's attitude toward
death.

Choragos. Like father, like daughter: both
    headstrong, deaf to reason!
    She has never learned to yield.

Creon.   She has much to learn.
    The inflexible heart breaks first, the toughest iron
    Cracks first, and the wildest horses bend their necks
    At the pull of the smallest curb.
                        Pride? In a slave?
80   This girl is guilty of a double insolence,
    Breaking the given laws and boasting of it.
    Who is the man here,
    She or I, if this crime goes unpunished?
    Sister's child, or more than sister's child,
85   Or closer yet in blood—she and her sister
    Win bitter death for this!
             (*to* Servants) Go, some of you,
    Arrest Ismene. I accuse her equally.
    Bring her: you will find her sniffling in the house
      there.
    Her mind's a traitor: crimes kept in the dark
90   Cry for light, and the guardian brain shudders;
    But how much worse than this
    Is brazen boasting of barefaced anarchy!

Antigone. Creon, what more do you want than my
    death?

Creon.   Nothing.
    That gives me everything.

Antigone.   Then I beg you: kill me.
95   This talking is a great weariness: your words
    Are distasteful to me, and I am sure that mine
    Seem so to you. And yet they should not seem so:
    I should have praise and honor for what I have done.
    All these men here would praise me
100 Were their lips not frozen shut with fear of you.
    (*bitterly*) Ah the good fortune of kings,
    Licensed to say and do whatever they please!

Creon. You are alone here in that opinion.

Antigone. No, they are with me. But they keep their
    tongues in leash.

105 **Creon.** Maybe. But you are guilty, and they are not.

Lines 82–83: Think about how Creon's perception of Antigone as a threat to his manhood heightens the conflict.

Antigone. There is no guilt in reverence for the dead.

Creon. But Eteocles—was he not your brother too?

Antigone. My brother too.

Creon. And you insult his memory?

Antigone (*softly*). The dead man would not say that I insult it.

110 **Creon.** He would: for you honor a traitor as much as him.

Antigone. His own brother, traitor or not, and equal in blood.

Creon. He made war on his country. Eteocles defended it.

Antigone. Nevertheless, there are honors due all the dead.

Creon. But not the same for the wicked as for the just.

115 **Antigone.** Ah Creon, Creon,
Which of us can say what the gods hold wicked?

Creon. An enemy is an enemy, even dead.

Antigone. It is my nature to join in love, not hate.

Creon (*finally losing patience*). Go join them, then; if you must have your love,
120 Find it in hell!

Choragos. But see, Ismene comes:

(*Enter* Ismene, *guarded.*)

Those tears are sisterly, the cloud
That shadows her eyes rains down gentle sorrow.

Creon. You too, Ismene,
125 Snake in my ordered house, sucking my blood
Stealthily—and all the time I never knew
That these two sisters were aiming at my throne!
Ismene,
Do you confess your share in this crime, or deny it?
Answer me.

130 **Ismene.** Yes, if she will let me say so. I am guilty.

◆ **Lines 113–116:** Unlike Creon, Antigone holds that humans cannot understand the thinking of the gods.

Antigone (*coldly*). No, Ismene. You have no right to say so.
> You would not help me, and I will not have you help me.

Ismene. But now I know what you meant; and I am here
> To join you, to take my share of punishment.

135 **Antigone.** The dead man and the gods who rule the dead
> Know whose act this was. Words are not friends.

Ismene. Do you refuse me, Antigone? I want to die with you:
> I too have a duty that I must discharge to the dead.

Antigone. You shall not lessen my death by sharing it.

140 **Ismene.** What do I care for life when you are dead?

Antigone. Ask Creon. You're always hanging on his opinions.

Ismene. You are laughing at me. Why, Antigone?

Antigone. It's a joyless laughter, Ismene.

Ismene.   But can I do nothing?

Antigone. Yes. Save yourself. I shall not envy you.
145 > There are those who will praise you; I shall have honor, too.

Ismene. But we are equally guilty!

Antigone.   No more, Ismene.
> You are alive, but I belong to death.

Creon (*to the* Chorus). Gentlemen, I beg you to observe these girls:
> One has just now lost her mind; the other,
150 > It seems, has never had a mind at all.

Ismene. Grief teaches the steadiest minds to waver, King.

Creon. Yours certainly did, when you assumed guilt with the guilty!

Ismene. But how could I go on living without her?

◆ **Lines 131–142:** Evaluate Antigone's treatment of her sister.

Creon. You are.
She is already dead.

Ismene.   But your own son's bride!

155 **Creon.** There are places enough for him to push his
      plow.
      I want no wicked women for my sons!

Ismene. O dearest Haemon, how your father wrongs
      you!

Creon. I've had enough of your childish talk of
      marriage!

Choragos. Do you really intend to steal this girl from
      your son?

160 **Creon.** No; death will do that for me.

Choragos.   Then she must die?

Creon (*ironically*). You dazzle me.
                    —But enough of this talk!
      (*to* Guards) You, there, take them away and guard
                    them well:
      For they are but women, and even brave men run
      When they see death coming.

            (*Exeunt* Ismene, Antigone, *and* Guards.)

ODE 2

165 **Chorus.** Fortunate is the man who has never tasted
            God's vengeance!
      Where once the anger of heaven has struck, that
            house is shaken
      Forever: damnation rises behind each child
      Like a wave cresting out of the black northeast,
      When the long darkness under sea roars up
170   And bursts drumming death upon the wind-whipped
            sand.

      I have seen this gathering sorrow from time long past
      Loom upon Oedipus' children: generation from
            generation
      Takes the compulsive rage of the enemy god.
      So lately this last flower of Oedipus' line
175   Drank the sunlight! but now a passionate word

♦ **Line 154:** Ismene's line adds
a complication to the plot:
Creon's son, Haemon, is
betrothed to Antigone. In
punishing Antigone, Creon
will punish his son as
well. Creon's love of his
immediate family is now
an issue in his conflict with
Antigone.

And a handful of dust have closed up all its beauty.
What mortal arrogance
Transcends the wrath of Zeus?
Sleep cannot lull him, nor the effortless long months
180 Of the timeless gods: but he is young forever,
And his house is the shining day of high Olympus.[1]
And that is and shall be,
And all the past, is his.
No pride on earth is free of the curse of heaven.

1. Olympus (ō lim′ pəs): a mountain in northern Greece, the home of the gods and goddesses.

185 The straying dreams of men
May bring them ghosts of joy:
But as they drowse, the waking embers burn them;
Or they walk with fixed eyes, as blind men walk.
But the ancient wisdom speaks for our own time:
190   *Fate works most for woe*
        With folly's fairest show.
Man's little pleasure is the spring of sorrow.

◆ **Line 192:** Consider how this line might apply to Creon.

SCENE 3

Choragos. But here is Haemon, King, the last of all
   your sons.
   Is it grief for Antigone that brings him here,
   And bitterness at being robbed of his bride?

(*Enter* Haemon.)

Creon. We shall soon see, and no need of diviners.[1]
                                                    —Son,
5   You have heard my final judgment on that girl:
   Have you come here hating me, or have you come
   With deference and with love, whatever I do?

1. diviners (də vīn′ ərz): those who predict the future.

Haemon. I am your son, Father, You are my guide.
   You make things clear for me, and I obey you.
10 No marriage means more to me than your continuing
      wisdom.

Creon. Good. That is the way to behave: subordinate
   Everything else, my son, to your father's will.
   This is what a man prays for, that he may get
   Sons attentive and dutiful in his house,
15 Each one hating his father's enemies,
   Honoring his father's friends. But if his sons
   Fail him, if they turn out unprofitably,

◆ **Lines 11–19:** Consider what Creon's words suggest about his relationship with his son.

What has he fathered but trouble for himself
And amusement for the malicious?
                                        So you are right
20   Not to lose your head over this woman.
Your pleasure with her would soon grow cold,
      Haemon,
And then you'd have a hellcat in bed and elsewhere.
Let her find her husband in hell!
Of all the people in this city, only she
25   Has had contempt for my law and broken it.

Do you want me to show myself weak before the
      people?
Or to break my sworn word? No, and I will not.
The woman dies.
I suppose she'll plead "family ties." Well, let her.
30   If I permit my own family to rebel,
How shall I earn the world's obedience?
Show me the man who keeps his house in hand,
He's fit for public authority.
                              I'll have no dealings
With lawbreakers, critics of the government:
35   Whoever is chosen to govern should be obeyed—
Must be obeyed, in all things, great and small,
Just and unjust! O Haemon,
The man who knows how to obey, and that man only,
Knows how to give commands when the time comes.
40   You can depend on him, no matter how fast
The spears come: he's a good soldier, he'll stick it out.

Anarchy, anarchy! Show me a greater evil!
This is why cities tumble and the great houses rain
      down,
This is what scatters armies!

45   No, no: good lives are made so by discipline.
We keep the laws then, and the lawmakers,
And no woman shall seduce us. If we must lose,
Let's lose to a man, at least! Is a woman stronger than
      we?

♦ **Lines 47–48:** Again Creon hints that he perceives Antigone as a threat to his manhood.

Choragos. Unless time has rusted my wits,
50   What you say, King, is said with point and dignity.

Haemon (*boyishly earnest*). Father:

Reason is God's crowning gift to man, and you are
  right
To warn me against losing mine. I cannot say—
I hope that I shall never want to say!—that you

55 Have reasoned badly. Yet there are other men
Who can reason, too; and their opinions might be
  helpful.
You are not in a position to know everything
That people say or do, or what they feel:
Your temper terrifies them—everyone

60 Will tell you only what you like to hear.
But I, at any rate, can listen; and I have heard them
Muttering and whispering in the dark about this girl.
They say no woman has ever, so unreasonably,
Died so shameful a death for a generous act:

65 "She covered her brother's body. Is this indecent?
She kept him from dogs and vultures. Is this a crime?
Death?—She should have all the honor that we can
  give her!"

This is the way they talk out there in the city.

You must believe me:

70 Nothing is closer to me than your happiness.
What could be closer? Must not any son
Value his father's fortune as his father does his?
I beg you, do not be unchangeable:
Do not believe that you alone can be right.

75 The man who thinks that,
The man who maintains that only he has the power
To reason correctly, the gift to speak, the soul—
A man like that, when you know him, turns out
  empty.

It is not reason never to yield to reason!

80 In flood time you can see how some trees bend,
And because they bend, even their twigs are safe,
While stubborn trees are torn up, roots and all.
And the same thing happens in sailing:
Make your sheet fast, never slacken—and over you go,

85 Head over heels and under: and there's your voyage.
Forget you are angry! Let yourself be moved!
I know I am young; but please let me say this:
The ideal condition

◆ **Lines 61–68:** Haemon's lines suggest that Creon is causing the very thing he most wants to prevent—anarchy.

◆ **Lines 79–85:** Compare Haemon's words to Creon with Creon's words to Antigone in Scene 2, beginning "The inflexible heart breaks first, . . ." (page 219, line 77)

Would be, I admit, that men should be right by
    instinct;
90   But since we are all too likely to go astray,
The reasonable thing is to learn from those who can
    teach.

Choragos. You will do well to listen to him, King,
If what he says is sensible. And you, Haemon,
Must listen to your father—both speak well.

95   **Creon.** You consider it right for a man of my years and
    experience
To go to school to a boy?

Haemon.   It is not right.
If I am wrong. But if I am young, and right,
What does my age matter?

Creon. You think it right to stand up for an anarchist?

100   **Haemon.** Not at all. I pay no respect to criminals.

Creon. Then she is not a criminal?

Haemon. The city would deny it, to a man.

Creon. And the city proposes to teach me how to rule?

Haemon. Ah. Who is it that's talking like a boy now?

105   **Creon.** My voice is the one voice giving orders in this
    city!

Haemon. It is no city if it takes orders from one
    voice.

Creon. The state is the king!

Haemon.   Yes, if the state is a desert.

(*Pause*)

Creon. This boy, it seems, has sold out to a woman.

Haemon. If you are a woman: my concern is only for
    you.

110   **Creon.** So? Your "concern"! In a public brawl with
    your father!

Haemon. How about you, in a public brawl with
    justice?

Creon. With justice, when all that I do is within my
    rights?

Haemon. You have no right to trample on God's
    right.

Creon (*completely out of control*). Fool, adolescent
    fool!
115   Taken in by a woman!

Haemon. You'll never see me taken in by anything
    vile.

Creon. Every word you say is for her!

Haemon (*quietly, darkly*).   And for you.
    And for me. And for the gods under the earth.

Creon. You'll never marry her while she lives.

120 **Haemon.** Then she must die—But her death will
    cause another.

Creon. Another?
    Have you lost your senses? Is this an open threat?

Haemon. There is no threat in speaking to emptiness.

Creon. I swear you'll regret this superior tone of yours!
    You are the empty one!

Haemon.   If you were not my father,
125   I'd say you were perverse.[2]

Creon. You girl-struck fool, don't play at words with
    me!

Haemon. I am sorry. You prefer silence.

Creon.   Now, by God—!
    I swear, by all the gods in heaven above us,
    You'll watch it, I swear you shall!
              (*to the* Servants) Bring her out!
130 Bring the woman out! Let her die before his eyes!
    Here, this instant, with her bridegroom beside her!

Haemon. Not here, no; she will not die here, King.
    And you will never see my face again.
    Go on raving as long as you've a friend to endure you.

                      (*Exit* Haemon.)

135 **Choragos.** Gone, gone.

2. perverse (pər vʉrs′):
stubbornly contrary.

Creon, a young man in a rage is dangerous!

Creon. Let him do, or dream to do, more than a man
   can.
   He shall not save these girls from death.

Choragos.   These girls?
   You have sentenced them both?

Creon.   No, you are right.
140   I will not kill the one whose hands are clean.

Choragos. But Antigone?

Creon (*somberly*).   I will carry her far away
   Out there in the wilderness and lock her
   Living in a vault of stone. She shall have food,
   As the custom is, to absolve the state of her death.
145   And there let her pray to the gods of hell:
   They are her only gods:
   Perhaps they will show her an escape from death,
   Or she may learn,
                    though late,
   That pity shown the dead is pity in vain.

                            (*Exit* Creon.)

◆ **Lines 141–149:** Consider
Creon's decision to bury a
person who is still alive
when he has steadfastly
refused to bury a dead one.

ODE 3

150   **Chorus.** Love, unconquerable
      Waster of rich men, keeper
      Of warm lights and all-night vigil
      In the soft face of a girl:
      Sea-wanderer, forest-visitor!
155   Even the pure Immortals cannot escape you,
      And mortal man, in his one day's dusk,
      Trembles before your glory.

      Surely you swerve upon ruin
      The just man's consenting heart,
160   As here you have made bright anger
      Strike between father and son—
      And none has conquered but love!
      A girl's glance working the will of Heaven:
      Pleasure to her alone who mocks us,
165   Merciless Aphrodite.[1]

1. Aphrodite (af rə dīt′ ē):
goddess of love and beauty.

SCENE 4

Choragos (*as Antigone enters, guarded*). But I can no
    longer stand in awe of this,
  Nor, seeing what I see, keep back my tears.
  Here is Antigone, passing to that chamber
  Where all find sleep at last.

5 **Antigone.** Look upon me, friends, and pity me
  Turning back at the night's edge to say
  Goodbye to the sun that shines for me no longer;
  Now sleepy death
  Summons me down to Acheron,[1] that cold shore:
10 There is no bride song there, nor any music.

  Chorus. Yet not unpraised, not without a kind of
    honor,
  You walk at last into the underworld;
  Untouched by sickness, broken by no sword.
  What woman has ever found your way to death?

15 **Antigone.** How often I have heard the story of Niobe,
  Tantalus' wretched daughter, how the stone
  Clung fast about her, ivy-close; and they say
  The rain falls endlessly
  And sifting soft snow; her tears are never done.
20 I feel the loneliness of her death in mine.

  Chorus. But she was born of heaven, and you
  Are woman, woman-born. If her death is yours,
  A mortal woman's, is this not for you
  Glory in our world and in the world beyond?

25 **Antigone.** You laugh at me. Ah, friends, friends,
  Can you not wait until I am dead? O Thebes,
  O men many-charioted, in love with fortune,
  Dear springs of Dirce, sacred Theban grove,
  Be witnesses for me, denied all pity,
30 Unjustly judged! and think a word of love
  For her whose path turns
  Under dark earth, where there are no more tears.

  Chorus. You have passed beyond human daring and
    come at last
  Into a place of stone where justice sits.
35 I cannot tell
  What shape of your father's guilt appears in this.

1. Acheron (ak′ ər än′): in Greek mythology, one of the rivers bordering the underworld.

◆ **Lines 15–20:** Niobe (nī′ ō bē), as you may recall from an explanatory note in *The Iliad*, was the queen of Thebes who boasted that she was greater than the goddess Leto because she had more children. When the gods killed all of Niobe's children, she was turned to stone but continued to shed tears. Her father Tantalus (tan′ tə ləs), was doomed in the underworld to stand in water that receded when he tried to drink it and under branches of fruit that remained just out of reach. Think about why Antigone might compare herself to the grieving Niobe.

From the 1960 movie *Antigone,* starring Irene Papas.
Culver Pictures, New York.

Antigone. You have touched it at last: that bridal bed
   Unspeakable, horror of son and mother mingling:
   Their crime, infection of all our family!
40   O Oedipus, father and brother!
   Your marriage strikes from the grave to murder mine.
   I have been a stranger here in my own land:
   All my life
   The blasphemy of my birth has followed me.

45   **Chorus.** Reverence is a virtue, but strength
   Lives in established law: that must prevail.
   You have made your choice,
   Your death is the doing of your conscious hand.

Antigone. Then let me go, since all your words are
      bitter,
50   And the very light of the sun is cold to me.
   Lead me to my vigil, where I must have
   Neither love nor lamentation;[2] no song, but silence.

2. **lamentation** (lam′ ən tā′ shən): wailing because of grief.

(Creon *interrupts impatiently.*)

Creon. If dirges and planned lamentations could put
      off death,
   Men would be singing forever.

            (*to the* Servants) Take her, go!
55   You know your orders: take her to the vault
   And leave her alone there. And if she lives or dies,
   That's her affair, not ours: our hands are clean.

Antigone. O tomb, vaulted bride-bed in eternal rock,
   Soon I shall be with my own again
60   Where Persephone[3] welcomes the thin ghosts
      underground:
   And I shall see my father again, and you, Mother,
   And dearest Polyneices—
                dearest indeed
   To me, since it was my hand
   That washed him clean and poured the ritual wine;
65   And my reward is death before my time!

3. **Persephone** (pər sef′ ə nē): the wife of Hades and queen of the underworld.

   And yet, as men's hearts know, I have done no wrong,
   I have not sinned before God. Or if I have,
   I shall know the truth in death. But if the guilt
   Lies upon Creon who judged me, then, I pray,
70   May his punishment equal my own.

Choragos.   O passionate heart,
  Unyielding, tormented still by the same winds!

Creon. Her guards shall have good cause to regret
    their delaying.

Antigone. Ah! That voice is like the voice of death!

Creon. I can give you no reason to think you are
    mistaken.

75 **Antigone.** Thebes, and you my fathers' gods,
      And rulers of Thebes, you see me now, the last
      Unhappy daughter of a line of kings,
      Your kings, led away to death. You will remember
      What things I suffer, and at what men's hands,
80   Because I would not transgress the laws of heaven.
      (*to the* Guards, *simply*) Come: let us wait no longer.

                (*Exit Antigone, left, guarded.*)

ODE 4

Chorus. All Danae's beauty was locked away
      In a brazen cell where the sunlight could not come:
      A small room, still as any grave, enclosed her.
85   Yet she was a princess, too,
      And Zeus in a rain of gold poured love upon her.
      O child, child,
      No power in wealth or war
      Or tough sea-blackened ships
90   Can prevail against untiring destiny!

      And Dryas' son also, that furious king,
      Bore the god's prisoning anger for his pride:
      Sealed up by Dionysus in deaf stone,
      His madness died among echoes.
95   So at the last he learned what dreadful power
      His tongue had mocked:
      For he had profaned the revels,
      And fired the wrath of the nine
      Implacable Sisters that love the sound of the flute.

100   And old men tell a half-remembered tale
      Of horror done where a dark ledge splits the sea
      And a double surf beats on the gray shores:
      How a king's new woman, sick

◆ **Lines 75–81:** Consider what these lines suggest about what Antigone values most.

◆ **Lines 82–86:** Danae (dan′ ā ē) was a princess imprisoned in a bronze tower by her father because of the prediction that her son would one day kill him. Zeus visited Danae in the form of a shower of gold, and later she gave birth to his son Perseus, who eventually did kill his grandfather.

◆ **Lines 91–99:** King Lycurgus (lī kʉr′ gəs), the son of Dryas (drī′ əs), was driven mad and then imprisoned in stone for objecting to the worship of Dionysus (dī′ ə nī′ səs), the god of wine and fertility. The nine implacable Sisters are the muses, the goddesses who preside over literature, the arts, and the sciences. Once offended, they cannot be appeased.

With hatred for the queen he had imprisoned,
105 Ripped out his two sons' eyes with her bloody hands
While grinning Ares watched the shuttle plunge
Four times: four blind wounds crying for revenge,

Crying, tears and blood mingled—piteously born,
Those sons whose mother was of heavenly birth!
110 Her father was the god of the North Wind
And she was cradled by gales,
She raced with young colts on the glittering hills
And walked untrammeled in the open light;
But in her marriage deathless Fate found means
115 To build a tomb like yours for all her joy.

SCENE 5

(*Enter blind* Teiresias, *led by a* Boy. *The opening speeches
of* Teiresias *should be in singsong contrast to the realistic
lines of* Creon.)

Teiresias. This is the way the blind man comes,
Princes, Princes,
Lock step, two heads lit by the eyes of one.

Creon. What new thing have you to tell us, old
Teiresias?

Teiresias. I have much to tell you: listen to the
prophet, Creon.

5 **Creon.** I am not aware that I have ever failed to listen.

Teiresias. Then you have done wisely, King, and ruled
well.

Creon. I admit my debt to you. But what have you to
say?

Teiresias. This, Creon: you stand once more on the
edge of fate.

Creon. What do you mean? Your words are a kind of
dread.

10 **Teiresias.** Listen, Creon:
I was sitting in my chair of augury, at the place
Where the birds gather about me. They were all
a-chatter,
As is their habit, when suddenly I heard

◆ **Lines 100–115:** According
to an ancient myth, King
Phineus (fī′ nōōs) imprisoned
his first wife, who was the
daughter of the North Wind,
and then permitted his new
wife to blind his sons from
his first marriage.

◆ **Lines 1–17:** The blind
Teiresias is physically blind
but spiritually sighted. As a
prophet, he functions as an
agent of the gods in their
dealings with humans. By
helping Oedipus to see the
truth about himself and thus
leave Thebes, Teiresias
indirectly helped Creon to
become king. The chair of
augury is the place where
Teiresias sits to hear the
birds, whose sounds reveal
the future to him. The
fighting among the birds
suggests that the anarchy
infecting Thebes has spread
even to the natural world.

A strange note in their jangling, a scream, a
15   Whirring fury; I knew that they were fighting,
Tearing each other, dying
In a whirlwind of wings clashing. And I was afraid.
I began the rites of burnt offering at the altar,
But Hephaestus[1] failed me: instead of bright flame,
20   There was only the sputtering slime of the fat thigh
        flesh
Melting: the entrails dissolved in gray smoke,
The bare bone burst from the welter. And no blaze!

This was a sign from heaven. My boy described it,
Seeing for me as I see for others.

25   I tell you, Creon, you yourself have brought
This new calamity upon us. Our hearths and altars
Are stained with the corruption of dogs and carrion
        birds
That glut themselves on the corpse of Oedipus' son.

The gods are deaf when we pray to them, their fire
30   Recoils from our offering, their birds of omen
Have no cry of comfort, for they are gorged
With the thick blood of the dead.
                                         O my son,
These are no trifles! Think: all men make mistakes,
But a good man yields when he knows his course is
        wrong,
35   And repairs the evil. The only crime is pride.

Give in to the dead man, then: do not fight with a
        corpse—
What glory is it to kill a man who is dead?
Think, I beg you:
It is for your own good that I speak as I do.
40   You should be able to yield for your own good.

Creon. It seems that prophets have made me their
        especial province.
All my life long
I have been a kind of butt for the dull arrows
Of doddering fortunetellers!
                                    No, Teiresias:
45   If your birds—if the great eagles of God himself
Should carry him stinking bit by bit to heaven,

1. **Hephaestus** (hē fes′ təs):
the god of fire.

◆ **Lines 21–32:** The birds and
dogs that have eaten the
corpse of Polyneices have
become corrupt offerings
rejected by the gods.

◆ **Lines 44–48:** Ask yourself
what these lines suggest
about Creon's view of
himself and the gods.

I would not yield. I am not afraid of pollution:
No man can defile the gods.

        Do what you will,
Go into business, make money, speculate
50 In India gold or that synthetic gold from Sardis,[2]
Get rich otherwise than by my consent to bury him.
Teiresias, it is a sorry thing when a wise man
Sells his wisdom, lets out his words for hire!

Teiresias. Ah Creon! Is there no man left in the
  world—

55 **Creon.** To do what?—Come, let's have the aphorism!

Teiresias. No man who knows that wisdom outweighs
  any wealth?

Creon. As surely as bribes are baser than any baseness.

Teiresias. You are sick, Creon! You are deathly sick!

Creon. As you say: it is not my place to challenge a
  prophet.

60 **Teiresias.** Yet you have said my prophecy is for sale.

Creon. The generation of prophets has always loved gold.

Teiresias. The generation of kings has always loved
  brass.

Creon. You forget yourself! You are speaking to your
  king.

Teiresias. I know it. You are a king because of me.

65 **Creon.** You have a certain skill; but you have sold out.

Teiresias. King, you will drive me to the words that—

Creon.   Say them, say them!
  Only remember: I will not pay you for them.

Teiresias. No, you will find them too costly.

Creon.   No doubt. Speak:
  Whatever you say, you will not change my will.

70 **Teiresias.** Then take this, and take it to heart!
  The time is not far off when you shall pay back
  Corpse for corpse, flesh of your own flesh.
  You have thrust the child of this world into living
   night,

2. Sardis (sär′ dis): the
capital of ancient Lydia,
where metal coins first
were produced.

◆ **Lines 71–78:** Speculate
about how this prophecy
might be fulfilled.

You have kept from the gods below the child that is
        theirs:
75   The one in a grave before her death, the other,
     Dead, denied the grave. This is your crime;
     And the Furies[3] and the dark gods of hell
     Are swift with terrible punishment for you.

     Do you want to buy me now, Creon?
                                    Not many days,
80   And your house will be full of men and women
        weeping,
     And curses will be hurled at you from far
     Cities grieving for sons unburied, left to rot
     Before the walls of Thebes.

     These are my arrows, Creon: they are all for you.

85   (*to* Boy) But come, child: lead me home.
     Let him waste his fine anger upon younger men.
     Maybe he will learn at last
     To control a wiser tongue in a better head.

                              (*Exit* Teiresias.)

Choragos. The old man has gone, King, but his words
90   Remain to plague us. I am old, too,
     But I cannot remember that he was ever false.

Creon. That is true . . . It troubles me.
     Oh it is hard to give in! But it is worse
     To risk everything for stubborn pride.

95   **Choragos.** Creon: take my advice.

Creon.   What shall I do?

Choragos. Go quickly: free Antigone from her vault
     And build a tomb for the body of Polyneices.

Creon. You would have me do this?

Choragos.   Creon, yes!
     And it must be done at once: God moves
100 Swiftly to cancel the folly of stubborn men.

Creon. It is hard to deny the heart! But I
     Will do it: I will not fight with destiny.

Choragos. You must go yourself, you cannot leave it
        to others.

3. **Furies** (fyo͞or′ ēz): three
goddesses who avenge
crimes, especially those
that violate family ties.

Creon. I will go.

              —Bring axes, servants:

105   Come with me to the tomb. I buried her, I
Will set her free.

             Oh quickly!

My mind misgives—
The laws of the gods are mighty, and a man must
   serve them
To the last day of his life!

                          (*Exit* Creon.)

EXODUS

(*Enter* Messenger, *left.*)

Messenger. Men of the line of Kadmos, you who live
   Near Amphion's[1] citadel:

                 I cannot say
Of any condition of human life "This is fixed,
This is clearly good, or bad." Fate raises up,

5   And fate casts down the happy and unhappy alike:
No man can foretell his fate.

                 Take the case of Creon:
Creon was happy once, as I count happiness;
Victorious in battle, sole governor of the land,
Fortunate father of the children nobly born.

10   And now it has all gone from him! Who can say
That a man is still alive when his life's joy fails?
He is a walking dead man. Grant him rich,
Let him live like a king in his great house:
If his pleasure is gone, I would not give

15   So much as the shadow of smoke for all he owns.

Choragos. Your words hint at sorrow; what is your
   news for us?

Messenger. They are dead. The living are guilty of
   their death.

Choragos. Who is guilty? Who is dead? Speak!

Messenger.   Haemon.
   Haemon is dead; and the hand that killed him

20   Is his own hand.

Choragos.   His father's? or his own?

Messenger. His own, driven mad by the murder his
   father had done.

♦ **Lines 1–15:** The exodus is the last episode in the play. It is followed by a final speech made by the Chorus and addressed directly to the audience. As you read, compare the messenger with the sentry who appeared in Scenes 1 and 2.

1. Amphion (am fī′ ən): Niobe's husband, who built a wall around Thebes by charming the stones into place with a lyre.

Choragos. Teiresias, Teiresias, how clearly you saw it all!

Messenger. This is my news; you must draw what conclusions you can from it.

Choragos. But look: Eurydice, our queen:
25   Has she overheard us?

(*Enter* Eurydice *from the palace, center.*)

Eurydice. I have heard something, friends:
       As I was unlocking the gate of Pallas'[2] shrine,
       For I needed her help today, I heard a voice
       Telling of some new sorrow. And I fainted
30   There at the temple with all my maidens about me.
       But speak again; whatever it is, I can bear it:
       Grief and I are not strangers.

Messenger.   Dearest lady,
       I will tell you plainly all that I have seen.
       I shall not try to comfort you: what is the use,
35   Since comfort could lie only in what is not true?
       The truth is always best.
                              I went with Creon
       To the outer plain where Polyneices was lying,
       No friend to pity him, his body shredded by dogs.
       We made our prayers in that place to Hecate
40   And Pluto,[3] that they would be merciful. And we
         bathed
       The corpse with holy water, and we brought
       Fresh-broken branches to burn what was left of it,
       And upon the urn we heaped up a towering barrow
       Of earth of his own land.
                              When we were done, we ran
45   To the vault where Antigone lay on her couch of
         stone.
       One of the servants had gone ahead,
       And while he was yet far off he heard a voice
       Grieving within the chamber, and he came back
       And told Creon. And as the king went closer,
50   The air was full of wailing, the words lost,
       And he begged us to make all haste. "Am I a
         prophet?"
       He said weeping. "And must I walk this road,
       The saddest of all that I have gone before?
       My son's voice calls me on. Oh quickly, quickly!

2. **Pallas** (pal′ əs): the goddess of wisdom.

◆ **Line 32:** Megareus (meg′ ə roos), the older son of Eurydice and Creon, had died in the battle for Thebes.

3. **Hecate and Pluto** (hek′ ə tē), (ploot′ ō): the goddess and god of the underworld.

◆ **Lines 40–44:** Note the contrast between the barrow erected by Creon and the handful of dirt used by Antigone to cover her brother.

55   Look through the crevice there, and tell me
  If it is Haemon, or some deception of the gods!"
  We obeyed; and in the cavern's farthest corner
  We saw her lying:
  She had made a noose of her fine linen veil
60   And hanged herself. Haemon lay beside her,
  His arms about her waist, lamenting her,
  His love lost underground, crying out
  That his father had stolen her away from him.

  When Creon saw him the tears rushed to his eyes
65   And he called to him: "What have you done, child?
    Speak to me.
  What are you thinking that makes your eyes so
    strange?
  O my son, my son, I come to you on my knees!"
  But Haemon spat in his face. He said not a word,
  Staring—
         And suddenly drew his sword
70   And lunged. Creon shrank back, the blade missed;
    and the boy,
  Desperate against himself, drove it half its length
  Into his own side and fell. And as he died
  He gathered Antigone close in his arms again,
  Choking, his blood bright red on her white cheek.
75   And now he lies dead with the dead, and she is his
  At last, his bride in the houses of the dead.

                (*Exit* Eurydice *into the palace.*)

Choragos. She has left us without a word. What can
  this mean?

Messenger. It troubles me, too; yet she knows what is
  best.
  Her grief is too great for public lamentation,
80   And doubtless she has gone to her chamber to weep
  For her dead son, leading her maidens in his dirge.

Choragos. It may be so; but I fear this deep silence.

(*Pause.*)

Messenger. I will see what she is doing. I will go in.

                  (*Exit* Messenger *into the palace.*)

(*Enter* Creon *with attendants, bearing* Haemon's *body.*)

Choragos. But here is the king himself: oh look at
    him,
85   Bearing his own damnation in his arms.

Creon. Nothing you say can touch me any more.
    My own blind heart has brought me
    From darkness to final darkness. Here you see
    The father murdering, the murdered son—
90   And all my civic wisdom!

    Haemon my son, so young, so young to die,
    I was the fool, not you; and you died for me.

Choragos. That is the truth; but you were late in
    learning it.

Creon. This truth is hard to bear. Surely a god
95   Has crushed me beneath the hugest weight of heaven,
    And driven me headlong a barbaric way
    To trample out the thing I held most dear.
    The pains that men will take to come to pain!

(*Enter* Messenger *from the palace.*)

Messenger. The burden you carry in your hands is
    heavy,
100   But it is not all: you will find more in your house.

Creon. What burden worse than this shall I find
    there?

Messenger. The queen is dead.

Creon. O port of death, deaf world,
    Is there no pity for me? And you, angel of evil,
105   I was dead, and your words are death again.
    Is it true, boy? Can it be true?
    Is my wife dead? Has death bred death?

Messenger. You can see for yourself.

(*The doors are opened, and the body of* Eurydice *is
    disclosed within.*)

Creon. Oh pity!
110   All true, all true, and more than I can bear!
    O my wife, my son!

Messenger. She stood before the altar, and her heart
    Welcomed the knife her own hand guided,

115 And a great cry burst from her lips for Megareus dead,
And for Haemon dead, her sons; and her last breath
Was a curse for their father, the murderer of her sons.
And she fell, and the dark flowed in through her
    closing eyes.

Creon. O God, I am sick with fear.
Are there no swords here? Has no one a blow for me?

120 **Messenger.** Her curse is upon you for the deaths of
    both.

Creon. It is right that it should be. I alone am guilty.
I know it, and I say it. Lead me in
Quickly, friends.
I have neither life nor substance. Lead me in.

125 **Choragos.** You are right, if there can be right in so
    much wrong.
The briefest way is best in a world of sorrow.

Creon. Let it come,
Let death come quickly, and be kind to me.
I would not ever see the sun again.

130 **Choragos.** All that will come when it will; but we,
    meanwhile,
Have much to do. Leave the future to itself.

Creon. All my heart was in that prayer!

Choragos. Then do not pray any more: the sky is deaf.

Creon. Lead me away. I have been rash and foolish.
135 I have killed my son and my wife.
I look for comfort; my comfort lies here dead.
Whatever my hands have touched has come to
    nothing.
Fate has brought all my pride to a thought of dust.

(*As Creon is being led into the house, the Choragos
advances and speaks directly to the audience.*)

Choragos. There is no happiness where there is no
    wisdom;
140 No wisdom but in submission to the gods.
Big words are always punished,
And proud men in old age learn to be wise.

Thinking About the Play

A PERSONAL RESPONSE

sharing impressions

1. How do you feel about what happens at the end of this play? Jot down your impressions in your journal.

constructing interpretations

2. How much do you think Creon is to blame for the suicides of Antigone, Haemon, and Eurydice?

Think about
- Creon's judgment of himself at the end of the play
- how Haemon and Eurydice feel about Creon at the moment of death
- Creon's attempt to rescue Antigone from the stone vault
- whether someone can be held accountable for another's suicide

3. What do you think is the main reason that Creon and Antigone cannot resolve their conflict?

Think about
- what Polyneices means to each character
- each character's view of what is right.
- the attitude of each character toward the gods

4. How would you rank each of the main characters in this play on the basis of his or her depth of love?

5. Who do you think suffers the most in this play, and why?

A CREATIVE RESPONSE

6. How do you think the effect of the last scene would be different if the deaths of Antigone, Haemon, and Eurydice occurred on stage instead of being described by the messenger?

A CRITICAL RESPONSE

7. What effect did the Choragos and the Chorus have on your interpretation of the events in this play? Go back to the play and find evidence to support your analysis.

8. Which of the messages conveyed by Sophocles do you think is most relevant for people today? Explain.

Think about
- Antigone's devotion to Polyneices
- Creon's way of ruling
- Creon's loss of his son and wife

9. Compare Antigone and Socrates as heroes.

Analyzing the Writer's Craft

DRAMATIC IRONY

Consider the following line spoken by Creon to Antigone: "That [your death] gives me everything." Now that you know the outcome of the play, this line conveys a different and more complex meaning to you than to the character who speaks it.

Building a Literary Vocabulary. Irony is a contrast between what is expected and what actually exists or happens. Dramatic irony is a type of irony that occurs when the reader or viewer is aware of information of which the character is unaware. Once you know the outcome of the play, you realize that Antigone's death will not give Creon everything. On the contrary, it will take from

Creon all that is meaningful in his life. This contrast between Creon's limited knowledge and your fuller understanding generates dramatic irony.

Application: Identifying Dramatic Irony. Get together with a small group of classmates and read aloud a few scenes from the play, looking for examples of dramatic irony. List each example that you find and write a brief explanation of why you consider it ironic. After you have completed your list, share your findings with another group and speculate about why Sophocles used this technique.

Connecting Reading and Writing

1. Think about how one of the less important figures in this play, such as Ismene, the sentry, or Teiresias, might view what happens to Antigone and Creon. Write a **diary entry** expressing the thoughts and feelings of one of these characters.

Option: Write an **interview** with the character to be published in a local paper, *The Thebes Sentinel.*

2. Imagine that you have been asked to address a women's group on this topic: "Women of Courage in Classic Literature." Write the portion of your **lecture** that concerns Antigone.

Option: Write a **eulogy** of Antigone that emphasizes her courage.

3. If you were going to direct a movie of this play, who would be your choices to play Antigone and Creon? Write a **memo** to the producer.

Option: Write a **press release** for movie reviewers describing your choices for the leading roles.

4. With a group of classmates, perform a few scenes from this play. Tape-record your performance. Then write a **program note** explaining your interpretation of the role you enacted.

Option: Write a **character sketch** for your classmates of the character that you played.

5. Early in the play, the Choragos comments on Antigone: "Like father, like daughter: both headstrong, deaf to reason!" Read Sophocles' play *Oedipus the King*, and then write a **review** in which you compare father and daughter.

Option: Write **notes** for a classroom presentation comparing Oedipus and Antigone.

Antigone

CZESLAW MILOSZ   born 1911   POLAND/U.S.

A biography of Milosz appears on page 747.

Approaching the Poem

In the following poem by Czeslaw Milosz (ches' wäs mē' lôsh), Antigone and
Ismene from Sophocles' play reappear in Hungary in 1949. Hungary was one of
the countries that suffered terribly during and after World War II. In March 1944,
Hitler seized Hungary, shipping more than 500,000 Hungarian Jews to concentration camps. Later that same year, Stalin's troops invaded the country. By 1949,
a political takeover occurred in which communists fashioned a new constitution
patterned on that of the Soviet Union.

Connecting Writing and Reading

What past events and circumstances do you consider tragedies? What attitudes do
you think people might have toward terrible ordeals of the past? Write your ideas
in your journal. As you read Milosz's poem, compare your ideas with the attitudes
expressed by Antigone and Ismene toward the sufferings of the past.

This fragment, written in 1949, is in remembrance of the Hungarian workers, students, and soldiers.

ANTIGONE:
Accepting everything in this way, as one accepts
Summer after spring, winter after fall,
Accepting man's lot in the same way
As one accepts the seasons, without thought?
As long as I live, I will cry out: no.
Do you hear, Ismene? I cry out: no.
And I do not want any of your consolations,
Not flowers of the spring night, nor the nightingale,
Sun nor clouds, nor pleasant rivers.
Nothing. May it persist unappeased
This, which remains and this, which will remain
Is the one thing worthy of memory: our hurt.
The rusted ruins, Ismene,
Know everything. With its black wing the raven
Death separated us from those years
When we thought that our country
Was like other countries, our people
The same as other people.
Fate's curse demands a victim.
The victim returns fate's curse.
When this happens, it is not the time
To preserve one's own insignificant life
And it is not the time to weep for oneself.
There is time for nothing. May devastation
Engulf the entire pitiless world,
May those who laugh at our sorrow
Turn their own cities into ashes.
Creon's law! And Creon's command!
What is Creon, when the world is disappearing?

ISMENE:
Yes, but our parents are dead
And our brothers are dead. And their revolution
Will not return. Why reach out to the past?
The old man with a cane cannot find his way
Vainly seeking slain sons in the deaf city.
Old women, quiet mourners,
Pace in the dust with bowed heads.
But already the greenery of dark places
Wormwood, thistle, is forcing its way through the
   smoldering ruins,

The butterfly, like a paper wafer in the inferno,
40 Flies among sheared stony chasms,
Tattered children again are going to school,
Lovers again are entwining hands,
And within this is a rhythm, believe me, a compelling
    rhythm,
Sorrow mingled with rapture—as though Persephone[1]
45 Were newly returned to the world.

ANTIGONE:
Fools believe that when they sacrifice
Memories of the past, they will live contentedly.
And fools believe: the death of one city
Is not a sentencing for other cities.

ISMENE:
50 Do not make light of the difficulty, Antigone,
With which we force our lips and hearts
Into silence. For this kind of triumph
Is also a triumph and gives hope.

ANTIGONE:
I do not need your hope.
55 For I saw the remains of Polynices[2]
There, on the threshold of the crumbling cathedral.
This skull, small as a child's,
With a strand of light hair. A handful of bones
Wrapped in crumbling, dark cloth
60 And the stench of a corpse. This then is our brother,
Whose heart beat like ours,
Who was happy and sang songs
And knew fear before death, because in him the same
    voices
Called that call within us.
65 And he conquered the voices summoning him
To life's bright, remote expanses,
And he went willingly to the sacrifice,
Faithful to his word and oath.
Twenty years old, beautiful and high-spirited,
70 How many plans, unspoken thoughts
By strength of will he offered up for destruction.
And this was the man who, by Creon's command
Was proclaimed a traitor. For him
Some dark corner in a barren place outside the city

1. Persephone (pər sef′ ə nē):
According to Greek myth-
ology, Persephone was
abducted by Hades, lord of
the underworld, to be his wife
and queen of the underworld.
Persephone stayed in the
underworld only four months
of the year, however, and her
return to the earth each year
brought spring.

2. Polynices (päl′ i nī′ sēz′):
alternate spelling of
Polyneices, brother of
Antigone and Ismene.

75 And in an empty helmet a moaning wind.
    But for others, for the glory of villains,
    Monuments will be erected
    Young girls will place wreaths on their graves
    The luster of torches illumines their names.
80 Here nothing, here darkness. With frightened hand
    Writers, compelled by fear
    Are lavish in praise of villains.
    And so he departs, exiled from legend
    Into the oblivion of eternity—traitor or hero?

ISMENE:
85 Words can enflame the hurt.
    One who remains silent does not suffer less, perhaps more.

ANTIGONE:
    Not only words, Ismene, not only words.
    Creon will not build his kingdom
    On our graves. He will not establish his order
90 With the power of the sword.
    Great is the power of the dead. No one is safe.
    Even though he surrounds himself
    With a crowd of spies and a million guards,
    The dead will reach him. They await the hour.
95 They are ironic, laughingly striding
    Around the lunatic, who does not believe in them.
    And when he adds up his accounts
    Suddenly the mistake is obvious.
    A little mistake, but multiplied,
100 Enough! And this mistake grows in magnitude,
    Villages and cities are consumed by the fire of iniquity.
    Blood! Blood! With crimson ink, he strives
    To eradicate the mistake. Too late. It is finished.
    Hapless Creon in this way intends to rule
105 As though we were a barbaric country.
    As though here every stone did not remember
    Tears of sorrow and tears of hope.

Thinking About the Poem

A PERSONAL RESPONSE

*sharing
impressions*

1. What picture of Antigone is created in this poem? Jot down a description in your journal.

*constructing
interpretations*

2. Whose attitude toward the sufferings of the past, Antigone's or Ismene's, appeals to you more?

Think about
- Antigone's attitude toward accepting her lot
- Ismene's idea about "Sorrow mingled with rapture"
- which sister might cope better with life after the war
- the ideas that you wrote in your journal before reading the poem

3. What lines in the poem have the greatest impact for you? Explain.

Think about
- Antigone's description of her brother (lines 55–75)
- Ismene's image of the old man with a cane (lines 33–34)
- Antigone's lines: "Blood! Blood! With crimson ink, he strives / To eradicate the mistake." (lines 102–103)

4. What do you think is the main reason that Antigone scorns Creon?

Think about
- Creon's attitude toward Antigone's country
- the power that Creon believes in
- what Antigone believes will happen to Creon

A CREATIVE RESPONSE

5. How do you think survivors of the Holocaust or of other wartime horrors generally would react to Antigone's character?

A CRITICAL RESPONSE

6. Why do you think Milosz used the ancient legend about Antigone in a poem dedicated to Hungarian workers, students, and soldiers in 1949?

Think about
- what effect Sophocles' play might have had on Milosz
- any similarities between the legend and the situation in Hungary in 1949

7. Whom do you admire more, Milosz's Antigone or Sophocles'? Support your opinion with details from both the poem and the play.

Hecuba's Testament

ROSARIO CASTELLANOS 1925–1974 MEXICO

A biography of Castellanos appears on page 740.

*A*pproaching the Poem

You may recall from *The Iliad* and *The Aeneid* that Hecuba was the wife of Priam,
king of Troy, and the mother of many children, including the princes Hector and
Paris. Hecuba saw Hector's dead body defiled by Achilles and later saw her
husband killed during the fall of Troy. All of her children died or were enslaved
by the conquering Greeks. She herself was made to serve the Greek captain
Odysseus. Hecuba is the speaker in this poem by Rosario Castellanos (rô sä′ rē ô
käs te yä′ nôs), a modern Mexican writer known for her exploration of women's
concerns.

*B*uilding Vocabulary

The following essential words are defined alongside the poem.

chaste (chāst): Unmarried, I lived **chaste** while that was right. (page 250, line 23)

reproach (rē prōch′): a widow without **reproach**, a queen made slave (page 251,
line 48)

docility (dō sil′ ə tē): Makes me / drink down a harsh **docility**, / which I more and
more learn to accept (page 251, lines 61–63)

*C*onnecting Writing and Reading

Consider what you've learned about Hecuba and the losses she has experienced.
What would you imagine this woman to be like in old age? In your journal,
speculate about the thoughts and feelings she might have. As you read, compare
your ideas about Hecuba with her portrayal by the poet. Pay particular attention
to the way Hecuba seems to feel about her sufferings.

Hecuba's Testament

A tower, no ivy, I. The wind was powerless,
horns lunging round and round me like a bull's.
It stirred up clouds of dust to north and south
and in quarters I've forgotten or never knew.
5   But I endured, foundations deep in earth,
walls broad, heart strong
and warm within, defending my own brood.

Sorrow was closer kin than any of those.
Not the favorite; not the eldest. But a kinsman
10   agreeable in the chores, humble at table,
a shadowy teller of tales beside the fire.
There were times he went off hunting far away
at the masculine call
of his steady pulse, his eye sharp on the target.
15   He returned with game, consigned it
to a helper shrewd with the knife
and the zealous care of women.

◆ **Lines 8–17:** Notice the comparison of sorrow to a relative who is part of daily life. Think about what it might mean for sorrow to go "off hunting" and to return "with game."

On retiring I'd say: What a fine
piece of work my hands are weaving out of the hours.
20   From girlhood on I kept before my eyes
a handsome sampler;
was ambitious to copy its figure; wished no more.

Unmarried, I lived chaste[1] while that was right;
later was loyal to one, to my own husband.
25   Never a dawn that found me still asleep,
never a night that overtook me till
the beehive hum of my home had sunk to rest.
The house of my lord was rich with works of my hand;
his lands stretched out to horizons.

1. chaste (chāst): pure; not engaging in sexual activity.

30   And so that his name would not die
when his body died,
he had sons of me; they were valiant sons; had stamina.
Of me he had virtuous girls
that all made a suitable match
35   (except for one, a virgin, that held aloof,
as offering, it well may be, to a god himself).

◆ **Lines 35–36:** These lines refer to Hecuba's daughter Polyxena, whom the Greeks sacrificed to appease the ghost of Achilles.

Those who knew me called me fortunate.
Not satisfied with receiving
the happy praise of my equals,
40 I leaned to the little ones,
to sow in these a harvest of gratitude.

When the lightning bolt came probing
that tree of the conversations,
he who was struck by it raged about injustice.

45 I said not a word, for my way is
to listen to one thing only: bounden duty.
Disaster spoke; I obeyed:
a widow without <u>reproach</u>,[2] a queen made slave
without loss to her queenly pride,
50 and mother, ah, and mother
orphaned of all her brood.

I dragged along old age like a tunic
too heavy to wear.
I was blind with years and weeping
55 and in my blindness saw
the vision that sustained my soul at its post.

Helplessness came, the cold, the cold,
and I had to surrender myself to the charity
of those alive. As before I had
60 surrendered myself to love, and to misfortune.

Someone cares for me in my final sufferings. Makes me
drink down a harsh <u>docility</u>,[3]
which I more and more learn to accept
so that all be fulfilled in me: those ultimate mysteries.

◆ **Lines 42–45:** The "tree of the conversations" may represent Hecuba's family. The "lightning bolt" that strikes the tree probably refers to the Trojan War, sent by the gods. The "he" who rages may be a male family member, most likely Priam, but perhaps Paris or Hector.

2. reproach (rē prōch′): shame or disgrace.

◆ **Lines 50–51:** Reflect on the seemingly contradictory idea of a mother being "orphaned" and on what this idea might suggest about Hecuba's sufferings.

3. docility (dō sil′ ə tē): obedience; surrendering one's will to another.

Thinking About the Poem

*sharing
impressions*

1. What are your feelings about Hecuba after reading about her life? Record your feelings in your journal.

*constructing
interpretations*

2. What kind of woman is Hecuba? Use lines from the poem to support your opinion.

3. How greatly does Hecuba's way of life change after the "disaster," the Trojan War?

Think about
- her characterization of sorrow
- her relationship to her husband and children, described in lines 24–34
- the response she calls "my way" and her description of herself in lines 45–51
- her repetition of the words "surrender[ed] myself" in lines 58–60

4. What do you think enables Hecuba to endure suffering?

Think about
- what the sustaining vision in line 56 might be
- the reason she gives in the last line for accepting docility

A CREATIVE RESPONSE

5. What might have happened to Hecuba had she not silently endured but instead "raged about injustice"?

A CRITICAL RESPONSE

6. Analyze the poem in relation to this quotation from an essay written in 1971 by Castellanos: "Self-sacrifice is the Mexican woman's most famous virtue. But I am going to be presumptuous enough to say something that, worse than a question, is a doubt: Is self-denial really a virtue?"

Think about
- your opinion of Hecuba's character
- whether the poem confirms or raises doubt that self-sacrifice is a virtue

7. Do you think that Hecuba's silent endurance of suffering makes her as heroic as Socrates, St. Catherine, and Antigone or less so? Cite examples from the selections to support your opinion.

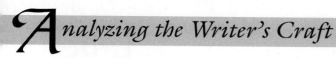

FIGURATIVE LANGUAGE

Think about the first words of the poem: "A tower, no ivy, I." What human qualities does this image suggest?

Building a Literary Vocabulary. These words are an example of figurative language, language that communicates ideas beyond the literal meanings of the words. The words in a figurative expression are not literally true; rather, they create impressions in the reader's mind.

Two of the most common forms of figurative language are metaphor and simile, which are introduced in Unit 1. "A tower, no ivy, I" is a metaphor that compares Hecuba to a tower, suggesting her qualities of strength and endurance. The first stanza of the poem is actually an extended metaphor, in which two things are compared at length and in various ways. The comparison to a tower is reinforced in the images "foundations deep in earth, / walls broad," which again suggest Hecuba's protective power. "Horns lunging round and round me like a bull's" is an example of a simile, which compares the troubles that beset Hecuba to the bull's horns that imperil a matador.

Personification is a figure of speech in which human qualities are attributed to an object, animal, or idea. "Disaster spoke; I obeyed" is an example of personification.

Application: Interpreting Figurative Language. Stanzas 2, 3, 4, 6, 7, 9, and 11 of this poem are rich in figurative language. Divide into seven small groups, with each group analyzing the figurative language in one of these stanzas. Identify the figurative language and classify it as simile, metaphor, or personification. Discuss the ideas it suggests. Each group should summarize its discussion for the rest of the class.

Lilies

RU ZHIJUAN   born 1925   CHINA

A biography of Zhijuan appears on page 751.

Approaching the Story

Ru Zhijuan (rōō jər sh̄üan'), a contemporary writer in China, views her writing as a tool for teaching the masses. In her story "Lilies," first published in 1958, she depicts the bond between the people and the Communist army during the civil war in China in 1946 and the heroism that the war inspired. In this war, the Communists, led by Mao Zedong (mɑu dsɑo' dôŋ'), eventually defeated the Nationalists, who fled from the mainland of China and settled in Taiwan. The narrator of "Lilies" is a woman serving in the Communist army. She uses the term *comrade* to refer to other Communist loyalists.

MID-AUTUMN 1946. The decision was made that day that the troops fighting in the coastal region would launch a general offensive that evening. The other comrades from the production office of our arts ensemble were all assigned work in various combat companies by the commander of the main offensive regiment, but, probably because I was a woman, the commander scratched his head in perplexity for a long time before finally calling a courier to lead me to a first-aid post near the front lines.

I didn't mind being assigned to a first-aid post. Just as long as I wasn't being ushered into a strongbox, I was willing to do anything. I shouldered my pack and set off after the courier.

That morning there had been a shower of rain, and although the sky was now clear, the road was still extremely slippery. But the crops on either side of the track had been washed a brilliant emerald-green and sparkled like jewels in the sunlight. The air carried a fresh, moist fragrance. If it hadn't been for the intermittent explosions of the enemy's blind cannon fire, I might have imagined myself on the way to market.

The courier walked ahead of me with rapid strides, and right from the start I lagged behind him some fifty or sixty meters. My feet were festering and the road so slippery that no matter how hard I tried, I couldn't catch up with him. I thought of calling to him to wait for me, but I was afraid he would laugh at me for being a frightened coward, and didn't dare. I really was afraid that I wouldn't be able to find the first-aid post on my own. I began to feel angry with him.

But strange to say, he seemed to have eyes in the back of his head and stopped at the roadside of his own accord, though he kept his face to the front and didn't even glance at me. When I had almost struggled up to where he stood, he set off again by himself and in a short time had once more left me far behind. I genuinely didn't have the strength to keep up, so simply staggered on slowly behind him. However, it was not so bad this time; he didn't let me lag too far back, but he never let me get close to him either, always maintaining the distance between us. If I walked quickly, he would stride on ahead, and if I walked slowly, he would vacillate[1] to the right and left before me. What was strange was that I never saw him look back once. I couldn't help feeling rather intrigued by this courier.

I hadn't paid him any attention at the regiment headquarters just now, but by the look of his tall, slender figure and broad shoulders he was a strong young fellow. He wore a faded yellow uniform and puttees[2] that reached to his knees. Several leafy twigs stuck into the barrel of the rifle on his shoulder seemed more a decoration than a means of camouflage.

I hadn't caught up with him, but my swollen feet were burning like twin fires. I suggested to him that we rest for a while and sat down on a stone at the edge of a field. He sat down with his back to me on another stone a good distance away, acting as if I simply didn't exist. From experience I knew that this was because I was a woman. Women comrades who worked at company level always had these problems. Slightly irritated, I displayed my spirit of resistance by walking over and sitting down directly opposite him. Now I could see his round, childish face. He must have been eighteen at the most. Seeing me sit down near him, he immediately became as alarmed as if a time bomb had been planted nearby. He was clearly ill at ease, knowing that to turn his head away would be impolite, but too embarrassed to face in my direction. He thought of standing up, but then felt that that would make things even more awkward. Fighting hard not to laugh, I casually asked him where he was from. He didn't answer immediately. He blushed a deep crimson like the painted face of the god of war, and only after stuttering incoherently for a while did he manage to make it clear that he was from the Tianmu[3] Mountains. So we were from the same area!

"What do you do at home?"

"I haul bamboo."

Looking at his broad shoulders, a vision of a green, misty sea of bamboo floated before my eyes. Through the trees a narrow, stone-stepped mountain path wound upward out of sight. A broad-shouldered young man with an old piece of blue cloth cushioning his shoulder was hauling several thick bamboos down the mountain. The tips of the bamboos trailed on the ground far behind him, issuing a rhythmic thud as they fell from step to step. This was the hometown life with which I was so familiar! My heart immediately warmed toward him. I questioned him further.

"How old are you?"

"Nineteen."

"When did you join the revolution?"

"A year ago."

"How did you come to join the revolution?" At this point I suddenly felt that this was more like an interrogation than a conversation, but I still couldn't resist questioning him.

"When the Communist troops pulled out of Jiangnan,[4] I followed them."

"How many in your family?"

"Mum, Dad, younger brothers and sisters,

---

1. **vacillate** (vas′ ə lāt): to move back and forth.

2. **puttees** (pu tēz′): cloth or leather leggings or cloth strips wound round the leg from the ankle to the knee.

3. **Tianmu** (tyen mōō′).

4. **Jiangnan** (jyäŋ nän′).

and another girl who lives with us."

"You're not married yet?"

He blushed scarlet and became even more disconcerted, his fingers endlessly counting the eyelets on his belt. After a long pause, he lowered his head with a bashful grin, and shook his head. I was going to ask him if he had a fiancée, but seeing the flustered state he was in, swallowed my words.

We sat in silence for a while, then he raised his head and looked at the sky, glancing at me to indicate that we should be on our way.

When I stood up to go, I saw him take off his cap and covertly mop the sweat with a towel. This was all my fault—he hadn't shed a drop of perspiration marching along the road, but his conversation with me had brought the sweat pouring off him.

When we arrived at the first-aid station, it was already past two in the afternoon. The first-aid post had been set up in a primary school about a mile from the battle front. Six buildings of various sizes were arranged in a rough triangle with a yard in the center overgrown with weeds. Obviously the school had been closed for some time. When we arrived, several health workers were preparing gauze bandages and cotton wool. The rooms were filled with doors propped up on piles of bricks that were to serve as hospital beds.

We hadn't been there long when a county cadre[5] arrived. His eyes were heavily bloodshot from lack of sleep, and he had stuck a piece of card under the front of his tattered felt cap to shade them from the sunlight. He came in puffing and panting, with a rifle on one shoulder and a steelyard[6] on the other, a basket of eggs in his left hand and a large cooking pot in his right. Putting down the things he had brought, he apologized to us and at the same time poured out his troubles. Gulping breathlessly from drinking down a cup of water, he pulled a lump of cooked rice from inside his jacket and took a large bite. I was so aston-

ished by the speed with which he did all this that I didn't catch what he was saying. He seemed to be saying that we would have to go and borrow cotton quilts ourselves. One of the health workers told me that the army quilts had still not been issued, but because it was essential that the wounded be kept warm, we would have to borrow quilts from the villagers. Even if we could get only a dozen or so strips of quilt padding, that would be better than nothing. I had been feeling frustrated at not being able to lend a hand, so I volunteered to undertake the task and, afraid that I wouldn't have time to complete it on my own, randomly asked my townsman to help me mobilize a few households before he went back. After a moment's hesitation, he followed me out of the door.

We went first to a nearby village, he covering the eastern side and I the western. In a short time I had written out three receipts and borrowed two strips of cotton padding and one cotton quilt. My arms were full and I was elated. I was just going to take the bedding back to the first-aid post and come back for more when the courier, his arms empty, came up from the opposite direction.

"What? You couldn't borrow any?" I was puzzled. I felt that the villagers' political awareness here was very high. They were also very openhearted. How could he possibly have not borrowed any?

"Comrade, you go and borrow them . . . the villagers here are strictly feudal . . ."

"Which house? You take me there." I guessed that he had certainly said something inappropriate and put the people's back up. Not being able to borrow a cotton quilt was a trifling matter, but to offend the ordinary people was of serious concern. I called him to take

---

5. cadre (ka' drē'): a member of a small military or political group around which a larger unit is built.

6. steelyard: a kind of balance or scale.

me to have a look, but he stubbornly lowered his head and stood as if nailed to the spot, unwilling to move. I went over to him and in a low voice explained to him the importance of making a good impression on the masses. Hearing what I said, without further ado, he led me to the house.

When we entered the courtyard, we found the main room of the house empty. The door to the inner room, which was screened by a piece of blue cloth on a red yoke, was framed to the right and left with an antithetical couplet written on bright red paper. We had no choice but to stand outside calling out "Elder Sister," "Sister-in-law." There was no answer, but there was the sound of movement within. After a moment the curtain was flicked aside, and a young woman appeared. She was very attractive: her eyebrows curved gracefully above a high-bridged nose, and a soft fringe covered her forehead. Although her clothes were of coarse cloth, they were all new.

Seeing that her hair was done up in the stiff bun of a married woman, I addressed her as "Elder Sister-in-law" and apologized to her, asking her not to take offense if this comrade had said something out of turn when he was here just now. She stood there listening with her face turned away slightly and a smile on her tightly closed lips. She didn't make a sound, even when I stopped speaking, but kept her head down, biting her lips as if holding back gales of laughter about something incredibly amusing. Now I began to feel awkward. What should I say next? I glanced at the courier at my side and saw him gazing at me unblinkingly as if watching the company commander giving a demonstration. All I could do was brace myself and somewhat sheepishly ask if we could borrow the quilt, explaining that the troops of the Communist Party were fighting for the ordinary people. As I talked, she stopped smiling and listened carefully, glancing toward the house now and then. When I

fell silent, she looked first at me and then at the courier, as if weighing up my words, then after long consideration, turned and went into the house to fetch the quilt.

The courier seized this opportunity to express his indignation. "That's exactly what I said just now, but she wouldn't lend it to me. Don't you think it's strange?"

I hastily threw him a disdainful glance to stop him talking, but it was already too late. The young woman with the quilt had already reached the doorway. As soon as I saw the quilt I understood why she had been so reluctant to lend it just now: it was completely new. The cover was of wine-colored synthetic satin, patterned all over with white lilies. As if deliberately wanting to annoy the courier, she held the quilt out to me saying, "Here, take it!"

My arms were already full of quilts, so I motioned to the courier with my lips that he should take it. Quite unexpectedly, he gazed up at the sky, pretending that he hadn't seen, and I was obliged to call to him before he finally took it with eyes cast down and a look of displeasure on his face. Highly flustered, he turned on his heel and shot out of the street door. But as he passed the door, we heard a sharp ripping sound as his uniform caught on the door hook, leaving a sizable piece of torn cloth hanging down from his shoulder. The young woman burst out laughing and hastily searched out a needle and cotton to stitch it up for him, but he wouldn't allow it on any account and left with the quilt under his arm.

We hadn't gone far when someone told us that the young woman was a new bride of only three days. This quilt was her entire dowry. I began to feel sorry that we had borrowed it, and the courier knitted his brows too, gazing silently at the quilt in his arms. I guessed he felt the same way as I did. Sure enough, as we walked along he began to mutter, "We didn't understand the situation. It's really not right to borrow someone's bridal quilt!" I couldn't resist playing a joke on him, and deliberately assumed a serious air. "You're right! Who knows how many mornings she got up early and how many evenings she stayed up late doing extra jobs to save up for this quilt? For all we know she might have spent sleepless nights on account of it. But some people still curse her as strictly feudal . . ."

Hearing this, he suddenly halted, and after a moment's silence said, "Then . . . then let's take it back to her!"

"Since we've already borrowed it, to take it back now would only hurt her feelings." His earnest, embarrassed expression was both amusing and endearing. Unaccountably, I had already given my heart to this simple young townsfellow of mine.

Hearing that my explanation seemed reasonable, he thought for a moment, then said resolutely, "OK, then we'll leave it at that, but when we've finished with it, we must wash it really clean for her." Having made this decision, he grabbed all the quilts out of my arms and with them hung over his shoulders went striding off at a rapid pace.

Back at the first-aid post, I told him to return to the regimental headquarters. He brightened up immediately, and after giving me a farewell salute, raced off. He had only gone a few paces when he suddenly thought of something and, feeling around in his shoulder bag, pulled out two steamed bread rolls which he waved at me, then placed on a boulder at the roadside. "Have something to eat!" he called, then sped off, his feet scarcely touching the ground. I went over to pick up the two hard, dry rolls and noticed that at some time a wild chrysanthemum had been added to the greenery in his rifle barrel and was now nodding at his ear.

He was already disappearing into the distance, but I could still see that torn patch of cloth hanging from his shoulder flapping in the breeze. I regretted not stitching it up for him before he had left. Now he would have to spend at least one night with a bared shoulder.

There were very few staff to run the first-aid post, so the county cadre mobilized several of the village women to fetch water, boil the cauldrons and do various other odd jobs. Our young woman came as well, smiling with closed lips as she had before. She occasionally stole a glance at me from the corner of her eye, but she frequently looked around her as if searching for something. Finally she asked me outright, "Where has that little comrade gone?" I told her he wasn't a member of the staff here and had gone to the front lines. She laughed in embarrassment and said, "When he came to borrow the quilt just now, I'm afraid he felt the sharp edge of my tongue!" She closed her lips in another smile, then set to work to lay the borrowed quilts and cotton padding out neatly on the doors and tables (two tables side by side served as a bed). I saw her put her own new lily-patterned quilt on a door outside under the eaves.

Night fell and a full moon rose above the horizon. Our general offensive had not yet been launched. As usual the enemy, dreading the night, had set great patches of the countryside ablaze and was continuing its barrage of blind shelling. Flare after flare was fired into the sky, nakedly exposing everything on the ground as if countless kerosene lamps had been lit under the moon. To launch an attack on a bright night like this presented enormous difficulties and would have to be paid for at considerable cost. I even began to hate that clear, bright moon.

The county cadre returned, bringing us several homemade dried-vegetable moon-cakes as a reward for our labors. It had slipped my mind that today was Mid-autumn Festival.

Ah—Mid-autumn Festival! At this moment outside every door in my home village would be placed a table on which was arranged incense, candles and several dishes of candied melon moon-cakes. The children would be impatiently longing for the incense to burn out so as to divide the things laid out for the enjoyment of the Moon Girl as soon as possible. They would be hopping and skipping beside the table and singing, "Moon, moon, bright and dandy, beat the gongs and buy some candy" . . . or perhaps, "Moon, moon is our nanny, shines on you and shines on me . . ." Thinking of the children, my thoughts turned to my young fellow townsman; several years ago the young man who hauled bamboos might very well have sung just those songs! . . . I took a bite of the delicious homemade mooncake and thought that he was probably at this moment lying behind the fortifications or at the regimental command post—or maybe he was running through those winding communication trenches.

A short time later our cannons sounded and several red signal flares streaked through the sky. The attack had begun. Not long afterward an intermittent stream of wounded men began to arrive at the first-aid post, and the atmosphere immediately became tense.

I took a notebook and began to register their names and units. Those with light wounds I could ask, but for the severely wounded I had to find their identification tags or look for a name on the inside of their jackets. Pulling out the identification tag of one badly wounded soldier, the word "courier" sent a sudden shiver down my spine, and my heart began to pound. Only after I had pulled myself together did I see below it "X Battalion." Ah! It wasn't him. My townsfellow was the regimental headquarters courier. But I felt an unaccountable desire to ask someone: might there be any wounded on the battlefield who had been missed? Apart from carrying messages, what else did couriers do on the battlefield? I didn't know myself why I should be asking these meaningless questions.

For the first hour or so of battle everything went smoothly. The wounded brought with them news that we had crossed the abatis[7]; we had crossed the wire entanglement; we had

occupied the enemy's front-line fortifications and driven the assault into the town. But then the news suddenly stopped. The wounded coming in would only answer briefly, "We're still fighting," or, "We're fighting in the streets." But from their mud-covered bodies, their look of utter exhaustion and even from the stretchers that looked as if they had been just dug out of a mud pit, everyone was well aware just what kind of battle was being fought at the front.

The first-aid post ran out of stretchers, and several badly wounded men who should have been sent immediately to the rear area hospital were unavoidably delayed. We could do nothing to relieve their pain; all we could do was wash their hands and faces with the aid of the village women, feed the ones who could eat, and put dry clothes on those who still carried their knapsacks. For some of them we also had to undo their clothing and wipe their bodies clean of mud and clotting blood.

I was accustomed to this kind of work, but the village women were both bashful and frightened. They were unwilling to touch the wounded men and vied[8] for the task of boiling the cauldrons—particularly that young bride. I talked to her for a long time before she assented with a blush, but she would only agree to be my assistant.

The sound of gunfire from the front had already become sporadic,[9] and it felt as if dawn should soon break, yet it was only midnight. Outside the moon shone brilliantly and seemed to have risen higher in the sky than usual. Another badly wounded soldier was brought in from the front. The beds inside were all filled, so I directed that he be put on

---

7. abatis (ab′ ə tis): a barricade of felled trees and barbed wire with branches pointed toward the enemy.

8. vied (vīd): competed.

9. sporadic (spə rad′ ik): happening from time to time; not regular.

the door outside under the eaves. The stretcher bearers lifted him on to the makeshift bed but remained at his side, unwilling to leave. An elderly stretcher bearer seized me by the shoulder, thinking I was a doctor. "Doctor! Whatever happens you must find a way to save this comrade. If you can save him, I . . . our whole stretcher-bearer corps will publicly commend you . . ." As he spoke, I discovered that all the other stretcher bearers were also gazing at me unblinkingly, as if a nod of my head would bring the wounded man instantaneous recovery. I wanted to explain the situation to them, but the young bride who had just approached the bed-head with a bowl of water suddenly gave a short scream. I pushed them aside and found myself looking down at a round, childish face, its once ruddy brown skin now an ashen yellow. His eyes were serenely closed, and at his shoulder, below the gaping hole in his uniform, that piece of torn cloth was still hanging limply.

"He did it all for us." The elderly stretcher bearer spoke with a heavy burden of guilt. "A dozen of us stretcher bearers were crowded into a small alley waiting for the chance to move forward. He was behind us. Then all of a sudden, from God knows which rooftop, one of those bastard reactionaries dropped a hand grenade right on top of us. While it was still smoking and rolling around, this comrade shouted to us to duck down, and leapt on top of it, covering it with his body."

The young woman gave another short scream. I fought back my tears and spoke to the stretcher bearers, sending them on their way. Turning back, I saw that the young bride had already quietly moved an oil lamp to the bedside and had undone his clothing; her recent bashfulness had completely disappeared and she was solemnly and piously washing his body. The tall young courier lay there without uttering a sound.

I suddenly came to my senses and leaping up, stumbled off to fetch the doctor. When the doctor and I hurried up with needle and syringe, the young woman was sitting down facing the bed.

Her head was lowered as stitch by stitch she repaired the hole in the shoulder of his uniform. The doctor listened to the courier's heart, then stood up slowly. "There's no need to give him an injection." I went forward and felt his hand: it was icy cold. But the young woman, as if seeing and hearing nothing, continued with her work, finely and closely stitching up the hole. I really couldn't stand the sight of it and said in a low voice, "Don't stitch it!" She threw me a peculiar glance, then lowered her head and continued to sew methodically, stitch after stitch. I wanted to pull her away, wanted to break through this cloying[10] atmosphere, wanted to see him sit up, see him bashfully smile. But unwittingly my hand knocked against something next to me. I stretched out my hand to feel it. It was the meal he had left me—two hard, dry, steamed rolls.

A health worker called someone to bring a coffin and took the quilt from the courier's body ready to place him inside. At this the young woman, her face ashen, seized the quilt from his hands and, glaring at him fiercely, laid half of the quilt smoothly over the bottom of the coffin and folded the remainder to cover the length of the courier's body. The health worker protested awkwardly, "The quilt . . . was borrowed from the people."

"It's mine," she shouted furiously, then wrenched her head away. In the moonlight I saw the tears shining in her eyes. I saw too that wine-colored quilt with its sprinkling of lilies—the symbols of purity and love—covering the face of that ordinary young man who hauled bamboo.

---

10. cloying (klo͝i′ iŋ): stifling; choking.

Reviewing Concepts

THE HERO: QUALITIES OF CHARACTER

*making
connections*

Each selection in this unit focuses on a character who is recognized in one way or another as heroic. Rama, Achilles, Aeneas, and Gassire, all heroes of cultural epics, have certain positive and negative qualities in common. Heroes as different as Socrates, St. Catherine, Antigone, Hecuba, and the courier in "Lilies" share characteristics with one another and with their epic counterparts as well. However, other character traits are unique to each hero.

Think back over the selections in this unit. Review the actions of each hero and the positive and negative qualities that stand out in your mind. Then copy the diagram that follows, adding more qualities and names as necessary.

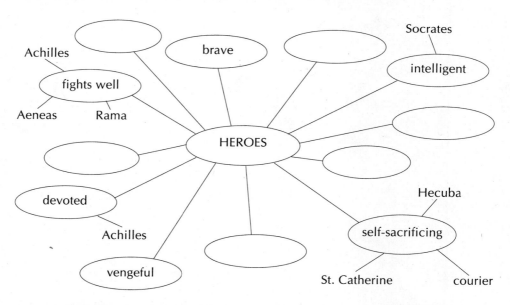

*describing
connections*

Review the information you have gathered on your diagram, looking for similarities and differences among the heroes depicted. Write an **essay** on the hero in literature. Compare and contrast your findings with those of your classmates.

Nostalgia, 1983, RAUL ANGUIANO.
Collection of René Arceo.

Hearts and Minds:

Literature of Self-Expression

*"Great literature, past or present,
is the expression of great knowledge
of the human heart."*

EDITH HAMILTON

Praising Nature

*I*n all times and places, individuals have marveled at the beauty and mystery of nature. In literature too, especially in poetry, nature has long played a significant role. For centuries, poets from around the world have attempted to express their intense personal feelings about the natural world: their love of nature and their joy and wonder in it.

For some poets, nature is simply a subject for descriptive poetry. Their poems may describe the peace and comfort found in quiet scenes of trees, rivers, and changing seasons. For other poets, nature is a retreat from the demands and restrictions of society or from the bustle and confusion of city life. Through their poetry, these poets may convey an intense longing for the pastoral scenes of their youth or joyfulness upon returning to those same landscapes.

For still other poets, nature is a compelling force that deeply affects their hearts and minds.

For them nature has the power to soothe a broken heart, nourish the soul, or create a spiritual experience. These poets appear to have a special bond or oneness with nature. Their poems describe feelings such as awe, humility, breathlessness, and exhilaration—intense feelings evoked by ordinary occurrences in nature, perhaps a rainbow or a sunset.

Although the feelings about nature expressed by poets vary dramatically, virtually all poets use imagery to convey their perceptions of the natural world. Poets may rely on simple description to paint pictures of the natural world, or they may employ more elaborate imagery. Occasionally, poets personify an aspect of nature, such as the sea, a storm, the moon, the morning, or the evening.

As you read the poems that follow, notice how the poets differ in the intensity of their feelings toward nature and in their use of imagery to express those feelings.

*L*iterary Vocabulary

INTRODUCED IN THIS SECTION

Mood. Mood is the feeling, or atmosphere, that a writer creates for the reader. One element that contributes to the mood of a poem is its imagery, that is, words and phrases that re-create sensory experiences for the reader. In the poem "Antigone," for example, Czeslaw Milosz reinforces a mood of despair in this image of Polynices' death: "For him / Some dark corner in a barren place outside the city / And in an empty helmet a moaning wind."

REVIEWED IN THIS SECTION

Imagery

Poem on Returning to Dwell in the Country

T'AO CH'IEN   A.D. 365–427   CHINA

My Heart Leaps Up

WILLIAM WORDSWORTH   1770–1850   ENGLAND

Biographies of T'ao Ch'ien and Wordsworth appear on pages 753 and 754.

Approaching the Poems

These two poems by T'ao Ch'ien (tou chyen) and William Wordsworth, written in times and places quite distant from each other, touch on a common theme: the human impulse to find harmony with nature. The speaker of the first poem, who has been living in the city, begins by recalling youthful feelings about the countryside. In the second poem the speaker expresses a deeply felt response to the sudden sight of a rainbow.

Building Vocabulary

These essential words are defined alongside the poems.

vulgar (vul′ gər): In youth I had nothing / that matched the **vulgar** tone, (page 267, lines 1–2)

piety (pī′ ə tē): And I could wish my days to be / Bound each to each by natural **piety**. (page 268, lines 8–9)

Connecting Writing and Reading

Imagine what your responses would be if you could be transported suddenly to each of the following natural settings:

a windswept ocean beach at night   a desert landscape in the Southwest
a mountain cabin in a snowstorm   a wooded hillside in autumn
a tropical rain forest   a Kansas wheat field in summer

Choose from this list two or three scenes that evoke strong positive or negative feelings, and describe these feelings in your journal. As you read the poems, compare the feelings about nature you recorded with those of each speaker.

Poem on Returning to Dwell in the Country

In youth I had nothing
    that matched the <u>vulgar</u>[1] tone,
For my nature always
    loved the hills and mountains.
5   Inadvertently I fell
    into the Dusty Net,[2]
Once having gone
    it was more than thirteen years.
The tame bird
10   longs for his old forest—
The fish in the house-pond
    thinks of his ancient pool.
I too will break the soil
    at the edge of the southern moor,
15   I will guard simplicity
    and return to my fields and garden.
My land and house—
    a little more than ten acres,
In the thatched cottage—
20   only eight or nine rooms.
Elms and willows
    shade the back verandah,
Peach and plum trees
    in rows before the hall.
25   Hazy and dimly seen
    a village in the distance,
Close in the foreground
    the smoke of neighbors' houses.
A dog barks
30   amidst the deep lanes,
A cock is crowing
    atop a mulberry tree.
No dust and confusion
    within my doors and courtyard;
35   In the empty rooms,
    more than sufficient leisure.
Too long I was held
    within the barred cage.
Now I am able
40   to return again to Nature.

1. **vulgar** (vul′ gər): coarse; lacking culture and refinement; indecent.

2. **Dusty Net:** phrase referring to worldliness and materialism.

My Heart Leaps Up

My heart leaps up when I behold
A rainbow in the sky:
So was it when my life began;
So is it now I am a man;
5 So be it when I shall grow old,
Or let me die!
The Child is father of the Man;
And I could wish my days to be
Bound each to each by natural piety.[1]

1. **piety** (pī′ ə tē): religious feeling and devotion.

Thinking About the Poems

A PERSONAL RESPONSE

sharing impressions

1. After reading the two poems, what impressions remain in your mind? Describe these impressions briefly in your journal.

constructing interpretations

2. How would you describe both speakers' views of nature?
Think about
- what each speaker gains from close contact with nature
- the feelings about nature experienced by each speaker when young
- the feelings of the speakers as revealed in the poems
- the ideas expressed about human nature by each speaker

3. Do you agree or disagree with T'ao Ch'ien about the superiority of country life? Cite details from the poem.

A CREATIVE RESPONSE

4. If instead of the word *leap* Wordsworth had used some synonym of that word, how would the meaning or the effect of the poem be changed?

5. If you were going to write a poem about one of the natural settings you responded to in your journal, would your tone be closer to that of T'ao Ch'ien or Wordsworth? Or would your tone be quite different? Explain.

> *Think about*
> - the definition of tone as the attitude a writer takes toward a subject
> - your own feelings about the natural setting
> - words, phrases, and punctuation marks in both poems that suggest the attitudes of the speakers toward their subjects

6. How do you think these two poets would react to life in the 1990's? Explain your answer, using details from the poems.

 nalyzing the Writer's Craft

MOOD AND IMAGERY

Reread the two poems, paying close attention to the way they make you feel. Then suggest words and phrases that describe the feeling, or mood, you associate with each poem.

Building a Literary Vocabulary. Mood is the feeling, or atmosphere, that a writer creates for the reader. One element that contributes to the mood of a poem is its imagery, that is, words and phrases that re-create sensory experiences for the reader. For example, in lines 21–22 of "Poem on Returning to Dwell in the Country," the visual image of elms and willows shading a verandah creates a quiet, peaceful mood.

Application: Analyzing Mood and Imagery. Working with a partner, identify four or five images in the second half of "Poem on Returning to Dwell in the Country." Then change the images in these lines so that they create a different mood. Have another pair of students review the new images and identify the mood that they create.

Time

GABRIELA MISTRAL   1889–1957   CHILE

Three Dawns

JEAN-JOSEPH RABÉARIVELO   1901–1937   MADAGASCAR

Biographies of Mistral and Rabéarivelo appear on pages 747 and 750.

Approaching the Poems

Each of these poems describes the passing of time, giving separate moments their own distinct character. It is noteworthy that poems so similar in subject and form are by writers from two different continents: Gabriela Mistral (gä′ brē ā′ lä mēs träl′) from South America and Jean-Joseph Rabéarivelo (rä bä ä re ve′ lô) from Africa.

Building Vocabulary

These essential words are defined alongside the poems.

grace: For **grace** lost and recovered / I stand humble. (page 271, lines 7–8)

poaching (pōch′ iŋ): Have you already seen the dawn / **poaching** in night's orchard? (page 273, lines 1–2)

suffused (sə fyo͞ozd′): from hills **suffused** with stars (page 274, line 16)

crucible (kro͞o′ sə bəl): Melted in the **crucible** of time (page 274, line 25)

lapidary (lap′ ə der′ ē): The **lapidary** night, ever so reluctantly / expiring, feels its millstones crumbling, (page 274, lines 28–29)

luminous (lo͞o′ mə nəs): A **luminous** slab / the artist would set / above his invisible tomb. (page 274, lines 32–34)

Connecting Writing and Reading

Think about the following times of day—daybreak, morning, afternoon, and night. In your journal, make a chart with four columns, one for each of these parts of the day. In each column of the chart, write a phrase or two describing visual or emotional qualities that you associate with that particular part of the day. For example, you might associate night with darkness or loneliness. As you read, add to your chart the qualities that the speakers in the poems give to parts of the day.

Time

Daybreak

My heart swells that the Universe
like a fiery cascade may enter.
The new day comes. Its coming
leaves me breathless.
5   I sing. Like a cavern brimming
I sing my new day.

For <u>grace</u>[1] lost and recovered
I stand humble. Not giving. Receiving.
Until the Gorgon[2] night,
10   vanquished, flees.

1. grace: love and mercy shown toward a person without that person earning or deserving it.

2. Gorgon (gôr′ gən): referring to any one of three sisters from Greek mythology who were so horrible-looking that anyone looking at them was turned to stone.

Morning

She has returned! She has returned!
Each morning the same and new.
Awaited every yesterday,
she must return this morning.

15 Mornings of empty hands
that promised and betrayed.
Behold this new morning unfold,
leap like a deer from the East,
awake, happy and new,
20 alert, eager and rich with deeds.

Brother, raise up your head
fallen to your breast. Receive her.
Be worthy of her who leaps up,
soars and darts like a halcyon,[3]
25 golden halcyon plunging earthward singing
Alleluia,[4] alleluia, alleluia!

3. halcyon (hal′ sē ən): bird like a kingfisher that, according to Greek legend, has a calming effect.
4. alleluia (al′ ə lōō′ yə): exclamation meaning "praise the Lord"; same as *hallelujah.*

Afternoon

I feel my heart melt like wax
in this sweetness:
slow oil, not wine,
30 my veins,
I feel my life fleeting
silent and sweet as a gazelle.

Night

Mountain ranges dissolve,
cattle wander astray,
35   the sun returns to its forge,
all the world slips away.
Orchard and garden are fading,
the farmhouse already immersed.
My mountains submerge their crests
40   and their living cry.

All creatures are sliding aslant
down toward forgetfulness and sleep.
You and I, also, my baby,
tumble down toward night's keep.

Three Dawns

Daybreak

Have you already seen the dawn
poaching[1] in night's orchard?
Here she comes homeward from the East
on pathways overgrown with iris;
5   she's all stained with milk
like those children of old raised by heifers;
her hands, carrying a torch,
are blue and black
like the lips of a girl
10   munching grapes.

One by one, the birds she has ensnared
escape, and fly before her.

1. poaching (pōch′ iŋ): trespassing, especially to hunt or steal.

Another Daybreak

Whether the first call came
from East or West no one knows;
15   but now,
from hills suffused[2] with stars
and shafts of darkness,
roosters sound the roll,
blowing into conch shells
20   and echoing from everywhere
until he-who-went-to-sleep-in-the-ocean
returns, and the lark rises to meet him
singing
songs drenched in dew.

Another

25   Melted in the crucible[3] of time
then frozen in the sea
the stars become a gem of many facets.
The lapidary[4] night, ever so reluctantly
expiring, feels its millstones crumbling,
30   crumbling like ashes in the wind
as lovingly they carve the prism,

A luminous[5] slab
the artist would set
above his invisible tomb.

2. suffused (sə fyo͞ozd′):
spread over so as to be filled
with something; covered.

3. crucible (kro͞o′ sə bəl): a
container made of a heat-
resistance substance, used to
melt ores, metals, and so on.

4. lapidary (lap′ ə der′ ē): of
or connected to the art of
cutting and engraving precious stones.

5. luminous (lo͞o′ mə nəs):
giving off light; shining;
bright.

Thinking About the Poems

A PERSONAL RESPONSE

sharing impressions

1. Which images from these poems linger in your mind? Respond in your journal.

constructing interpretations

2. Compare the qualities that the speakers in the poems associate with various times of day with those you associate with these same times of day.

Think about
- the emotional state of the speaker in each section of "Time"
- the opposing ideas in "Time": "grace lost and recovered" (line 7), "Each morning the same and new" (line 12), "empty hands/that promised and betrayed" (lines 15–16)
- visual and emotional qualities suggested by the images in "Three Dawns"
- similarities and differences between the details listed in each column of your prereading chart

3. When you consider each poem as a whole, what ideas about time come to mind?

A CREATIVE RESPONSE

4. How would rearranging the sections affect each poem?

A CRITICAL RESPONSE

5. What do you think about the way these poets personify the sun and parts of the day?

Think about
- personification as the attribution of human qualities to an object, animal, or idea
- qualities of the sun or parts of the day brought out through personification
- whether it is valid to attribute such qualities to nonhuman things

Connecting Reading and Writing

1. Drawing on your prereading chart, write a **poem** that brings out the qualities of your favorite time of day. Use personification if you wish. Read this poem aloud to your classmates.

Option: Write an **invitation** to a friend asking him or her to take a walk with you during your favorite time of day.

2. Imagine that you and a partner are making a short film inspired by one of these poems. Choose a piece of music to accompany a particular section and write a **note** to your partner explaining your choice.

Option: Illustrate a section of one of these poems and write a brief **artist's statement** to explain your work to viewers.

3. Draw up a **lesson plan** to show points about personification, tone, and mood that you would cover when comparing "Time," "Three Dawns," and "Adoration of the Disk," the ancient Egyptian poem in Unit 1.

Option: For display in your classroom, show common and unique elements of the three poems in a large **Venn diagram** with three interlocking circles.

Leaving Crete

SAPPHO   610–580 B.C.   ANCIENT GREECE

Drinking the Corinthian Sun

ODYSSEUS ELYTIS   born 1911   GREECE

Biographies of Sappho and Elytis appear on pages 751 and 742.

Approaching the Poems

The poets Sappho (saf′ ō) and Odysseus Elytis (ō dis′ ē əs e lē′ tis) lived 2,500 years apart but share the same homeland. Both poets celebrate nature in the special setting of Greece: specifically, in Corinth, a seaport in the southeast of the country, and in Crete, an island in the Aegean Sea. To read these poems is to imagine a land of legends and landscapes, timeless ruins in the clear Greek sunlight, the aroma of roses and lemon trees, vineyards close to the sea, and ancient sacred places important in history and myth.

Leaving Crete

Leaving Crete, come visit again our temple,
please, for me. So holy a place, a pleasant
stand of apple trees, and the altar wreathed in cedary
   incense.
Once within, you've water that chuckles cool through
5   mazy apple paths, with a dusk of roses
overgrown. There's sleep in the air: the wind and leaves
   are like magic.
Once within, you've pasture for horses grazing;
Maytime flowers are rich in the grass, the friendly
heavens breathe. . . .

Drinking the Corinthian Sun

Drinking the Corinthian sun
Reading the marble ruins
Striding over vineyard seas
Aiming with my harpoon
5   At votive[1] fish that elude[2] me
I found those leaves that the psalm[3] of the sun memorizes
The living land that desire rejoices
To open

I drink water, cut fruit
10   Plunge my hands through the wind's foliage
Lemon trees quicken the pollen of summer days
Green birds cut through my dreams
And I leave, my eyes filled
With a boundless gaze where the world becomes
15   Beautiful again from the beginning according to the heart's
     measure.

1. votive (vō′ tiv): offered in fulfillment of a vow.

2. elude (ē lo͞od′): to avoid or escape from by quickness or cunning.

3. psalm (säm): sacred poem or hymn.

© John Veltri, San Geronimo, California.

Expressing Love

The emotional nature of poetry has made it the most popular literary form for the celebration of love. Inspired by the joys and the sorrows of love, creative minds across cultures have turned to poetry to express their sentiments.

Some poems are unqualified declarations of love. In eloquent, often exaggerated language, they praise the virtues of a particular person and proclaim in great detail the profound effect that the person has had on the speaker's heart and mind. Occasionally, the object of the speaker's affection is glorified in such a manner as to assume nearly divine characteristics. Other poems describe unrequited love, a one-sided relationship in which the speaker longs for the attention of a loved one but receives little or no notice. Still others describe thwarted love, a disruption in a relationship brought about when loved ones are separated by war, misunderstanding, or death.

Poets throughout time have turned to images from nature to help them convey their feelings. At times, nature is used to mirror emotion. One poet, for example, uses the pallor of a flower and the sorrowful song of a bird to echo the speaker's own sadness over forsaken love. In other instances, nature appears to mock the speaker. For example, in one poem the cheerful sights and sounds of spring stand in sharp contrast to the speaker's dejection over a lengthy separation from her husband.

As you read the following poems about love, notice the feelings expressed by each speaker and the specific imagery used to convey those feelings. Consider why poetry has become the vehicle of self-expression for so many writers.

Literary Vocabulary

Sonnet. A sonnet is a poem of fourteen lines that follows a set rhyme scheme. The two main types of sonnets are the Italian, or Petrarchan, and the English, or Shakespearean. In this part of the book, you will learn about both types.

Rhyme Scheme. Rhyme scheme is the pattern of end rhyme in a poem. The pattern is charted by assigning a letter of the alphabet, beginning with the letter *a,* to each line. Lines that rhyme are given the same letter. In "The spring returns," a sonnet that you will study, the rhyme scheme of the first four lines is *abba.*

Couplet. A couplet is a rhymed pair of lines. The Shakespearean sonnets you will read in this part of the book make use of couplets.

The Song of a Soldier's Wife

ĐẶNG TRẦN CÔN   1710–1745   AND   PHAN HUY ÍCH   1750–1822   VIETNAM

Written in Behalf of My Wife

LI PO   A.D. 701–762   CHINA

A biography of Li Po appears on page 746.

Approaching the Poems

Both of the following poems express the feelings of a wife separated from her husband. "The Song of a Soldier's Wife" was written by the eighteenth-century Vietnamese poet Phan Huy Ích (fän hwē i), who based his writing on a poem written by Đặng Trần Côn (däŋ truŋ kōn) in classical Chinese. The theme of separation caused by war has made the poem popular among the Vietnamese, whose history has been a turbulent one. Li Po (lē bô) writes "in behalf of" his wife, making her the speaker of a poem in which he imagines what her thoughts might be at a time when he is away from home.

Building Vocabulary

These essential words are defined alongside "The Song of a Soldier's Wife."
assuaged (ə swājd′): Hearts won't feel **assuaged**. (page 283, line 30)
hoary (hôr′ ē): United, they can't part till **hoary** age. (page 292, line 352)

Connecting Writing and Reading

Using the following list, make a bar graph showing the relative strength of the various emotions you have experienced when separated from someone you love.

anger or bitterness	loss of self-esteem
self-pity	resentment at having to carry on alone
regret	pride in what the loved one was accomplishing
loneliness	longing to be reunited
fear and worry	indifference to the absence of the loved one

As you read these poems, take notes on the sometimes shifting feelings expressed by each of the speakers as she endures separation from her loved one.

The Song of a Soldier's Wife

When all through earth and heaven rise dust storms,
how hard and rough, the road a woman walks!
O thou that rulest in yonder blue above,
who is the cause and maker of this woe?

5 In our Ch'ang-an[1] drums beat and moonlight throbs.
On Mount Kan-ch'üan[2] fires burn and clouds glow red.
The Emperor, leaning on his precious sword,
at midnight calls for war and sets the day.

The realm has known three hundred years of peace—
10 now soldiers don their battle dress once more.
At daybreak heralds speed them through the mists—
the law outweighs what they may feel inside.

Full armed with bows and arrows, they fare forth,
from wives and children wrenching their numb hearts.
15 As banners wave and drums resound far off,
grief spreads from chamber door to mountain pass.

Born to a race of heroes, you, my love,
discard your brush and ink for tools of war.
You vow to capture citadels for the throne—
20 your sword will spare no foe of Heaven's sway.

A man will win a horseskin for his shroud;
his life he'll drop in battle like goose down.
In war attire you leave and cross the Wei,[3]
cracking your whip while roars the autumn wind.

25 Beneath the bridge the brook flows crystal-clear.
Along the nearby path thrives grass, still young.
I see you off and sorrow—oh, to be
your horse on land, your vessel on the stream!

The water flows, yet grief won't wash away.
30 The grass smells sweet, yet hearts won't feel assuaged.[4]
We say goodbye, then we hold hands again—
we try to part, keep halting at each step.

1. Ch' ang-an (chän än): the former capital of China.

2. Mount Kan-ch' üan (gän chüan): a mountain two hundred miles from Ch'ang-an, where beacon fires were lit and smoke signals sent up to warn the capital of impending attacks by barbarians.

♦ **Line 21:** A shroud is a cloth used to wrap the body of a dead person. To be buried in the skin of a horse was considered a soldier's destiny.

3. Wei (wā): a river often crossed by Chinese troops on expeditions against barbarians.

4. assuaged (ə swājd'): lessened or eased.

My heart pursues you like the moon on high.
Your heart leaps space, bound for the Thousand Peaks.[5]
35 The wine once drained, you wave the Lung-ch'üan sword[6]
and thrust it toward the lair of those wild beasts.

You'll tread in Chieh-tzu's steps and seize Lou-lan.[7]
You'll reach Man-hsi, discussing old Fu-po.[8]
Your coat is red like sunglow from the clouds;
40 your horse is white as if all soaked with snow.

A jumbled din of drums and horses' bells—
we huddle face to face, then have to part.
Here at this bridge we'll go our separate ways—
forlorn beside the road, I watch flags fly.

45 Carts form the van, approaching Willow Camp.
Horsemen bring up the rear at Poplar Field.
In haste the troops escort you on your way—
do willows and poplars know I break inside?

Flutes pipe and send faint echoes from afar.
50 Flags file and stir vague shadows to and fro.
Your tracks pursue the trail of clouds on clouds—
I watch the mountain range and mourn our home.

Your way leads you to lands of rain and wind—
mine takes me back to our old room, our bed.
55 We turn and look, but all has come between—
green mountains and blue clouds roll on and on.

You in Han-yang[9] still turn your head and gaze.
Here at Hsiao-hsiang[10] I still stare after you.
Between, the Hsiao-hsiang mists shut off Han-yang.
60 Between, the Han-yang trees shut off Hsiao-hsiang.

We look to find each other but see none—
we only see those green mulberry groves.
Mulberry groves all share one shade of green—
of your own grief and mine, which hurts the more?

65 Since you left for the realm of wind and sand,
where are you resting on this moonlit night?
Of old and now, such are all battlegrounds,
those endless wastes the elements strike at.

5. Thousand Peaks: Ch'ien-shan, a mountain near the Korean border.

6. Lung-ch'üan sword (lʊʊŋ chüan): a magic sword, the ancient Chinese equivalent of King Arthur's Excalibur.

7. Chieh-tzu (jye dzə) . . . **Lou-lan** (lô län): Chieh-tzu was a famous general who returned from battle with the head of the king of Lou-lan.

8. Man-hsi (män Hē) . . . **Fu-po** (fōō bô̂): Fu-po was a general who in A.D. 43 put down resistance to Chinese control of Man-hsi, an area in northern Vietnam.

◆ **Lines 56–64:** Notice here and in later passages how nature imagery is used to suggest the separation of the lovers.

9. Han-yang (hän yäŋ): a city that was the western capital.

10. Hsiao-hsiang (Hyʊu Hyäŋ): the meeting place of the Hsiao and Hsiang rivers. In Chinese tradition, the Hsiang River is associated with lovelorn grief.

Men's faces shrivel under raw wind blasts,
70   and horses' knees will buckle fording streams.
For pillows all hug saddles or clasp drums—
all lie asleep on white sand or green moss.

Today Han troops pitch camp inside Pai-teng.[11]
Tomorrow Huns will watch from their Blue Sea.[12]
75   A scene of streams and mountains, near and far—
they roll on and break off, they rise and fall.

From mountain peaks dew drops like rain at dusk,
and down in streams the fords still lie waist-deep.
Pity those who've long worn their coats of mail—[13]
80   their homesick faces bear a world of gloom.

Inside brocaded curtains, does He know?
A soldier's portrait who can paint for Him?
I think of you who've wandered all these years,
from the Vast Desert to the Lonesome Pass.[14]

85   You've braved the wilds where snakes and tigers lurk;
you've shivered dwelling with chill dew and wind.
I climb on high and watch the pall of clouds—
whose heart can stay unstirred by longing pangs?

You left and traveled toward the far Southeast—
90   who knows where you are fighting at this hour?
All those who for so long have gone to war
have learned to treat their lives like leaves of grass.

With valiant spirit they'll pay off great debts—
how many, courting peril, will die old?
95   The moon shines dangling over hushed Mount Ch'i.[15]
Winds blow on lonesome tombs along the Fei.[16]

Winds howl and howl at ghosts of those war's killed—
on soldiers' faces shines the stalking moon.
O men, alive or dead, has anyone
100   portrayed your faces or invoked your souls?

The brand of war has marked old streams and hills—
a traveler, passing by, feels wrung at heart.
A man must spend his prime on battlegrounds:
with hair all streaked with frost, Pan Ch'ao[17] came home.

11. Pai-teng (bī deŋ): a fortress where Emperor Han Kao-tsu was besieged for seven days by Tartars in 200 B.C.

12. Blue Sea: the Koko Nor, a large lake.

13. mail: flexible body armor made of small linked chains.

◆ **Lines 81–82:** Note the cynical reference to the Emperor ("He"), seen as unaware of the suffering of soldiers.

14. Vast Desert . . . Lonesome Pass: the Gobi desert and a mountain pass known as Hsiao-kuan.

15. Mount Ch'i (chē): Mount Ch'i-lien, scene of a historic victory over the Tartars.

16. Fei (fā): a river on whose banks a crushing military defeat took place in A.D. 384.

17. Pan Ch'ao (bän chou): a soldier who for thirty-one years had fought against various tribes and returned home only to die soon afterward.

105 I think of you as you bear pains and hurts—
armed with a sword, a saddle, you rush through
windswept shores, moonlit woods, as arrows whiz
past horses' heads and spears attack the walls.

A hundred dangers strew the path of fame—
110 you toil and struggle, never taking rest.
To whom can you confide what moves your heart?
I'm here at home, you're there at heaven's edge.

Inside this door I live my fated life,
but were you born to roam at heaven's edge?
115 We hoped to join like fish and water once:
instead, we're split apart—a stream, a cloud.

I never thought I'd be a soldier's wife,
you never aped rich playboys wandering far.
Why are those streams and hills dividing us
120 and causing us to sorrow day and night?

Endowed with grace and charm in youthful bloom,
we formed a couple bound by bonds of love.
Who has the heart to break young lovers up
and build a mountain wall between the two?

125 No orioles yet on willows—you set out
and promised you'd come back when cuckoos sang.
Cuckoos have followed orioles grown old—
before the house, some swallows chirp and peep.

Plum trees were still wind-shy when you set forth
130 and promised you'd come back as peaches bloomed.
Peach blossoms now have fled with their east wind—
beside the river, roses fall to shreds.

You told me once you'd meet me in Lung-hsi—[18]
since dawn I looked for you but saw no trace.
135 I choked back tears as leaves fell on my hair—
at noon the village woke to birds' shrill cries.

You pledged to meet me by the Han-yang bridge.
Till nightfall I awaited you in vain.
I choked back tears as winds lashed at my gown—
140 the evening tide was surging over shore.

♦ **Lines 125–132:** In these
lines, nature imagery is used
to convey the passage of time
during which the lovers have
been separated.

18. Lung-hsi (lʊʊŋ Hē): a
district in Kansu in northwest
China.

I've sent you word but I haven't seen you back—
the poplar's catkins, wilted, strew green moss.
Green moss in many patches spreads around—
I pace the courtyard, turmoil in my heart.

♦ **Lines 142–144:** Here images
from nature suggest the mood
of the speaker. Catkins are
drooping, spike-like flowers
without petals.

145   Your letters have come home, but you're not home.
The sun sends tilted beams through my thin blinds.
The sun keeps shining through day after day—
why have you failed nine pledges out of ten?

Let's reckon—ever since you went away
150   the lotus leaves like coins have thrice peeped forth.
Pity those who must man such distant posts,
with shelter far from home, near Mount Huang-hua.[19]

19. Mount Huang-hua (hwäŋ
hwä): the scene of a famous
victory over barbarian
invaders.

Who has no kin or family to love?
All long and miss old parents or young wives.
155   Your mother's hair is covered now with frost—
Your son who's still at suck needs tender care.

The mother waits heart-weary at the door.
The child in hunger cries for his chewed rice.
I feed your mother, serving as her son,
160   and like a father teach your child to read.

Alone, I feed the old and teach the young—
I bear all burdens, yearning for my man.
I long for you while stars will whirl away
as spring's passed by and winter's drawing near.

165   Let's count those years of parting—three or four.
My heart has grown a thousand more snarled threads.
If only I could nestle by your side,
revealing all the bitterness I've felt!

This hairpin from the Han, your wedding gift,
170   and that Ch'in mirror jointly we looked in—
by whom could I transmit both there to you
and let you know how much I'm missing you?

The ring my finger wears I've so admired,
the emerald comb I toyed with as a child—
175   by whom could I dispatch both there to you
as tender keepsakes from the one you love?

For many springs news traveled back and forth—
this spring's still bare of any sign from you.
In vain I've hoped for letters seeing geese—
180   in vain I've made a quilt at the first frost.

The wester thwarts the path of geese in flight.
Alas, out there you're drenched by snow and rain.
You live with rain as screen, with snow as tent—
I think of you and feel your cold out there.

185   My message on brocade[20] I seal, unseal.
I toss the coins and dread what they portend.
At dusk, I stand beneath the eaves, forlorn—
the midnight moon lights pillowed hair, unkempt.

Have I a mind gone crazy, addled wits?
190   Bedazed, I drift and wander in a void.
With shame I set my hairpin, don my skirt—
my raveled hair's awry, my waistband's loose.

In staggering steps I pace a lonesome porch.
I often raise and drop a diaphanous shade.
195   Outside the shade no magpie brings glad news—
inside, perhaps, the lamp knows how I feel.

The lamp may know, but nothing can it do—
my heart must bear its anguish all alone.
Its sorrow finds no utterance in words—
200   pity the shadow by the lamp's bright flame.

Cocks crow the night's fifth watch as dewdrops fall.
Sophoras[21] flutter tossing shadows down.
An hour of waiting drags and seems a year—
my grief lies deep and sullen like the sea.

205   Incense I burn—my soul, enraptured, roams.
The mirror I look in—my tears stream forth.
I try to pluck the lute, but I so dread
to break its strings or disarray its frets.

If with the easter[22] I could send this heart,
210   I'd pay pure gold and send it to Mount Yen.[23]
It grieves me that Mount Yen cannot be reached—
in thought I search for you through vast, vast skies.

20. **message on brocade:** a reference to the story of a wife who embroidered a poem on brocade and sent it to her husband, who had been fighting against barbarians for many years in the Gobi desert. The king, moved by her love for her husband, allowed him to come home.

21. **Sophoras** (sə fō′ rəz): plants which belong to the genus *sophora* and are native to warm climates.

22. **easter:** the east wind.
23. **Mount Yen:** a mountain in Outer Mongolia.

The sky's too vast to search from end to end—
My sorrowed yearn for you will never cease.
215 As nature mourns, a human heart knows grief—
hoarfrost soaks trees, rain mutes grasshoppers' cries.

Frost hammers willows wearing them away.
Rain saws plane-trees destroying withered boughs.
On high birds chill their wings amidst dense mists.
220 Insects on walls lament—far off bells toll.

A cricket's chirps, with moonbeams, strew the yard.
Outside the porch winds blast the plantain leaves.
A sudden gust bursts through—the curtain stirs.
The moon casts shades of flowers upon the blind.

225 Flowers bask in floods of moonlight smooth as silk—
the moon enfolds each flower, sets it aglow.
A play of moon and flower, of flower and moon—
watching the moon, the flower, I hurt within.

How can I tell them all, the pains I feel?
230 A woman's skills I have neglected since.
I've shunned the sewing needle, spurned the loom—
I've stopped embroidering orioles in pairs.

I loathe to paint my face, I hate to talk,
leaning against the window morn and eve.
235 Against the window, brooding, I just lean.
You're gone—whom would my rouge and powder charm?

I groom myself no more—grief fills my heart.
I grieve for you who're rambling far from home.
I'm like Ch'ang O[24] who pines there in the moon,
240 the Weaver-Maid who sobs by Heaven's Stream.[25]

Who'd make a pillow heaping grief on grief?
Who'd cook a dinner boiling gloom and gloom?
I would allay my pain with flowers and wine,
but sorrow stales the wine and wilts the flowers.

245 I clap jade castanets—they give no sound.
I hug the zither—frets fall off my hand.
I grieve for you whom duty sent away
to tread long trails with hunger in your bag.

♦ **Lines 213–228:** This is another passage in which nature images are used to reflect the speaker's feelings.

24. Ch'ang O: a woman who, according to Chinese mythology, stole the elixir of life from her husband and fled to the moon, where she has been living without a mate ever since.

25. Weaver-Maid . . . Heaven's Stream: In Chinese mythology, the Herdboy and the Weaver-Maid are heavenly lovers who have been separated. They are seen as stars separated by "Heaven's Stream," the Milky Way.

The mocking cuckoo's song makes me shed tears.
250 The watchman's drumbeats tug at my heart's strings.
My lovely looks have changed, turned drawn and pale.
How bitter parting is! I know the taste.

I taste of bitterness and know my heart.
Who's given it to me, this bitter taste?
255 Because of you tears flow in two long streams.
Because of you I shiver all alone.

I'm not to join you there inside your tent—
my tears are not to wet your battle cap.
I can come near you only in a dream—
260 At night I prowl all riverbanks for you.

I look for you on the road to Yang Tower.[26]
I find you at the harbor of the Hsiang.
When happy chance brings us together thus,
we share an hour of love, a spring night's dream.

265 I curse my lot unequal to my dream,
each time I've met you there in Lung or Han.
How I regret[27] each dream on waking up!
All love amounts to nothing, in a dream.

Still, my true heart can't be torn off from you—
270 it ever follows you each day, each hour.
It follows you, yet nowhere are you seen
when on a height I peer for your cart's wheels.

Southward I look, but duckweeds[28] hide the stream.
Grass jasper blue, mulberry leaves bright green.
275 Some village huts that totter with the wind.
Below the twilit cliff, a flock of storks.

Northward I look—some groups of traveler's inns.
Clouds, flush with trees, block out the soaring hills.
Wild rice grows scattered at the ramparts' foot.
280 Rain sprinkles—in a chamber sighs a flute.

On the eastern hills I see but leaves and leaves.
A pheasant flaps its wings, plum branches dance.
Thick mists like billows surge above the woods—
a wind-blown bird, astray, cries piteous cries.

26. Yang Tower: the mountain where a legendary king met the goddess of love in his dreams.

27. regret: miss; mourn the loss of.

◆ **Lines 272–292:** In this passage the speaker, always watching for the return of her husband, stands upon a height and looks out in all four directions. The imagery used to describe the landscape suggests much about her mood.

28. duckweeds: clover ferns, plants that symbolize longing and homesickness.

285 Westward the river turns and twists its course.
Geese sail on high, waves steer an angler's boat.
Reed swamps lie snugly tucked among the pines—
across the stream, some man is going home.

I look around exploring earth and sky—
290 I often go upstairs, come down again.
Cloud rises after cloud to stop my gaze—
where is Jade Pass,[29] the field of men at war?

How could I get that wand[30] and shrink the earth,
or find that magic scarf[31] and bridge far shores?
295 I'd turn to stone,[32] but then I'd have no tears
to weep for you, awaiting you upstairs.

When I gaze back at willows, how I wish
I'd counseled you to spurn a noble's rank.
I wonder—while you're traveling your long road,
300 does it, your heart, feel what my own heart feels?

If only it would feel that way, your heart!
Then I'd not let my mind pursue wild thoughts.
My heart turns toward the sun just like that flower—
as roams your heart, I dread the sun will set.

305 The sun has spurned his flower and let her wilt.
The flower's wilted as the sun won't shine.
Wilted, she drops her petals by the wall—
I've often watched them drop on dew-cold nights.

The garden's orchids all have been plucked off—
310 now duckweeds near the bank are breathing scent.
Clad in my robe, I stroll before the house,
my languid gaze on heaven's glorious vault.

The Silver River[33] gleams and dims by fits.
The Strider[34] will appear and disappear.
315 The clouds now glow all bright, now turn pale.
The Dipper's handle shifts from east to west.

My looks and charms keep fading year by year,
and still my man keeps wandering far away.
We were a body and its shadow once—
320 now we stand worlds apart like Shen and Shang.[35]

29. Jade Pass: a place that commanded the road to Central Asia.

30. wand: a legendary bamboo walking staff with which one could travel a great distance quickly.

31. magic scarf: in a fairy tale, a scarf that could serve as a bridge in an emergency.

32. turn to stone: an allusion to a folk tale in which a woman stood waiting for her absent husband and eventually turned to stone.

♦ **Lines 303–308:** Here the speaker draws an analogy between her heart and a sunflower.

♦ **Lines 313–316:** Again a sense of the passing of time is conveyed, this time through images describing the night sky.

33. Silver River: Milky Way.

34. Strider: a constellation that stands for manly ambition.

35. Shen and Shang: evening and morning stars that never appear in the same sky and thus symbolize the separation of lovers.

You're galloping your horse on cloud-wrapped trails—
I'm shuffling slippers through moss-covered paths.
Day after day the spring wind's brought no news—
How many happy seasons we have missed!

325 They come to mind, those flowers of Yao and Wei,[36]
wedding their gold and crimson on spring winds.
And lo the Herdboy and his Weaver-Maid
who cross the Stream beneath the autumn moon.

I mourn the wife inside an empty room
330 who lets her finest seasons go to waste.
The days and months like shuttles hurtle by,
and youth is springtide ebbing in a flash.

In spring I brood, in fall I seethe with rage—
I've known more parting sorrow than shared joy.
335 Anger and grief entangle all their threads—
how can a reed, a willow stop spring's flight?

There was Wen-chün,[37] a beauty in the past:
afraid that age would gray her head, she grieved.
And there was P'an whose face shone like a flower:
340 as he feared frost would mar his hair, he wept.

I weep my looks, a flower in its full bloom,
and mourn fleet time which slides and slips away.
I weep a thankless fate, mourn blossom years—
a fresh young maiden turns a matron soon.

345 Upon this moonlit tower I dream your face.
Inside that flower-decked room scents waft about.
On Heaven I must blame our life gone wrong—
I grieve and grieve for you, for my own self.

Haven't you seen those mandarin ducks afield?
350 They go in pairs as mates and won't soon split.
Haven't you watched those swallows on a roof?
United, they can't part till hoary[38] age.

Two ch'iung-ch'iung beasts[39] stay close, head touching
   head.
Two chien-chien birds[40] fly jointly, wing to wing.
355 The willow and the lotus are mere plants,
yet each boasts wedded leaves and coupled flowers.

36. Yao and Wei (you, wā): in ancient China, two aristocratic clans that adopted the yellow peony and red peony, respectively, as their heraldic emblems.

37. Wen-chün (wən jün): a woman who, when aged, regained her husband's interest by writing a moving poem.

38. hoary (hôr′ ē): having white or gray hair because very old; ancient.

39. *ch'iung-ch'iung* (chyooŋ chyooŋ) **beasts**: in Chinese mythology, white horse-like creatures that could run, male and female together, for a hundred miles at a stretch.

40. *chien-chien* (jyen jyen) **birds**: fabulous birds with only one wing, so that two must join their wings in order to fly.

That's how in nature ties of love will bind—
why keep two humans severed, here and there?
May we in future lives become two birds
360   that join their wings, two trees that twine their boughs!

No doubt, a thousand lifetimes love shall last,
but life together here and now is best.
To silver may age never turn your hair!
And may I ever keep the looks of youth!

365   Oh, let me be your shadow, follow you!
Where you're to go, you'll find me by your side.
I wish you will remain out in the sun
as you perform all duties of a man.

Serve well your country with a true-red heart.
370   Defend your people with an iron will.
The Chun-yü's blood and Jou-chih heads[41] will sate
your thirst and hunger as your drink and meat.

Time after time you rush at swords and spears,
but Heaven will protect a loyal man.
375   You'll win all battles, and from our north pass
to our west hills all arms will be laid down.

Banners and flags will leave the border posts—
bound for the Capital, men will sing of triumph.
Mount Yen will bear your name in stone-writ odes.
380   Your trophies you will offer to the throne.

You'll wash your weapons in the Silver Stream.[42]
They will make music and intone your praise.
In merit you'll compare with Ch'in and Huo—[43]
your fame will grace Mist Tower, Unicorn Hall.[44]

385   A state grandee, you'll shine in sash and cap—
on monuments public joy will be engraved.
Your son will share in bounty from above—
with you your wife will bask in Heaven's grace.

I'm not a foolish woman like Su's wife.
390   and you're as clever as those Lo-yang men.
When you come home and bear that seal of gold,
will I stay at the loom and show disdain?

41. Chun-yü's blood and Jou-chih heads (joon yü, yoo ji): a reference to rebel forces.

42. Silver Stream: the Milky Way. In a well-known antiwar poem, the Chinese poet Tu Fu (A.D. 712–770) wished that "some great man could pull Heaven's Stream down and wash all weapons clean, never to be used again."

43. Ch'in and Huo (hwô): famous generals.

44. Mist Tower, Unicorn Hall: places where heroes were honored.

♦ **Lines 389–392:** These lines allude to a poor, unknown scholar named Su Ch'in, who had lived in the city of Lo-yang. According to legend, his wife disregarded him, refusing to leave her weaving loom when she saw him come home.

I'll take off you the soldier's coat of mail.
I'll shake off you the wanderer's dew and dust.
395 For you I'll fill a golden cup with wine.
For you I'll wear enchanting scent and powder.

You'll view my tear-stained kerchiefs one by one.
You'll read my song of grief line after line.
We'll substitute gay lines for doleful lines
400 while sipping wine, we'll tell each other all.

We'll slowly fill and drain cup after cup;
we'll softly sing one stanza, then the next.
We'll hum linked verse and face to face we'll drink,
staying together till a ripe old age.

405 This parting grief—we'll make up for it all:
we'll have and hold each other, blessing peace.
I sing and with my love send you this wish:
thus may you act and live, a gallant man!

Written in Behalf of My Wife

To cleave a running stream with a sword,
The water will never be severed.
My thoughts that follow you in your wanderings
Are as interminable as the stream.
5   Since we parted, the grass before our gate
In the autumn lane has turned green in spring.
I sweep it away but it grows back,
Densely it covers your footprints.
The singing phoenixes were happy together;
10 Startled, the male and the female each flies away.
On which mountaintop have the drifting clouds stayed?
Once gone, they never are seen to return.
From a merchant traveling to Ta-lou,[1]
I learn you are there at Autumn Cove.
15 In the Liang Garden[2] I sleep in an empty embroidered bed;
On the Yang Terrace[3] you dream of the drifting rain.
Three times my family has produced a prime minister;
Then moved to west Ch'in[4] since our decline.
We still have our old flutes and songs,
20 Their sad notes heard everywhere by neighbors.
When the music rises to the purple clouds,
I cry for the absence of my beloved.
I am like a peach tree at the bottom of a well,
For whom will the blossoms smile?
25 You are like the moon high in the sky,
Unwilling to cast your light on me.
I cannot recognize myself when I look in the mirror,
I must have grown thin since you left home.
If only I could own the fabled parrot[5]
30 To tell you of the feelings in my heart!

Guide for Interpretation

◆ **Line 3:** The speaker here is Li Po's wife; the wandering poet is speaking in her behalf.

1. **Ta-lou** (dä lō): a mountain area in southwest China.

2. **Liang** (lyäŋ) **Garden:** a region in Honan in northeast China.

3. **On the Yang Terrace:** in the area of the Yangtze River.

4. **Ch'in:** formerly a feudal state in northwest China.

◆ **Lines 23–26:** The speaker describes the relationship with her husband in terms of nature imagery.

5. **fabled parrot:** in folklore, a bird that could carry messages to a loved one.

Thinking About the Poems

sharing impressions

1. What overall feeling are you left with after reading these poems? Record this feeling in your journal.

constructing interpretations

2. How would you describe the relationship in each poem between the speaker and the loved one?

> **Think about**
> - the image in lines 1–2 of "Written in Behalf of My Wife": "To cleave a running stream with a sword, / The water will never be severed."
> - shifting or conflicting feelings expressed by the speaker in "The Song of a Soldier's Wife"

3. In what ways do the speakers of these poems express some of the same feelings that you have experienced when separated from a loved one? Refer to your prereading notes.

A CREATIVE RESPONSE

4. How would these poems be different if the speakers were men left behind by women?

A CRITICAL RESPONSE

5. What opinions do you think these poets have about war, love, nature, marriage, or any of the other subjects dealt with in these poems? Express these opinions as thematic statements.

6. From the two poems, select ten nature images that you find especially striking and explain any connections you see between the images and the themes in the poems.

Rapt in the one fond thought
The spring returns

FRANCESCO PETRARCH   1304–1374   ITALY

No longer mourn for me
When in the chronicle of wasted time

WILLIAM SHAKESPEARE   1564–1616   ENGLAND

Biographies of Petrarch and Shakespeare appear on pages 749 and 752.

Approaching the Poems

The sonnet is a form of poetry used by poets since the thirteenth century to express deep and intense feelings. In the fourteenth century Francesco Petrarch perfected the form in Italian. More than two centuries later, William Shakespeare, using a modified form, perfected the sonnet in English. Each of the following sonnets expresses deep feelings about the experience of love. Petrarch's two sonnets show his longing for Laura, with whom he fell in love on Good Friday, April 6, 1327. He wrote the second sonnet after her death. Scholars have not identified conclusively the person or persons who inspired Shakespeare's sonnets.

Building Vocabulary

These essential words are defined alongside "When in the chronicle of wasted time."

chronicle (krän′ i kəl): When in the **chronicle** of wasted time (page 299, line 1)

prefiguring (prē fig′ yər iŋ): So all their praises are but prophecies / Of this our time, all you **prefiguring**; (page 299, lines 9–10)

divining (də vīn′ iŋ): And, for they looked but with **divining** eyes, / They had not skill enough your worth to sing: (page 299, lines 11–12)

Connecting Writing and Reading

Imagine someone, such as a movie, television, or rock star, with whom you would love to have a date. In your journal describe your feelings for that person. As you read, compare your feelings with the feelings expressed in each of the sonnets.

Rapt in the one fond thought

Rapt in the one fond thought that makes me stray
from other men and walk this world alone,
sometimes I have escaped myself and flown
to seek the very one that I should flee;
5   so fair and fell[1] I see her passing by
that the soul trembles to take flight again,
so many armèd sighs are in her train,
this lovely foe to Love himself and me!
And yet, upon that high and clouded brow
10   I seem to see a ray of pity shine,
shedding some light across the grieving heart:
so I call back my soul, and when I vow
at last to tell her of my hidden pain,
I have so much to say I dare not start.

Guide for Interpretation

1. fell: cruel; devastating.

◆ **Line 7:** *Train* can mean "a group of persons following as attendants in a procession." *Train* also means "the persons or vehicles that carry supplies, ammunition, and food for combat troops." Consider how this second meaning applies to the poem and look for other words or phrases in the poem that reinforce this interpretation.

The spring returns

The spring returns, the spring wind softly blowing
Sprinkles the grass with gleam and glitter of showers,
Powdering pearl and diamond, dripping with flowers,
Dropping wet flowers, dancing the winter's going;
5   The swallow twitters, the groves of midnight are glowing
With nightingale music and madness; the sweet fierce
   powers
Of love flame up through the earth; the seed-soul towers
And trembles; nature is filled to overflowing . . .
The spring returns, but there is no returning
10   Of spring for me. O heart with anguish burning!
She that unlocked all April in a breath
Returns not . . . And these meadows, blossoms, birds,
These lovely gentle girls—words, empty words,
As bitter as the black estates of death!

No longer mourn for me

No longer mourn for me when I am dead
Than you shall hear the surly sullen bell
Give warning to the world that I am fled
From this vile world, with vilest worms to dwell.
5 Nay, if you read this line, remember not
The hand that writ it, for I love you so
That I in your sweet thoughts would be forgot
If thinking on me then should make you woe.
O, if, I say, you look upon this verse
10 When I, perhaps, compounded am with clay,
Do not so much as my poor name rehearse,
But let your love even with my life decay,
   Lest the wise world should look into your moan
   And mock you with me after I am gone.

When in the chronicle
of wasted time

When in the chronicle[1] of wasted time
I see descriptions of the fairest wights,[2]
And beauty making beautiful old rime
In praise of ladies dead and lovely knights;
5 Then, in the blazon[3] of sweet beauty's best,
Of hand, of foot, of lip, of eye, of brow,
I see their antique pen would have expressed
Even such a beauty as you master now.
So all their praises are but prophecies
10 Of this our time, all you prefiguring;[4]
And, for they looked but with divining[5] eyes,
They had not skill enough your worth to sing:
   For we, which now behold these present days,
   Have eyes to wonder, but lack tongues to praise.

1. chronicle (krän′ i kəl): a history or record of things that happened.

2. wights (wīts): people.

3. blazon (blā′ zən): record honoring the memory of the dead.

4. prefiguring (prē fig′ yər iŋ): picturing in advance.

5. divining (də vīn′ iŋ): discovering or understanding through supernatural insight.

Thinking About the Poems

sharing
impressions

1. What impressions do you have about the experience of love, based on how it is described in these sonnets? Note your impressions in your journal.

constructing
interpretations

2. How would you describe the speakers and their feelings?
   Think about
   • the speaker's frustrations in "Rapt in the one fond thought"
   • the speaker's responses to nature in "The spring returns"
   • the speaker's concern for the person addressed in "No longer mourn for me"
   • the speaker's attitude toward the beauty of the person addressed in "When in the chronicle of wasted time"
   • the speakers' attitudes toward bereavement in "The spring returns" and "No longer mourn for me"

3. Which of the speakers do you think seems most deeply in love? Explain your answer.

A CREATIVE RESPONSE

4. How would "The spring returns" be different if the speaker had described winter rather than spring?

A CRITICAL RESPONSE

5. Why do you think both Petrarch and Shakespeare use contrast in these sonnets?
   Think about
   • the speaker's feelings and actions in "Rapt in the one fond thought"
   • nature and the speaker's feelings in "The spring returns"
   • the speaker's description of the world as "vile" in line 4 and "wise" in line 13 in "No longer mourn for me"
   • descriptions of past beauty and the reality of the speaker's beloved in "When in the chronicle of wasted time"

6. Identify those aspects of the sonnets that you think appeal as strongly today as in the poets' own times.

Analyzing the Writer's Craft

SONNET

Reread "The spring returns." What relationship do you detect between the first eight lines and the last six?

Building a Literary Vocabulary. A sonnet is a poem of fourteen lines that follows a set rhyme scheme. The two main types of sonnets are the Italian, or Petrarchan, and the English, or Shakespearean. The Petrarchan sonnet is divided into two parts: an octave, the first eight lines, and a sestet, the last six lines. The rhyme scheme for the octave is usually *abbaabba*. The rhyme scheme for the sestet may be *cdecde, cdcdcd,* or some other variation.

Generally, the octave tells a story, introduces a situation, or raises a question. The sestet, in turn, comments on the story, situation, or question. For example, in the octave of "The spring returns," the speaker describes the rebirth of nature in spring. In the sestet the speaker contrasts this rebirth with his own desolation.

Application: Analyzing a Shakespearean Sonnet. Get together with a partner and reread "No longer mourn for me" and "When in the chronicle of wasted time." Identify the rhyme scheme and then use it to decide which lines you would group together. Pay special attention to the use of couplets, or rhymed pairs of lines. Finally write a definition of a Shakespearean sonnet in which you explain the relationship among the groups of lines according to both rhyme and meaning. Use examples from the sonnets in your explanation.

Song

HEINRICH HEINE 1797–1856 GERMANY

I Was Born at Birth of Blossoms

ROSALÍA DE CASTRO 1837–1885 SPAIN

Biographies of Heine and de Castro appear on pages 743 and 740.

*A*pproaching the Poems

In these two poems, the speakers express feelings they have when rejected by a loved one. The first poem is by the German writer Heinrich Heine (hīn' *r*iH hī'nə), perhaps the best-known European love poet since Petrarch. The second poem is by the Galician Rosalía de Castro (rô̄ sä lē' ä de käs' trô̄). Though Galicia lies within the borders of Spain, Galicians retain their own language and a strong cultural identity.

*B*uilding Vocabulary

This essential word is defined alongside "Song."

languishing (laŋ' gwi*sh* iŋ): And why it is that I myself / So **languishing** should be? (page 303, lines 13–14)

*C*onnecting Writing and Reading

Recall a time when you were rejected by someone you thought you were in love with. How did this experience affect the way you saw yourself and the world? Record a few memories in your journal. Compare your experience of rejection with the experiences of the speakers in these poems.

Song

O dearest, canst thou tell me why
  The rose should be so pale?
And why the azure violet
  Should wither in the vale?

5 And why the lark should in the cloud
  So sorrowfully sing?
And why from loveliest balsam buds
  A scent of death should spring?

And why the sun upon the mead
10 So chillingly should frown?
And why the earth should, like a grave,
  Be moldering and brown?

And why it is that I myself
  So languishing[1] should be?
15 And why it is, my heart of hearts,
  That thou forsakest[2] me?

1. **languishing** (laŋ′ gwish iŋ): suffering with longing.
2. **forsakest** (for sāk′ əst): to desert; leave.

I Was Born at Birth
of Blossoms

I was born at birth of blossoms,
born when all the gardens grew,
on so very soft a morning,
on a morning April-blue.
5   So I'm Rosa—that's the reason—
of the lonely smile, it's true.
I'm a thorny rose for others;
never had a thorn for you.
When I fell in love—and little
10   thanks I had of it—I threw
all my life away, believing
you my earth and heaven too.
Why then this complaining, Mauro?
Why are loving looks so few?
15   If my dying made you happy,
dying's what I'd learn to do.
All these bitter words about me,
bitter, barbed! I never knew
what it was you really wanted.
20   Lunacies you've put me through!
All I had I gave to you. Couldn't
dull my hungering for you.

Even now, my heart I'm sending,
with the one key fits it true.
25   *Nothing left to give you, nothing;*
nothing you could ask me to.

$\mathcal{T}$hinking About the Poems

A PERSONAL RESPONSE

sharing impressions

1. What are your feelings toward the speakers in these poems? Jot down these feelings in your journal.

constructing interpretations

2. How would you say each speaker is affected by the loved one's rejection?
Think about
- the speaker's view of nature in "Song"
- the speaker's descriptions of herself and her actions in "I Was Born at Birth of Blossoms"
- the questions each speaker asks
- each speaker's attitude toward the loved one

3. What would you want to say to the speakers, based on your own experience of rejection?

A CREATIVE RESPONSE

4. Why might the speakers' loved ones have rejected them?

A CRITICAL RESPONSE

5. "Song" and many other poems by Heine have been set to music. De Castro's poems recall the melancholy love songs sung by Galician troubadours. What do you find songlike about these two poems?

6. According to her biographer, V. García Martí, de Castro uses language that is "the most simple and direct imaginable." Does the translation of "I Was Born at Birth of Blossoms" seem simple and direct to you? Offer examples to support your view.

7. Based on these two poems and on the other poems about love presented in this part of Unit 3, what generalizations can you make about love and the experience of rejection or loss?

Connecting Reading and Writing

1. Imagine that you are the loved one addressed in one of these poems. Write a **letter** in response to the speaker, explaining your rejection of the speaker.

Option: Respond to the speaker in a **poem** similar in form to the original work. This could be a serious poem or a parody.

2. In an **essay** for a literature class, analyze the ways that nature imagery is used in "Song" and in either "I Was Born at Birth of Blossoms," "The spring returns," "Written in Behalf of My Wife," or "The Song of a Soldier's Wife."

Option: To help students who will study these poems next year, create a set of **annotations** for "Song" and "I Was Born at Birth of Blossoms" that comment on the nature imagery in the poems.

3. Compare these two poems, written over one hundred years ago, with a contemporary song about the experience of rejection. Make your comparisons in an **article** for a popular magazine such as *Rolling Stone.*

Option: Write an imagined **conversation** between the two poets and the composer.

I Will Pronounce Your Name

LÉOPOLD SÉDAR SENGHOR   born 1906   SENEGAL

A biography of Senghor appears on page 752.

Approaching the Poem

In this poem, Léopold Sédar Senghor (lā ô pôld′ sā där′ sän gôr′) celebrates the wonders of Naëtt (nä et′), his first wife. The images associate her name with the aromas, sights, and sounds of the Senegalese countryside Senghor knew as a child, an Africa untouched by European influences. Senghor indicated that the poem should be read to the accompaniment of the African *tama,* or "drum," the instrument of a Senegalese troubadour, or singer.

I will pronounce your name, Naëtt, I will declaim you,
    Naëtt!
Naëtt, your name is mild like cinnamon, it is the fragrance
    in which the lemon grove sleeps,
Naëtt, your name is the sugared clarity of blooming coffee
    trees
And it resembles the savannah,[1] that blossoms forth under
    the masculine <u>ardor</u>[2] of the midday sun.
5 Name of dew, fresher than shadows of tamarind,[3]
Fresher even than the short dusk, when the heat of the day
    is silenced.
Naëtt, that is the dry tornado, the hard clap of lightning
Naëtt, coin of gold, shining coal, you my night, my sun! . .

I am your hero, and now I have become your sorcerer, in
    order to pronounce your names.
10 Princess of Elissa, banished from Futa on the fateful day.

1. savannah (sə van′ ə): a treeless plain or grassland.
2. ardor (är′ dər): enthusiasm; zeal.
3. tamarind (tam′ ə rind′): a tree with bright red-striped yellow flowers.

Sharing Ideas

*J*ust as writers throughout time have expressed their feelings about nature and love, they have also used writing as a means of expressing their ideas. The ideas may be philosophical, political, or personal in nature; they may reveal a positive outlook on life, or they may focus on a more negative subject. Although diverse, such works of literature share a common purpose: they celebrate the human mind and the world of ideas.

Throughout history, many writers have shared their insights about world events and social conditions. Some writers have chosen the essay form to discuss injustices experienced by their people. Other writers have shared ideas about war and destruction in novels set during crucial periods of history. Speeches, too, have been a popular tool for delivering opinions about the world, and as a result they have become an integral part of the literature of ideas.

Literary artists have reflected not only upon society but also upon their own place in society.

Some have conveyed ideas about their role as writers, perhaps in a poem about the power of poetry or in a speech or essay on the principal function of literature. Certain writers have viewed themselves as eccentrics—unique personalities who do not fit into the mainstream of society. They seem compelled to express through writing their particular isolation or discomfort within society.

Writers from different countries and time periods have sometimes shared similar ideas despite the varying circumstances that may have inspired those ideas. Writings about the swift passing of time, about the inevitability of death, and about the limitations and flaws of human nature speak to all people.

Some writers present their ideas about life and human nature directly. Their opinions and attitudes cannot be misconstrued. Other writers are more subtle; they imply certain ideas and opinions through their tone. As you read the selections that follow notice the many ways in which the writers share ideas about themselves, their work, and the world around them.

$\mathcal{L}$*iterary Vocabulary*

INTRODUCED IN THIS SECTION

Theme. Theme is the central idea or message communicated by a work of literature. It is a perception about life or human nature that the writer chooses to share with the reader. For example, a theme of the story "How Much Land Does a Man Need?" in Unit 1 is that excessive desire for wealth and possessions will lead to calamity. Figurative language often helps convey theme in poetry. In "Written in Behalf of My Wife," for example, the theme concerns the frustration and futility brought on by separation from a loved one. The simile "I am like a peach tree at the bottom of a well" reinforces this idea.

Fable. A fable is a brief tale, either in prose or verse, told to illustrate a moral. The characters are most frequently animals, but people and inanimate objects are sometimes the central figures. In Aesop's fable "The Fox and the Goat," the fox, who is stuck at the bottom of a well, convinces the goat to jump down into the well for water, all the time intending to use her as a way to climb out of the well. The goat, of course, is left trapped at the bottom of the well. The moral of this fable might be stated: "Never trust the advice of a person in difficulties."

Aphorism. An aphorism is a brief statement that expresses a general observation about life in a clever or pointed way. An aphorism is often a sentence that is still meaningful when taken out of its original context. For example, the phrase "Virtue attracts sin as complement" from "Seraphim, come" in Unit 2 could be called an aphorism because it makes an observation about life that is meaningful outside the context of the poem.

REVIEWED IN THIS SECTION

Metaphor

from The Rubáiyát

OMAR KHAYYÁM   1050?–1123?   PERSIA

Translated by Edward FitzGerald

A biography of Omar Khayyám appears on page 748.

Approaching the Poems

The work of Arabic literature best known in the West is probably *The Rubáiyát* (roo′ bī yät′) of Omar Khayyám (ō′ mär kī yäm′). The word *rubáiyát* is the plural of *rubai*, a Persian poetic form. A *rubai* is a quatrain, or four-line poem, in which the first, second, and fourth lines rhyme. Although the entire collection of poems is attributed to Omar Khayyám, a twelfth-century Persian astronomer and mathematician, scholars now believe that he wrote only a fraction of the poems.

In 1859 the British writer Edward FitzGerald loosely translated 75 of these poems into English. FitzGerald kept their overall theme and general form but modified the images to fit the tastes of his Victorian audience. His version of *The Rubáiyát* became enormously popular, and in later years FitzGerald published revised editions containing 101 poems.

Building Vocabulary

These essential words are defined alongside the poems.

repentance (ri pen′ təns): Your Winter-garment of **Repentance** fling (page 311)

myriads (mir′ ē ədz): Strange, is it not? that of the **myriads** who / Before us passed the door of Darkness through (page 311)

Connecting Writing and Reading

You may have heard expressions such as "Life is a bowl of cherries" or "Life's a beach." In your journal complete this sentence with an original comparison that expresses your view of life: "Life is a(n) _____." Briefly explain why you think the comparison is valid. As you read these poems, be aware that this speaker too uses comparisons to express a philosophy of life.

1

Wake! For the Sun, who scattered into flight
The Stars before him from the Field of Night,
   Drives Night along with them from Heav'n
    and strikes
The Sultán's Turret[1] with a Shaft of Light.

7

Come, fill the Cup, and in the fire of Spring
Your Winter-garment of <u>Repentance</u>[2] fling;
   The Bird of Time has but a little way
To flutter—and the Bird is on the Wing.

12

A Book of Verses underneath the Bough,
A Jug of Wine, a Loaf of Bread—and Thou
   Beside me singing in the Wilderness—
Oh, Wilderness were Paradise enow![3]

63

Oh threats of Hell and Hopes of Paradise!
One thing at least is certain—*This* Life
    flies;
   One thing is certain and the rest is Lies—
The Flower that once has blown forever dies.

64

Strange, is it not? that of the <u>myriads</u>[4] who
Before us passed the door of Darkness
    through,
   Not one returns to tell us of the Road,
Which to discover we must travel too.

68

We are no other than a moving row
Of Magic Shadow-shapes that come and go
   Round with the Sun-illumined Lantern held
In Midnight by the Master of the Show;

69

But helpless Pieces of the Game He plays
Upon this Checker-board of Nights and Days;
   Hither and thither[5] moves, and checks, and
    slays,
And one by one back in the Closet lays.

1. Sultán's Turret (sōol tänz′ tυr′ it): the tower of a Moslem ruler's palace.

2. repentance (ri pen′ təns): remorse; feeling of sorrow for a wrongdoing.

3. enow (ē nou′): enough.

4. myriads (mir′ ē ədz): countless numbers of people.

5. hither and thither: here and there.

96

Yet Ah, that Spring should vanish with the
    Rose!
That Youth's sweet-scented manuscript
    should close!
  The Nightingale that in the branches sang,
Ah whence, and whither flown again, who
    knows!

99

Ah, Love! could you and I with Him conspire
To grasp this sorry Scheme of Things entire,
  Would not we shatter it to bits—and then
Remold it nearer to the Heart's Desire!

Thinking About the Poems

A PERSONAL RESPONSE

sharing impressions

1. Jot down in your journal some of the thoughts triggered by these poems.

constructing interpretations

2. How would you describe the philosophy of life presented in *The Rubáiyát?*

Think about
- what time is compared to in poem 7
- actions the speaker advocates in poems 1, 7, and 12
- the view of death in poems 63 and 64
- what humans are compared to in poems 68 and 69

3. Which idea expressed in the poems seems to come closest to your own philosophy of life? Explain.

A CREATIVE RESPONSE

4. Whom is the speaker addressing, and what might this person's response be?

A CRITICAL RESPONSE

5. How might the speaker's philosophy of life apply to situations affecting students your age? Give examples.

6. Here is a literal translation of the Persian quatrain that inspired poem 12.

If hand should give of the pith of the wheat a loaf, and of wine a two-maunder jug, of sheep a thigh, with a little sweetheart seated in a desolation, a pleasure it is that is not the attainment of any sultan.

Discuss the changes that FitzGerald made in his reworking of the poem. Which version do you prefer, and why?

Think about
- the images in each version
- the feelings expressed
- capitalization and other elements of style

7. *The Rubáiyát* expresses a popular theme of lyric poetry known as *carpe diem*. The term, which literally means "seize the day," comes from a Latin poem by Horace that advocates enjoying life fully because death is inevitable. Here is the beginning of a famous seventeenth-century poem that illustrates the *carpe diem* philosophy, Robert Herrick's "To the Virgins, to Make Much of Time":

> Gather ye rosebuds while ye may,
>   Old Time is still a-flying;
> And this same flower that smiles today,
>   Tomorrow will be dying.

Which verses from *The Rubáiyát* do you feel are especially close to Herrick's stanza? Cite details to support your answer.

Analyzing the Writer's Craft

METAPHOR AND THEME

What ideas about time do you get from the lines "The Bird of Time has but a little way/ To flutter—and the Bird is on the Wing"?

Building a Literary Vocabulary. This statement is a metaphor, a figure of speech that makes a comparison between two things that have something in common. Unlike a simile, a metaphor makes a comparison without using *like* or *as*. The comparison may be directly stated, as in "Life is a broken-winged bird," or it may be implied, as in "The Bird of Time," and "*This* Life flies." In poetry a metaphor often helps convey a theme, or message. A theme is a perception about life or human nature that a writer chooses to share with the reader. For exam-

ple, in poem 7, time is compared to a bird that has already completed part of a short journey. This comparison expresses the theme that time is limited and passes quickly.

Application: Relating Metaphor to Theme. On the front of an index card or a folded sheet of paper, write another metaphor from these poems. On the back of the card or paper, write the two things that are being compared and the theme that is expressed through the metaphor. Do the same for two additional metaphors. As a class, discuss your interpretations and decide which metaphor is most memorable and effective.

from Facing Mount Kenya

JOMO KENYATTA   1890?–1978   KENYA

A biography of Kenyatta appears on page 744.

Approaching the Selection

Kenya, a country in central East Africa, became independent from British rule in 1964 and chose Jomo Kenyatta (jô′ mô̂ ki nyä′ tä) as its first president. African-born and the grandson of a medicine man, Kenyatta had a deep understanding of Africa and its people. In the following excerpt from his masterpiece _Facing Mount Kenya,_ Kenyatta tells how his ancestors, the Gikuyu (gi kᴏᴏ′ yᴏᴏ), or Kikuyu, became an oppressed people. He begins this account with the story of a Gikuyu medicine man who has a prophetic dream.

Building Vocabulary

These essential words are footnoted within the selection.

supplication (sup′ lə kā′ shən): The ceremonial elders . . . recited ritual songs as **supplication** to Ngai. (page 316)

cant (kant): Misled by European **cant,** the Gikuyu thought that the Europeans with their caravans did not mean any harm. (page 317)

estranged (e strānjd′): "The people became **estranged,** and presently murdered several porters." (page 318)

magnanimity (mag′ nə nim′ ə tē): The Gikuyu lost most of their lands through their **magnanimity.** (page 319)

unbiased (un bī′ əst): "We have already heard the circumstances from various **unbiased** sources." (page 320)

embroiled (em broild′): While they were all **embroiled** together, the man set the hut on fire. (page 321)

Connecting Writing and Reading

Think back to a time when, as a young person, you had difficulty dealing with a neighborhood or school bully. How did you feel as a person oppressed by someone else? In your journal jot down your recollections. As you read, compare your own experience and Kenyatta's account of his oppressed people.

from Facing Mount Kenya

ONCE UPON A time there lived in Gikuyuland a great medicine man known as Mogo or Moro wa Kebiro.[1] His national duty was to foretell future events and to advise the nation how to prepare for what was in store. We are told that one early morning the prophet woke up trembling and unable to speak, his body covered with bruises. His wives on seeing him were very frightened and in a state of hysteria, not knowing what had happened to their husband, who went to bed in perfect health the previous evening. Horror-stricken, the family summoned the ceremonial elders to his side with a view to offer a sacrifice to Ngai[2] (God) and to inquire what the great man had foreseen that had so frightened him.

When the ceremonial elders arrived, a male goat _(thenge)_ [3] was immediately slaughtered, and Mogo wa Kebiro was seated on the raw skin. The senior elder among the gathering took the blood of the animal, mixed it with oil, and then this mixture was poured on the head of the great seer as an anointment. At the same time the ceremonial elders, saturated with religious beliefs, recited ritual songs as supplication[4] to Ngai. Soon Mogo wa Kebiro regained his power of speech. With his usual prophetic voice he began to narrate what he had experienced during the previous night. He told the elders that during his sleep Ngai had taken him away to an unknown land. There the Ngai had revealed to him what would happen to the Gikuyu people in the near future. On hearing this he was horrified, and in his endeavor to persuade Ngai to avert the evil events coming to the Gikuyu, he was badly bruised and exhausted and could not do anything but obey the Ngai's command to come back and tell the people what would happen.

After a little pause, Mogo wa Kebiro continued his prophetic narrative. In a low and sad voice he said that strangers would come to Gikuyuland from out of the big water; the color of their body would resemble that of a small, light-colored frog _(kiengere)_ [5] which lives in water; their dress would resemble the wings of butterflies; that these strangers would carry magical sticks which would produce fire. That these sticks would be very much worse in killing than the poisoned arrows. The strangers, he said, would later bring an iron snake with as many legs as _monyongoro_ [6] (centipede); that this iron snake would spit fires and would stretch from the big water in the east to another big water in the west of the Gikuyu country. Further, he said that a big famine would come, and this would be the sign to show that the strangers with their iron snake were near at hand. He went on to say that when this came to pass, the Gikuyu, as well as their neighbors, would suffer greatly. That the nations would mingle with a merciless attitude toward each other, and the result would seem as though they were eating one another. He also said that sons and daughters would abuse their parents in a way unknown hitherto by the Gikuyu.

Mogo wa Kebiro urged the people not to

---

1. Mogo or Moro wa Kebiro (mʊ gô′, mʊ rô′ wä ki bē′ rʊ).

2. Ngai (ŋgī).

3. _thenge_ (the′ ŋge).

4. supplication (sup′ lə kā′ shən): a humble request or prayer.

5. _kiengere_ (kē e′ ŋge re).

6. _monyongoro_ (mʊ nyô′ ŋgô rô′).

take arms against the coming strangers, that the result of such actions would be annihilation of the tribe, because the strangers would be able to kill the people from a far distance with their magical sticks which spit deadly fires. The warriors were very angry when they heard this statement and said that they would take up arms and kill the iron snake and the strangers. But the great seer calmed them and told the warriors that the best thing would be to establish friendly relations with the coming strangers, because the spears and arrows would not be able to penetrate the iron snake, and therefore the warriors' attempt to fight the strangers and their snake would be futile.

The great medicine man advised the people that when these strangers arrived it would be the best policy to treat them with courtesy mingled with suspicion, and above all to be careful not to bring them too close to their homesteads, for these strangers are full of evil deeds and would not hesitate to covet the Gikuyu homeland and in the end would want to take everything from the Gikuyu.

When the people heard what Mogo wa Kebiro had predicted, they were very disturbed and did not know what to do except wait and face the coming danger. Many moons afterwards, about 1890 or thereabout, the predicted danger began to appear, for sure enough, the strangers dressed in clothes resembling the wings of butterflies started to arrive in small groups; this was expected, for prior to their arrival a terrible disease, called *ndigana* or *nyongo*,[7] had broken out and destroyed a great number of Gikuyu cattle as well as those of the neighboring tribes, the Masai and Wakamba.[8] The incident was followed by a great famine, which also devastated thousands of the tribesmen.

The first few Europeans who passed near the Gikuyu country were more or less harmless, for they passed through along the borderline of the country between the Gikuyu and Masai or between Wakamba and the Gikuyu. They were thus directed according to the prediction of the great medicine man. The Europeans with their caravans kept coming and going the same way from the coast to Lake Victoria and Uganda. In their upward and downward journeys they traded with the Gikuyu with little or no conflict. At last, misled by European <u>cant</u>,[9] the Gikuyu thought that the Europeans with their caravans did not mean any harm and befriended them. Forgetting the words of Mogo wa Kebiro to treat the Europeans with courtesy mingled with suspicion and not to bring them near their homesteads, the Gikuyu began to welcome the Europeans in close proximity to their homesteads.

At this stage it is interesting to give a short narrative of how the Gikuyu came to lose their best lands. When the Europeans first came into the Gikuyuland, the Gikuyu looked upon them as wanderers (*orori* or *athongo*)[10] who had deserted from their homes and were lonely and in need of friends. The Gikuyu, in their natural generosity and hospitality, welcomed the wanderers and felt pity for them. As such the Europeans were allowed to pitch their tents and to have a temporary right of occupation on the land in the same category as those Gikuyu *mohoi* or *mothami*[11] who were given only cultivation or building rights. The Europeans were treated in this way in the belief that one day they would get tired of wandering and finally return to their own country.

These early empire builders, knowing what they were after, played on the ignorance and

---

7. *ndigana* or *nyongo* (ndē gä′ nä, nyɔɔ′ ŋgɔɔ).

8. **Masai and Wakamba** (mä sī′, wä kä′ mbä).

9. **cant** (kant): insincere talk, especially pious remarks by hypocrites.

10. *orori* or *athongo* (ō′ rɔɔ rē, ä *th*ɔɔ′ ŋgɔɔ).

11. *mohoi* or *mothami* (mɔɔ hô′ ē, mɔɔ *th*ä′ mē).

sincere hospitable nature of the people. They agreed to the terms of a *mohoi* or *mothami*, and soon started to build small forts or camps, saying that "the object of a station is to form a center for the purchase of food for caravans proceeding to Uganda," etc. For "Kikuyu was reported a country where food was extraordinarily abundant and cheap."

The Gikuyu gave the Europeans building rights in places like Dagoretti, Fort Smith and others, with no idea of the motives which were behind the caravans, for they thought that it was only a matter of trading and nothing else. Unfortunately, they did not realize that these places were used for the preliminary preparations for taking away their land from them. They established friendly relations with the Europeans and supplied them with food for their caravans, taking it for granted that naturally the white wanderers must undoubtedly have their own country and therefore could not settle for good in a foreign land, that they would feel homesick and, after selling their goods, would go back to live in their homesteads with parents and relatives.

The belief that the Europeans were not going to live permanently in Africa was strengthened by the fact that none of them seemed to stay very long in one place. Therefore, reasoning from this, the Gikuyu naturally came to the conclusion that one day all the Europeans in Africa would pack up bag and baggage and return to their own country in the same way as they came. It was a common saying among the Gikuyu until a few years ago that *"Gotire ondo wa ndereri, nagowo Coomba no okainoka,"*[12] which means that there is no mortal thing or act that lives for eternity; the Europeans will, no doubt, eventually go back to their own country. This saying was taken up as a lamenting slogan and was sung in various songs, especially when the wanderers started to show their real motive for wandering.

The early travellers reported that "Kikuyu promised to be the most progressive station between the coast and the lake. The natives were very friendly, and even enlisted as porters to go to the coast, but these good relations received a disastrous check. Owing largely to the want of discipline in the passing caravans, whose men robbed the crops and otherwise made themselves troublesome, the people became estranged,[13] and presently murdered several porters." This was the beginning of the suffering and the use of the sticks which produced killing fire, as Mogo wa Kebiro had predicted in his prophecy of the coming of the white men. For soon after the above incident, we are told that the Gikuyu were "taught a lesson": they were compelled to make "the payment of fifty goats daily, and the free work of three hundred men to build the fort they had destroyed."

After this event the Gikuyu, with bitterness in their hearts, realized that the strangers they had given hospitality to had planned to plunder and subjugate them by brute force. The chief, Waiyaki,[14] who had entered into a treaty of friendship with the strangers, was afterward deported and died on his way to the coast. People were indignant for these acts of ingratitude on the part of the Europeans and declined to trade with them, thinking that the Europeans and their caravans would get hungry and move away from the Gikuyu country; but soon the Gikuyu were made to know that "might is right," for it is reported that "from this country of teeming abundance, where in a few days I obtained many thousand pounds of food, the officer finds it impossible to purchase

---

12. *Gotire ondo wa ndereri, nagowo Coomba no okainoka* (goo tē′ ri oo ndoo wä nde′ ri rē, nä gwô′ chô′ mbä nô oo kī′ noo′ kä).

13. estranged (e strānjd′): newly unfriendly and hostile.

14. Waiyaki (wī yä′ kē).

a single bag of grain," and parties were sent out regularly to take it by force!—and "large armed parties were necessary to procure firewood and water."

The prediction of Mogo wa Kebiro was slowly being fulfilled, for soon afterward the Kenya-Uganda railway (the iron snake) was completed. And the Europeans, having their feet firm on the soil, began to claim the absolute right to rule the country and to have the ownership of the lands under the title of "Crown Lands," where the Gikuyu, who are the original owners, now live as "tenants at will of the Crown." The Gikuyu lost most of their lands through their magnanimity,[15] for the Gikuyu country was never wholly conquered by force of arms, but the people were put under the ruthless domination of European imperialism through the insidious trickery of hypocritical treaties.

The relation between the Gikuyu and the Europeans can well be illustrated by a Gikuyu story which says that: once upon a time an elephant made a friendship with a man. One day a heavy thunderstorm broke out. The elephant went to his friend, who had a little hut at the edge of the forest, and said to him: "My dear good man, will you please let me put my trunk inside your hut to keep it out of this torrential rain?" The man, seeing what situation his friend was in, replied: "My dear good elephant, my hut is very small, but there is room for your trunk and myself. Please put your trunk in gently." The elephant thanked his friend, saying: "You have done me a good deed, and one day I shall return your kindness." But what followed? As soon as the elephant put his trunk inside the hut, slowly he pushed his head inside and finally flung the man out in the rain, and then lay down comfortably inside his friend's hut, saying: "My dear good friend, your skin is harder than mine, and as there is not enough room for both of us, you can afford to remain in the rain while I am protecting my delicate skin from the hailstorm."

The man, seeing what his friend had done to him, started to grumble; the animals in the nearby forest heard the noise and came to see what was the matter. All stood around listening to the heated argument between the man and his friend the elephant. In this turmoil the lion came along roaring and said in a loud voice: "Don't you all know that I am the King of the Jungle! How dare anyone disturb the peace of my kingdom?" On hearing this the elephant, who was one of the high ministers in the jungle kingdom, replied in a soothing voice and said: "My Lord, there is no disturbance of the peace in your kingdom. I have only been having a little discussion with my friend here as to the possession of this little hut which your lordship sees me occupying." The lion, who wanted to have "peace and tranquillity" in his kingdom, replied in a noble voice, saying: "I command my ministers to appoint a Commission of Enquiry to go thoroughly into this matter and report accordingly." He then turned to the man and said: "You have done well by establishing friendship with my people, especially with the elephant who is one of my honorable ministers of state. Do not grumble any more; your hut is not lost to you. Wait until the sitting of my Imperial Commission, and there you will be given plenty of opportunity to state your case. I am sure that you will be pleased with the findings of the Commission." The man was very pleased by these sweet words from the King of the Jungle and innocently waited for his opportunity, in the belief that, naturally, the hut would be returned to him.

The elephant, obeying the command of his master, got busy with other ministers to appoint the Commission of Enquiry. The following elders of the jungle were appointed to

---

15. magnanimity (mag′ nə nim′ ə tē): generosity in overlooking injury or insult.

sit in the Commission: (1) Mr. Rhinoceros, (2) Mr. Buffalo, (3) Mr. Alligator, (4) The Rt. Hon. Mr. Fox to act as chairman, and (5) Mr. Leopard to act as secretary to the Commission. On seeing the personnel, the man protested and asked if it was not necessary to include in this Commission a member from his side. But he was told that it was impossible, since no one from his side was well enough educated to understand the intricacy of jungle law. Further, that there was nothing to fear, for the members of the Commission were all men of repute for their impartiality in justice, and as they were gentlemen chosen by God to look after the interests of races less adequately endowed with teeth and claws, he might rest assured that they would investigate the matter with the greatest care and report impartially.

The Commission sat to take the evidence. The Rt. Hon. Mr. Elephant was first called. He came along with a superior air, brushing his tusks with a sapling which Mrs. Elephant had provided, and in an authoritative voice said: "Gentlemen of the Jungle, there is no need for me to waste your valuable time in relating a story which I am sure you all know. I have always regarded it as my duty to protect the interests of my friends, and this appears to have caused the misunderstanding between myself and my friend here. He invited me to save his hut from being blown away by a hurricane. As the hurricane had gained access owing to the unoccupied space in the hut, I considered it necessary, in my friend's own interests, to turn the undeveloped space to a more economic use by sitting in it myself, a duty which any of you would undoubtedly have performed with equal readiness in similar circumstances."

After hearing the Rt. Hon. Mr. Elephant's conclusive evidence, the Commission called Mr. Hyena and other elders of the jungle, who all supported what Mr. Elephant had said. They then called the man, who began to give his own account of the dispute. But the Commission cut him short, saying: "My good man, please confine yourself to relevant issues. We have already heard the circumstances from various <u>unbiased</u>[16] sources; all we wish you to tell us is whether the undeveloped space in your hut was occupied by anyone else before Mr. Elephant assumed his position." The man began to say: "No, but—" But at this point the Commission declared that they had heard sufficient evidence from both sides and retired to consider their decision. After enjoying a delicious meal at the expense of the Rt. Hon. Mr. Elephant, they reached their verdict, called the man, and declared as follows: "In our opinion this dispute has arisen through a regrettable misunderstanding due to the backwardness of your ideas. We consider that Mr. Elephant has fulfilled his sacred duty of protecting your interests. As it is clearly for your good that the space should be put to its most economic use, and as you yourself have not yet reached the stage of expansion which would enable you to fill it, we consider it necessary to arrange a compromise to suit both parties. Mr. Elephant shall continue his occupation of your hut, but we give you permission to look for a site where you can build another hut more suited to your needs, and we will see that you are well protected."

The man, having no alternative and fearing that his refusal might expose him to the teeth and claws of members of the Commission, did as they suggested. But no sooner had he built another hut than Mr. Rhinoceros charged in with his horn lowered and ordered the man to quit. A Royal Commission was again appointed to look into the matter, and the same finding was given. This procedure was repeated until Mr. Buffalo, Mr. Leopard, Mr. Hyena and the rest were all accommodated with new

---

16. unbiased (un bī′ əst): without prejudice; impartial; fair.

huts. Then the man decided that he must adopt an effective method of protection, since Commissions of Enquiry did not seem to be of any use to him. He sat down and said: *"Ng'enda thi ndeagaga motegi,"*[17] which literally means "There is nothing that treads on the earth that cannot be trapped," or, in other words, you can fool people for a time, but not for ever. Early one morning, when the huts already occupied by the jungle lords were all beginning to decay and fall to pieces, he went out and built a bigger and better hut a little distance away. No sooner had Mr. Rhinoceros seen it than he came rushing in, only to find that Mr. Elephant was already inside, sound asleep. Mr. Leopard next came in at the window, Mr. Lion, Mr. Fox, and Mr. Buffalo entered the doors, while Mr. Hyena howled for a place in the shade and Mr. Alligator basked on the roof. Presently they all began disputing about their rights of penetration, and from disputing they came to fighting, and while they were all <u>embroiled</u>[18] together, the man set the hut on fire and burnt it to the ground, jungle lords and all. Then he went home, saying: "Peace is costly, but it's worth the expense," and lived happily ever after.

---

17. *Ng'enda thi ndeagaga motegi* (ŋe' ndä *th*i ndi ä' gä gä mʊʊ te' gē).

18. embroiled (em brɔild'): drawn into a conflict or fight.

Thinking About the Selection

A PERSONAL RESPONSE

sharing impressions

1. How do you feel about what happened to the Gikuyu people? Jot down your impressions in your journal.

constructing interpretations

2. Do you think the man in the Gikuyu story is justified in burning down his hut?
Think about
- the conduct of the jungle lords
- whether peaceful means might have resolved the situation
- whether using violence against an oppressor is ever right

3. What connections do you see between the man and the jungle lords in the Gikuyu story and the Gikuyu and their oppressors in real life?

4. To what extent do you think the Gikuyu are responsible for becoming an oppressed people?
Think about
- the warnings and advice of Mogo wa Kebiro
- the way in which the Europeans first gained a foothold in Kenya
- what might have happened if the Gikuyu had treated the Europeans with "courtesy mingled with suspicion"
- the experience you recalled in your journal

A CREATIVE RESPONSE

5. How might your interpretation of this selection be different if any of the three parts of the selection were not included?

A CRITICAL RESPONSE

6. How objective do you consider Kenyatta's account of the oppressed people and their oppressors? Cite details from the selection to support your views.

7. What do you think Kenyatta might be saying that would apply to all peoples?

Analyzing the Writer's Craft

Recall the acts of the man and the jungle lords in the Gikuyu story that concludes Kenyatta's account.

Building a Literary Vocabulary. A fable is a brief tale, either in prose or verse, told to illustrate a moral. The characters are most frequently animals, but people and inanimate objects are sometimes the central figures. For example, consider Aesop's fable of the race between the speedy but arrogant hare and the plodding but persevering tortoise. The events of that fable dramatize the moral "Slow and steady wins the race."

Application: Analyzing a Fable. Get together with a small group of classmates and make a chart with two columns, labeled "Man" and "Jungle lords." In the first column list three or more qualities that the man in the fable shows and the actions that convey these qualities. In the second column list three or more qualities that the jungle animals show and their corresponding actions. After you have completed the chart, discuss what it reveals about the relationship between the man and the jungle lords. Then decide how you would state the moral of the fable.

Connecting Reading and Writing

1. Write a **fable** for your classmates that illustrates a moral relating to an important issue at school.

Option: Rewrite Jomo Kenyatta's **fable** so that it dramatizes a different moral.

2. Imagine that a group of citizens wants the local library to ban Kenyatta's book on the grounds that the concluding fable advocates violence as a tool for social change. Defend or challenge this contention in a **letter** to the library board.

Option: Express your views on this issue in **notes** for an address to the library board.

3. Research the history of a Native American tribe and, in a **report** for your classmates, compare the tribe's experience of being invaded with the experience of the Gikuyu people.

Option: Create a classroom **chart** or some other visual aid that shows the comparison between the Gikuyu and a Native American tribe.

Nobel Acceptance Speeches

ALBERT CAMUS   1913–1960   ALGERIA/FRANCE

IVO ANDRIĆ   1892–1975   YUGOSLAVIA

Biographies of Camus and Andrić appear on pages 740 and 738.

*A*pproaching the Speeches

Every year in Stockholm, Sweden, the Nobel Prize Foundation honors individuals for outstanding achievements in chemistry, physics, medicine, economics, literature, and peace. The following are the acceptance speeches of two winners of the Nobel Prize in literature. Novelist and essayist Albert Camus (ka mōō′) received the Nobel Prize in 1957. Ivo Andrić (ē′ vô än′ drēch) was the first Yugoslav to receive a Nobel Prize. He received the award in 1961.

*B*uilding Vocabulary

These essential words are footnoted within the selections.

resound (ri zound′): He manages . . . to make it **resound** by means of his art. (page 326)

legitimacy (lə jit′ ə mə sē): But the fact remains that most of us . . . have engaged upon a quest for **legitimacy.** (page 326)

ineluctable (in ē luk′ tə bəl): This story attempts to . . . suspend the **ineluctable** decree of the fate that threatens us. (page 329)

gratuitous (grə tōō′ i təs): A writer of historical stories and novels could not in my opinion accept such a **gratuitous** judgment. (page 329)

*C*onnecting Writing and Reading

In your journal jot down the following goals that a writer might have and mark the two or three that you think are most important: to teach, to express himself or herself, to entertain, to leave a record for posterity, to influence events, to serve humanity, to offer escape, and to create beauty.

As you read the speeches of these two honored writers, compare your ideas about the role of the writer with their ideas.

Albert Camus

IN RECEIVING THE distinction with which your free Academy has so generously honored me, my gratitude has been profound, particularly when I consider the extent to which this recompense has surpassed my personal merits. Every man, and for stronger reasons, every artist, wants to be recognized. So do I. But I have not been able to learn of your decision without comparing its repercussions to what I really am. A man almost young, rich only in his doubts and with his work still in progress, accustomed to living in the solitude of work or in the retreats of friendship: how would he not feel a kind of panic at hearing the decree that transports him all of a sudden, alone and reduced to himself, to the center of a glaring light? And with what feelings could he accept this honor at a time when other writers in Europe, among them the very greatest, are condemned to silence, and even at a time when the country of his birth is going through unending misery?

I felt that shock and inner turmoil. In order to regain peace I have had, in short, to come to terms with a too generous fortune. And since I cannot live up to it by merely resting on my achievement, I have found nothing to support me but what has supported me through all my life, even in the most contrary circumstances: the idea that I have of my art and of the role of the writer. Let me only tell you, in a spirit of gratitude and friendship, as simply as I can, what this idea is.

For myself, I cannot live without my art. But I have never placed it above everything. If, on the other hand, I need it, it is because it cannot be separated from my fellow men, and it allows me to live, such as I am, on one level with them. It is a means of stirring the greatest number of people by offering them a privileged picture of common joys and sufferings. It obliges the artist not to keep himself apart; it subjects him to the most humble and the most universal truth. And often he who has chosen the fate of the artist because he felt himself to be different soon realizes that he can maintain neither his art nor his difference unless he admits that he is like the others. The artist forges himself to the others, midway between the beauty he cannot do without and the community he cannot tear himself away from. That is why true artists scorn nothing: they are obliged to understand rather than to judge. And if they have to take sides in this world, they can perhaps side only with that society in which, according to Nietzsche's[1] great words, not the judge but the creator will rule, whether he be a worker or an intellectual.

By the same token, the writer's role is not free from difficult duties. By definition he cannot put himself today in the service of those

Guide for Interpretation

When Camus received this award, the Communist regimes in several Eastern European countries were imposing harsh restrictions on authors who criticized the government. It is to this that Camus alludes when he describes other European writers as being "condemned to silence." Also at the time of this award, violent civil war plagued Camus's country of birth, Algeria, which accounts for his reference to "unending misery."

---

1. Nietzsche (nē′ chə): Friedrich Nietzsche, a late-nineteenth-century German philosopher and poet noted for his theory that specially gifted individuals should be regarded as supermen who are not bound by traditional values and morals.

who make history; he is at the service of those who suffer it. Otherwise, he will be alone and deprived of his art. Not all the armies of tyranny with their millions of men will free him from his isolation, even and particularly if he falls into step with them. But the silence of an unknown prisoner, abandoned to humiliations at the other end of the world, is enough to draw the writer out of his exile, at least whenever, in the midst of the privileges of freedom, he manages not to forget that silence, and to transmit it in order to make it resound[2] by means of his art.

None of us is great enough for such a task. But in all circumstances of life, in obscurity or temporary fame, cast in the irons of tyranny or for a time free to express himself, the writer can win the heart of a living community that will justify him, on the one condition that he will accept to the limit of his abilities the two tasks that constitute the greatness of his craft: the service of truth and the service of liberty. Because his task is to unite the greatest possible number of people, his art must not compromise with lies and servitude, which, wherever they rule, breed solitude. Whatever our personal weaknesses may be, the nobility of our craft will always be rooted in two commitments, difficult to maintain: the refusal to lie about what one knows and the resistance to oppression.

For more than twenty years of an insane history, hopelessly lost like all the men of my generation in the convulsions of time, I have been supported by one thing: by the hidden feeling that to write today was an honor because this activity was a commitment—and a commitment not only to write. Specifically, in view of my powers and my state of being, it was a commitment to bear, together with all those who were living through the same history, the misery and the hope we shared. These men, who were born at the beginning of the First World War,

who were twenty when Hitler came to power and the first revolutionary trials were beginning, who were then confronted as a completion of their education with the Spanish Civil War, the Second World War, the world of concentration camps, a Europe of torture and prisons—these men must today rear their sons and create their works in a world threatened by nuclear destruction. Nobody, I think, can ask them to be optimists. And I even think that we should understand—without ceasing to fight it—the error of those who in an excess of despair have asserted their right to dishonor and have rushed into the nihilism of the era. But the fact remains that most of us, in my country and in Europe, have refused this nihilism and have engaged upon a quest for legitimacy.[3] They have had to forge for themselves an art of living in times of catastrophe in order to be born a second

---

2. resound (ri zound′): to echo; be filled with sound.
3. legitimacy (lə jit′ ə mə sē): the state of being justifiable.

time and to fight openly against the instinct of death at work in our history.

Each generation doubtless feels called upon to reform the world. Mine knows that it will not reform it, but its task is perhaps even greater. It consists in preventing the world from destroying itself. Heir to a corrupt history, in which are mingled fallen revolutions, technology gone mad, dead gods, and worn-out ideologies, where mediocre powers can destroy all yet no longer know how to convince, where intelligence has debased itself to become the servant of hatred and oppression, this generation starting from its own negations has had to reestablish, both within and without, a little of that which constitute the dignity of life and death. In a world threatened by disintegration, in which our grand inquisitors[4] run the risk of establishing forever the kingdom of death, it knows that it should, in an insane race against the clock, restore among the nations a peace that is not servitude, reconcile anew labor and culture, and remake with all men the Ark of the Covenant.[5] It is not certain that this generation will ever be able to accomplish this immense task, but already it is rising everywhere in the world to the double challenge of truth and liberty and, if necessary, knows how to die for it without hate. Wherever it is found, it deserves to be saluted and encouraged, particularly where it is sacrificing itself. In any event, certain of your complete approval, it is to this generation that I should like to pass on the honor that you have just given me.

At the same time, after having outlined the nobility of the writer's craft, I should have put him in his proper place. He has no other claims but those which he shares with his comrades in arms: vulnerable but obstinate, unjust but impassioned for justice, doing his work without shame or pride in view of everybody, not ceasing to be divided between sorrow and beauty, and devoted finally to drawing from his double

existence the creations that he obstinately tries to erect in the destructive movement of history. Who after all this can expect from him complete solutions and high morals? Truth is mysterious, elusive, always to be conquered. Liberty is dangerous, as hard to live with as it is elating. We must march toward these two goals, painfully but resolutely, certain in advance of our failings on so long a road. What writer would from now on in good conscience dare set himself up as a preacher of virtue? For myself, I must state once more that I am not of this kind. I have never been able to renounce the light, the pleasure of being, and the freedom in which I grew up. But although this nostalgia explains many of my errors and my faults, it has doubtless helped me toward a better understanding of my craft. It is helping me still to support unquestioningly all those silent men who sustain the life made from them in the world only through memory of the return of brief and free happiness.

Thus reduced to what I really am, to my limits and debts as well as to my difficult creed, I feel freer, in concluding, to comment upon the extent and the generosity of the honor you have just bestowed upon me, freer also to tell you that I would receive it as an homage rendered to all those who, sharing in the same fight, have not received any privilege but have on the contrary known misery and persecution. It remains for me to thank you from the bottom of my heart and to make before you publicly, as a personal sign of my gratitude, the same and ancient promise of faithfulness which every true artist repeats to himself in silence every day.

---

4. grand inquisitors: those officials who can condemn someone to death for holding political or philosophical beliefs that are contrary to the established doctrine.
5. Ark of the Covenant: in the Jewish religion, a sacred object representing God's commitment to protect his people.

Ivo Andrić

IN CARRYING OUT the high duties entrusted to it, the Nobel Committee of the Swedish Academy has this year awarded the Nobel Prize in literature, a signal mark of honor on the international scene, to a writer from a small country, as it is commonly called. In receiving this honor, I should like to make a few remarks about this country and to add a few considerations of a more general character about the storyteller's work to which you have graciously awarded your prize.

My country is indeed a "small country between the worlds," as it has aptly been characterized by one of our writers, a country which, at breakneck speed and at the cost of great sacrifices and prodigious efforts, is trying in all fields, including the field of culture, to make up for those things of which it has been deprived by a singularly turbulent and hostile past. In choosing the recipient of this award you have cast a shining light upon the literary activity of that country, at the very moment when, thanks to a number of new names and original works, that country's literature is beginning to gain recognition through an honest endeavor to make its contribution to world literature. There is no doubt that your distinction of a writer of this country is an encouragement which calls for our gratitude; I am happy to have the opportunity to express this gratitude to you in this place and at this time, simply but sincerely.

It is a more difficult and more delicate task to tell you about the storyteller's work which you have honored with your prize. In fact, when it comes down to a writer and his work, can we expect him to be able to speak of that work, when in reality his creation is but a part of himself? Some among us would rather consider the authors of works of art either as mute and absent contemporaries or as famous writers of the past, and think that the work of art speaks with a clearer and purer voice if the living voice of the author does not interfere. This attitude is neither uncommon nor particularly new. Even in his day Montesquieu[1] contended that authors are not good judges of their own works. I remember reading with understanding admiration Goethe's[2] rule: "The artist's task is to create, not to talk"; and many years later I was moved to find the same thought brilliantly expressed by the greatly mourned Albert Camus.[3]

Let me then, as seems fitting to me, concentrate in this brief statement on the story and the storyteller in general. In thousands of languages, in the most diverse climes, from century to century, beginning with the very old stories told around the hearth in the huts of our remote ancestors down to the works of modern storytellers which are appearing at this moment in the publishing houses of the great cities of the world, it is the story of the human condition that is being spun and that men never weary of telling to one another. The manner of telling and the form of the story vary according to periods and circumstances, but the taste for telling and retelling a story remains the same: the narrative flows

---

1. Montesquieu: a seventeenth-century French political philosopher. (See the selection from *The Persian Letters,* Unit 1, page 83.)

2. Goethe: Johann Wolfgang von Goethe (1749–1832), a German poet, novelist, dramatist, and philosopher who helped give birth to the Romantic Movement.

3. Albert Camus: Andrić's fellow Nobel Prize winner had been killed in a car crash just a year before.

endlessly and never runs dry. Thus, at times, one might almost believe that from the first dawn of consciousness throughout the ages, mankind has constantly been telling itself the same story, though with infinite variations, to the rhythm of its breath and pulse. And one might say that after the fashion of the legendary and eloquent Scheherazade,[4] this story attempts to stave off[5] the executioner, to suspend the ineluctable[6] decree of the fate that threatens us, and to prolong the illusion of life and of time. Or should the storyteller by his work help man to know and to recognize himself? Perhaps it is his calling to speak in the name of all those who did not have the ability or who, crushed by life, did not have the power to express themselves. Or could it be that the storyteller tells his own story to himself, like the child who sings in the dark in order to assuage his own fear? Or finally, could the aim of these stories be to throw some light on the dark paths into which life hurls us at times and to tell us about this life, which we live blindly and unconsciously, something more than we can apprehend and comprehend in our weakness? And thus the words of a good storyteller often shed light on our acts and on our omissions, on what we should do and on what we should not have done. Hence one might wonder whether the true history of mankind is not to be found in these stories, oral or written, and whether we might not at least dimly catch the meaning of that history. And it matters little whether the story is set in the present or in the past.

Guide for Interpretation

Notice that Andrić suggests five possible desires that might motivate storytellers: to pretend that life can go on forever, to teach human beings about themselves, to speak for those who would not otherwise be heard from, to ease their own fears, or to illuminate the mystery of life itself. As you read, consider why Andrić suggests that storytelling can convey humankind's "true" history.

Nevertheless, some will maintain that a story dealing with the past neglects, and to a certain degree turns its back on, the present. A writer of historical stories and novels could not in my opinion accept such a gratuitous[7] judgment. He would rather be inclined to confess that he does not himself know very well when or how he moves from what is called the present into what we call the past, and that he crosses easily—as in a dream—the threshold of centuries. But in the end, do not past and present confront us with similar phenomena and with the same problems: to be a man, to have been born without knowing it or wanting it, to be thrown into the ocean of existence, to be obliged to swim, to exist; to have an identity; to resist the pressure and shocks from the outside and the unforeseen and unforeseeable acts—one's own and those of others—which so often exceed one's capacities? And what is more, to endure one's own thoughts about all this: in a word, to be human.

So it happens that beyond the imaginary demarcation line between past and present the writer still finds himself eye to eye with the human condition, which he is bound to observe and understand as best he can, with which he must identify, giving it the strength of his breath and the warmth of his blood, which he must attempt to turn into the living texture of the story that he intends to translate for his readers, in such a way that the result be

---

4. Scheherazade (shə her′ ə zä′ də): the clever wife in *One Thousand and One Arabian Nights* who kept putting off her own execution by telling stories each night for three years. (See *The Tale of the Anklet,* Unit 1, page 72.)
5. stave off: to ward off or hold off, as by force or cleverness.
6. ineluctable (in ē luk′ tə bəl): inevitable; not to be avoided or escaped.
7. gratuitous (grə to͞o′ i təs): without cause or reason; uncalled for.

as beautiful, as simple, and as persuasive as possible.

How can a writer arrive at this aim, by what ways, by what means? For some it is by giving free rein[8] to their imagination, for others it is by studying with long and painstaking care the instructions that history and social evolution afford. Some will endeavor to assimilate the substance and meaning of past epochs; others will proceed with the capricious and playful nonchalance of the prolific French novelist who once said, "What is history but a peg to hang my novels on?" In a word, there are a thousand ways and means for the novelist to arrive at his work, but what alone matters and alone is decisive is the work itself.

The author of historical novels could put as an epigraph to his works, in order to explain everything to everyone, once and for all, the old saying: "Cogitavi dies antiquos et annos aeternos in mente habui" ("I have pondered the days of yore and I have kept in mind the years of eternity"). But with or without epigraph, his work, by its very existence, suggests the same idea.

Still, these are ultimately nothing but questions of technique, tastes, and methods, a fascinating intellectual pastime concerning a work or having vaguely to do with it. In the end it matters little whether the writer evokes the past, describes the present, or even plunges boldly into the future. The main thing is the spirit which informs his story, the message that his work conveys to mankind; and it is obvious that rules and regulations do not avail here. Each builds his story according to his own inward needs, according to the measure of his inclinations, innate or acquired, according to his conceptions and to the power of his means of expression. Each assumes the moral responsibility for his own story, and each must be allowed to tell it freely. But, in conclusion, it is to be hoped that the story told by today's author to his contemporaries, irrespective of its form and content, should be neither tarnished by hate nor obscured by the noise of homicidal machines, but that it should be born out of love and inspired by the breadth of ideas of a free and serene human mind. For the storyteller and his work serve no purpose unless they serve, in one way or another, man and humanity. That is the essential point. And that is what I have attempted to bring out in these brief reflections inspired by the occasion and which, with your permission, I shall conclude as I began them, with the repeated expression of a profound and sincere gratitude.

---

8. **free rein:** freedom to act without restraint.

Thinking About the Speeches

A PERSONAL RESPONSE

sharing impressions

1. How did you react to these two speeches? Jot down some notes in your journal that reflect your reaction.

constructing interpretations

2. Now that you have read the speeches, in what ways have your ideas about the role of the writer changed or expanded?

Think about

- Andrić's ideas about the human condition and the art of storytelling
- Camus's view of the two most important tasks of the writer
- Camus's statement that writers should serve not those who make history but those who suffer it
- your prereading journal entry

3. If each of these writers were offered a choice of two successful careers, writing popular romantic novels or writing dramatically effective political speeches, which career do you think he would choose? In explaining your answer, refer to the statements in the two speeches.

A CREATIVE RESPONSE

4. If Camus and Andrić had been painters or musicians instead of writers, how might they have defined their mission or purpose?

A CRITICAL RESPONSE

5. Ivo Andrić described five desires that might motivate a person to be a storyteller. Think of one of the narrative selections in this book that you particularly enjoyed and decide which of these motivations was probably most important for the writer of that selection. Refer to aspects of the story in your answer.

Analyzing the Writer's Craft

APHORISM

Imagine that you are a television news editor who must choose a thirty-second "sound bite" for the evening news from either of these speeches. How difficult would it be to find a sentence that seems particularly quotable?

Building a Literary Vocabulary. An aphorism is a brief statement that expresses a general observation about life in a clever or pointed way. An aphorism is often a sentence that is still meaningful when taken out of its original context. For example, Andrić quotes an aphorism by the German writer Goethe: "The artist's task is to create, not to talk." Both of the speeches you have just read include statements that could serve as aphorisms, that is, concise statements expressing general truths.

Application: Identifying Aphorisms. With several classmates pretend that you are on a committee doing fieldwork to develop a *Nobel Prize Winner's Dictionary of Aphorisms and Quotations.* From each speech, select a minimum of three statements that you believe should be considered for the dictionary. At times you may need to edit a sentence slightly or to use only part of it. For each aphorism identify the key word under which it should be indexed. (To see a sample format, you may wish to consult a dictionary of quotations in the library.) Then, because the editors of the dictionary are not sure how much space they will have, select the two aphorisms from each writer that you consider most worthy of being included.

Connecting Reading and Writing

1. Imagine that you are a consultant for a wealthy foundation that is considering whether to honor outstanding achievements in literature or science. Write a **memo** to your board of directors recommending one of these fields for the awards.

Option: Imagine that you wish to bequeath part of your large fortune to fund an award in science or literature. Write a paragraph or two of your **will,** setting forth how you wish the money to be spent.

2. Read a short story by one of these two writers, perhaps "The Guest" by Camus or "Summer in the South" by Andrić. Then write a **letter** to the Nobel Committee supporting or opposing the author's selection as a Nobel Prize winner.

Option: Write a **review** of the story to be shared with other students who have read it.

3. Read the acceptance speech that was delivered by the American writer William Faulkner when he received the Nobel Prize in literature in 1950. Write a **report** for the class comparing Faulkner's understanding of the role of the writer with the views of Camus and Andrić.

Option: Imagine hosting a radio talk show with Camus, Andrić, and Faulkner as guests. Write a series of **questions** that you could ask these writers on the air to bring out their ideas on the role of the writer and what an aspiring writer should do.

The Albatross

CHARLES BAUDELAIRE   1821–1867   FRANCE

Poem

JOSÉ MARTÍ   1853–1895   CUBA

1996

RABINDRANATH TAGORE   1861–1941   INDIA

Biographies of Baudelaire, Martí, and Tagore appear on pages 738, 746, and 753.

Approaching the Poems

Each of the following poems is a literary mirror—a poem that expresses the poet's ideas about poetry. In the first poem the French poet Charles Baudelaire (bōd ler') compares a poet to a large bird. In the second poem the Cuban poet José Martí (hô se' mär tē') uses several comparisons to express his view of his poems. In the third poem the Indian poet Rabindranath Tagore (rə bēn' drə nät' tə gôr') explores the connection between poet and reader.

Building Vocabulary

These essential words are defined alongside the poems.

indolent (in' də lənt): that **indolent** companion of voyage (page 334, line 3)

azure (azh' ər), **gauche** (gōsh): When that king of **azure,** shameful and **gauche,** / Piteously lets his great wings wreck (page 334, lines 6–7)

impetuous (im pech' ōō əs): think of the young spring day / wild, **impetuous** and free; (page 337, lines 19–20)

Connecting Writing and Reading

What is your immediate response when you are given an assignment to write a poem? In your journal jot down several words that describe your ideas about being a poet and about your past experiences with writing poetry. As you read, compare your ideas and the views about poets and poetry expressed in the following poems.

The Albatross

Sometimes, for sport, the men of the crew
Will snare a bird, the vast albatross,
that <u>indolent</u>[1] companion of voyage, who
follows their glide through bitter gulfs.

5   Scarcely is their victim decoyed to deck
When that king of <u>azure</u>,[2] shameful and <u>gauche</u>,[3]
Piteously lets his great wings wreck
Like oars that trail an unmanned boat.

The winged voyager grows clumsy and weak.
10   The beautiful swimmer now seems a clown.
One, to torment, props a pipe in his beak,
Another limps him high and down.

The Poet is like that prince of the clouds
Who frequents the storm, the archer mocks;
15   Exiled aground in sporting crowds,
His giant wings will not let him walk.

1. indolent (in′ də lənt): idle; lazy.

2. azure (azh′ ər): in poetry, the blue sky.

3. gauche (gōsh): awkward; clumsy.

Woodcut, LYND WARD. From *Storyteller Without Words* by Lynd Ward.
Courtesy of May McNeer Ward.

Poem

Should you see a hill of foam,
It is my poetry you see;
My poems are mountains
And feather fans.

5   My poems are daggers
Sprouting blossoms from the hilts;
My poems are fountains
Spraying jets of coral.

My poems are palest green
10   And flaming scarlet;
A wounded deer that searches for
A refuge in the forest.

My poems please the valiant;
Sincere and brief, my poetry
15   Is rugged as the steel they use
To forge a sword.

Poema

Si ves un monte de espumas,
Es mi verso lo que ves:
Mi verso es un monte, y es
Un abanico de plumas.

5   Mi verso es como un puñal
Que por el puño echa flor:
Mi verso es un surtidor
Que da un agua de coral.

Mi verso es de un verde claro
10   Y de un carmín encendido:
Mi verso es un ciervo herido
Que busca en el monte amparo.

Mi verso al valiente agrada:
Mi verso, breve y sincero,
15   Es del vigor del acero
Con que se funde la espada.

1996

Who are you reading curiously this poem of mine
a hundred years from now?
Shall I be able to send to you
—steeped in the love of my heart—
5   the faintest touch of this spring morning's joy,
the scent of a flower,
a bird-song's note,
a spark of today's blaze of color
a hundred years from now?

10   Yet, for once, open your window on the south
and from your balcony
gaze at the far horizon.
Then, sinking deep in fancy
think of the ecstasies of joy
15   that came floating down
from some far heaven of bliss
to touch the heart of the world
a hundred years ago;
think of the young spring day
20   wild, impetuous[1] and free;
and of the south wind
—fragrant with the pollen of flowers—
rushing on restless wings to paint the earth
with the radiant hues of youth
25   a hundred years before your day.

And think, how his heart aflame,
his whole being rapt in song,
a poet was awake that day
to unfold like flowers
30   his myriad thoughts
with what wealth of love!—
one morning a hundred years ago.

1. impetuous (im pech′ oō əs): impulsive; acting suddenly with little thought.

A hundred years from now
who is the new poet singing his songs to you?
35   Across the years I send him
the joyous greeting of this spring.
May my song echo for a while,
on your spring day,
in the beating of your heart,
40   in the murmur of bees,
in the rustling of leaves,—
a hundred years from today.

February, 1896

Thinking About the Poems

A PERSONAL RESPONSE

sharing
impressions

1. What impressions of poetry do you have after reading these poems? Write your thoughts and feelings in your journal.

constructing
interpretations

2. How would you explain each poet's view of poetry?
   Think about
   • Tagore's ideas about his poem and a future reader
   • the comparisons made by Martí
   • Baudelaire's contrast between the bird in flight and the bird in captivity

3. Which ideas conveyed by these poets come closest to your own ideas about poets and poetry?

A CREATIVE RESPONSE

4. How do you think either Tagore or Martí might have responded to Baudelaire's choice of an albatross to represent the poet?

5. Which examples of figurative language in these poems had the most impact on you? Explain your choices.

> ***Think about***
> - the extended metaphor of the albatross in the poem of the same name
> - the metaphors comparing "my poems" to such objects as mountains and a wounded deer in "Poem"
> - the simile in "1996" in which the poet's thoughts "unfold like flowers"

6. Select one of the three poems and compare the ideas it expresses about poets and poetry with the ideas on the role of the writer expressed by either Camus or Andrić in his Nobel acceptance speech.

Connecting Reading and Writing

1. Write a **poem** to express your ideas about poets and poetry.

Option: Create **lyrics** for a song about a poet and his or her life and work.

2. Tape-record a reading of one of these poems. Then listen to the reading and identify what it brings out that a silent reading might not. Express your ideas in an **advertisement** that might appear in a teacher's catalog of poetry cassettes.

Option: Write **program notes** that a radio announcer might read to enhance an audience's appreciation of the oral reading.

3. Imagine that your school is planning to publish a literary journal to showcase student poems. Write an **introduction** for that journal, expressing your ideas on poets and poetry and referring to some of the views expressed by Baudelaire, Martí, and Tagore.

Option: Write a **letter** to one of the three poets, explaining your own ideas about poets and poetry.

4. If you know French, Spanish, or Bengali, examine "The Albatross," "Poem," or "1996" in its original language and try to translate a few lines into your own words. Then write a **job description** identifying the skills necessary for translating poetry.

Option: In an **essay** for your classmates, describe your experiences with trying to translate a poem.

Pride

DAHLIA RAVIKOVITCH   born 1936   ISRAEL

A biography of Ravikovitch appears on page 750.

Approaching the Poem

"Pride" is a translation from Hebrew of a poem by Dahlia Ravikovitch (dä′ lē ə ru vē kō′ vich), the leading woman poet in Israel. Like the works that precede it, this poem expresses the writer's ideas on a topic; however, the ideas are not formally defined or analyzed. Rather, they are implied through imagery and metaphor. It is up to you, the reader, to discover how the details in this description of a scene from nature convey ideas about pride.

———————

      I tell you, even rocks crack,
      and not because of age.
      For years they lie on their backs
      in the heat and the cold,
5   so many years,
      it almost seems peaceful.
      They don't move, so the cracks stay hidden.
      A kind of pride.
      Years pass over them, waiting there.
10   Whoever is going to shatter them
      hasn't come yet.
      And so the moss flourishes, the seaweed
      whips around,
      the sea pushes through and rolls back—
15   the rocks seem motionless.
      Till a little seal comes to rub against them,
      comes and goes away.
      And suddenly the rock has an open wound.
      I told you, when rocks break, it happens by surprise.
20   And people, too.

LITERATURE OF SELF-EXPRESSION

Reviewing Concepts

IMAGERY AND TONE: ELEMENTS OF SELF-EXPRESSION

making connections

The writers represented in this unit all share a purpose: to express themselves through their writing. Although some of the writers' works focus on feelings and others on ideas, all of the writers depend to some degree on imagery to convey their tone, or attitude toward a subject. This attitude influences the readers' perceptions of what the writer is saying, both directly and indirectly.

In "Poem on Returning to Dwell in the Country," T'ao Ch'ien uses images of the countryside to convey a tone of both joy and longing. In "Song," Heine employs unlikely images of nature, such as pale and withering flowers and a lark's mournful singing, to convey a tone of sorrow. In his Nobel acceptance speech, Camus uses the image of "a glaring light" in describing his surprise at being chosen for the award; this image helps convey a tone of humility and wonder at the beginning of the speech.

To understand the importance of imagery and tone in works of self-expression, think back over the selections in this unit. For at least six selections, decide on the tone of the writer and identify two or more images that help create the tone. Make a chart similar to the one below and record your findings. You may find in certain selections that more than one tone is conveyed.

Selection	Tone	Images
"Poem on Returning to Dwell in the Country"	joy, longing	"A cock is crowing/atop a mulberry tree." "The tame bird/longs for his old forest"

describing connections

Note whether your chart reveals any similarities in tone between two or more selections. Also look for sharp contrasts in tone. Compare your chart with those of several classmates. Take **notes** on your discussion and use the notes to prepare an oral group presentation on the importance of imagery and tone in literature of self-expression.

Hunting Scene, 1966, ADEBISI AKANJI.
Section of a cement screen around a gas station in Nigeria. The Studio Museum in Harlem, New York; gift of Ronald and Jacqueline Springwater.

The Way of the World:

Literature as Observation

*"Let observation with extensive view,
Survey mankind, from China to Peru;
Remark each anxious toil, each eager strife
And watch the busy scenes of crowded life."*

SAMUEL JOHNSON

Recording Events

*T*he present, the here and now, is ever elusive. Each moment, as it is lived, slips inevitably into the past, never to be experienced again. A moment can no more be captured and held than light on the water can be caught in a net. And yet it seems to be part of the human condition to try. We take photographs or make videotapes of people, places, and events. We fill diaries and store away mementos of special occasions, all in an attempt to keep in touch with the present as it rapidly turns into the past. In this endless attempt to capture time in a bottle, writers hold a special place. They have been honored and rewarded in almost every society, in part because they have been able to record life, keeping moments from being forever lost.

Even before written language existed, bards sang about the history of their people, using rhymes and other tricks of language to help their memories hold onto the past. Through the use of detail and mood, the bards were able to convey the significance of characters' actions. Early historians learned from the bards and carried on the tradition. The histories they wrote convey not only events but also details of setting and the motivations of historic figures. In many instances, these well-conceived portrayals of earlier times are the only sources of information about important historical periods.

Other historical writings have also found a place in the world of literature. They are personal writings, such as memoirs, diaries, and letters, that are executed with such skill, grace, or sincerity that they interest and move readers centuries after their authors died. The personal view of everyday life and of historical events that these writings provide is often more absorbing, and sometimes more accurate, than the more detached view found in the works of professional historians.

Glimpses into the past can be both entertaining and rewarding, giving new insights into the history of civilization and into human nature itself. As you read the selections that follow, consider the information you gain about events of the past. Also think about the lessons to be learned from the mistakes of others.

Literary Vocabulary

Historical Writing. Historical writing is the systematic telling, often in narrative form, of the past of a nation or group of people. Historical writing generally has the following characteristics: (1) it is concerned with real events rather than mythological ones; (2) it uses chronological order; and (3) it is usually an objective retelling of the facts rather than a personal interpretation of them. In this unit you will read a piece of historical writing by the ancient Roman historian Tacitus.

Description. Description is writing that helps a reader to picture scenes, events, and characters. It helps a reader understand exactly what someone or something is like. An effective description is often like a good painting, providing visual details that create a clear impression of the person, place, object, or event being described. For example, in "The Silver Mine," a story in Unit 1, the reader learns through description what the King sees: "fairly large meadows and villages . . . between thick rows of alder bushes."

Setting. Setting refers to the time and place of the action of a literary work. Setting often plays an important part in what happens and why. For example, the setting of "Mussoco," a story in Unit 1, is a small village in Africa in which the people work hard for what little they receive. In the context of this setting, the significance of Donana's lost money is magnified.

The Burning of Rome

TACITUS   c. A.D. 56–c. 120   ANCIENT ROME

A biography of Tacitus appears on page 752.

Approaching the History

Tacitus was probably the greatest of the Roman historians. One of his most famous works is called the *Annals* because it records events year by year from A.D. 14 to 68. This excerpt from the *Annals* tells of the destructive fire that swept through Rome in A.D. 64 during the reign of the emperor Nero. At first a wise and serious ruler, Nero turned unpredictable and brutal. Nero's reputation at the time contributed to widespread suspicion about his role in the fire.

Building Vocabulary

These essential words are footnoted within the selection.

inextricable (in eks′ tri kə bəl): All made up a scene of **inextricable** confusion. (page 347)

prodigious (prō dij′ əs): The labor would have been **prodigious,** and no object served. (page 348)

propitiate (prō pish′ ē āt′): Means were taken to **propitiate** the gods. (page 349)

incendiarism (in sen′ dē ə riz′ əm): A vast number were condemned, not so much on the charge of **incendiarism** as for their hatred of the human race. (page 349)

direst (dīr′ est), **glut:** But guilty as these men were and worthy of **direst** punishment, the fact that they were being sacrificed . . . only to **glut** the cruelty of one man, aroused a feeling of pity on their behalf. (page 350)

Connecting Writing and Reading

Think about television or newspaper reports of a calamity such as a tornado, earthquake, hurricane, flood, or fire. In your journal describe how individual citizens and government officials responded during and after the calamity. As you read this selection, compare the responses you noted in your journal with the response of the Roman people and government to the calamity of fire.

ND NOW CAME a calamitous fire—whether it was accidental or purposely contrived by the Emperor remains uncertain: for on this point authorities are divided—more violent and more destructive than any that ever befell our city. It began in that part of the Circus[1] which adjoins the Palatine and Caelian[2] hills. Breaking out in shops full of inflammable merchandise, it took hold and gathered strength at once; and, being fanned by the wind, soon embraced the entire length of the Circus, where there were no mansions with protective walls, no temple enclosures, nor anything else to arrest its course. Furiously the destroying flames swept on, first over the level ground, then up the heights, then again plunging into the hollows, with a rapidity that outstripped all efforts to cope with them, the ancient city lending itself to their progress by its narrow, tortuous streets and its misshapen blocks of buildings. The shrieks of panic-stricken women; the weakness of the aged and the helplessness of the young; the efforts of some to save themselves, of others to help their neighbors; the hurrying of those who dragged their sick along, the lingering of those who waited for them—all made up a scene of inextricable[3] confusion.

Many persons, while looking behind them, were enveloped from the front or from the side; or, having escaped to the nearest place of safety, found this too in possession of the flames, and even places which they had thought beyond their reach in the same plight with the rest. At last, not knowing where to turn or what to avoid, they poured into the roads or threw themselves down in the fields: some having lost their all, not having even food for the day; others, though with means of escape open to them, preferring to perish for love of the dear ones whom they could not save. And none dared to check the flames; for there were many who threatened and forced back those who would extinguish them, while others openly flung in torches, saying that they had their orders—whether it was really so or only that they wanted to plunder undisturbed.

At this moment Nero was at Antium.[4] He did not return to the city until the flames were approaching the mansion which he had built to connect the Palatine with the Gardens of Maecenas,[5] nor could they be stopped until the whole Palatine, including the palace and everything around it, had been consumed. Nero assigned the Campus Martius and the Agrippa monuments[6] for the relief of the fugitive and houseless multitude. He threw open his own gardens also and put up temporary buildings for the accommodation of the destitute; he brought up provisions from Ostia[7] and the neighboring towns; and he reduced the price of corn to three sesterces the peck. But popular as these measures were, they aroused no gratitude; for a rumor had got abroad that at the moment when the city was in flames, Nero had mounted upon a stage in his own house and, by way of likening modern calamities to ancient, had sung the tale of the sack of Troy.

Not until the sixth day was the fire got under, at the foot of the Esquiline[8] hill, by demolishing a vast extent of buildings, so as to

---

1. Circus: reference to the Circus Maximus, a large stadium used for chariot races.
2. Palatine (pa′ lə tīn) . . . **Caelian** (sē′ lē ən).
3. inextricable (in eks′ tri kə bəl): too complicated or involved to clear up.
4. Antium (an′ tē əm): city just south of Rome.
5. Maecenas (mī sē′ nəs).

6. Campus Martius (kam′ pəs mär′ shē əs) . . . **monuments:** an area containing public buildings, including the public baths built by Agrippa, Roman military leader and statesman.
7. Ostia (äs′ tē ə): the part of Rome at the mouth of the Tiber River.
8. Esquiline (es′ kwə līn).

present nothing but the ground—and, as it were, the open sky—to its continued fury. But scarcely had the alarm subsided or the populace recovered from their despair when it burst out again in the more open parts of the city; and though here the loss of life was less, the destruction of temples and porticoes of pleasure was still more complete. And the scandal attending this new fire was the greater that it broke out in the property owned by Tigellinus,[9] in the Aemilian[10] quarter, the general belief being that Nero had the ambition to build a new city to be called after his own name. For of the fourteen regions into which Rome was divided only four remained intact. Three were burned to the ground; in the other seven, nothing remained save a few fragments of ruined and half-burned houses.

To count up the number of mansions, of tenements, and of temples that were destroyed would be no easy matter. Among the oldest of the sacred buildings burned was that dedicated by Servius Tullius of the Moon, and the Great Altar and fane raised by Evander to the Present Hercules. The temple vowed by Romulus to Jupiter, the Stayer of Flight; the Royal Palace of Numa; the Temple of Vesta,[11] with the household gods of the Roman people, were all destroyed; added to these were the treasures won in numerous battles, and masterpieces of Greek art, as well as ancient and genuine monuments of Roman genius which were remembered by the older generation amid all the splendor of the restored city, and which could never be replaced. Some noted that the nineteenth of July, the day on which the fire began, was also the day on which the Senonian Gauls had taken and burned the city; others were so curious in their calculations as to discover that the two burnings

were separated from one another by exactly the same number of years, of months, and of days.

Nero profited by the ruin of his country to erect a palace in which the marvels were not to be gold and jewels, the usual and commonplace objects of luxury, so much as lawns and lakes and mock wildernesses, with woods on one side and open glades and vistas on the other. His engineers and masters-of-works were Severus and Celer,[12] men who had the ingenuity and the impudence to fool away the resources of the empire in the attempt to provide by art what nature had pronounced impossible.

For these men undertook to dig a navigable canal, along the rocky shore and over the hills, all the way from Lake Avernus[13] to the mouths of the Tiber. There was no other water for supplying such a canal than that of the Pontine marshes, and even if practicable, the labor would have been prodigious,[14] and no object served. But Nero had a thirst for the incredible, and traces of his vain attempt to excavate the heights adjoining Lake Avernus are to be seen to this day.

The parts of the city unoccupied by Nero's palace were not built over without divisions, or indiscriminately, as after the Gallic fire, but

---

9. **Tigellinus** (ti gə lī′ nəs): Nero's chief adviser.

10. **Aemilian** (i mē′ lē ən).

11. **Servius Tullius** (sʉr′ vē əs tōō′ lē əs) . . . **Vesta:** references to various temples and altars dedicated by important Romans to certain gods and heroes of Roman civilization.

12. **Severus and Celer** (sə ver′ us, se′ ler).

13. **Avernus** (ə vʉr′ nəs).

14. **prodigious** (prō dij′ əs): enormous; huge.

in blocks of regular dimensions, with broad streets between. A limit was placed to the height of houses; open spaces were left; and colonnades were added to protect the fronts of tenements, Nero undertaking to build these at his own cost and to hand over the building sites, cleared of rubbish, to the proprietors. He offered premiums also, in proportion to the rank and means of the owners, on condition of mansions' or tenements' being completed within a given time; and he assigned the marshes of Ostia for the reception of the rubbish, which was taken down the Tiber in the same vessels which had brought up the corn. Certain parts of the houses were to be built without beams and of solid stone, Gabian or Alban, those stones being impervious to fire. Then, as water had often been improperly intercepted by individuals, inspectors were appointed to secure a more abundant supply, and over a larger area, for public use; owners were required to keep appliances for quenching fire in some open place; party walls were forbidden, and every house had to be enclosed within walls of its own.

These useful measures added greatly to the appearance of the new city; and yet there were not wanting persons who thought that the plan of the old city was more conducive to health, as the narrow streets and high roofs were a protection against the rays of the sun, which now beat down with double fierceness upon broad and shadeless thoroughfares.

Such were the measures suggested by human counsels; after which means were taken to propitiate[15] the Gods. The Sibylline Books[16] were consulted, and prayers were offered, as prescribed by them, to Vulcan, to Ceres, and to Proserpine. Juno[17] was supplicated by the matrons, in the Capitol first and afterwards at the nearest point upon the sea, from which water was drawn to sprinkle the temple and image of the goddess; banquets to the goddesses and all-night festivals were celebrated by married women.

But neither human aid nor imperial bounty nor atoning offerings to the gods could remove the sinister suspicion that the fire had been brought about by Nero's order. To put an end, therefore, to this rumor, he shifted the charge on to others and inflicted the most cruel tortures upon a body of men detested for their abominations and popularly known by the name of Christians. This name came from one Christus, who was put to death in the reign of Tiberius[18] by the Procurator Pontius Pilate; but though checked for the time, the detestable superstition broke out again, not in Judea only, where the mischief began, but even in Rome, where every horrible and shameful iniquity, from every quarter of the world, pours in and finds a welcome.

First those who acknowledged themselves of this persuasion were arrested; and upon their testimony a vast number were condemned, not so much on the charge of incendiarism[19] as for

> **Guide for Interpretation**
>
> Notice Tacitus' description of the early Christians. As you read, look for other signs of Tacitus' attitude toward this group of people.

---

15. **propitiate** (prō pish′ ē āt′): to win or regain the goodwill of; to calm the anger of.
16. **Sibylline** (si′ bə lῑn) **Books:** books containing the prophecies of Apollo's priestesses.
17. **Vulcan** (vul′ kən): god of fire and metalwork; **Ceres** (sē′ rēz): goddess of agriculture; **Proserpine** (präs′ ər pῑn′): daughter of Ceres and wife of Pluto; **Juno:** queen of the gods and goddess of marriage.

18. **Tiberius** (tῑ bir′ ē əs): Roman emperor from 42 B.C. to A.D. 37.
19. **incendiarism** (in sen′ dē ə riz′ əm): the act of starting a fire with the intent to destroy property; arson.

their hatred of the human race. Their death was turned into a diversion. They were clothed in the skins of wild beasts and torn to by dogs; they were fastened to crosses, or set up to be burned so as to serve the purpose of lamps when daylight failed. Nero gave up his own gardens for this spectacle; he provided also Circensian games,[20] during which he mingled with the populace or took his stand upon a chariot, in the garb of a charioteer. But guilty as these men were and worthy of direst[21] pun-ishment, the fact that they were being sacrificed for no public good, but only to glut[22] the cruelty of one man, aroused a feeling of pity on their behalf.

c. A.D. 117

---

20. Circensian (sər sen′ sē ən) **games:** chariot games in the Circus Maximus.
21. direst (dīr′ est): most dreadful; most terrible.
22. glut: to feed or fill to excess.

Coin of Nero. Photo Courtesy Weidenfeld & Nicolson, Publishers, London.

Thinking About the History

A PERSONAL RESPONSE

sharing impressions

1. How do you feel about Nero's response to the fire that engulfed Rome?

constructing interpretations

2. Explain whether you think the Romans were right to suspect Nero of causing the fire.

Think about
- the measures Nero took for the relief of the victims
- the rumors that spread about him both during and after the fire
- the way he accuses and punishes the Christians
- possible motives suggested by his actions

3. What picture of Rome and the Roman people do you get from this selection?

Think about
- how the people respond during the calamity
- how quickly rumors about Nero spread throughout the city
- the people's reaction to the executions of the Christians
- details that describe the city of Rome

4. Compare the response of the Roman people and government to the fire with the response of individuals and governments to similar calamities today.

A CREATIVE RESPONSE

5. If there had not been any suspicions about Nero, how do you think people might have explained the cause of the calamity?

A CRITICAL RESPONSE

6. The Greek philosopher Aristotle assigns a low position to history as a form of literature because it deals with particulars—details of time and place—and not with things of universal or lasting importance. Do you think this evaluation applies to Tacitus' account? Go back through the selection to find evidence that supports your position.

7. Compare Tacitus' description of the burning of Rome with Aeneas' description in *The Aeneid* of the sack of Troy (page 165). Account for the major differences.

Analyzing the Writer's Craft

HISTORICAL WRITING

Based on this account, what do you think is Tacitus' opinion of Nero?

Building a Literary Vocabulary. Historical writing is the systematic telling, often in narrative form, of the past of a nation or group of people. Historical writing generally has the following characteristics: (1) It is concerned with real events rather than mythological ones; (2) it uses chronological order; and (3) it is usually an objective re-telling of the facts rather than a personal interpretation of them.

Tacitus' work is a form of historical writing known as the annal, a narrative of historical events recorded year by year. Tacitus believed in the ideals of the Roman republic, a form of government that had no emperor. In spite of this bias, Tacitus does attempt to be fair in expressing both sides of the question of whether Nero started the fire of Rome.

Thus, it is difficult to determine his own opinion about Nero from this account alone.

Application: Analyzing Historical Writing. Using passages from "The Burning of Rome" as evidence, work together with your entire class to hold a trial of Nero for the burning of Rome. The prosecution team, composed of three or four students, will need to go through the excerpt to find evidence that incriminates Nero. The members of the defense team will have to prepare themselves to refute the prosecution's charges by finding evidence that vindicates Nero. There should also be witnesses—Tigellinus, surviving Romans, the workmen on Nero's canal, and Nero himself—to testify at the trial and a judge to ensure the justice of the proceedings. The remainder of the class could serve as the jury.

Connecting Reading and Writing

1. Write a **transcript** of one person's testimony from the trial of Nero to be shared with the class.

Option: Write a **newspaper account** of the trial for your school newspaper.

2. Interview someone in your family or community who has experienced a tornado, earthquake, hurricane, flood, or other calamity. Write up your **interview** and include it with the interviews of several classmates in a news magazine.

Option: Prepare for an interview by researching a specific calamity and writing a set of **questions** you would like to ask someone who experienced that event.

3. Read a modern account of Nero and the fire at Rome, such as chapter fourteen of *Nero, Emperor of Rome* by Arthur Weigall. As you read, take **notes** in your journal comparing Tacitus' account with the modern account. Share your notes with your classmates.

Option: Imagine that you work for a publisher who must decide which account of the fire to print in a textbook. Write a **memo** to your boss stating your opinion.

4. Research another fire that engulfed an entire city, such as the Great Fire of London in 1666 or the Chicago Fire of 1871. Compare that fire with the fire of Rome in terms of origin, firefighting techniques, extent of damage and injury, and fire-prevention measures taken as a result of the fire. Then create a **chart** that could be displayed in your school during fire-prevention week.

Option: Compare and contrast the two fires in an **essay** to be featured in a history book.

from Memoirs of Madame Vigée Lebrun

ÉLISABETH VIGÉE LEBRUN   1755–1842   FRANCE

A biography of Lebrun appears on page 745.

*A*pproaching the Memoir

A gifted artist commissioned to paint portraits of French nobles, Élisabeth Vigée Lebrun (e lē za bet′ vē′ zhe lə brën′) recalls in her memoirs events of her own life amidst the turmoil of the French Revolution (1789–95). In this excerpt, Lebrun focuses on two of her best-known subjects: Marie Antoinette (mȧ rē′ än′ twȧ net′), the French queen who became a symbol for the idle aristocracy, and Madame Du Barry (dü bȧ rē′), the infamous mistress of Louis XV. Thousands of people, including the deposed King Louis XVI, Marie Antoinette, and Madame Du Barry, were executed by guillotine in the violent struggle to end the monarchy.

*B*uilding Vocabulary

These essential words are footnoted within the selection.

mien (mēn): Her majestic **mien** . . . [did] not . . . diminish . . . the sweetness and amiability of her face. (page 355)

vouchsafed (vouch sāft′): Louis XVI **vouchsafed** to talk to me at some length. (page 357)

execrable (ek′ si krə bəl), **fortitude** (fôrt′ ə tood): If the victims of that period of **execrable** memory had not had the noble pride of dying with **fortitude,** the Terror would have ceased long before it did. (page 358)

*C*onnecting Writing and Reading

Imagine a society divided between a few extremely rich aristocrats and many desperately poor people. If you lived among the rich, how might you feel about the poor? How might they feel about you? Describe these possible feelings in your journal. Then, as you read, compare them with those feelings of the rich and the poor as revealed in Lebrun's memoirs of revolutionary France.

*I*T WAS IN the year 1779 that I painted the Queen for the first time; she was then in the heyday of her youth and beauty. Marie Antoinette was tall and admirably built, being somewhat stout, but not excessively so. Her arms were superb, her hands small and perfectly formed, and her feet charming. She had the best walk of any woman in France, carrying her head erect with a dignity that stamped her queen in the midst of her whole court, her majestic mien[1] however, not in the least diminishing the sweetness and amiability of her face. To anyone who has not seen the Queen it is difficult to get an idea of all the graces and all the nobility combined in her person. Her features were not regular; she had inherited that long and narrow oval peculiar to the Austrian nation. Her eyes were not large; in color they were almost blue, and they were at the same time merry and kind. Her nose was slender and pretty, and her mouth not too large, though her lips were rather thick. But the most remarkable thing about her face was the splendor of her complexion. I never have seen one so brilliant, and brilliant is the word, for her skin was so transparent that it bore no umber in the painting. Neither could I render the real effect of it as I wished. I had no colors to paint such freshness, such delicate tints, which were hers alone, and which I had never seen in any other woman.

At the first sitting the imposing air of the Queen at first frightened me greatly, but Her Majesty spoke to me so graciously that my fear was soon dissipated. It was on that occasion that I began the picture representing her with a large basket, wearing a satin dress, and holding a rose in her hand. This portrait was destined for her brother, Emperor Joseph II, and the Queen ordered two copies besides—one for the Empress of Russia, the other for her own apartments at Versailles or Fontainebleau.[2]

I painted various pictures of the Queen at different times. In one I did her to the knees, in a pale orange-red dress, standing before a table on which she was arranging some flowers in a vase. It may be well imagined that I preferred to paint her in a plain gown and especially without a wide hoop skirt. She usually gave these portraits to her friends or to foreign diplomatic envoys. One of them shows her with a straw hat on and a white muslin dress, whose sleeves are turned up, though quite neatly. When this work was exhibited at the Salon, malignant folk did not fail to make the remark that the Queen had been painted in her chemise, for we were then in 1786, and calumny was already busy concerning her. Yet in spite of all this, the portraits were very successful.

Toward the end of the exhibition, a little piece was given at the Vaudeville Theatre, bearing the title, I think, "The Assembling of the Arts." Brongniart,[3] the architect, and his wife, whom the author had taken into his confidence, had taken a box on the first tier, and called for me on the day of the first performance. As I had no suspicion of the surprise in store for me, judge of my emotion when Painting appeared on the scene and I saw the actress representing that art copy me in the act of painting a portrait of the Queen. The same moment everybody in the parterre and the boxes turned toward me and applauded to bring the roof down. I can hardly believe that anyone was ever more moved and more grateful than I was that evening.

I was so fortunate as to be on very pleasant terms with the Queen. When she heard that I had something of a voice, we rarely had a sit-

---

1. **mien** (mēn): a way of carrying and conducting oneself; manner.
2. **Versailles or Fontainebleau** (ver sä′ y′, fôn ten blō′).
3. **Brongniart** (brôn nyär′).

ting without singing some duets by Grétry[4] together, for she was exceedingly fond of music, although she did not sing very true. As for her conversation, it would be difficult for me to convey all its charm, all its affability. I do not think that Queen Marie Antoinette ever missed an opportunity of saying something pleasant to those who had the honor of being presented to her, and the kindness she always bestowed upon me has ever been one of my sweetest memories.

One day I happened to miss the appointment she had given me for a sitting; I had suddenly become unwell. The next day I hastened to Versailles to offer my excuses. The Queen was not expecting me; she had had her horses harnessed to go out driving, and her carriage was the first thing I saw on entering the palace yard. I nevertheless went upstairs to speak with the chamberlains on duty. One of them, M. Campan,[5] received me with a stiff and haughty manner and bellowed at me in his stentorian voice, "It was yesterday, madame, that Her Majesty expected you, and I am very sure she is going out driving, and I am very sure she will give you no sitting today!" Upon my reply that I had simply come to take Her Majesty's orders for another day, he went to the Queen, who at once had me conducted to her room. She was finishing her toilet[6] and was holding a book in her hand, hearing her daughter repeat a lesson. My heart was beating violently, for I knew that I was in the wrong. But the Queen looked up at me and said most amiably, "I was waiting for you all the morning yesterday; what happened to you?"

"I am sorry to say, Your Majesty," I replied, "I was so ill that I was unable to comply with Your Majesty's commands. I am here to receive more now, and then I will immediately retire."

"No, no! Do not go!" exclaimed the Queen. "I do not want you to have made your journey for nothing!" She revoked the order for her carriage and gave me a sitting. I remember

that, in my confusion and my eagerness to make a fitting response to her kind words, I opened my paint box so excitedly that I spilled my brushes on the floor. I stooped down to pick them up. "Never mind, never mind," said the Queen, and, for aught I could say, she insisted on gathering them all up herself.

When the Queen went for the last time to Fontainebleau, where the court, according to custom, was to appear in full gala, I repaired there to enjoy that spectacle. I saw the Queen in her grandest dress; she was covered with diamonds, and as the brilliant sunshine fell upon her, she seemed to me nothing short of dazzling. Her head, erect on her beautiful Greek neck, lent her as she walked such an imposing, such a majestic air, that one seemed to see a goddess in the midst of her nymphs. During the first sitting I had with Her Majesty after this occasion, I took the liberty of mentioning the impression she had made upon me and of saying to the Queen how the carriage of her head added to the nobility of her bearing. She answered in a jesting tone, "If I were not Queen, they would say I looked insolent, would they not?"

The Queen neglected nothing to impart to her children the courteous and gracious manners which endeared her so to all her surroundings. I once saw her make her six-year-old daughter dine with a little peasant girl and attend to her wants. The Queen saw to it that the little visitor was served first, saying to her daughter, "You must do the honors."

The last sitting I had with Her Majesty was given me at Trianon,[7] where I did her hair for the large picture in which she appeared with

---

4. Grétry (gre′ trē): eighteenth-century French composer of operas.
5. Campan (kän pän′).
6. toilet: the act of dressing or grooming oneself.
7. Trianon (trē′ à nōn).

her children. After doing the Queen's hair, as well as separate studies of the Dauphin,[8] Madame Royale, and the Duke de Normandie, I busied myself with my picture, to which I attached great importance, and I had it ready for the Salon of 1788. The frame, which had been taken there alone, was enough to evoke a thousand malicious remarks. "That's how the money goes," they said, and a number of other things which seemed to me the bitterest comments. At last I sent my picture, but I could not muster up the courage to follow it and find out what its fate was to be, so afraid was I that it would be badly received by the public. In fact, I became quite ill with fright. I shut myself in my room, and there I was, praying to the Lord for the success of my "Royal Family," when my brother and a host of friends burst in to tell me that my picture had met with universal acclaim. After the Salon, the King having had the picture transferred to Versailles, M. d'Angevilliers,[9] then minister of the fine arts and director of royal residences, presented me to His Majesty. Louis XVI vouchsafed[10] to talk to me at some length and to tell me that he was very much pleased. Then he added, still looking at my work, "I know nothing about painting, but you make me like it."

The picture was placed in one of the rooms at Versailles, and the Queen passed it going to mass and returning. After the death of the Dauphin, which occurred early in the year 1789, the sight of this picture reminded her so keenly of the cruel loss she had suffered that she could not go through the room without shedding tears. She then ordered M. d'Angevilliers to have the picture taken away, but with her usual consideration she informed me of the fact as well, apprising me of her motive for the removal. It is really to the Queen's sensitiveness that I owed the preservation of my picture, for the fishwives[11] who soon afterward came to Versailles for Their Majesties would certainly have destroyed it, as

they did the Queen's bed, which was ruthlessly torn apart.

I never had the felicity of setting eyes on Marie Antoinette after the last court ball at Versailles. The ball was given in the theater, and the box where I was seated was so situated that I could hear what the Queen said. I observed that she was very excited, asking the young men of the court to dance with her, such as M. Lameth,[12] whose family had been overwhelmed with kindness by the Queen, and others, who all refused, so that many of the dances had to be given up. The conduct of these gentlemen seemed to me exceedingly improper; somehow their refusal likened a sort of revolt—the prelude to revolts of a more serious kind. The Revolution was drawing near; it was, in fact, to burst out before long. . . .

It was in 1786 that I went for the first time to Louveciennes,[13] where I had promised to paint Mme. Du Barry. She might then have been about forty-five years old. She was tall without being too much so; she had a certain roundness, her throat being rather pronounced but very beautiful; her face was still attractive, her features were regular and graceful; her hair was ashy, and curly like a child's. But her complexion was beginning to fade. She received me with much courtesy and seemed to me very well behaved, but I found her more spontaneous in mind than in manner: her glance was

---

8. **Dauphin** (dō fan′): the eldest son and heir to the throne of the king of France

9. **d'Angevilliers** (dän zh ə vēl ye′).

10. **vouchsafed** (vouch sāft′): was kind or gracious enough to give or grant.

11. **fishwives:** coarse, scolding women, in this case the common women who supported the French Revolution.

12. **Lameth** (là met′).

13. **Louveciennes** (loov syen′).

that of a coquette,[14] for her long eyes were never quite open, and her pronunciation had something childish, which no longer suited her age.

She lodged me in a part of the building where I was greatly put out by the continual noise. Under my room was a gallery, sadly neglected, in which busts, vases, columns, the rarest marbles, and a quantity of other valuable articles were displayed without system or order. These remains of luxury contrasted with the simplicity adopted by the mistress of the house, with her dress and her mode of life. Summer and winter Mme. Du Barry wore only a dressing robe of cotton cambric or white muslin, and every day, whatever the weather might be, she walked in her park, or outside of it, without ever incurring disastrous consequences, so sturdy had her health become through her life in the country. She had maintained no relations with the numerous court that surrounded her so long. In the evening we were usually alone at the fireside, Mme. Du Barry and I. She sometimes talked to me about Louis XV and his court. She showed herself a worthy person by her actions as well as her words and did a great deal of good at Louveciennes, where she helped all the poor. Every day after dinner we took coffee in the pavilion, which was so famous for its rich and tasteful decorations. The first time Mme. Du Barry showed it to me, she said: "It is here that Louis XV did me the honor of coming to dinner. There was a gallery above for musicians and singers, who performed during the meal."

When Mme. Du Barry went to England, before the Terror,[15] to get back her stolen diamonds, which, in fact, she recovered there, the English received her very well. They did all they could to prevent her from returning to France. But it was not long before she succumbed to the fate in store for everybody who had some possessions. She was informed against and betrayed by a little Negro called Zamore, who is mentioned in all the memoirs of the period as having been overwhelmed with kindness by her and Louis XV. Being arrested and thrown into prison, Mme. Du Barry was tried and condemned to death by the Revolutionary tribunal at the end of 1793. She was the only woman among all who perished in those dreadful days unable to face the scaffold[16] with firmness; she screamed, she sued for pardon to the hideous mob surrounding her, and that mob became moved to such a degree that the executioner hastened to finish his task. This has always confirmed my belief that if the victims of that period of execrable[17] memory had not had the noble pride of dying with fortitude[18] the Terror would have ceased long before it did.

I made three portraits of Mme. Du Barry. In the first I painted her at half-length, in a dressing gown and straw hat. In the second she is dressed in white satin; she holds a wreath in one hand, and one of her arms is leaning on a pedestal. The third portrait I made of Mme. Du Barry is in my own possession. I began it about the middle of September 1789. From Louveciennes we could hear shooting in the distance, and I remember the poor woman saying, "If Louis XV were alive, I am sure this would not be happening." I had done the head and outlined the body and arms, when I was

---

14. coquette (kō ket′): a girl or woman who tries to get men to notice and admire her; a flirt.

15. the Terror: the Reign of Terror, a period of violence, lawlessness, and terror that occurred during the French Revolution as a result of the savage measures taken by the temporary rulers.

16. scaffold: raised platform on which people were executed.

17. execrable (ek′ si krə bəl): that deserves to be hated or detested; very bad.

18. fortitude (fôrt′ ə tōōd): the strength to bear misfortune or pain calmly and patiently; firm courage.

obliged to make an expedition to Paris. I hoped to be able to return to Louveciennes to finish my work, but heard that Berthier and Foulon[19] had been murdered. I was now frightened beyond measure and thenceforth thought of nothing but leaving France. The fearful year 1789 was well advanced, and all decent people were already seized with terror. I remember perfectly that one evening when I had gathered some friends about me for a concert, most of the arrivals came into the room with looks of consternation; they had been walking at Longchamps[20] that morning, and the populace assembled at the Étoile gate had cursed at those who passed in carriages in a dreadful manner. Some of the wretches had clambered on the carriage steps, shouting, "Next year you will be behind your carriages, and we shall be inside!" and a thousand other insults.

As for myself, I had little need to learn fresh details in order to foresee what horrors impended. I knew beyond doubt that my house in the Rue Gros Chenet,[21] where I had settled but three months since, had been singled out by the criminals. They threw sulphur into our cellars through the air holes. If I happened to be at my window, vulgar ruffians would shake their fists at me. Numberless sinister rumors reached me from every side; in fact, I now lived in a state of continual anxiety and sadness. My health became sensibly affected, and two of my best friends, the architect Brongniart and his wife, when they came to see me, found me so thin and so changed that they besought me to come and spend a few days with them, which invitation I thankfully accepted. Brongniart had his lodgings at the Invalides, whither I was conducted by a physician attached to the Palais Royal, whose servants wore the Orléans livery, the only one then held in any respect. There I was given everything of the best. As I was unable to eat, I was nourished on excellent Burgundy wine and soup, and Mme. Brongniart was in constant attendance upon me. All this solicitude ought to have quieted me, especially as my friends took a less black view of things than I did. Nevertheless, they did not succeed in banishing my evil forebodings. "What is the use of living; what is the use of taking care of oneself?" I would often ask my good friends, for the fears that the future held over me made life distasteful to me. But I must acknowledge that even with the farthest stretch of my imagination I guessed only at a fraction of the crimes that were to be committed. . . .

I had made up my mind to leave France. For some years I had cherished the desire to go to Rome. The large number of portraits I had engaged to paint had, however, hindered me from putting my plan into execution. But I could now paint no longer; my broken spirit, bruised with so many horrors, shut itself entirely to my art. Besides, dreadful slanders were pouring upon my friends, my acquaintances and myself, although, Heaven knows, I had never hurt a living soul. I thought like the man who said, "I am accused of having stolen the towers of Notre Dame; they are still in their usual place, but I am going away, as I am evidently to blame." I left several portraits I had begun, among them Mlle. Contat's. At the same time I refused to paint Mlle. de Laborde (afterward Duchess de Noailles),[22] brought to me by her father. She was scarcely sixteen, and very charming, but it was no longer a question of success or money—it was only a question of saving one's head. I had my carriage loaded and my passport ready so that I might leave next day with my daughter and

---

19. Berthier (ber tye′): French soldier and aristocrat; **Foulon** (foo lôn′): government minister of war and finance; increased his own wealth at the expense of the poor.

20. Longchamps (lôn shän′).

21. Rue Gros Chenet (rü grô shə ne′).

22. Contat's (kôn täz′) . . . **Noailles** (nô ä′ yə).

her governess, when a crowd of national guardsmen burst into my room with their muskets. Most of them were drunk and shabby and had terrible faces. A few of them came up to me and told me in the coarsest language that I must not go, but that I must remain. I answered that since everybody had been called upon to enjoy his liberty, I intended to make use of mine. They would barely listen to me, and kept on repeating, "You will not go, citizeness; you will not go!" Finally they went away. I was plunged into a state of cruel anxiety when I saw two of them return. But they did not frighten me, although they belonged to the gang, so quickly did I recognise that they wished me no harm. "Madame," said one of them, "we are your neighbors, and we have come to advise you to leave, and as soon as possible. You cannot live here; you are changed so much that we feel sorry for you. But do not go in your carriage: go in the stagecoach; it is much safer." I thanked them with all my heart and followed their good advice. I had three places reserved, as I still wanted to take my daughter, who was then five or six years old, was unable to secure them until a fortnight later, because all who exiled themselves chose the stagecoach, like myself. At last came the long-expected day.

It was the 5th of October, and the King and Queen were conducted from Versailles to Paris surrounded by pikes. The events of that day filled me with uneasiness as to the fate of Their Majesties and that of all decent people, so that I was dragged to the stagecoach at midnight in a dreadful state of mind. I was very much afraid of the Faubourg Saint Antoine, which I was obliged to traverse to reach the Barrière du Trône.[23] My brother and my husband escorted me as far as this gate without leaving the door of the coach for a moment; but the suburb that I was so frightened of was perfectly quiet. All its inhabitants, the workmen and the rest, had been to Versailles after the royal family, and fatigue kept them all in bed.

Opposite me in the coach was a very filthy man who stunk like the plague and told me quite simply that he had stolen watches and other things. Luckily he saw nothing about me to tempt him, for I was only taking a small amount of clothing and eighty louis for my journey. I had left my principal effects and my jewels in Paris, and the fruit of my labors was in the hands of my husband, who spent it all. I lived abroad solely on the proceeds of my painting.

Not satisfied with relating his fine exploits to us, the thief talked incessantly of stringing up such and such people on lampposts, naming a number of my own acquaintances. My daughter thought this man very wicked. He frightened her, and this gave me the courage to say, "I beg you, sir, not to talk of killing before this child." That silenced him, and he ended by playing at battle with my daughter. On the bench I occupied there also sat a mad Jacobin[24] from Grenoble, about fifty years old, with an ugly, bilious[25] complexion, who each time we stopped at an inn for dinner or supper made violent speeches of the most fearful kind. At all of the towns a crowd of people stopped the coach to learn the news from Paris. Our Jacobin would then exclaim: "Everything is going well, children! We have the baker and his wife safe in Paris. A constitution will be drawn up, they will be forced to accept it, and then it will be all over." There were plenty of ninnies and flatheads who believed this man as if he had been an oracle. All this made my journey a very melancholy one. I had no fur-

---

23. Faubourg Saint Antoine (fō bō͞or′ san tän twàn′) ... **Barrière du Trône** (bàr yer′ dü trōn′).
24. Jacobin (zhȧk ô̂ ban′): any member of a society of radical democrats during the French Revolution.
25. bilious (bil′ yəs): having a yellowish color resulting from a disorder of the liver.

ther fears for myself, but I feared greatly for everybody else—for my mother, for my brother, and for my friends. I also had the gravest apprehensions concerning Their Majesties, for all along the route, nearly as far as Lyons, men on horseback rode up to the coach to tell us that the King and Queen had been killed and that Paris was on fire. My poor little girl got all a-tremble; she thought she saw her father dead and our house burned down, and no sooner had I succeeded in reassuring her than another horseman appeared and told us the same stories.

I cannot describe the emotions I felt in passing over the Beauvoisin[26] Bridge. Then only did I breathe freely. I had left France behind, that France which nevertheless was the land of my birth and which I reproached myself with quitting with so much satisfaction. The sight of the mountains, however, distracted me from all my sad thoughts. I had never seen high mountains before; those of the Savoy seemed to touch the sky and seemed to mingle with it in a thick vapor. My first sensation was that of fear, but I unconsciously accustomed myself to the spectacle and ended by admiring it. A certain part of the road completely entranced me;

I seemed to see the "Gallery of the Titans," and I have always called it so since. Wishing to enjoy all these beauties as fully as possible, I got down from the coach, but after walking some way I was seized with a great fright, for there were explosions being made with gunpowder, which had the effect of a thousand cannon shots, and the din echoing from rock to rock was truly infernal.

I went up Mount Cenis,[27] as other strangers were doing, when a postilion approached me, saying, "The lady ought to take a mule; to climb up on foot is too fatiguing." I answered that I was a workwoman and quite accustomed to walking. "Oh! no!" was the laughing reply. "The lady is no workwoman; we know who she is!" "Well, who am I, then?" I asked him. "You are Mme. Lebrun, who paints so well, and we are all very glad to see you safe from those bad people." I never guessed how the man could have learned my name, but it proved to me how many secret agents the Jacobins must have had. Happily I had no occasion to fear them any longer.

---

26. **Beauvoisin** (bō vwä za*n*′).
27. **Cenis** (se nēs′).

Thinking About the Memoir

A PERSONAL RESPONSE

sharing impressions

1. How did you feel about the situation Lebrun found herself in? Jot down your reactions in your journal.

constructing interpretations

2. Explain Lebrun's feelings about the French Revolution, as revealed in her comments about the rich and the poor.

Think about
- encounters she has with the aristocracy and the revolutionaries
- terms that she uses to refer to the aristocracy and the revolutionaries
- her acceptance by the French aristocracy

3. What impression of Marie Antoinette's character do you think Lebrun wishes to convey, and why? Explain your opinion using examples from the selection.

4. Did you find Lebrun a sympathetic person? Explain why or why not.

A CREATIVE RESPONSE

5. If Lebrun had not been an artist able to associate with the rich but a poor workwoman instead, how might her attitude toward the revolution be different?

A CRITICAL RESPONSE

6. How does Lebrun's tone influence the way you feel about the people and events she describes?

Think about
- tone as the attitude a writer takes toward the subject
- the people in the memoir whom you feel sympathetic toward and why
- the values of the rich portrayed by Lebrun

7. Lebrun's account is considered a memoir, while Tacitus' *Annals* is called a history. Based on these two works, compare the characteristics of memoir and history. Use specific examples from both selections to support your response.

Analyzing the Writer's Craft

DESCRIPTION

What impression of Madame Du Barry do you get from Lebrun's account?

Building a Literary Vocabulary. Description is writing that helps a reader to picture scenes, events, and characters. It helps a reader understand exactly what someone or something is like. An effective description is often like a good painting: it provides visual details such as color, size, and shape that give the reader a clear impression of the person, place, object, or event being described. For example, Lebrun portrays Madame Du Barry as an attractive, aging coquette with a "regular and graceful" face, "ashy" hair, and an inappropriately flirtatious and childish manner.

Application: Examining Description. Working in a small group, go back through the selection and identify words and phrases that describe Marie Antoinette's physical appearance. On a separate sheet of paper, sketch a full-length picture of a person to represent Marie Antoinette and write the descriptive words and phrases on the appropriate parts of the sketch. For example, Lebrun uses the terms "majestic mien" and "sweetness" to describe the queen's face, so those terms should be written on the face of the picture. Then, based on the descriptive details identified, reach a group consensus on what contemporary actress could best play the stage role of Marie Antoinette.

Connecting Reading and Writing

1. Locate a reproduction of one of Lebrun's portraits and, using Lebrun's descriptive style, write a **catalog entry** on that painting for visitors to a museum. Include information such as the year the painting was done and the subject's name, and point out distinctive qualities of the painting.

Option: Prepare the **speech** that an art auctioneer might give to persuade a collector to purchase the painting for several million dollars.

2. Imagine that you are in revolutionary France and are among a crowd in the streets clamoring for the heads of Marie Antoinette and Madame Du Barry. Based on what you know from Lebrun's memoirs, do you think the two women should be pardoned or executed? Write **notes** for a speech defending or condemning them.

Option: Interview ten of your classmates to learn whether they would defend or condemn Marie Antoinette and Madame Du Barry, and why. Present your results in a **chart** with accompanying summary.

3. Keeping in mind Lebrun's use of detailed description to portray the events of her time in her memoirs, write your own **memoir** of a contemporary historical event or of a more personal experience—for example, a town celebration or school event—that could be read two centuries from now.

Option: Write about that historical event or personal experience in the more factual, objective form of a **news report** for the school newspaper.

from Child of the Dark

CAROLINA MARIA DE JESUS   1913–1977   BRAZIL

A biography of de Jesus appears on page 744.

_A_pproaching the Diary

Born into a life of grueling poverty, Carolina Maria de Jesus (jē′ jā zōōs′) had only two years of formal education. Even so, her diary became the best selling book in Brazilian history. Written on blank pages of notebooks de Jesus found in the garbage, the diary tells of her struggle to support her three children and herself in the poorest slum of São Paulo (soun pou′ lōō) by collecting and selling scrap paper and metal. By chance, a newspaper reporter heard about her diary and arranged to have it serialized in a newspaper and later published as a book under the title _Child of the Dark._

_B_uilding Vocabulary

These essential words are footnoted within the selection.

indigo (in′ di gō′): The sky was the color of **indigo.** (page 366)

malice (mal′ is): The worst thing about it is that **malice** is the main subject. (page 367)

incalculable (in kal′ kyōō lə bəl): A sack . . . for me has an **incalculable** value, because I earn my daily bread with it. (page 368)

_C_onnecting Writing and Reading

If you were facing a personal struggle, such as a change in your family structure, a poor relationship with a family member, or a long-lasting feeling of depression, what would you do? Would you seek professional advice? confide in a friend? write about your troubles? Record your response in your journal. As you read, compare what you would do with what Carolina Maria de Jesus does as she faces personal struggles.

July 15, 1955

THE BIRTHDAY OF my daughter Vera Eunice. I wanted to buy a pair of shoes for her, but the price of food keeps us from realizing our desires. Actually, we are slaves to the cost of living. I found a pair of shoes in the garbage, washed them, and patched them for her to wear. . . .

I was ill all day. I thought I had a cold. At night my chest pained me. I started to cough. I decided not to go out at night to look for paper. I searched for my son João.[1] He was . . . near the market. A bus had knocked a boy into the sidewalk, and a crowd had gathered. João was in the middle of it all. I poked him a couple of times, and within five minutes he was home.

I washed the children, put them to bed, then washed myself and went to bed . . . When I awoke the sun was sliding in space. My daughter, Vera Eunice, said: "Go get some water, Mother!"

July 16

I got up and obeyed Vera Eunice. I went to get the water. I made coffee. I told the children that I didn't have any bread, that they would have to drink their coffee plain . . . I thought of the worrisome life that I led. Carrying paper, washing clothes for the children, staying in the streets all day long. Yet I'm always lacking things, Vera doesn't have shoes, and she doesn't like to go barefoot. For at least two years I've wanted to buy a meat grinder. And a sewing machine.

I came home and made lunch for the two boys. Rice, beans, and meat, and I'm going out to look for paper. I left the children, told them to play in the yard and not go into the street, because the terrible neighbors I have won't leave my children alone. I was feeling ill and wished I could lie down. But the poor don't rest, nor are they permitted the pleasure of relaxation. I was nervous inside, cursing my luck. I collected two full sacks of paper. Afterward I went back and gathered up some scrap metal, some cans, and some kindling wood. . . .

When I came home there was a crowd at my door. Children and women claiming José[2] Carlos had thrown stones at their houses. They wanted me to punish him.

July 18

I got up at 7. Happy and content. Weariness would be here soon enough. . . .

Dona Silvia came to complain about my children. That they were badly educated. I don't look for defects in children. Neither in mine nor in others. I know that a child is not born with sense. When I speak with a child, I use pleasant words. What infuriates me is that the parents come to my door to disrupt my rare moments of inner tranquillity. But when they upset me, I write. I know how to dominate my impulses. I only had two years of schooling, but I got enough to form my character. The only thing that does not exist in the *favela*[3] is friendship. . . .

My kids are not kept alive by the church's bread. I take on all kinds of work to keep them. And those women have to beg or even steal. At night when they are begging, I peacefully sit in my shack listening to Viennese waltzes. While their husbands break the boards of the shack, I and my children sleep peacefully. I don't envy the married women of the *favelas* who lead lives like Indian slaves.

I never got married and I'm not unhappy. Those who wanted to marry me were mean and the conditions they imposed on me horrible.

---

1. João (jô oun′).

2. José (jô zā′).

3. *favela* (fä vä′ lä) *Portuguese:* ghetto; slum.

. . . When those female witches invade my shack, my children throw stones at them. The women scream:

"What uneducated brats!"

I reply:

"My children are defending me. You are ignorant and can't understand that. I'm going to write a book about the *favela*, and I'm going to tell everything that happened here. And everything that you do to me. I want to write a book, and you with these disgusting scenes are furnishing me with the material."

Silvia asked me to take her name out of my book. . . .

July 21

I woke with the voice of Dona Maria asking me if I wanted to buy bananas or lettuce. . . . Then I went to wash clothes. While the clothes were bleaching, I sat on the sidewalk and wrote. A man passed by and asked me:

"What are you writing?"

"All the cheating that the *favela* dwellers practice. Those human wrecks."

He said:

"Write it and give it to an editor so he can make revisions."

. . . I spent the rest of the afternoon writing. At 4:30 . . . I gave the children a bath and got ready to go out. I went out to pick up paper but I felt ill. I hurried because it was cold. When I got home it was 10:30. I turned on the radio, took a bath, and heated some food. I read a little. I don't know how to sleep without reading. I like to leaf through a book. The book is man's best invention so far.

July 27

I am writing a book to sell. I am hoping that with this money I can buy a place and leave the *favela*. . . .

May 15, 1958

. . . I classify São Paulo this way: The Governor's Palace is the living room. The mayor's office is the dining room and the city is the garden. And the *favela* is the back yard where they throw the garbage.

May 19

. . . What our President Senhor Juscelino[4] has in his favor is his voice. He sings like a bird and his voice is pleasant to the ears. And now the bird is living in a golden cage called Catete[5] Palace. Be careful, little bird, that you don't lose this cage, because cats when they are hungry think of birds in cages. The *favelados*[6] are the cats, and they are hungry. . . .

I washed the floor because I am expecting a visit from the future deputy, and he wants me to make some speeches for him. He says he wants to know the *favelas* and if he is elected, he's going to abolish them.

The sky was the color of indigo,[7] and I understood that I adore my Brazil. My glance went over to the trees . . . the leaves moved by themselves. I thought: they are applauding my gesture of love to my country. I went on looking for paper. . . .

May 20

. . . My children ran to tell me that they had found some macaroni in the garbage. As the food supply was low, I cooked some of the macaroni with beans. And my son João said to me:

"Uh, huh. You told me you weren't going to

---

4. **Senhor Juscelino** (se nyōr′ jōō sä lē′ nōō).

5. **Catete** (kä tä′ chē).

6. *favelados* (fä vä lä′ dōōs) *Portuguese:* inhabitants of a *favela*.

7. **indigo** (in′ di gō′): a deep violet-blue dye obtained from certain plants.

eat any more things from the garbage."

It was the first time I had failed to keep my word. I said:

"I had faith in President Kubitschek."[8]

"You had faith, and now you don't have it any more?"

"No, my son, democracy is losing its followers. In our country everything is weakening. The money is weak. Democracy is weak, and the politicians are very weak. Everything that is weak dies one day."

The politicians know that I am a poetess. And that a poet will even face death when he sees his people oppressed.

June 1

. . . I haven't said anything about my dear mother. She was very good. She wanted me to study to be a teacher. It was the uncertainties of life that made it impossible for her to realize her dream. But she formed my character, taught me to like the humble and the weak. That's why I have pity on the *favelados* . . .

June 7

. . . When I was a girl my dream was to be a man to defend Brazil, because I read the history of Brazil and became aware that war existed. I read the masculine names of the defenders of the country, then I said to my mother:

"Why don't you make me become a man?"
She replied:
"If you walk under a rainbow, you'll become a man."

When a rainbow appeared I went running in its direction. But the rainbow was always a long way off. Just as the politicians are far from the people. I got tired and sat down. Afterward I started to cry. But the people must not get tired. They must not cry. They must fight to improve Brazil so that our children don't suffer as we are suffering. I returned and told my mother:

"The rainbow ran away from me."

June 23

I stopped at the butcher's to buy a half kilo[9] of beef. . . I was confused about the differences in prices. The butcher explained to me that filet was more expensive. I thought of the bad luck of the cow, the slave of man. Those that live in the woods eat vegetation, they like salt, but man doesn't give it because it's too expensive. After death they are divided, weighed, and selected. And they die when man wants them to. In life they give money to man. Their death enriches the man. Actually, the world is the way the whites want it. I'm not white, so I don't have anything to do with this disorganized world. . . .

July 30

I got 15 *cruzeiros*[10] and went by the shoemaker to see if Vera's shoes were ready, because she complains when she has to go barefoot. They were, and she put on the shoes and began to smile. I stood watching my daughter's smile, because I myself don't know how to smile.

. . . I started thinking about the unfortunate children who, even being tiny, complain about their condition in the world. They say that princess Margaret of England doesn't like being a princess. Those are the breaks in life.

August 12

I left my bed at 6:30 and went to get water. There was a long line. The worst thing about it is that malice[11] is the main subject. There was a Negress there who acted as if she'd been vaccinated by a phonograph needle. She

---

8. **Kubitschek** (kōō′ bit chek).

9. **kilo** (kē′ lō): kilogram, a metric unit of measure equivalent to about 2.2 pounds.

10. *cruzeiros* (krōō zā′ rōōs) Portuguese: dollars, the former basic monetary unit of Brazil.

11. **malice** (mal′ is): ill will; desire to harm another; spite.

talked about her daughter and son-in-law who were constantly fighting. And Dona Clara had to listen to it because she was the only one paying attention.

Lately it has become very difficult to get water, because the amount of people in the *favela* has doubled. And there is only one spigot.

September 8

Today I'm happy. I'm laughing without any reason. I'm singing. When I sing, I make up the verses. I sing until I get tired of the song. Today I made this song:

> There is a voodoo curse on you
> And who did it, I know who.
> It was little Mary.
> The one you loved before.
> She said she loved you too
> But you showed her the door.

January 16, 1959

I went to the post office to take out the notebooks that returned from the United States. I came back to the *favela* as sad as if they had cut off one of my arms. *Reader's Digest* returned my novels. The worst slap for those who write is the return of their works. . . .

May 6

At 9:30 the reporter appeared. I exclaimed: "You said you would be here at 9:30 and not one minute late!"

He said that many people wanted to see him because they liked his articles. We got into a taxi. Vera was happy because she was in an automobile. We went to Arouche[12] Square, and the reporter started to photograph me. He took me to the São Paulo Academy of Letters. I sat in the doorway and put the sack of paper beside me. The janitor came and told me to get away from the door. He grabbed my sack. A sack that for me has an <u>incalculable</u>[13] value,

because I earn my daily bread with it. The reporter said that it was he who had told me to sit in the doorway. The janitor said that he wasn't allowed to let just anybody who wanted to sit in the front of the entrance.

We went to Seventh of April Street and the reporter bought a doll for Vera. I told the sales-girls that I had written a diary that was going to be published in O *Cruzeiro*.[14]

June 8

When I got home and opened the door I found a note. I recognized the reporter's writing. . . . The note said that the article on me would come out on the 10th, in O *Cruzeiro*. That the book was going to be published. I filled with emotion.

Senhor Manuel[15] arrived. . . .

"They earn money from your work and won't pay you. They're tricking you. You should never have given him the book."

I was not impressed with the skepticism of Senhor Manuel.

June 9

. . . I was reading stories to the children when there was a knock at the window. João said:

"Mama, there is a man here with glasses."

I went to see. It was Vera's father.

"Come in!"

"Where do you get in?"

"Go around front."

He came inside. He let his eyes wander around the shack.

He asked:

"Aren't you cold here? Doesn't it rain in?"

"It rains, but I'm used to it."

---

12. Arouche (ä r$\overline{oo}$′ chä).
13. incalculable (in kal′ ky$\overline{oo}$ lə bəl): that cannot be calculated; usually too great to be measured.
14. *O Cruzeiro:* "The Dollar," name of publication.
15. Senhor Manuel (se ny$\overline{o}$r′ män wel′).

"You wrote me that the girl was ill, I came to see her. Thank you for the letters. I thank you because you promised to protect me and not reveal my name in your diary."

. . . He gave 100 *cruzeiros*. José Carlos thought that was very little, because he had other bills of 1,000.

June 10

. . . When João returned, he said the story was out. I searched all my pockets for money. I had 13 *cruzeiros*. I lacked two. Senhor Luiz loaned them to me. And João went to get it. My heart was beating just like the springs in a watch. What would they write about me? When João came back with the magazine, I read it—"A Picture of the Favela in Carolina's Diary."

I read the article and smiled. . . .

June 11

. . . I fed the children and sat on the bed to write. There was a knock at the door. I sent João to see who it was and shouted:

"Enter, black woman!"

"She isn't a black woman, Mama. It's a white woman, and she has a copy of *O Cruzeiro* in her hands."

She came in. A very pretty blonde. She said that she had read the article in *O Cruzeiro* and wanted to take me to the *Diário da Noite*[16] newspaper office to get help for me.

At the newspaper I got choked with emotion. The boss, Senhor Antonio, was on the third floor. He gave me a magazine to read. Afterward he went to get lunch for me—steak, potatoes and a salad. I was eating what I had dreamed about! I was in a pretty room.

Reality was much prettier than a dream.

. . . I am so happy! It feels as if my dirty life is now being washed.

July 13

. . . We went to a shoe shop, and I bought a pair of shoes for Vera. When Senhor Manuel, a *nortista*,[17] tried the shoes on her, she said:

"Shoes, please don't wear out! Because later Mama has to work hard to buy another pair, and I don't like to walk barefoot."

January 1, 1960

I got up at 5 and went to get water.

---

16. *Diário da Noite* (jē ä′ rē o͞o dä nô̂ ē′ chē).
17. *nortista* (nô̂r tēs′ tä) *Portuguese:* a person from the north of Brazil.

Thinking About the Diary

A PERSONAL RESPONSE

sharing impressions

1. How do you feel after reading de Jesus's diary entries? Describe your feelings in your journal.

constructing interpretations

2. Why do you think de Jesus chooses to write?
Think about
- the personal struggles she faces
- why she writes when others upset her
- her view of how a poet reacts to oppression
- why she thinks that books are man's best invention
- why she feels "as if my dirty life is now being washed" when she is published

3. Which character traits and personal beliefs of de Jesus seem to help her the most in facing her personal struggles?
Think about
- how she supports herself and her family
- her relationships with her neighbors
- her reflections about economic conditions and politics in São Paulo
- her attitude about writing
- her opinions about herself

4. What picture of poverty emerges from de Jesus's diaries?

A CREATIVE RESPONSE

5. If de Jesus had never learned to read and write, how might her life have been different?

A CRITICAL RESPONSE

6. Discuss how well de Jesus uses metaphors and similes to express her opinions about people and political situations.
Think about
- metaphors and similes as comparisons between two things that are actually unlike yet have something in common
- the people and situations described with similes and metaphors
- the qualities emphasized by the metaphors and similes
- your own response to the descriptions

7. What similarities and differences do you see in the poverty de Jesus experiences and the kinds of poverty that exist in America today?

8. What opinion do you think Madame Vigée Lebrun and Carolina Maria de Jesus would have of each other?

> ***Think about***
> - how social class affects their experiences and their viewpoints
> - the political opinions they express
> - the problems each faces
> - why each of them writes
> - how each relates to other people

Analyzing the Writer's Craft

SETTING

Much of de Jesus's writing reveals what life was like in the *favela* of São Paulo. What details of *favela* life stand out in your mind?

Building a Literary Vocabulary. Setting refers to the time and place of the action of a literary work. Often setting plays an important part in what happens and why. The crowded conditions and lack of resources in the *favela* were directly responsible for many of de Jesus's actions. For example, she had to get up at 5 A.M. to avoid waiting in a long line to get water from the only spigot in the *favela*.

Application: Evaluating Setting. Imagine that you are going to produce a television screenplay based on de Jesus's diaries. Your first job is to determine the settings you will use. In a small group, go through the diary excerpts and identify specific details of time and physical surroundings. Then write a proposal describing the locations you would portray on film. Share your proposal with the class.

from From Emperor to Citizen

AISIN-GIORO P'U YI   1906–1967   CHINA

A biography of P'u Yi appears on page 750.

Approaching the Selection

Many people are intrigued by the lifestyles of the rich and famous. This chapter from Aisin-Gioro P'u Yi's (ā Hin jüe lō pōō yē) autobiography tells of the extravagant life led by the boy destined to be the last emperor of China. P'u Yi became emperor under a regency at the age of three but as a result of the Republican Revolution was forced to abdicate in 1912. Under the Favorable Treatment Agreement, P'u Yi was allowed to keep his title, his court, a large pension, and possession of the Forbidden City, a walled area within the Imperial Palace that was restricted to the emperor and his household.

In 1924 P'u Yi was forced to leave the Imperial Palace by the army of the Chinese Nationalist Party and for a time took refuge outside of China. The success of the communist forces of Mao Zedong in 1949 put a final end to the dynastic rule of China. When P'u Yi's autobiography was published in 1960—with the help of an official government editor—readers believed that P'u Yi had been forced by Mao's government to criticize the dynastic system in order to show that even a former emperor could change his opinion of communist government. Regardless of value judgments made in the autobiography, evidence suggests that P'u Yi's depiction of his life is an accurate one.

THE "ARTICLES FOR Favorable Treatment" stipulated that I could live temporarily in the Imperial Palace without fixing any definite time limit. Apart from three large halls that were handed over to the Republic, the rest of the Forbidden City continued to belong to the Imperial Palace. It was in this tiny world that I was to spend the most absurd childhood possible until I was driven out by the soldiers of the National Army in 1924. I call it absurd because at a time when China was called a republic and mankind had advanced into the twentieth century, I was still living the life of an emperor, breathing the dust of the nineteenth century.

Whenever I think of my childhood, my head fills with a yellow mist. The glazed tiles were yellow, my sedan chair was yellow, my chair cushions were yellow, the linings of my hats and clothes were yellow, the girdle round my waist was yellow, the dishes and bowls from which I ate and drank, the padded cover of the rice-gruel saucepan, the material in which my books were wrapped, the window curtains, the bridle of my horse . . . everything was yellow. This color, the so-called "brilliant yellow," was used exclusively by the imperial household and made me feel from my earliest years that I was unique and had a "heavenly" nature different from that of everybody else.

When I was ten, my grandmother and mother started to come and visit me on the orders of the High Consorts,[1] and they brought my brother P'u Chieh[2] and my first sister to play with me for a few days. Their first visit started off very drearily: I and my grandmother sat on the *kang*,[3] and she watched me playing dominoes while my brother and sister stood below us very properly, gazing at me with a fixed stare like attendants on duty in a *yamen*.[4] Later it occurred to me to take them along to the part of the palace in which I lived, where I asked P'u Chieh, "What games do you play at home?"

"P'u Chieh can play hide-and-seek," said my brother, who was a year younger than I, in a very respectful way.

"So you play hide-and-seek too? It's a jolly good game." I was very excited. I had played it with the eunuchs[5] but never with children younger than myself. So we started to play hide-and-seek, and in the excitement of the game, my brother and sister forgot their inhibitions. We deliberately let down the blinds to make the room very dark. My sister, who was two years younger than I, was at the same time enraptured and terrified, and as my brother and I kept giving her frights, we got so carried away that we were laughing and shouting. When we were exhausted, we climbed up onto the *kang* to get our breath back, and I told them to think of some new game. P'u Chieh was thoughtful for a while, then started to gaze at me wordlessly, a silly smile on his face.

"What are you grinning at?"

He went on grinning.

"Tell me! Tell me!" I urged him impatiently, thinking that he must certainly have thought out some new game. To my surprise he came out with, "I thought, oh, P'u Chieh thought that Your Majesty would be different from ordinary people. The emperors on the stage have long beards. . . ." As he spoke, he pretended to be stroking his beard.

This gesture was his undoing. As he raised his hand, I noticed that the lining of his sleeve was a very familiar color. My face blackened.

"P'u Chieh, are you allowed to wear that color?"

"But . . . bu . . . but isn't it apricot?"

"Nonsense! It's imperial brilliant yellow."

"Yes, sire, yes, sire . . . ." P'u Chieh stood away from me, his arms hanging respectfully by his sides. My sister slipped over to stand with him, frightened to the point of tears.

"It's brilliant yellow. You have no business to be wearing it."

"Yes, sire."

With his "yes, sire" my brother reverted to being my subject. The sound "yes, sire" died out long ago, and it seems very funny when one thinks of it today. But I got used to it from early childhood, and if people did not use the words when replying to me, I would not stand for it. It was the same with kneeling and kowtowing.[6]

---

1. **High Consorts:** widows of two previous emperors.
2. **P'u Chieh** (pō͞o jye).
3. *kang:* a kind of brick platform built along one end of a room, used to sleep on; in the winter it is heated by a fire.
4. *yamen* (yä′ mən): the office or residence of a mandarin, or public official, in China.
5. **eunuchs** (yō͞o′ nəks): castrated men employed as servants.
6. **kowtowing** (kou′ tou′ iŋ): kneeling and touching one's forehead on the ground in a show of humble respect.

Young emperor being pulled in sedan chair in Peking.
Peabody Museum of Salem, Massachusetts.

From my infancy I was accustomed to having people kowtow to me, particularly people over ten times my own age. They included old officials of the Ch'ing Dynasty and the elders of my own clan, men in the court robes of the Ch'ing Dynasty and officials of the Republic in Western dress.

Another strange thing which seemed quite normal at the time was the daily pomp.

Every time I went to my schoolroom to study, or visited the High Consorts to pay my respects, or went for a stroll in the garden, I was always followed by a large <u>retinue</u>.[7] Every trip I made to the Summer Palace must have cost thousands of Mexican dollars: the Republic's police had to be asked to line the roads to protect me, and I was accompanied by a motorcade consisting of dozens of vehicles.

Whenever I went for a stroll in the garden, a procession had to be organized. In front went a eunuch from the Administrative Bureau whose function was roughly that of a motor horn: he walked twenty or thirty yards ahead of the rest of the party intoning the sound "chir . . . chir . . ." as a warning to anyone who might be in the vicinity to go away at once. Next came two chief eunuchs, advancing crabwise on either side of the path; ten paces behind them came the center of the procession—the Empress Dowager[8] or myself. If I was being carried in a chair, there would be two junior eunuchs walking beside me to attend to my wants at any moment; if I was walking, they would be supporting me. Next came a eunuch with a large silk canopy followed by a large group of eunuchs of whom some were empty-handed and others were holding all sorts of things: a seat in case I wanted to rest, changes of clothing, umbrellas and parasols. After these eunuchs of the imperial presence came eunuchs of the imperial tea bureau with boxes of various kinds of cakes and delicacies and, of course, jugs of hot water and a tea service; they were followed by

eunuchs of the imperial dispensary bearing cases of medicine and first-aid equipment suspended from carrying poles. The medicines carried always included potions prepared from lampwick sedge, chrysanthemums, the roots of reeds, bamboo leaves, and bamboo skins; in summer there were always Essence of Betony[9] Pills for Rectifying the Vapor, Six Harmony Pills for Stabilizing the Center, Gold coated, Heat-dispersing Cinnabar,[10] Fragrant Herb Pills, Omnipurpose Bars, colic medicine and anti-plague powder; and throughout all four seasons there would be the Three Immortals Beverage to aid the digestion, as well as many other medicaments. At the end of the procession came the eunuchs who carried commodes and chamber pots. If I was walking, a sedan chair, open or covered according to the season, would bring up the rear. This <u>motley</u>[11] procession of several dozen people would proceed in perfect silence and order.

But I would often throw it into confusion. When I was young, I liked to run around when I was in high spirits just as any child does. At first they would all scuttle along after me puffing and panting with their procession reduced to chaos. When I grew a little older and knew how to give orders, I would tell them to stand and wait for me; then, apart from the junior eunuchs of the imperial presence who came with me, they would all stand there waiting in silence with their loads. After I had finished running around, they would form up again

---

7. retinue (ret′ 'n yo͞o′): the servants and followers of a person of rank or importance.

8. Empress Dowager (dou′ ə jər): widow of the deceased emperor, who still holds a title.

9. betony (bet′ 'n ē): plant belonging to the mint family.

10. cinnabar (sin′ ə bär′): the mineral mercuric sulfide.

11. motley (mät′ lē): of many different or clashing elements.

behind me. When I learn to ride a bicycle and ordered the removal of all the upright wooden thresholds in the palace so that I could ride around without obstruction, the procession was no longer able to follow me, and so it had to be temporarily abolished. But when I went to pay my respects to the High Consorts or to my schoolroom, I still had to have something of a retinue, and without it I would have felt rather odd. When I heard people telling the story of the last emperor of the Ming Dynasty who had only one eunuch left with him at the end, I felt very uncomfortable.

The type of extravagant display that wasted the most effort, money and material was meals. There were special terms to refer to the emperor's eating, and it was absolutely forbidden to fail to use them correctly. Food was called not "food" but "viands";[12] eating was called "consuming viands"; serving the meal was "transmitting the viands"; and the kitchen was the "imperial viands room." When it was time to eat (and the times of the meals were not set but were whenever the emperor felt like eating), I would give the command "Transmit the viands!" The junior eunuchs of the presence would then repeat "Transmit the viands" to the eunuchs standing in the main hall of the palace in which I lived, and they would pass it on to the eunuchs standing on duty outside the hall; these would in turn call it out to the eunuchs of the "imperial viands room" waiting in the Western Avenue of the Forbidden City. Thus my order went straight to the kitchens, and before its echoes had died away a procession rather of the sort that used to take a bride's trousseau to her groom's house had already issued from the "viands room." It was made up of an imposing column of several dozen neatly dressed eunuchs hurrying to the Mind Nurture Palace with seven tables of various sizes and scores of red-lacquered boxes painted with golden dragons. When they reached the main hall, they handed their bur-

dens over to young eunuchs wearing white sleeves, who laid out the meal in an eastern room of the palace.

Usually there were two tables of main dishes with another one of chafing dishes added in winter; there were three tables with cakes, rice and porridge, respectively; and there was another small table of salted vegetables. All the crockery was imperial yellow porcelain with dragon designs and the words "Ten thousand long lives without limit" painted on it. In winter I ate from silver dishes placed on top of porcelain bowls of hot water. Every dish or bowl had a strip of silver on it as a precaution against poison, and for the same reason all the food was tasted by a eunuch before it was brought in. This was called "appraising the viands." When everything had been tasted and laid out, and before I took my place, a young eunuch would call out "Remove the covers." This was the signal for four or five other junior eunuchs to take the silver lids off all the food dishes, put them in a large box and carry them out. I then began to "use the viands."

And what was the food laid out "ten cubits square"?[13] The empress dowager Lung Yu[14] would have about a hundred main dishes on six tables, an extravagance inherited from the empress dowager Tzu Hsi.[15] I had about thirty. But these dishes which were brought in with such ceremonial were only for show. The reason why the food could be served almost as soon as I gave the word was that it had been prepared several hours or even a whole day in advance and was being kept warm over the kitchen stoves. The cooks knew that at least since the time of Kuang Hsu,[16] the emperor

---

12. viands (vīʹ əndz): choice dishes of food.
13. ten cubits square: about sixteen to eighteen feet on each side.
14. Lung Yu (lʊʊŋ yü).
15. Tzu Hsi (dzə Hē).
16. Kuang Hsu (gwäŋ Hü).

had not eaten this food. The food I ate was sent over by the Empress Dowager, and after her death, by the High Consorts. She and each of the High Consorts had kitchens of their own staffed by highly skilled chefs who produced twenty or more really delicious dishes for every meal. This was the food that was put in front of me, while that prepared by the imperial kitchens was set some distance away as it was only there for the sake of appearances.

To show how they loved and cared for me, the High Consorts also sent a responsible eunuch to report on how I had "consumed viands." This too was a pure formality. No matter what I had really eaten, the eunuch would go to the quarters of the High Consorts, kneel before them and say:

"Your slave reports to his masters: the Lord of Ten Thousand Years consumed one bowl of old rice viands (or white rice viands), one steamed breadroll (or a griddle cake) and a bowl of congee. He consumed it with relish."

At Chinese New Year and other festivals and on the birthdays of the High Consorts, my kitchen sent a spread of food to the Consorts as a mark of my filial piety. This food could be described as expensive and showy without being good, and was neither nutritious nor tasty.

According to the record of one month of the second year of my reign, the empress dowager Lung Yu, the four High Consorts and myself used up 3,960 catties of meat (over two tons) and 388 chickens and ducks every month, of which 810 catties and 240 chickens and ducks were for me, a four-year-old child. In addition there was a monthly allocation for the numerous people in the palace who served us: members of the Grand Council, imperial bodyguards, tutors, Hanlin academicians, painters, men who drew the outlines of characters for others to fill in, important eunuchs, shaman[17] magicians who came every day to sacrifice to the spirits, and many others.

Including the Dowager, the Consorts and myself, the monthly consumption of pork was 14,642 catties at a cost of 2,342.72 taels[18] of silver. On top of this there were the extra dishes we had every day, which often cost several times as much again. In the month in question there were 31,844 catties of extra meat, 814 catties of extra pork fat and 4,786 extra chickens and ducks, to say nothing of the fish, shrimps and eggs. All these extras cost 11,641.07 taels, and with miscellaneous items added, the total expenditure came to 14,794.19 taels. It is obvious that all this money (except what was embezzled) was wasted in order to display the grandeur of the emperor. This figure, moreover, does not include the cost of the cakes, fruit, sweets and drinks that were constantly being devoured.

Just as food was cooked in huge quantities but not eaten, so was a vast amount of clothing made which was never worn. I cannot now remember much about this, but I do know that while the Dowager and the High Consorts had fixed yearly allocations, there were no limits for the emperor, for whom clothes were constantly made throughout the year. I do not know what exactly was made, but everything I wore was always new. I have before me an account from an unspecified year headed "List of materials actually used in making clothes for His Majesty's use from the sixth day of the eleventh month." According to this list the following garments were made for me that month: eleven fur jackets, six fur inner and outer gowns, two fur waistcoats, and thirty padded waistcoats and pairs of trousers. Leaving aside the cost of the main materials and of the labor, the bill for such minor items as the edgings, pockets, buttons and thread came to 2,137.6335 silver dollars.

My changes of clothing were all laid down

---

17. **shaman** (shä′ mən): priest or medicine man.
18. **taels** (tālz): a tael is a Chinese unit of money.

in regulations and were the responsibility of the eunuchs of the clothing storerooms. Even my everyday gowns came in twenty-eight different styles, from the one in black and white inlaid fur that I started wearing on the nineteenth of the first lunar month to the sable one I changed into on the first day of the eleventh month. Needless to say, my clothes were far more complicated on festivals and ceremonial occasions.

To manage all this extravagant pomp there was, of course, a suitable proliferation of offices and personnel. The Household Department, which administered the domestic affairs of the emperor, had under its control seven bureaus and forty-eight offices. The seven bureaus—the storage bureau, the guard bureau, the protocol, the counting house, the stock-raising bureau, the disciplinary bureau and the construction bureau—all had storerooms, workshops and so on under them. The storage bureau, for example, was for stores for silver, fur, porcelain, satin, clothes and tea. According to a list of officials dating from 1909, the personnel of the Household Department numbered 1,023 (excluding the Palace Guard, the eunuchs and the servants known as "sulas"); in the early years of the Republic, this number was reduced to something over 600, and at the time I left the Imperial Palace there were still more than 300. It is not hard to imagine an organization as large as this with so many people in it, but the triviality of some of its functions was almost unthinkable. One of the forty-eight offices, for example, was the As You Wish Lodge (Ju Yi Kuan).[19] Its only purpose was to paint pictures and do calligraphy for the Empress Dowager and the High Consorts; if the Dowager wanted to paint something, the As You Wish Lodge would outline a design for her so that all she had to do was to fill in the colors and write a title on it. The calligraphy for large tablets was sketched out by the experts of the Great Diligence Hall or else

done by the Hanlin academicians. Nearly all late Ching inscriptions that purport to be the brushwork of a dowager or an emperor were produced in this way.

The buildings all around me and the furniture of the palace were all a part of my indoctrination. Apart from the golden-glazed tiles that were exclusively for the use of the emperor, the very height of the buildings was an imperial prerogative[20] that served to teach me from an early age that not only was everything under heaven the emperor's land but even the sky above my head belonged to nobody else. Every piece of furniture was "direct method" teaching material for me. It was said that the emperor Chien Lung[21] once laid it down that nothing in the palace, not even a blade of grass, must be lost. To put this principle into practice, he put some blades of grass on a table in the palace and gave orders that they were to be counted every day to see that not a single one of them was missing. This was called "taking the grass as a standard." Even in my time these thirty-six withered blades of grass were still preserved in a cloisonné[22] canister in the Mind Nurture Palace. This grass filled me with unbounded admiration for my ancestor and unbridled hatred for the Revolution of 1911.

There is no longer any way of calculating exactly the enormous cost of the daily life of an emperor, but a record called "A comparison between the expenditure of the seventh year of Hsuan Tung[23] (1915) and the past three years" compiled by the Household Department shows that expenditure in 1915 topped 2,790,000 taels and that, while it dropped in

---

19. Ju Yi Kuan (jə yē gwän).
20. prerogative (prē räg′ ə tiv): a special privilege, especially of rank, class, etc.
21. Chien Lung (jyen lʊʊŋ).
22. cloisonné (klɔi′ zə nā′): a decorative form of enamel work.
23. Hsuan Tung (Hüan dʊʊŋ).

each of the following three years, it was always over 1,890,000 taels. Thus it was that with the connivance[24] of the Republican authorities we continued our prodigious[25] waste of the sweat and blood of the people in order to maintain our former pomp and continue our parasitic way of life.

Some of the rules in the palace were originally not simply for the sake of show. The system by which all the food dishes had strips of silver on them and the food was tasted before the emperor ate it and the large-scale security precautions [were taken] whenever he went out was basically to protect him against any attempt on his life. It was said that the reason why emperors had no outside privies was that one emperor had been set upon by an assassin when going out to relieve himself. These stories and all the display had the same effect on me: they made me believe that I was a very important and august person, a man apart who ruled and owned the universe.

---

24. connivance (kə nīv' əns): secret cooperation, especially in a wrongdoing.
25. prodigious (prō dij' əs): enormous; huge.

Painting Pictures with Words

*W*ords have remarkable powers. We use them to communicate needs, make demands, and express feelings. Words can comfort, threaten, inform, or amuse. Like the paints of an artist's palette, they offer an almost infinite variety of possibilities. In the hands of a skilled writer, words can create images that echo forever in the mind.

The writers in this section of the book are artists with words. They have chosen not merely to record what they have seen but to lay out, as on a canvas, the shapes, tints, and textures of life. They stretch the limits of language to present pictures of worlds most of us will never see. These worlds may be distant in space or in time, but through words they become part of our own experience of life.

PORTRAITS

To most of us, a portrait is a painting or a photograph of a person posed and usually looking straight ahead, perhaps somewhat formal. Such a portrait records what a person looks like and, if created by an artist of talent, gives some hint of the subject's personality. What is important about a portrait is that it communicates clearly what the artist feels is significant about that person.

Literary portraits must accomplish the same task, and they are particularly suited for it. A writer can draw on a dazzling array of forms and approaches to reveal the subject's personality and character. There is descriptive vocabulary—words such as *honest, creative, compassionate, level-headed, intense*. There are stories and anecdotes that reveal, rather than tell, who the person is. There are complex analyses of motivations and accounts of relationships with other people. All of these can go into creating a vivid literary portait, one that makes the reader feel that someone has been added to his or her personal circle of acquaintances.

LANDSCAPES

Almost everyone has handed a snapshot to a friend and said, "This doesn't really show you what it's like." There, on a small square of paper, is an image bearing the outlines of a lake backed by towering mountains. What is not conveyed is the rich, clean smell of earth after a rain; the rustle of leaves as a sweet, mild breeze stirs the trees; the sudden light that falls on the water and breaks up into flashing darts of silver as that same breeze ripples the surface. How does a photographer capture, on a bit of paper, the scale of the mountains and their majesty—and the feeling of awe when one looks up at them and an eagle sweeps across the sky?

Often what comes closest to communicating the true spirit of a place is not a photograph at all. It is the picture in words created by a truly talented writer. Words can engage all of the reader's senses, as image after image captures the imagination, allowing the reader to bring into play his or her own memories. Words can communicate to the reader the feeling of time passing, the echoes of lives lived. Words, well used, can make a place come alive. They enable readers to experience the harmony and din, the stench and fragrance, the scene and spectacle of times and places they would otherwise never know.

Literary Vocabulary

INTRODUCED IN THIS SECTION

Soliloquy. In drama, a soliloquy is a speech in which a character utters thoughts aloud. Usually the character is on the stage alone, not speaking to other characters and perhaps not even consciously addressing the audience. Soliloquies reveal the character's inner thoughts, feelings, and plans. In *Mozart and Salieri,* a play you will read in this section of the book, writer Alexander Pushkin makes use of several soliloquies.

REVIEWED IN THIS SECTION

Tone

Mozart and Salieri

ALEXANDER PUSHKIN   1799–1837   RUSSIA

A biography of Pushkin appears on page 749.

*A*pproaching the Play

Alexander Pushkin is considered the greatest poet in Russian literature. *Mozart and Salieri* (mō′ tsärt′, sål yer′ ē) is one of four brief verse plays in which he explores the effect of a single strong emotion on human behavior. The composers Wolfgang Amadeus Mozart and Antonio Salieri lived in Vienna in the late 1700's. During their lifetime, Mozart was recognized as being the more gifted of the two. Salieri's reputation as a composer began to fade even before his death, whereas Mozart is now considered one of the greatest musical geniuses of all time.

*B*uilding Vocabulary

These essential words are defined alongside the play.

assay (as′ ā): It was then / . . . I first dared / to **assay** the bliss of the creative dream. (page 383, lines 21–23)

ignoble (ig nō′ bəl), **parody** (par′ ə dē): Nothing's for laughter when some base / buffoon in an **ignoble parody** / degrades the name of Dante. (page 385, lines 84–86)

untrammeled (un tram′ əld): No one would / trouble about life's grosser cares—and all / would dedicate themselves to **untrammeled** art! (page 389, lines 212–214)

*C*onnecting Writing and Reading

Imagine that you have spent months preparing for a competition—either in sports, academics, or music. You are in top form, but at the actual event someone who has been working only a week or two completely outclasses you. In your journal list words and phrases that express how you would feel about your rival. As you read the play, compare your feelings about a rival with Salieri's feelings about Mozart.

SCENE 1   (*A room.*)

Salieri. Everyone says, there's no truth in this world;
there's no truth either, even higher up.
This is as plain to me as a simple scale.
Ever since birth, my love has been for art;
5   I remember, as a child, our ancient church,
on high the organ pealing, and I listened,
listened with all my ears; in spite of me
the sweet tears flowed. And from the earliest age
I shunned all vain enjoyment; any science
10   that had no link with music, I detested;
I found it hateful—turned my face away
from it in obstinacy and in pride;
music was all my life. But the first step
was hard; the first road, boring. I withstood
15   the opening trials, I built up craftsmanship
as pedestal for art, became a craftsman;
I taught my fingers a fluency that was
expressionless and docile; trained my ear
to truth. I murdered sounds, and then dissected
20   music like a cadaver. Harmony
became for me an algebra. It was then
that, tempted out from science, I first dared
to <u>assay</u>[1] the bliss of the creative dream.
Embarked upon creation, but in silence,
25   in secrecy, I never ventured yet
to think of glory. Often, having sat
two or three days long in my silent cell,
forgetting sleep and food, tasting the joys
and tears of inspiration, I would burn
30   my handiwork, and coldly watch my thought,
and all the notes I'd given birth to, blaze
and vanish in a thread of smoke! . . . But no;
when the great Gluck[2] appeared, when he revealed
to us new secrets—deep and captivating!—
35   did I not then abandon all I knew,
all that I'd loved so much, all I believed
so fervently, did I not boldly march
without a murmur after him, just like
a lost wayfarer meeting with someone
40   who sets him on a different path? At length,
by force of effort and the most intense
perseverance, I reached a high degree

◆ **Lines 1–4:** Note that Salieri doesn't believe in any absolute value, or truth, either on earth or in heaven. He lives for art.

◆ **Lines 15–23:** Salieri studied the craft and science of music before starting to create his own compositions. Note especially his cold-blooded approach in lines 19–20.
   1. assay (as' ā): to attempt.

◆ **Lines 29–32:** Think about why Salieri burned his early compositions.
   2. Gluck (glo͝ok): Christoph Willibald Gluck (1714–1787), German composer. He is credited with having established certain reforms in operatic style that emphasize simplicity of expression. Salieri was one of Gluck's followers.

in the frontierless realms of art. And fame
already smiled on me; in people's hearts
45   I found a chord that echoed my creations.
My life was happy; I enjoyed in peace
labor, success and glory, yes, also
the labor and successes of my friends,
of my companions in the marvelous art.
50   No, never once did I experience envy!
Oh, never, never!—neither when Piccini[3]
managed to captivate the boorish ear
of the Parisian, nor when first I heard
the opening phrases of *Iphigenia*.[4]
55   Who could have forecast that the proud Salieri
would one day change to a contemptible
envier, to a serpent that men crush
as it gnaws feebly at the dust and sand?
No one! . . . But now—I'll say the word myself—
60   I am an envier! . . . Yes, I envy deeply
and agonizingly. O God in Heaven!
Where's justice, when the consecrated gift,
when genius the immortal is not sent
as prize for blazing love, and self-denial,
65   labor, and zeal, and prayer, but comes down
to shine upon the forehead of a madman,
a trivial idler? . . . Oh, Mozart, Mozart!

(*Enter* Mozart.)

Mozart. Ah, so you've seen me! But I had been hoping
to treat you to a joke you didn't expect.

70   **Salieri.** You're here! Since when?

Mozart.   This minute. On my way,
bringing along something I had to show you,
just as I passed the inn, all of a sudden
I heard a violin . . . No, dear Salieri!
Never in all my lifetime have I listened
75   to anything more comic! . . . At the inn
a blind violinist, playing, I swear it's true,
voi che sapete![5] No, I couldn't wait,
I've brought the fiddler with me, to entertain
you with his art. Come in.

(*Enter an old man with a violin.*)

                      Now play something

◆ **Lines 44–45:** Note the musical metaphor "in people's hearts / I found a chord that echoed my creations" used to describe Salieri's popular appeal.

3. Piccini (pi chē′ nē): Niccolo Piccini (also spelled Piccinni) (1728-1800), another follower of Gluck.

4. *Iphigenia* (if′ ə jə nī′ ə): reference to one of two operas—one by Gluck, the other by Piccini—on the subject of Iphigenia, a female character in Greek mythology.

◆ **Lines 61–67:** Salieri admits that he envies Mozart because genius is given to such a "trivial idler" and not to a hard worker like himself.

5. *voi che sapete* (vȯi kā sä pā′ tā) *Italian:* phrase meaning "what do you know!"

80   from Mozart!

(*The old man plays an aria from Don Giovanni:*[6] Mozart *laughs.*)

Salieri.   And you have the face to laugh?

Mozart. But you, Salieri, aren't you laughing?

Salieri.   No.
To me, nothing's for laughter when a useless
dauber is botching up Raphael's Madonna;[7]
to me, nothing's for laughter when some base
85   buffoon in an <u>ignoble</u>[8] <u>parody</u>[9]
degrades the name of Dante.[10] Old man, go!

Mozart. Wait just a minute: here—to drink my health!

(*The old man goes.*)

Salieri, you're in a bad mood just now.
I'll come to visit you another time.

90   **Salieri.** What have you brought me?

Mozart.   Nothing—just a trifle.
The other night I couldn't sleep; a few
ideas came to me. Today I've sketched them out.
I wanted your opinion; but just now
you're out of humor.

Salieri.   Oh, Mozart, Mozart!
95   For you, when am I ever out of humor?
Sit down. I'll listen.

Mozart (*at the piano*). Picture to yourself . . .
Who shall it be? Me, if you like, but younger;
in love—but not too much, just very slightly;
I'm with a beauty, or a friend—perhaps
100   with you; I'm cheerful. But then all at once:
a spectacle of death, a sudden darkness,
something of that sort. Listen.

(*He plays.*)

Salieri.   And with this
you came to me, then had the strength to stop
in front of the inn, to hear the blind violinist!—
105   By God, Mozart, you don't deserve yourself.

Mozart. What, is it good?

6. ***Don Giovanni*** (dän jô vä′ nē): an opera by Mozart.

7. Raphael's Madonna: reference to a famous painting by the Italian master Raphael.

◆ **Lines 82–86:** Consider why Salieri and Mozart have different reactions to the blind musician's poor playing.

8. ignoble (ig nō′ bəl): not noble in character or quality; dishonorable.

9. parody (par′ ə dē): a poor or weak imitation.

10. Dante (dän′ tā): Italian poet Dante Alighieri (1265–1321).

Salieri.   Such boldness! Such profundity!
And such proportion! Mozart, you're a god;
you don't know it yourself—it's I who know!

Mozart. Bah! Could that be the truth? Well, I suppose . . .
110 But my godhead is starving.

Salieri.   Listen, we
could go together to the Golden Lion.

Mozart. By all means. I'd be delighted. Give me time
just to go home and tell my wife she's not
to expect me there for dinner.

(*He goes.*)

Salieri.   I'll wait here;
115 be sure you come!
                    No, I can't fight my fate;
I've been picked out to stop him, otherwise
we'll all be ruined, music's priests, its servants,
not I alone, with my dull reputation . . .
No, what use is it, if Mozart lives on
120 and reaches a new summit? By so doing
will he raise art up higher? No! As soon
as he is gone, it will sink down again:
he leaves no heir behind him. So whatever
use can he be? Just like some cherub.[11]
125 he's brought us a few songs of paradise,
only to rouse in us wingless desires,
a smoke of dust—and then to fly away!
Then off you fly! The sooner so, the better!
                    Here is a poison, my Isaure's[12] last gift.
130 For eighteen years I've carried it with me;
often my life meanwhile has seemed a wound
too painful to be borne; often I've sat
at the same table with some unconcerned
enemy and never yielded to temptation's
135 whispered address, although I'm not a coward,
however deeply I may feel affronts,
however little I may value life.
Yet I delayed, although a thirst for death
tormented me—why die? I thought, perhaps
140 life may yet bring me unpredicted gifts;
perhaps delight will come, and a creative
midnight, and inspiration; or perhaps
another Haydn[13] will create some marvel

◆ **Lines 105–109:** Compare Salieri's praise of Mozart with Mozart's reaction to the praise. Think about which composer seems more concerned with reputation.

11. cherub (cher′ əb): angel.

◆ **Lines 115–128:** Notice why Salieri believes that he has been chosen to kill Mozart.

12. Isaure (ē soʊ′ rā): possible reference to Salieri's loved one.

13. Haydn (hīd′ ′n): Austrian composer Franz Joseph Haydn (1732–1809), a friend of Salieri.

for my enchantment . . . so as I sat feasting
145   with my unlovely guest, I thought, one day
perhaps I'll find a mortal enemy;
perhaps some mortal outrage will project me
headlong from pride's high mountain—ah, but then
you won't desert me, gift of my Isaure.
150   And I was right! I have both found at last
my enemy, and have been quite transported
with wonder and delight by a new Haydn!
Yes, now it's time. You hallowed gift of love,
you must this day pass into friendship's cup.

◆ **Lines 129–149:** Note the reasons Salieri gives for refraining from using the poison that Isaure gave him.

SCENE 2   (*A private room in an inn: a piano.* Mozart *and* Salieri *at table.*)

155   **Salieri.** Why so cast down today?

Mozart.   I? No.

Salieri.   Mozart,
I'm certain that there's something which disturbs you.
The dinner's good, and there's a glorious wine,
yet you sit silent, scowling . . .

Mozart.   I admit it,
I'm worried by my Requiem.[14]

Salieri.   So it's
160   a Requiem you've been writing. For some time?

Mozart. Oh, yes a good three weeks. But something
strange . . . Have I not told you?

Salieri.   Never.

Mozart.   Well, just listen:
three weeks ago, I came home late. They said
someone had called for me. Why, I don't know,
165   but all night long I wondered who it was
and what he wanted from me. The next day
he called again, again he found me absent.
The third day I was playing on the floor
with my small lad. They called me; I went out.
170   A man, dressed all in black, bowed deeply to me,
commissioned me to write a Requiem and
vanished. So I at once sat down and started
to write—and since that day my man in black

14. **Requiem** (rā′ kwē em′): any grand musical service or hymn in honor of the dead.

175 has not returned; but I've been glad: it would
have been a sorrow to be parted from
my Requiem, although by now it's quite
ready and finished. But meanwhile I . . .

Salieri.   What?

Mozart. I'm quite ashamed to admit it . . .

Salieri.   To admit what?

Mozart. My man in black, by day or night he gives me
180 no minute's peace. He trails me everywhere
just like a shadow. Even now I think
he's sitting here between us.

Salieri.   No, enough!
What childish terrors! You must chase away
such idle thoughts. Beaumarchais [15] said to me:
185 "Listen, my dear Salieri, when ideas
of gloom attack you, then uncork champagne
or else reread *The Marriage of Figaro*."[16]

Mozart. Well, yes! Beaumarchais was of course your friend;
it was for him you composed *Tarara*,[17]
190 that glorious work. There's a motif in it . . .
when I feel happy, I sing it constantly . . .
La la la la . . . But is it true, Salieri,
that Beaumarchais once poisoned someone?

Salieri. No, I doubt it; he was too much of a joker
195 for such a trade.

Mozart.   In fact he was a genius
like you and me. Genius and villainy
don't go together, do they?

Salieri.   Don't you think so?

(*He drops poison in* Mozart's *glass.*)

Well, drink.

Mozart.   Here's to your health, my friend,
to the true link uniting Mozart and
200 Salieri, those two sons of harmony.

(*He drinks.*)

Salieri. But wait, but wait! . . . you've drunk alone . . .
without me?

Lines 170–174: Speculate about who the man in black is and why he commissioned Mozart to write a Requiem.

15. Beaumarchais (bō màr she′): French dramatist (1732-1799).

16. *The Marriage of Figaro* (fi′ gà rô): A play written by Beaumarchais. Eventually, Mozart wrote an opera based on this play.

17. *Tarara* (tà rà′ rà): a French opera written by Salieri, considered his best work.

Lines 196–197: Note the dramatic irony: Mozart does not realize he is being poisoned by the man who questions his statement that "Genius and villainy / don't go together."

(Mozart *throws his napkin on the table.*)

Enough, I've finished. (*He goes to the piano.*)
　　　　　　　　　　Now, Salieri, listen,
my Requiem . . . (*He plays.*)
　　　　　　　You're weeping?

Salieri.　　　　　　　　　　Yes, these tears
　　are the first ones I've shed: there's pain, there's pleasure,
205　as if I'd carried out some heavy task,
　　as if some salutary knife had severed
　　an ailing member! Dear Mozart, these tears . . .
　　don't notice them. Continue, hurry on,
　　pour still more sounds into my soul . . .

Mozart.　　　　　　　　　　If only
210　everybody could so feel the strength
　　of harmony! But no: for in that case
　　the world could not continue: no one would
　　trouble about life's grosser cares—and all
　　would dedicate themselves to <u>untrammeled</u>[18] art!
215　How few of us there are, we happy idlers,
　　we chosen ones who spurn the ignoble call
　　of mere utility, priests dedicated
　　only to beauty. But just now I feel
　　a sickness, something weighing heavy on me;
220　I'll go and sleep. Farewell.

Salieri.　　　　　　　　　　Till our next meeting.

(*Alone.*)

　　Yes, go to your long sleep, Mozart! . . .
　　　　　　　　　　　　　But was he
　　not right? and am I not a genius too?
　　Genius and villainy don't go together.
　　That's wrong: take Buonarroti? . . . Or is that
225　a fable of the thoughtless herd—and was
　　the Vatican's creator no assassin?

◆ **Lines 203–207:** Speculate about why Salieri weeps as he listens to Mozart's Requiem.

18. untrammeled (un tram′ əld): not entangled, handicapped, or limited.

◆ **Lines 215–218:** Compare Mozart's attitude about music, expressed in these lines, with Salieri's earlier statement "I murdered sounds, and then dissected / music like a cadaver" (lines 19–20).

◆ **Lines 221–226:** Salieri is referring to the allegation that the great sculptor Michelangelo Buonarroti (mī′ kəl an′ jə lō′ bwô̂ när *r*ô̂′ tē) killed another sculptor in a brawl. Think about why Salieri uses this example to prove that genius and villainy can go together.

Thinking About the Play

*sharing
impressions*

1. How do you feel about Mozart and Salieri? In your journal, describe your response to them.

*constructing
interpretations*

2. What do you think drives Salieri to the extreme step of murdering his rival?

Think about
- why his response to Mozart differs from his response to Gluck and Haydn
- how he justifies killing Mozart
- what his choice of poison as his weapon might represent
- your own feelings about a rival who succeeds without much effort

3. Compare Mozart's and Salieri's attitudes toward music and explain the difference between them.

4. What insight into himself and his talent, if any, do you think Salieri shows?

Think about
- his question "Who could have forecast that the proud Salieri / would one day change to a contemptible / envier?"
- why he decides to use the poison on Mozart after having refrained from using it on himself or other enemies
- why he compares himself to Buonarroti at the end of the play

A CREATIVE RESPONSE

5. If Mozart had had to work harder to write better music than Salieri, do you think Salieri would have poisoned him?

A CRITICAL RESPONSE

6. Evaluate the impact this drama might have on an audience.

Think about
- the dramatic irony in the play
- the development of the characters
- the development of the plot
- how suspenseful the play is

7. Like Mozart, Pushkin was recognized as an artistic genius when he was very young but was accused of not being serious enough. Why do you suppose he did not feature Mozart as the central character of this play?

Analyzing the Writer's Craft

SOLILOQUY

Several times in the play Salieri talks to himself. How do those speeches differ from his speeches to Mozart?

Building a Literary Vocabulary. In drama, a soliloquy is a speech in which a character utters thoughts aloud. Usually the character is on the stage alone, not speaking to other characters and perhaps not even consciously addressing the audience. Soliloquies reveal the character's inner thoughts, feelings, and plans. In the first soliloquy,

Salieri speaks openly of his envy, an emotion that he tries to mask as soon as Mozart enters.

Application: Analyzing Soliloquies. In a small group, carefully read Salieri's three soliloquies. Create a chart that lists the thoughts, feelings, and plans that Salieri conveys in each soliloquy. Then, as a group, decide whether the three soliloquies give similar portrayals of Salieri or show changes in his character. Share your analysis with the class.

Connecting Reading and Writing

1. This play is from a collection titled *Little Tragedies.* Write an **essay** for your teacher in which you explore whether *Mozart and Salieri* is a tragedy. Include both a definition of tragedy and examples from the play to support your opinion.

Option: Create **program notes** for a production of *Mozart and Salieri.* Name the actors you would cast in the title roles, describe the sets, and explain whether the play is a tragedy.

2. Another play that implicates Salieri in Mozart's death is *Amadeus* by Peter Schaffer. Either read the play or watch the movie version of *Amadeus* and then compare the two plays in a **review** to be published in the arts section of a newspaper.

Option: Write an **outline** for an oral report to be delivered to your class comparing the two plays on the basis of both literary merit and audience appeal.

3. Imagine that you are a psychiatrist and that Salieri has repeated his three soliloquies to you. Write a **psychological profile** for your files in which you describe Salieri's personality and the major conflicts he feels.

Option: Write a new **scene** for the play in which a friend who knows of Salieri's plan tries to talk him out of it.

4. Write a **parody** of *Mozart and Salieri* in which a comic book hero, sports figure, or rock star expresses envy of a more gifted rival. Read your parody to your class.

Option: Using your prereading notes, write a **soliloquy** expressing the feelings you would have toward a rival who does not have to work hard to be better than you. Read your soliloquy to a friend.

from Earthly Paradise

COLETTE   1873–1954   FRANCE

A biography of Colette appears on page 740.

*A*pproaching the Selection

The French novelist Colette lovingly remembers her mother, Sido (sē dô′), in these two excerpts from her autobiography. The excerpt titled "I could live in Paris. . ." describes Colette's childhood memories of Sido when they lived together in a French country village. The excerpt titled "The time came . . ." presents Sido many years later when she was an old woman living alone and Colette would come back to visit, leaving her own home and family in Paris.

*B*uilding Vocabulary

These essential words are footnoted within the autobiography.

vindictive (vin dik′ tiv): She would harden her heart, frown, and answer "No" with a **vindictive** look. (page 394)

carmine (kär′ min): He . . . tore off the petals, as curved and **carmine** as his own lips. (page 394)

bohemian (bō hē′ mē ən): My biographers . . . sometimes make her out to be a "whimsical **bohemian**." (page 395)

lucidity (lo͞o sid′ ə tē): I sing her praises as best I may, and celebrate the native **lucidity** . . . in her. (page 395)

*C*onnecting Writing and Reading

What is your most vivid early memory of a parent or other adult? In your journal describe that memory and explain why it has lingered in your mind for so long. As you read, compare your memory with the memories Colette has of her mother and the French countryside.

*I*COULD LIVE in Paris only if I had a beautiful garden," [my mother] would confess to me. "And even then! I can't imagine a Parisian garden where I could pick those big bearded oats I sew on a bit of cardboard for you because they make such sensitive barometers." I chide myself for having lost the very last of those rustic barometers made of oat grains whose two awns,[1] as long as a shrimp's feelers, crucified on a card, would turn to the left or the right according to whether it was going to be fine or wet.

No one could equal Sido, either, at separating and counting the talc-like skins of onions. "One—two—three coats; three coats on the onions!" And letting her spectacles or her lorgnette[2] fall on her lap, she would add pensively: "That means a hard winter. I must have the pump wrapped in straw. Besides, the tortoise has dug itself in already, and the squirrels round about Guillemette[3] have stolen quantities of walnuts and cobnuts for their stores. Squirrels always know everything."

If the newspapers foretold a thaw, my mother would shrug her shoulders and laugh scornfully. "A thaw? Those Paris meteorologists can't teach me anything about that! Look at the cat's paws!" Feeling chilly, the cat had indeed folded her paws out of sight beneath her, and shut her eyes tight. "When there's only going to be a short spell of cold," went on Sido, "the cat rolls herself into a turban with her nose against the root of her tail. But when it's going to be really bitter, she tucks in the pads of her front paws and rolls them up like a muff."

All the year round she kept racks full of plants in pots standing on green-painted wooden steps. There were rare geraniums, dwarf rose bushes, spireas with misty white and pink plumes, a few "succulents," hairy and squat as crabs, and murderous cacti. Two warm walls formed an angle which kept the harsh winds from her trial ground, which consisted of some red earthenware bowls in which I could see nothing but loose, dormant earth.

"Don't touch!"

"But nothing's coming up!"

"And what do you know about it? Is it for you to decide? Read what's written on the labels stuck in the pots! These are seeds of blue lupin; that's a narcissus bulb from Holland; those are seeds of winter cherry; that's a cutting of hibiscus—no, of course it isn't a dead twig!—and those are some seeds of sweet peas whose flowers have ears like little hares. And that . . . and that . . ."

"Yes, and that?"

My mother pushed her hat back, nibbled the chain of her lorgnette, and put the problem frankly to me:

"I'm really very worried. I can't remember whether it was a family of crocus bulbs I planted there, or the chrysalis of an emperor moth."

"We've only got to scratch to find out."

A swift hand stopped mine. Why did no one ever model or paint or carve that hand of Sido's, tanned and wrinkled early by household tasks, gardening, cold water, and the sun, with its long, finely tapering fingers and its beautiful, convex, oval nails?

"Not on your life! If it's the chrysalis, it'll die as soon as the air touches it, and if it's the crocus, the light will shrivel its little white shoot and we'll have to begin all over again.

---

1. awns (ônz): the slender bristles that form at the top of certain grains and grasses.

2. lorgnette (lôrn yet′): a pair of eyeglasses attached to a handle.

3. Guillemette (gē yə met′).

Are you taking in what I say? You won't touch it?"

"No, Mother."

As she spoke, her face, alight with faith and an all-embracing curiosity, was hidden by another, older face, resigned and gentle. She knew that I should not be able to resist, any more than she could, the desire to know, and that like herself I should ferret in the earth of that flowerpot until it had given up its secret. I never thought of our resemblance, but she knew I was her own daughter and that, child though I was, I was already seeking for that sense of shock, the quickened heartbeat, and the sudden stoppage of the breath—symptoms of the private ecstasy of the treasure seeker. A treasure is not merely something hidden under the earth or the rocks or the sea. The vision of gold and gems is but a blurred mirage. To me the important thing is to lay bare and bring to light something that no human eye before mine has gazed upon.

She knew then that I was going to scratch on the sly in her trial ground until I came upon the upward-climbing claw of the cotyledon, the sturdy sprout urged out of its sheath by the spring. I thwarted the blind purpose of the bilious-looking, black-brown chrysalis, and hurled it from its temporary death into a final nothingness.

"You don't understand . . . you can't understand. You're nothing but a little eight-year-old murderess—or is it ten? You just can't understand something that wants to live." That was the only punishment I got for my misdeeds; but that was hard enough for me to bear.

Sido loathed flowers to be sacrificed. Although her one idea was to give, I have seen her refuse a request for flowers to adorn a hearse or a grave. She would harden her heart, frown, and answer "No" with a <u>vindictive</u>[4] look.

"But it's for poor Monsieur Enfert,[5] who died last night! Poor Madame Enfert's so pathetic, she says if she could see her husband depart covered with flowers, it would console her! And you've got such lovely moss roses, Madame Colette."

"My moss roses on a corpse! What an outrage!"

It was an involuntary cry, but even after she had pulled herself together she still said: "No. My roses have not been condemned to die at the same time as Monsieur Enfert."

But she gladly sacrificed a very beautiful flower to a very small child, a child not yet able to speak, like the little boy whom a neighbor to the east proudly brought into the garden one day, to show him off to her. My mother found fault with the infant's swaddling clothes, for being too tight, untied his three-piece bonnet and his unnecessary woolen shawl, and then gazed to her heart's content on his bronze ringlets, his cheeks, and the enormous, stern black eyes of a ten months' old baby boy, really so much more beautiful than any other boy of ten months! She gave him a *cuisse-de-nymphe-émue*[6] rose, and he accepted it with delight, put it in his mouth, and sucked it; then he kneaded it with his powerful little hands and tore off the petals, as curved and <u>carmine</u>[7] as his own lips.

"Stop it, you naughty boy!" cried his young mother.

But mine, with looks and words, applauded his massacre of the rose, and in my jealousy I said nothing.

She also regularly refused to lend double geraniums, pelargoniums, lobelias, dwarf rose bushes and spirea for the wayside altars on Corpus Christi day, for although she was bap-

---

4. **vindictive** (vin dik′ tiv): said or done in revenge.

5. **Monsieur Enfert** (mə syö′ än fer′).

6. *cuisse-de-nymphe-émue* (küēs′ də nanf e mü′) French: a variety of rose.

7. **carmine** (kär′ min): red or purplish-red.

tized and married in church, she always held aloof from Catholic trivialities and pageantries. But she gave me permission, when I was between eleven and twelve, to attend catechism classes and to join in the hymns at the evening service.

On the first of May, with my comrades of the catechism class, I laid lilac, chamomile, and roses before the altar of the Virgin, and returned full of pride to show my "blessed posy." My mother laughed her irreverent laugh and, looking at my bunch of flowers, which was bringing the May bugs into the sitting room right under the lamp, she said: "Do you suppose it wasn't already blessed before?"

I do not know where she got her aloofness from any form of worship. I ought to have tried to find out. My biographers, who get little information from me, sometimes depict her as a simple farmer's wife and sometimes make her out to be a "whimsical bohemian."[8] One of them, to my astonishment, goes so far as to accuse her of having written short literary works for young persons!

In reality, this Frenchwoman spent her childhood in the Yonne,[9] her adolescence among painters, journalists, and musicians in Belgium, where her two elder brothers had settled, and then returned to the Yonne, where she married twice. But whence, or from whom, she got her sensitive understanding of country matters and her discriminating appreciation of the provinces, I am unable to say. I sing her praises as best I may, and celebrate the native lucidity[10] which, in her, dimmed and often extinguished the lesser lights painfully lit through the contact of what she called "the common run of mankind."

I once saw her hang up a scarecrow in a cherry tree to frighten the blackbirds, because our kindly neighbor of the west, who always had a cold and was shaken with bouts of sneezing, never failed to disguise his cherry trees as old tramps and crown his currant bushes with battered opera hats. A few days later I found my mother beneath the tree, motionless with excitement, her head turned toward the heavens in which she would allow human religions no place.

"Sssh! Look!"

A blackbird, with a green and violet sheen on his dark plumage, was pecking at the cherries, drinking their juice and lacerating their rosy pulp.

"How beautiful he is!" whispered my mother. "Do you see how he uses his claw? And the movements of his head and that arrogance of his? See how he twists his beak to dig out the stone! And you notice that he only goes for the ripest ones."

"But, Mother, the scarecrow!"

"Sssh! The scarecrow doesn't worry him!"

"But, Mother, the cherries!"

My mother brought the glance of her rain-colored eyes back to earth: "The cherries? Yes, of course, the cherries."

In those eyes there flickered a sort of wild gaiety, a contempt for the whole world, a lighthearted disdain which cheerfully spurned me along with everything else. It was only momentary, and it was not the first time I had seen it. Now that I know her better, I can interpret those sudden gleams in her face. They were, I feel, kindled by an urge to escape from everyone and everything, to soar to some high place where only her own writ ran.[11] If I am mistaken, leave me to my delusion.

But there, under the cherry tree, she returned to earth once more among us, weighed down with anxieties, and love, and a husband and children who clung to her. Faced with the

---

8. bohemian (bō hē′ mē ən): an artist or poet who lives in a free, unconventional way.

9. Yonne (yôn).

10. lucidity (lōō sid′ ə tē): state of being clearheaded or rational.

11. writ ran: law was enforced.

common round of life, she became good and comforting and humble again.

"Yes, of course, the cherries . . . you must have cherries too."

The blackbird, gorged, had flown off, and the scarecrow waggled his empty opera hat in the breeze.

The time came . . .

The time came when all her strength left her. She was amazed beyond measure and would not believe it. Whenever I arrived from Paris to see her, as soon as we were alone in the afternoon in her little house, she had always some sin to confess to me. On one occasion she turned up the hem of her dress, rolled her stocking down over her shin, and displayed a purple bruise, the skin nearly broken.

"Just look at that!"

"What on earth have you done to yourself this time, Mother?"

She opened wide eyes, full of innocence and embarrassment.

"You wouldn't believe it, but I fell downstairs!"

"How do you mean—'fell'?"

"Just what I said. I fell, for no reason. I was going downstairs and I fell. I can't understand it."

"Were you going down too quickly?"

"Too quickly? What do you call too quickly? I was going down quickly. Have I time to go downstairs majestically like the Sun King? And if that were all . . . But look at this!"

On her pretty arm, still so young above the faded hand, was a scald forming a large blister.

"Oh goodness! Whatever's that!"

"My foot warmer."

"The old copper foot warmer? The one that holds five quarts?"

"That's the one. Can I trust anything, when that foot warmer has known me for forty years? I can't imagine what possessed it, it was boiling fast, I went to take it off the fire, and crack,

something gave in my wrist. I was lucky to get nothing worse than the blister. But what a thing to happen! After that I let the cupboard alone. . . ."

She broke off, blushing furiously.

"What cupboard?" I demanded severely.

My mother fenced, tossing her head as though I were trying to put her on a lead.

"Oh, nothing! No cupboard at all!"

"Mother! I shall get cross!"

"Since I've said, 'I let the cupboard alone,' can't you do the same for my sake? The cupboard hasn't moved from its place, has it? So, shut up about it!"

The cupboard was a massive object of old walnut, almost as broad as it was high, with no carving save the circular hole made by a Prussian bullet that had entered by the right-hand door and passed out through the back panel.

"Do you want it moved from the landing, Mother?"

An expression like that of a young she-cat, false and glittery, appeared on her wrinkled face.

"I? No, it seems to me all right there—let it stay where it is!"

All the same, my doctor brother and I agreed that we must be on the watch. He saw my mother every day, since she had followed him and lived in the same village, and he looked after her with a passionate devotion which he hid. She fought against all her ills with amazing elasticity, forgot them, baffled them, inflicted on them signal if temporary defeats, recovered, during entire days, her vanished strength; and the sound of her battles, whenever I spent a few days with her, could be heard all over the house till I was irresistibly reminded of a terrier tackling a rat.

At five o'clock in the morning I would be awakened by the clank of a full bucket being set down in the kitchen sink immediately opposite my room.

"What are you doing with that bucket, Mother? Couldn't you wait until Josephine arrives?"

And out I hurried. But the fire was already blazing, fed with dry wood. The milk was boiling on the blue-tiled charcoal stove. Nearby, a bar of chocolate was melting in a little water for my breakfast, and, seated squarely in her cane armchair, my mother was grinding the fragrant coffee which she roasted herself. The morning hours were always kind to her. She wore their rosy colors in her cheeks. Flushed with a brief return to health, she would gaze at the rising sun, while the church bell rang for early Mass, and rejoice at having tasted, while we still slept, so many forbidden fruits.

The forbidden fruits were the overheavy bucket drawn up from the well, the firewood split with a billhook on an oaken block, the spade, the mattock, and above all the double steps propped against the gable window of the woodhouse. There were the climbing vine whose shoots she trained up to the gable windows of the attic, the flowery spikes of the too-tall lilacs, the dizzy cat that had to be rescued from the ridge of the roof. All the accomplices of her old existence as a plump and sturdy little woman, all the minor rustic divinities who once obeyed her and made her so proud of doing without servants, now assumed the appearance and position of adversaries. But they reckoned without that love of combat which my mother was to keep till the end of her life. At seventy-one, dawn still found her undaunted, if not always undamaged. Burnt by the fire, cut with the pruning knife, soaked by melting snow or spilled water, she had always managed to enjoy her best moments of independence before the earliest risers had opened their shutters. She was able to tell us of the cats' awakening, of what was going on in the nests, of news gleaned, together with the morning's milk and the warm loaf, from the milkmaid and the baker's girl, the record in fact of the birth of a new day.

It was not until one morning when I found the kitchen unwarmed, and the blue enamel saucepan hanging on the wall, that I felt my mother's end to be near. Her illness knew many respites, during which the fire flared up again on the hearth, and the smell of fresh bread and melting chocolate stole under the door together with the cat's impatient paw. These respites were periods of unexpected alarms. My mother and the big walnut cupboard were discovered together in a heap at the foot of the stairs, she having determined to transport it in secret from the upper landing to the ground floor. Whereupon my elder brother insisted that my mother should keep still and that an old servant should sleep in the little house. But how could an old servant prevail against a vital energy so youthful and mischievous that it contrived to tempt and lead astray a body already half-fettered by death? My brother, returning before sunrise from attending a distant patient, one day caught my mother red-handed in the most wanton of crimes. Dressed in her nightgown, but wearing heavy gardening sabots, her little gray septuagenarian's plait of hair turning up like a scorpion's tail on the nape of her neck, one foot firmly planted on the crosspiece of the beech trestle, her back bent in the attitude of the expert jobber, my mother, rejuvenated by an indescribable expression of guilty enjoyment, in defiance of all her promises and of the freezing morning dew, was sawing logs in her own yard.

Colette at her desk.
The Granger Collection, New York.

Thinking About the Selection

A PERSONAL RESPONSE

sharing impressions

1. What incident from Colette's memories of her mother impressed you the most? Explain your response in your journal.

constructing interpretations

2. What does the final image of Sido—happily sawing logs in her nightgown—convey about the kind of woman she was throughout her life? Use examples from both excerpts to support your response.

3. Why does Sido sacrifice the rose to the child and the cherries to the blackbird, yet refuse to give flowers for funerals or for the church?

4. What do you learn about Colette from these memories of her mother?
   Think about
   • qualities Colette says she shares with her mother
   • feelings Colette reveals about her childhood
   • Colette's attitude toward her mother's aging

5. What do you think Sido teaches her daughter about life?

A CREATIVE RESPONSE

6. If Colette and her mother had lived in Paris rather than in a country village, how might Colette's account of her childhood memories differ?

A CRITICAL RESPONSE

7. Locate two or three brief passages describing Sido and explain the impression of Sido that you formed from those passages.

8. Identify several contemporary problems of the aged that you are aware of and indicate which of those problems Sido experiences and which problems she escapes.

9. Some critics describe Colette's writing style as sensitive and sensuous. How might her country childhood with Sido have contributed to the development of that style?

Analyzing the Writer's Craft

TONE

Colette says about her mother, "I sing her praises as best I may." How can you tell that Colette loves and admires her mother?

Building a Literary Vocabulary. Tone is the attitude a writer takes toward a subject. Colette's warm and loving tone is revealed in her choice of memories to relate and in the words she uses to describe Sido. For example, comments such as "Why did no one ever model or paint or carve that hand of Sido's?" and "her one idea was to give" clearly convey Colette's admiration for her mother.

Application: Understanding Tone. In a small group, choose one incident from the selection and identify key words and phrases that create Colette's tone. Then develop a dramatic reading of the incident, preserving Colette's tone throughout your performance.

Connecting Reading and Writing

1. Write a **character sketch** of a parent or other adult who was important to you as a child. Use your prereading journal entry as a starting point, keeping in mind Colette's depiction of Sido in her autobiography.

Option: Write a **letter** to that parent or other adult explaining the impact that person has had on your life.

2. Do you think Sido was a good mother? Express your opinion in a **persuasive speech** that you can imagine giving before a task force of child development experts. Be sure to support your opinion with details from the selection.

Option: Conduct and then write up several **interviews** with your classmates in which you ask their opinion of Sido's parenting.

3. Contemporary problems of the aged include difficulties related to health, mobility, friendship, and finance. Write a **pamphlet** that communicates Sido's advice for dealing with these problems. Base the pamphlet on Sido's own life, as described in the selection.

Option: Have Sido write an **advice column** response to an elderly person who has asked for suggestions to make his or her life more meaningful.

Haiku

MATSUO BASHŌ 1644–1694 JAPAN

KOBAYASHI ISSA 1763–1828 JAPAN

TAKARAI KIKAKU 1661–1707 JAPAN

YOSA BUSON 1716–1784 JAPAN

Biographies of Bashō, Issa, Kikaku, and Buson appear on pages 738, 744, 745, and 739.

Approaching the Poems

Haiku (hī′ ko͞o′) is a form of Japanese poetry that embodies qualities highly valued in Japanese art: precision, economy, and delicacy. The traditional haiku form dates from the seventeenth century and has very narrowly defined rules. The poet must create a single, clear picture of an aspect of nature that evokes a strong emotional response in the reader—using in the original language only seventeen syllables in three lines with a pattern of five, seven, and five syllables per line. The brevity of haiku can be misleading: their powerful effect comes as much from what is suggested as from what is directly said.

Connecting Writing and Reading

Close your eyes and picture yourself in a natural setting such as a park, the woods, or mountains. In your journal describe the emotions that you associate with that scene. As you read, compare the emotions you described with the emotions the haiku evoke in you.

Haiku

Year's end,
all corners
of this floating world, swept.
　　　　　—BASHŌ

Autumn—
even the birds
and clouds look old.
　　　　　—BASHŌ

Autumn wind—
mountain's shadow
wavers.
　　　　　—ISSA

Leaf
of the yam—
raindrop's world.
　　　　　—KIKAKU

What a world,
where lotus flowers
are ploughed into a field.
　　　　　—ISSA

Nightingale's song
this morning,
soaked with rain.
　　　　　—ISSA

A sudden chill—
in our room my dead wife's
comb, underfoot.
　　　　　—BUSON

Dew on the bramble,
thorns
sharp white.
　　　　　—BUSON

Thinking About the Poems

A PERSONAL RESPONSE

sharing impressions

1. Did you enjoy reading these haiku? Briefly explain why or why not in your journal.

constructing interpretations

2. What emotions do the haiku evoke in you?

3. What impressions of nature do the haiku poets seem to share?
   Think about
   • words used to describe the natural world
   • seasons referred to or that may be inferred

A CREATIVE RESPONSE

4. If the two haiku about autumn were to be about spring instead, what images might be used?

A CRITICAL RESPONSE

5. The modern architect Mies van der Rohe describes his theory of design as "Less is more." Using examples from the poems, explain how this statement might apply to the haiku form.

6. Compare and contrast the ways in which Colette and the haiku poets portray nature. Choose examples to illustrate your points.

A Gazelle

from Out of Africa

ISAK DINESEN   1885–1962   DENMARK

A biography of Dinesen appears on page 742.

Approaching the Selection

"A Gazelle" is a word portrait, done from memory, of an African antelope deer. Karen Blixen, who used the pen name Isak Dinesen (ē′ säk dē′ nə sən), went to Africa at age twenty-nine and spent the next seventeen years running a coffee plantation in Kenya. Although managing her property occupied much of her time, she also pursued painting and writing.

The book from which this excerpt is taken, *Out of Africa,* was written several years after the failure of the plantation forced Dinesen to return to her native Denmark. The memory of Kenya and her life there continued to have psychological and emotional importance to her, as revealed in her vivid descriptions.

LULU CAME TO my house from the woods as Kamante[1] had come to it from the plains.

To the east of my farm lay the Ngong[2] Forest Reserve, which then was nearly all virgin forest. To my mind it was a sad thing when the old forest was cut down, and eucalyptus and grevillea planted in its place; it might have made a unique pleasure ground and park for Nairobi.[3]

An African native forest is a mysterious region. You ride into the depths of an old tapestry, in places faded and in others darkened with age, but marvelously rich in green shades. You cannot see the sky at all in there, but the sunlight plays in many strange ways, falling through the foliage. The gray fungus, like long drooping beards, on the trees, and the creepers hanging down everywhere, give a secretive, recondite[4] air to the native forest. I used to ride here with Farah on Sundays, when there was nothing to do on the farm, up and down the slopes, and across the little winding forest streams. The air in the forest was cool like water, and filled with the scent of plants, and in the beginning of the long rains when the creepers flowered, you rode through sphere after sphere of fragrance. One kind of African Daphne of the woods, which flowers with a small cream-colored sticky blossom, had an overwhelming sweet perfume, like lilac, and wild lily of the valley. Here and there, hollow tree stems were hung up in ropes of hide on a

---

1. **Kamante** (kä män′ te).
2. **Ngong** (ŋgôŋ).
3. **Nairobi** (nī rō′ bē): capital of Kenya.
4. **recondite** (rek′ ən dīt′): hard to see; hidden.

branch; the Kikuyu[5] hung them there to make the bees build in them, and to get honey. Once as we turned a corner in the forest, we saw a leopard sitting on the road, a tapestry animal.

Here, high above the ground, lived a garrulous restless nation, the little gray monkeys. Where a pack of monkeys had travelled over the road, the smell of them lingered for a long time in the air, a dry and stale, mousy smell. As you rode on you would suddenly hear the rush and whizz over your head, as the colony passed along on its own ways. If you kept still in the same place for some time you might catch sight of one of the monkeys sitting immovable in a tree, and, a little after, discover that the whole forest round you was alive with his family, placed like fruits on the branches, grey or dark figures according to how the sunlight fell on them, all with their long tails hanging down behind them. They gave out a peculiar sound, like a smacking kiss with a little cough to follow it; if from the ground you imitated it, you saw the monkeys turn their heads from one side to the other in an affected manner, but if you made a sudden movement they were all off in a second, and you could follow the decreasing swash as they clove the treetops, and disappeared in the wood like a shoal of fishes in the waves.

In the Ngong Forest I have also seen, on a narrow path through thick growth, in the middle of a very hot day, the Giant Forest Hog, a rare person to meet. He came suddenly past me, with his wife and three young pigs, at a great speed, the whole family looking like uniform, bigger and smaller figures cut out in dark paper, against the sunlit green behind them. It was a glorious sight, like a reflection in a forest pool, like a thing that had happened a thousand years ago.

Lulu was a young antelope of the bushbuck tribe, which is perhaps the prettiest of all the African antelopes. They are a little bigger than the fallow deer; they live in the woods, or in the bush, and are shy and fugitive, so that they are not seen as often as the antelopes of the plains. But the Ngong Hills, and the surrounding country, were good places for bushbuck, and if you had your camp in the hills, and were out hunting in the early morning, or at sunset, you would see them come out of the bush into the glades, and as the rays of the sun fell upon them their coats shone red as copper. The male has a pair of delicately turned horns.

Lulu became a member of my household in this way:

I drove one morning from the farm to Nairobi. My mill on the farm had burnt down a short time before, and I had had to drive into town many times to get the insurance settled and paid out; in this early morning I had my head filled with figures and estimates. As I came driving along the Ngong Road a little group of Kikuyu children shouted to me from the roadside, and I saw that they were holding a very small bushbuck up for me to see. I knew that they would have found the fawn in the bush, and that now they wanted to sell it to me, but I was late for an appointment in Nairobi, and I had no thought for this sort of thing, so I drove on.

When I was coming back in the evening and was driving past the same place, there was again a great shout from the side of the road and the small party was still there, a little tired and disappointed, for they may have tried to sell the fawn to other people passing by in the course of the day, but keen now to get the deal through before the sun was down, and they held up the fawn high to tempt me. But I had had a long day in town, and some adversity about the insurance, so that I did not care to stop or talk, and I just drove on past them. I

---

5. **Kikuyu** (ki ko͞o′ yo͞o); also spelled **Gikuyu.**

did not even think of them when I was back in my house, and dined and went to bed.

The moment that I had fallen asleep I was woken up again by a great feeling of terror. The picture of the boys and the small buck, which had now collected and taken shape, stood out before me, clearly, as if it had been painted, and I sat up in bed as appalled as if someone had been trying to choke me. What, I thought, would become of the fawn in the hands of the captors who had stood with it in the heat of the long day, and had held it up by its joined legs? It was surely too young to eat on its own. I myself had driven past it twice on the same day, like the priest and the Levite in one,[6] and had given no thought to it, and now, at this moment, where was it? I got up in a real panic and woke up all my houseboys. I told them that the fawn must be found and brought me in the morning, or they would all of them get their dismissal from my service. They were immediately up to the idea. Two of my boys had been in the car with me the same day, and had not shown the slightest interest in the children or the fawn; now they came forward, and gave the others a long list of details of the place and the hour and of the family of the boys. It was a moonlight night; my people all took off and spread in the landscape in a lively discussion of the situation; I heard them expatiating[7] on the fact that they were all to be dismissed in case the bushbuck were not found.

Early next morning when Farah brought me in my tea, Juma came in with him and carried the fawn in his arms. It was a female, and we named her Lulu, which I was told was the Swahili[8] word for a pearl.

Lulu by that time was only as big as a cat, with large quiet purple eyes. She had such delicate legs that you feared they would not bear being folded up and unfolded again, as she lay down and rose up. Her ears were smooth as silk and exceedingly expressive. Her nose was as black as a truffle.[9] Her diminutive hoofs gave her all the air of a young Chinese lady of the old school, with laced feet. It was a rare experience to hold such a perfect thing in your hands.

Lulu soon adapted herself to the house and its inhabitants and behaved as if she were at home. During the first weeks the polished floors in the rooms were a problem in her life, and when she got outside the carpets her legs went away from her to all four sides; it looked catastrophic but she did not let it worry her much and in the end she learnt to walk on the bare floors with a sound like a succession of little angry finger taps. She was extraordinarily neat in all her habits. She was headstrong already as a child, but when I stopped her from doing the things she wanted to do, she behaved as if she said: Anything rather than a scene.

Kamante brought her up on a sucking bottle, and he also shut her up at night, for we had to be careful of her as the leopards were up round the house after nightfall. So she held to him and followed him about. From time to time when he did not do what she wanted, she gave his thin legs a hard butt with her young head, and she was so pretty that you could not help, when you looked upon the two together, seeing them as a new paradoxical illustration to the tale of the Beauty and the Beast. On the strength of this great beauty and gracefulness, Lulu obtained for herself a commanding posi-

---

6. priest and the Levite in one: In the story of the Good Samaritan, an injured man, lying by the side of the road, is passed first by a priest and then by a Levite, or holy man, before a Samaritan stops to help him.
7. expatiating (eks pā′ shē at′ iŋ): speaking in great detail.
8. Swahili (swä hē′ lē): language of people inhabiting Zanzibar and the nearby mainland.
9. truffle (truf′ əl): a mushroomlike plant that grows underground.

Isak Dinesen and Lulu. The Royal Library of Copenhagen.

tion in the house, and was treated with respect by all.

In Africa I never had dogs of any other breed than the Scotch deerhound. There is no more noble or gracious kind of dog. They must have lived for many centuries with men to understand and fall in with our life and its conditions the way they do. You will also find them in old paintings and tapestries, and they have in themselves a tendency to change, by their looks and manners, their surroundings into tapestry; they bring with them a feudal atmosphere.

The first of my tribe of deerhounds, who was named Dusk, had been given to me as a wedding present, and had come out with me when I began my life in Africa, on "The Mayflower," so to say. He was a gallant, generous character. He accompanied me when, during the first months of the war, I did transport for the government, with ox wagons in the Masai[10] Reserve. But a couple of years later he was killed by zebra. By the time that Lulu came to live in my house I had two of his sons there.

The Scotch deerhound went well with African scenery and the African native. It may be due to the altitude—the highland melody in all three—for he did not look so harmonious at sea level in Mombasa.[11] It was as if the great, spare landscape, with the plains, hills and rivers, was not complete until the deerhounds were also in it. All the deerhounds were great hunters and had more nose than the greyhounds, but they hunted by sight and it was a highly wonderful thing to see two of them working together. I took them with me when I was out riding in the game reserve, which I was not allowed to do, and there they would spread the herds of zebra and wildebeest over the plain, as if it were all the stars of heaven running wild over the sky. But when I was out in the Masai Reserve shooting I never lost a wounded head of game, if I had the deerhounds with me.

They looked well in the native forests too, dark gray in the sombre green shades. One of them, in here, all by himself, killed a big old male baboon, and in the fight had his nose bitten straight through, which spoilt his noble profile but by everybody on the farm was considered an honorable scar, for the baboons are destructive beasts and the Natives detest them.

The deerhounds were very wise, and knew who amongst my houseboys were Mohammedans,[12] and not allowed to touch dogs.

During my first years in Africa I had a Somali[13] gun bearer named Ismail,[14] who died while I was still out there. He was one of the old-time gun bearers and there are no such people now. He had been brought up by the great old big-game hunters of the beginning of the century, when all Africa was a real deer park. His acquaintance with civilization was entirely of the hunting fields, and he spoke an English of the hunting world, so that he would talk of my big and my young rifle. After Ismail had gone back to Somaliland, I had a letter from him which was addressed to *Lioness Blixen*, and opened: *Honorable Lioness.* Ismail was a strict Mohammedan, and would not for the life of him touch a dog, which caused him much worry in his profession. But he made an exception with Dusk and never minded my taking him with us in the mule trap;[15] he would even let Dusk sleep in his tent. For Dusk, he said, would know a Mohammedan when he saw him, and would

---

10. **Masai** (mä sī′).
11. **Mombasa** (mäm bä′ sä): seaport on the southeast coast of Kenya.
12. **Mohammedans** (mō häm′ i dənz): people of the Muslim religion.
13. **Somali** (sō mä′ lē): of Somalia, an East African country.
14. **Ismail** (is′ mä ēl).
15. **mule trap**: a small carriage pulled by a mule.

never touch him. Indeed, Ismail assured me, Dusk could see at once who was a sincere Mohammedan at heart. He once said to me: "I know now that the Dusk is of the same tribe as you yourself. He laughs at the people."

Now my dogs understood Lulu's power and position in the house. The arrogance of the great hunters was like water with her. She pushed them away from the milk bowl and from their favorite places in front of the fire. I had tied a small bell on a rein round Lulu's neck, and there came a time when the dogs, when they heard the jingle of it approaching through the rooms, would get up resignedly from their warm beds by the fireplace, and go and lie down in some other part of the room. Still nobody could be of a gentler demeanor than Lulu was when she came and lay down, in the manner of a perfect lady who demurely gathers her skirts about her and will be in no one's way. She drank the milk with a polite, pernickety mien, as if she had been pressed by an overkind hostess. She insisted on being scratched behind the ears, in a pretty forbearing way, like a young wife who pertly permits her husband a caress.

When Lulu grew up and stood in the flower of her young loveliness she was a slim delicately rounded doe, from her nose to her toes unbelievably beautiful. She looked like a minutely painted illustration to Heine's[16] song of the wise and gentle gazelles by the flow of the river Ganges.[17]

But Lulu was not really gentle; she had the so called devil in her. She had, to the highest degree, the feminine trait of appearing to be exclusively on the defensive, concentrated on guarding the integrity of her being, when she was really, with every force in her, bent upon the offensive. Against whom? Against the whole world. Her moods grew beyond control or computation, and she would go for my horse, if he displeased her. I remembered old Hagenbeck in Hamburg, who had said that of all animal races, the carnivora included, the deer are the least to be relied on, and that you may trust a leopard, but if you trust a young stag, sooner or later he falls upon you in the rear.

Lulu was the pride of the house even when she behaved like a real shameless young coquette; but we did not make her happy. Sometimes she walked away from the house for hours, or for a whole afternoon. Sometimes when the spirit came upon her and her discontent with her surroundings reached a climax, she would perform, for the satisfaction of her own heart, on the lawn in front of the house, a war dance, which looked like a brief zigzagged prayer to Satan.

"Oh Lulu," I thought, "I know that you are marvelously strong and that you can leap higher than your own height. You are furious with us now, you wish that we were all dead, and indeed we should be so if you could be bothered to kill us. But the trouble is not as you think now, that we have put up obstacles too high for you to jump, and how could we possibly do that, you great leaper? It is that we have put up no obstacles at all. The great strength is in you, Lulu, and the obstacles are within you as well, and the thing is, that the fullness of time has not yet come."

One evening Lulu did not come home and we looked out for her in vain for a week. This was a hard blow to us all. A clear note had gone out of the house and it seemed no better than other houses. I thought of the leopards by the river and one evening I talked about them to Kamante.

As usual he waited some time before he answered, to digest my lack of insight. It was not till a few days later that he approached me

---

16. **Heine** (hī′ nə): German poet (1797-1856). (See page 302.)
17. **Ganges** (gan′ jēz): river in North India and Bangladesh.

upon the matter. "You believe that Lulu is dead, Msabu,"[18] he said.

I did not like to say so straight out, but I told him I was wondering why she did not come back.

"Lulu," said Kamante, "is not dead. But she is married."

This was pleasant, surprising news, and I asked him how he knew of it.

"Oh yes," he said, "she is married. She lives in the forest with her *bwana*,"[19]—her husband, or master. "But she has not forgotten the people; most mornings she is coming back to the house. I lay out crushed maize to her at the back of the kitchen, then just before the sun comes up, she walks round there from the woods and eats it. Her husband is with her, but he is afraid of the people because he has never known them. He stands below the big white tree by the other side of the lawn. But up to the houses he dares not come."

I told Kamante to come and fetch me when he next saw Lulu. A few days later before sunrise he came and called me out.

It was a lovely morning. The last stars withdrew while we were waiting, the sky was clear and serene but the world in which we walked was sombre still, and profoundly silent. The grass was wet; down by the trees where the ground sloped it gleamed with the dew like dim silver. The air of the morning was cold, it had that twinge in it which in northern countries means that the frost is not far away. However often you make the experience, I thought, it is still impossible to believe, in this coolness and shade, that the heat of the sun and the glare of the sky, in a few hours' time, will be hard to bear. The gray mist lay upon the hills, strangely taking shape from them; it would be bitterly cold on the buffalo if they were about there now, grazing on the hillside, as in a cloud.

The great vault over our heads was gradually filled with clarity like a glass with wine.

Suddenly, gently, the summits of the hills caught the first sunlight and blushed. And slowly, as the earth leaned toward the sun, the grassy slopes at the foot of the mountain turned a delicate gold, and the Masai woods lower down. And now the tops of the tall trees in the forest, on our side of the river, blushed like copper. This was the hour for the flight of the big purple wood pigeons which roosted by the other side of the river and came over to feed on the Cape chestnuts in my forest. They were here only for a short season in the year. The birds came surprisingly fast, like a cavalry attack of the air. For this reason the morning pigeon shooting on the farm was popular with my friends in Nairobi; to be out by the house in time, just as the sun rose, they used to come out so early that they rounded my drive with the lamps of their cars still lighted.

Standing like this in the limpid shadow, looking up toward the golden heights and the clear sky, you would get the feeling that you were in reality walking along the bottom of the sea, with the currents running by you, and were gazing up toward the surface of the ocean.

A bird began to sing, and then I heard, a little way off in the forest, the tinkling of a bell. Yes, it was a joy, Lulu was back, and about in her old places! It came nearer, I could follow her movements by its rhythm; she was walking, stopping, walking on again. A turning round one of the boys' huts brought her upon us. It suddenly became an unusual and amusing thing to see a bushbuck so close to the house. She stood immovable now, she seemed to be prepared for the sight of Kamante, but not for that of me. But she did not make off, she looked at me without fear and without any remembrance of our skirmishes of the past or

---

18. Msabu (msä′ boo): name used by Kamante to address Dinesen.
19. *bwana* (bwä′ nä).

of her own ingratitude in running away without warning.

Lulu of the woods was a superior, independent being, a change of heart had come upon her, she was in possession. If I had happened to have known a young princess in exile, and while she was still a pretender to the throne, and had met her again in her full queenly estate after she had come into her rights, our meeting would have had the same character. Lulu showed no more meanness of heart than King Louis Philippe did, when he declared that the King of France did not remember the grudges of the Duke of Orléans.[20] She was now the complete Lulu. The spirit of offensive had gone from her; for whom, and why, should she attack? She was standing quietly on her divine rights. She remembered me enough to feel that I was nothing to be afraid of. For a minute she gazed at me; her purple smoky eyes were absolutely without expression and did not wink, and I remembered that the gods or goddesses never wink, and felt that I was face to face with the ox-eyed Hera.[21] She lightly nipped a leaf of grass as she passed me, made one pretty little leap, and walked on to the back of the kitchen, where Kamante had spread maize on the ground.

Kamante touched my arm with one finger and then pointed it toward the woods. As I followed the direction, I saw, under a tall Cape chestnut tree, a male bushbuck, a small tawny silhouette at the outskirt of the forest, with a fine pair of horns, immovable like a tree stem. Kamante observed him for some time, and then laughed.

"Look here now," he said, "Lulu has explained to her husband that there is nothing up by the houses to be afraid of, but all the same he dares not come. Every morning he thinks that today he will come all the way, but, when he sees the house and the people, he gets a cold stone in the stomach"—this is a common thing in the native world, and often gets in the way of the work on the farm—"and then he stops by the tree."

For a long time Lulu came to the house in the early mornings. Her clear bell announced that the sun was up on the hills; I used to lie in bed, and wait for it. Sometimes she stayed away for a week or two, and we missed her and began to talk of the people who went to shoot in the hills. But then again my houseboys announced: "Lulu is here," as if it had been the married daughter of the house on a visit. A few times more I also saw the bushbuck's silhouette amongst the trees, but Kamante had been right, and he never collected enough courage to come all the way to the house.

One day, as I came back from Nairobi, Kamante was keeping watch for me outside the kitchen door, and stepped forward, much excited, to tell me that Lulu had been to the farm the same day and had had her Toto—her baby—with her. Some days after, I myself had the honor to meet her amongst the boys' huts, much on the alert and not to be trifled with, with a very small fawn at her heels, as delicately tardive[22] in his movements as Lulu herself had been when we first knew her. This was just after the long rains, and, during those summer months, Lulu was to be found near the houses, in the afternoon, as well as at daybreak. She would even be round there at midday, keeping in the shadow of the huts.

Lulu's fawn was not afraid of the dogs, and would let them sniff him all over, but he could not get used to the natives or to me, and if we ever tried to get hold of him, the mother and the child were off.

---

20. King Louis Philippe . . . Duke of Orléans: as king, King Louis Philippe felt he was above the more commonplace dealings he had been involved in as a duke.

21. Hera (hē′ rə): queen of the gods, and goddess of women and marriage.

22. tardive (tär′ div): late in developing.

Lulu herself would never, after her first long absence from the house, come so near to any of us that we could touch her. In other ways she was friendly, she understood that we wanted to look at her fawn, and she would take a piece of sugarcane from an outstretched hand. She walked up to the open dining-room door, and gazed thoughtfully into the twilight of the rooms, but she never again crossed the threshold. She had by this time lost her bell, and came and went away in silence.

My houseboys suggested that I should let them catch Lulu's fawn, and keep him as we had once kept Lulu. But I thought it would make a boorish return to Lulu's elegant confidence in us.

It also seemed to me that the free union between my house and the antelope was a rare, honorable thing. Lulu came in from the wild world to show that we were on good terms with it, and she made my house one with the African landscape, so that nobody could tell where the one stopped and the other began. Lulu knew the place of the Giant Forest Hog's lair and had seen the rhino. In Africa there is a cuckoo which sings in the middle of the hot days in the midst of the forest, like the sonorous heartbeat of the world; I had never had the luck to see her, neither had anyone that I knew, for nobody could tell me how she looked. But Lulu had perhaps walked on a narrow green deer path just under the branch on which the cuckoo was sitting. I was then reading a book about the old great Empress of China, and of how after the birth of her son, young Yahanola came on a visit to her old home; she set forth from the Forbidden City[23] in her golden, green-hung palanquin.[24] My house, I thought, was now like the house of the young Empress's father and mother.

The two antelopes, the big and the small, were round by my house all that summer; sometimes there was an interval of a fortnight, or three weeks, between their visits, but at other times we saw them every day. In the beginning of the next rainy season my houseboys told me that Lulu had come back with a new fawn. I did not see the fawn myself, for by this time they did not come up quite close to the house, but later I saw three bushbucks together in the forest.

The league between Lulu and her family and my house lasted for many years. The bushbucks were often in the neighborhood of the house, they came out of the woods and went back again as if my grounds were a province of the wild country. They came mostly just before sunset, and first moved in amongst the trees like delicate dark silhouettes on the dark trees, but when they stepped out to graze on the lawn in the light of the afternoon sun their coats shone like copper. One of them was Lulu, for she came up near to the house, and walked about sedately, pricking her ears when a car arrived, or when we opened a window; and the dogs would know her. She became darker in color with age. Once I came driving up in front of my house with a friend and found three bushbucks on the terrace there, round the salt that was laid out for my cows.

It was a curious thing that apart from the first big bushbuck, Lulu's *bwana,* who had stood under the Cape chestnut with his head up, no male bushbuck was amongst the antelopes that came to my house. It seemed that we had to do with a forest matriarchy.

The hunters and naturalists of the colony took an interest in my bushbucks, and the game warden drove out to the farm to see them, and did see them there. A correspondent wrote about them in the *East African Standard.*

---

23. Forbidden City: in the Chinese city of Beijing, the walled-in section that contains the Imperial Palace; so named because it was closed to the public.
24. palanquin (pal′ ən kēn′): an enclosed carriage, carried on the shoulders of several people.

The years in which Lulu and her people came round to my house were the happiest of my life in Africa. For that reason, I came to look upon my acquaintance with the forest antelopes as a great <u>boon</u>,[25] and a token of friendship from Africa. All the country was in it, good omens, old covenants, a song:

"Make haste, my beloved and be thou like to a roe or to a young hart[26] upon the mountain of spices."[27]

During my last years in Africa I saw less and less of Lulu and her family. Within the year before I went away I do not think that they ever came. Things had changed; south of my farm, land had been given out to farmers and the forest had been cleared here, and houses built. Tractors were heaving up and down where the glades had been. Many of the new settlers were keen sportsmen and the rifles sang in the landscape. I believe that the game withdrew to the West and went into the woods of the Masai Reserve.

I do not know how long an antelope lives; probably Lulu has died a long time ago.

Often, very often, in the quiet hours of day-break, I have dreamed that I have heard Lulu's clear bell, and in my sleep my heart has run full of joy, I have woken up expecting something very strange and sweet to happen, just now, in a moment.

When I have then lain and thought of Lulu, I have wondered if in her life in the woods she ever dreamed of the bell. Would there pass in her mind, like shadows upon water, pictures of people and dogs?

If I know a song of Africa, I thought—of the Giraffe, and the African new moon lying on her back, of the ploughs in the fields, and the sweaty faces of the coffee pickers—does Africa know a song of me? Would the air over the plain quiver with a color that I had on, or the children invent a game in which my name was, or the full moon throw a shadow over the gravel of the drive that was like me, or would the eagles of Ngong look out for me?

---

25. boon: a welcome benefit; a blessing.

26. roe . . . hart: a small female deer and a male deer.

27. "Make haste, . . . spices": a quotation from the Bible's Song of Solomon, 8:14.

Confronting the Past

The character of every individual, in every time and place, is rooted to some degree in past experiences. Through literature, individuals from around the world have shared past events that have had a profound effect upon their lives.

For many writers, recalling the past evokes warm memories of a happy childhood or adolescence. For others, confronting the past has been a personal challenge, a time of coming to terms with a painful memory such as an unpleasant family relationship, a terrifying childhood experience, or a youth overshadowed by poverty, prejudice, or war. Some writers have indicated that writing about the past has provided them with an emotional outlet. Writing has given them an opportunity for introspection about a past event and, in some cases, has enabled them to cope with feelings of sorrow and anger that they have harbored for many years.

A variety of literary forms have been used by writers confronting their pasts. Some have chosen poetry or the personal essay to describe a memorable event. Others, desiring to reveal their pasts in detail, have written autobiographies. Certain writers, in an attempt to distance themselves from the past, have dealt with personal recollections through fiction, allowing their characters to communicate the intensity of the past.

Some writers have been able to find humor in formerly unpleasant situations and have injected this humor into their writing. In contrast, writers recalling extremely sad experiences have sometimes produced works having a bitter and remorseful tone. Occasionally, writers employ a detached tone that allows readers to judge an experience for themselves.

Certain themes tend to recur in literature that reflects upon the past. One theme common to many works deals with the topic of parent-child relationships. Another common theme concerns the conflict between traditional and contemporary values. Literature that describes historical events often presents themes about the effects of tyranny on individuals and a culture.

As you read the literary works in this section of the book, consider the themes being conveyed. Compare the feelings revealed by the writers as they confront vivid and often painful moments of the past.

Literary Vocabulary

INTRODUCED IN THIS SECTION

Dialogue. Dialogue is written conversation between two or more characters. The use of dialogue brings characters to life and gives the reader insights into their qualities, or personality traits. For example, in the selection from *Earthly Paradise,* Colette reveals her mother's lively spirit and respect for the natural world in this dialogue:

> "Don't touch!"
> "But nothing's coming up!"
> "And what do you know about it? Is it for you to decide?"

Conflict. The plot of a story generally involves some sort of conflict, or struggle between opposing forces. A conflict may be external, involving a character pitted against an outside force—nature, a physical obstacle, another character, or society. A conflict may also be internal, occurring within a character. In the *Memoirs of Madame Vigée Lebrun,* Lebrun experiences both external conflict—caused by the revolution that threatens her safety—and internal conflict—her struggle to decide whether to leave France.

Plot Structure. Plot refers to the actions and events in a literary work. A plot moves forward because of a conflict, or struggle between opposing forces. Plot structure consists of the **exposition,** the **rising action,** the **climax,** and the **falling action.** The exposition is the explanation that lays groundwork and provides necessary background information. In "Mussoco" in Unit 1, the exposition begins when Mussoco finds the money, the foundation of the story's conflict. Next follows the **rising action,** in which complications of the conflict build to a **climax,** or turning point. In "Mussoco," Donana's discovery that her money is missing begins the rising action, which then proceeds as her threats affect Mussoco, her family, and the community. Interest and intensity reach their peak at this point. The climax occurs when Mussoco dies. The **falling action** comes after the climax and shows forces acting against the main characters. The falling action in "Mussoco" occurs as other people in the community, including Donana, die.

REVIEWED IN THIS SECTION

Theme

Hiccups

LÉON DAMAS   1912–1978   FRENCH GUIANA

A biography of Damas appears on page 741.

Approaching the Poem

One of the most important human relationships is that between parent and child. In "Hiccups" by Léon Damas (le ôn' dà mà'), the speaker tells about his relationship with his mother when he was a child. In the poem, Damas uses words of his mother's that still live in his memory. Léon Damas sought to affirm black values in his poetry. He grew up in French Guiana, a former French colony in South America populated mostly by blacks and Creoles of mixed black and white ancestry. Damas, a Creole, was sensitive to the rejection of blackness and African heritage he perceived in the dominant French culture of his country.

Connecting Writing and Reading

What qualities do you think characterize a good relationship between a parent and child? In your journal complete the following sentences with several possibilities:

A good parent always _____.
A good parent never _____.
A good parent sometimes _____.

Discuss your sentences with your classmates and try to draw some generalizations about what makes a good parent. As you read, compare your ideas with those expressed by the speaker about a relationship between a parent and child.

I gulp down seven drinks of water
several times a day
and all in vain
instinctively
5   like the criminal to the crime
my childhood returns
in a rousing fit of hiccups

Talk about calamity
talk about disasters
10   I'll tell you

My mother wanted her son to have good manners at the table:
            keep your hands on the table
            we don't cut bread
            we break it
15   we don't gobble it down
            the bread your father sweats for
            our daily bread

            eat the bones carefully and neatly
            a stomach has to have good manners too
20   and a well-bred stomach never
            burps
            a fork is not a tooth-pick
            don't pick your nose
            in front of the whole world
25   and sit up straight
            a well-bred nose
            doesn't sweep the plate

And then
and then
30   and then in the name of the Father
                    and the Son
                    and the Holy Ghost
at the end of every meal

And then and then
35   talk about calamity
talk about disasters
I'll tell you

My mother wanted her son to have the very best marks
                 if you don't know your history
40   you won't go to mass
                 tomorrow
                 in your Sunday suit

This child will disgrace our family name
This child will be our . . . in the name of God
45   be quiet
                 have I or have I not
                 told you to speak French
                 the French of France
                 the French that Frenchmen speak
50   French French

Talk about calamity
talk about disasters
I'll tell you

My mother wanted her son to be a mama's boy:
55   you didn't say good evening to our neighbor
                 what—dirty shoes again
                 and don't let me catch you any more
                 playing in the street or on the grass or in the park
                 underneath the War Memorial
60   playing
                 or picking a fight with what's-his-name
                 what's-his-name who isn't even baptized

Talk about calamity
talk about disasters
65   I'll tell you

My mother wanted her son to be
                 very *do*
                 very *re*
                 very *mi*
70   very *fa*
                 very *sol*
                 very *la*
                 very *ti*
                 very *do-re-mi*
75   *fa-sol-la-ti-*
                        do

I see you haven't been to your vi-o-lin lesson
                    a banjo
                    did you say a banjo
80   what do you mean
                    a banjo
                    you really mean
                    a banjo
                    no indeed young man
85   you know there won't be any
                            ban-or
                                jo
                                    or
                                gui-or
90   tar
                                        in our house
        They are not for *colored* people
        Leave them to the *black* folks!

Thinking About the Poem

A PERSONAL RESPONSE

sharing impressions

1. In your journal, jot down words and phrases that describe your feelings about the speaker's mother.

constructing interpretations

2. What is your opinion of the relationship between the parent and child in this poem?

Think about
- the musical instruments each one prefers
- the values of the speaker and the values of the mother
- the ideas you wrote in your journal before reading

3. Do you think the speaker is justified in using the words *calamity* and *disasters* to refer to his childhood?

   Think about
   - the reprimands of the mother
   - the speaker's use of the simile "like the criminal to the crime" to describe his recollection of childhood
   - why the speaker refers to himself as "her son" instead of "me"

A CREATIVE RESPONSE

4. If the speaker had grown up to be exactly what his mother wanted, what do you think he might have gained and lost?

A CRITICAL RESPONSE

5. The poet Léopold Sédar Senghor said that the poems of Léon Damas are "charged with an emotion concealed by humor." To what extent does this evaluation apply to the poem "Hiccups"? Support your answer by citing lines from the poem.

Connecting Reading and Writing

1. Imagine that the mother in the poem "Hiccups" had asked you how she might improve her relationship with her son. Express your views in an imagined **question/answer column** for a magazine about parenting.

Option: Write a **letter** to the mother, advising her about her relationship with her son.

2. Read Langston Hughes's poem "Mother to Son." Then write an **essay** for your classmates comparing what the two mothers seem to value.

Option: Imagine that the children of the two mothers are discussing their mothers' reactions to a real-life situation, such as their receiving a low grade on a test or quitting an after-school job. Create the **dialogue** that the two children might have in which they compare their mothers' values.

3. Read three or four other poems by Damas, such as "They Came That Night," "The Black Man's Lament," "Their Thing," and "Sleepless Night." Then write a **memo** to your teacher recommending which poem might be studied along with "Hiccups."

Option: Explore Damas's major issues in **annotations** to be given to your classmates to review as they prepare to listen to an oral interpretation of these poems.

from Kaffir Boy

MARK MATHABANE   born 1960   SOUTH AFRICA / U.S.

A biography of Mathabane appears on page 746.

_A_pproaching the Selection

In _Kaffir Boy,_ Mark Mathabane (mä tä bä′ ne) describes what it was like to be a black growing up in Johannesburg, South Africa in the 1960's. The South African government had established its policy of apartheid, which legalizes segregation and discrimination against blacks, forcing them to live in overcrowded, disease-ridden townships and severely limiting the opportunities for meaningful work and a better life. The word _kaffir_ (ka′ fər), a term used to refer to blacks, means "infidel" in Arabic, reflecting this racist attitude. In this excerpt from his autobiography, Mathabane tells about the day on which he made an important decision.

_B_uilding Vocabulary

These essential words are footnoted within the selection.

coteries (kōt′ ər ēz): Workless men and women were beginning to assemble in their usual **coteries.** (page 424)

austere (ô stir′), **inscrutable** (in skr<del>oo</del>t′ ə bəl): His **austere,** shiny face, **inscrutable** and imposing, reminded me of my father. (page 425)

mores (mōr′ ēz): Many tribal women questioned her sanity in daring to question well-established **mores.** (page 428)

_C_onnecting Writing and Reading

Imagine yourself ten to fifteen years from now. Where will you live? What kind of job will you have? How important do you think your education will be in helping you create the kind of life that you want? Jot down your ideas in your journal. As you read, compare your thoughts about the value of education with the different characters' views on the value of education.

from Kaffir Boy

"Education will open doors where none seem to exist."

HEN MY mother began dropping hints that I would soon be going to school, I vowed never to go, because school was a waste of time. She laughed and said, "We'll see. You don't know what you're talking about." My philosophy on school was that of a gang of ten-, eleven- and twelve-year-olds whom I so revered that their every word seemed that of an oracle.

These boys had long left their homes and were now living in various neighborhood junkyards, making it on their own. They slept in abandoned cars, smoked glue and benzene, ate pilchards[1] and brown bread, sneaked into the white world to caddy and, if unsuccessful, came back to the township to steal beer and soda bottles from shebeens,[2] or goods from the Indian traders on First Avenue. Their lifestyle was exciting, adventurous and full of surprises; and I was attracted to it. My mother told me that they were no-gooders, that they would amount to nothing, that I should not associate with them, but I paid no heed. What does she know? I used to tell myself. One thing she did not know was that the gang's way of life had captivated me wholly, particularly their philosophy on school: they hated it and considered an education a waste of time.

They, like myself, had grown up in an environment where the value of an education was never emphasized; where the first thing a child learned was not how to read and write and spell but how to fight and steal and rebel; where the money to send children to school was grossly lacking, for survival was first priority. I kept my membership in the gang, knowing that for as long as I was under its influence, I would never go to school.

One day my mother woke me up at four in the morning.

"Are they here? I didn't hear any noises," I asked in the usual way.

"No," my mother said. "I want you to get into that washtub over there."

"What!" I balked, upon hearing the word *washtub*. I feared taking baths like one feared the plague. Throughout seven years of hectic living the number of baths I had taken could be counted on one hand with several fingers missing. I simply had no natural inclination for water; cleanliness was a trait I still had to acquire. Besides, we had only one bathtub in the house, and it constantly sprung a leak.

"I said get into that tub!" My mother shook a finger in my face.

Reluctantly, I obeyed, yet wondered why all of a sudden I had to take a bath. My mother, armed with a scropbrush and a piece of Lifebuoy soap, purged me of years and years of grime till I ached and bled. As I howled, feeling pain shoot through my limbs as the thistles of the brush encountered stubborn calluses, there was a loud knock at the door.

Instantly my mother leaped away from the tub and headed, on tiptoe, toward the bedroom. Fear seized me as I, too, thought of the police. I sat frozen in the bathtub, not

---

1. **pilchards** (pilʹ chərdz): small, oily fishes.
2. **shebeens** (shi bēnzʹ): establishments where liquor is sold without a license.

knowing what to do.

"Open up, Mujaji[3] (my mother's maiden name)," Granny's voice came shrilling through the door. "It's me."

My mother heaved a sigh of relief; her tense limbs relaxed. She turned and headed to the kitchen door, unlatched it and in came Granny and Aunt Bushy.

"You scared me half to death," my mother said to Granny. "I had forgotten all about your coming."

"Are you ready?" Granny asked my mother.

"Yes—just about," my mother said, beckoning me to get out of the washtub.

She handed me a piece of cloth to dry myself. As I dried myself, questions raced through my mind: What's going on? What's Granny doing at our house this ungodly hour of the morning? And why did she ask my mother, "Are you ready?" While I stood debating, my mother went into the bedroom and came out with a stained white shirt and a pair of faded black shorts.

"Here," she said, handing me the togs, "put these on."

"Why?" I asked.

"Put them on I said!"

I put the shirt on; it was grossly loosefitting. It reached all the way down to my ankles. Then I saw the reason why: it was my father's shirt!

"But this is Papa's shirt," I complained. "It don't fit me."

"Put it on," my mother insisted. "I'll make it fit."

"The pants don't fit me either," I said. "Whose are they anyway?"

"Put them on," my mother said. "I'll make them fit."

Moments later I had the garments on; I looked ridiculous. My mother started working on the pants and shirt to make them fit. She folded the shirt in so many intricate ways and stashed it inside the pants, they too having been folded several times at the waist. She then choked the pants at the waist with a piece of sisal rope to hold them up. She then lavishly smeared my face, arms and legs with a mixture of pig's fat and vaseline. "This will insulate you from the cold," she said. My skin gleamed like the morning star and I felt as hot as the center of the sun and I smelled God knows like what. After embalming me, she headed to the bedroom.

"Where are we going, Gran'ma?" I said, hoping that she would tell me what my mother refused to tell me. I still had no idea I was about to be taken to school.

"Didn't your mother tell you?" Granny said with a smile. "You're going to start school."

"What!" I gasped, leaping from the chair where I was sitting as if it were made of hot lead. "I am not going to school!" I blurted out and raced toward the kitchen door.

My mother had just reappeared from the bedroom and guessing what I was up to, she yelled, "Someone get the door!"

Aunt Bushy immediately barred the door. I turned and headed for the window. As I leaped for the windowsill, my mother lunged at me and brought me down. I tussled, "Let go of me! I don't want to go to school! Let me go!" but my mother held fast onto me.

"It's no use now," she said, grinning triumphantly as she pinned me down. Turning her head in Granny's direction, she shouted, "Granny! Get a rope quickly!"

Granny grabbed a piece of rope nearby and came to my mother's aid. I bit and clawed every hand that grabbed me and howled protestations against going to school; however, I was no match for the two determined matriarchs. In a jiffy they had me bound, hands and feet.

"What's the matter with him?" Granny,

_____

3. **Mujaji** (mōō jä′ jē).

bewildered, asked my mother. "Why did he suddenly turn into an imp when I told him you're taking him to school?"

"You shouldn't have told him that he's being taken to school," my mother said. "He doesn't want to go there. That's why I requested you come today, to help me take him there. Those boys in the streets have been a bad influence on him."

As the two matriarchs hauled me through the door, they told Aunt Bushy not to go to school but stay behind and mind the house and the children.

The sun was beginning to rise from beyond the veld when Granny and my mother dragged me to school. The streets were beginning to fill with their everyday traffic: old men and women—wizened, bent and ragged—were beginning their rambling; workless men and women were beginning to assemble in their usual <u>coteries</u>[4] and head for shebeens in the backyards, where they discussed how they escaped the morning pass raids and contemplated the conditions of life amidst intense beer drinking and vacant, uneasy laughter; young boys and girls, some as young as myself, were beginning their aimless wanderings along the narrow, dusty streets in search of food, carrying bawling infants piggyback.

As we went along some of the streets, boys and girls who shared the same fears about school as I were making their feelings known in a variety of ways. They were howling their protests and trying to escape. A few managed to break loose and make a mad dash for freedom, only to be recaptured in no time, admonished or whipped, or both, and ordered to march again.

As we made a turn into Sixteenth Avenue, the street leading to the tribal school I was being taken to, a short, chubby black woman came along from the opposite direction. She had a scuttle overflowing with coal on her *doek*-covered (cloth-covered) head. An infant,

bawling deafeningly, was loosely swathed with a piece of sheepskin onto her back. Following closely behind the woman and picking up pieces of coal as they fell from the scuttle and placing them in a small plastic bag was a half-naked, potbellied and thumb-sucking boy of about four. The woman stopped abreast. For some reason we stopped too.

"I wish I had done the same to my oldest son," the strange woman said in a regretful voice, gazing at me. I was confounded by her stopping and offering her unsolicited opinion.

"I wish I had done that to my oldest son," she repeated, and suddenly burst into tears; amidst sobs, she continued, "before . . . the street claimed him . . . and . . . turned him into a *tsotsi*."[5]

Granny and my mother offered consolatory remarks to the strange woman.

"But it's too late now," the strange woman continued, tears now streaming freely down her puffy cheeks. She made no attempt to dry them. "It's too late now," she said for the second time; "he's beyond any help. I can't help him even if I wanted to. *Uswile*[6] (He is dead)."

"How did he die?" my mother asked in a sympathetic voice.

"He shunned school and, instead, grew up to live by the knife. And the same knife he lived by ended his life. That's why whenever I see a boy child refuse to go to school, I stop and tell the story of my dear little *mbitsini*[7] (heartbreak)."

Having said that, the strange woman left as mysteriously as she had arrived.

"Did you hear what that woman said!" my

---

4. coteries (kōt′ ər ēz): close circles of friends with common interests or backgrounds; cliques.
5. tsotsi (tsô̂′ tsē): a thug armed with a knife or other weapon.
6. Uswile (σōs wē′ le).
7. mbitsini (mbē tsē′ nē).

mother screamed into my ears. "Do you want the same to happen to you?"

I dropped my eyes. I was confused.

"Poor woman," Granny said ruefully. "She must have truly loved her son."

Finally, we reached the school and I was ushered into the principal's office, a tiny cubicle facing a row of privies[8] and a patch of yellowed grass.

"So this is the rascal we'd been talking about," the principal, a tall, wiry man, foppishly dressed in a black pin-striped suit, said to my mother as we entered. His austere,[9] shiny face, inscrutable[10] and imposing, reminded me of my father. He was sitting behind a brown table upon which stood piles of dust and cobweb-covered books and papers. In one upper pocket of his jacket was arrayed a variety of pens and pencils; in the other nestled a lily-white handkerchief whose presence was more decorative than utilitarian. Alongside him stood a disproportionately portly black woman, fashionably dressed in a black skirt and a white blouse. She had but one pen, and this she held in her hand. The room was hot and stuffy and buzzing with flies.

"Yes, Principal," my mother answered, "this is he."

"I see he's living up to his notoriety," remarked the principal, noticing that I had been bound. "Did he give you too much trouble?"

"Trouble, Principal," my mother sighed. "He was like an imp."

"He's just like the rest of them, Principal," Granny sighed. "Once they get out into the streets, they become wild. They take to the many vices of the streets like an infant takes to its mother's milk. They begin to think that there's no other life but the one shown them by the *tsotsis*. They come to hate school and forget about the future."

"Well," the principal said, "We'll soon remedy all that. Untie him."

"He'll run away," my mother cried.

"I don't think he's that foolish to attempt that with all of us here."

"He *is* that foolish, Principal," my mother said as she and Granny began untying me. "He's tried it before. Getting him here was an ordeal in itself."

The principal rose from his seat, took two steps to the door and closed it. As the door swung closed, I spotted a row of canes of different lengths and thicknesses hanging behind it. The principal, seeing me staring at the canes, grinned and said, in a manner suggesting that he had wanted me to see them, "As long as you behave, I won't have to use any of those on you."

Use those canes on me? I gasped. I stared at my mother—she smiled; at Granny—she smiled too. That made me abandon any inkling of escaping.

"So they finally gave you the birth certificate and the papers," the principal addressed my mother as he returned to his chair.

"Yes, Principal," my mother said, "they finally did. But what a battle it was. It took me nearly a year to get all them papers together." She took out of her handbag a neatly wrapped package and handed it to the principal. "They've been running us around for so long that there were times when I thought he would never attend school, Principal," she said.

"That's pretty much standard procedure, Mrs. Mathabane," the principal said, unwrapping the package. "But you now have the papers and that's what's important.

"As long as we have the papers," he continued, minutely perusing the contents of the package, "we won't be breaking the law in

---

8. privies: outhouses.

9. austere (ô stir′): having a severe or stern manner.

10. inscrutable (in skro͞ot′ ə bəl): that cannot be easily understood; completely mysterious.

admitting your son to this school, for we'll be in full compliance with the requirements set by the authorities in Pretoria."[11]

"Sometimes I don't understand the laws from Pitori,"[12] Granny said. "They did the same to me with my Piet[13] and Bushy. Why, Principal, should our children not be allowed to learn because of some piece of paper?"

"The piece of paper you're referring to, Mrs. Mabaso[14] (Granny's maiden name)," the principal said to Granny, "is as important to our children as a pass is to us adults. We all hate passes; therefore, it's only natural we should hate the regulations our children are subjected to. But as we have to live with passes, so our children have to live with the regulations, Mrs. Mabaso. I hope you understand, that is the law of the country. We would have admitted your grandson a long time ago, as you well know, had it not been for the papers. I hope you understand."

"I understand, Principal," Granny said, "but I don't understand," she added paradoxically.

One of the papers caught the principal's eye and he turned to my mother and asked, "Is your husband a Shangaan,[15] Mrs. Mathabane?"

"No, he's not, Principal," my mother said. "Is there anything wrong? He's Venda[16] and I'm Shangaan."

The principal reflected for a moment or so and then said, concernedly, "No, there's nothing seriously wrong. Nothing that we can't take care of. You see, Mrs. Mathabane, technically, the fact that your child's father is a Venda makes him ineligible to attend this tribal school because it is only for children whose parents are of the Shangaan tribe. May I ask what language the children speak at home?"

"Both languages," my mother said worriedly, "Venda and Shangaan. Is there anything wrong?"

The principal coughed, clearing his throat,

then said, "I mean which language do they speak more?"

"It depends, Principal," my mother said, swallowing hard. "When their father is around, he wants them to speak only Venda. And when he's not, they speak Shangaan. And when they are out at play, they speak Zulu and Sisotho."[17]

"Well," the principal said, heaving a sigh of relief. "In that case, I think an exception can be made. The reason for such an exception is that there's currently no school for Vendas in Alexandra. And should the authorities come asking why we took in your son, we can tell them that. Anyway, your child is half-half."

Everyone broke into a nervous laugh, except me. I was bewildered by the whole thing. I looked at my mother, and she seemed greatly relieved as she watched the principal register me; a broad smile broke across her face. It was as if some enormously heavy burden had finally been lifted from her shoulders and her conscience.

"Bring him back two weeks from today," the principal said as he saw us to the door. "There're so many children registering today that classes won't begin until two weeks hence. Also, the school needs repair and cleaning up after the holidays. If he refuses to come, simply notify us, and we'll send a couple of big boys to come fetch him, and he'll be very sorry if it ever comes to that."

As we left the principal's office and headed home, my mind was still against going to school. I was thinking of running away from home and joining my friends in the junkyard.

---

11. **Pretoria** (pre tôr′ ē ə): capital of South Africa.
12. **Pitori** (pi tō′ rē): another name for Pretoria.
13. **Piet** (pēt).
14. **Mabaso** (mä bä′ sô).
15. **Shangaan** (shäŋ gän′).
16. **Venda** (ven′ dä).
17. **Zulu and Sisotho** (zōō′ lōō, si sōō′ tōō).

I didn't want to go to school for three reasons: I was reluctant to surrender my freedom and independence over to what I heard every school-going child call "tyrannous discipline." I had heard many bad things about life in tribal school—from daily beatings by teachers and mistresses who worked you like a mule to long school hours—and the sight of those canes in the principal's office gave ample credence to rumors that school was nothing but a torture chamber. And there was my allegiance to the gang.

But the thought of the strange woman's lamentations over her dead son presented a somewhat strong case for going to school: I didn't want to end up dead in the streets. A more compelling argument for going to school, however, was the vivid recollection of all that humiliation and pain my mother had gone through to get me the papers and the birth certificate so I could enroll in school. What should I do? I was torn between two worlds.

But later that evening something happened to force me to go to school.

I was returning home from playing soccer when a neighbor accosted me by the gate and told me that there had been a bloody fight at my home.

"Your mother and father have been at it again," the neighbor, a woman, said.

"And your mother left."

I was stunned.

"Was she hurt badly?"

"A little bit," the woman said. "But she'll be all right. We took her to your grandma's place."

I became hot with anger.

"Is anyone in the house?" I stammered, trying to control my rage.

"Yes, your father is. But I don't think you should go near the house. He's raving mad. He's armed with a meat cleaver. He's chased out your brother and sisters, also. And some of the neighbors who tried to intervene—he's threatened to carve them to pieces. I have never seen him this mad before."

I brushed aside the woman's warnings and went. Shattered windows convinced me that there had indeed been a skirmish of some sort. Several pieces of broken bricks, evidently broken after being thrown at the door, were lying about the door. I tried opening the door; it was locked from the inside. I knocked. No one answered. I knocked again. Still no one answered, until, as I turned to leave:

"Who's out there?" my father's voice came growling from inside.

"It's me, Johannes," I said.

"Go away, you bastard!" he bellowed. "I don't want you or that mother of yours setting foot in this house. Go away before I come out there and kill you!"

"Let me in!" I cried. "Dammit, let me in! I want my things!"

"What things? Go away, you black swine!"

I went to the broken window and screamed obscenities at my father, daring him to come out, hoping that if he as much as ever stuck his black face out, I would pelt him with the half-a-loaf brick in my hand. He didn't come out. He continued launching a tirade of obscenities at my mother and her mother. He was drunk, but I wondered where he had gotten the money to buy beer, because it was still the middle of the week and he was dead broke. He had lost his entire wage for the past week in dice and had had to borrow bus fare.

"I'll kill you someday for all you're doing to my mother," I threatened him, overwhelmed with rage. Several nosey neighbors were beginning to congregate by open windows and doors. Not wanting to make a spectacle of myself, which was something many of our neighbors seemed to always expect from our family, I backtracked away from the door and vanished into the dark street. I ran, without stopping, all the way to the other end of the township where Granny lived. There I found my mother, her face swollen and bruised and her eyes puffed up to the point where she could scarcely see.

"What happened, Mama?" I asked, fighting to hold back the tears at the sight of her disfigured face.

"Nothing, child, nothing," she mumbled, almost apologetically, between swollen lips. "Your papa simply lost his temper, that's all."

"But why did he beat you up like this, Mama?" Tears came down my face. "He's never beaten you like this before."

My mother appeared reluctant to answer me. She looked searchingly at Granny, who was pounding millet with pestle and mortar and mixing it with sorghum and nuts for an African delicacy. Granny said, "Tell him, child, tell him. He's got a right to know. Anyway, he's the cause of it all."

"Your father and I fought because I took you to school this morning," my mother began. "He had told me not to, and when I told him that I had, he became very upset. He was drunk. We started arguing, and one thing led to another."

"Why doesn't he want me to go to school?"

"He says he doesn't have money to waste paying for you to get what he calls a useless white man's education," my mother replied. "But I told him that if he won't pay for your schooling, I would try and look for a job and pay, but he didn't want to hear that, also. 'There are better things for you to work for,' he said. 'Besides, I don't want you to work. How would I look to other men if you, a woman I owned, were to start working?' When I asked him why shouldn't I take you to school, seeing that you were now of age, he replied that he doesn't believe in schools. I told him that school would keep you off the streets and out of trouble, but still he was belligerent."

"Is that why he beat you up?"

"Yes, he said I disobeyed his orders."

"He's right, child," Granny interjected. "He paid *lobola*[18] (bride price) for you. And your father ate it all up before he left me."

To which my mother replied, "But I desperately want to leave this beast of a man. But with his *lobola* gone I can't do it. That worthless thing you call your husband shouldn't have sold Jackson's scrawny cattle and left you penniless."

"Don't talk like that about your father, child," Granny said. "Despite all, he's still your father, you know. Anyway, he asked for *lobola* only because he had to get back what he spent raising you. And you know it would have been taboo for him to let you or any of your sisters go without asking for *lobola*."

"You and Papa seemed to forget that my sisters and I have minds of our own," my mother said. "We didn't need you to tell us whom to marry, and why, and how. If it hadn't been for your interference, I could have married that schoolteacher."

Granny did not reply; she knew well not to. When it came to the act of "selling" women as marriage partners, my mother was vehemently opposed to it. Not only was she opposed to this one aspect of tribal culture, but to others as well, particularly those involving relations between men and women and the upbringing of children. But my mother's sharply differing opinion was an exception rather than the rule among tribal women. Most times, many tribal women questioned her sanity in daring to question well-established <u>mores</u>.[19] But my mother did not seem to care; she would always scoff at her opponents and call them fools in letting their husbands enslave them completely.

Though I disliked school, largely because I knew nothing about what actually went on there, and the little I knew had painted a

---

18. *lobola* (lô bō′ lä).

19. mores (môr′ ēz): folkways that seem favorable to the welfare of a society and are followed by most people; often become incorporated into law.

dreadful picture, the fact that a father would not want his son to go to school, especially a father who didn't go to school, seemed hard to understand.

"Why do you want me to go to school, Mama?" I asked, hoping that she might, somehow, clear up some of the confusion that was building in my mind.

"I want you to have a future, child," my mother said. "And, contrary to what your father says, school is the only means to a future. I don't want you growing up to be like your father."

The latter statement hit me like a bolt of lightning. It just about shattered every defense mechanism and every pretext I had against going to school.

"Your father didn't go to school," she continued, dabbing her puffed eyes to reduce the swelling with a piece of cloth dipped in warm water. "That's why he's doing some of the bad things he's doing. Things like drinking, gambling and neglecting his family. He didn't learn how to read and write; therefore, he can't find a decent job. Lack of any education has narrowly focused his life. He sees nothing beyond himself. He still thinks in the old, tribal way and still believes that things should be as they were back in the old days when he was growing up as a tribal boy in Louis Trichardt.[20] Though he's my husband, and your father, he doesn't see any of that."

"Why didn't he go to school, Mama?"

"He refused to go to school because his father led him to believe that an education was a tool through which white people were going to take things away from him, like they did black people in the old days. And that a white man's education was worthless insofar as black people were concerned because it prepared them for jobs they can't have. But I know it isn't totally so, child, because times have changed somewhat. Though our lot isn't any better today, an education will get you a

decent job. If you can read and write you'll be better off than those of us who can't. Take my situation: I can't find a job because I don't have papers, and I can't get papers because white people mainly want to register people who can read and write. But I want things to be different for you, child. For you and your brother and sisters. I want you to go to school because I believe that an education is the key you need to open up a new world and a new life for yourself, a world and life different from that of either your father's or mine. It is the only key that can do that, and only those who seek it earnestly and perseveringly will get anywhere in the white man's world. Education will open doors where none seem to exist. It'll make people talk to you, listen to you and help you, people who otherwise wouldn't bother. It will make you soar, like a bird lifting up into the endless blue sky, and leave poverty, hunger, and suffering behind. It'll teach you to learn to embrace what's good and shun what's bad and evil. Above all, it'll make you a somebody in this world. It'll make you grow up to be a good and proud person. That's why I want you to go to school, child, so that education can do all that, and more, for you."

A long, awkward silence followed, during which I reflected upon the significance of my mother's lengthy speech. I looked at my mother; she looked at me.

Finally, I asked, "How come you know so much about school, Mama? You didn't go to school, did you?"

"No, child," my mother replied. "Just like your father, I never went to school." For the second time that evening, a mere statement of fact had a thunderous impact on me. All the confusion I had about school seemed to leave my mind, like darkness giving way to light. And what had previously been a dark, yawn-

---

20. Louis Trichardt (tri′ chärt): town in northern South Africa.

ing void in my mind was suddenly transformed into a beacon of light that began to grow larger and larger, until it had swallowed up, blotted out, all the blackness. That beacon of light seemed to reveal things and facts, which, though they must have always existed in me, I hadn't been aware of up until now.

"But unlike your father," my mother went on, "I've always wanted to go to school, but couldn't because my father, under the sway of tribal traditions, thought it unnecessary to educate females. That's why I so much want you to go, child, for if you do, I know that someday I too would come to go, old as I would be then. Promise me, therefore, that no matter what, you'll go back to school. And I, in turn, promise that I'll do everything in my power to keep you there."

With tears streaming down my cheeks and falling upon my mother's bosom, I promised her that I would go to school "forever." That night, at seven and a half years of my life, the battle lines in the family were drawn. My mother on the one side, illiterate but determined to have me drink, for better or for worse, from the well of knowledge. On the other side, my father, he too illiterate, yet determined to have me drink from the well of ignorance. Scarcely aware of the magnitude of the decision I was making or, rather, the decision which was being emotionally thrust upon me, I chose to fight on my mother's side, and thus my destiny was forever altered.

Classroom, Rooigrond, 1984, WENDY SCHWEGMANN. From *South Africa: The Cordoned Heart,* edited by Omar Badsha.

Thinking About the Selection

A PERSONAL RESPONSE ────────────────────────

sharing impressions

1. What feelings do you have after reading this account? Jot down your impressions in your journal.

constructing interpretations

2. What do you think is the greatest challenge that the narrator's mother faces in getting her son an education?

> **Think about**
> - regulations that discourage blacks from registering at school
> - her husband's brutal opposition to her plans for her son
> - the tribal traditions about the status of a married woman
> - the influence of the gang on her son's attitude toward school

3. Do you agree with the narrator's mother that "education will open doors where none seem to exist"?

> **Think about**
> - what an education might do for the narrator
> - what you wrote in your journal about the value of education
> - any possible situations in which education would not "open doors"

A CREATIVE RESPONSE ────────────────────────

4. How might this excerpt be different if the father shared the mother's views on the value of an education?

A CRITICAL RESPONSE ────────────────────────

5. What do you think is the most important message that Mathabane wants to share in this selection?

> **Think about**
> - Mathabane's views about the junkyard and the school
> - descriptions of the people in the township
> - why Mathabane's father acts the way he does

6. What do you think a crusader against apartheid might especially value in this excerpt? Go back to the selection and find details to support your opinion.

Analyzing the Writer's Craft

Think about what Mathabane gains by presenting the exact words spoken by the characters to each other.

Building a Literary Vocabulary. Dialogue is written conversation between two or more characters. The use of dialogue brings characters to life and gives the reader insights into their qualities, or personality traits. For example, consider the dialogue between the strange woman and the narrator's mother. This conversation between a mother who has lost her son and a mother fighting heroically to keep hers dramatizes the regret and sorrow of the one and the sympathy and determination of the other.

Application: Interpreting Dialogue. Get together with two classmates. Identify an episode in which dialogue is used, such as the scene with the narrator and his mother and grandmother at the end of the excerpt. First identify the characters' qualities that are reflected in the dialogue. Then each of you should choose one of the characters and as a group prepare a dramatic reading to convey those qualities.

Connecting Reading and Writing

1. Imagine that you are young Mark Mathabane and that a gang member accosts you after you have started attending school. Write a **monologue** in which you defend the value of an education.

Option: Create the **script** for a public announcement on South African television in which Mark Mathabane as an adult implores young South African blacks to go to school.

2. In the preface to *Kaffir Boy,* Mark Mathabane wrote that his purpose in writing about his experiences was to make the rest of the world "understand why apartheid cannot be reformed: it has to be abolished." Research what others have said about the effects of apartheid. In an **expository** **essay** for your classmates, summarize what you learned about apartheid from your research and from reading the excerpt from *Kaffir Boy.*

Option: Write **notes** for a panel discussion on apartheid, summarizing what you have learned.

3. Read Alice Walker's poem "Women," noting how Walker's images of women compare with Mathabane's portrayal of his mother in the excerpt from *Kaffir Boy.* Discuss the two works in a **letter** to a friend who you think would enjoy reading them.

Option: Using "Women" as a model, write a **poem** about Mathabane's mother.

from When Heaven and Earth Changed Places

LE LY HAYSLIP   born 1949   VIETNAM / U.S.

A biography of Hayslip appears on page 743.

Approaching the Selection

Vietnam is a country with a long history of war. In the third century B.C., Vietnam was conquered by the Chinese under the Han dynasty. The Vietnamese maintained their resistance to Chinese rule for over twelve hundred years. During the late nineteenth and early twentieth centuries, the French attempted to colonize Vietnam but were finally defeated by Ho Chi Minh and his communist organization, the Viet Minh. After World War II, the country was divided into communist North Vietnam and noncommunist South Vietnam. Republican forces in South Vietnam, supported by Americans, fought against the Viet Cong, communist rebels who were backed by the North Vietnamese government. It is at this point in time that the selection takes place.

In this excerpt from her autobiography, Le Ly Hayslip (lā lē hā′ slip) shares childhood memories of her father and reveals the impact of war on Vietnamese families. Bay Ly (bī lē) is the writer's childhood nickname, *Bay* meaning "six." She was the youngest of six children.

Connecting Writing and Reading

Get together with another student and brainstorm associations with the word *Vietnam.* In your journal create a cluster diagram that shows these associations. As you read, note whether the selection confirms or contradicts your impressions of Vietnam.

from When Heaven and Earth Changed Places

Fathers and Daughters

AFTER MY BROTHER Bon went North, I began to pay more attention to my father.

He was built solidly—big-boned—for a Vietnamese man, which meant he probably had well-fed, noble ancestors. People said he had the body of a natural-born warrior. He was a year younger and an inch shorter than my mother, but just as good-looking. His face was round, like a Khmer or Thai,[1] and his complexion was brown as soy from working all his life in the sun. He was very easygoing about everything and seldom in a hurry. Seldom, too, did he say no to a request—from his children or his neighbors. Although he took everything in stride, he was a hard and diligent worker. Even on holidays, he was always mending things or tending to our house and animals. He would not wait to be asked for help if he saw someone in trouble. Similarly, he always said what he thought, although he knew, like most honest men, when to keep silent. Because of his honesty, his empathy, and his openness to people, he understood life deeply. Perhaps that is why he was so easygoing. Only a half-trained mechanic thinks everything needs fixing.

He loved to smoke cigars and grew a little tobacco in our yard. My mother always wanted him to sell it, but there was hardly ever enough to take to market. I think for her it was the principle of the thing: smoking cigars was like burning money. Naturally, she had a song for such gentle vices—her own habit of chewing betel nuts included:

Get rid of your tobacco,
And you will get a water buffalo.

Give away your betel,
And you will get more paddy land.

Despite her own good advice, she never abstained from chewing betel, nor my father from smoking cigars. They were rare luxuries that life and the war allowed them.

My father also liked rice wine, which we made, and enjoyed an occasional beer, which he purchased when there was nothing else we needed. After he'd had a few sips, he would tell jokes and happy stories and the village kids would flock around. Because I was his youngest daughter, I was entitled to listen from his knee—the place of honor. Sometimes he would sing funny songs about whoever threatened the village and we would feel better. For example, when the French or Moroccan soldiers were near, he would sing:

There are many kinds of vegetables,
Why do you like spinach?
There are many kinds of wealth,
Why do you use Minh money?
There are many kinds of people,
Why do you love terrorists?

We laughed because these were all the things the French told us about the Viet Minh fighters, whom we favored in the war. Years later, when the Viet Cong were near, he would sing:

There are many kinds of vegetables,
Why do you like spinach?
There are many kinds of money,

---

1. Khmer or Thai (kə mer′, tī): one of the native races of Cambodia; natives of Thailand.

Why do you use Yankee dollars?
There are many kinds of people,
Why do you disobey your ancestors?

This was funny because the words were taken from the speeches the North Vietnamese cadres delivered to shame us for helping the Republic. He used to have a song for when the Viet Minh were near too, which asked in the same way, "Why do you use francs?" and "Why do you love French traitors?" Because he sang these songs with a comical voice, my mother never appreciated them. She couldn't see the absurdity of our situation as clearly as we children. To her, war and real life were different. To us, they were all the same.

Even as a parent, my father was more lenient than our mother, and we sometimes ran to him for help when she was angry. Most of the time it didn't work, and he would lovingly rub our heads as we were dragged off to be spanked. The village saying went: "A naughty child learns more from a whipping stick than a sweet stick." We children were never quite sure about that but agreed the whipping stick was an eloquent teacher. When he absolutely had to punish us himself, he didn't waste time. Wordlessly, he would find a long, supple bamboo stick and let us have it behind our thighs. It stung, but he could have whipped us harder. I think seeing the pain in his face hurt more than receiving his half-hearted blows. Because of that, we seldom did anything to merit a father's spanking—the highest penalty in our family. Violence in any form offended him. For this reason, I think, he grew old before his time.

One of the few times my father ever touched my mother in a way not consistent with love was during one of the yearly floods, when people came to our village for safety from the lower ground. We sheltered many in our house, which was nothing more than a two-room hut with woven mats for a floor. I came home one day in winter rain to see refugees and Republican soldiers milling around outside. They did not know I lived there, so I had to elbow my way inside. It was nearly supper time, and I knew my mother would be fixing as much food as we could spare.

In the part of the house we used as our kitchen, I discovered my mother crying. She and my father had gotten into an argument outside a few minutes before. He had assured the refugees he would find something to eat for everyone, and she insisted there would not be enough for her children if everyone was fed. He repeated his order to her, this time loud enough for all to hear. Naturally, he thought this would end the argument. She persisted in contradicting him, so he had slapped her.

This show of male power—we called it *do danh vo*[2]—was usual behavior for Vietnamese husbands but unusual for my father. My mother could be as strict as she wished with his children, and he would seldom interfere. Now, I discovered there were limits even to his great patience. I saw the glowing red mark on her cheek and asked if she was crying because it hurt. She said no. She said she was crying because her action had caused my father to lose face in front of strangers. She promised that if I ever did what she had done to a husband, I would have both cheeks glowing: one from his blow and one from hers.

Once, when I was the only child at home, my mother went to Da Nang[3] to visit Uncle Nhu, and my father had to take care of me. I woke up from my nap in the empty house and cried for my mother. My father came in from the yard and reassured me, but I was still cranky and continued crying. Finally, he gave me a rice cookie to shut me up. Needless to

----

2. ***do danh vo*** (dỗ zäny vỗ).

3. **Da Nang** (dä naŋ): seaport in central Vietnam.

say, this was a tactic my mother never used.

The next afternoon I woke up, and although I was not feeling cranky, I thought a rice cookie might be nice. I cried a fake cry, and my father came running in.

"What's this?" he asked, making a worried face. "Little Bay Ly doesn't want a cookie?"

I was confused again.

"Look under your pillow," he said with a smile.

I twisted around and saw that, while I was sleeping, he had placed a rice cookie under my pillow. We both laughed, and he picked me up like a sack of rice and carried me outside while I gobbled the cookie.

In the yard, he plunked me down under a tree and told me some stories. After that, he got some scraps of wood and showed me how to make things: a doorstop for my mother and a toy duck for me. This was unheard of—a father doing these things with a child that was not a son! Where my mother would instruct me on cooking and cleaning and tell stories about brides, my father showed me the mystery of hammers and explained the customs of our people.

His knowledge of the Vietnamese went back to the Chinese Wars in ancient times. I learned how one of my distant ancestors, a woman named Phung Thi Chinh,[4] led Vietnamese fighters against the Han. In one battle, even though she was pregnant and surrounded by Chinese, she delivered the baby, tied it to her back, and cut her way to safety wielding a sword in each hand. I was amazed at this warrior's bravery and impressed that I was her descendant. Even more, I was amazed and impressed by my father's pride in her accomplishments (she was, after all, a humble female) and his belief that I was worthy of her example. *Con phai theo got chan co ta*[5] ("follow in her footsteps"), he said. Only later would I learn what he truly meant.

Never again did I cry after my nap. Phung

Thi women were too strong for that. Besides, I was my father's daughter, and we had many things to do together.

On the eve of my mother's return, my father cooked a feast of roast duck. When we sat down to eat it, I felt guilty and my feelings showed on my face. He asked why I acted so sad.

"You've killed one of mother's ducks," I said. "One of the fat kind she sells at the market. She says the money buys gold, which she saves for her daughters' weddings. Without gold for a dowry—*con o gia*[6]—I will be an old maid!"

My father looked suitably concerned, then brightened and said, "Well, Bay Ly, if you can't get married, you will just have to live at home forever with me!"

I clapped my hands at the happy prospect.

My father cut into the rich, juicy bird and said, "Even so, we won't tell your mother about the duck, okay?"

I giggled and swore myself to secrecy.

The next day, I took some water out to him in the fields. My mother was due home any time, and I used every opportunity to step outside and watch for her. My father stopped working, drank gratefully, then took my hand and led me to the top of a nearby hill. It had a good view of the village and the land beyond it, almost to the ocean. I thought he was going to show me my mother coming back, but he had something else in mind.

He said, "Bay Ly, you see all this here? This is the Vietnam we have been talking about. You understand that a country is more than a lot of dirt, rivers, and forests, don't you?"

I said, "Yes, I understand." After all, we had learned in school that one's country is as sacred as a father's grave.

---

4. **Phung Thi Chinh** (fʊʊŋ ti chiny).
5. ***Con phai theo got chan co ta*** (kôn fĩ teô′ gô chän kô̂ tä).
6. ***con o gia*** (kôn u yä).

"Good. You know, some of these lands are battlefields where your brothers and cousins are fighting. They may never come back. Even your sisters have all left home in search of a better life. You are the only one left in my house. If the enemy comes back, you must be both a daughter and a son. I told you how the Chinese used to rule our land. People in this village had to risk their lives diving in the ocean just to find pearls for the Chinese emperor's gown. They had to risk tigers and snakes in the jungle just to find herbs for his table. Their payment for this hardship was a bowl of rice and another day of life. That is why Le Loi,[7] Gia Long,[8] the Trung Sisters, and Phung Thi Chinh fought so hard to expel the Chinese. When the French came, it was the same old story. Your mother and I were taken to Da Nang to build a runway for their airplanes. We labored from sunup to sundown and well after dark. If we stopped to rest or have a smoke, a Moroccan would come up and whip our behinds. Our reward was a bowl of rice and another day of life. Freedom is never a gift, Bay Ly. It must be won and won again. Do you understand?"

I said that I did.

"Good." He moved his finger from the patchwork of brown dikes, silver water, and rippling stalks to our house at the edge of the village. "This land here belongs to me. Do you know how I got it?"

I thought a moment, trying to remember my mother's stories, then said honestly, "I can't remember."

He squeezed me lovingly. "I got it from your mother."

"What? That can't be true!" I said. Everyone in the family knew my mother was poor and my father's family was wealthy. Her parents were dead, and she had to work like a slave for her mother-in-law to prove herself worthy. Such women don't have land to give away!

"It's true." My father's smile widened. "When I was a young man, my parents needed someone to look after their lands. They had to be very careful about whom they chose as wives for their three sons. In the village, your mother had a reputation as the hardest worker of all. She raised herself and her brothers without parents. At the same time, I noticed a beautiful woman working in the fields. When my mother said she was going to talk to the matchmaker about this hard-working village girl she'd heard about, my heart sank. I was too attracted to this mysterious tall woman I had seen in the rice paddies. You can imagine my surprise when I found out the girl my mother heard about and the woman I admired were the same.

"Well, we were married and my mother tested your mother severely. She not only had to cook and clean and know everything about children, but she had to be able to manage several farms and know when and how to take the extra produce to the market. Of course, she was testing her other daughters-in-law as well. When my parents died, they divided their several farms among their sons, but you know what? They gave your mother and me the biggest share because they knew we would take care of it best. That's why I say the land came from her, because it did."

I suddenly missed my mother very much and looked down the road to the south, hoping to see her. My father noticed my sad expression.

"Hey." He poked me in the ribs. "Are you getting hungry for lunch?"

"No. I want to learn how to take care of the farm. What happens if the soldiers come back? What did you and Mother do when the soldiers came?"

My father squatted on the dusty hilltop and

---

7. **Le Loi** (lā lō′ ē).
8. **Gia Long** (zä lôŋ).

wiped the sweat from his forehead. "The first thing I did was to tell myself that it was my duty to survive—to take care of my family and my farm. That is a tricky job in wartime. It's as hard as being a soldier. The Moroccans were very savage. One day the rumor passed that they were coming to destroy the village. You may remember the night I sent you and your brothers and sisters away with your mother to Da Nang."

"You didn't go with us!" My voice still held the horror of the night I thought I had lost my father.

"Right! I stayed near the village—right on this hill—to keep an eye on the enemy and on our house. If they really wanted to destroy the village, I would save some of our things so that we could start over. Sure enough, that was their plan.

"The real problem was to keep things safe and avoid being captured. Their patrols were everywhere. Sometimes I went so deep in the forest that I worried about getting lost, but all I had to do was follow the smoke from the burning huts and I could find my way back.

"Once, I was trapped between two patrols that had camped on both sides of a river. I had to wait in the water for two days before one of them moved on. When I got out, my skin was shriveled like an old melon's. I was so cold I could hardly move. From the waist down, my body was black with leeches. But it was worth all the pain. When your mother came back, we still had some furniture and tools to cultivate the earth. Many people lost everything. Yes, we were very lucky."

My father put his arms around me. "My brother Huong[9]—your uncle Huong—had three sons and four daughters. Of his four daughters, only one is still alive. Of his three sons, two went north to Hanoi[10] and one went south to Saigon.[11] Huong's house is very empty. My other brother, your uncle Luc, had only two sons. One went north to Hanoi, the other was killed in the fields. His daughter is deaf and dumb. No wonder he has taken to drink, eh? Who does he have to sing in his house and tend his shrine when he is gone? My sister Lien had three daughters and four sons. Three of the four sons went to Hanoi and the fourth went to Saigon to find his fortune. The girls all tend their in-laws and mourn slain husbands. Who will care for Lien when she is too feeble to care for herself? Finally, my baby sister Nhien lost her husband to French bombers. Of her two sons, one went to Hanoi and the other joined the Republic, then defected, then was murdered in his house. Nobody knows which side killed him. It doesn't really matter."

My father drew me out to arm's length and looked me squarely in the eye. "Now, Bay Ly, do you understand what your job is?"

I squared my shoulders and put on a soldier's face. "My job is to avenge my family. To protect my farm by killing the enemy. I must become a woman warrior like Phung Thi Chinh!"

My father laughed and pulled me close. "No, little peach blossom. Your job is to stay alive—to keep an eye on things and keep the village safe. To find a husband and have babies and tell the story of what you've seen to your children and anyone else who'll listen. Most of all, it is to live in peace and tend the shrine of our ancestors. Do these things well, Bay Ly, and you will be worth more than any soldier who ever took up a sword."

---

9. **Huong** (hoo ôŋ').

10. **Hanoi** (hä noi'): capital of North Vietnam (1954–1976), now capital of the unified country of Vietnam.

11. **Saigon** (sī' gän'): capital of South Vietnam (1954–1976), now called Ho Chi Minh City.

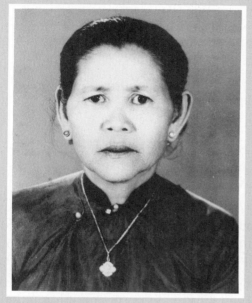

Mother, 1960

Father, 1960

Le Ly Hayslip, 1990

Sister Lan, 1960

Brother Sau Ban, 1960

Le Ly's
Family Photos

Father, 1960

Thinking About the Selection

A PERSONAL RESPONSE

sharing
impressions

1. What is your impression of Bay Ly's father? Describe your response to him in your journal.

constructing
interpretations

2. How well does Bay Ly's family seem to maintain its unity in a time of war?

Think about
- the relationships among Bay Ly, her father, and her mother
- the story Bay Ly is told about her ancestor Phung Thi Chinh
- the father's actions when the Moroccan soldiers return
- the fates of Bay Ly's brothers, sisters, uncles, and aunts

3. Compare what you have learned about Vietnam from this selection with the associations you recorded on your prereading diagram. Add to the diagram any new associations with the word *Vietnam.*

4. Bay Ly's father tells her that her job is not to fight but to stay alive and raise a family. Reflect on why he might believe this. What do you think of this advice?

A CREATIVE RESPONSE

5. If Bay Ly had not been the youngest daughter and the only child left at home, how do you think her relationship with her father might have been different?

A CRITICAL RESPONSE

6. What makes you aware of the writer's attitude toward her father?

7. What does this selection reveal to you about the values of the Vietnamese people? Give examples to support your conclusions.

8. Bay Ly's father, Mark Mathabane's mother, and Carolina Maria de Jesus all raised families under difficult circumstances. Talk about the conditions affecting each parent and compare their approaches to child rearing.

Analyzing the Writer's Craft

THEME

Which ideas from this selection do you think are worth remembering?

Building a Literary Vocabulary. Theme is a central idea or message in a work of literature. Theme should not be confused with subject, or what the work is about. Rather, theme is a perception about life or humanity that a writer expresses in relation to a subject. Most works communicate several themes, one of which usually predominates. In this autobiography the writer shares many insights about life. One theme of this excerpt is that in wartime the most important task

for an individual is to survive. This theme is stated directly. Often, however, themes are expressed indirectly and become clear only after careful reading and thinking about a work.

Application: Identifying Themes. Reread this selection, copying statements that communicate themes directly. Then think about the piece and write down other messages expressed indirectly. Working as a whole class, make a list of the themes on the board and choose the three you believe are most important.

Connecting Reading and Writing

1. Write a **nomination** giving reasons why the writer's father should receive a parenting award.

Option: In a **guest column** for *Parents* magazine, have the writer's father share child-rearing advice.

2. Do research to find out more information about modern Vietnamese culture. Present the information in a **chart** that compares Vietnamese and American cultures in terms of values, family unity, types of work, economy, and social customs.

Option: In a **letter** to a Vietnamese pen pal, explain what you have learned about the similarities and differences in the two cultures. Ask your pen pal to share his or her ideas.

3. Both this selection and the poem "The Song of a Soldier's Wife" in Unit 3 concern the effects of war

on the Vietnamese. Based on the anti-war messages conveyed in both works, create an anti-war **handbill** that reveals the impact of war on families and family life.

Option: Write **song lyrics** that convey the anti-war themes of both works.

4. Read Le Ly Hayslip's entire autobiography. In a **book review,** explain whether she followed in the footsteps of her warrior ancestor, Phung Thi Chinh.

Option: Answer this question in a **biographical sketch** of Hayslip intended for a reference book on notable women.

from A Dakar Childhood

NAFISSATOU DIALLO   1941–1982   SENEGAL

A biography of Diallo appears on page 742.

Approaching the Selection

This selection is a chapter from the autobiography of a woman who grew up in Dakar, the capital of Senegal in West Africa. Nafissatou Diallo (nä fi sä′ tōō dē ä′ lō) was an ordinary woman—a midwife and nurse—who wrote to show a new generation of young people what her own generation was like when young. Diallo, nicknamed Safi (sä′ fē) as a child, lost her mother at an early age and was raised by her father and her grandmother Mame (mum). The family was Muslim, as are most of the people in Senegal, though the country includes Christians and followers of traditional African religions. There is a strong Muslim influence on cultural life. There is also a strong French influence, as Senegal was formerly a colony of France.

Building Vocabulary

These essential words are footnoted within the selection.

reprobation (rep′ rə bā′ shən): His dominant expression was of merciless and severe **reprobation.** (page 444)

propitiatory (prō pish′ ē ə tôr′ ē): I recited the formula seven times and then buried the **propitiatory** piece of charcoal in my hair. (page 445)

recourse (rē′ kôrs′), **protocol** (prōt′ ō kôl′), **reconciliation** (rek′ ən sil′ ē ā′ shən): We had to have **recourse** to **protocol** for our **reconciliation.** (page 446)

Connecting Writing and Reading

Often young people find that having a romance creates tension within their families. In your journal, write down some of the reasons why this happens, based on your experiences and those of people you know. As you read this account of a high-school romance, think about why it causes family tension.

OR SOME TIME now I had noticed a very light-complexioned boy on the beach; he had delicate, almost feminine features but was by no means lacking in masculinity. He used to sit in his corner buried in his books, apparently oblivious of us girls. He behaved as if we simply were not there and naturally he turned all our heads, including mine; but I would not have let him suspect this for anything in the world. Some of the girls, even the shy and the well-bred ones, had gone so far as to write notes to him. For my part I looked the picture of indifference and let no one into the secret of what I felt.

"I wonder if he's a man or if he's got a stone in place of a heart. He's always there with his head shaved like Yul Brynner[1] and his caftans[2] and with eyes for nothing except his books," said the girls, unable to imagine the real state of affairs.

"For all his effeminate looks, you're dying for him to talk to you," I said. "Leave the poor boy alone; he's a saint." But for all my apparent indifference I would have been in seventh heaven if he had cast those magnificent eyes in my direction.

What was my excitement when one day as I went out to buy bread I saw him posted at the corner of our street. My heart beat fit to burst, but I walked past him with my nose in the air without a glance. A little while later my young sister passed a note secretly to me, which I read in the lavatory. I was flooded with joy.

"Mademoiselle," he wrote . . .

"My heart can no longer keep its secret. I have tried to no avail to keep silent, but I feel I shall choke if I do not speak. I love you. I have loved you from the first time I saw you on the beach. I dared not write for fear of seeming ridiculous. What indeed could a wretched high-school boy mean to you, compared with those students who are the real big noises in

your school? For my part love must know no prejudice. Intelligent as I imagine you to be, you must surely share this opinion. Have pity on me. I will wait for you on Thursday in the gardens of the Council Chamber.

"If you come I shall be the happiest of mortals; your absence will plunge me into the deepest despair."

I was carried away on a wave of delight. I breathed deeply, gulping in air under the stress of my emotion. I felt blissfully happy. The next day I met him at the appointed place, in the park opposite the palace, where the military headquarters are now. We understood each other immediately without need for words. We sat on a bench under the trees, hand in hand, with no word coming from our lips but our hearts brimming over with identical feelings. I could now observe him at leisure: he was really handsome. Like all girls of my age, I was very impressed by good looks. But he combined great intelligence with his charm; he was often the first in his class and shone in several subjects. We saw a lot of each other. The same little park was our meeting place. If he was the slightest bit late, I was plunged in despair. Later he tried, unsuccessfully, to get me to take an interest in mathematics.

I was intrigued by his caftans and his shaved head. "My father runs a Koranic[3] school," he told me. "He has very strict religious principles. He shaves our heads to make it easier for our ablutions and obliges us to dress like this, as is laid down for prayer. I'm the first one in the family to find this an embarrassment, as hardly anyone else in high school dresses like

---

1. Yul Brynner (yo͞ol brə′ nər): leading man of numerous American movies; he had a shaved head.
2. caftans (kaf′ tənz): long-sleeved robes with belts, worn in eastern Mediterranean countries.
3. Koranic (kə ran′ ik): of or having to do with the Koran, the sacred book of the Muslim religion.

this. As soon as I go to university, I shall dress as I please."

He was my guest to Marie-Louise's First Communion. My school friends, seeing us together for the first time, were most surprised. How their tongues wagged! Some of the girls tried to get him away from me, but I knew how to look after my own interests. He had borrowed a European outfit for the occasion from a friend, and it suited him down to the ground.

Marie-Louise's party was as elaborate as if it had been a wedding. She was an only child, and her mother spoilt her and spared no expense to please her. All the young people of the Plateau had been invited. There was plenty to eat and lots to drink. A *gumbe* band from Bayeux[4] Street played for dancing.

Dancing started at half-past five. My cousin Ami had taken particular trouble over my appearance. She had straightened my hair with a hot comb and then arranged it in curls. She made me up, managing to darken my eyebrows symmetrically, a thing I could never do for myself. I had a new dress for the occasion—very short. Ami lent me her shoes with stiletto heels and a black leather bag with a long handle that I wore over my shoulder in the fashion of the time. She would have nothing to do with Mame's oily *kiki*[5] and scented me with a light toilet water whose aroma floated around me, intoxicating me before anyone else.

My holidays in Saint-Louis had made me expert in modern dances. So many young men wanted to dance with me that my school friends were furious, but eventually, after I had agreed to dance out of courtesy with various other partners, I danced all the rest of the evening with *him*; I felt for the first time that I could abandon myself to the rhythm in arms that I would have liked to have around me forever. What a feast for heart and body. But this intoxicating evening was to end disastrously.

After the dance, which finished as was customary about eight o'clock, I had only a very short walk to get home, but he and I took it into our heads to go the long way round. We wandered about for some time, holding hands, but sooner or later we had to find our way back to the corner of my street and say goodbye. He kissed me good night. Even so close to the house I wasn't afraid of being seen. No one in our family or in our street put their noses out of doors at that hour; and Father would be at the mosque[6] with the older members of the congregation. So I was just returning his kiss when a powerfully-built figure passed very close to us, wrapped in a brown jellaba[7] which, it's true, looked very like Father's. But I felt so safe that it didn't bother me in the slightest. Besides, the figure passed us by with his face hidden by the hood, without taking any notice of us. At that moment I stepped back and waved goodbye to my sweetheart, saying, "Good night, darling!"

The man in the jellaba stopped and turned around. Father's eyes were upon me; in the half darkness I could see the thick lenses of his spectacles glinting. He froze like a statue, the picture of utter astonishment. I thought I saw the expression of his face change to one of disillusionment and contempt. Then he pulled himself up to his full height, and his form seemed to fill the whole street. I could see his face better now, and while his features still registered stupefaction, his dominant expression was of merciless and severe <u>reprobation</u>.[8] He had been surprised in the middle of his prayers and could not speak; the hand that he lifted to his lips held his rosary. He did not say a word,

---

4. **Bayeux** (bȧ yö′).

5. *kiki* (kē′ kē): a heavy scent with an oily base.

6. **mosque** (mäsk): a Muslim temple or place of worship.

7. **jellaba** (jə lä′ bä): a man's heavy overgarment; a sort of cloak with a hood.

8. **reprobation** (rep′ rə bā′ shən): strong disapproval.

but a hissing sound broke involuntarily from his lips as if he were spitting.

He still did not speak a word, but it was worse than if he had shouted at me. I was trembling from head to foot. Then he walked purposefully back to the house, his bitter anger manifest in his bearing.

I lingered on in the street, a prey to a thousand contradictory thoughts. Well, this was it! Father could only assume, from what he had seen and heard, that I was thoroughly depraved. So, in the first place he was deeply hurt because of his exclusive, profound, jealous love for me. But what was worse, to find his daughter kissing a young man in the street meant dishonor. In those days honor was very important: the honor of the family, of the clan. And this was no imported virtue, something learned from books: it was an inherent part of our traditional past. Our tales and legends were full of chaste girls, heroic warriors, mothers whose nobility endured to their dying day. The distance between Father and myself suddenly seemed like a cold, unbearable wilderness. He was going to despise me, was already despising me. In a trice his trust in me would be lost; he would never be able to look at me again without that expression of contempt round his mouth that I had just witnessed.

Why did not something happen to me at that moment? Why did I not fall ill, become crippled? Why was I not struck by a thunderbolt? Everything was at an end for me; I couldn't go on living. Perhaps I could kill myself, throw myself in the sea? Perhaps I should run away?

Mame came and made me go home, but her words only added another fear to my worries about moral issues. "Whatever have you done, Safi?" she said. "I've never seen your father in such a state. He's going to beat you within an inch of your life, and no one will be able to restrain him."

So now, added to everything else, there was the dread of a thrashing. I took off my shoes and followed Mame home, ready to make off if I saw Father approaching. I ran to the kitchen to get a piece of charcoal over which I recited the familiar incantation: "He who strikes me strikes the daughter of the Prophet; he who lays a hand on me lays a hand on God; I seek the protection of Fatou Binetou, the daughter of the Prophet!" I recited the formula seven times and then buried the propitiatory[9] piece of charcoal in my hair. Then I waited, more or less reassured, but this did not prevent me from clinging to Mame, following her about like a shadow. But I had to go to the lavatory alone. I managed to get there safely, but though I dashed back like lightning, I was not quick enough. Father seized hold of me, more or less carried me to his room and locked the door.

His face was disfigured with anger. Having contained himself for more than an hour, he was now about to explode. I even think that his long habit of self-control and moderation that he had acquired over the years made him all the more liable to fly into a paroxysm of unbridled rage when he did let himself go.

He thrashed me. Mercilessly . . . .

The neighbors who had heard my screams looked at me with commiseration but not without some malice. My school friends came to see me, and they too could be divided into the true friends, those who were totally sincere in their sympathy, and those who I could feel were inwardly delighted. "He," for his part, sent me secret little notes that reduced me to tears. He felt himself responsible for what had happened. My boy cousins spitefully took every opportunity of reminding me of my punishment. Mame was my guiding light through this time of trial. Always stable and kind, she showed me the way through her firmness and gentleness, and I felt that with her help I had

---

9. propitiatory (prō pish′ ē ə tôr′ ē): intended to win or regain goodwill or to calm anger.

served an apprenticeship for life.

I resumed my normal activities. Nevertheless I maintained my stubborn attitude toward my father. I would mutter a forced greeting and then go out of my way to avoid him. And yet I could tell that he was embarrassed and unhappy. He was sorry for what he had done, and I could not bear to read in his eyes the reflection of his remorse. It was the mute flicker in his eyes that made me forget my resolution to remain unmoved, and I decided to put an end to this cold war. We had to have recourse[10] to protocol[11] for our reconciliation.[12] Mame sent for Aunt Safi, and both of them accompanied me to his room. I knelt down in front of Father and with bowed head begged his forgiveness.

---

10. recourse (rē′ kôrs′): a turning to for aid or safety.

11. protocol (prōt′ ō kôl′): a code of procedures and courtesies that are accepted as polite and proper, used to assure that none of the parties in a given situation is offended.

12. reconciliation (rek′ ən sil′ ē ā′ shən): the act of settling a dispute or making friendly again.

Thinking About the Selection

A PERSONAL RESPONSE

sharing impressions

1. How do you feel about what happens to Safi? Describe your feelings in your journal.

constructing interpretations

2. Do you think Safi should have asked her father for forgiveness? Explain.

3. Who or what is most to blame for the family tension in Safi's household?
Think about
- Safi's flaws and virtues
- her father's reasons for punishing her
- her boyfriend's feelings of responsibility
- the traditional values of her father
- the social values of the young people

4. Is Safi's romance worth the problems it causes? Explain your answer.

A CREATIVE RESPONSE

5. How is Safi's romance likely to turn out?

A CRITICAL RESPONSE

6. How universal are the experiences depicted in this selection?
Think about
- your experiences with romance
- what you wrote in your journal about family tensions
- contemporary social values

7. What attitudes do you think the writer displays—toward herself as an adolescent, toward the people in her life, and toward the events that happen to her? Explain your answer.

Analyzing the Writer's Craft

CONFLICT

Think about all the forces that conspire against Safi as she tries to conduct her romance.

Building a Literary Vocabulary. Plot always involves some sort of conflict, or struggle between opposing forces. A conflict may be external, involving a character pitted against an outside force—nature, a physical obstacle, another character, or society. Safi's father's violent opposition to her romance is an external conflict. A conflict may also be internal, occurring within a character. Safi's wish to avoid her father and yet to be reconciled with him is an internal conflict.

Application: Analyzing Conflict. Reread this selection, looking for passages that reveal conflict. Next to each passage, on an attached tag, summarize the conflict and identify it as internal or external. As a class, discuss the different conflicts and decide whether or not they are resolved.

Connecting Reading and Writing

1. Imagine that Safi, her father, and her grandmother are discussing this troubling incident in the office of a family counselor. Create a **transcript** of the counseling session that includes the counselor's advice on ways to resolve the family tensions.

Option: Assume the viewpoint of Safi's father or grandmother and reflect on the incident in a **memoir.**

2. From your reading of this selection, make a set of **notes** that you would use to write an article about cultural conflicts in modern Senegal. Include in your notes aspects of modern French culture and aspects of traditional Muslim culture evident in the selection.

Option: In an **essay** for a social studies class, compare the cultural conflicts evident in Senegal with those present in the United States, another multicultural society.

3. In a **speech** to the school parents' association, state your views about the extent to which parents should control teenagers' personal lives and the methods that should or should not be used.

Option: Present your opinions in a **letter to the editor** of your local newspaper.

4. Nafissatou Diallo wrote her book to remind "today's youngsters of what we were like when we were their age." Write a **letter** to her telling what you think modern American students can learn from her story.

Option: Write a **recommendation** of this book to the school librarian explaining why students should read it.

The Name

AHARON MEGGED   born 1920   POLAND / ISRAEL

A biography of Megged appears on page 747.

*A*pproaching the Story

One of the enduring concerns of literature is the effort of different generations to get along. This story by Aharon Megged (u hu rōn′ me′ ged) is about an elderly Jew who left his Ukrainian village in Eastern Europe before World War II to join his daughter and her family in what later became Israel. Here, settlers from many places came together to make a new life. But here, as elsewhere, the past and the future often have conflicting claims. The following story is about some of the decisions people must make when struggling with those claims.

*B*uilding Vocabulary

These essential words are footnoted within the story.

placatingly (plā′ kāt′ iŋ lē): She would smile at him **placatingly.** (page 451)

commiseration (kə miz′ ər ā′ shən): A strained silence of **commiseration** would descend. (page 452)

wont (wänt): Grandfather sat down on the chair and placed the palm of his hand on the edge of the table, as was his **wont.** (page 456)

chasm (kaz′ əm): It was as if a **chasm** gaped between a world that was passing and a world that was born. (page 459)

*C*onnecting Writing and Reading

Think of any customs or traditions, such as using certain family names, that have been kept alive in your family or in the family of someone you know. Then imagine that you are about to start a family of your own. Describe in your journal one tradition you would like to continue and one that you cannot easily identify with, explaining how you feel about these traditions. As you read the following story, compare your feelings about family traditions with those expressed by the characters.

GRANDFATHER ZISSKIND lived in a little house in a southern suburb of the town. About once a month, on a Saturday afternoon, his granddaughter Raya and her young husband, Yehuda,[1] would go and pay him a visit.

Raya would give three cautious knocks on the door (an agreed signal between her and her grandfather ever since her childhood, when he had lived in their house together with the whole family), and they would wait for the door to be opened. "Now he's getting up," Raya would whisper to Yehuda, her face glowing, when the sound of her grandfather's slippers was heard from within, shuffling across the room. Another moment, and the key would be turned and the door opened.

"Come in," he would say somewhat absently, still buttoning up his pants, with the rheum of sleep in his eyes. Although it was very hot, he wore a yellow winter vest with long sleeves, from which his wrists stuck out—white, thin, delicate as a girl's, as was his bare neck with its taut skin.

After Raya and Yehuda had sat down at the table, which was covered with a white cloth showing signs of the meal he had eaten alone—crumbs from the Sabbath loaf, a plate with meat leavings, a glass containing some grape pips, a number of jars, and so on—he would smooth the crumpled pillows, spread a cover over the narrow bed, and tidy up. It was a small room, and its obvious disorder aroused pity for the old man's helplessness in running his home. In the corner was a shelf with two sooty kerosene burners, a kettle, and two or three saucepans, and next to it a basin containing plates, knives, and forks. In another corner was a stand holding books with thick leather bindings, leaning and lying on each other. Some of his clothes hung over the backs of the chairs. An ancient walnut cupboard with an empty buffet stood exactly opposite the door. On the wall hung a clock that had long since stopped.

"We ought to make Grandfather a present of a clock," Raya would say to Yehuda as she surveyed the room and her glance lighted on the clock; but every time the matter slipped her memory. She loved her grandfather, with his pointed white silky beard, his tranquil face from which a kind of holy radiance emanated, his quiet, soft voice that seemed to have been made only for uttering words of sublime wisdom. She also respected him for his pride, which had led him to move out of her mother's house and live by himself, accepting the hardship and trouble and the affliction of loneliness in his old age. There had been a bitter quarrel between him and his daughter. After Raya's father had died, the house had lost its grandeur and shed the trappings of wealth. Some of the antique furniture that they had retained—along with some crystalware and jewels, the dim luster of memories from the days of plenty in their native city—had been sold, and Rachel, Raya's mother, had been compelled to support the home by working as a dentist's nurse. Grandfather Zisskind, who had been supported by the family ever since he came to the country, wished to hand over to his daughter his small capital, which was deposited in a bank. She was not willing to accept it. She was stubborn and proud like

---

1. Raya . . . Yehuda (rä′ yə, ye hoo′ də).

him. Then, after a prolonged quarrel and several weeks of not speaking to each other, he took some of the things in his room and the broken clock and went to live alone. That had been about four years ago. Now Rachel would come to him once or twice a week, bringing with her a bag full of provisions, to clean the room and cook some meals for him. He was no longer interested in expenses and did not even ask about them, as though they were of no more concern to him.

"And now . . . what can I offer you?" Grandfather Zisskind would ask when he considered the room ready to receive guests. "There's no need to offer us anything, Grandfather; we didn't come for that," Raya would answer crossly.

But protests were of no avail. Her grandfather would take out a jar of fermenting preserves and put it on the table, then grapes and plums, biscuits and two glasses of strong tea, forcing them to eat. Raya would taste a little of this and that just to please the old man, while Yehuda, for whom all these visits were unavoidable torment, the very sight of the dishes arousing his disgust, would secretly indicate to her by making a sour face that he just couldn't touch the preserves. She would smile at him placatingly,[2] stroking his knee. But Grandfather insisted, so he would have to taste at least a teaspoonful of the sweet and nauseating stuff.

Afterwards Grandfather would ask about all kinds of things. Raya did her best to make the conversation pleasant in order to relieve Yehuda's boredom. Finally would come what Yehuda dreaded most of all and on account of which he had resolved more than once to refrain from these visits. Grandfather Zisskind would rise, take his chair and place it next to the wall, get up on it carefully, holding on to the back so as not to fall, open the clock, and take out a cloth bag with a black cord tied around it. Then he would shut the clock, get

off the chair, put it back in its place, sit down on it, undo the cord, take out of the cloth wrapping a bundle of sheets of paper, lay them in front of Yehuda, and say:

"I would like you to read this."

"Grandfather," Raya would rush to Yehuda's rescue, "but he's already read it at least ten times. . . ."

But Grandfather Zisskind would pretend not to hear and would not reply, so Yehuda was compelled each time to read there and then that same essay, spread over eight, long sheets in a large, somewhat shaky handwriting, which he almost knew by heart. It was a lament for Grandfather's native town in the Ukraine, which had been destroyed by the Germans, and all its Jews slaughtered. When he had finished, Grandfather would take the sheets out of his hand, fold them, sigh, and say:

"And nothing of all this is left. Dust and ashes. Not even a tombstone to bear witness. Imagine, of a community of twenty thousand Jews not even one survived to tell how it happened . . . Not a trace."

Then out of the same cloth bag, which contained various letters and envelopes, he would draw a photograph of his grandson Mendele,[3] who had been twelve years old when he was killed; the only son of his son Ossip, chief

2. **placatingly** (plā′ kat′ iŋ lē): in a manner intended to calm or soothe.

3. **Mendele** (men′ də le).

engineer in a large chemical factory. He would show it to Yehuda and say:

"He was a genius. Just imagine, when he was only eleven, he had already finished his studies at the Conservatory, won a scholarship from the government, and was considered an outstanding violinist. A genius! Look at that forehead. . . ." And after he had put the photograph back he would sigh and repeat, "Not a trace."

A strained silence of commiseration[4] would descend on Raya and Yehuda, who had already heard these same things many times over and no longer felt anything when they were repeated. And as he wound the cord around the bag the old man would muse: "And Ossip was also a prodigy. As a boy he knew Hebrew well and could recite Bialik's poems by heart. He studied by himself. He read endlessly, Gnessin, Frug, Bershadsky[5] . . . You didn't know Bershadsky; he was a good writer . . . He had a warm heart, Ossip had. He didn't mix in politics, he wasn't even a Zionist,[6] but even when they promoted him there, he didn't forget that he was a Jew . . . He called his son Mendele, of all names, after his dead brother, even though it was surely not easy to have a name like that among the Russians . . . Yes, he had a warm, Jewish heart . . . "

He would turn to Yehuda as he spoke, since in Raya he always saw the child who used to sit on his knee listening to his stories, and for him she had never grown up, while he regarded Yehuda as an educated man who could understand someone else, especially inasmuch as Yehuda held a government job.

Raya remembered how the change had come about in her grandfather. When the war was over he was still sustained by uncertainty and hoped for some news of his son, for it was known that very many had succeeded in escaping eastward. Wearily he would visit all those who had once lived in his town, but none of them had received any sign of life from relatives. Nevertheless he continued to hope, for Ossip's important position might have helped to save him. Then Raya came home one evening and saw him sitting on the floor with a rent in his jacket.[7] In the house they spoke in whispers, and her mother's eyes were red with weeping. She, too, had wept at Grandfather's sorrow, at the sight of his stricken face, at the oppressive quiet in the rooms. For many weeks afterward it was as if he had imposed silence on himself. He would sit at his table from morning to night, reading and rereading old letters, studying family photographs by the hour as he brought them close to his shortsighted eyes, or leaning backward on his chair, motionless, his hand touching the edge of the table and his eyes staring through the window in front of him, into the distance, as if he had turned to stone. He was no longer the same talkative, wise, and humorous grandfather who interested himself in the house, asked what his granddaughter was doing,

---

4. **commiseration** (kə miz′ ər ā′ shən): the act of feeling or showing sorrow or pity for another's troubles; the act of showing sympathy.

5. **Bialik . . . Gnessin, Frug, Bershadsky** (bē ä′ lik, gne′ sin, froog, bər shäd′ skē): The Russian-born Hayyim Nahman Bialik (1873–1934) was a leading and influential poet in modern Hebrew literature. The other writers mentioned are less well-known.

6. **Zionist:** a follower of the movement to establish and maintain the Jewish national state of Israel.

7. **rent in his jacket:** A rent is a tear in a cloth. It is a practice among some Jews to tear their clothing as an act of mourning for the loss of a loved one.

instructed her, tested her knowledge, proving boastfully like a child that he knew more than her teachers. Now he seemed to cut himself off from the world and entrench himself in his thoughts and his memories, which none of the household could penetrate. Later, a strange perversity had taken hold of him that was hard to tolerate. He would insist that his meals be served at his table, apart, that no one should enter his room without knocking at the door, or close the shutters of his window against the sun. When anyone disobeyed these prohibitions, he would flare up and quarrel violently with his daughter. At times it seemed that he hated her.

When Raya's father died, Grandfather Zisskind did not show any signs of grief and did not even console his daughter. But when the days of mourning were past, it was as if he had been restored to new life, and he emerged from his silence. Yet he did not speak of his son-in-law, nor of his son Ossip, but only of his grandson Mendele. Often during the day he would mention the boy by name as if he were alive and would speak of him familiarly, although he had seen him only in photographs—as though deliberating aloud and turning the matter over, he would talk of how Mendele ought to be brought up. It was hardest of all when he started criticizing his son and his son's wife for not having foreseen the impending disaster, for not having rushed the boy away to a safe place, not having hidden him with non-Jews, not having tried to get him to the Land of Israel in good time. There was no logic in what he said; this would so infuriate Rachel that she would burst out with, "Oh, do stop! Stop it! I'll go out of my mind with your foolish nonsense!" She would rise from her seat in anger, withdraw to her room, and afterward, when she had calmed down, would say to Raya, "Sclerosis,[8] apparently. Loss of memory. He no longer knows what he's talking about."

One day—Raya would never forget this—

she and her mother saw that Grandfather was wearing his best suit, the black one, and under it a gleaming white shirt; his shoes were polished, and he had a hat on. He had not worn these clothes for many months, and the family was dismayed to see him. They thought that he had lost his mind. "What holiday is it today?" her mother asked. "Really, don't you know?" asked her grandfather. "Today is Mendele's birthday!" Her mother burst out crying. She too began to cry and ran out of the house.

After that, Grandfather Zisskind went to live alone. His mind, apparently, had become settled, except that he would frequently forget things that had occurred a day or two before, though he clearly remembered, down to the smallest detail, things that had happened in his town and to his family more than thirty years ago. Raya would go and visit him, at first with her mother and, after her marriage, with Yehuda. What bothered them was that they were compelled to listen to his talk about Mendele his grandson and to read that same lament for his native town that had been destroyed.

Whenever Rachel happened to come there during their visit, she would scold Grandfather rudely. "Stop bothering them with your masterpiece," she would say, and would herself remove the papers from the table and put them back in their bag. "If you want them to keep on visiting you, don't talk to them about the dead. Talk about the living. They're young people, and they have no mind for such things." And as they left his room together she would say, turning to Yehuda in order to placate him, "Don't be surprised at him. Grandfather's already old. Over seventy. Loss of memory."

---

8. sclerosis (skli rō′ sis); an abnormal hardening of body tissues, especially of the nervous system or the walls of major arteries.

When Raya was seven months pregnant, Grandfather Zisskind had in his absent-mindedness not yet noticed it. But Rachel could no longer refrain from letting him share her joy and hope, and told him that a great-grandchild would soon be born to him. One evening the door of Raya and Yehuda's apartment opened, and Grandfather himself stood on the threshold in his holiday clothes, just as on the day of Mendele's birthday. This was the first time he had visited them at home, and Raya was so surprised that she hugged and kissed him as she had not done since she was a child. His face shone, his eyes sparkled with the same intelligent and mischievous light they had in those far-off days before the calamity. When he entered, he walked briskly through the rooms, giving his opinion on the furniture and its arrangement and joking about everything around him. He was so pleasant that Raya and Yehuda could not stop laughing all the time he was speaking. He gave no indication that he knew what was about to take place, and for the first time in many months he did not mention Mendele.

"Ah, you naughty children," he said, "is this how you treat Grandfather? Why didn't you tell me you had such a nice place?"

"How many times have I invited you here, Grandfather?" asked Raya.

"Invited me? You ought to have *brought* me here, dragged me by force!"

"I wanted to do that too, but you refused."

"Well, I thought that you lived in some dark den, and I have a den of my own. Never mind, I forgive you."

And when he took leave of them he said:

"Don't bother to come to me. Now that I know where you're to be found and what a palace you have, I'll come to you . . . if you don't throw me out, that is."

Some days later, when Rachel came to their home and they told her about Grandfather's amazing visit, she was not surprised:

"Ah, you don't know what he's been contemplating during all these days, ever since I told him that you're about to have a child . . . He has one wish—that if it's a son, it should be named . . . after his grandson."

"Mendele?" exclaimed Raya, and involuntarily burst into laughter. Yehuda smiled as one smiles at the fond fancies of the old.

"Of course, I told him to put that out of his head," said Rachel, "but you know how obstinate he is. It's some obsession and he won't think of giving it up. Not only that, but he's sure that you'll willingly agree to it, and especially you, Yehuda."

Yehuda shrugged his shoulders. "Crazy. The child would be unhappy all his life."

"But he's not capable of understanding that," said Rachel, and a note of apprehension crept into her voice.

Raya's face grew solemn. "We have already decided on the name," she said. "If it's a girl, she'll be called Osnath, and if it's a boy—Ehud."[9]

Rachel did not like either.

The matter of the name became almost the sole topic of conversation between Rachel and the young couple when she visited them, and it infused gloom into the air of expectancy that filled the house.

Rachel, midway between the generations, was of two minds about the matter. When she spoke to her father, she would scold and contradict him, flinging at him all the arguments she had heard from Raya and Yehuda as though they were her own; but when she

> **Guide for Interpretation**
>
> In Israel, Hebrew—not Yiddish—is the official language. Raya and Yehuda, who were born in Israel and have Hebrew names, associate Yiddish names with ghetto life and a troubled past and think this association will affect the child's happiness. Notice as you read how different characters in this story feel about tradition and the significance of names.

9. **Osnath . . . Ehud** (ôs′ nät, e′ hood).

spoke to the children, she sought to induce them to meet his wishes and would bring down their anger on herself. As time went on, the question of a name, to which in the beginning she had attached little importance, became a kind of mystery, concealing something preordained, fearful, and pregnant with life and death. The fate of the child itself seemed in doubt. In her innermost heart she prayed that Raya would give birth to a daughter.

"Actually, what's so bad about the name Mendele?" she asked her daughter. "It's a Jewish name like any other."

"What are you talking about, Mother"— Raya rebelled against the thought—"a ghetto name, ugly, horrible! I wouldn't even be capable of letting it cross my lips. Do you want me to hate my child?"

"Oh, you won't hate your child. At any rate, not because of the name . . ."

"I should hate him. It's as if you'd told me that my child would be born with a hump! And anyway—why should I? What for?"

"You have to do it for Grandfather's sake," Rachel said quietly, although she knew that she was not speaking the whole truth.

"You know, Mother, that I am ready to do anything for Grandfather," said Raya. "I love him, but I am not ready to sacrifice my child's happiness on account of some superstition of his. What sense is there in it?"

Rachel could not explain the "sense in it" rationally, but in her heart she rebelled against her daughter's logic, which had always been hers too and now seemed very superficial, a symptom of the frivolity afflicting the younger generation. Her old father now appeared to her like an ancient tree whose deep roots suck up the mysterious essence of existence, of which neither her daughter nor she herself knew anything. Had it not been for this argument about the name, she would certainly never have got to meditating on the transmi-

gration of souls[10] and the eternity of life. At night she would wake up covered in cold sweat. Hazily, she recalled frightful scenes of bodies of naked children, beaten and trampled under the jackboots of soldiers, and an awful sense of guilt oppressed her spirit.

Then Rachel came with a proposal for a compromise: that the child should be named Menahem. A Hebrew name, she said; an Israeli one, by all standards.[11] Many children bore it, and it occurred to nobody to make fun of them. Even Grandfather had agreed to it after much urging.

Raya refused to listen.

"We have chosen a name, Mother," she said, "which we both like, and we won't change it for another. Menahem is a name that reeks of old age, a name that for me is connected with sad memories and people I don't like. Menahem you could call only a boy who is short, weak, and not good-looking. Let's not talk about it any more, Mother."

Rachel was silent. She almost despaired of convincing them. At last she said:

"And are you ready to take the responsibility of going against Grandfather's wishes?"

Raya's eyes opened wide, and fear was reflected in them:

"Why do you make such a fateful thing of it? You frighten me!" she said, and burst into

---

10. transmigration of souls: Some Jews believe that a soul transmigrates, or moves from a dead person to a living person. The tradition of naming a child after a deceased person is sometimes seen as a way to guarantee this transmigration.

11. Menahem . . . standards (me nä′ khem): *Mendel* and *Menahem* are Yiddish and Hebrew versions of the same name; both mean "comforter." Jews often adapt the tradition of naming a child after a loved one who is deceased by giving the child a different name that begins with the same letter. This allows for the use of more modern names.

tears. She began to fear for her offspring as one fears the evil eye.[12]

"And perhaps there *is* something fateful in it . . ." whispered Rachel without raising her eyes. She flinched at her own words.

"What is it?" insisted Raya, with a frightened look at her mother.

"I don't know . . . ," she said. "Perhaps all the same we are bound to retain the names of the dead . . . in order to leave a remembrance of them . . ." She was not sure herself whether there was any truth in what she said or whether it was merely a stupid belief, but her father's faith was before her, stronger than her own doubts and her daughter's simple and understandable opposition.

"But I don't always want to remember all those dreadful things, Mother. It's impossible that this memory should always hang about this house and that the poor child should bear it!"

Rachel understood. She, too, heard such a cry within her as she listened to her father talking, sunk in memories of the past. As if to herself, she said in a whisper:

"I don't know . . . at times it seems to me that it's not Grandfather who's suffering from loss of memory, but ourselves. All of us."

About two weeks before the birth was due, Grandfather Zisskind appeared in Raya and Yehuda's home for the second time. His face was yellow, angry, and the light had faded from his eyes. He greeted them, but did not favor Raya with so much as a glance, as if he had pronounced a ban upon the sinner. Turning to Yehuda he said, "I wish to speak to you."

They went into the inner room. Grandfather sat down on the chair and placed the palm of his hand on the edge of the table, as was his <u>wont</u>,[13] and Yehuda sat, lower than he, on the bed.

"Rachel has told me that you don't want to call the child by my grandchild's name," he said.

"Yes . . . ," said Yehuda diffidently.

"Perhaps you'll explain to me why?" he asked.

"We . . . ," stammered Yehuda, who found it difficult to face the piercing gaze of the old man. "The name simply doesn't appeal to us."

Grandfather was silent. Then he said, "I understand that Mendele doesn't appeal to you. Not a Hebrew name. Granted! But Menahem—what's wrong with Menahem?" It was obvious that he was controlling his feelings with difficulty.

"It's not . . . ," Yehuda knew that there was no use explaining; they were two generations apart in their ideas. "It's not an Israeli name . . . it's from the *Golah*."

"*Golah*," repeated Grandfather. He shook with rage, but somehow he maintained his self-control. Quietly he added, "We all come from the *Golah*. I, and Raya's father and mother. Your father and mother. All of us."

"Yes . . . ," said Yehuda. He resented the fact that he was being dragged into an argument that was distasteful to him, particularly with this old man whose mind was already not quite clear. Only out of respect did he restrain himself from shouting: That's that, and it's done with! . . . "Yes, but we were born in this country," he said aloud; "that's different."

---

12. the evil eye: a look which, in superstitious belief, is able to harm or bewitch the one stared at.

13. wont (wänt): usual practice; habit.

Grandfather Zisskind looked at him contemptuously. Before him he saw a wretched boor, an empty vessel.

"You, that is to say, think that there's something new here," he said, "that everything that was there is past and gone. Dead, without sequel. That you are starting everything anew."

"I didn't say that. I only said that we were born in this country . . ."

"You were born here. Very nice . . . ," said Grandfather Zisskind with rising emotion. "So what of it? What's so remarkable about that? In what way are you superior to those who were born *there*? Are you cleverer than they? More cultured? Are you greater than they in Torah[14] or good deeds? Is your blood redder than theirs?" Grandfather Zisskind looked as if he could wring Yehuda's neck.

"I didn't say that either. I said that *here* it's different . . ."

Grandfather Zisskind's patience with idle words was exhausted.

"You good-for-nothing!" he burst out in his rage. "What do you know about what was there? What do you know of the *people* that were there? The communities? The cities? What do you know of the *life* they had there?"

"Yes," said Yehuda, his spirit crushed, "but we no longer have any ties with it."

"You have no ties with it?" Grandfather Zisskind bent toward him. His lips quivered in fury. "With what . . . with what *do* you have ties?"

"We have . . . with this country," said Yehuda and gave an involuntary smile.

"Fool!" Grandfather Zisskind shot at him. "Do you think that people come to a desert and make themselves a nation, eh? That you are the first of some new race? That you're not the son of your father? Not the grandson of your grandfather? Do you want to forget them? Are you ashamed of them for having had a hundred times more culture and education than you have? Why . . . why, everything

here"—he included everything around him in the sweep of his arm—"is no more than a puddle of tap water against the big sea that was there! What have you here? A mixed multitude! Seventy languages! Seventy distinct groups! Customs? A way of life? Why, every home here is a nation in itself, with its own customs and its own names! And with this you have ties, you say . . ."

Yehuda lowered his eyes and was silent.

"I'll tell you what ties are," said Grandfather Zisskind calmly. "Ties are remembrance! Do you understand? The Russian is linked to his people because he remembers his ancestors. He is called Ivan, his father was called Ivan, and his grandfather was called Ivan, back to the first generation. And no Russian has said: 'From today onward I shall not be called Ivan because my fathers and my fathers' fathers were called that; I am the first of a new Russian nation which has nothing at all to do with the Ivans.' Do you understand?"

"But what has that got to do with it?" Yehuda protested impatiently. Grandfather Zisskind shook his head at him.

"And you—you're ashamed to give your son the name Mendele lest it remind you that there were Jews who were called by that name. You believe that his name should be wiped off the face of the earth. That not a trace of it should remain . . ."

He paused, heaved a deep sigh, and said:

"O children, children, you don't know what you're doing . . . You're finishing off the work which the enemies of Israel began. They took the bodies away from the world, and you—the name and the memory . . . No continuation, no evidence, no memorial, and no name. Not a trace . . ."

And with that he rose, took his stick, and with long strides went toward the door and left.

---

14. in Torah (tō′ rə): in the study of Jewish religious teachings.

The newborn child was a boy, and he was named Ehud, and when he was about a month old, Raya and Yehuda took him in the carriage to Grandfather's house.

Raya gave three cautious knocks on the door, and when she heard a rustle inside she could also hear the beating of her anxious heart. Since the birth of the child, Grandfather had not visited them even once. "I'm terribly excited," she whispered to Yehuda with tears in her eyes. Yehuda rocked the carriage and did not reply. He was now indifferent to what the old man might say or do.

The door opened, and on the threshold stood Grandfather Zisskind, his face weary and wrinkled. He seemed to have aged. His eyes were sticky with sleep, and for a moment it seemed as if he did not see the callers.

"Good Sabbath, Grandfather," said Raya with great feeling. It seemed to her now that she loved him more than ever.

Grandfather looked at them as if surprised and then said absently, "Come in, come in."

"We've brought the baby with us!" said Raya, her face shining, and her glance traveled from Grandfather to the infant sleeping in the carriage.

"Come in, come in," repeated Grandfather Zisskind in a tired voice. "Sit down," he said as he removed his clothes from the chairs and turned to tidy the disordered bedclothes.

Yehuda stood the carriage by the wall and whispered to Raya, "It's stifling for him here." Raya opened the window wide.

"You haven't seen our baby yet, Grandfather!" she said with a sad smile.

"Sit down, sit down," said Grandfather, shuffling over to the shelf, from which he took the jar of preserves and the biscuit tin, putting them on the table.

"There's no need, Grandfather, really there's no need for it. We didn't come for that," said Raya.

"Only a little something. I have nothing to offer you today . . . ," said Grandfather in a dull, broken voice. He took the kettle off the kerosene burner and poured out two glasses of tea, which he placed before them. Then he too sat down, said, "Drink, drink," and softly tapped his fingers on the table.

"I haven't seen Mother for several days now," he said at last.

"She's busy . . . ," said Raya in a low voice, without raising her eyes to him. "She helps me a lot with the baby . . ."

Grandfather Zisskind looked at his pale, knotted, and veined hands lying helplessly on the table; then he stretched out one of them and said to Raya, "Why don't you drink? The tea will get cold."

Raya drew up to the table and sipped the tea.

"And you—what are you doing now?" he asked Yehuda.

"Working as usual," said Yehuda, and added with a laugh, "I play with the baby when there's time."

Grandfather again looked down at his hands, the long thin fingers of which shook with the palsy of old age.

"Take some of the preserves," he said to Yehuda, indicating the jar with a shaking finger. "It's very good." Yehuda dipped the spoon in the jar and put it to his mouth.

There was a deep silence. It seemed to last a very long time. Grandfather Zisskind's fingers gave little quivers on the white tablecloth. It was hot in the room, and the buzzing of a fly could be heard.

Suddenly the baby burst out crying, and Raya started from her seat and hastened to quiet him. She rocked the carriage and crooned, "Quiet, child, quiet, quiet . . ." Even after he had quieted down, she went on rocking the carriage back and forth.

Grandfather Zisskind raised his head and said to Yehuda in a whisper:

"You think it was impossible to save him . . .

it was possible. They had many friends. Ossip himself wrote to me about it. The manager of the factory had a high opinion of him. The whole town knew them and loved them . . . How is it they didn't think of it . . . ?" he said, touching his forehead with the palm of his hand. "After all, they knew that the Germans were approaching . . . It was still possible to do something . . ." He stopped a moment and then added, "Imagine that a boy of eleven had already finished his studies at the Conservatory—wild beasts!" He suddenly opened eyes filled with terror. "Wild beasts! To take little children and put them into wagons and deport them . . ."

When Raya returned and sat down at the table, he stopped and became silent, and only a heavy sigh escaped from deep within him.

Again there was a prolonged silence, and as it grew heavier Raya felt the oppressive weight on her bosom increasing till it could no longer be contained. Grandfather sat at the table tapping his thin fingers, and alongside the wall the infant lay in his carriage; it was as if a chasm[15] gaped between a world that was passing and a world that was born. It was no longer a single line to the fourth generation. The aged father did not recognize the great-grandchild whose life would be no memorial.

Grandfather Zisskind got up, took his chair, and pulled it up to the clock. He climbed on to it to take out his documents.

Raya could no longer stand the oppressive atmosphere.

"Let's go," she said to Yehuda in a choked voice.

"Yes, we must go," said Yehuda, and rose from his seat. "We have to go," he said loudly as he turned to the old man.

Grandfather Zisskind held the key of the clock for a moment more, then he let his hand fall, grasped the back of the chair, and got down.

"You have to go . . . ," he said with a tortured grimace. He spread his arms out helplessly and accompanied them to the doorway.

When the door had closed behind them, the tears flowed from Raya's eyes. She bent over the carriage and pressed her lips to the baby's chest. At that moment it seemed to her that he was in need of pity and of great love, as though he were alone, an orphan in the world.

---

15. **chasm** (kaz′ əm): a deep crack in the earth's surface.

Thinking About the Story

A PERSONAL RESPONSE

sharing impressions

1. What are your thoughts and feelings at the end of the story? Describe them briefly in your journal.

constructing interpretations

2. Do you think Raya and Yehuda do the right thing in choosing the name that they do?

Think about
- Raya's seeing her baby, at the end of the story, as "an orphan in the world"
- Raya's unwillingness to "sacrifice my child's happiness on account of some superstition" of her grandfather's
- the desire of the couple to dissociate from the past and identify with Israel

3. Why do you think that Grandfather Zisskind and the young couple are so divided in their feelings about the family tradition? Explain.

Think about
- Rachel's comparison of her father to "an ancient tree whose deep roots suck up the mysterious essence of existence"
- what you would have done in a similar situation

A CREATIVE RESPONSE

4. If Raya and Yehuda had named their son Mendele according to the family tradition, how do you think they would have felt about it in later life?

A CRITICAL RESPONSE

5. In what way do you think the clock belonging to the grandfather works as a symbol in this story?

Think about
- the definition of symbol as a person, place, object, or activity that stands for something beyond itself
- what the clock means to the characters in the story

6. Which of the themes, or messages, that can be drawn from "The Name" seems most relevant to your life?

Think about
- the effect of the past on the present
- the issue of cultural identity
- differences between youth and age
- questions of independence
- the possibility of compromise

7. Compare Raya and Yehuda's situation with those of the young people in the other selections in **Confronting the Past.** In which cases do you see similarities?

Think about
- the relationship between mother and son in "Hiccups"
- the decision the boy makes in *Kaffir Boy*
- the relationship of Bay Ly to her ancestors in *When Heaven and Earth Changed Places*
- the family tensions in *A Dakar Childhood*

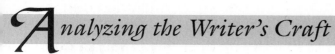

Analyzing the Writer's Craft

PLOT STRUCTURE

What are the key events in this story?

Building a Literary Vocabulary. Plot refers to the actions and events in a literary work. The plot moves forward because of a conflict, or struggle between opposing forces. In a traditional narrative, plot structure consists of the exposition, the rising action, the climax, and the falling action. The **exposition** is the explanation that lays the groundwork for the narrative and provides necessary background information. In "The Name," for example, exposition occurs in the first several pages so that the reader understands who the characters are, where they live, and what happened in the past to lead up to the present action. During the **rising action** of the plot, complications of the conflict build to a **climax,** or turning point. Interest and intensity reach their peak at this point. The events that follow the climax, called the **falling action,** show the results of the major events and resolve loose ends in the plot.

Application: Analyzing Plot Structure. Work in a small group to diagram the plot structure of "The Name." The main task will be to decide where the climax of the story occurs and where the falling action begins. Compare your findings with the findings of other groups in the class.

Connecting Reading and Writing

1. In this story Rachel sympathizes with the viewpoints of both her father and her daughter. Write a series of **diary entries** that Rachel might have written during the time this crisis was taking place.

Option: Create a **transcript** of a telephone conversation that Rachel might have with a friend shortly after the birth of her grandson.

2. Imagine that Grandfather writes a letter to his great-grandson Ehud. He puts this letter inside the old clock and tells Raya that the boy should read it when he grows into his teens. Write this **letter** as you imagine it would be.

Option: Create an **oral history** recorded by Grandfather that Ehud can listen to when he is twelve years old and curious about his ancestors.

3. To learn more about the culture of Russian and Ukrainian Jews in the late nineteenth and early twentieth centuries, read a few stories from one of Sholom Aleichem's collections, such as *Some Laughter, Some Tears.* Prepare a **report** for your class, explaining what these stories teach about the life that Grandfather Zisskind left behind in his native town.

Option: Using information from Sholom Aleichem's stories, create a **passage** to be added to "The Name" in which Grandfather describes life in his native town.

When in Early Summer

NELLY SACHS 1891–1970 GERMANY/SWEDEN

A biography of Sachs appears on page 751.

Approaching the Poem

Looming in the background of this poem is the Holocaust. Nelly Sachs nearly
became one of its victims before escaping from Germany in 1940. Her poem opens
with tender images of the beauty and enchantment of awakening nature. An interrupting voice, however, discloses other realities, horrors perpetrated in the midst of
loveliness. The poem thus points to a terrible irony and asks an unanswerable
question.

When in early summer the moon sends out secret signs,
the chalices of lilies scent of heaven,
some ear opens to listen
beneath the chirp of the cricket
5   to earth turning and the language of spirits set free.

But in dreams fish fly in the air
and a forest takes firm root in the floor of the room.

But in the midst of enchantment a voice speaks clearly and amazed:
World, how can you go on playing your games
10   and cheating time—
World, the little children were thrown like butterflies,
wings beating into the flames—

and your earth has not been thrown like a rotten apple
into the terror-roused abyss—

15   And sun and moon have gone on walking—
two cross-eyed witnesses who have seen nothing.

Reviewing Concepts

CONFLICT AND SETTING: OBSERVING LIFE

*making
connections*

As observers of life, writers frequently focus on the conflicts that are part of all people's lives. Several selections in this unit present conflicts that arise out of the setting. In the excerpt from *Kaffir Boy,* for example, the setting, an impoverished South African town, is a major cause of the conflict Mark Mathabane feels between going to school and taking to the streets. This setting also enters into the conflict between Mathabane's mother and father. The father, a victim of poverty and apartheid, takes out his anger on his wife.

Think back over the selections you have read in this unit and decide which selections portray settings that are sources of conflict. Then create a chart like the one that follows, noting for each selection the setting(s) and setting-related conflict(s).

	Setting	**Conflict caused by setting**
from *Kaffir Boy*	impoverished town in South Africa where apartheid is practiced	1. the lure of the streets *vs.* the mother's pressure on the boy to go to school 2. father's sense of futility *vs.* mother's hopes for son

*describing
connections*

Review the information on your chart, comparing the effects of setting in various selections. Write **notes** for an oral presentation in which you discuss the connection between setting and conflict as demonstrated in at least five selections in this unit. Prepare a concluding statement about human beings and their environment.

Hand With Reflecting Sphere, 1935, M. C. ESCHER.
National Gallery of Art, Washington, D.C.

The Critical Eye:

Literature of Insight

"It is the function of art to renew our perception. What we are familiar with we cease to see. The writer shakes up the familiar scene, and as if by magic, we see a new meaning in it."

ANAÏS NIN

Revealing
the Human Condition

*I*n every age and country, writers have created literature that holds a mirror to human nature. The characters depicted in this literature demonstrate noble or base qualities, or combinations of both. Unlike cultural heroes, who are exceptionally grand and courageous, these characters are ordinary people facing the complexities of life. By focusing on such people and their experiences, writers give insights into the human condition.

Some writers have examined the darker side of human nature, seeking to understand qualities such as cowardice, deceit, prejudice, vanity, selfishness, and greed. Other writers have examined the relationship between humans and the universe, sometimes emphasizing the powerlessness of the ordinary individual. Fundamental questions explored by writers include What does being an adult really mean? Why do actions often fall short of ideals? How can I make a difference in the world?

In dealing with these questions, writers generally take their readers inside the mind of one or more characters. The characters are involved in plots that may feature symbolic journeys, rites of passage, or tests of courage. Sometimes, the plot builds to a moment of keen insight, revealing the truth about the main character's situation. This truth sheds light on the human condition as well.

As you read the selections that follow, look for insights about the main characters, yourself, and all human beings.

Literary Vocabulary

INTRODUCED IN THIS SECTION

Allusion. An allusion is a reference to a historical or literary person, place, or event with which the reader is assumed to be familiar. Understanding the allusions in a work can give the reader a better understanding of it. For example, in the excerpt from *Memoirs of Madame Vigée Lebrun,* Lebrun alludes to several historical figures from the French Revolution, two of whom, Berthier and Foulon, were beheaded for their aristocratic sympathies. By knowing who these figures are, the reader comes to understand the impact that the revolution had on Lebrun.

First-Person Point of View. Point of view refers to the narrative method, or kind of narrator, used in a short story, novel, or nonfiction selection. First-person point of view exists when a character in a literary work is also the narrator. Events are seen through his or her eyes. The excerpt from *Kaffir Boy* is an example of first-person point of view. Through the childhood recollections of Mathabane, the reader feels the intensity of his situation first-hand.

REVIEWED IN THIS SECTION

Symbol

Simile

Metaphor

Conflict

Mood

Setting

from # The Inferno

DANTE ALIGHIERI   1265–1321   ITALY

Translated by John Ciardi

A biography of Dante appears on page 741.

Approaching the Poem

The Inferno is one of three sections that make up Dante Alighieri's (dän′ tä′ äl′ ēg yer′ ē) famous work, *The Divine Comedy*. *The Divine Comedy* is considered one of the greatest poems in all of European literature. It is a fantastic story in which Dante himself is the main character, a traveler who represents all of humanity. The 14,000-line poem follows the story of Dante as he journeys down into the Inferno, or Hell, then to Purgatory, a place of temporary punishment, and finally to Heaven, where at last he stands before the throne of God. There he receives a dazzling glimpse of eternal glory, beauty, and truth.

The Inferno is divided into parts called *cantos*, from the Latin word for *song*. Canto I begins as Dante, halfway through his life, awakens in a dark wood and realizes that he has lost his way.

Building Vocabulary

These essential words are defined alongside the poem.

attrition (ə trish′ ən): all tears and **attrition** / I wavered back (page 470, lines 57–58)

lamentation (lam′ ən tā′ shən): "There you shall see the ancient spirits tried / in endless pain, and hear their **lamentation**" (page 472, lines 108–109)

debauchery (dē bôch′ ər ē), **depravity** (dē prav′ ə tē): "to hide the guilt of her **debauchery** / she licensed all **depravity** alike" (page 479, lines 317–318)

Connecting Writing and Reading

In your journal list various actions that you consider wrong and suggest the appropriate punishment for each. As you read, compare your ideas about wrongdoing and punishment with those of this medieval writer.

Canto I
The Dark Wood of Error

Guide for Interpretation

Midway in our life's journey, I went astray
   from the straight road and woke to find myself
   alone in a dark wood. How shall I say

what wood that was! I never saw so drear,
5   so rank, so arduous a wilderness!
   Its very memory gives a shape to fear.

Death could scarce be more bitter than that place!
   But since it came to good, I will recount
   all that I found revealed there by God's grace.

10   How I came to it I cannot rightly say,
   so drugged and loose with sleep I had become
   when I first wandered there from the True Way.

But at the far end of that valley of evil
   whose maze had sapped my very heart with fear!
15   I found myself before a little hill

and lifted up my eyes. Its shoulders glowed
   already with the sweet rays of that planet[1]
   whose virtue leads men straight on every road,

and the shining strengthened me against the fright
20   whose agony had wracked the lake of my heart[2]
   through all the terrors of that piteous night.

Just as a swimmer, who with his last breath
   flounders ashore from perilous seas, might turn
   to memorize the wide water of his death—

25   so did I turn, my soul still fugitive
   from death's surviving image, to stare down
   that pass that none had ever left alive.

And there I lay to rest from my heart's race
   till calm and breath returned to me. Then rose
30   and pushed up that dead slope at such a pace

1. that planet . . . every road: the sun, which medieval astronomers considered a planet. This image is thought to symbolize God, who lights the way for human beings.

2. lake of my heart: reflects the medieval belief that the heart was a reservoir for blood.

each footfall rose above the last. And lo!
  almost at the beginning of the rise
  I faced a spotted Leopard, all tremor and flow

and gaudy pelt. And it would not pass, but stood
35 so blocking my every turn that time and again
  I was on the verge of turning back to the wood.

This fell at the first widening of the dawn
  as the sun was climbing Aries with those stars
  that rode with him to light the new creation.

40 Thus the holy hour and the sweet season
  of commemoration did much to arm my fear
  of that bright murderous beast with their good omen.

Yet not so much but what I shook with dread
  at sight of a great Lion that broke upon me
45 raging with hunger, its enormous head

held high as if to strike a mortal terror
  into the very air. And down his track,
  a She-Wolf drove upon me, a starved horror

ravening and wasted beyond all belief.
50 She seemed a rack for avarice, gaunt and craving.
  Oh many the souls she has brought to endless grief!

She brought such heaviness upon my spirit
  at sight of her savagery and desperation,
  I died from every hope of that high summit.

55 And like a miser—eager in acquisition
  but desperate in self-reproach when Fortune's wheel³
  turns to the hour of his loss—all tears and <u>attrition</u>⁴

I wavered back; and still the beast pursued,
  forcing herself against me bit by bit
60 till I slid back into the sunless wood.

And as I fell to my soul's ruin, a presence
  gathered before me on the discolored air,
  the figure of one who seemed hoarse from long silence.

◆ **Lines 31–36:** Dante will encounter three beasts that block his path. They are believed by critics to stand for the main forces of evil in the world: lust, pride, and covetousness, or greed.

◆ **Lines 37–42:** Interpreted according to medieval astronomical beliefs, the story begins at dawn in the Easter season of 1300. This "holy hour" comforts Dante in his encounter with the first beast. Consider what Dante seems to be saying about the power of his religious belief.

3. Fortune's wheel: medieval image describing the inevitable cycle of good and bad fortune encountered by every human being.

4. attrition (ə trish′ ən): repentance that is not perfect because it is not prompted solely by sorrow for having offended God.

◆ **Lines 61–84:** This opening scene, with its mood of dream or nightmare, leads to the miraculous appearance of the ghost of Virgil, the long-dead Roman poet (70 B.C.– 19 B.C.) who will now be Dante's guide.

At sight of him in that friendless waste I cried:
65 "Have pity on me, whatever thing you are,
 whether shade or living man." And it replied:

"Not man, though man I once was, and my blood
 was Lombard, both my parents Mantuan.[5]
 I was born, though late, *sub Julio*,[6] and bred

70 in Rome under Augustus[7] in the noon
 of the false and lying gods. I was a poet
 and sang of old Anchises' noble son

who came to Rome after the burning of Troy.[8]
 But you—why do *you* return to these distresses
75 instead of climbing that shining Mount of Joy

which is the seat and first cause of man's bliss?"
 "And are you then that Virgil and that fountain
 of purest speech?" My voice grew tremulous:

"Glory and light of poets! Now may that zeal
80 and love's apprenticeship that I poured out
 on your heroic verses serve me well!

For you are my true master and first author,
 the sole maker from whom I drew the breath
 of that sweet style whose measures have brought me
  honor.

85 See there, immortal sage, the beast I flee.
 For my soul's salvation, I beg you, guard me from her,
 for she has struck a mortal tremor through me."

And he replied, seeing my soul in tears:
 "He must go by another way who would escape
90 this wilderness, for that mad beast that fleers[9]

before you there, suffers no man to pass.
 She tracks down all, kills all, and knows no glut,
 but, feeding, she grows hungrier than she was.

She mates with any beast, and will mate with more
95 before the Greyhound comes to hunt her down.
 He will not feed on lands nor loot, but honor

5. Lombard . . . Mantuan (läm′ bärd′; man′ tyo͞o ən): of the region in northern Italy called Lombardy; Mantua is a province of Lombardy.

6. *sub Julio*: during the reign of Julius Caesar.

7. Augustus: the first emperor of Rome.

◆ **Lines 69–71:** Virgil introduces himself as one who was born in the era of "false" gods, that is, before the time of Jesus Christ.

8. old Anchises' (an kī′ sēz′) **noble son . . . Troy:** Aeneas, whose travels and deeds, including the founding of Rome, are described in Virgil's *The Aeneid*. (See pages 162–174.)

◆ **Lines 85–87:** Many scholars believe that, for Dante, Virgil symbolizes reason. Think about the significance of Dante's asking Virgil for help in overcoming the forces of evil as represented by the She-Wolf, who symbolizes greed.

9. fleers: sneers; laughs at derisively.

◆ **Lines 89–91:** Dante must choose a longer and harder road if he is to reach his final destination. He must first visit Hell and Purgatory.

and love and wisdom will make straight his way.
　　He will rise between Feltro and Feltro,[10] and in him
　　shall be the resurrection and new day

100　of that sad Italy for which Nisus died,
　　and Turnus, and Euryalus, and the maid Camilla.[11]
　　He shall hunt her through every nation of sick pride

　　till she is driven back forever to Hell
　　whence Envy first released her on the world.
105　Therefore, for your own good, I think it well

　　you follow me and I will be your guide
　　and lead you forth through an eternal place.
　　There you shall see the ancient spirits tried

　　in endless pain, and hear their <u>lamentation</u>[12]
110　as each bemoans the second death of souls.[13]
　　Next you shall see upon a burning mountain[14]

　　souls in fire and yet content in fire,
　　knowing that whensoever it may be
　　they yet will mount into the blessed choir.[15]

115　To which, if it is still your wish to climb,
　　a worthier spirit shall be sent to guide you.
　　With her shall I leave you, for the King of Time,

　　who reigns on high, forbids me to come there
　　since, living, I rebelled against his law.
120　He rules the waters and the land and air

　　and there holds court, his city and his throne.
　　Oh blessed are they he chooses!" And I to him:
　　"Poet, by that God to you unknown,

　　lead me this way. Beyond this present ill
125　and worse to dread, lead me to Peter's gate
　　and be my guide through the sad halls of Hell."

　　And he then: "Follow." And he moved ahead
　　in silence, and I followed where he led.

10. Greyhound . . . Feltro and Feltro: The Greyhound who will hunt down the She-Wolf is believed to stand for an Italian political leader of the time who Dante believed would help the cause of social order in Italy. "Feltro and Feltro" refers to the leader's birthplace, somewhere between the towns of Feltre and Montefeltro.

11. Nisus . . . Camilla (nī′ səs; tʉr′ nəs; yoō rī′ə ləs; kə mil′ ə): in Virgil's *The Aeneid* characters who die.

12. lamentation (lam′ ən tā′ shən): weeping or wailing because of grief.

13. second death of souls: the suffering of the spirits in Hell.

14. burning mountain: Purgatory.

15. blessed choir: Heaven, where those who suffer in Purgatory will go once they have repented their sins.

◆ **Lines 115–119:** Virgil explains that if Dante wants to visit Heaven also, he will need a different guide, since Virgil lived before Christ and cannot enter Heaven.

◆ **Lines 124–126:** Peter's gate was in Purgatory. Dante is asking Virgil to accompany him as far as he can.

At first, Dante wonders whether he is too cowardly and unworthy to make the trip that Virgil proposes. Virgil then explains that Beatrice, the woman Dante had idealized and loved from afar when she was alive, descended from Heaven in order to ask Virgil to guide Dante on his journey. Hearing this, Dante follows Virgil willingly. The two poets arrive at the Gate of Hell and read what is inscribed above the gate.

Canto III
The Vestibule of Hell: The Opportunists

I AM THE WAY INTO THE CITY OF WOE.
130 I AM THE WAY TO A FORSAKEN PEOPLE.
I AM THE WAY INTO ETERNAL SORROW.

SACRED JUSTICE MOVED MY ARCHITECT.
I WAS RAISED HERE BY DIVINE OMNIPOTENCE,
PRIMORDIAL LOVE AND ULTIMATE INTELLECT.

135 ONLY THOSE ELEMENTS TIME CANNOT WEAR
WERE MADE BEFORE ME, AND BEYOND TIME I STAND.
ABANDON ALL HOPE YE WHO ENTER HERE.

These mysteries I read cut into stone
    above a gate. And turning I said: "Master,
140   what is the meaning of this harsh inscription?"

And he then as initiate to novice:
    "Here must you put by all division of spirit
    and gather your soul against all cowardice.

This is the place I told you to expect.
145   Here you shall pass among the fallen people,
    souls who have lost the good of intellect."[16]

So saying, he put forth his hand to me,
    and with a gentle and encouraging smile
    he led me through the gate of mystery.

150 Here sighs and cries and wails coiled and recoiled
    on the starless air, spilling my soul to tears.
    A confusion of tongues and monstrous accents toiled

16. souls . . . intellect: those who have lost sight of God.

in pain and anger. Voices hoarse and shrill
    and sounds of blows, all intermingled, raised
155   tumult and pandemonium that still

whirls on the air forever dirty with it
    as if a whirlwind sucked at sand. And I,
    holding my head in horror, cried: "Sweet Spirit,

what souls are these who run through this black haze?"
160   And he to me: "These are the nearly soulless
    whose lives concluded neither blame nor praise.

They are mixed here with that despicable corps
    of angels who were neither for God nor Satan,
    but only for themselves. The High Creator

165   scourged them from Heaven for its perfect beauty,
    and Hell will not receive them since the wicked
    might feel some glory over them." And I:

"Master, what gnaws at them so hideously
    their lamentation stuns the very air?"
170   "They have no hope of death," he answered me,

"and in their blind and unattaining state
    their miserable lives have sunk so low
    that they must envy every other fate.

No word of them survives their living season.
175   Mercy and Justice deny them even a name.
    Let us not speak of them: look, and pass on."

I saw a banner there upon the mist.
    Circling and circling, it seemed to scorn all pause.
    So it ran on, and still behind it pressed

180 a never-ending rout of souls in pain.
    I had not thought death had undone so many
    as passed before me in that mournful train.

And some I knew among them; last of all
    I recognized the shadow of that soul
185   who, in his cowardice, made the Great Denial.[17]

Lines 160–176: Here, confined to the Vestibule of Hell, are those souls who in life acted neither for good nor evil but only for themselves. They are unfit for Heaven and barely admitted to Hell.

17. shadow of . . . Great Denial: believed to refer to either Celestine V, who resigned the office of Pope in 1294, or Pontius Pilate, who took a neutral position at the trial of Christ.

At once I understood for certain: these
    were of that retrograde and faithless crew
    hateful to God and to His enemies.

These wretches never born and never dead
190   ran naked in a swarm of wasps and hornets
    that goaded them the more the more they fled,

and made their faces stream with bloody gouts
    of pus and tears that dribbled to their feet
    to be swallowed there by loathsome worms and maggots.

195   Then looking onward I made out a throng
    assembled on the beach of a wide river,
    whereupon I turned to him: "Master, I long

to know what souls these are, and what strange usage
    makes them as eager to cross as they seem to be
200   in this infected light." At which the Sage:

"All this shall be made known to you when we stand
    on the joyless beach of Acheron."[18] And I
    cast down my eyes, sensing a reprimand

in what he said, and so walked at his side
205   in silence and ashamed until we came
    through the dead cavern to that sunless tide.

There, steering toward us in an ancient ferry
    came an old man with a white bush of hair,[19]
    bellowing: "Woe to you depraved souls! Bury

210   Here and forever all hope of Paradise:
    I come to lead you to the other shore,
    into eternal dark, into fire and ice.

And you who are living yet, I say begone
    from these who are dead." But when he saw me stand
215   against his violence he began again:

"By other windings and by other steerage
    shall you cross to that other shore. Not here! Not here!
    A lighter craft than mine must give you passage."

18. Acheron (ak′ ər än′): a river in Hell that serves as its outer boundary.

19. old man . . . hair: Charon (ker′ ən) who, in classical mythology, ferries souls of the dead across the river of death.

♦ **Lines 213–221:** Charon recognizes Dante as a living man and refuses to carry him on his boat, which is meant only for souls of the damned. Dante, who is destined eventually for Purgatory and Paradise, must take a different passage. Virgil, however, insists that God has willed Dante's journey and Charon must not question the order.

And my Guide to him: "Charon, bite back your spleen:
220   this has been willed where what is willed must be,
       and is not yours to ask what it may mean."

The steersman of that marsh of ruined souls,
       who wore a wheel of flame around each eye,
       stifled the rage that shook his woolly jowls.

225   But those unmanned and naked spirits there
       turned pale with fear and their teeth began to chatter
       at the sound of his crude bellow. In despair

they blasphemed God, their parents, their time on earth,
       the race of Adam, and the day and the hour
230   and the place and the seed and the womb that gave
          them birth.

But all together they drew to that grim shore
       where all must come who lose the fear of God.
       Weeping and cursing they come for evermore,

and demon Charon with eyes like burning coals
235   herds them in, and with a whistling oar
       flails on the stragglers to his wake of souls.

As leaves in autumn loosen and stream down
       until the branch stands bare above its tatters
       spread on the rustling ground, so one by one

240   the evil seed of Adam in its Fall
       cast themselves, at his signal, from the shore
       and streamed away like birds who hear their call.

So they are gone over that shadowy water,
       and always before they reach the other shore
245   a new noise stirs on this, and new throngs gather.

"My son," the courteous Master said to me,
       "all who die in the shadow of God's wrath
       converge to this from every clime and country.

And all pass over eagerly, for here
250   Divine Justice transforms and spurs them so
       their dread turns wish: they yearn for what they fear.

◆ **Lines 227–230:** The souls of the damned are without divine grace and are not permitted to repent; they can only curse.

◆ **Lines 237–245:** Notice the simile that compares the souls being swept away to leaves falling from a tree. As you continue to read, look for other similes used by Dante.

◆ **Lines 250–251:** Because in life the sinners hardened their hearts against grace, thus working out their own damnation, they are now required by divine justice to wish for Hell, which stands for sin.

No soul in Grace comes ever to this crossing;
   therefore if Charon rages at your presence
   you will understand the reason for his cursing."

255 When he had spoken, all the twilight country
   shook so violently, the terror of it
   bathes me with sweat even in memory:

the tear-soaked ground gave out a sigh of wind
   that spewed itself in flame on a red sky,
260   and all my shattered senses left me. Blind,

like one whom sleep comes over in a swoon,
   I stumbled into darkness and went down.

◆ **Lines 260–262:** Dante, about to be carried across the Acheron, falls down in a faint. When he awakes, he will be on the other side of the river, in Hell itself.

Dante awakens to find himself now with Virgil on the brink of Hell itself—a huge, funnel-shaped pit running down to the center of the earth. Around the sides of the pit is a series of ledges, or Circles, arranged in a descending order. The lower the ledge, the more serious the kind of sin assigned to it. Virgil leads Dante into Limbo, the First Circle of Hell. Here they meet the virtuous pagans, souls who did not sin but who did not have the Christian faith. Present are Homer, Aristotle, Plato, and some of the other great poets, philosophers, heroes, and heroines of antiquity. They are not tormented, but they are limited by human reason and can never come into the light of God. Dante and Virgil now descend to the Second Circle, where the real torments of Hell begin.

Canto V
Circle Two: The Carnal

So we went down to the second ledge alone;
   a smaller circle of so much greater pain
265   the voice of the damned rose in a bestial moan.

There Minos[20] sits, grinning, grotesque, and hale.
   He examines each lost soul as it arrives
   and delivers his verdict with his coiling tail.

That is to say, when the ill-fated soul
270   appears before him it confesses all,
   and that grim sorter of the dark and foul

20. Minos (mī′ näs′): the judge of the dead in classical mythology, and here a monster that assigns each soul to its proper depth in Hell.

decides which place in Hell shall be its end,
    then wraps his twitching tail about himself
    one coil for each degree it must descend.

275   The soul descends and others take its place:
    each crowds in its turn to judgment, each confesses,
    each hears its doom and falls away through space.

"O you who come into this camp of woe,"
    cried Minos when he saw me turn away
280   without awaiting his judgment, "watch where you go

once you have entered here, and to whom you turn!
    Do not be misled by that wide and easy passage!"
    And my Guide to him: "That is not your concern;

it is his fate to enter every door.
285   This has been willed where what is willed must be,
    and is not yours to question. Say no more."

Now the choir of anguish, like a wound,
    strikes through the tortured air. Now I have come
    to Hell's full lamentation, sound beyond sound.

290 I came to a place stripped bare of every light
    and roaring on the naked dark like seas
    wracked by a war of winds. Their hellish flight

of storm and counterstorm through time foregone,
    sweeps the souls of the damned before its charge.
295 Whirling and battering it drives them on,

and when they pass the ruined gap of Hell
    through which we had come, their shrieks begin anew.
    There they blaspheme the power of God eternal.

And this, I learned, was the never ending flight
300 of those who sinned in the flesh, the carnal and lusty
    who betrayed reason to their appetite.

As the wings of wintering starlings bear them on
    in their great wheeling flights, just so the blast
    wherries[21] these evil souls through time foregone.

◆ **Lines 292–310:** In the Second Circle, those guilty of lust are punished by whirling about in unceasing winds that represent the passions to which they submitted during their lives. Perhaps because this is the sin most nearly associated with love, the poet Dante has given it the lightest of punishments to be found in Hell proper.

21. wherries (hwer′ ēz): transports by boat.

305 Here, there, up, down, they whirl and, whirling, strain
    with never a hope of hope to comfort them,
    not of release, but even of less pain.

    As cranes go over sounding their harsh cry,
      leaving the long streak of their flight in air,
310   so come these spirits, wailing as they fly.

    And watching their shadows lashed by wind, I cried:
      "Master, what souls are these the very air
      lashes with its black whips from side to side?"

    "The first of these whose history you would know,"
315   he answered me, "was Empress of many tongues.
      Mad sensuality corrupted her so

    that to hide the guilt of her debauchery[22]
      she licensed all depravity[23] alike,
      and lust and law were one in her decree.

320 She is Semiramis[24] of whom the tale is told
      how she married Ninus and succeeded him
      to the throne of that wide land the Sultans hold.

    The other is Dido;[25] faithless to the ashes
      of Sichaeus, she killed herself for love.
325   The next whom the eternal tempest lashes

    is sense-drugged Cleopatra.[26] See Helen[27] there,
      from whom such ill arose. And great Achilles,[28]
      who fought at last with love in the house of prayer.

    And Paris.[29] And Tristan."[30] As they whirled above
330   he pointed out more than a thousand shades
      of those torn from the mortal life by love.

    I stood there while my Teacher one by one
      named the great knights and ladies of dim time;
      and I was swept by pity and confusion.

335 At last I spoke: "Poet, I should be glad
      to speak a word with those two swept together
      so lightly on the wind and still so sad."

22. **debauchery** (dē bôch′ ər ē): the satisfying of one's desires and appetites in a bad or wild way.

23. **depravity** (dē prav′ ə tē): corruption; wickedness.

24. **Semiramis** (si mir′ ə mis): Assyrian princess of the ninth century B.C. who was said to have founded Babylon.

25. **Dido** (dī′ dō): queen of Carthage who, according to *The Aeneid*, vowed to remain faithful to the memory of her dead husband, Sichaeus, but fell in love with Aeneas. When Aeneas left for Italy, the abandoned Dido committed suicide.

26. **Cleopatra:** the queen of Egypt and a mistress of Julius Caesar and Mark Antony.

27. **Helen:** in Greek mythology, the most beautiful of women. She was abducted by Paris, an action that set off the Trojan War.

28. **Achilles:** hero of the Trojan War who, according to one legend, deserted the Greeks when he fell in love with Polyxena (pō lik′ sə nə), daughter of King Priam of Troy. On his way to meet her in a temple, he was slain by Paris.

29. **Paris:** son of King Priam and Queen Hecuba of Troy. When asked to decide which goddess was the fairest, he chose Aphrodite, goddess of love, over Athena and Hera, the goddesses of wisdom and of marriage. He is placed here in Hell because he chose love over reason.

30. **Tristan:** in medieval romance, the lover of Isolde. (See "Chevrefoil," page 656.)

And he to me: "Watch them. When next they pass,
    call to them in the name of love that drives
340   and damns them here. In that name they will pause."

Thus, as soon as the wind in its wild course
    brought them around, I called: "O wearied souls!
    if none forbid it, pause and speak to us."

As mating doves that love calls to their nest
345   glide through the air with motionless raised wings,
    borne by the sweet desire that fills each breast—

Just so those spirits turned on the torn sky
    from the band where Dido whirls across the air;
    such was the power of pity in my cry.

350 "O living creature, gracious, kind, and good,
    going this pilgrimage through the sick night,
    visiting us who stained the earth with blood,

were the King of Time our friend, we would pray His peace
    on you who have pitied us. As long as the wind
355   will let us pause, ask of us what you please.

The town where I was born lies by the shore
    where the Po descends into its ocean rest
    with its attendant streams in one long murmur.

Love, which in gentlest hearts will soonest bloom
360   seized my lover with passion for that sweet body
    from which I was torn unshriven to my doom.

Love, which permits no loved one not to love,
    took me so strongly with delight in him
    that we are one in Hell, as we were above.

365 Love led us to one death. In the depths of Hell
    Caïna waits for him who took our lives."
    This was the piteous tale they stopped to tell.

And when I had heard those world-offended lovers
    I bowed my head. At last the Poet spoke:
370   "What painful thoughts are these your lowered brow
      covers?"

◆ **Lines 336–355:** Dante here notices two souls who are "swept together." These are the lovers Paolo (pä′ ô lô) and Francesca (frän ches′ kä), two people of Dante's time. The sympathetic treatment of their story in this poem has inspired many legends. Francesca was married to Giovanni Malatesta in 1275 but fell in love with Giovanni's younger brother Paolo. The affair continued for many years until Giovanni happened upon them and killed them both. When Dante calls out to them in pity, they come gliding down to him like doves, still impelled by desire. Francesca expresses gratitude to Dante for his pity.

◆ **Line 361:** Francesca explains that she was "torn unshriven to my doom," meaning that because she was killed suddenly, there was no time for her to confess her sin and be absolved, or shriven, for it.

◆ **Line 366:** Giovanni Malatesta was still alive when Dante wrote *The Inferno*. His fate is already decided, however, according to this passage. Francesca explains that his soul will fall to Caïna (kä ē′ nä), a section within Hell where those who performed acts of treachery against their kin are punished.

When at length I answered, I began: "Alas!
    What sweetest thoughts, what green and young desire
    led these two lovers to this sorry pass."

Then turning to those spirits once again,
375   I said: "Francesca, what you suffer here
    melts me to tears of pity and of pain.

But tell me: in the time of your sweet sighs
    by what appearances found love the way
    to lure you to his perilous paradise?"

380 And she: "The double grief of a lost bliss
    is to recall its happy hour in pain.
    Your Guide and Teacher knows the truth of this.

But if there is indeed a soul in Hell
    to ask of the beginning of our love
385   out of his pity, I will weep and tell:

On a day for dalliance we read the rhyme
    of Lancelot, how love had mastered him.
    We were alone with innocence and dim time.

Pause after pause that high old story drew
390   our eyes together while we blushed and paled;
    but it was one soft passage overthrew

our caution and our hearts. For when we read
    how her fond smile was kissed by such a lover,
    he who is one with me alive and dead

395 breathed on my lips the tremor of his kiss.
    That book, and he who wrote it, was a pander.
    That day we read no further." As she said this,

the other spirit, who stood by her, wept
    so piteously, I felt my senses reel
400   and faint away with anguish. I was swept

by such a swoon as death is, and I fell,
    as a corpse might fall, to the dead floor of Hell.

◆ **Lines 387–396:** In the Arthurian legends, Lancelot was the bravest of the knights of King Arthur. He became the lover of Guinevere, the king's wife. Reading about Lancelot had a strong effect on Paolo and Francesca; Francesca describes both the story and its author as a "pander," a go-between who arranges a love affair.

Thinking About the Poem

A PERSONAL RESPONSE

sharing impressions

1. What feelings are you left with after experiencing Dante's vision of Hell? In your journal jot down words and phrases that describe your feelings.

constructing interpretations

2. Do you think the system of punishments described in this poem is fair? Explain.

Think about
- how each type of wrongdoing or sin described in this excerpt is punished
- the fact that illicit lovers are punished more leniently than other sinners
- the fact that the punishments last forever

3. How would you describe Dante's view of life and the human condition?

Think about
- the way Paolo and Francesca are punished in Canto V
- Dante's vision of the Vestibule of Hell in Canto III
- his encounter with the three beasts in Canto I

A CREATIVE RESPONSE

4. What differences would occur in *The Inferno* if Hell were described from the viewpoint of a condemned sinner rather than of a traveler passing through?

A CRITICAL RESPONSE

5. *The Divine Comedy* is an allegory, or work in which characters and actions stand for or illustrate abstract ideas. Dante's work portrays the individual's attempts to strive for spirituality, perfection, and eventual union with God. Select details from the poem and interpret them in light of this overall meaning.

Think about
- the significance of the dark wood
- the signficance of the three beasts
- Virgil as a symbol of reason
- other details that might have an allegorical meaning

6. Based on what you have read in this excerpt, to what extent do you think *The Inferno* is relevant to readers today? Explain.

Analyzing the Writer's Craft

ALLUSION

What might have been Virgil's reasons for referring to various legendary figures in his speech to Dante in Canto I, lines 100–101?

Building a Literary Vocabulary. An allusion is a reference to a historical or literary person, place, or event with which the reader is assumed to be familiar. When Virgil speaks of "that sad Italy for which Nisus died, / and Turnus, and Euryalus, and the maid Camilla," he is alluding to events described in *The Aeneid*. He is reminding the reader of legendary figures who were slain in the ancient time when Aeneas was leading his Trojan survivors into Italy to found Rome. Such allusions to heroic figures from early Roman history give additional weight to Virgil's remarks about the need for a leader (called "the Greyhound" in Line 95) who will rule Italy now in "honor and love and wisdom."

Application: Interpreting Allusions. Work with one or two other students to identify the allusions in the three cantos from *The Inferno*. Most of them will be in Canto V. In addition to reading the sidenotes, you may want to consult an encyclopedia. Decide why Dante might have included each of these allusions. Then do some library research on the subject of one of the allusions and share your findings with the rest of the class.

The Heir

SŎ KIWŎN   born 1930   KOREA

A biography of Sŏ Kiwŏn appears on page 752.

Approaching the Story

This story by Sŏ Kiwŏn (sô kē′ wôn) is set in Korea. For many centuries Korea was governed by one royal family and an elite group of civil servants chosen by examination. Most people lived in rural areas and upheld family-centered values, particularly ancestor worship. In 1910 the Japanese took control of the government, seizing farmlands and so forcing many young people to leave the countryside and find work in cities. Japanese rule ended after World War II, but political and social turmoil remained.

"The Heir" was first published in 1963. In the story, an adolescent boy from Seoul, the capital of South Korea, goes to live with country relatives after his father dies.

Building Vocabulary

These essential words are footnoted within the story.

dissolute (dis′ ə loot′): Later he found out that his grandfather as a youth had led a **dissolute** life. (page 486)

keening (kēn′ iŋ): He started **keening,** followed by everybody else. The grandfather's . . . was the loudest and the saddest. (page 489)

surreptitiously (sʉr′ əp tish′ əs lē): He half opened his eyes and looked up **surreptitiously.** (page 489)

punctilious (puŋk til′ ē əs): He heard the voice of his **punctilious** grandfather. (page 494)

Connecting Writing and Reading

If you had to go live with another family member, such as a stepparent, grandparent, aunt, or uncle, what adjustments would you find difficult? Describe these potential problems in your journal. As you read, see if the boy in this story has some of the same difficulties adjusting to a new family situation.

*I*T WAS THE monsoon season; rain was pouring down heavily, but he did not hear it. As he read to Sŏkhŭi,[1] he was conscious of the smell of straw emanating from his cousin's hair.

"Why did the man leave his home? Sŏgun,[2] brother Sŏgun?" asked Sŏkhŭi. They had come to the part of the story—the end of the first chapter—where the hero leaves home.

"Won't you let me break off here for today?" he asked her, closing the book. But she pestered him to go on, twisting at her waist.

He opened the book again and trained his eyes on the printed letters. On his cheeks he felt a blush appearing. He wished she would leave his room now. To be alone in a room with her made him uncomfortable.

Through the driving rain, he heard his grandfather's voice calling from across the courtyard.

"I think Grandfather's calling me." He raised his eyes from the book and strained his ears. Sŏkhŭi seemed not to care, whatever the old man might be wanting. She stared at his half-turned face intently. The call came louder.

"Coming!" he answered with a formal, grown-up voice and, leaving the room, put on the polite manner of a boy called to the presence of his elders. His name, Sŏgun, sounded much the same in the inarticulate pronunciation of the paralytic old man as those of his two other cousins, Sŏkpae[3] and Sŏkkŭn.[4] Often they answered to the old man's call together. His cousins, however, had not been seen around the house since morning.

"Greet the gentleman here," ordered the old man in the smoke-filled room, even before Sŏgun finished closing the double door. He bowed to the stranger who, like his grandfather, was wearing the old-style horsehair headgear. Sŏgun blushed as he did so, for he could never perform a kowtow without feeling embarrassment. He could not help feeling a momentary sense of disgrace whenever he had to kneel down on the floor with hands folded on his forehead.

"A fine-looking boy he is! Sit down." The stranger spoke in a low voice, caressing his long beard, which looked like the silk of an ear of corn.

"He takes after his father. Do you remember my son?"

"Yes," answered the stranger, and then, to express his sympathy, he clucked his tongue.

Seated respectfully with bowed head, Sŏgun listened to them while they talked about his dead father. He stole a glance at his grandfather. The old man seemed to be reluctant to satisfy the other man's curiosity. The old man seemed to have mixed feelings of pity and resentment about his son, who had died in a strange place.

"You may retire now," said Grandfather.

The rainwater had gathered into a mud pool in the courtyard. The rain was not likely to let up soon. Standing in the gloom of the entrance, he looked across toward his room, where Sŏkhŭi was waiting for his return. He had a pale forehead and long black eyebrows. Bashfulness lingered between his brows, which he narrowly knit, as if from biting a sour fruit.

To shelter himself from the rain, he stepped gingerly along the narrow strip of dry ground under the eaves. He entered the storeroom next to the room that stood beyond the garden, filled with the tepid warmth of straw decaying in the damp. The rafters stood out darkly from the mud-coated ceiling. He could smell the acrid odor of mud as the rats raced about the room. He looked up at the window set high in the wall. The paper was torn here and there, and a gray

---

1. **Sŏkhŭi** (sôk' hwē).
2. **Sŏgun** (sô' goon).
3. **Sŏkpae** (sôk' pa).
4. **Sŏkkŭn** (sôk' koon).

shaft of soft light entered, as at the dawn of a rainy day. The storehouse was divided into two sections. One of them served as a barn, where farming tools lay scattered all around. Winnows and baskets hung on the wall where the cornstalk wattles showed amidst the mud plaster. It was damp and stuffy in the poorly ventilated storehouse.

Sŏgun picked up a weeding hoe and made a hoeing motion in the air a few times. A weeding hoe with its long, curved neck always amused him. He thought there was something attractive in its curious curve. Looking around the room, he saw the connecting door to the other section of the storehouse. There used to be an iron lock on the door ring. To his surprise, however, the rusty lock had come loose. His heart throbbed.

This room had been an object of curiosity ever since he came to the country house—a vague fear and mysterious expectation mixed in his curiosity. Perhaps it was not right for him to enter the room without his grandfather's or uncle's permission. He hesitated a moment in front of the half-locked door, then finally took the lock off and stepped into the room. He assured himself that he was the heir of the family and was entitled to have a look at what was lawfully his. In fact, the word *heir* as it was said by Grandfather did not sound quite real to him. But now the boy once again uttered the word to himself.

Inside this part of the storehouse, it was darker than in the barn. There was a window the size of a portable table, but it opened on the dark entrance, providing no more illumination than a pale square of light like the night sky. There were soot-colored paper chests stacked one upon another on a corner of the shelf. He tiptoed to the shelf. At every stealthy step, the floor squeaked. Old books, tied up in small bundles with string and stacked high, were keeping a precarious balance. But the books interested him little. His attention was on the soot-colored paper chests. He did not hear the rain outside. The day after his arrival here, Grandfather had taken him to this room. From among the paper chests, the old man opened the one that best kept its shape. Taking out a scroll, he said:

"This is a *hongp'ae*,[5] which the king issued to those who passed the civil service examination."

"What is a civil service examination?" asked Sŏgun.

"You had to pass it if you were to get an official position."

"Did you take it, Grandfather?"

"No, I did not."

"Why not?"

"By the time I was old enough for the examination, the Japanese were here, and the examination was banned."

There was embarrassment in the old man's tone. Later he found out that his grandfather as a youth had led a <u>dissolute</u>[6] life and did not apply himself to study. It was not because of the Japanese but because of his own laziness that the old man failed to take the examination. All this he learned from his aunt, who, having heard it from her mother-in-law, passed it on to him like a family secret. The boy had a good laugh out of it.

"You are the ninth heir of a family with as many as five *hongp'aes*," the old man would say. But hearing his grandfather, the boy would picture a young man with a rambunctious crew of his schoolmates who abhorred books, juxtaposed with the present figure of his grandfather. Thinking about this amusing incongruity when he was alone, he would laugh to himself.

He carefully took down the paper chest his grandfather had shown him. It was full of scrolls. He ransacked them to see if there was anything else in the chest. But there was noth-

---

5. **hongp'ae** (hôŋ′ pa).
6. **dissolute** (dis′ ə lo͞ot′): wasted and immoral.

ing except the grimy scrolls. He unrolled the one his grandfather had called *hongp'ae*, which looked like a sheet of flooring paper dyed red. A precocious boy who read difficult books beyond his age, he deciphered the faded characters. He found the three characters which made up his ancestor's name. They looked familiar to him.

He rolled up the paper and put it where it had been and shut the lid of the chest. Then he took down a leather case from a peg on the wall. It was a roughly made thing, heavy as an iron trunk. The old man told him it was a quiver. There was a broken brass lock on it like the one on the rice chest, though smaller. The key was hanging on the corner of the case, but he did not need to use it.

Among various trinkets and knickknacks, he caught sight of a small wooden box. Out of the box he took a pair of jade rings strung together. The jade was a soft, milky color.

He had no idea what these rings were for. The holes in the center would be too small even for the little finger of Sŏkhŭi. Maybe a kind of ornament for ladies, he thought.

He clicked the pieces of jade one against the other. They gave off a clear, sharp sound. Repeating the clicking several times, he listened to the sound intently. Then he strung the pieces together and put them into his pocket. His legs trembled. But hadn't he been told that everything there in the room was lawfully his? As he closed the leather case, his pale hands shook. He did not look into the other relics. He stole out of the room. The rain was beginning to turn to a drizzle.

At every mealtime, Sŏgun sat alone with Sŏkpae at the same table with his grandfather. The country cooking, which was so different from what he had been used to in the city, tasted bitter. What was more, the boy hated to sit close to Sŏkpae, their shoulders nearly touching. He felt repelled by the occasional contact with the other boy's skin. Sŏkpae, two

years his junior, was an epileptic. That his cousin looked like him disgusted him. As he looked at Sŏkpae, a secret shame seemed to stir in him.

It was not until a week after his arrival that he had found out about Sŏkpae's condition; the fit occurred at dinner time. The shredded squash seasoned with marinated shrimp gave off a foul smell. The soy sauce in the dark earthenware dish was no better. To swallow the squash, he had to hold his breath. A sense of loneliness choked him when he thought that he would be spending countless days from now on in this house, eating this food. Suddenly Sŏkpae fell over on his back, his spoon flung to the floor with a jangling sound. His eyes showing white, his foaming mouth thrust sideways, he struggled for air. Frightened, Sŏgun sat back from the table. The old man put his spoon down and sighed, turning away. The veins stood out in his eyes, either for grief or anger. Perhaps he was trying to keep the tears back.

Sŏkhŭi came in to serve the rice tea. Sŏgun felt pity for her. Perhaps the pity in his eyes touched her. He could see her eyes become moist. She hurriedly turned away and went out of the room.

Suddenly his uncle shouted angrily: "Take away the table!" He was moaning.

"What's the matter with you? Is he not your son, sick as he is?" Grandfather checked the outburst of the uncle. The uncle sat silently; a blue vein showed in the middle of his forehead.

"Don't be frightened, Sŏgun. He worries me so." His aunt tried to placate him in a tearful voice. Sŏgun wanted to run out of the room. But he felt that he had to see it through with the other members of the family until the fit was over.

Stiffness began to go out of Sŏkpae's twisted limbs, and he was breathing with more ease, but was still unconscious. He became soft like an uncoiled snake or a lump of sticky substance liquefying.

The boy gulped down some of the rice tea and left the room. The midsummer sun was going down, the clouds glowing in the twilit sky. Clear water, bubbling up from the well in the courtyard, prattled along in a little stream. They said a huge carp lived in the well among the moss-covered rocks.

His great-grandfather, returning from a long exile, had settled down here by the water, as his grandfather told the boy the story. Five gingko trees stood in line, dividing the path leading to the village and outer yard.

"I wish he were dead!" Sŏkhŭi's sharp-edged voice came from behind his back. He wondered a moment whom she meant, but he did not care whom she wanted to be dead. He was feeling desolate enough to take it calmly, even if it was himself she was referring to. He watched Sŏkhŭi as she came near. He tried hard to be casual, but he felt as if he were choking; she looked grown-up, more grown-up than himself. She was smiling.

"Cousin Sŏgun, tell me about Seoul."

He did not answer. He merely smiled. Sŏkhŭi sat on one of the rocks by the well and stretched her skinny red legs.

"I am the second tallest girl in class." She giggled, ducking her head. He wanted to find out more about her brother's illness, but he felt she feared to be questioned about it.

"You will be going to middle school next year. Perhaps the one in the county seat, right?" he asked.

"Grandpa won't let me go," Sŏkhŭi said in a thin, angry voice.

"I suppose not," mumbled the boy.

"You don't know anything." Sŏkhŭi rolled her eyes and was going to add something, then seemed to give up. The air did not stir. Evening was coming on. A dry coughing broke the spell which had hovered over the scene. He recognized the dry coughs of his grandfa-ther, which he heard early mornings, while still in bed. His eyes searched around in the gathering dusk.

The smell of wild sesame-seed oil came drifting by; they must be frying something in the kitchen. He saw the white steam rising inside the dimly lighted kitchen. Grandpa had told him to get some sleep until called. Both his male cousins, Sŏkpae and Sŏkkŭn, seemed to like memorial services very much. They would poke their heads into the kitchen and get shouted at by their mother.

This was his first experience with sacrificial rites for the dead ancestors. He remembered his mother reminding his father about the rites and worrying. She would ask him if they shouldn't send some money to the country house to cover part of the expenses. Then his father would snap out sharply between his teeth: "How could we when they're having these rites every month of the year!" Sŏgun now seemed to understand why his father was so bitter about these rites. His uncle also looked angry and gloomy while getting the table and plates ready for the ritual. He could see his uncle considered these ancestral rites a burden.

Calming his restless spirit, he gazed at the tilted flame on top of the wooden lamp post. He made his bed and lay down, but sleep eluded him.

Sooty flames rose from the two candles burning in the discolored brass candlesticks set on either side of the sacrificial table. Through the thick wax paper covering the foods on the table came the pungent smell of fish. The grandfather, unwrapping a bundle of ancient hemp clothes, took out a long ceremonial robe and put it on.

The dusty robe wrapped around his thin, old body, the old man knelt down before the sacrificial table and respectfully kindled the incense in the burner. Thin wreaths of bluish smoke began to writhe up from the age-stained burner. The stink from the fish on the round, flat plate filled the room.

"The meat dishes should be set to the left. When will you learn the proper manner of setting the sacrificial table?" The man reprimanded his son and, holding up the sleeve of the robe with one hand, rearranged the dishes on the table with his free hand.

"This is for an ancestor of five generations ago," he told the boy for the third time this evening. The two elder men in the ceremonial robes made low bows; the children in the back rows did the same. Sŏgun nearly burst into laughter at the comic sight of the big flourish with which they brought their hands up to their foreheads before each kowtow. Yet his cousin Sŏkpae had a certain grace when he performed sacrificial bows. His soft and elastic body, unlike Sŏkkŭn's, fitted into the role with natural ease.

Sŏgun brought his hands up to his breast but dropped them; Sŏkpae was bowing away ecstatically, flourishing his two limbs, which looked longer than his torso, as if performing a dance.

Grandfather cleared his throat, coughing a few times, before he started reading the prayer to the dead in a low, tremulous voice. Finished, he started <u>keening</u>,[7] followed by everybody else. The grandfather's keening was the loudest and the saddest. The uncle was mumbling something in a low, indistinct voice.

Sŏgun remained still, his eyes and mouth shut tight. Yet he was not indifferent; he was tense and felt an unexplainable chill running down his spine. He half opened his eyes and looked up <u>surreptitiously</u>.[8] Insects had gathered around the candle flames, which cast their shadows over the sacrificial table. He had an illusion of a strange figure squatting in the gloom behind the tablet bearing the ancestral name.

When he died, his father became like a stranger, the way he heaved a last chilly breath toward him. Sŏgun had had to draw his hand by force out of his father's tightened grip. He feared that the hand would come and grip him again. He could not bring himself to touch his father. He could not cry. But when he came out of the death chamber, an inconsolable sorrow seized him, and he cried with abandon.

The boy closed his eyes again. The keening went on. His body shook from suppressed crying.

When the rite was over, Sŏgun went out to the well. Stars glittered in the night sky between the clouds. The pale starlight played on the ripples in the well. He dipped his hands in the cool water. He washed and rubbed his hands until he thought he had scrubbed the last odor of the rite from his hands.

"Sŏgun!" His grandfather called him.

In the hall were placed three tables, around which sat all the family. "We are going to partake of the ancestral food and receive the blessing of the ancestors," said the grandfather, pointing with his chin to the seat opposite him for Sŏgun. The bronze rice bowl that had been placed on the sacrificial table was now set in front of the old man, almost touching his beard. Sŏgun could still see, in the center of the heaped rice in the bowl, the hole which had been dug by the brass spoon in the course of the rite.

Sŏgun tried a sip from the brass wine cup his grandfather handed to him. He grimaced. Making much noise, everybody ate a bowl of soup with rice in it. The grandfather seemed displeased that Sŏgun did not eat like the others. He excused himself from the table, saying he had a stomachache, and returned to his room.

---

7. **keening** (kēn′ iŋ): wailing or crying for the dead.
8. **surreptitiously** (sʉr′ əp tish′ əs lē): secretly.

"How like his father!" he heard the old man say in a cracked voice.

The grandfather, donning the new ramie cloth coat the aunt had finished for him overnight, left for town early in the morning. The boy waited until he was sure his cousins were all safely out playing and then took his suitcase down from the attic storeroom. He took stock of its contents. The first time he was engaged with his things in the suitcase after he came here, his cousins stuck their noses in and pestered him. He wanted to keep his things to himself. In the suitcase were several novels, his school texts, a glass weight with a goldfish swimming in it, a telescope made of millboard, and a wallet which his father had given him the day before he died. They were all very dear to him. He placed on his palm the jade rings he had taken from the storeroom on that rainy day. He listened to the music the milky jade made when clicked together. The sound was as clear and sharp as before. The sound, in fact, had improved with the weather, which had cleared in the meantime.

Somebody came into the room, unannounced.

"What are you doing?" It was Sŏkpae.

"Just checking on my things," the boy answered, very much confused and concealing his hand with the jade rings behind his back.

"Are you going somewhere?" asked Sŏkpae, drawing near.

"No."

Sŏkpae sneaked an eager look into the suitcase and then, grabbing at something, said:

"Won't you draw a picture of me, please?" The object Sŏkpae took hold of was a half-empty case of pastels. Sŏkpae's slit eyes winked at him.

"Oh, well." Sŏgun was pleased; he wanted to boast of his artistic talent. He felt much relieved that his cousin did not suspect anything. He spread out a sheet of paper on top of his suitcase and made Sŏkpae sit facing the doorway. He picked up a yellow crayon, taking a close look at his cousin. Sŏkpae sat, putting on an air of importance with his lower lip solemnly protruding. Sŏgun looked into the other boy's eyes and sat unmoving for a while, absorbed.

He felt dismay at a face that was so like his own. If Sŏkpae's features were taken separately, they would not noticeably resemble those of anyone in the family, let alone Sŏgun's. However, when Sŏgun looked at the whole face, it wasn't as though he were looking at a face other than his own.

"Aren't you going to draw?" Sŏkpae asked, only lowering his eyes.

Sŏgun began to draw. Sŏkpae's skin was darker, his features duller and fatter. From time to time, he slipped out a red, pointed tongue and licked his lips. Suddenly Sŏgun found himself wishing that Sŏkpae would have his fit there and then. A mixture of fear and curiosity came over him. He deliberately took time with his drawing.

"Here you are." The boy handed the finished picture over to his cousin, blushing.

"Why, it's you, not me, you drew!" Sŏkpae muttered.

"It's not true. It looks exactly like you!" he retorted angrily.

"Will you write down my name on this?"

He picked up a black crayon and wrote down the name.

Finally the grandfather found out about the missing jade. Sŏgun was sitting with his legs dangling on the low porch in back. The air was filled with the fragrant scent of balsam flowers, and beyond the mud wall towered the jagged ridges of the Mountain of the Moon against the cloudy, gray sky. In the direction of the courtyard, he heard the grandfather's querulous voice. Now being used to the old man's intonation, he could follow the old man as he bawled out in fury:

"Why, you ignorant ones! You think it's a toy or something, eh?"

"Oh, please, Father. I will take it back from the boy as soon as he comes home." His uncle tried to pacify the old man.

"It is all because you are so ignorant. You should have raised your boys to act like a gentleman's offspring. Instead, what do you have now?"

The old man did not attempt to choose his words in chiding his son, even when children were present. Sŏgun's heart sank. It was clear that Sŏkpae was being suspected of stealing the jade rings from the storeroom.

"That he could get so upset over such trash, after he has sold off every bit of property of any worth!" his uncle muttered after the old man disappeared into his quarters. Sŏgun trembled all over. He could not walk out of his hiding place and face the family. When he thought of what would take place after Sŏkpae came home, he felt an impulse to rush out to his grandfather and tell him everything. But still he could not move.

"I say, do you know what that is?" Grandfather, coming back, said now in a mocking voice.

"You told us it was jade beads, didn't you?" his uncle said.

"So you think it is just like any other jade, eh? It is no less than *tori* jade,[9] you hear?" The old man did not spare his son in taking him to task, as if they were not father and son but strangers to each other. Sŏgun did not know what jade beads were. They would not bring much money on the market, but they must still mean a great deal to his grandfather, the boy guessed.

He went out to the yard, dragging the rubber shoes which were too big for him. He was counting in his mind the money his father had left him along with that wallet. He thought he had enough to pay for board and room for four

or five months. After his father died, his house, where he had a sunny study room, was sold by his uncle. He kept only the scuffed leather wallet and the bills in it.

"Let's go fishing together later on," said Sŏkhŭi, coming out to the yard with an armful of vegetables from the farm.

"It looks like rain again," he said.

Sŏkhŭi squatted down by the well and started washing the radishes.

"Pretty, isn't it?" Sŏkhŭi held out her wet hand, wiggling her pinkie to draw his attention to it. He noticed that it was dyed with balsam flowers. As he looked at the finger, she bobbed her head, puffing her cheeks, as she often did when she felt bashful. She was smiling. Sŏgun threw his head back and laughed like a grown-up. Looking at her from the back, in her white blouse and blue skirt, he could not think she was a cousin younger than himself.

"Do you know, Sŏkhŭi, what jade beads are?" asked Sŏgun, lowering his voice.

"Did you see the buttonlike things on Grandfather's headgear? They call them *kwanja*,"[10] Sŏkhŭi whispered back.

"They are not jade, are they?" He expressed his doubt.

"You hate my brother, don't you?" Sŏkhŭi, too, must be suspecting Sŏkpae of stealing the jade rings.

"Why should I?" Sŏgun feigned ignorance.

"I heard Grandpa once say there has been no one else like him in the family." Sŏkhŭi looked up from her work, stopping her washing for a moment.

Sŏgun did not say anything. What he had just heard hurt him somehow.

---

9. *tori* (tō′ dē) **jade:** jade rings or beads worn by those in the senior and junior first ranks of traditional Korean civil service.

10. *kwanja* (kwän′ jä): jade rings or beads worn on the hat of officials.

"Do you know he had his head cauterized with moxa?"[11] said Sŏkhŭi wearily.

Sŏgun stood up and, leaving Sŏkhŭi to her work, walked toward the stream. He kicked at the small rocks on the roadside.

Rain started again toward evening; thunder clapped and rain began to pour down in streaming showers. It was only then that the house became topsy-turvy. The old man kept pacing back and forth between the inner and the outer wings of the house, oblivious to the downpouring rain soaking his clothes.

"Where's your father? Of all the misfortunes of man!" The old man kept saying the same thing, wiping away the raindrops running down his beard. Sŏgun guessed the cause of all the commotion in the house. He saw in his imagination Sŏkpae's helpless body whirled in muddy torrents and then dashed against the rocks. His upturned eyes and foaming mouth were covered with the muddy water. "Grandfather, oh Grandfather! I didn't steal them!" But mud water filled his mouth, and not a moan came out of him. Sŏgun hugged his shaking knees. The uncle, who had just come back from the search, was going out again, this time taking Sŏkkŭn along with him.

"Let me go with you," asked Sŏgun.

"We don't need you." His uncle looked at him out of the corner of his eyes.

"I want to go," insisted Sŏgun.

"I said we didn't need you." His uncle flung back an answer with anger in his voice.

The old man groaned with agony and said, "You had better take several men along with you."

"All right, all right," answered the uncle, exasperated.

The moldy smell pervaded the room. A millipede crawled up the door frame and then down into the room. The sound of rain did not reach him. He thought he ought to walk over to the male quarters and keep the old man

company. He did not have the courage, however. He lit the lamp. He felt his forehead with his hand. Probably his hand was feverish, too. His forehead felt almost cold against his palm. He felt a chill running down his back. He was too sick to sit up and wait. He made the bed and lay down.

He could hear the light, pleasant music of the jade rings in the rain. For a moment, he wished Sŏkpae's wriggling body would stiffen into a chunk of wood. He wished that Sŏkpae would never show up again. Even after he was gone from this house, Sŏkpae must not show up before the grandfather.

When he awoke from sleep, Sŏkhŭi was sitting by him. Her body, outlined against the lamplight, was almost that of a woman. He felt a cool hand on his forehead. He did not shake it off. The palm grew warm and sticky.

"Anything new about Sŏkpae?" asked Sŏgun, turning toward her.

"Sŏkkŭn came back alone," answered Sŏkhŭi. "Father went to the Mountain of the Moon with the village people."

Sŏgun remained silent.

"This happened before," said Sŏkhŭi. "Everybody was terribly scared. Sŏkpae came back the next morning. Even he himself didn't know where he had been."

The uncle came back toward midnight, exhausted.

"Oh, that I might be struck dead!" The aunt wailed, beating the floor with her fists.

Sŏgun spent a sleepless night. Early in the morning, the villagers arrived with the news that Sŏmun[12] Bridge had been washed away overnight. It was a wooden bridge on the way from the village to the county seat.

It was hard to tell whether his uncle was laughing or crying. He was scowling darkly. He

---

11. moxa (mäks′ ə): a leafy herb whose leaves are burned on the skin for medicinal purposes.
12. Sŏmun (sô′ moon).

sat on the damp floor and ordered the kitchen staff to prepare drinks for the guests and called in the people who stood around in the yard.

"Did you look into Snake Valley?" demanded the uncle.

"He can't have gone that far," said a man from the searching party, "and it rained so hard last night."

"The last time the bridge was washed out was five years ago," said another man and suggested: "Hadn't we better notify the police?"

The uncle stood up abruptly and, rolling up his trousers, started out. The rest of the men stood up, too, and, drying their wet lips with their hands, followed him out. The uncle disappeared out the front gate. But he seemed to have given up all hope.

"Oh, that I might be struck dead!" The aunt wailed in the main room. Her usual heartburn had gotten worse, and she had been fasting the previous day. When the heartburn got too painful, she nearly fainted but never forgot to exclaim: "Oh, that I might be struck dead!" as though it were some charm she had to repeat. She was not likely to recover from her mania unless Sŏkpae came back alive. She would rather cling to her sobbing, cling to her suffering, than seek a release from it, Sŏgun thought.

Sŏgun could not help feeling that Sŏkpae had gone out in the rain because of him. If only he had not come here, everything would have gone on in this moldy house as it had before his arrival. He was responsible for the untoward change in it.

Dark shadow covered the courtyard. No one stirred in the house. The whole place looked deserted. There was only the sound of heavy raindrops falling in the garden. The boy took up the jade rings in his hand and stole across the courtyard into the storehouse, shaking with excitement and fear. The rotten planks creaked and groaned under his light body.

He stifled an exclamation of surprise; a new lock was hanging from the quiver in place of the rusty old lock. The silver gleam of the new lock mocked him. A white, mean mocking was spreading all over the place: we have been waiting for you; we knew all along that you would come here to open the quiver again.

Sŏgun felt dizzy and had to lean against the muddy wall.

Sŏkpae's body was found lying among the rocks after the flood receded. It had once been as light and supple as a snake crossing the highway, but it was now as stiff and heavy as a water-soaked wooden tub, his once sleek skin turned dirty yellow by the working of the muddy water. His uncle loaded the body on his A-frame and carried it down the slope with unsteady steps.

Sŏgun thought he must go away from this house before Sŏkpae's body should come home. He must get away quickly because he could not face the dead body of someone virtually killed by him.

Sŏgun ran to his room and took down his trunk. He fished out the wallet his father gave him and put it deep into his pocket.

"Are you going someplace?" Sŏkhŭi's voice called from behind. He was startled but did not turn his head.

"Don't go, please. Don't go." Sŏkhŭi implored with tears in her voice. Sŏgun turned his head around and looked into her eyes. He shook his head sadly. His lips were trembling, and his throat choked so hard that he could hardly breathe. Sŏkhŭi was crying with her head lowered.

The smell of dry straw drifted from Sŏkhŭi's hair. Sŏgun walked out, leaving her alone in the room. The rain suddenly poured down in torrents. All he carried with him was an umbrella, the wallet with the scuffed edges, and the pair of jade rings. He started slowly toward the highway, all the time feeling with one hand the cool jade rings in his pocket. Rain soaked him. He heard the voice of his punctilious[13] grandfather saying: "Everything in here is yours."

Once he reached the highway, Sŏgun started running.

---

13. punctilious (puŋk til′ ē əs): very careful about every detail of behavior, ceremony, and so on.

$\mathcal{T}$*hinking About the Story*

A PERSONAL RESPONSE

sharing impressions

1. How did you feel at the end of the story? Describe your feelings in your journal.

constructing interpretations

2. Why do you think Sŏgun leaves his relatives' home?

3. How would you describe Sŏgun's feelings toward his relatives?

Think about
- his relationships with his grandfather and his cousins Sŏkhŭi and Sŏkpae
- his thoughts as he kowtows to his grandfather's visitor
- his behavior during and after the sacrificial rites
- his decision to take the jade rings with him when he leaves

4. How would you characterize the grandfather?

> ***Think about***
> * what you learn about the relationship he had with Sŏgun's father
> * his views of the sacrificial rites
> * the exchange between the grandfather and uncle after the jade is discovered missing
> * the grandfather's comments about Sŏkpae
> * the reason that Sŏkhŭi will not attend school

5. Why do you think Sŏgun has difficulties adjusting to a new family situation?

6. Should Sŏgun feel responsible for Sŏkpae's death? Give reasons for your answer.

A CREATIVE RESPONSE

7. If Sŏkpae had returned home safely, would Sŏgun still have left?

A CRITICAL RESPONSE

8. What connections do you see between the setting and the emotional state of the characters? Cite examples from the story.

9. If Sŏgun were meant to represent an entire generation of youth, what might the writer be saying about Korea? Explain.

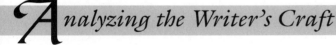
Analyzing the Writer's Craft

SYMBOL

Think about why the scuffed leather wallet is so important to Sŏgun.

Building a Literary Vocabulary. A symbol is a person, place, activity, or object that stands for something beyond itself. Cultural symbols are those that have meanings for people in the same culture. To many people in the United States, for example, an eagle symbolizes freedom and strength. Literary symbols take on meaning within the context of a literary work. To Sŏgun, the scuffed leather wallet symbolizes both the memory of his father and the means of surviving on his own.

Application: Interpreting Symbols. Form small groups and discuss the meaning of three other symbols in this story: the storehouse, the jade rings, and the rain. In a chart with three columns, write down ideas that each of these things might represent. Compare your group's ideas with those of other groups.

Connecting Reading and Writing

1. In a **character analysis** for a classmate who has also read the story, examine the character of Sŏgun, his grandfather, Sŏkpae, or Sŏkhŭi.

Option: Write a **dramatic monologue** for one of these characters, to be performed in front of the class.

2. Write a **short story** for an anthology of contemporary literature, adapting "The Heir" to a present-day American setting in which the main character has difficulties adjusting to a family situation.

Option: Write your adaptation as a **script** for television.

3. Draw a detailed **map** of the setting of this story to be displayed in your classroom. Label the features of the house and grounds and note what action occurs in each place.

Option: Create a set of **instructions** for a set designer who must reproduce the setting for a film.

4. Research one of the traditional Korean customs described in this story, such as the kowtow. Then create **notes** for a short lecture based on your findings.

Option: Write an **encyclopedia entry**, intended for an encyclopedia of Korean culture, explaining this custom.

Games at Twilight

ANITA DESAI   born 1937   INDIA

A biography of Desai appears on page 742.

Approaching the Story

"Games at Twilight" by Anita Desai (dā sī') is about Ravi (ru' vē), a young boy who is part of a large, wealthy family. Many families among the Indian upper classes still retain a preference for the Western values and social behaviors that they learned during Britain's long colonial rule in India, which ended in 1947. In this story, the children play games similar to those of English and American children. The rhyme that begins "Dip, Dip, Dip . . ." determines who will be "It," like the American rhyme "Eeny, Meeny, Miny, Mo."

Building Vocabulary

These essential words are footnoted within the story.

temerity (tə mer' ə tē): He chuckled aloud with astonishment at his own **temerity**. (page 500)

lugubrious (lə gōō' brē əs): The children trooped under it . . . in a **lugubrious** circle. (page 502)

ignominy (ig' nə min' ē): The **ignominy** of being forgotten—how could he face it? (page 502)

Connecting Writing and Reading

Think back to a time when, as a child, you played games such as hide-and-seek or tag. In your journal write down words and phrases that come to mind about events that occurred and feelings that you had. As you read, compare your experiences and feelings with those of Ravi.

Games at Twilight

IT WAS STILL too hot to play outdoors. They had had their tea, they had been washed and had their hair brushed, and after the long day of confinement in the house that was not cool but at least a protection from the sun, the children strained to get out. Their faces were red and bloated with the effort, but their mother would not open the door; everything was still curtained and shuttered in a way that stifled the children, made them feel that their lungs were stuffed with cotton wool and their noses with dust and if they didn't burst out into the light and see the sun and feel the air, they would choke.

"Please, Ma, please," they begged. "We'll play in the veranda and porch—we won't go a step out of the porch."

"You will, I know you will, and then—"

"No—we won't, we won't," they wailed so horrendously that she actually let down the bolt of the front door, so that they burst out like seeds from a crackling, overripe pod into the veranda with such wild, maniacal yells that she retreated to her bath and the shower of talcum powder and the fresh sari that were to help her face the summer evening.

They faced the afternoon. It was too hot. Too bright. The white walls of the veranda glared stridently in the sun. The bougainvillea[1] hung about it, purple and magenta, in livid balloons. The garden outside was like a tray made of beaten brass, flattened out on the red gravel and the stony soil in all shades of metal—aluminum, tin, copper and brass. No life stirred at this arid time of day—the birds still drooped, like dead fruit, in the papery tents of the trees; some squirrels lay limp on the wet earth under the garden tap. The outdoor dog lay stretched as if dead on the veranda mat, his paws and ears and tail all reaching out like dying travellers in search of water. He rolled his eyes at the children—two white marbles rolling in the purple sockets, begging for sympathy—and attempted to lift his tail in a wag but could not. It only twitched and lay still.

Then, perhaps roused by the shrieks of the children, a band of parrots suddenly fell out of the eucalyptus tree, tumbled frantically in the still, sizzling air, then sorted themselves out into battle formation and streaked away across the white sky.

The children, too, felt released. They too began tumbling, shoving, pushing against each other, frantic to start. Start what? Start their business. The business of the children's day which is—play.

"Let's play hide-and-seek."

"Who'll be It?"

"You be It."

"Why should I? You be—"

"You're the eldest—"

"That doesn't mean—"

The shoves became harder. Some kicked out. The motherly Mira[2] intervened. She pulled the boys roughly apart. There was a tearing sound of cloth, but it was lost in the heavy panting and angry grumbling, and no one paid attention to the small sleeve hanging loosely off a shoulder.

"Make a circle, make a circle!" she shouted, firmly pulling and pushing till a kind of vague

---

1. **bougainvillea** (bo͞o′ gən vil′ ē ə): a woody tropical vine of the four o'clock family.
2. **Mira** (mē′ rə).

circle was formed. "Now clap!" she roared, and clapping, they all chanted in melancholy unison: "Dip, dip, dip—my blue ship—" and every now and then one or the other saw he was safe by the way his hands fell at the crucial moment—palm on palm, or back of hand on palm—and dropped out of the circle with a yell and a jump of relief and jubilation.

Raghu[3] was It. He started to protest, to cry, "You cheated—Mira cheated—Anu[4] cheated—" but it was too late; the others had all already streaked away. There was no one to hear when he called out, "Only in the veranda—the porch—Ma said—Ma *said* to stay in the porch!" No one had stopped to listen; all he saw was their brown legs flashing through the dusty shrubs, scrambling up brick walls, leaping over compost heaps and hedges; and then the porch stood empty in the purple shade of the bougainvillea and the garden was as empty as before; even the limp squirrels had whisked away, leaving everything gleaming, brassy and bare.

Only small Manu[5] suddenly reappeared, as if he had dropped out of an invisible cloud or from a bird's claws, and stood for a moment in the center of the yellow lawn, chewing his finger and near to tears as he heard Raghu shouting, with his head pressed against the veranda wall, "Eighty-three, eighty-five, eighty-nine, ninety . . ." and then made off in a panic, half of him wanting to fly north, the other half counselling south. Raghu turned just in time to see the flash of his white shorts and the uncertain skittering of his red sandals and charged after him with such a blood-curdling yell that Manu stumbled over the hose pipe, fell into its rubber coils and lay there weeping, "I won't be It—you have to find them all—all—All!"

"I know I have to, idiot," Raghu said, superciliously kicking him with his toe. "You're dead," he said with satisfaction, licking the beads of perspiration off his upper lip, and then

stalked off in search of worthier prey, whistling spiritedly so that the hiders should hear and tremble.

Ravi heard the whistling and picked his nose in a panic, trying to find comfort by burrowing the finger deep—deep into that soft tunnel. He felt himself too exposed, sitting on an upturned flower pot behind the garage. Where could he burrow? He could run around the garage if he heard Raghu come—around and around and around—but he hadn't much faith in his short legs when matched against Raghu's long, hefty, hairy footballer legs. Ravi had a frightening glimpse of them as Raghu combed the hedge of crotons and hibiscus, trampling delicate ferns underfoot as he did so. Ravi looked about him desperately, swallowing a small ball of snot in his fear.

The garage was locked with a great, heavy lock to which the driver had the key in his room, hanging from a nail on the wall under his work shirt. Ravi had peeped in and seen him still sprawling on his string cot in his vest and striped underpants, the hair on his chest and the hair in his nose shaking with the vibrations of his phlegm-obstructed snores. Ravi had wished he were tall enough, big enough to reach the key on the nail, but it was impossible, beyond his reach for years to come. He had sidled away and sat dejectedly on the flower pot. That at least was cut to his own size.

But next to the garage was another shed with a big green door. Also locked. No one even knew who had the key to the lock. That shed wasn't opened more than once a year, when Ma turned out all the old broken bits of furniture and rolls of matting and leaking buckets, and the white ant hills were broken

---

3. **Raghu** (*ru′ gꝏ*).
4. **Anu** (u′ nꝏ).
5. **Manu** (mu′ nꝏ).

and swept away and Flit sprayed into the spider webs and rat holes so that the whole operation was like the looting of a poor, ruined and conquered city. The green leaves of the door sagged. They were nearly off their rusty hinges. The hinges were large and made a small gap between the door and the walls—only just large enough for rats, dogs and, possibly, Ravi to slip through.

Ravi had never cared to enter such a dark and depressing mortuary of defunct household goods seething with such unspeakable and alarming animal life, but, as Raghu's whistling grew angrier and sharper and his crashing and storming in the hedge wilder, Ravi suddenly slipped off the flower pot and through the crack and was gone. He chuckled aloud with astonishment at his own temerity[6] so that Raghu came out of the hedge, stood silent with his hands on his hips, listening, and finally shouted, "I heard you! I'm coming! *Got you*—" and came charging round the garage only to find the upturned flower pot, the yellow dust, the crawling of white ants in a mud hill against the closed shed door—nothing. Snarling, he bent to pick up a stick and went off, whacking it against the garage and shed walls as if to beat out his prey.

Ravi shook, then shivered with delight, with self-congratulation. Also with fear. It was dark, spooky in the shed. It had a muffled smell, as of graves. Ravi had once got locked into the linen cupboard and sat there weeping for half an hour before he was rescued. But at least that had been a familiar place and even smelt pleasantly of starch, laundry and, reassuringly, his mother. But the shed smelt of rats, ant hills, dust and spider webs. Also of less definable, less recognizable horrors. And it was dark. Except for the white-hot cracks along the door, there was no light. The roof was very low. Although Ravi was small, he felt as if he could reach up and touch it with his fingertips.

But he didn't stretch. He hunched himself into a ball so as not to bump into anything, touch or feel anything. What might there not be to touch him and feel him as he stood there, trying to see in the dark? Something cold or slimy—like a snake. Snakes! He leapt up as Raghu whacked the wall with his stick—then, quickly realizing what it was, felt almost relieved to hear Raghu, hear his stick. It made him feel protected.

But Raghu soon moved away. There wasn't a sound once his footsteps had gone around the garage and disappeared. Ravi stood frozen inside the shed. Then he shivered all over. Something had tickled the back of his neck. It took him a while to pick up the courage to lift his hand and explore. It was an insect—perhaps a spider—exploring *him*. He squashed it and wondered how many more creatures were watching him, waiting to reach out and touch him, the stranger.

There was nothing now. After standing in that position—his hand still on his neck, feeling the wet splodge of the squashed spider gradually dry—for minutes, hours, his legs began to tremble with the effort, the inaction. By now he could see enough in the dark to make out the large, solid shapes of old wardrobes, broken buckets and bedsteads piled on top of each other around him. He recognized an old bathtub—patches of enamel glimmered at him, and at last he lowered himself onto its edge.

He contemplated slipping out of the shed and into the fray. He wondered if it would not be better to be captured by Raghu and returned to the milling crowd as long as he could be in the sun, the light, the free spaces of the garden and the familiarity of his brothers, sisters and cousins. It would be evening soon. Their games would become legitimate. The

6. **temerity** (tə mer′ ə tē): foolish or rash boldness; recklessness.

parents would sit out on the lawn on cane basket chairs and watch them as they tore around the garden or gathered in knots to share a loot of mulberries or black, teeth-splitting *jamun*[7] from the garden trees. The gardener would fix the hose pipe to the water tap, and water would fall lavishly through the air to the ground, soaking the dry, yellow grass and the red gravel and arousing the sweet, the intoxicating, scent of water on dry earth—that loveliest scent in the world. Ravi sniffed for a whiff of it. He half rose from the bathtub, then heard the despairing scream of one of the girls as Raghu bore down upon her. There was the sound of a crash and of rolling about in the bushes, the shrubs, then screams and accusing sobs of "I touched the den—" "You did not—" "I did—" "You liar, you did *not*," and then a fading away and silence again.

Ravi sat back on the harsh edge of the tub, deciding to hold out a bit longer. What fun if they were all found and caught—he alone left unconquered! He had never known that sensation. Nothing more wonderful had ever happened to him than being taken out by an uncle and bought a whole slab of chocolate all to himself, or being flung into the soda man's pony cart and driven up to the gate by the friendly driver with the red beard and pointed ears. To defeat Raghu—that hirsute, hoarse-voiced football champion—and to be the winner in a circle of older, bigger, luckier children—that would be thrilling beyond imagination. He hugged his knees together and smiled to himself almost shyly at the thought of so much victory, such laurels.

There he sat smiling, knocking his heels against the bathtub, now and then getting up and going to the door to put his ear to the broad crack and listening for sounds of the game, the pursuer and the pursued, and then returning to his seat with the dogged determination of the true winner, a breaker of records, a champion.

It grew darker in the shed as the light at the door grew softer, fuzzier, turned to a kind of crumbling yellow pollen that turned to yellow fur, blue fur, gray fur. Evening. Twilight. The sound of water gushing, falling. The scent of earth receiving water, slaking its thirst in great gulps and releasing that green scent of freshness, coolness. Through the crack Ravi saw the long purple shadows of the shed and the garage lying still across the yard. Beyond that, the white walls of the house. The bougainvillea had lost its lividity, hung in dark bundles that quaked and twittered and seethed with masses of homing sparrows. The lawn was shut off from his view. Could he hear the children's voices? It seemed to him that he could. It seemed to him that he could hear them chanting, singing, laughing. But what about the game? What had happened? Could it be over? How could it when he was still not found?

It then occurred to him that he could have slipped out long ago, dashed across the yard to the veranda and touched the "den." It was necessary to do that to win. He had forgotten. He had only remembered the part of hiding and trying to elude the seeker. He had done that so successfully, his success had occupied him so wholly, that he had quite forgotten that success had to be clinched by that final dash to victory and the ringing cry of "Den!"

With a whimper he burst through the crack, fell on his knees, got up and stumbled on stiff, benumbed legs across the shadowy yard, crying heartily by the time he reached the veranda so that when he flung himself at the white pillar and bawled, "Den! Den! Den!" his voice broke with rage and pity at the disgrace of it all, and he felt himself flooded with tears and misery.

Out on the lawn, the children stopped chanting. They all turned to stare at him in amazement. Their faces were pale and triangular in the dusk. The trees and bushes around

---

7. *jamun* (jä′ mōōn): a kind of plum.

them stood inky and sepulchral, spilling long shadows across them. They stared, wondering at his reappearance, his passion, his wild animal howling. Their mother rose from her basket chair and came toward him, worried, annoyed, saying, "Stop it, stop it, Ravi. Don't be a baby. Have you hurt yourself?" Seeing him attended to, the children went back to clasping their hands and chanting, "The grass is green, the rose is red. . . ."

But Ravi would not let them. He tore himself out of his mother's grasp and pounded across the lawn into their midst, charging at them with his head lowered so that they scattered in surprise. "I won, I won, I won," he bawled, shaking his head so that the big tears flew. "Raghu didn't find me. I won, I won—"

It took them a minute to grasp what he was saying, even who he was. They had quite forgotten him. Raghu had found all the others long ago. There had been a fight about who was to be It next. It had been so fierce that their mother had emerged from her bath and made them change to another game. Then they had played another and another. Broken mulberries from the tree and eaten them. Helped the driver wash the car when their father returned from work. Helped the gardener water the beds till he roared at them and swore he would complain to their parents. The parents had come out, taken up their positions on the cane chairs. They had begun to play again, sing and chant. All this time no one had remembered Ravi. Having disappeared from the scene, he had disappeared from their minds. Clean.

"Don't be a fool," Raghu said roughly, pushing him aside, and even Mira said, "Stop howling, Ravi. If you want to play, you can stand at the end of the line," and she put him there very firmly.

The game proceeded. Two pairs of arms reached up and met in an arc. The children trooped under it again and again in a lugubrious[8] circle, ducking their heads and intoning

"The grass is green,
The rose is red;
Remember me
When I am dead, dead, dead, dead . . ."

And the arc of thin arms trembled in the twilight, and the heads were bowed so sadly, and their feet tramped to that melancholy refrain so mournfully, so helplessly, that Ravi could not bear it. He would not follow them; he would not be included in this funereal game. He had wanted victory and triumph—not a funeral. But he had been forgotten, left out and he would not join them now. The ignominy[9] of being forgotten—how could he face it? He felt his heart go heavy and ache inside him unbearably. He lay down full length on the damp grass, crushing his face into it, no longer crying, silenced by a terrible sense of his insignificance.

---

8. lugubrious (lə gōō′ brē əs): mournful, especially exaggeratedly or artificially mournful.

9. ignominy (ig′ nə min′ ē): shame and dishonor.

Thinking About the Story

A PERSONAL RESPONSE

sharing impressions

1. How do you feel about what happens to Ravi? Describe your feelings in your journal.

constructing interpretations

2. Why do you think Ravi's experience during the hide-and-seek game affects him so deeply?

Think about
- how this experience compares with the time he was locked in the linen cupboard
- his expectations about what winning will be like
- how the family reacts to his crying and to his declaration that he won
- why he refuses to join in the funeral game

3. How would you evaluate the way that Ravi's family behaves toward him?
Think about
- why the family forgets about him
- why they fail to respond according to his expectations

A CREATIVE RESPONSE

4. If Ravi came from a smaller family, how might his experience be different?

A CRITICAL RESPONSE

5. Describe the mood, or atmosphere, of this story and identify passages that you think are important in creating that mood.
Think about
- the children's feelings of being stifled inside the house at the beginning of the story
- what it is like inside the shed
- the references to death in the description of the dog and in both games the children play

6. One critic has written that the story conveys "Ravi's first experience of his own mortality, his sense of his own small, brief place in a vast and difficult universe." Using details from the story, explain whether you agree or disagree with this interpretation.

7. Who do you think feels more isolated from his family, Sŏgun in "The Heir" or Ravi? Use specific details from the stories to support your answer.

Analyzing the Writer's Craft

FIGURATIVE LANGUAGE: SIMILE AND METAPHOR

The children bursting out of the house to play are described as being "like seeds from a crackling, overripe pod." Jot down some words or phrases that this comparison brings to mind.

Building a Literary Vocabulary. Figurative language is language that communicates ideas beyond the literal meanings of the words. A simile compares two things in a phrase that contains *like* or *as*. Desai's comparison of the children to seeds bursting from a dry, brittle pod is a simile that conveys the exuberant sense of release with which the children escape the protective "pod" of the house. The children are like seeds in their youthful energy and potential for growth.

A metaphor is another figure of speech that makes a comparison between two things that have something in common. While a simile contains the word *like* or *as*, a metaphor either makes the comparison directly or implies it. The same idea in

Desai's simile could be expressed as a metaphor by saying, "The children were seeds bursting out from a crackling, overripe pod."

Application: Identifying Figures of Speech. Working in a group, find at least five similes and metaphors in the story. For each example, create a diagram similar to the one that follows.

Example from story:

Subject		**Simile (or metaphor)**
children going outside	⟶	seeds from a crackling, overripe pod

Idea communicated
sense of release, energy, youth, and potential growth

Choose the one simile or metaphor that your group likes best and diagram it for your class.

Connecting Reading and Writing

1. Write a **first-person narrative** recounting a situation like Ravi's in which your expectations were disappointed by the actual event. Share your narrative with a friend.

Option: Write about the event as a **diary entry.**

2. To what extent do you think children's games teach them to live in the adult world? Referring to both your own experience and the story, express your opinion in an **article** to be published in a magazine or newsletter for parents.

Option: Write on the topic of life lessons taught by children's games in a **memo** to be given to the teachers at a preschool.

3. Write an **episode** from a short story showing Ravi and his playmates playing games a week after the incident.

Option: Compose a **letter** that Ravi might write to either Raghu or Mira when they are adults, telling them how the experience of that afternoon affected him.

As the Night the Day

ABIOSEH NICOL   born 1924   SIERRA LEONE

A biography of Nicol appears on page 748.

*A*pproaching the Story

The following story concerns the relationships among high school students and teachers in a school in Sierra Leone (sē er′ ə lē ōn′). This nation, located in West Africa, on the Atlantic Ocean, was a British colony until 1961. The population of Sierra Leone consists primarily of Africans, with Indians, Lebanese, and Syrians in the minority.

*B*uilding Vocabulary

These essential words are footnoted within the story.

malevolence (mə lev′ ə ləns): The thin thread of quicksilver shot upward . . . with swift **malevolence**. (page 506)

protracted (prō trak′ təd), **recrimination** (ri krim′ ə na′ shən): They knew the matter would end there with no **protracted** interviews [and] moral **recrimination**. (page 507)

avuncular (ə vuŋ′ kyoo lər): [He was] a tall, thin, dignified Negro, with graying hair and silver-rimmed spectacles . . . making him look **avuncular**. (page 507)

enigmatically (e′ nig mat′ ə kal ē): "Ah! That is what is called research," he replied, **enigmatically**. (page 508)

stentorian (sten tôr′ ē ən): Mr. Abu's **stentorian** voice rang out. (page 508)

*C*onnecting Writing and Reading

What is the main lesson that you have learned about human relationships since you started high school? Write down your response in your journal. You may want to use the following list to get you thinking about issues that can be important in relationships.

friendship	love
respect	anger
generosity	peer pressure

As you read, compare what you have learned with what Kojo learns about human relationships in this story.

As The Night the Day

KOJO[1] AND Bandele[2] walked slowly across the hot, green lawn, holding their science manuals with moist fingers. In the distance they could hear the junior school collecting in the hall of the main school building, for singing practice. Nearer, but still far enough, their classmates were strolling toward them. The two reached the science block and entered it. It was a low building set apart from the rest of the high school, which sprawled on the hillside of the African savanna. The laboratory was a longish room, and at one end they saw Basu,[3] another boy, looking out of the window, his back turned to them. Mr. Abu,[4] the ferocious laboratory attendant, was not about. The rows of multicolored bottles looked inviting. A Bunsen burner soughed loudly in the heavy, weary heat. Where the tip of the light-blue triangle of flame ended, a shimmering plastic transparency started. One could see the restless hot air moving in the minute tornado. The two African boys watched it, interestedly, holding hands.

"They say it is hotter inside the flame than on its surface," Kojo said, doubtfully. "I wonder how they know."

"I think you mean the opposite; let's try it ourselves," Bandele answered.

"How?"

"Let's take the temperature inside."

"All right, here is a thermometer. You do it."

"It says ninety degrees now. I shall take the temperature of the outer flame first, then you can take the inner yellow one."

Bandele held the thermometer gently forward to the flame, and Kojo craned to see. The thin thread of quicksilver shot upward within the stem of the instrument with swift malevolence,[5] and there was a slight crack. The stem had broken. On the bench the small bulbous drops of mercury which had spilled from it shivered with glinting, playful malice and shuddered down to the cement floor, dashing themselves into a thousand shining pieces, some of which coalesced again and shook gaily as if with silent laughter.

"Oh my God!" whispered Kojo hoarsely.

"Shut up!" Bandele said, imperiously, in a low voice.

Bandele swept the few drops on the bench into his cupped hand and threw the blob of mercury down the sink. He swept those on the floor under an adjoining cupboard with his bare feet. Then, picking up the broken halves of the thermometer, he tiptoed to the waste bin and dropped them in. He tiptoed back to Kojo, who was standing petrified by the blackboard.

"See no evil, hear no evil, speak no evil," he whispered to Kojo.

It all took place in a few seconds. Then the rest of the class started pouring in, chattering and pushing each other. Basu, who had been at the end of the room with his back turned to them all the time, now turned round and limped laboriously across to join the class, his eyes screwed up as they always were.

The class ranged itself loosely in a semicircle around the demonstration platform. They

---

1. **Kojo** (kô′ jô).
2. **Bandele** (bän de′ le).
3. **Basu** (ba′ sōō).
4. **Abu** (ä′ bōō).
5. **malevolence** (mə lev′ ə ləns): hostility; spite.

were dressed in the school uniform of white shirt and khaki shorts. Their official age was around sixteen, although, in fact, it ranged from Kojo's fifteen years to one or two boys of twenty-one.

Mr. Abu, the laboratory attendant, came in from the adjoining store and briskly cleaned the blackboard. He was a retired African sergeant from the Army Medical Corps and was feared by the boys. If he caught any of them in any petty thieving, he offered them the choice of a hard smack on the bottom or of being reported to the science masters. Most boys chose the former, as they knew the matter would end there, with no protracted[6] interviews, moral recrimination,[7] and an entry in the conduct book.

The science master stepped in and stood on his small platform. A tall, thin, dignified Negro, with graying hair and silver-rimmed spectacles badly fitting on his broad nose and always slipping down, making him look avuncular.[8] "Vernier"[9] was his nickname, as he insisted on exact measurement and exact speech "as fine as a vernier scale," he would say, which measured, of course, things in thousandths of a millimeter. Vernier set the experiments for the day and demonstrated them, then retired behind the *Church Times*, which he read seriously in between walking quickly down the aisles of lab benches, advising boys. It was a simple heat experiment to show that a dark surface gave out more heat by radiation than a bright surface.

During the class, Vernier was called away to the telephone and Abu was not about, having retired to the lavatory for a smoke. As soon as a posted sentinel announced that he was out of sight, minor pandemonium broke out. Some of the boys raided the store. The wealthier ones swiped rubber tubing to make catapults and to repair bicycles and helped themselves to chemicals for developing photographic films. The poorer boys were in deadlier earnest

and took only things of strict commercial interest which could be sold easily in the market. They emptied stuff into bottles in their pockets. Soda for making soap, magnesium sulphate for opening medicine, salt for cooking, liquid paraffin for women's hairdressing, and fine yellow iodoform powder much in demand for sprinkling on sores. Kojo protested mildly against all this. "Oh, shut up!" a few boys said. Sorie,[10] a huge boy who always wore a fez[11] indoors and who, rumor said, had already fathered a child, commanded respect and some leadership in the class. He was sipping his favorite mixture of diluted alcohol and bicarbonate—which he called "gin and fizz"—from a beaker. "Look here, Kojo, you are getting out of hand. What do you think our parents pay taxes and school fees for? For us to enjoy—or to buy a new car every year for Simpson?" The other boys laughed. Simpson was the European headmaster, feared by the small boys, adored by the boys in the middle school, and liked, in a critical fashion, with reservations, by some of the senior boys and African masters. He had a passion for new motorcars, buying one yearly.

"Come to think of it," Sorie continued to Kojo, "you must take something yourself; then we'll know we are safe." "Yes, you must," the other boys insisted. Kojo gave in and, unwillingly, took a little nitrate for some gunpowder experiments which he was carrying out at home.

"Someone!" the lookout called.

---

6. protracted (prō trak' təd): drawn out; prolonged.

7. recrimination (ri krim' ə nā' sʰən): the act of answering an accuser by accusing him or her in return.

8. avuncular (ə vuŋ' kyo͞o lər): of or like an uncle.

9. Vernier (vʉr' nē ər).

10. Sorie: (sô̂' rē).

11. fez: a man's brimless hat, shaped like a cone, with a flat top and a black tassel.

The boys dispersed in a moment. Sorie swilled out his mouth at the sink with some water. Mr. Abu, the lab attendant, entered and observed the innocent collective expression of the class. He glared round suspiciously and sniffed the air. It was a physics experiment, but the place smelled chemical. However, Vernier came in then. After asking if anyone was in difficulty, and finding that no one could momentarily think up anything, he retired to his chair and settled down to an article on Christian reunion, adjusting his spectacles and thoughtfully sucking an empty tooth socket.

Toward the end of the period, the class collected around Vernier and gave in their results, which were then discussed. One of the more political boys asked Vernier: if dark surfaces gave out more heat, was that why they all had black faces in West Africa? A few boys giggled. Basu looked down and tapped his clubfoot embarrassedly on the floor. Vernier was used to questions of this sort from the senior boys. He never committed himself, as he was getting near retirement and his pension, and became more guarded each year. He sometimes even feared that Simpson had spies among the boys.

"That may be so, although the opposite might be more convenient."

Everything in science had a loophole, the boys thought, and said so to Vernier.

"Ah! That is what is called research," he replied, enigmatically.[12]

Sorie asked a question. Last time, they had been shown that an electric spark with hydrogen and oxygen atoms formed water. Why was not that method used to provide water in town at the height of the dry season when there was an acute water shortage?

"It would be too expensive," Vernier replied, shortly. He disliked Sorie, not because of his different religion, but because he thought that Sorie was a bad influence and also asked ridiculous questions.

Sorie persisted. There was plenty of water during the rainy season. It could be split by lightning to hydrogen and oxygen in October and the gases compressed and stored, then changed back to water in March during the shortage. There was a faint ripple of applause from Sorie's admirers.

"It is an impracticable idea," Vernier snapped.

The class dispersed and started walking back across the hot grass. Kojo and Bandele heaved sighs of relief and joined Sorie's crowd, which was always the largest.

"Science is a bit of a swindle," Sorie was saying. "I do not for a moment think that Vernier believes any of it himself," he continued, "because, if he does, why is he always reading religious books?"

"Come back, all of you, come back!" Mr. Abu's stentorian[13] voice rang out, across to them.

They wavered and stopped. Kojo kept walking on in a blind panic.

"Stop," Bandele hissed across. "You fool." He stopped, turned, and joined the returning crowd, closely followed by Bandele. Abu joined Vernier on the platform. The loose semicircle of boys faced them.

"Mr. Abu just found this in the waste bin," Vernier announced, gray with anger. He held up the two broken halves of the thermometer. "It must be due to someone from this class, as the number of thermometers was checked before being put out."

A little wind gusted in through the window and blew the silence heavily this way and that.

"Who?"

No one answered. Vernier looked round and waited.

"Since no one has owned up, I am afraid I shall have to detain you for an hour after school as punishment," said Vernier.

---

12. **enigmatically** (e′ nig mat′ ə kal ē): mysteriously.
13. **stentorian** (sten tôr′ ē ən): very loud.

There was a murmur of dismay and anger. An important soccer house-match was scheduled for that afternoon. Some boys put their hands up and said that they had to play in the match.

"I don't care," Vernier shouted. He felt, in any case, that too much time was devoted to games and not enough to work.

He left Mr. Abu in charge and went off to fetch his things from the main building.

"We shall play 'Bible and Key,'" Abu announced as soon as Vernier had left. Kojo had been afraid of this, and new beads of perspiration sprang from his troubled brow. All the boys knew the details. It was a method of finding out a culprit by divination. A large door key was placed between the leaves of a Bible at the New Testament passage where Ananias and Sapphira[14] were struck dead before the Apostles for lying and the Bible suspended by two bits of string tied to both ends of the key. The combination was held up by someone, and the names of all present were called out in turn. When that of the sinner was called, the Bible was expected to turn round and round violently and fall.

Now Abu asked for a Bible. Someone produced a copy. He opened the first page and then shook his head and handed it back. "This won't do," he said. "It's a Revised Version; only the genuine Word of God will give us the answer."

An Authorized King James Version was then produced, and he was satisfied. Soon he had the contraption fixed up. He looked round the semicircle, from Sorie at one end, through the others, to Bandele, Basu, and Kojo at the other, near the door.

"You seem to have an honest face," he said to Kojo. "Come and hold it." Kojo took the ends of the string gingerly with both hands, trembling slightly.

Abu moved over to the low window and stood at attention, his sharp profile outlined against the red hibiscus flowers, the green trees, and the molten sky. The boys watched anxiously. A black-bodied lizard scurried up a wall and started nodding its pink head with grave impartiality.

Abu fixed his ageing, bloodshot eyes on the suspended Bible. He spoke hoarsely and slowly:

"Oh, Bible, Bible, on a key,
Kindly tell it unto me,
By swinging slowly round and true,
To whom this sinful act is due. . . ."

He turned to the boys and barked out their names in a parade-ground voice, beginning with Sorie and working his way round, looking at the Bible after each name.

To Kojo, trembling and shivering as if ice-cold water had been thrown over him, it seemed as if he had lost all power and that some gigantic being stood behind him holding up his tired, aching elbows. It seemed to him as if the key and Bible had taken on a life of their own, and he watched with fascination the whole combination moving slowly, jerkily, and rhythmically in short arcs as if it had acquired a heartbeat.

"Ayo Sogbenri, Sonnir Kargbo, Oji Ndebu." Abu was coming to the end now. "Tommy Longe, Ajayi Cole, Bandele Fagb . . ."[15]

Kojo dropped the Bible. "I am tired," he said, in a small scream. "I am tired."

"Yes, he is," Abu agreed, "but we are almost finished; only Bandele and Basu are left."

"Pick up that book, Kojo, and hold it up again." Bandele's voice whipped through the

---

14. **Ananias and Sapphira** (an′ ə nī′ əs; sə fī′ rə): husband and wife who fell dead when Peter rebuked them for withholding from the apostles a part of the proceeds from a sale of their land.

15. **Ayo Sogbenri . . . Fagb** (ä′ yō sŏg ben′ rē; sŏn′ nēr kärg′ bō; ō′ jē nde′ bōō; lŏŋ ge; ä jä′ yē kōl; fägb).

air with cold fury. It sobered Kojo, and he picked it up.

"Will you continue, please, with my name, Mr. Abu?" Bandele asked, turning to the window.

"Go back to your place quickly, Kojo," Abu said. "Vernier is coming. He might be vexed. He is a strongly religious man and so does not believe in the Bible-and-Key ceremony."

Kojo slipped back with sick relief, just before Vernier entered.

In the distance the rest of the school was assembling for closing prayers. The class sat and stood around the blackboard and demonstration bench in attitudes of exasperation, resignation, and self-righteous indignation. Kojo's heart was beating so loudly that he was surprised no one else heard it.

"Once to every man and nation
Comes the moment to decide . . ."[16]

The closing hymn floated across to them, interrupting the still afternoon.

Kojo got up. He felt now that he must speak the truth, or life would be intolerable ever afterward. Bandele got up swiftly before him. In fact, several things seemed to happen all at the same time. The rest of the class stirred. Vernier looked up from a book review which he had started reading. A butterfly, with black and gold wings, flew in and sat on the edge of the blackboard, flapping its wings quietly and waiting too.

"Basu was here first before any of the class," Bandele said firmly.

Everyone turned to Basu, who cleared his throat.

"I was just going to say so myself, sir," Basu replied to Vernier's inquiring glance.

"Pity you had no thought of it before," Vernier said, dryly. "What were you doing here?"

"I missed the previous class, so I came straight to the lab and waited. I was over there

by the window, trying to look at the blue sky. I did not break the thermometer, sir."

A few boys tittered. Some looked away. The others muttered. Basu's breath always smelt of onions, but although he could play no games, some boys liked him and were kind to him in a tolerant way.

"Well, if you did not, someone did. We shall continue with the detention."

Vernier noticed Abu standing by. "You need not stay, Mr. Abu," he said to him. "I shall close up. In fact, come with me now and I shall let you out through the back gate."

He went out with Abu.

When he had left, Sorie turned to Basu and asked mildly:

"You are sure you did not break it?"

"No, I didn't."

"He did it," someone shouted.

"But what about the Bible-and-Key?" Basu protested. "It did not finish. Look at him." He pointed to Bandele.

"I was quite willing for it to go on," said Bandele. "You were the only one left."

Someone threw a book at Basu and said, "Confess!"

Basu backed on to a wall. "To God, I shall call the police if anyone strikes me," he cried fiercely.

"He thinks he can buy the police," a voice called.

"That proves it," someone shouted from the back.

"Yes, he must have done it," the others said, and they started throwing books at Basu. Sorie waved his arm for them to stop, but they did not. Books, corks, boxes of matches rained on Basu. He bent his head

---

16. Once to . . . decide: The words of the hymn are from "Present Crisis," a poem by the American poet James Russell Lowell (1819–1891). The theme of the poem is that a person must stand up for self or country when the need arises.

and shielded his face with his bent arm.

"I did not do it, I swear I did not do it. Stop it, you fellows," he moaned over and over again. A small cut had appeared on his temple, and he was bleeding. Kojo sat quietly for a while. Then a curious hum started to pass through him, and his hands began to tremble, his armpits to feel curiously wetter. He turned round and picked up a book and flung it with desperate force at Basu, and then another. He felt somehow that there was an awful swelling of guilt which he could only shed by punishing himself through hurting someone. Anger and rage against everything different seized him, because if everything and everyone had been the same, somehow he felt nothing would have been wrong and they would all have been happy. He was carried away now by a torrent which swirled and pounded. He felt that somehow Basu was in the wrong, must be in the wrong, and if he hurt him hard enough, he would convince the others and therefore himself that he had not broken the thermometer and that he had never done anything wrong. He groped for something bulky enough to throw, and picked up the Bible.

"Stop it," Vernier shouted through the open doorway. "Stop it, you hooligans, you beasts."

They all became quiet and shamefacedly put down what they were going to throw. Basu was crying quietly and hopelessly, his thin body shaking.

"Go home, all of you, go home. I am ashamed of you." His black face shone with anger. "You are an utter disgrace to your nation and to your race."

They crept away, quietly, uneasily, avoiding each other's eyes, like people caught in a secret passion.

Vernier went to the first-aid cupboard and started dressing Basu's wounds.

Kojo and Bandele came back and hid behind the door, listening. Bandele insisted that they should.

Vernier put Basu's bandaged head against his waistcoat and dried the boy's tears with his handkerchief, gently patting his shaking shoulders.

"It wouldn't have been so bad if I had done it, sir," he mumbled, snuggling his head against Vernier, "but I did not do it. I swear to God I did not."

"Hush, hush," said Vernier comfortingly.

"Now they will hate me even more," he moaned.

"Hush, hush."

"I don't mind the wounds so much; they will heal."

"Hush, hush."

"They've missed the football match and now they will never talk to me again; oh-ee, oh-ee, why have I been so punished?"

"As you grow older," Vernier advised, "you must learn that men are punished not always for what they do, but often for what people think they will do or for what they are. Remember that and you will find it easier to forgive them. 'To thine own self be true!'" Vernier ended with a flourish, holding up his clenched fist in a mock dramatic gesture, quoting from the Shakespeare examination set-book for the year and declaiming to the dripping taps and empty benches and still afternoon, to make Basu laugh.

Basu dried his eyes and smiled wanly and replied: "'And it shall follow as the night the day.' *Hamlet*, Act One, Scene Three, Polonius to Laertes."[17]

"There's a good chap. First Class Grade One. I shall give you a lift home."

17. **And it shall . . . the day:** The complete passage in Shakespeare's *Hamlet,* in which Polonius (pə lō′ nē əs) advises his son Laertes, (lā ur′ tēz), is "This above all—to thine own self be true,/And it must follow, as the night the day,/Thou can'st not then be false to any man." In other words, be honest with yourself and you will be honest with others.

Kojo and Bandele walked down the red laterite road together, Kojo dispiritedly kicking stones into the gutter.

"The fuss they made over a silly old thermometer," Bandele began.

"I don't know, old man, I don't know," Kojo said impatiently.

They had both been shaken by the scene in the empty lab. A thin, invisible wall of hostility and mistrust was slowly rising between them.

"Basu did not do it, of course," Bandele said.

Kojo stopped dead in his tracks. "Of course he did not do it," he shouted; "we did it."

"No need to shout, old man. After all, it was your idea."

"It wasn't," Kojo said furiously. "You suggested we try it."

"Well, you started the argument. Don't be childish." They tramped on silently, raising small clouds of dust with their bare feet.

"I should not take it too much to heart," Bandele continued. "That chap Basu's father hoards foodstuff like rice and palm oil until there is a shortage and then sells them at high prices. The police are watching him."

"What has that got to do with it?" Kojo asked.

"Don't you see, Basu might quite easily have broken that thermometer. I bet he has done things before that we have all been punished for." Bandele was emphatic.

They walked on steadily down the main road of the town, past the Syrian and Lebanese shops crammed with knickknacks and rolls of cloth, past a large Indian shop with dull red carpets and brass trays displayed in its windows, carefully stepping aside in the narrow road as the British officials sped by in cars to their hill-station bungalows for lunch and siesta.

Kojo reached home at last. He washed his feet and ate his main meal for the day. He sat about heavily and restlessly for some hours.

Night soon fell with its usual swiftness, at six, and he finished his homework early and went to bed. Lying in bed he rehearsed again what he was determined to do the next day. He would go up to Vernier:

"Sir," he would begin, "I wish to speak with you privately."

"Can it wait?" Vernier would ask.

"No, sir," he would say firmly, "as a matter of fact, it is rather urgent."

Vernier would take him to an empty classroom and say, "What is troubling you, Kojo Ananse?"[18]

"I wish to make a confession, sir. I broke the thermometer yesterday." He had decided he would not name Bandele; it was up to the latter to decide whether he would lead a pure life.

Vernier would adjust his slipping glasses up his nose and think. Then he would say:

"This is a serious matter, Kojo. You realize you should have confessed yesterday?"

"Yes, sir, I am very sorry."

"You have done great harm, but better late than never. You will, of course, apologize in front of the class and particularly to Basu, who has shown himself a finer chap than all of you."

"I shall do so, sir."

"Why have you come to me now to apologize? Were you hoping that I would simply forgive you?"

"I was hoping you would, sir. I was hoping you would show your forgiveness by beating me."

Vernier would pull his glasses up his nose again. He would move his tongue inside his mouth reflectively. "I think you are right. Do you feel you deserve six strokes or nine?"

"Nine, sir."

"Bend over!"

Kojo had decided he would not cry because he was almost a man.

---

18. **Ananse** (ä nän′ sē).

Whack! Whack!

Lying in bed in the dark thinking about it all as it would happen tomorrow, he clenched his teeth and tensed his buttocks in imaginary pain.

Whack! Whack! Whack!

Suddenly, in his little room, under his thin cotton sheet, he began to cry. Because he felt the sharp, lancing pain already cutting into him. Because of Basu and Simpson and the thermometer. For all the things he wanted to do and be which would never happen. For all the good men they had told them about—Jesus Christ, Mohammed, and George Washington, who never told a lie. For Florence Nightingale[19] and David Livingstone.[20] For Kagawa,[21] the Japanese man, for Gandhi,[22] and for Kwegyir Aggrey,[23] the African. Oh-ee, oh-ee. Because he knew he would never be as straight and strong and true as the school song said they should be. He saw, for the first time, what this thing would be like, becoming a man. He touched the edge of an inconsolable eternal grief. Oh-ee, oh-ee; always, he felt, always I shall be a disgrace to the nation and the race.

His mother passed by his bedroom door, slowly dragging her slippered feet as she always did. He pushed his face into his wet pillow to stifle his sobs, but she had heard him. She came in and switched on the light.

"What is the matter with you, my son?"

He pushed his face farther into his pillow.

"Nothing," he said, muffled and choking.

"You have been looking like a sick fowl all afternoon," she continued.

She advanced and put the back of her moist, cool fingers against the side of his neck.

"You have got fever," she exclaimed. "I'll get something from the kitchen."

When she had gone out, Kojo dried his tears and turned the dry side of the pillow up. His mother reappeared with a thermometer in one hand and some quinine mixture in the other.

"Oh, take it away, take it away," he shouted, pointing to her right hand and shutting his eyes tightly.

"All right, all right," she said, slipping the thermometer into her bosom.

He is a queer boy, she thought, with pride and a little fear as she watched him drink the clear, bitter fluid.

She then stood by him and held his head against her broad thigh as he sat up on the low bed, and she stroked his face. She knew he had been crying but did not ask him why, because she was sure he would not tell her. She knew he was learning, first slowly and now quickly, and she would soon cease to be his mother and be only one of the womenfolk in the family. Such a short time, she thought, when they are really yours and tell you everything. She sighed and slowly eased his sleeping head down gently.

The next day Kojo got to school early and set to things briskly. He told Bandele that he was going to confess but would not name him. He half hoped he would join him. But Bandele had said, threateningly, that he had better not mention his name, let him go and be a Boy Scout on his own. The sneer strengthened him, and he went off to the lab. He met Mr. Abu and asked for Vernier. Abu said Vernier was busy and what was the matter, anyhow.

---

19. **Florence Nightingale** (1820–1910): English nurse regarded as the founder of modern nursing.
20. **David Livingstone** (1813–1873): Scottish missionary and explorer in Africa.
21. **Kagawa** (kä′ gä wä′) (1888–1960): Japanese pacifist, social reformer, and Christian evangelist.
22. **Gandhi** (gän′ dē) (1869–1948): Hindu nationalist leader who preached nonviolence.
23. **Kwegyir Aggrey** (kweg′ yēr äg′ grā) (1875–1927): West African educator and orator.

"I broke the thermometer yesterday," Kojo said in a businesslike manner.

Abu put down the glassware he was carrying.

"Well, I never!" he said. "What do you think you will gain by this?"

"I broke it," Kojo repeated.

"Basu broke it," Abu said impatiently. "Sorie got him to confess, and Basu himself came here this morning and told the science master and myself that he knew now that he had knocked the thermometer by mistake when he came in early yesterday afternoon.

He had not turned round to look, but he had definitely heard a tinkle as he walked by. Someone must have picked it up and put it in the waste bin. The whole matter is settled, the palaver finished."

He tapped a barometer on the wall and, squinting, read the pressure. He turned again to Kojo.

"I should normally have expected him to say so yesterday and save you boys missing the game. But there you are," he added, shrugging and trying to look reasonable, "you cannot hope for too much from a Syrian boy."

Thinking About the Story

A PERSONAL RESPONSE

sharing impressions

1. How does the ending of this story make you feel? Jot down your impressions in your journal.

constructing interpretations

2. What do you think is the main reason that Basu confesses to breaking the thermometer?

Think about
- the kind of person he is
- his relationships with the other students

3. Who do you think suffers more from this experience, Basu or Kojo? Support your answer with references to the story.

4. Describe the lessons that you think Kojo learns about human relationships in this story.

5. How might this story have ended if Kojo had spoken to Mr. Vernier instead of to Mr. Abu?

6. Speculate about why the writer might have chosen a school laboratory as the setting of this story.

> **Think about**
> - a laboratory as a place where experiments and tests are conducted
> - your own experiences in a school laboratory

7. While comforting Basu, Vernier quotes a line from Shakespeare's play *Hamlet*: "To thine own self be true." Which character in this story do you think comes closest to living up to this standard of conduct? Support your view with details from the story.

Analyzing the Writer's Craft

CONFLICT

Think about Kojo's moments of decision in this story.

Building a Literary Vocabulary. Conflict is a struggle between opposing forces. An external conflict involves a character pitted against an outside force—nature, a physical obstacle, or another character. An internal conflict is one that occurs between opposing tendencies within a character. In "Games at Twilight," for example, the external conflict is between Ravi and Raghu, whom Ravi is trying to elude. An internal conflict is between Ravi's determination to win the game and his fear of staying in the shed.

Application: Analyzing Internal Conflict. Get together with a partner and go back through this story, looking for passages that suggest Kojo's internal conflicts. Identify the tendencies within Kojo that are in opposition. Then evaluate how Kojo's character develops as a result of his internal conflicts.

Connecting Reading and Writing

1. Write an **autobiographical essay** in which Kojo explains why he lets Mr. Abu have the final say at the end of the story.

Option: Have Kojo explain his conduct in a **journal entry** written after his confrontation with Mr. Abu.

2. Imagine that you are on a committee appointed to select the Teacher of the Year in Sierra Leone and that Mr. Vernier is a candidate for that honor. Write a **memo** to your committee chairperson expressing your views of the candidate.

Option: Write a **letter** to Mr. Vernier explaining why you chose or rejected him for this honor.

3. Write the **dialogue** that may have taken place between Sorie and Basu when Basu agrees to confess to breaking the thermometer.

Option: Write a **monologue** in which Sorie tells his followers about his talk with Basu.

4. Write a draft of a **speech** to be delivered to your class about peer pressure at school. Include examples from this story.

Option: Write an **article** for your high school newspaper in which you support your ideas about peer pressure with examples from this story.

No Dogs Bark

JUAN RULFO   1918–1986   MEXICO

A biography of Rulfo appears on page 751.

Approaching the Story

This story by Juan Rulfo (hwän $\overline{oo}$l' fô) is told almost completely through dialogue. From the characters' speech you must make inferences about their relationship and the events they have experienced. The beginning of the story finds a father in the unusual situation of carrying his son on his back.

Connecting Writing and Reading

If you found yourself in serious trouble—for example, if you hurt someone in a fight or caused a fatal automobile accident—what would you expect your parents or guardians to do?

disown you   turn you in to the police
comfort you   pay damages to the victim
shame you   blame themselves
take no action   get legal or medical help for you

In your journal, jot down as many of these answers as apply; add others if you wish. As you read, compare your expectations with the reactions of the parent in this story.

YOU UP THERE, Ignacio![1] Don't you hear something or see a light somewhere?"

"I can't see a thing."

"We ought to be near now."

"Yes, but I can't hear a thing."

"Look hard. Poor Ignacio."

The long black shadow of the men kept moving up and down, climbing over rocks, diminishing and increasing as it advanced along the edge of the arroyo.[2] It was a single, reeling shadow.

The moon came out of the earth like a round flare.

"We should be getting to that town, Ignacio. Your ears are uncovered, so try to see if you can't hear dogs barking. Remember they told us Tonaya[3] was right behind the mountain. And we left the mountain hours ago. Remember, Ignacio?"

"Yes, but I don't see a sign of anything."

"I'm getting tired."

"Put me down."

The old man backed up to a thick wall and shifted his load but didn't let it down from his shoulders. Though his legs were buckling on him, he didn't want to sit down, because then he would be unable to lift his son's body, which they had helped to sling on his back hours ago. He had carried him all this way.

"How do you feel?"

"Bad."

Ignacio didn't talk much. Less and less all the time. Now and then he seemed to sleep. At times he seemed to be cold. He trembled. When the trembling seized him, his feet dug into his father's flanks like spurs. Then his hands, clasped around his father's neck, clutched at the head and shook it as if it were a rattle.

The father gritted his teeth so he wouldn't bite his tongue, and when the shaking was over, he asked, "Does it hurt a lot?"

"Some," Ignacio answered.

First Ignacio had said, "Put me down here—leave me here—you go on alone. I'll catch up with you tomorrow or as soon as I get a little better." He'd said this some fifty times. Now he didn't say it.

There was the moon. Facing them. A large red moon that filled their eyes with light and stretched and darkened its shadow over the earth.

"I can't see where I'm going anymore," the father said.

No answer.

The son up there was illumined by the moon. His face, discolored, bloodless, reflected the opaque light. And he here below.

"Did you hear me, Ignacio? I tell you, I can't see very well."

No answer.

Falteringly, the father continued. He hunched his body over, then straightened up to stumble on again.

"This is no road. They told us Tonaya was behind the hill. We've passed the hill. And you can't see Tonaya or hear any sound that would tell us it is close. Why won't you tell me what you see up there, Ignacio?"

"Put me down, Father."

"Do you feel bad?"

---

1. **Ignacio** (ēg nä′ sē ô̂).
2. **arroyo** (ä rô̂′ yô̂): a narrow ravine where water once flowed.
3. **Tonaya** (tô̂ nä′ yä).

"Yes."

"I'll get you to Tonaya. There I'll find somebody to take care of you. They say there's a doctor in the town. I'll take you to him. I've already carried you for hours, and I'm not going to leave you lying here now for somebody to finish off."

He staggered a little. He took two or three steps to the side, then straightened up again.

"I'll get you to Tonaya."

"Let me down."

His voice was faint, scarcely a murmur. "I want to sleep a little."

"Sleep up there. After all, I've got a good hold on you."

The moon was rising, almost blue, in a clear sky. Now the old man's face, drenched with sweat, was flooded with light. He lowered his eyes so he wouldn't have to look straight ahead, since he couldn't bend his head, tightly gripped in his son's hands.

"I'm not doing all this for you. I'm doing it for your dead mother. Because you were her son. That's why I'm doing it. She would've haunted me if I'd left you lying where I found you and hadn't picked you up and carried you to be cured as I'm doing. She's the one who gives me courage, not you. From the first you've caused me nothing but trouble, humiliation, and shame."

He sweated as he talked. But the night wind dried his sweat. And over the dry sweat, he sweated again.

"I'll break my back, but I'll get to Tonaya with you so they can ease those wounds you got. I'm sure as soon as you feel well, you'll go back to your bad ways. But that doesn't matter to me anymore. As long as you go far away, where I won't hear anything more of you. As long as you do that—because as far as I'm concerned, you aren't my son anymore. I've cursed the blood you got from me. My part of it I've cursed. I said, 'Let the blood I gave him rot in his kidneys.' I said it when I heard you'd taken to the roads, robbing and killing people—good people. My old friend Tranquilino,[4] for instance. The one who baptized you. The one who gave you your name. Even he had the bad luck to run into you. From that time on I said, 'That one cannot be my son.'"

"See if you can't see something now. Or hear something. You'll have to do it from up there, because I feel deaf."

"I don't see anything."

"Too bad for you, Ignacio."

"I'm thirsty."

"You'll have to stand it. We must be near now. Because it's now very late at night, they must've turned out the lights in the town. But at least you should hear dogs barking. Try to hear."

"Give me some water."

"There's no water here. Just stones. You'll have to stand it. Even if there was water, I wouldn't let you down to drink. There's nobody to help me lift you up again, and I can't do it alone."

"I'm awfully thirsty and sleepy."

"I remember when you were born. You were that way then. You woke up hungry and ate and went back to sleep. Your mother had to give you water because you'd finished all her milk. You couldn't be filled up. And you were always mad and yelling. I never thought that in time this madness would go to your head. But it did. Your mother, may she rest in peace, wanted you to grow up strong. She thought when you grew up, you'd look after her. She only had you. The other child she tried to give birth to killed her. And you would've killed her again if she'd lived till now."

The man on his back stopped gouging with his knees. His feet began to swing loosely from side to side. And it seemed to the father that Ignacio's head, up there, was shaking as if he were sobbing.

---

4. Tranquilino (trän kē lē′ nô).

On his hair he felt thick drops fall.

"Are you crying, Ignacio? The memory of your mother makes you cry, doesn't it? But you never did anything for her. You always repaid us badly. Somehow your body got filled with evil instead of affection. And now you see? They've wounded it. What happened to your friends? They were all killed. Only they didn't have anybody. They might well have said, 'We have nobody to be concerned about.' But you, Ignacio?"

At last, the town. He saw roofs shining in the moonlight. He felt his son's weight crushing him as the back of his knees buckled in a final effort. When he reached the first dwelling, he leaned against the wall by the sidewalk. He slipped the body off, dangling, as if it had been wrenched from him.

With difficulty he unpried his son's fingers from around his neck. When he was free, he heard the dogs barking everywhere.

"And you didn't hear them, Ignacio?" he said. "You didn't even help me listen."

*T*hinking About the Story

A PERSONAL RESPONSE

sharing
impressions

1. How did you feel after reading this story? Jot down your impressions in your journal.

constructing
interpretations

2. Why do you think Ignacio does not tell his father that he hears dogs barking?

3. How would you judge Ignacio's father as a parent?

Think about

- the ordeal of carrying Ignacio to Tonaya
- what he feels toward Ignacio
- how the father's reactions to serious trouble compare with those you would expect from your parents or guardians

4. If Ignacio were to recover, do you think he would change? Explain your answer.

5. How would you describe the relationship between mood and setting in this story?

Think about
- mood as the feeling, or atmosphere, that the writer creates for the reader
- details of the setting, such as the rising moon, the arroyo, and the rocks that must be climbed

6. Most of what you learn about the characters is implied rather than stated. How successful did you find this method of storytelling?

7. George D. Schade, the translator of this story, describes a dominant theme of Rulfo's work in the following way: "Man is abject and lonely. He seeks communication but usually is thwarted." Discuss how this theme is brought out in "No Dogs Bark" and whether this view of the human condition is accurate in your opinion.

Connecting Reading and Writing

1. Write an **internal monologue** that reveals what Ignacio is thinking as his father carries him to Tonaya.

Option: Imagine that Ignacio recovers from his wounds. Compose a **letter** that he might write to his father shortly after his recovery.

2. Rewrite your own version of this **short story**, providing explanations of events and descriptions of characters that Rulfo does not. With your classmates create a collection of story variations to share with other English classes.

Option: Write your version of the story as a **screenplay**. Use flashbacks to depict the events that you have added to Rulfo's story.

3. Create an **editorial** that Rulfo might write about theories that attribute juvenile crime to parental neglect or about laws that would punish parents for their children's offenses.

Option: Write a **speech** that Rulfo might give to a group of youths at a juvenile detention center.

4. Compare this story with "Luvina" or another story from Rulfo's collection *The Burning Plain*. Design a **chart** for display in your school library that shows similarities and differences in plot, characters, setting, mood, and theme.

Option: Compare the two stories in a **report** for students interested in reading Rulfo's works.

The Interview

RUTH PRAWER JHABVALA   born 1927   GERMANY/INDIA

A biography of Jhabvala appears on page 744.

Approaching the Story

The narrator of this story by Ruth Prawer Jhabvala (prä′ wer jäb wä′ lä) is a young Indian man who belongs to a typical urban Indian family. Marriages in India are generally arranged for young people, who, after marrying, live with the husband's parents. In this highly traditional society, women are taught to be subservient to men, and women's roles outside the home are few. Within the home, the mother or the wife of an oldest son dominates the extended family, supervising the cooking, making decisions, and keeping the keys. Many educated Indian men seek work at government jobs that require fluent English, a lingering effect of the long British occupation of India.

Connecting Writing and Reading

Make a list of things that you do only because they are expected of you, not because you really want to do them. In your journal describe how it feels to be forced to meet someone else's expectations for you. As you read, compare your feelings to the narrator's feelings about his family's expectations for him.

I AM ALWAYS very careful of my appearance, so you could not say that I spent much more time than usual over myself that morning. I trimmed and oiled my mustache, but then I often do that; I always like it to look very neat, like Raj Kapoor's,[1] the film star's. My sister-in-law and my wife were watching me, my sister-in-law smiling and resting one hand on her hip and my wife only looking anxious. I knew why she was anxious. All night she had been whispering to me, saying, "Get this job and take me away to live somewhere alone—only you and I and the children." I had answered, "Yes," because I wanted to go to sleep. I don't know where and why she has taken this notion that we should go and live alone.

When I had finished combing my hair, I sat on the floor, and my sister-in-law brought me my food on a tray. It may sound strange that my sister-in-law, and not my wife, should serve me, but it is so in our house. It used to be my mother who brought me my food, even after I was married; she would never allow my wife to do this for me, though my wife wanted to very much. Then, when my mother got so old, my sister-in-law began to serve me. I know that my wife feels deeply hurt by this, but she doesn't dare say anything. My mother really doesn't notice things anymore; otherwise, she certainly would not allow my sister-in-law to serve me. She always used to be very jealous of this privilege, though she never cared who served my brother. Now she has become so old that she can hardly see anything, and most of the time she sits in the corner by the family trunks and folds and strokes her pieces of cloth. For years now she has been collecting pieces of cloth. Some of them are very old and dirty, but she doesn't care. Nobody else is allowed to touch them, and once, I remember, there was a great quarrel because my wife had taken one of them to make a dress for our child. My mother shouted at her—it was terrible to hear her, but then she has never liked my wife—and my wife was very much afraid and cried and tried to excuse herself. I hit her across the face, not very hard and not because I wanted to, but only to satisfy my mother. It seemed to quiet the old woman, and she went back to folding and stroking her pieces of cloth.

All the time I was eating, I could feel my sister-in-law looking at me and smiling. It made me uncomfortable. I thought she might be smiling because she knew I wouldn't get the job for which I had to go and be interviewed that day. I also knew I wouldn't get it, but I didn't like her smiling like that, as if she were saying, "You see, you will always have to be dependent on us." It is clearly my brother's duty to keep me and my family until I can get work and contribute my own earnings to the household, so there is no need for smiling. But it is true that I am more dependent on her now than on anyone else. Lately, my sister-in-law has become more and more the most important person in the house, and now she even keeps the keys and the household stores. At first, I didn't like this. As long as my mother was managing the household, I was sure of getting many extra tidbits. But now I find that my sister-in-law is also very kind to me—much more kind than she is to her husband. It is not for him that she saves the tidbits or for her children. She never says anything when she gives them to me, but she smiles, and then I feel confused and rather embarrassed. My wife has noticed what she does for me.

I have found that women are usually kind to me. I think they realize that I am a rather sensitive person and that therefore I must be treated gently. My mother has always treated me very gently. I am her youngest child, and I am fifteen years younger than my brother, who

---

1. **Raj Kapoor's** (räj ku poo̅rz′).

is next to me. (She did have several children in between us, but they all died.) Right from the time when I was a tiny baby, she understood that I needed greater care and tenderness than other children. She always made me sleep close beside her in the night, and in the day I usually sat with her and my grandmother and my widowed aunt, who were also very fond of me. When I got bigger, my father sometimes wanted to take me to help in his stall (he had a little grocer's stall, where he sold lentils and rice and cheap cigarettes and colored drinks in bottles), but my mother and grandmother and aunt never liked to let me go. Once, I remember, he did take me with him, and he made me pour some lentils out of paper bags into a tin. I rather liked pouring the lentils—they made such a nice noise as they landed in the tin—but suddenly my mother came and was very angry with my father for making me do this work. She took me home at once, and when she told my grandmother and aunt what had happened, they stroked me and kissed me, and then they gave me a beautiful hot fritter to eat. The fact is, right from childhood I have been a person who needs a lot of peace and rest, and my food, too, has to be rather more delicate than that of other people. I have often tried to explain this to my wife, but as she is not very intelligent, she doesn't seem to understand.

Now my wife was watching me while I ate. She was squatting on the floor, washing our youngest baby; the child's head was in her lap, and all one could see of it was the back of its naked legs. My wife did not watch me as openly as my sister-in-law did, but from time to time she raised her eyes to me, looking very worried and troubled. She, too, was thinking about the job for which I was going to be interviewed, but she was anxious that I should get it. I cannot imagine why she wanted us to go and live alone, when she knew that it was not possible and never would be.

And even if it were possible, I would not like it. I cannot leave my mother, and I do not think I would like to live away from my sister-in-law. I often look at her, and it makes me happy. Even though she is not young anymore, she is still beautiful. She is tall, with big hips and eyes that flash. She often gets angry, and then she is the most beautiful of all. Her eyes look like fire, and she shows all her teeth, which are very strong and white, and her head is proud, with the black hair flying loose. My wife is not beautiful at all. I was very disappointed in her when they first married me to her. Now I have grown used to her, and I even like her because she is so good and quiet and never troubles me at all. But I don't think anybody else in our house likes her. My sister-in-law always calls her "that beauty," and she makes her do all the most difficult household tasks. She shouts at her and abuses her, which is not right because my wife has never done anything to her and has always treated her with respect. But I cannot interfere in their quarrels.

I finished my meal and then I was ready to go, though I did not want to. My mother blessed me, and my sister-in-law looked at me over her shoulder, and her great eyes flashed with laughter. I did not look at my wife, who was still squatting on the floor, but I knew she was pleading with me to get the job. Even as I walked down the stairs, I knew what would happen at the interview. I had been to so many during the past few months, and the same thing always happened. Of course, I know I have to work. My last position was in an insurance office, and all day they made me sit at a desk and write figures. What pleasure could there be for me in that? I am a very thoughtful person, and I always like to sit and think my own thoughts. But in that office, my thinking sometimes caused me to make mistakes over the figures, and then they were very angry with me. I was always afraid of their anger, and I begged their forgiveness and admitted that I was much at fault. But the last time they would not forgive me again, although I begged many times and cried what a faulty, bad man I was and what good men they were, and how they were my mother and my father, and how I looked only to them for my life and the lives of my children. But when they still said I must go, I saw that the work there was really finished, so I stopped crying. I went into the cloakroom and combed my hair and folded my soap in my towel, and then I took my money from the accountant without a word and left the office with my eyes lowered. But I was no longer afraid, because what is finished is finished, and my brother still had work and probably one day I would get another job.

Ever since then, my brother has been trying to get me into government service. He himself is a clerk in government service and enjoys many advantages. Every five years, he gets an increase of ten rupees[2] in his salary. He has ten days' sick leave in the year, and when he retires he will get a pension. It would be good for me to have such a job, but it is difficult to get, because first there is an interview, at which important people sit at a desk and ask many questions. Because I am afraid of them, I cannot understand properly what they are saying, but I answer what I think they want me to answer. But it seems that my answers are somehow not the right ones, because they have not given me a job.

Now, as I walked down the stairs, I wished I could go to the cinema instead. If I had had ten annas,[3] perhaps I would have gone; it was just time for the morning show. The young clerks and the students would be collecting in a queue outside the cinema now. They would be standing and not talking much, holding their ten annas and waiting for the box office to open. I enjoy those morning shows, perhaps because the people who come to them are all young men, like myself—all silent and rather

sad. I am often sad; it would even be right to say that I am sad most of the time. But when the film begins, I am happy. I love to see the beautiful women dressed in golden clothes, with heavy earrings, and necklaces, and bracelets covering their arms, and to see their handsome lovers, who are all the things I would like to be. And when they sing their love songs, so full of deep feelings, the tears sometimes come into my eyes because I am so happy. After the film is over, I never go home straightway, but I walk around the streets and think about how wonderful life could be.

When I arrived at the place where the interview was, I had to walk down many corridors and ask directions from many peons before I could find the right room. The peons were all rude to me because they knew what I had come for. They lounged back on benches outside the offices, and when I asked them, they looked me up and down before answering and sometimes made jokes about me to one another. But I was very polite to them, for even though they were only peons, they had uniforms and jobs and belonged here, whereas I did not. At last I came to the room where I had to wait. Many others were already sitting there, on chairs drawn up against the wall all around the room. No one was talking. I found a chair, and after a while an official came in with a list and asked if anyone else had come. I got up and he asked my name, and then he looked down the list and made a tick with a pencil. "Why are you late?" he asked me very sternly. I begged pardon and told him the bus in which I had come had had an accident. He said, "When you are called for an interview, you have to be here exactly on time or your

<hr />

2. **rupees** (r$\overline{oo}$ pēz′): The rupee is the basic monetary unit of India.

3. **annas** (a′ nəz): The anna is a former monetary unit of India equal to one-sixteenth of a rupee.

name is crossed off the list." I begged pardon again and asked him very humbly please not to cross me off this time. I knew that all the others were listening, even though none of them looked at us. He said some more things to me very scornfully, but in the end he said, "Wait here. When your name is called, you must go in at once."

I didn't count the number of people waiting in the room, but there were a great many. Perhaps there was one job free, perhaps two or three. As I sat there, I began to feel the others all hoping anxiously that they might get the job, so I became worried and anxious, too. I stared around and tried to put my mind on something else. The walls of the room were painted green halfway up and white above that, and were quite bare. There was a fan turning from the ceiling, but it didn't give much breeze. An interview was going on behind the big door. One by one, we would all be called in there and have the door closed behind us.

I began to worry desperately. It always happens like this. When I come to an interview, I never want the job at all, but when I see all the others waiting and worrying, I want it terribly. Yet at the same time I know, deep down, that I don't want it. I know it would only be the same thing over again: writing figures and making mistakes and then being afraid when they found out. And there would be a superior officer in my office to whom I would have to be very deferential, and every time I saw him or heard his voice, I would begin to be afraid that he had found out something against me. For weeks and months I would sit and write figures, getting wearier of it and wearier, and thinking my own thoughts more and more. Then the mistakes would come, and my superior officer would be angry.

My brother never makes mistakes. For years he has been sitting in the same office, writing figures, being deferential to his superior officer, and concentrating very hard on his work. But, nevertheless, he is afraid of the same thing—a mistake that will make them angry with him and cost him his job. I think it is right for him to be afraid, for what would become of us all if he also lost his job? It is not the same with me. I believe I am afraid to lose my job only because that is a thing of which one is expected to be afraid. When I have actually lost it, I am really relieved. But this is not surprising, because I *am* very different from my brother; even in appearance I am different. As I have said, he is fifteen years older than I, but even when he was my age, he never looked as I do. My appearance has always attracted others; and right up to the time I was married, my mother used to stroke my hair and my face and say many tender things to me. Once when I was walking on my way to school through the bazaar, a man called to me very softly; and when I came, he gave me a ripe mango and said, "You are beautiful, beautiful." He looked at me in an odd, kind way and wanted me to go with him to his house, in another part of the city. I love wearing fine clothes—especially very thin white muslin kurtas[4] that have been freshly washed and starched and are embroidered at the shoulders. Sometimes I also use scent—a fine khas[5] smell—and my hair oil also smells of khas. Several years ago, just after I was married, there was a handsome teenage girl who lived in the tailor's shop opposite our house and who used to wait for me and follow me whenever I went out. But it is my brother, not I, who is married to a beautiful wife, and this has always seemed most unfair.

The big closed door opened, and the man who had been in there for an interview came out. We all looked at him, but he walked out

---

4. kurtas (kʉrt′ əz): knee-length collarless shirts worn over pajamas by men in India.
5. khas (kus): fragrant grass used in scented oil.

in a great hurry, with a preoccupied expression on his face. I could feel the anxiety in the other men getting stronger, and mine, too. The official with the list came, and we all looked up at him. He read off another name, and the man whose name was called jumped up from his chair. He started forward, but then he was brought up short by his dhoti,[6] which had got caught on a nail in the chair. As soon as he realized what had happened, he became very agitated, and when he tried to disentangle himself, his fingers shook so much that he could not get the dhoti off the nail. The official watched him coldly and said, "Hurry, now! Do you think the gentlemen will wait for as long as you please?" In his confusion, the man dropped his umbrella, and then he tried to disentangle the dhoti and pick up the umbrella at the same time. When he could not get the dhoti loose, he became so desperate that he pulled at the cloth and ripped it free. It was a pity to see the dhoti torn, because it was a new one, which he was probably wearing for the first time and had put on specially for the interview. He clasped his umbrella to his chest and scurried into the interviewing room with his dhoti hanging about his legs and his face swollen with embarrassment and confusion.

We all sat and waited. The fan, which seemed to be a very old one, made a creaking noise. One man kept cracking his finger joints—*tik*, we heard, *tik*. All the rest of us kept very still. From time to time, the official with the list came in and walked around the room very slowly, tapping his list, and then we all looked down at our feet, and the man even stopped cracking his fingers. A faint and muffled sound of voices came from behind the closed door. Sometimes a voice was raised, but even then I could not make out what was being said, though I strained hard.

My previous interview was very unpleasant for me. One of the people who were interviewing took a dislike to me and shouted at me

very loudly. He was a large, fat man who wore an English suit. His teeth were quite yellow, and when he became angry and shouted he showed them all, and even though I was very upset, I couldn't help looking at them and wondering how they had become so yellow. I don't know why he was angry. He shouted, "Good God, man! Can't you understand what's said to you?" It was true I could not understand, but I had been trying hard to answer well. What else did he expect of me? Probably there was something in my appearance he did not like. It happens that way sometimes—they take a dislike to you, and then, of course, there is nothing you can do.

Now the thought of the man with the yellow teeth made me more anxious than ever. I need great calm in my life. Whenever anything worries me too much, I have to cast the thought of it off immediately; otherwise, there is a danger that I may become ill. I felt now as if I were about to become very ill. All my limbs were itching, so that it was difficult for me to sit still, and I could feel blood rushing into my brain. I knew it was this room that was doing me so much harm—the waiting, silent men; the noise from the fan; the official with the list, walking up and down, tapping his list or striking it against his thigh; and the big closed door behind which the interview was going on. I felt a great need to get up and go away. I *didn't* want the job. I wasn't even thinking about it anymore—only about how to avoid having to sit here and wait.

Now the door opened again, and the man with the torn dhoti came out. He was biting his lip and scratching the back of his neck, and he, too, walked straight out without looking at us at all. The big door of the interviewing room was left slightly open for a moment, and

---

6. dhoti (dō′ tē): typical garment worn by Indian men, consisting of cloth tied around the waist and extending down to the ankles.

I could see a man's arm in a white shirt sleeve and part of the back of his head. His shirt was very white and of good material, and his ears stood away from his head so that one could see how his spectacles fitted over the backs of his ears. I suddenly realized that this man would be my enemy and that he would make things very difficult for me and perhaps even shout at me. Then I knew it was no use for me to stay there. The official with the list came back, and a panic seized me that he would read out my name. I rose quickly, murmuring, "Please excuse me—bathroom," and went out. I heard the official with the list call after me, "Hey, Mister, where are you going?" so I lowered my head and walked faster. I would have started to run, but that might have caused some kind of suspicion, so I just walked as fast as I could down the stairs and right out of the building. There, at last, I was able to stop and take a deep breath, and I felt much better.

I stood still only for a minute, and then I started off again, though not in any particular direction. There were a great many clerks and peons moving past me in the street, hurrying from one office building to another, with files and papers under their arms. Everyone seemed to have something to do. In the next block, I found a little park, and I was glad to see people like myself, who had nothing to do, sitting under the trees or in any other patch of shade they could find. But I couldn't sit there; it was too close to the office blocks, and any moment someone might come up and say to me, "Why did you go away?" So I walked farther. I was feeling quite lighthearted with relief over having escaped the interview.

At last I came to a row of eating stalls, and I sat down on a wooden bench outside one of them, which was called the Paris Hotel, and asked for tea. I felt badly in need of tea, and since I intended to walk part of the way home, I was in a position to pay for it. There were two Sikhs[7] sitting at the end of my bench who were eating with great appetite, dipping their hands very rapidly into brass bowls. Between mouthfuls, they exchanged remarks with the proprietor of the Paris Hotel, who sat high up inside his stall, stirring a big brass pot in which he was cooking the day's food. He was chewing a betel leaf, and from time to time he very skillfully spat the red betel juice far over the cooking pot and onto the ground between the wooden benches and tables.

I sat quietly at my end of the bench and drank my tea. The food smelled good, and it made me realize that I was hungry. I made a calculation and decided that if I walked all the way home, I could afford a little cake. (I am very fond of sweet things.) The cake was not very new, but it had a beautiful piece of bright orange peel inside it. What I wanted to do when I got home was to lie down at once and not wake up again until the next morning. That way, no one would be able to ask me any questions. By not looking at my wife at all I would be able to avoid the question in her eyes. I would not look at my sister-in-law, either, but she would be smiling—that I knew—leaning against the wall, with her hand on her hip, and looking at me and smiling. She would know that I had run away, but she would not say anything.

Let her know! What did it matter? It was true I had no job and no immediate prospect of getting one. It was true that I was dependent on my brother. Everybody knew that. There is no shame in it; there are many people without jobs. And she had been so kind to me up till now that there was no reason she should not continue to be kind to me.

The Sikhs at the end of the bench had finished eating. They licked their fingers and

---

7. Sikhs (sēks): members of a Hindu religious sect based on belief in one God and on rejection of the caste system, a rigid system of class distinctions.

belched deeply, the way one does after a good meal. They started to joke and laugh with the proprietor. I sat quiet and alone at my end of the bench. Of course, they did not laugh and joke with me, for they knew that I was superior to them; they work with their hands, whereas I am a lettered man who does not have to sweat for a living but sits on a chair in an office and writes figures and can speak in English. My brother is very proud of his superiority, and he has great contempt for carpenters and mechanics and such people. I, too, am proud of being a lettered man, but when I listened to the Sikhs laughing and joking, it occurred to me that perhaps their life was happier than mine. It was a thought that had come to me before. There is a carpenter who lives downstairs in our house, and though he is poor, there is always great eating in his house, and many people come, and I hear them laughing and singing and even dancing. The carpenter is a big, strong man, and he always looks happy, never anxious and sick with worry the way my brother does. To be sure, he doesn't wear shoes and clean, white clothes as my brother and I do, nor does he speak any English, but all the same he is happy. I don't think he gets weary of his work, and he doesn't look like a man who is afraid of his superior officers.

I put the ignorant carpenter out of my mind and thought again of my sister-in-law. If I were kind to her, I decided, she would really be kind to me someday. I became quite excited at this idea. Then I would know whether she is as soft and yet as strong as she looks. And I would know about her mouth, with the big, strong teeth. Her tongue and palate are very pink—just the color of the pink satin blouse she wears on festive occasions. And this satin has often made me think also of how smooth and warm her skin would feel. Her eyes would be shut and perhaps there would be tears on the lashes, and she would be smiling but in a different sort of way. I became very excited when I thought of it, but then the excitement passed and I was sad. I thought of my wife, who is thin and not beautiful and is without excitement. But she does whatever I want and always tries to please me. I thought of her whispering to me in the night, "Take me away to live somewhere alone—only you and I and the children." That can never be, and so always she will have to be unhappy.

Sitting on that bench, I grew more and more sad when I thought of her being unhappy, because it is not only she who is unhappy but I also and many others. Everywhere there is unhappiness. I thought of the man whose new dhoti had been torn and who would now have to go home and sew it carefully, so that the tear would not be seen. I thought of all those other men sitting and waiting to be interviewed, all but one or two of whom would not get the job for which they had come and so would have to go on to another interview and another and another, to sit and wait and be anxious. And my brother, who has a job but is frightened that he will lose it—and my mother, who is so old that she can only sit on the floor and stroke her pieces of cloth—and my sister-in-law, who is warm and strong and does not care for her husband. Yet life could be so different. When I go to the cinema and hear the beautiful songs they sing, I know how different it could be; and also sometimes, when I sit alone and think my thoughts, I have a feeling that everything could be truly beautiful. But now my tea was finished and also my cake, and I wished I had not bought them, because it was a long way to walk home and I was tired.

Thinking About the Story

A PERSONAL RESPONSE

*sharing
impressions*

1. How do you feel about the narrator of the story? Jot down your reaction in your journal.

*constructing
interpretations*

2. How well do you think the narrator understands himself?
   Think about
   • qualities he directly ascribes to himself
   • qualities indirectly revealed in his internal monologue
   • the reasons he gives for avoiding the interview
   • the things that give him pleasure

3. Evaluate the narrator's family relationships.
   Think about
   • the expectations of his family
   • his role as a dependent brother in the household
   • the nature of his relationship with his wife
   • his comments about his sister-in-law

4. How do you account for the narrator's fascination with movies? Cite examples to support your response.

5. Is the narrator's tendency to be a "thoughtful person" a strength or weakness in his case?

A CREATIVE RESPONSE

6. If the narrator had gone through the interview and been hired for the job, how might the story have ended?

A CRITICAL RESPONSE

7. Use details from "The Interview" to explain the story's message about human nature.

8. Which stories that you have read so far in this unit seem most similar to this story in their views of the human condition? Explain.

Analyzing the Writer's Craft

POINT OF VIEW AND NARRATOR

Think about the information the narrator provides about himself and his family and whether his observations seem accurate.

Building a Literary Vocabulary. Point of view refers to the narrative method, or kind of narrator, used in a short story, novel, or nonfiction selection. "The Interview" is written from the first-person point of view. The narrator is the main character in the story, and the events in the story are seen through his eyes. Because the first-person point of view reveals only the narrator's view—of himself, his family relationships, and events in the story—the reader may find that the observations are colored or distorted by his perspective.

Application: Understanding Point of View and Narrator. Read the following statements that the narrator makes. With a classmate, discuss how the narrator's perceptions in each statement compare with your own.

1. "I am always very careful of my appearance. . . . I always like it [my mustache] to look very neat, like Raj Kapoor's, the film star's."

2. "I think they [women] realize that I am a rather sensitive person and that therefore I must be treated gently."

3. "I believe I am afraid to lose my job only because that is a thing of which one is expected to be afraid. When I have actually lost it, I am really relieved."

4. "I, too, am proud of being a lettered man, but when I listened to the Sikhs laughing and joking, it occurred to me that perhaps their life was happier than mine."

Connecting Reading and Writing

1. Put yourself in the role of an employment counselor to whom the young man in the story comes for advice. Write a **dialogue** to share with the class in which you and the young man discuss his interests, skills, and goals.

Option: Imagine that the young man has decided to apply for a vocational program and needs a reference. Write a **recommendation** for him.

2. Write a **narrative** for your teacher and classmates from the point of view of the wife in the story. Include such information as her thoughts and feelings about being in that household, her goals for her husband, and her own dreams.

Option: Record the thoughts and feelings of the narrator's wife in a **diary entry** that she might write.

3. Read more about contemporary Indian society and write an **expository essay** for publication in a travel magazine in which you discuss the impact of Western values, such as ambition, on traditional Indian life.

Option: Write **notes** for an oral presentation on this subject for your class.

The Happy Man

NAGUIB MAHFOUZ   born 1911   EGYPT

A biography of Mahfouz appears on page 746.

Approaching the Story

Imagine that you awake one morning to find that a magical change has occurred within you. Suddenly, you feel so incredibly happy that all worries and troubles have lost their power to affect you. The main character in the following story by Naguib Mahfouz (nu gēb′ màh foōz′) finds himself in this situation.

H E WOKE UP in the morning and discovered that he was happy. "What's this?" he asked himself. He could not think of any word which described his state of mind more accurately and precisely than *happy*. This was distinctly peculiar when compared with the state he was usually in when he woke up. He would be half-asleep from staying so late at the newspaper office. He would face life with a sense of strain and contemplation. Then he would get up, whetting his determination to face up to all inconveniences and withstand all difficulties.

Today he felt happy, full of happiness, as a matter of fact. There was no arguing about it. The symptoms were quite clear, and their vigor and obviousness were such as to impose themselves on his senses and mind all at once. Yes, indeed; he was happy. If this was not happiness, then what was? He felt that his limbs were well proportioned and functioning per-fectly. They were working in superb harmony with each other and with the world around him. Inside him, he felt a boundless power, an imperishable energy, an ability to achieve anything with confidence, precision, and obvious success. His heart was overflowing with love for people, animals, and things and with an all-engulfing sense of optimism and joy. It was as if he were no longer troubled or bothered by fear, anxiety, sickness, death, argument, or the question of earning a living. Even more important than that, and something he could not analyze, it was a feeling which penetrated to every cell of his body and soul; it played a tune full of delight, pleasure, serenity, and peace and hummed in its incredible melodies the whispering sound of the world which is denied to the unhappy.

He felt drunk with ecstasy and savored[1] it slowly with a feeling of surprise. He asked him-

---

1. savored (sā′ vərd): dwelt upon with delight; relished.

self where it had come from and how; the past provided no explanation, and the future could not justify it. Where did it come from, then, and how? How long would it last? Would it stay with him till breakfast? Would it give him enough time to get to the newspaper office? Just a minute though, he thought . . . it won't last because it can't. If it did, man would be turned into an angel or something even higher. So he told himself that he should devote his attention to savoring it, living with it, and storing up its nectar before it became a mere memory with no way of proving it or even being sure that it had ever existed.

He ate his breakfast with relish, and this time nothing distracted his attention while he was eating. He gave "Uncle" Bashir,[2] who was waiting on him, such a beaming smile that the poor man felt rather alarmed and taken aback. Usually he would only look in his direction to give orders or ask questions, although on most occasions he treated him fairly well.

"Tell me, Uncle Bashir," he asked the servant, "am I a happy man?"

The poor man was startled. He realized why his servant was confused; for the first time ever he was talking to him as a colleague or friend. He encouraged his servant to forget about his worries and asked him with unusual insistence to answer his question.

"Through God's grace and favor, you are happy," the servant replied.

"You mean, I should be happy. Anyone with my job, living in my house, and enjoying my health should be happy. That's what you want to say. But do you think I'm really happy?"

The servant replied, "You work too hard, Sir"; after yet more insistence, "It's more than any man can stand. . . ."

He hesitated, but his master gestured to him to continue with what he had to say.

"You get angry a lot," he said, "and have fierce arguments with your neighbors. . . ."

He interrupted him by laughing loudly.

"What about you," he asked, "don't you have any worries?"

"Of course, no man can be free of worry."

"You mean that complete happiness is an impossible quest?"

"That applies to life in general. . . ."

How could he have dreamed up this incredible happiness? He or any other human being? It was a strange, unique happiness, as though it were a private secret he had been given. In the meeting hall of the newspaper building, he spotted his main rival in this world sitting down thumbing through a magazine. The man heard his footsteps but did not look up from the magazine. He had undoubtedly noticed him in some way and was therefore pretending to ignore him so as to keep his own peace of mind. At some circulation meetings, they would argue so violently with each other that sparks would begin to fly and they would exchange bitter words. One stage more, and they would come to blows. A week ago, his rival had won in the union elections and he had lost. He had felt pierced by a sharp, poisoned arrow, and the world had darkened before his eyes. Now here he was approaching his rival's seat; the sight of him sitting there did not make him excited, nor did the memories of their dispute spoil his composure. He approached him with a pure and carefree heart, feeling drunk with his incredible happiness; his face showed an expression full of tolerance and forgiveness. It was as though he were approaching some other man toward whom he had never had any feelings of enmity,[3] or perhaps he might be renewing a friendship again. "Good morning!" he said without feeling any compunction.

The man looked up in amazement. He was silent for a few moments until he recovered,

---

2. **Bashir** (bu shēr′).
3. **enmity** (en′ mə tē): the hatred one feels toward an enemy.

and then returned the greeting curtly. It was as though he did not believe his eyes and ears.

He sat down alongside the man. "Marvelous weather today . . . ," he said.

"Okay . . . ," the other replied guardedly.

"Weather to fill your heart with happiness."

His rival looked at him closely and cautiously. "I'm glad that you're so happy . . . ," he muttered.

"Inconceivably happy . . . ," he replied with a laugh.

"I hope," the man continued in a rather hesitant tone of voice, "that I shan't spoil your happiness at the meeting of the administrative council. . . ."

"Not at all. My views are well known, but I don't mind if the members adopt your point of view. That won't spoil my happiness!"

"You've changed a great deal overnight," the man said with a smile.

"The fact is that I'm happy, inconceivably happy."

The man examined his face carefully. "I bet your dear son has changed his mind about staying in Canada?" he asked.

"Never, never, my friend," he replied, laughing loudly. "He is still sticking to his decision. . . ."

"But that was the principal reason for your being so sad. . . ."

"Quite true. I've often begged him to come back out of pity for me in my loneliness and to serve his country. But he told me that he's going to open an engineering office with a Canadian partner; in fact, he's invited me to join him in it. Let him live where he'll be happy. I'm quite happy here—as you can see, inconceivably happy. . . ."

The man still looked a little doubtful. "Quite extraordinarily brave!" he said.

"I don't know what it is, but I'm happy in the full meaning of the word."

Yes indeed, this was full happiness; full, firm, weighty, and vital. As deep as absolute power, widespread as the wind, fierce as fire, bewitching as scent, transcending[4] nature. It could not possibly last.

The other man warmed to his display of affection. "The truth is," he said, "that I always picture you as someone with a fierce and violent temperament which causes him a good deal of trouble and leads him to trouble other people."

"Really?"

"You don't know how to make a truce, you've no concept of intermediate solutions. You work with your nerves, with the marrow in your bones. You fight bitterly, as though any problem is a matter of life and death!"

"Yes, that's true."

He accepted the criticism without any difficulty and with an open heart. His wave expanded into a boundless ocean of happiness. He struggled to control an innocent, happy laugh which the other man interpreted in a way far removed from its pure motives.

"So then," he asked, "you think it's necessary to be able to take a balanced view of events, do you?"

"Of course. I remember, by way of example, the argument we had the day before yesterday about racism. We both had the same views on the subject; it's something worth being zealous about, even to the point of anger. But what kind of anger? An intellectual anger, abstract to a certain extent; not the type which shatters your nerves, ruins your digestion, and gives you palpitations. Not so?"

"That's obvious; I quite understand. . . ." He struggled to control a second laugh and succeeded. His heart refused to renounce[5] one drop of its joy. Racism, Vietnam, Palestine, . . . no problem could assail that fortress of happi-

---

4. transcending (tran send′ iŋ): going beyond the limits of.

5. renounce (ri nouns′): give up (a pursuit, practice, claim, or belief).

ness which was encircling his heart. When he remembered a problem, his heart guffawed. He was happy. It was a tyrannical happiness, despising all misery and laughing at any hardship; it wanted to laugh, dance, sing, and distribute its spirit of laughter, dancing, and singing among the various problems of the world.

He could not bear to stay in his office at the newspaper; he felt no desire to work at all. He hated the very idea of thinking about his daily business and completely failed to bring his mind down from its stronghold in the kingdom of happiness. How could he possibly write about a trolley bus falling into the Nile when he was so intoxicated by this frightening happiness? Yes, it really was frightening. How could it be anything else, when there was no reason for it at all, when it was so strong that it made him exhausted and paralyzed his will—apart from the fact that it had been with him for half a day without letting up in the slightest degree?

He left the pages of paper blank and started walking backwards and forwards across the room, laughing and cracking his fingers. . . .

He felt slightly worried; it did not penetrate deep enough to spoil his happiness but paused on the surface of his mind like an abstract idea. It occurred to him that he might recall the tragedies of his life so that he could test their effect on his happiness. Perhaps they would be able to bring back some idea of balance or security, at least until his happiness began to flag a little. For example, he remembered his wife's death in all its various aspects and details. What had happened? The event appeared to him as a series of movements without any meaning or effect, as though it had happened to some other woman, the wife of another man, in some distant historical age. In fact, it had a contagious effect which prompted a smile and then even provoked laughter. He could not stop himself laughing,

and there he was guffawing, ha . . . ha . . .ha!

The same thing happened when he remembered the first letter his son had sent him saying that he wanted to emigrate to Canada. The sound of his guffaws as he paraded the bloody tragedies of the world before him would have attracted the attention of the newspaper workers and passersby in the street had it not been for the thickness of the walls. He could do nothing to dislodge his happiness. Memories of unhappy times hit him like waves being thrown onto a sandy beach under the golden rays of the sun.

He excused himself from attending the administrative council and left the newspaper office without writing a word. After lunch, he lay down on his bed as usual but could not sleep. In fact, sleep seemed an impossibility to him. Nothing gave him any indication that it was coming, even slowly. He was in a place alight and gleaming, resounding with sleeplessness and joy. He had to calm down and relax, to quiet his senses and limbs, but how could he do it? He gave up trying to sleep and got up. He began to hum as he was walking around his house. If this keeps up, he told himself, I won't be able to sleep, just as I can't work or feel sad. It was almost time for him to go to the club, but he did not feel like meeting any friends. What was the point of exchanging views on public affairs and private worries? What would they think if they found him laughing at every major problem? What would they say? How would they picture things? How would they explain it? No, he did not need anyone, nor did he want to spend the evening talking. He should be by himself and go for a long walk to get rid of some of his excess vitality and think about his situation. What had happened to him? How was it that this incredible happiness had overwhelmed him? How long would he have to carry it on his shoulders? Would it keep depriving him of work, friends, sleep and peace of mind? Should he resign himself to it?

Should he abandon himself to the flood to play with him as the whim took it? Or should he look for a way out for himself through thought, action, or advice?

When he was called into the examination room in the clinic of his friend, the specialist in internal medicine, he felt a little alarmed. The doctor looked at him with a smile. "You don't look like someone who's complaining about being ill," he said.

"I haven't come to see you because I'm ill," he told the doctor in a hesitant tone of voice, "but because I'm happy!"

The doctor looked piercingly at him with a questioning air.

"Yes," he repeated to underline what he had said, "because I'm happy!"

There was a period of silence. On one side there was anxiety, and on the other, questioning and amazement.

"It's an incredible feeling which can't be defined in any other way, but it's very serious. . . ."

The doctor laughed. "I wish your illness was contagious," he said, prodding him jokingly.

"Don't treat it as a joke. It's very serious, as I told you. I'll describe it to you. . . ."

He told him all about his happiness from the time he had woken up in the morning till he had felt compelled to visit him.

"Haven't you been taking drugs, alcohol, or tranquilizers?"

"Absolutely nothing like that."

"Have you had some success in an important sphere of your life—work . . . love . . . money?"

"Nothing like that either. I've twice as much to worry about as I have to make me feel glad. . . ."

"Perhaps if you were patient for a while. . . ."

"I've been patient all day. I'm afraid I'll be spending the night wandering around. . . ."

The doctor gave him a precise, careful, and comprehensive examination and then shrugged his shoulders in despair. "You're a picture of health," he said.

"And so?"

"I could advise you to take a sleeping pill, but it would be better if you consulted a nerve specialist. . . ."

The examination was repeated in the nerve specialist's clinic with the selfsame precision, care, and comprehensiveness. "Your nerves are sound," the doctor told him. "They're in enviable condition!"

"Haven't you got a plausible explanation for my condition?" he asked hopefully.

"Consult a gland specialist!" the doctor replied, shaking his head.

The examination was conducted for a third time in the gland specialist's clinic with the same precision, care, and comprehensiveness. "I congratulate you!" the doctor told him. "Your glands are in good condition."

He laughed. He apologized for laughing, laughing as he did so. Laughter was his way of expressing his alarm and despair.

He left the clinic with the feeling that he was alone; alone in the hands of his tyrannical happiness with no helper, no guide, and no friend. Suddenly, he remembered the doctor's sign he sometimes saw from the window of his office in the newspaper building. It was true that he had no confidence in psychiatrists even though he had read about the significance of psychoanalysis. Apart from that, he knew that their tentacles were very long and they kept their patients tied in a sort of long association. He laughed as he remembered the method of cure through free association and the problems which it eventually uncovers. He was laughing as his feet carried him toward the psychiatrist's clinic, and imagined the doctor listening to his incredible complaints about feeling happy, when he was used to hearing people complain about hysteria, schizophrenia, anxiety, and so on.

"The truth is, Doctor, that I've come to see you because I'm happy!"

He looked at the doctor to see what effect his statement had had on him but noticed that he was keeping his composure. He felt ridiculous. "I'm inconceivably happy . . . ," he said in a tone of confidence.

He began to tell the doctor his story, but the latter stopped him with a gesture of his hand. "An overwhelming, incredible, debilitating[6] happiness?" he asked quietly.

He stared at him in amazement and was on the point of saying something, but the doctor spoke first. "A happiness which has made you stop working," he asked, "abandon your friends, and detest going to sleep? . . ."

"You're a miracle!" he shouted.

"Every time you get involved in some misfortune," the psychiatrist continued quietly, "you dissolve into laughter? . . ."

"Sir . . . are you familiar with the invisible?"

"No!" he said with a smile. "Nothing like that. But I get a similar case in my clinic at least once a week!"

"Is it an epidemic?" he asked.

"I didn't say that, and I wouldn't claim that it's been possible to analyze one case into its primary elements as yet."

"But is it a disease?"

"All the cases are still under treatment."

"But are you satisfied without any doubt that they aren't natural cases? . . ."

"That's a necessary assumption for the job; there's only . . ."

"Have you noticed any of them to be deranged in . . . ," he asked anxiously, pointing to his head.

"Absolutely not," the doctor replied convincingly. "I assure you that they're all intelligent in every sense of the word. . . ."

The doctor thought for a moment. "We should have two sessions a week, I think," he said.

"Very well . . . ," he replied in resignation.

"There's no sense in getting alarmed or feeling sad. . . ."

Alarmed, sad? He smiled, and his smile kept on getting broader. A laugh slipped out, and before long, he was dissolving into laughter. He was determined to control himself, but his resistance collapsed completely. He started guffawing loudly. . . .

---

6. debilitating (dē bil′ ə tāt′ iŋ): making weak or feeble.

Illuminating the Faults of Society

The literature of most countries includes works that spotlight the faults of society. These works take a critical look at how people act and what they believe. Some writers make the reader laugh at their characters and situations. Other writers touch the reader's heart and stir deep emotions.

A work that examines the faults of society ultimately has a positive purpose: to criticize weakness so that people can learn to live wisely. Such a work reinforces the values that guide human conduct.

SOCIAL CRITICISM

Generally in works of social criticism, the characters and the situations have something laughable about them. The reader does not identify with the characters but rather observes them from a distance. Through their interactions, often in a realistic but sometimes in an imaginary setting, the writer conveys a message or lesson. This message raises questions about the conduct of the characters and the values important to them.

As you read the first group of selections in this section, remember that each one conveys a message about society. Look for that message or lesson and think about how the writer communicates it to you. Then consider why the writer might have written the work.

POLITICAL PROTEST

Like the literature of social criticism, the literature of political protest examines conduct and values that the writer wants changed. Literature of political protest, though, has an urgency about it. It generally concerns a terrible injustice already existing or likely to happen. The writer calls for drastic changes in the social order to remedy this injustice.

As you read the second group of works in this section, identify the injustice targeted by the writer. Ask yourself how the writer makes you feel about the situation presented.

Literary Vocabulary

Characterization in Drama. The techniques of characterization used in fiction and in drama are different in some ways and similar in others. In a short story or novel, a writer can describe a character's physical appearance and behavior. In the script of a play, the writer provides some of the same information through stage directions, so that when the play is performed, the audience learns about the characters by observing them onstage. The writer of fiction can also show what a character is like by describing the character's inner thoughts. In a play, characters' thoughts are made known only when characters talk to themselves in monologues or to the audience in asides. In *Mozart and Salieri* in Unit 4, Pushkin makes extensive use of monologue to develop the character of Salieri. In both fiction and drama, characters are revealed through their own actions and words—as well as through the actions and words of other characters.

Satire. Satire is a literary technique in which ideas or customs are ridiculed for the purpose of improving society. Satire may be gently witty, mildly abrasive, or bitterly critical. In "The Happy Man," for example, writer Naguib Mahfouz satirizes the modern way of life by creating a character who is surprised and puzzled to wake one day and find that he is happy.

Science Fiction. Science fiction is prose writing in which a writer explores unexpected possibilities of the past or the future, using known scientific data and theories as well as his or her creative imagination. Most science fiction writers create a believable world, although some create a fantasy world that has familiar elements. In this section of the book, you will read "Tale of the Computer That Fought a Dragon," an example of science fiction.

Experimental Fiction. Experimental fiction breaks with the conventions, or accepted rules, of traditional fiction. For example, an experimental work might have a beginning and end but no middle. It might be a set of incomplete notes instead of a sustained narrative. The selection you will read titled "Vocational Counselling" is an example of experimental fiction.

REVIEWED IN THIS SECTION

Characterization

Tone

Point of View

Theme

Conflict

Tartuffe

MOLIÈRE   1622–1673   FRANCE

Translated by Richard Wilbur

A biography of Molière appears on page 748.

Approaching the Play

Molière (mōl yer′) believed that the function of comedy is to "correct men's vices." His method was satire: exposing and ridiculing human follies. Often he would base a play on a particular vice or failing, shown in an exaggerated way in one character. In this play his target is the hypocrite, the person who pretends to virtue without actually possessing the quality. As the action of this play begins, the character Tartuffe (tar tüf′) is living in the household of a man named Orgon (ôr gôn′) and acting as a "director of conscience"—a person who gives spiritual guidance to the family. As the curtain rises, Orgon's mother defends Tartuffe.

Building Vocabulary

These essential words are footnoted within the play.

pious (pī′ əs): If I were / . . . this lady's good and **pious** spouse, / I wouldn't make you welcome in my house. (page 542)

censoriousness (sen sôr′ ē əs nes): They think **censoriousness** a mark of pride. (page 549)

insolent (in′ sə lənt): She's so upset me by her **insolent** talk. (page 554)

mortify (môrt′ ə fī′): I perceive that Heaven, outraged by me, / Has chosen this occasion to **mortify** me. (page 567)

unconscionable (un kän′ shən ə bəl): And meanwhile the **unconscionable** knave / Tries to induce my wife to misbehave. (page 579)

Connecting Writing and Reading

Have you ever known someone who seemed to be kind and good but who was really just the opposite? In your journal make a note of the way you felt about this person, or describe how you would likely feel if you encountered such a person. Then compare those feelings with the way you respond to Tartuffe's hypocrisy.

CHARACTERS

Madame Pernelle (mả dảm′ per nel′), Orgon's mother
Orgon (ôr gōn′), Elmire's husband
Elmire (el mēr′), Orgon's wife
Damis (dả mē′), Orgon's son, Elmire's stepson
Mariane (màr yän′), Orgon's daughter, Elmire's stepdaughter, in love with Valère
Valère (và ler′), in love with Mariane
Cléante (kle änt′), Orgon's brother-in-law
Tartuffe (tàr tüf′), a hypocrite
Dorine (dô rēn′), Mariane's lady's maid
Monsieur Loyal (mə syö′ lwà yàl′), a bailiff
A Police Officer
Flipote (flē pôt′), Madame Pernelle's maid

The scene throughout: Orgon's *house in Paris.*

ACT ONE

SCENE 1

MADAME PERNELLE *and* FLIPOTE, *her maid,* ELMIRE, MARIANE, DORINE, DAMIS, CLÉANTE.

Madame Pernelle. Come, come, Flipote; it's time I left this place.

Elmire. I can't keep up, you walk at such a pace.

Madame Pernelle. Don't trouble, child; no need to show me out.
It's not your manners I'm concerned about.

Elmire. We merely pay you the respect we owe.
But, Mother, why this hurry? Must you go?

Madame Pernelle. I must. This house appalls me. No one in it

Will pay attention for a single minute.
Children, I take my leave much vexed in spirit.
I offer good advice, but you won't hear it.
You all break in and chatter on and on.
It's like a madhouse with the keeper gone.

Dorine. If . . .

Madame Pernelle. Girl, you talk too much, and I'm afraid
You're far too saucy for a lady's-maid.
You push in everywhere and have your say.

Damis. But . . .

Madame Pernelle. You, boy, grow more foolish every day.
To think my grandson should be such a dunce!
I've said a hundred times, if I've said it once,
That if you keep the course on which you've started,

You'll leave your worthy father broken-
  hearted.

Mariane. I think . . .

Madame Pernelle. And you, his sister,
  seem so pure,
So shy, so innocent, and so demure.
But you know what they say about still
  waters.
I pity parents with secretive daughters.

Elmire. Now, Mother . . .

Madame Pernelle. And as for you, child,
  let me add
That your behavior is extremely bad,
And a poor example for these children, too.
Their dear, dead mother did far better
  than you.
You're much too free with money, and I'm
  distressed
To see you so elaborately dressed.
When it's one's husband that one aims to
  please,
One has no need of costly fripperies.

Cléante. Oh, Madam, really . . .

Madame Pernelle.   You are her
  brother, Sir,
And I respect and love you; yet if I were
My son, this lady's good and pious[1] spouse,
I wouldn't make you welcome in my
  house.
You're full of worldly counsels which, I
  fear,
Aren't suitable for decent folk to hear.
I've spoken bluntly, Sir; but it behooves us
Not to mince words when righteous fervor
  moves us.

Damis. Your man Tartuffe is full of holy
  speeches . . .

Madame Pernelle. And practices precisely
  what he preaches.
He's a fine man, and should be listened to.

I will not hear him mocked by fools like
  you.

Damis. Good God! Do you expect me to
  submit
To the tyranny of that carping hypocrite?
Must we forgo all joys and satisfactions
Because that bigot censures all our actions?

Dorine. To hear him talk—and he talks all
  the time—
There's nothing one can do that's not a
  crime.
He rails at everything, your dear Tartuffe.

Madame Pernelle. Whatever he reproves
  deserves reproof.
He's out to save your souls, and all of you
Must love him, as my son would have you
  do.

Damis. Ah no, Grandmother, I could
  never take
To such a rascal, even for my father's sake.
That's how I feel, and I shall not dissemble.
His every action makes me seethe and
  tremble
With helpless anger, and I have no doubt
That he and I will shortly have it out.

Dorine. Surely it is a shame and a disgrace
To see this man usurp the master's place—
To see this beggar who, when first he came,
Had not a shoe or shoestring to his name
So far forget himself that he behaves
As if the house were his, and we his slaves.

Madame Pernelle. Well, mark my words,
  your souls would fare far better
If you obeyed his precepts to the letter.

Dorine. You see him as a saint. I'm far less
  awed;
In fact, I see right through him. He's a
  fraud.

---

1. **pious** (pī′ əs): having religious devotion.

Madame Pernelle. Nonsense!

Dorine. His man Laurent's the same, or
    worse;
  I'd not trust either with a penny purse.

Madame Pernelle. I can't say what his
    servant's morals may be;
  His own great goodness I can guarantee.
  You all regard him with distaste and fear
  Because he tells you what you're loath to
    hear,
  Condemns your sins, points out your
    moral flaws,
  And humbly strives to further Heaven's
    cause.

Dorine. If sin is all that bothers him, why
    is it
  He's so upset when folk drop in to visit?
  Is Heaven so outraged by a social call
  That he must prophesy against us all?
  I'll tell you what I think: if you ask me,
  He's jealous of my mistress' company.

Madame Pernelle. Rubbish! (*to* Elmire)
  He's not alone, child, in complaining
  Of all your promiscuous entertaining.
  Why, the whole neighborhood's upset, I
    know,
  By all these carriages that come and go,
  With crowds of guests parading in and out
  And noisy servants loitering about.
  In all of this, I'm sure there's nothing
    vicious;
  But why give people cause to be suspicious?

Cléante. They need no cause; they'll talk
    in any case.
  Madam, this world would be a joyless place
  If, fearing what malicious tongues might
    say,
  We locked our doors and turned our
    friends away.
  And even if one did so dreary a thing,
  D'you think those tongues would cease
    their chattering?

One can't fight slander; it's a losing battle;
  Let us instead ignore their tittle-tattle.
  Let's strive to live by conscience' clear
    decrees,
  And let the gossips gossip as they please.

Dorine. If there is talk against us, I know
    the source:
  It's Daphne and her little husband, of
    course.
  Those who have greatest cause for guilt
    and shame
  Are quickest to besmirch a neighbor's
    name.
  When there's a chance for libel, they
    never miss it;
  When something can be made to seem
    illicit
  They're off at once to spread the joyous
    news,
  Adding to fact what fantasies they choose.
  By talking up their neighbor's indiscretions
  They seek to camouflage their own trans-
    gressions,
  Hoping that others' innocent affairs
  Will lend a hue of innocence to theirs,
  Or that their own black guilt will come to
    seem
  Part of a general shady color scheme.

Madame Pernelle. All that is quite
    irrelevant. I doubt
  That anyone's more virtuous and devout
  Than dear Orante;[2] and I'm informed that
    she
  Condemns your mode of life most
    vehemently.

Dorine. Oh, yes, she's strict, devout, and
    has no taint
  Of worldliness; in short, she seems a saint.
  But it was time which taught her that
    disguise.
  She's thus because she can't be otherwise.

---

2. **Orante** (ô ränt′).

So long as her attractions could enthrall,
She flounced and flirted and enjoyed it
    all,
But now that they're no longer what they
    were
She quits a world which fast is quitting
    her,
And wears a veil of virtue to conceal
Her bankrupt beauty and her lost appeal.
That's what becomes of old coquettes
    today.
Distressed when all their lovers fall away,
They see no recourse but to play the prude,
And so confer a style on solitude.
Thereafter, they're severe with everyone,
Condemning all our actions, pardoning
    none,
And claiming to be pure, austere, and
    zealous
When, if the truth were known, they're
    merely jealous,
And cannot bear to see another know
The pleasures time has forced them to
    forgo.

Madame Pernelle (*initially to* Elmire).
That sort of talk is what you like to
    hear;
Therefore you'd have us all keep still, my
    dear,
While Madam rattles on the livelong day.
Nevertheless, I mean to have my say.
I tell you that you're blest to have Tartuffe
Dwelling, as my son's guest, beneath this
    roof;
That Heaven has sent him to forestall its
    wrath
By leading you, once more, to the true
    path;
That all he reprehends is reprehensible,
And that you'd better heed him, and be
    sensible.
These visits, balls, and parties in which
    you revel
Are nothing but inventions of the Devil.

One never hears a word that's edifying:
Nothing but chaff and foolishness and
    lying,
As well as vicious gossip in which one's
    neighbor
Is cut to bits with épée, foil, and saber.[3]
People of sense are driven half-insane
At such affairs, where noise and folly reign
And reputations perish thick and fast.
As a wise preacher said on Sunday last,
Parties are Towers of Babylon,[4] because
The guests all babble on with never a
    pause;
And then he told a story which, I think . . .

(*to* Cléante)

I heard that laugh, Sir, and I saw that wink!
Go find your silly friends and laugh some
    more!
Enough; I'm going; don't show me to the
    door.
I leave this household much dismayed and
    vexed;
I cannot say when I shall see you next.

(*slapping* Flipote)

Wake, don't stand there gaping into space!
I'll slap some sense into that stupid face.
Move, move, you slut.

SCENE 2

CLÉANTE, DORINE.

Cléante.   I think I'll stay behind;
I want no further pieces of her mind.
How that old lady . . .

---

3. **épée** (ā pā′), **foil, and saber:** types of swords.
4. **Towers of Babylon:** a misuse of words, or
malapropism. Madame Pernelle is confusing Babylon
with the Tower of Babel, described in the Bible as a
tower whose construction was interrupted by the
confusion of sounds and voices. Her mistake
apparently amuses Cléante.

Dorine. Oh, what wouldn't she say
  If she could hear you speak of her that way!
  She'd thank you for the *lady*, but I'm sure
  She'd find the *old* a little premature.

Cléante. My, what a Scene she made, and what a din!
  And how this man Tartuffe has taken her in!

Dorine. Yes, but her son is even worse deceived;
  His folly must be seen to be believed.
  In the late troubles,[5] he played an able part
  And served his king with wise and loyal heart,
  But he's quite lost his senses since he fell
  Beneath Tartuffe's infatuating spell.
  He calls him brother, and loves him as his life,
  Preferring him to mother, child, or wife.
  In him and him alone will he confide;
  He's made him his confessor and his guide;
  He pets and pampers him with love more tender
  Than any pretty mistress could engender,
  Gives him the place of honor when they dine,
  Delights to see him gorging like a swine.
  Stuffs him with dainties till his guts distend,
  And when he belches, cries "God bless you, friend!"
  In short, he's mad; he worships him; he dotes;
  His deeds he marvels at, his words he quotes,
  Thinking each act a miracle, each word
  Oracular as those that Moses heard.
  Tartuffe, much pleased to find so easy a victim,
  Has in a hundred ways beguiled and tricked him,
  Milked him of money, and with his permission
  Established here a sort of Inquisition.
  Even Laurent, his lackey, dares to give
  Us arrogant advice on how to live;
  He sermonizes us in thundering tones
  And confiscates our ribbons and colognes.
  Last week he tore a kerchief into pieces
  Because he found it pressed in a *Life of Jesus*:
  He said it was a sin to juxtapose
  Unholy vanities and holy prose.

SCENE 3

ELMIRE, MARIANE, DAMIS, CLÉANTE, DORINE.

Elmire (*to* Cléante). You did well not to follow; she stood in the door
  And said *verbatim* all she'd said before.
  I saw my husband coming. I think I'd best
  Go upstairs now, and take a little rest.

Cléante. I'll wait and greet him here; then I must go.
  I've really only time to say hello.

Damis. Sound him about my sister's wedding, please.
  I think Tartuffe's against it, and that he's
  Been urging Father to withdraw his blessing.
  As you well know, I'd find that most distressing.
  Unless my sister and Valère can marry,
  My hopes to wed *his* sister will miscarry,
  And I'm determined . . .

Dorine. He's coming.

SCENE 4

ORGON, CLÉANTE, DORINE.

Orgon. Ah, Brother, good day.

---

5. **the late troubles:** a reference to civil strife that had broken out in France a few years earlier.

Cléante. Well, welcome back. I'm sorry I
can't stay.
How was the country? Blooming, I trust,
and green?

Orgon. Excuse me, Brother; just one
moment.

(*to* Dorine)

Dorine . . .

(*to* Cléante)

To put my mind at rest, I always learn
The household news the moment I return.

(*to* Dorine)

Has all been well, these two days I've been
gone?
How are the family? What's been going on?

Dorine. Your wife, two days ago, had a bad
fever,
And a fierce headache which refused to
leave her.

Orgon. Ah. And Tartuffe?

Dorine.   Tartuffe?
Why,
he's round and red,
Bursting with health, and excellently fed.

Orgon. Poor fellow!

Dorine.   That night, the mistress was unable
To take a single bite at the dinner table.
Her headache pains, she said, were simply
hellish.

Orgon. Ah. And Tartuffe?

Dorine.   He ate his meal
with relish,
And zealously devoured in her presence
A leg of mutton and a brace of pheasants.

Orgon. Poor fellow!

Dorine.   Well, the pains contin-
ued strong,
And so she tossed and tossed the whole
night long,
Now icy cold, now burning like a flame.
We sat beside her bed till morning came.

Orgon. Ah. And Tartuffe?·

Dorine.   Why, having
eaten, he rose
And sought his room, already in a doze,
Got into his warm bed, and snored away
In perfect peace until the break of day.

Orgon. Poor fellow!

Dorine.   After much ado, we
talked her
Into dispatching someone for the doctor.
He bled her, and the fever quickly fell.

Orgon. Ah. And Tartuffe?

Dorine.   He bore it very
well.
To keep his cheerfulness at any cost,
And make up for the blood *Madame* had
lost,
He drank, at lunch, four beakers full of
port.

Orgon. Poor fellow!

Dorine.   Both are doing well, in
short.
I'll go and tell *Madame* that you've expressed
Keen sympathy and anxious interest.

SCENE 5

ORGON, CLÉANTE.

Cléante. That girl was laughing in your
face, and though
I've no wish to offend you, even so
I'm bound to say that she had some excuse.

How can you possibly be such a goose?
Are you so dazed by this man's hocus-pocus
That all the world, save him, is out of
     focus?
You've given him clothing, shelter, food,
     and care;
Why must you also . . .

Orgon.   Brother, stop right
     there.
You do not know the man of whom you
     speak.

Cléante. I grant you that. But my judg-
     ment's not so weak
That I can't tell, by his effect on others . . .

Orgon. Ah, when you meet him, you two
     will be like brothers!
There's been no loftier soul since time
     began.
He is a man who . . . a man who . . . an
     excellent man.
To keep his precepts is to be reborn.
And view this dunghill of a world with
     scorn.
Yes, thanks to him I'm a changed man
     indeed.
Under his tutelage my soul's been freed
From earthly loves, and every human tie:
My mother, children, brother, and wife
     could die,
And I'd not feel a single moment's pain.

Cléante. That's a fine sentiment, Brother;
     most humane.

Orgon. Oh, had you seen Tartuffe as I first
     knew him,
Your heart, like mine, would have surren-
     dered to him.
He used to come into our church each day
And humbly kneel nearby, and start to
     pray.
He'd draw the eyes of everybody there
By the deep fervor of his heartfelt prayer:
He'd sigh and weep, and sometimes with a
     sound
Of rapture he would bend and kiss the
     ground;
And when I rose to go, he'd run before
To offer me holy water at the door.
His serving man, no less devout than he,
Informed me of his master's poverty;
I gave him gifts, but in his humbleness
He'd beg me every time to give him less.
"Oh, that's too much," he'd cry, "too
     much by twice!
I don't deserve it. The half, Sir, would
     suffice."
And when I wouldn't take it back, he'd
     share
Half of it with the poor, right then and
     there.
At length, Heaven prompted me to take
     him in
To dwell with us, and free our souls from
     sin.
He guides our lives, and to protect our
     honor
Stays by my wife, and keeps an eye upon
     her;
He tells me whom she sees, and all she
     does,
And seems more jealous than I ever was!
And how austere he is! Why, he can
     detect
A mortal sin where you would least suspect;
In smallest trifles, he's extremely strict.
Last week, his conscience was severely
     pricked
Because, while praying, he had caught a
     flea
And killed it, so he felt, too wrathfully.

Cléante. Good God, man! Have you lost
     your common sense—
Or is this all some joke at my expense?
How can you stand there and in all
     sobriety . . .

Orgon. Brother, your language savors of
     impiety.

Too much freethinking's made your faith
  unsteady,
And as I've warned you many times already,
'Twill get you into trouble before you're
  through.

Cléante. So I've been told before by dupes
  like you:
Being blind, you'd have all others blind as
  well;
The cleareyed man you call an infidel,
And he who sees through humbug and
  pretense
Is charged, by you, with want of reverence.
Spare me your warnings, Brother; I have
  no fear
Of speaking out, for you and Heaven to
  hear,
Against affected zeal and pious knavery.
There's true and false in piety, as in bravery,
And just as those whose courage shines
  the most
In battle, are the least inclined to boast,
So those whose hearts are truly pure and
  lowly
Don't make a flashy show of being holy.
There's a vast difference, so it seems to me,
Between true piety and hypocrisy:
How do you fail to see it, may I ask?
Is not a face quite different from a mask?
Cannot sincerity and cunning art,
Reality and semblance, be told apart?
Are scarecrows just like men, and do you
  hold
That a false coin is just as good as gold?
Ah, Brother, man's a strangely fashioned
  creature
Who seldom is content to follow Nature,
But recklessly pursues his inclination
Beyond the narrow bounds of moderation,
And often, by transgressing Reason's laws,[6]
Perverts a lofty aim or noble cause.
A passing observation, but it applies.

Orgon. I see, dear Brother, that you're profoundly wise;

You harbor all the insight of the age.
You are our one clear mind, our only sage,
The era's oracle, its Cato[7] too.
And all mankind are fools compared to
  you.

Cléante. Brother, I don't pretend to be a
  sage,
Nor have I all the wisdom of the age.
There's just one insight I would dare to
  claim:
I know that true and false are not the
  same;
And just as there is nothing I more
  revere
Than a soul whose faith is steadfast and
  sincere,
Nothing that I more cherish and admire
Than honest zeal and true religious fire,
So there is nothing that I find more base
Than specious piety's dishonest face—
Than these bold mountebanks, these
  histrios
Whose impious mummeries[8] and hollow
  shows
Exploit our love of Heaven, and make a
  jest
Of all that men think holiest and best;
These calculating souls who offer prayers
Not to their Maker, but as public wares,
And seek to buy respect and reputation
With lifted eyes and sighs of exaltation;
These charlatans, I say, whose pilgrim
  souls
Proceed, by way of Heaven, toward earth-
  ly goals,

---

6. to follow Nature . . . Reason's laws: a characteristic neoclassical point of view. Nature is seen as a
source of order; human beings should use their reason
to discern natural laws and find virtue and happiness.

7. Cato: the Roman statesman and philosopher
Marcus Porcius Cato (95–46 B.C.), who had a reputation for great honesty and incorruptibility.

8. mountebanks . . . histrios . . . mummeries: fakers,
actors, and ridiculous performances.

Who weep and pray and swindle and
  extort,
Who preach the monkish life, but haunt
  the court,
Who make their zeal the partner of their
  vice—
Such men are vengeful, sly, and cold as ice,
And when there is an enemy to defame
They cloak their spite in fair religion's
  name,
Their private spleen[9] and malice being
  made
To seem a high and virtuous crusade,
Until, to mankind's reverent applause,
They crucify their foe in Heaven's cause.
Such knaves are all too common; yet, for
  the wise,
True piety isn't hard to recognize,
And, happily, these present times provide
  us
With bright examples to instruct and
  guide us.
Consider Ariston and Périandre;
Look at Oronte, Alcidamas, Clitandre;[10]
Their virtue is acknowledged; who could
  doubt it?
But you won't hear them beat the drum
  about it.
They're never ostentatious, never vain,
And their religion's moderate and humane;
It's not their way to criticize and chide:
They think censoriousness[11] a mark of
  pride,
And therefore, letting others preach and
  rave,
They show, by deeds, how Christians
  should behave.
They think no evil of their fellow man,
But judge of him as kindly as they can.
They don't intrigue and wangle and con-
  spire;
To lead a good life is their one desire;
The sinner wakes no rancorous hate in
  them;

It is the sin alone which they condemn;
Nor do they try to show a fiercer zeal
For Heaven's cause than Heaven itself
  could feel.
These men I honor, these men I advocate
As models for us all to emulate.
Your man is not their sort at all, I fear:
And, while your praise of him is quite
  sincere,
I think that you've been dreadfully deluded.

Orgon. Now then, dear Brother, is your
  speech concluded?

Cléante. Why, yes.

Orgon.   Your servant, Sir.

(*He turns to go.*)

Cléante.   No, Brother; wait.
  There's one more matter. You agreed of
  late
  That young Valère might have your
  daughter's hand.

Orgon. I did.

Cléante.   And set the date, I understand.

Orgon. Quite so.

Cléante.   You've now postponed it;
  is that true?

Orgon. No doubt.

Cléante.   The match no longer

---

9. **spleen:** malice; spite; bad temper. This definition
of the word originates from an earlier belief that the
spleen was the part of the body from which certain
emotions derived.

10. **Ariston** (ăr ēs tōn′) **and Périandre** (per yän′ drə);
Oronte (ô rōnt′), **Alcidamas** (ăl sē dả mả′), **Clitandre**
(klē tän′ drə): fictitious names resembling the Greek
and Roman names found in the elegant literature of
the day.

11. **censoriousness** (sen sôr′ ē əs nes): being harshly
critical.

pleases you?

Orgon. Who knows?

Cléante. D'you mean to go back on your word?

Orgon. I won't say that.

Cléante. Has anything occurred
Which might entitle you to break your pledge?

Orgon. Perhaps.

Cléante. Why must you hem, and haw, and hedge?
The boy asked me to sound you in this affair . . .

Orgon. It's been a pleasure.

Cléante. But what shall I tell Valère?

Orgon. Whatever you like.

Cléante. But what have you decided?
What are your plans?

Orgon. I plan, Sir, to be guided By Heaven's will.

Cléante. Come, Brother, don't talk rot.
You've given Valère your word; will you keep it, or not?

Orgon. Good day.

Cléante. This looks like poor Valère's undoing;
I'll go and warn him that there's trouble brewing.

ACT TWO

SCENE 1

ORGON, MARIANE.

Orgon. Mariane.

Mariane. Yes, Father?

Orgon. A word with you; come here.

Mariane. What are you looking for?

Orgon (*peering into a small closet*). Eavesdroppers, dear.
I'm making sure we shan't be overheard.
Someone in there could catch our every word.
Ah, good, we're safe. Now, Mariane, my child,
You're a sweet girl who's tractable and mild,
Whom I hold dear, and think most highly of.

Mariane. I'm deeply grateful, Father, for your love.

Orgon. That's well said, Daughter; and you can repay me
If, in all things, you'll cheerfully obey me.

Mariane. To please you, Sir, is what delights me best.

Orgon. Good, good. Now, what d'you think of Tartuffe, our guest?

Mariane. I, Sir?

Orgon. Yes. Weigh your answer; think it through.

Mariane. Oh, dear. I'll say whatever you wish me to.

Orgon. That's wisely said, my Daughter.
   Say of him, then,
That he's the very worthiest of men,
And that you're fond of him, and would
   rejoice
In being his wife, if that should be my
   choice.
Well?

Mariane. What?

Orgon.   What's that?

Mariane.   I . . .

Orgon.   Well?

Mariane.   Forgive me, pray.

Orgon. Did you not hear me?

Mariane.   Of *whom*, Sir,
   must I say
That I am fond of him, and would rejoice
In being his wife, if that should be your
   choice?

Orgon. Why, of Tartuffe.

Mariane.   But, Father, that's
   false, you know.
Why would you have me say what isn't so?

Orgon. Because I am resolved it shall be
   true.
That it's my wish should be enough for you.

Mariane. You can't mean, Father . . .

Orgon.   Yes,
   Tartuffe shall be
Allied by marriage to this family,
And he's to be your husband, is that clear?
It's a father's privilege . . .

SCENE 2

DORINE, ORGON, MARIANE.

Orgon (*to* Dorine).   What

are you doing in here?
Is curiosity so fierce a passion
With you, that you must eavesdrop in
   this fashion?

Dorine. There's lately been a rumor going
   about—
Based on some hunch or chance remark,
   no doubt—
That you mean Mariane to wed Tartuffe.
I've laughed it off, of course, as just a spoof.

Orgon. You find it so incredible?

Dorine.   Yes, I do.
I won't accept that story, even from you.

Orgon. Well, you'll believe it when the
   thing is done.

Dorine. Yes, yes, of course. Go on and have
   your fun.

Orgon. I've never been more serious in my
   life.

Dorine. Ha!

Orgon.   Daughter, I mean it; you're to
   be his wife.

Dorine. No, don't believe your father; it's
   all a hoax.

Orgon. See here, young woman . . .

Dorine.   Come,
   Sir, no more jokes; You can't fool us.

Orgon. How dare you talk that way?

Dorine. All right, then: we believe you, sad
   to say.
But how a man like you, who looks so
   wise
And wears a moustache of such splendid
   size,
Can be so foolish as to . . .

Orgon.   Silence, please!
My girl, you take too many liberties.

I'm master here, as you must not forget.

Dorine. Do let's discuss this calmly; don't
  be upset.
  You can't be serious, Sir, about this plan.
  What should that bigot want with
    Mariane?
  Praying and fasting ought to keep him
    busy.
  And then, in terms of wealth and rank,
    what is he?
  Why should a man of property like you
  Pick out a beggar son-in-law?

Orgon.   That will do.
  Speak of his poverty with reverence.
  His is a pure and saintly indigence
  Which far transcends all worldly pride and
    pelf.
  He lost his fortune, as he says himself,
  Because he cared for Heaven alone, and so
  Was careless of his interests here below.
  I mean to get him out of his present straits
  And help him to recover his estates—
  Which, in his part of the world, have no
    small fame.
  Poor though he is, he's a gentleman just
    the same.

Dorine. Yes, so he tells us; and, Sir, it
  seems to me
  Such pride goes very ill with piety.
  A man whose spirit spurns this dungy
    earth
  Ought not to brag of lands and noble
    birth;
  Such worldly arrogance will hardly square
  With meek devotion and the life of prayer.
  . . . But this approach, I see, has drawn a
    blank;
  Let's speak, then, of his person, not his
    rank.
  Doesn't it seem to you a trifle grim
  To give a girl like her to a man like him?
  When two are so ill-suited, can't you see
  What the sad consequence is bound to be?

A young girl's virtue is imperiled, Sir,
When such a marriage is imposed on her;
For if one's bridegroom isn't to one's taste,
It's hardly an inducement to be chaste,
And many a man with horns[1] upon his
  brow
Has made his wife the thing that she is
  now.
It's hard to be a faithful wife, in short,
To certain husbands of a certain sort,
And he who gives his daughter to a man
  she hates
Must answer for her sins at Heaven's gates.
Think, Sir, before you play so risky a role.

Orgon. This servant girl presumes to save
  my soul!

Dorine. You would do well to ponder what
  I've said.

Orgon. Daughter, we'll disregard this
  dunderhead.
  Just trust your father's judgment. Oh, I'm
    aware
  That I once promised you to young Valère;
  But now I hear he gambles, which greatly
    shocks me;
  What's more, I've doubts about his
    orthodoxy.
  His visits to church, I note, are very few.

Dorine. Would you have him go at the
  same hours as you,
And kneel nearby, to be sure of being seen?

Orgon. I can dispense with such remarks,
  Dorine.

(*to* Mariane)

  Tartuffe, however, is sure of Heaven's
    blessing,
  And that's the only treasure worth
    possessing.

---

1. horns: a common symbol in Molière's time for a
man whose wife is unfaithful.

This match will bring you joys beyond all
    measure;
Your cup will overflow with every pleasure;
You two will interchange your faithful
    loves
Like two sweet cherubs, or two turtledoves.
No harsh word shall be heard, no frown be
    seen,
And he shall make you happy as a queen.

Dorine. And she'll make him a cuckold,
    just wait and see.

Orgon. What language!

Dorine.   Oh, he's a man of
    destiny;
He's *made* for horns, and what the stars
    demand
Your daughter's virtue surely can't with-
    stand.

Orgon. Don't interrupt me further. Why
    can't you learn
That certain things are none of your
    concern?

Dorine. It's for your own sake that I
    interfere.

(*She repeatedly interrupts* Orgon *just as he is
    turning to speak to his daughter.*)

Orgon. Most kind of you. Now, hold your
    tongue, d'you hear?

Dorine. If I didn't love you . . .

Orgon.   Spare me
    your affection.

Dorine. I'll love you, Sir, in spite of your
    objection.

Orgon. Blast!

Dorine.   I can't bear, Sir, for your
    honor's sake,
To let you make this ludicrous mistake.

Orgon. You mean to go on talking?

Dorine.   If I
    didn't protest
This sinful marriage, my conscience
    couldn't rest.

Orgon. If you don't hold your tongue, you
    little shrew . . .

Dorine. What, lost your temper? A pious
    man like you?

Orgon. Yes! Yes! You talk and talk. I'm
    maddened by it.
Once and for all, I tell you to be quiet.

Dorine. Well, I'll be quiet. But I'll be
    thinking hard.

Orgon. Think all you like, but you had
    better guard
That saucy tongue of yours, or I'll . . .

(*turning back to* Mariane)

                                    Now,
    child.
I've weighed this matter fully.

Dorine (*aside*).   It drives me
    wild
That I can't speak.

(Orgon *turns his head, and she is silent.*)

Orgon.   Tartuffe is no young
    dandy.
But, still his person . . .

Dorine (*aside*).   Is as sweet as candy.

Orgon. Is such that, even if you shouldn't
    care
For his other merits . . .

(*He turns and stands facing* Dorine, *arms
    crossed.*)

Dorine (*aside*).   They'll make a
    lovely pair.

If I were she, no man would marry me
Against my inclination, and go scot-free.
He'd learn, before the wedding day was
over,
How readily a wife can find a lover.

Orgon (*to* Dorine). It seems you treat my
orders as a joke.

Dorine. Why, what's the matter? 'Twas not
to you I spoke.

Orgon. What *were* you doing?

Dorine.   Talking to
myself, that's all.

Orgon. Ah! (*aside*) One more bit of impudence and gall,
And I shall give her a good slap in the face.

(*He puts himself in a position to slap her;
Dorine, whenever he glances at her, stands
immobile and silent.*)

Daughter, you shall accept, and with good
grace,
The husband I've selected . . . Your wedding day . . .

(*to* Dorine)

Why don't you talk to yourself?

Dorine.   I've nothing
to say.

Orgon. Come, just one word.

Dorine.   No thank
you, Sir. I pass.

Orgon. Come, speak; I'm waiting.

Dorine.   I'd not be
such an ass.

Orgon (*turning to* Mariane). In short, dear
Daughter, I mean to be obeyed,
And you must bow to the sound choice
I've made.

Dorine (*moving away*). I'd not wed such a
monster, even in jest.

(Orgon *attempts to slap her, but misses.*)

Orgon. Daughter, that maid of yours is a
thorough pest;
She makes me sinfully annoyed and nettled.
I can't speak further; my nerves are too
unsettled.
She's so upset me by her insolent[2] talk,
I'll calm myself by going for a walk.

SCENE 3

DORINE, MARIANE.

Dorine (*returning*). Well, have you lost
your tongue, girl? Must I play
Your part, and say the lines you ought to
say?
Faced with a fate so hideous and absurd,
Can you not utter one dissenting word?

Mariane. What good would it do? A
father's power is great.

Dorine. Resist him now, or it will be too
late.

Mariane. But . . .

Dorine.   Tell him one cannot love
at a father's whim;
That you shall marry for yourself, not him;
That since it's you who are to be the bride,
It's you, not he, who must be satisfied;
And that if his Tartuffe is so sublime,
He's free to marry him at any time.

Mariane. I've bowed so long to Father's
strict control,
I couldn't oppose him now, to save my
soul.

Dorine. Come, come, Mariane. Do listen
to reason, won't you?

---

2. **insolent** (in′ sə lənt): extremely rude.

Valère has asked your hand. Do you love
   him, or don't you?

Mariane. Oh, how unjust of you! What
   can you mean
   By asking such a question, dear Dorine?
   You know the depth of my affection for
   him;
   I've told you a hundred times how I adore
   him.

Dorine. I don't believe in everything I
   hear;
   Who knows if your professions were sincere?

Mariane. They were, Dorine, and you do
   me wrong to doubt it;
   Heaven knows that I've been all too frank
   about it.

Dorine. You love him, then?

Mariane.   Oh, more than
   I can express.

Dorine. And he, I take it, cares for you no
   less?

Mariane. I think so.

Dorine.   And you both, with
   equal fire,
   Burn to be married?

Mariane.   That is our one desire.

Dorine. What of Tartuffe, then? What of
   your father's plan?

Mariane. I'll kill myself, if I'm forced to
   wed that man.

Dorine. I hadn't thought of that recourse.
   How splendid!
   Just die, and all your troubles will be ended!
   A fine solution. Oh, it maddens me
   To hear you talk in that self-pitying key.

Mariane. Dorine, how harsh you are! It's
   most unfair.
   You have no sympathy for my despair.

Dorine. I've none at all for people who talk
   drivel!
   And, faced with difficulties, whine and
   snivel.

Mariane. No doubt I'm timid, but it would
   be wrong . . .

Dorine. True love requires a heart that's
   firm and strong.

Mariane. I'm strong in my affection for
   Valère,
   But coping with my father is his affair.

Dorine. But if your father's brain has grown
   so cracked
   Over his dear Tartuffe that he can retract
   His blessing, though your wedding day was
   named,
   It's surely not Valère who's to be blamed.

Mariane. If I defied my father, as you suggest,
   Would it not seem unmaidenly, at best?
   Shall I defend my love at the expense
   Of brazenness and disobedience?
   Shall I parade my heart's desires, and
   flaunt . . .

Dorine. No, I ask nothing of you. Clearly
   you want
   To be Madame Tartuffe, and I feel bound
   Not to oppose a wish so very sound.
   What right have I to criticize the match?
   Indeed, my dear, the man's a brilliant
   catch.
   Monsieur Tartuffe! Now, there's a man of
   weight!
   Yes, yes, Monsieur Tartuffe, I'm bound to
   state,
   Is quite a person; that's not to be denied;
   'Twill be no little thing to be his bride.
   The world already rings with his renown;
   He's a great noble—in his native town;
   His ears are red, he has a pink complexion,
   And all in all, he'll suit you to perfection.

Mariane. Dear God!

Dorine. Oh, how triumphant you will feel
At having caught a husband so ideal!

Mariane. Oh, do stop teasing, and use your cleverness
To get me out of this appalling mess.
Advise me, and I'll do whatever you say.

Dorine. Ah, no, a dutiful daughter must obey
Her father, even if he weds her to an ape.
You've a bright future; why struggle to escape?
Tartuffe will take you back where his family lives,
To a small town aswarm with relatives—
Uncles and cousins whom you'll be charmed to meet.
You'll be received at once by the elite,
Calling upon the bailiff's wife, no less—
Even, perhaps, upon the mayoress,
Who'll sit you down in the *best* kitchen chair.
Then, once a year, you'll dance at the village fair
To the drone of bagpipes—two of them, in fact—
And see a puppet show, or an animal act.
Your husband . . .

Mariane. Oh, you turn my blood to ice!
Stop torturing me, and give me your advice.

Dorine (*threatening to go*). Your servant, Madam.

Mariane. Dorine, I beg of you . . .

Dorine. No, you deserve it; this marriage must go through.

Mariane. Dorine!

Dorine. No.

Mariane. Not Tartuffe! You know I think him . . .

Dorine. Tartuffe's your cup of tea, and you shall drink him.

Mariane. I've always told you everything, and relied . . .

Dorine. No. You deserve to be tartuffified.

Mariane. Well, since you mock me and refuse to care,
I'll henceforth seek my solace in despair:
Despair shall be my counsellor and friend,
And help me bring my sorrows to an end.

(*She starts to leave.*)

Dorine. There now, come back; my anger has subsided.
You do deserve some pity, I've decided.

Mariane. Dorine, if Father makes me undergo
This dreadful martyrdom, I'll die, I know.

Dorine. Don't fret; it won't be difficult to discover
Some plan of action . . . But here's Valère, your lover.

SCENE 4

VALÈRE, MARIANE, DORINE.

Valère. Madam, I've just received some wondrous news
Regarding which I'd like to hear your views.

Mariane. What news?

Valère. You're marrying Tartuffe.

Mariane. I find
That Father does have such a match in mind.

Valère. Your father, Madam . . .

Mariane. . . . has just

this minute said
That it's Tartuffe he wishes me to wed.

Valère. Can he be serious?

Mariane.   Oh, indeed he
can;
He's clearly set his heart upon the plan.

Valère. And what position do you propose
to take, Madam?

Mariane. Why—I don't know.

Valère.   For heaven's
sake—
You don't know?

Mariane.   No.

Valère.   Well, well!

Mariane.   Advise me,
do.

Valère. Marry the man. That's my advice
to you.

Mariane. That's your advice?

Valère.   Yes.

Mariane.   Truly?

Valère.   Oh,
absolutely.
You couldn't choose more wisely, more
astutely.

Mariane. Thanks for this counsel; I'll
follow it, of course.

Valère. Do, do; I'm sure 'twill cost you no
remorse.

Mariane. To give it didn't cause your heart
to break.

Valère. I gave it, Madam, only for your sake.

Mariane. And it's for your sake that I take
it, Sir.

Dorine (*withdrawing to the rear of the stage*).

Let's see which fool will prove the stub-
borner.

Valère. So! I am nothing to you, and it was
flat
Deception when you . . .

Mariane.   Please, enough of that.
You've told me plainly that I should agree
To wed the man my father's chosen for me,
And since you've deigned to counsel me
so wisely,
I promise, Sir, to do as you advise me.

Valère. Ah, no, 'twas not by me that you
were swayed.
No, your decision was already made;
Though now, to save appearances, you
protest
That you're betraying me at my behest.

Mariane. Just as you say.

Valère.   Quite so. And I
now see
That you were never truly in love with me.

Mariane. Alas, you're free to think so if
you choose.

Valère. I choose to think so, and here's a
bit of news:
You've spurned my hand, but I know
where to turn
For kinder treatment, as you shall quickly
learn.

Mariane. I'm sure you do. Your noble
qualities
Inspire affection . . .

Valère.   Forget my qualities,
please.
They don't inspire you overmuch, I find.
But there's another lady I have in mind
Whose sweet and generous nature will not
scorn
To compensate me for the loss I've borne.

Mariane. I'm no great loss, and I'm sure
   that you'll transfer
Your heart quite painlessly from me to her.

Valère. I'll do my best to take it in my
   stride.
The pain I feel at being cast aside
Time and forgetfulness may put an end to.
Or if I can't forget, I shall pretend to.
No self-respecting person is expected
To go on loving once he's been rejected.

Mariane. Now, that's a fine, high-minded
   sentiment.

Valère. One to which any sane man would
   assent.
Would you prefer it if I pined away
In hopeless passion till my dying day?
Am I to yield you to a rival's arms
And not console myself with other charms?

Mariane. Go then: console yourself; don't
   hesitate.
I wish you to; indeed, I cannot wait.

Valère. You wish me to?

Mariane.   Yes.

Valère.   That's the final straw.
Madame, farewell. Your wish shall be my
   law.

(*He starts to leave, and then returns: this
repeatedly.*)

Mariane. Splendid.

Valère (*coming back again*). This breach,
   remember, is of your making;
It's you who've driven me to the step
   I'm taking.

Mariane. Of course.

Valère (*coming back again*). Remember,
   too, that I am merely
Following your example.

Mariane.   I see that clearly.

Valère. Enough. I'll go and do your bid-
   ding, then.

Mariane. Good.

Valère (*coming back again*). You shall never
   see my face again.

Mariane. Excellent.

Valère (*walking to the door, then turning
   about*).
                          Yes?

Mariane.   What?

Valère. What's that? What did you say?

Mariane. Nothing. You're dreaming.

Valère.   Ah. Well,
   I'm on my way.
Farewell, *Madame*. (*He moves slowly away.*)

Mariane.   Farewell.

Dorine (*to* Mariane).   If you ask me,
Both of you are as mad as mad can be.
Do stop this nonsense, now. I've only let
   you
Squabble so long to see where it would get
   you.
Whoa there, Monsieur Valère!

(*She goes and seizes* Valère *by the arm; he
makes a great show of resistance.*)

Valère.   What's this,
   Dorine?

Dorine. Come here.

Valère.   No, no, my heart's too
   full of spleen.
Don't hold me back; her wish must be
   obeyed.

Dorine. Stop!

Valère.   It's too late now; my decision's made.

Dorine. Oh, pooh!

Mariane (*aside*). He hates the sight of me, that's plain.
  I'll go, and so deliver him from pain.

Dorine (*leaving* Valère, *running after* Mariane).
  And now *you* run away! Come back.

Mariane.   No, no.
  Nothing you say will keep me here. Let go!

Valère (*aside*). She cannot bear my presence, I perceive.
  To spare her further torment, I shall leave.

Dorine (*leaving* Mariane, *running after* Valère). Again! You'll not escape,
  Sir; don't you try it.
  Come here, you two. Stop fussing and be quiet.

(*She takes* Valère *by the hand, then* Mariane, *and draws them together.*)

Valère (*to* Dorine). What do you want of me?

Mariane (*to* Dorine). What is the point of this?

Dorine. We're going to have a little armistice.
  (*to* Valère)
  Now, weren't you silly to get so overheated?

Valère. Didn't you see how badly I was treated?

Dorine (*to* Mariane). Aren't you a simpleton, to have lost your head?

Mariane. Didn't you hear the hateful things he said?

Dorine (*to* Valère). You're both great fools. Her sole desire, Valère,
  Is to be yours in marriage. To that I'll swear.

(*to* Mariane)
  He loves you only, and he wants no wife
  But you, Mariane. On that I'll stake my life.

Mariane (*to* Valère). Then why you advised me so, I cannot see.

Valère (*to* Mariane). On such a question, why ask advice of *me*?

Dorine. Oh, you're impossible. Give me your hands, you two.

(*to* Valère)
  Yours first.

Valère (*giving* Dorine *his hand*). But why?

Dorine (*to* Mariane).   And now a hand from you.

Mariane (*also giving* Dorine *her hand*).
  What are you doing?

Dorine.   There: a perfect fit.
  You suit each other better than you'll admit.

(Valère *and* Mariane *hold hands for some time without looking at each other.*)

Valère (*turning toward* Mariane). Ah, come, don't be so haughty. Give a man
  A look of kindness, won't you, Mariane?

(Mariane *turns toward* Valère *and smiles.*)

Dorine. I tell you, lovers are completely mad!

Valère (*to* Mariane). Now come, confess that you were very bad
  To hurt my feelings as you did just now.
  I have a just complaint, you must allow.

Mariane. *You* must allow that you were most unpleasant . . .

Dorine. Let's table that discussion for the present;

Your father has a plan which must be
stopped.

Mariane. Advise us, then; what means
must we adopt?

Dorine. We'll use all manner of means, and
all at once.

(*to* Mariane)

Your father's addled; he's acting like a
dunce.
Therefore you'd better humor the old fossil.
Pretend to yield to him, be sweet and
docile,
And then postpone, as often as necessary,
The day on which you have agreed to
marry.
You'll thus gain time, and time will turn
the trick.
Sometimes, for instance, you'll be taken
sick,
And that will seem good reason for delay;
Or some bad omen will make you change
the day—
You'll dream of muddy water, or you'll pass
A dead man's hearse, or break a looking
glass.
If all else fails, no man can marry you
Unless you take his ring and say "I do."
But now, let's separate. If they should find
Us talking here, our plot might be divined.

(*to* Valère)

Go to your friends, and tell them what's
occurred,
And have them urge her father to keep his
word.
Meanwhile, we'll stir her brother into
action,
And get Elmire, as well, to join our faction.
Goodbye.

Valère (*to* Mariane). Though each of us
will do his best,
It's your true heart on which my hopes
shall rest.

Mariane (*to* Valère). Regardless of what
Father may decide,
None but Valère shall claim me as his bride.

Valère. Oh, how those words content me!
Come what will . . .

Dorine.   Oh, lovers, lovers! Their
tongues are never still.
Be off, now.

Valère (*turning to go, then turning back*).
One last word . . .

Dorine.   No time to chat:
You leave by this door; and *you* leave by
that.

(Dorine *pushes them, by the shoulders,
toward opposing doors.*)

ACT THREE

SCENE 1

DAMIS, DORINE.

Damis. May lightning strike me even as I
speak,
May all men call me cowardly and weak,
If any fear or scruple holds me back

From settling things, at once, with that
great quack!

Dorine. Now, don't give way to violent
emotion.
Your father's merely talked about this
notion,
And words and deeds are far from being
one.
Much that is talked about is left undone.

Damis. No, I must stop that scoundrel's machinations;
I'll go and tell him off; I'm out of patience.

Dorine. Do calm down and be practical. I had rather
My mistress dealt with him—and with your father.
She has some influence with Tartuffe, I've noted.
He hangs upon her words, seems most devoted,
And may, indeed, be smitten by her charm.
Pray Heaven it's true! 'Twould do our cause no harm.
She sent for him, just now, to sound him out
On this affair you're so incensed about;
She'll find out where he stands, and tell him, too,
What dreadful strife and trouble will ensue
If he lends countenance to your father's plan.
I couldn't get in to see him, but his man
Says that he's almost finished with his prayers.
Go, now. I'll catch him when he comes downstairs.

Damis. I want to hear this conference, and I will.

Dorine. No, they must be alone.

Damis.   Oh, I'll keep still.

Dorine. Not you. I know your temper. You'd start a brawl,
And shout and stamp your foot and spoil it all.
Go on.

Damis. I won't; I have a perfect right . . .

Dorine. Lord, you're a nuisance! He's coming; get out of sight.

(Damis *conceals himself in a closet at the rear of the stage.*)

SCENE 2

TARTUFFE, DORINE.

Tartuffe (*observing* Dorine, *and calling to his manservant offstage*).

Hang up my hair shirt, put my scourge[1] in place,
And pray, Laurent, for Heaven's perpetual grace.
I'm going to the prison now, to share
My last few coins with the poor wretches there.

Dorine (*aside*). Dear God, what affectation! What a fake!

Tartuffe. You wished to see me?

Dorine.   Yes . . .

Tartuffe (*taking a handkerchief from his pocket*).
                    For mercy's sake,
Please take this handkerchief, before you speak.

Dorine. What?

Tartuffe.   Cover that bosom, girl. The flesh is weak.
And unclean thoughts are difficult to control.
Such sights as that can undermine the soul.

Dorine. Your soul, it seems, has very poor defenses,
And flesh makes quite an impact on your senses.

---

1. **hair shirt . . . scourge:** a shirt of rough haircloth and a whip or strap, used by monks in doing penance.

Culver Pictures, New York.

It's strange that you're so easily excited;
My own desires are not so soon ignited,
And if I saw you naked as a beast,
Not all your hide would tempt me in the
    least.

Tartuffe. Girl, speak more modestly; unless
    you do,
I shall be forced to take my leave of you.

Dorine. Oh, no, it's I who must be on my
    way;
I've just one little message to convey.

Madame is coming down, and begs you, Sir,
To wait and have a word or two with her.

Tartuffe. Gladly.

Dorine (*aside*). *That* had a softening effect!
I think my guess about him was correct.

Tartuffe. Will she be long?

Dorine.   No: that's her
    step I hear.
Ah, here she is, and I shall disappear.

SCENE 3

ELMIRE, TARTUFFE.

Tartuffe. May Heaven, whose infinite goodness we adore
Preserve your body and soul forevermore,
And bless your days, and answer thus the plea
Of one who is its humblest votary.

Elmire. I thank you for that pious wish. But please,
Do take a chair and let's be more at ease.

(*They sit down.*)

Tartuffe. I trust that you are once more well and strong?

Elmire. Oh, yes: the fever didn't last for long.

Tartuffe. My prayers are too unworthy, I am sure,
To have gained from Heaven this most gracious cure;
But lately, Madam, my every supplication
Has had for object your recuperation.

Elmire. You shouldn't have troubled so. I don't deserve it.

Tartuffe. Your health is priceless, Madam, and to preserve it
I'd gladly give my own, in all sincerity.

Elmire. Sir, you outdo us all in Christian charity.
You've been most kind. I count myself your debtor.

Tartuffe. 'Twas nothing, Madam. I long to serve you better.

Elmire. There's a private matter I'm anxious to discuss.
I'm glad there's no one here to hinder us.

Tartuffe. I too am glad; it floods my heart with bliss
To find myself alone with you like this.
For just this chance I've prayed with all my power—
But prayed in vain, until this happy hour.

Elmire. This won't take long, Sir, and I hope you'll be
Entirely frank and unconstrained with me.

Tartuffe. Indeed, there's nothing I had rather do
Than bare my inmost heart and soul to you.
First, let me say that what remarks I've made
About the constant visits you are paid
Were prompted not by any mean emotion,
But rather by a pure and deep devotion,
A fervent zeal . . .

Elmire. No need for explanation.
Your sole concern, I'm sure, was my salvation.

Tartuffe (*taking* Elmire's *hand and pressing her fingertips*).
Quite so; and such great fervor do I feel . . .

Elmire. Ooh! Please! You're pinching!

Tartuffe. 'Twas from excess of zeal.
I never meant to cause you pain, I swear.
I'd rather . . .

(*He places his hand on* Elmire's *knee*.)

Elmire. What can your hand be doing there?

Tartuffe. Feeling your gown; what soft, fine-woven stuff!

Elmire. Please, I'm extremely ticklish. That's enough.

(*She draws her chair away;* Tartuffe *pulls his after her.*)

Tartuffe (*fondling the lace collar of her gown*). My, my, what lovely lacework

on your dress!
The workmanship's miraculous, no less.
I've not seen anything to equal it.

Elmire. Yes, quite. But let's talk business for
    a bit.
They say my husband means to break his
    word
And give his daughter to you, Sir. Had
    you heard?

Tartuffe. He did once mention it. But I
    confess
I dream of quite a different happiness.
It's elsewhere, Madam, that my eyes discern
The promise of that bliss for which I yearn.

Elmire. I see: you care for nothing here
    below.

Tartuffe. Ah, well—my heart's not made
    of stone, you know.

Elmire. All your desires mount heaven-
    ward, I'm sure,
In scorn of all that's earthly and impure.

Tartuffe. A love of heavenly beauty does
    not preclude
A proper love for earthly pulchritude;
Our senses are quite rightly captivated
By perfect works our Maker has created.
Some glory clings to all that Heaven has
    made;
In you, all Heaven's marvels are displayed.
On that fair face, such beauties have been
    lavished,
The eyes are dazzled and the heart is
    ravished;
How could I look on you, O flawless
    creature,
And not adore the Author of all Nature,
Feeling a love both passionate and pure
For you, his triumph of self-portraiture?
At first, I trembled lest that love should
    be
A subtle snare that Hell had laid for me;
I vowed to flee the sight of you, eschewing

A rapture that might prove my soul's
    undoing;
But soon, fair being, I became aware
That my deep passion could be made to
    square
With rectitude, and with my bounden
    duty.
I thereupon surrendered to your beauty.
It is, I know, presumptuous on my part
To bring you this poor offering of my
    heart,
And it is not my merit, Heaven knows,
But your compassion on which my hopes
    repose.
You are my peace, my solace, my
    salvation;
On you depends my bliss—or desolation;
I bide your judgment and, as you think
    best,
I shall be either miserable or blest.

Elmire. Your declaration is most gallant,
    Sir,
But don't you think it's out of character?
You'd have done better to restrain your
    passion
And think before you spoke in such a
    fashion.
It ill becomes a pious man like you . . .

Tartuffe. I may be pious, but I'm human
    too:
With your celestial charms before his eyes,
A man has not the power to be wise.
I know such words sound strangely,
    coming from me,
But I'm no angel, nor was meant to be,
And if you blame my passion, you must
    needs
Reproach as well the charms on which it
    feeds.
Your loveliness I had no sooner seen
Than you became my soul's unrivaled
    queen;
Before your seraph glance, divinely sweet,
My heart's defenses crumbled in defeat,

And nothing fasting, prayer, or tears might do
Could stay my spirit from adoring you.
My eyes, my sighs have told you in the past
What now my lips make bold to say at last,
And if, in your great goodness, you will deign
To look upon your slave, and ease his pain,—
If, in compassion for my soul's distress,
You'll stoop to comfort my unworthiness,
I'll raise to you, in thanks for that sweet manna,[2]
An endless hymn, an infinite hosanna.[3]
With me, of course, there need be no anxiety,
No fear of scandal or of notoriety.
These young court gallants, whom all the ladies fancy,
Are vain in speech, in action rash and chancy;
When they succeed in love, the world soon knows it;
No favor's granted them but they disclose it
And by the looseness of their tongues profane
The very altar where their hearts have lain.
Men of my sort, however, love discreetly,
And one may trust our reticence completely.
My keen concern for my good name ensures
The absolute security of yours;
In short, I offer you, my dear Elmire,
Love without scandal, pleasure without fear.

Elmire. I've heard your well-turned speeches to the end,
And what you urge I clearly apprehend.
Aren't you afraid that I may take a notion
To tell my husband of your warm devotion,
And that, supposing he were duly told,
His feelings toward you might grow rather cold?

Tartuffe. I know, dear lady, that your exceeding charity
Will lead your heart to pardon my temerity;
That you'll excuse my violent affection
As human weakness, human imperfection;
And that—O fairest!—you will bear in mind
That I'm but flesh and blood, and am not blind.

Elmire. Some women might do otherwise, perhaps,
But I shall be discreet about your lapse:
I'll tell my husband nothing of what's occurred
If, in return, you'll give your solemn word
To advocate as forcefully as you can
The marriage of Valère and Mariane,
Renouncing all desire to dispossess
Another of his rightful happiness,
And . . .

SCENE 4

DAMIS, ELMIRE, TARTUFFE.

Damis (*emerging from the closet where he has been hiding*). No! We'll not hush up this vile affair;
I heard it all inside that closet there,
Where Heaven, in order to confound the pride
Of this great rascal, prompted me to hide.
Ah, now I have my long-awaited chance
To punish his deceit and arrogance,
And give my father clear and shocking proof

---

2. **manna:** from the Bible, spiritual sustenance.
3. **hosanna** (hō zan′ ə): an exclamation of praise to God.

Of the black character of his dear Tartuffe.

Elmire. Ah no, Damis; I'll be content if he
Will study to deserve my leniency.
I've promised silence—don't make me
break my word;
To make a scandal would be too absurd.
Good wives laugh off such trifles, and for-
get them;
Why should they tell their husbands, and
upset them?

Damis. You have your reasons for taking
such a course,
And I have reasons, too, of equal force.
To spare him now would be insanely
wrong.
I've swallowed my just wrath for far too
long
And watched this insolent bigot bringing
strife
And bitterness into our family life.
Too long he's meddled in my father's
affairs,
Thwarting my marriage hopes, and poor
Valère's.
It's high time that my father was un-
deceived,
And now I've proof that can't be dis-
believed—
Proof that was furnished me by Heaven
above.
It's too good not to take advantage of.
This is my chance, and I deserve to lose it
If, for one moment, I hesitate to use it.

Elmire. Damis . . .

Damis.   No, I must do what I
think right.
Madam, my heart is bursting with delight,
And, say whatever you will, I'll not consent
To lose the sweet revenge on which I'm
bent.
I'll settle matters without more ado;
And here, most opportunely, is my cue.

SCENE 5

ORGON, DAMIS, TARTUFFE, ELMIRE.

Damis. Father, I'm glad you've joined us.
Let us advise you
Of some fresh news which doubtless will
surprise you.
You've just now been repaid with interest
For all your lovingkindness to our guest.
He's proved his warm and grateful feelings
toward you;
It's with a pair of horns he would reward
you.
Yes, I surprised him with your wife, and
heard
His whole adulterous offer, every word.
She, with her all too gentle disposition,
Would not have told you of his proposi-
tion;
But I shall not make terms with brazen
lechery,
And feel that not to tell you would be
treachery.

Elmire. And I hold that one's husband's
peace of mind
Should not be spoilt by tattle of this kind.
One's honor doesn't require it: to be pro-
ficient
In keeping men at bay is quite sufficient.
These are my sentiments, and I wish,
Damis,
That you had heeded me and held your
peace.

SCENE 6

ORGON, DAMIS, TARTUFFE.

Orgon. Can it be true, this dreadful thing I
hear?

Tartuffe. Yes, Brother, I'm a wicked man, I
fear:
A wretched sinner, all depraved and twisted,

The greatest villain that has ever existed.
My life's one heap of crimes, which grows
    each minute;
There's naught but foulness and corrup-
    tion in it;
And I perceive that Heaven, outraged by
    me,
Has chosen this occasion to mortify[4] me.
Charge me with any deed you wish to
    name;
I'll not defend myself, but take the blame.
Believe what you are told, and drive
    Tartuffe
Like some base criminal from beneath
    your roof;
Yes, drive me hence, and with a parting
    curse:
I shan't protest, for I deserve far worse.

Orgon (*to* Damis). Ah, you deceitful boy,
    how dare you try
To stain his purity with so foul a lie?

Damis. What! Are you taken in by such a
    bluff?
Did you not hear . . . ?

Orgon.   Enough, you rogue,
    enough!

Tartuffe. Ah, Brother, let him speak: you're
    being unjust.
Believe his story; the boy deserves your
    trust.
Why, after all, should you have faith in me?
How can you know what I might do, or be?
Is it on my good actions that you base
Your favor? Do you trust my pious face?
Ah, no, don't be deceived by hollow shows;
I'm far, alas, from being what men suppose;
Though the world takes me for a man of
    worth,
I'm truly the most worthless man on earth.

(*to* Damis)

Yes, my dear son, speak out now: call me
    the chief

Of sinners, a wretch, a murderer, a thief;
Load me with all the names men most
    abhor;
I'll not complain; I've earned them all,
    and more;
I'll kneel here while you pour them on my
    head
As a just punishment for the life I've led.

Orgon (*to* Tartuffe). This is too much, dear
    Brother.
(*to* Damis) Have you no heart?

Damis. Are you so hoodwinked by this
    rascal's art . . . ?

Orgon. Be still, you monster.
(*to* Tartuffe)
                        Brother, I
    pray you, rise.
(*to* Damis)
    Villain!

Damis.   But . . .

Orgon.   Silence!

Damis.   Can't you
    realize . . . ?

Orgon. Just one word more, and I'll tear
    you limb from limb.

Tartuffe. In God's name, Brother, don't be
    harsh with him.
I'd rather far be tortured at the stake
Than see him bear one scratch for my
    poor sake.

Orgon (*to* Damis). Ingrate!

Tartuffe.   If I must beg you,
    on bended knee,
To pardon him . . .

Orgon (*falling to his knees, addressing*
    Tartuffe).

---

4. mortify (môrt′ ə fī′): to shame or humiliate.

Such goodness cannot be!

(*to* Damis)

Now, *there's* true charity!

Damis. What, you . . . ?

Orgon.   Villain, be still!
I know your motives; I know you wish him
    ill;
Yes, all of you—wife, children, servants,
    all—
Conspire against him and desire his fall.
Employing every shameful trick you can
To alienate me from this saintly man.
Ah, but the more you seek to drive him
    away,
The more I'll do to keep him. Without
    delay,
I'll spite this household and confound its
    pride
By giving him my daughter as his bride.

Damis. You're going to force her to accept
    his hand?

Orgon. Yes, and this very night, d'you
    understand?
I shall defy you all, and make it clear
That I'm the one who gives the orders
    here.
Come, wretch, kneel down and clasp his
    blessed feet,
And ask his pardon for your black deceit.

Damis. I ask that swindler's pardon? Why,
    I'd rather . . .

Orgon. So! You insult him, and defy your
    father!
A stick! A stick! (*to* Tartuffe) No, no—
    release me, do.

(*to* Damis)

Out of my house this minute! Be off with
    you,
And never dare set foot in it again.

Damis. Well, I shall go, but . . .

Orgon.   Well, go
    quickly, then.
I disinherit you; an empty purse
Is all you'll get from me—except my curse!

SCENE 7

ORGON, TARTUFFE.

Orgon. How he blasphemed your good-
    ness! What a son!

Tartuffe. Forgive him, Lord, as I've already
    done.
(*to* Orgon)
    You can't know how it hurts when some
    one tries
    To blacken me in my dear Brother's eyes.

Orgon. Ahh!

Tartuffe. The mere thought of such
    ingratitude
Plunges my soul into so dark a mood . . .
Such horror grips my heart . . . I gasp for
    breath,
And cannot speak, and feel myself near
    death.

Orgon (*he runs, in tears, to the door through
    which he has just driven his son.*) You
    blackguard! Why did I spare you? Why
        did I not
Break you in little pieces on the spot?
Compose yourself, and don't be hurt, dear
    friend.

Tartuffe. These scenes, these dreadful
    quarrels, have got to end.
I've much upset your household, and I
    perceive
That the best thing will be for me to leave.

Orgon. What are you saying!

Tartuffe.   They're all
    against me here;

They'd have you think me false and
  insincere.

Orgon. Ah, what of that? Have I ceased
  believing in you?

Tartuffe. Their adverse talk will certainly
  continue,
And charges which you now repudiate
You may find credible at a later date.

Orgon. No, Brother, never.

Tartuffe.   Brother, a wife
  can sway
Her husband's mind in many a subtle way.

Orgon. No, no.

Tartuffe.   To leave at once is the
  solution;
Thus only can I end their persecution.

Orgon. No, no, I'll not allow it; you shall
  remain.

Tartuffe. Ah, well; 'twill mean much martyrdom and pain,
But if you wish it . . .

Orgon.   Ah!

Tartuffe.   Enough; so be it.
But one thing must be settled, as I see it.
For your dear honor, and for our friend-
  ship's sake,
There's one precaution I feel bound to
  take.
I shall avoid your wife, and keep away . . .

Orgon. No, you shall not, whatever they
  may say.
It pleases me to vex them, and for spite
I'd have them see you with her day and
  night.
What's more, I'm going to drive them to
  despair
By making you my only son and heir;
This very day, I'll give to you alone
Clear deed and title to everything I own.
A dear, good friend and son-in-law-to-be
Is more than wife, or child, or kin to me.
Will you accept my offer, dearest son?

Tartuffe. In all things, let the will of
  Heaven be done.

Orgon. Poor fellow! Come, we'll go draw
  up the deed.
Then let them burst with disappointed
  greed!

ACT FOUR

SCENE 1

CLÉANTE, TARTUFFE.

Cléante. Yes, all the town's discussing it,
  and truly,
Their comments do not flatter you unduly.
I'm glad we've met, Sir, and I'll give my
  view
Of this sad matter in a word or two.
As for who's guilty, that I shan't discuss;
Let's say it was Damis who caused the fuss;
Assuming, then, that you have been ill-used
By young Damis, and groundlessly accused,
Ought not a Christian to forgive, and
  ought
He not to stifle every vengeful thought?
Should you stand by and watch a father
  make
His only son an exile for your sake?
Again I tell you frankly, be advised:
The whole town, high and low, is scandal-
  ized;
This quarrel must be mended, and my
  advice is
Not to push matters to a further crisis.

No, sacrifice your wrath to God above,
And help Damis regain his father's love.

Tartuffe. Alas, for my part I should take
    great joy
In doing so. I've nothing against the boy.
I pardon all, I harbor no resentment;
To serve him would afford me much con-
    tentment.
But Heaven's interest will not have it so:
If he comes back, then I shall have to go.
After his conduct—so extreme, so
    vicious—
Our further intercourse would look
    suspicious.
God knows what people would think!
    Why, they'd describe
My goodness to him as a sort of bribe;
They'd say that out of guilt I made pretense
Of lovingkindness and benevolence—
That, fearing my accuser's tongue, I strove
To buy his silence with a show of love.

Cléante. Your reasoning is badly warped
    and stretched.
And these excuses, Sir, are most far-fetched.
Why put yourself in charge of Heaven's
    cause?
Does Heaven need our help to enforce its
    laws?
Leave vengeance to the Lord, Sir; while
    we live,
Our duty's not to punish, but forgive;
And what the Lord commands, we should
    obey
Without regard to what the world may say.
What! Shall the fear of being misunder-
    stood
Prevent our doing what is right and good?
No, no; let's simply do what Heaven
    ordains,
And let no other thoughts perplex our
    brains.

Tartuffe. Again, Sir, let me say that I've
    forgiven

Damis, and thus obeyed the laws of Heaven;
But I am not commanded by the Bible
To live with one who smears my name
    with libel.

Cléante. Were you commanded, Sir, to
    indulge the whim
Of poor Orgon, and to encourage him
In suddenly transferring to your name
A large estate to which you have no claim?

Tartuffe. 'Twould never occur to those
    who know me best
To think I acted from self-interest.
The treasures of this world I quite despise;
Their specious glitter does not charm my
    eyes;
And if I have resigned myself to taking
The gift which my dear Brother insists on
    making,
I do so only, as he well understands,
Lest so much wealth fall into wicked
    hands,
Lest those to whom it might descend in
    time
Turn it to purposes of sin and crime,
And not, as I shall do, make use of it
For Heaven's glory and mankind's benefit.

Cléante. Forget these trumped-up fears.
    Your argument
Is one the rightful heir might well resent;
It *is* a moral burden to inherit
Such wealth, but give Damis a chance to
    bear it.
And would it not be worse to be accused
Of swindling, than to see that wealth
    misused?
I'm shocked that you allowed Orgon to
    broach
This matter, and that you feel no self-
    reproach;
Does true religion teach that lawful heirs
May freely be deprived of what is theirs?
And if the Lord has told you in your heart

That you and young Damis must dwell
   apart,
Would it not be the decent thing to beat
A generous and honorable retreat,
Rather than let the son of the house be
   sent,
For your convenience, into banishment?
Sir, if you wish to prove the honesty
Of your intentions . . .

Tartuffe.   Sir, it is half past
   three.
I've certain pious duties to attend to,
And hope my prompt departure won't
   offend you.

Cléante (*alone*). Damn.

SCENE 2

ELMIRE, MARIANE, CLÉANTE, DORINE.

Dorine.   Stay, Sir, and help
   Mariane, for Heaven's sake!
She's suffering so, I fear her heart will
   break.
Her father's plan to marry her off tonight
Has put the poor child in a desperate
   plight.
I hear him coming. Let's stand together,
   now,
And see if we can't change his mind,
   somehow,
About this match we all deplore and fear.

SCENE 3

ORGON, ELMIRE, MARIANE, CLÉANTE, DORINE.

Orgon. Hah! Glad to find you all
   assembled here.

(*to Mariane*)

   This contract, child, contains your happi-
      ness,

And what it says I think your heart can
   guess

Mariane (*falling to her knees*). Sir, by that
   Heaven which sees me here distressed,
And by whatever else can move your
   breast,
Do not employ a father's power, I pray you,
To crush my heart and force it to obey you,
Nor by your harsh commands oppress me
   so
That I'll begrudge the duty which I owe—
And do not so embitter and enslave me
That I shall hate the very life you gave me.
If my sweet hopes must perish, if you refuse
To give me to the one I've dared to choose,
Spare me at least—I beg you, I implore—
The pain of wedding one whom I abhor;
And do not, by a heartless use of force,
Drive me to contemplate some desperate
   course.

Orgon (*feeling himself touched by her*). Be
   firm, my soul. No human weakness,
   now.

Mariane. I don't resent your love for him.
   Allow
Your heart free rein. Sir; give him your
   property,
And if that's not enough, take mine from
   me;
He's welcome to my money; take it, do,
But don't, I pray, include my person too.
Spare me, I beg you; and let me end the
   tale
Of my sad days behind a convent veil.

Orgon. A convent! Hah! When crossed in
   their amours,
All lovesick girls have the same thought
   as yours.
Get up! The more you loathe the man,
   and dread him,
The more ennobling it will be to wed him.

Marry Tartuffe, and mortify your flesh!
Enough; don't start that whimpering
    afresh.

Dorine. But why . . . ?

Orgon.   Be still, there. Speak
    when you're spoken to.
Not one more bit of impudence out of
    you.

Cléante. If I may offer a word of counsel
    here . . .

Orgon. Brother, in counseling you have no
    peer;
All your advice is forceful, sound, and
    clever;
I don't propose to follow it, however.

Elmire (*to* Orgon). I am amazed, and don't
    know what to say;
Your blindness simply takes my breath
    away.
You are indeed bewitched, to take no
    warning
From our account of what occurred this
    morning.

Orgon. Madam, I know a few plain facts,
    and one
Is that you're partial to my rascal son;
Hence, when he sought to make Tartuffe
    the victim
Of a base lie, you dared not contradict
    him.
Ah, but you underplayed your part, my
    pet;
You should have looked more angry, more
    upset.

Elmire. When men make overtures, must
    we reply
With righteous anger and a battle cry?
Must we turn back their amorous
    advances
With sharp reproaches and with fiery
    glances?

Myself, I find such offers merely amusing,
And make no scenes and fusses in refusing;
My taste is for good-natured rectitude,
And I dislike the savage sort of prude
Who guards her virtue with her teeth and
    claws,
And tears men's eyes out for the slightest
    cause:
The Lord preserve me from such honor as
    that,
Which bites and scratches like an alley cat!
I've found that a polite and cool rebuff
Discourages a lover quite enough.

Orgon. I know the facts, and I shall not be
    shaken.

Elmire. I marvel at your power to be mis-
    taken.
Would it, I wonder, carry weight with you
If I could *show* you that our tale was true?

Orgon. Show me?

Elmire.   Yes.

Orgon.   Rot.

Elmire.   Come, what if I
    found a way
To make you see the facts as plain as day?

Orgon. Nonsense.

Elmire.   Do answer me; don't be
    absurd.
I'm not now asking you to trust our word.
Suppose that from some hiding place in
    here
You learned the whole sad truth by eye
    and ear—
What would you say of your good friend,
    after that?

Orgon. Why, I'd say . . . nothing, by
    Jehoshaphat![1]

---

1. Jehoshaphat (ji hăsh′ ə făt′): the name of a
biblical king, used as an exclamation.

It can't be true.

Elmire. You've been too long deceived,
And I'm quite tired of being disbelieved.
Come now: let's put my statements to the test,
And you shall see the truth made manifest.

Orgon. I'll take that challenge. Now do your uttermost.
We'll see how you make good your empty boast.

Elmire (*to* Dorine). Send him to me.

Dorine. He's crafty; it may be hard
To catch the cunning scoundrel off his guard.

Elmire. No, amorous men are gullible. Their conceit
So blinds them that they're never hard to cheat.
Have him come down. (*to* Cléante *and* Mariane) Please leave us, for a bit.

SCENE 4

ELMIRE, ORGON.

Elmire. Pull up this table, and get under it.

Orgon. What?

Elmire. It's essential that you be well hidden.

Orgon. Why there?

Elmire. Oh, Heavens! Just do as you are bidden.
I have my plans; we'll soon see how they fare.
Under the table, now; and once you're there,
Take care that you are neither seen nor heard.

Orgon. Well, I'll indulge you, since I gave my word
To see you through this infantile charade.

Elmire. Once it is over, you'll be glad we played.

(*to her husband, who is now under the table*)

I'm going to act quite strangely, now, and you
Must not be shocked at anything I do.
Whatever I may say, you must excuse
As part of that deceit I'm forced to use.
I shall employ sweet speeches in the task
Of making that imposter drop his mask;
I'll give encouragement to his bold desires,
And furnish fuel to his amorous fires.
Since it's for your sake, and for his destruction,
That I shall seem to yield to his seduction,
I'll gladly stop whenever you decide
That all your doubts are fully satisfied.
I'll count on you, as soon as you have seen
What sort of man he is, to intervene,
And not expose me to his odious lust
One moment longer than you feel you must.
Remember; you're to save me from my plight
Whenever . . . He's coming! Hush! Keep out of sight!

SCENE 5

TARTUFFE, ELMIRE, ORGON.

Tartuffe. You wish to have a word with me, I'm told.

Elmire. Yes. I've a little secret to unfold.
Before I speak, however, it would be wise
To close that door, and look about for spies.

(Tartuffe *goes to the door, closes it, and returns.*)

The very last thing that must happen now
Is a repetition of this morning's row.
I've never been so badly caught off guard.

Oh, how I feared for you! You saw how
 hard
I tried to make that troublesome Damis
Control his dreadful temper, and hold his
 peace.
In my confusion, I didn't have the sense
Simply to contradict his evidence;
But as it happened, that was for the best,
And all has worked out in our interest.
This storm has only bettered your position;
My husband doesn't have the least suspicion,
And now, in mockery of those who do,
He bids me be continually with you.
And that is why, quite fearless of reproof,
I now can be alone with my Tartuffe,
And why my heart—perhaps too quick to
 yield—
Feels free to let its passion be revealed.

Tartuffe. Madam, your words confuse me.
 Not long ago,
You spoke in quite a different style, you
 know.

Elmire. Ah, Sir, if that refusal made you
 smart,
It's little that you know of woman's heart,
Or what the heart is trying to convey
When it resists in such a feeble way!
Always, at first, our modesty prevents
The frank avowal of tender sentiments;
However high the passion which inflames
 us,
Still, to confess its power somehow
 shames us.
Thus we reluct, at first, yet in a tone
Which tells you that our heart is over-
 thrown,
That what our lips deny, our pulse con-
 fesses,
And that, in time, all noes will turn to
 yesses.
I fear my words are all too frank and free,
And a poor proof of woman's modesty;
But since I'm started, tell me, if you will—
Would I have tried to make Damis be still,

Would I have listened, calm and unof-
 fended,
Until your lengthy offer of love was ended,
And been so very mild in my reaction,
Had your sweet words not given me satis-
 faction?
And when I tried to force you to undo
The marriage plans my husband has in
 view,
What did my urgent pleading signify
If not that I admired you, and that I
Deplored the thought that someone else
 might own
Part of a heart I wished for mine alone?

Tartuffe. Madam, no happiness is so com-
 plete
As when, from lips we love, come words
 so sweet;
Their nectar floods my every sense, and
 drains
In honeyed rivulets through all my
 veins.
To please you is my joy, my only goal;
Your love is the restorer of my soul;
And yet I must beg leave, now, to confess
Some lingering doubts as to my happiness.
Might this not be a trick? Might not the
 catch
Be that you wish me to break off the
 match
With Mariane, and so have feigned to
 love me?
I shan't quite trust your fond opinion of
 me
Until the feelings you've expressed so
 sweetly
Are demonstrated somewhat more con-
 cretely,
And you have shown, by certain kind
 concessions,
That I may put my faith in your professions.

Elmire (*she coughs, to warn her husband*).
 Why be in such a hurry? Must my heart
Exhaust its bounty at the very start?

To make that sweet admission cost me
   dear,
But you'll not be content, it would appear,
Unless my store of favors is disbursed
To the last farthing, and at the very first.

Tartuffe. The less we merit, the less we
   dare to hope,
And with our doubts, mere words can
   never cope.
We trust no promised bliss till we receive
   it;
Not till a joy is ours can we believe it.
I, who so little merit your esteem,
Can't credit this fulfillment of my dream,
And shan't believe it, Madam, until I
   savor
Some palpable assurance of your favor.

Elmire. My, how tyrannical your love can
   be.
And how it flusters and perplexes me!
How furiously you take one's heart in hand,
And make your every wish a fierce com-
   mand!
Come, must you hound and harry me to
   death?
Will you not give me time to catch my
   breath?
Can it be right to press me with such force,
Give me no quarter, show me no remorse,
And take advantage, by your stern insis-
   tence,
Of the fond feelings which weaken my
   resistance?

Tartuffe. Well, if you look with favor upon
   my love,
Why, then, begrudge me some clear proof
   thereof?

Elmire. But how can I consent without
   offense
To Heaven, toward which you feel such
   reverence?

Tartuffe. If Heaven is all that holds you

back, don't worry.
I can remove that hindrance in a hurry.
Nothing of that sort need obstruct our
   path.

Elmire. Must one not be afraid of Heaven's
   wrath?

Tartuffe. Madam, forget such fears, and be
   my pupil,
And I shall teach you how to conquer
   scruple.
Some joys, it's true, are wrong in Heaven's
   eyes
Yet Heaven is not averse to compromise;
There is a science, lately formulated,
Whereby one's conscience may be liberated,
And any wrongful act you care to mention
May be redeemed by purity of intention.
I'll teach you, Madam, the secrets of that
   science;
Meanwhile, just place on me your full
   reliance.
Assuage my keen desires, and feel no
   dread:
The sin, if any, shall be on my head.

(Elmire *coughs, this time more loudly.*)

You've a bad cough.

Elmire.   Yes, yes. It's bad indeed.

Tartuffe (*producing a little paper bag*). A
   bit of licorice may be what you need.

Elmire. No, I've a stubborn cold, it seems.
   I'm sure it
Will take much more than licorice to cure
   it.

Tartuffe. How aggravating.

Elmire.   Oh, more than
   I can say.

Tartuffe. If you're still troubled, think of
   things this way:
No one shall know our joys, save us alone,

And there's no evil till the act is known;
It's scandal, Madam, which makes it an
  offense,
And it's no sin to sin in confidence.

Elmire (*having coughed once more*).
Well, clearly I must do as you require,
And yield to your importunate desire.
It is apparent, now, that nothing less
Will satisfy you, and so I acquiesce.
To go so far is much against my will;
I'm vexed that it should come to this; but
  still,
Since you are so determined on it, since
  you
Will not allow mere language to convince
  you,
And since you ask for concrete evidence, I
See nothing for it, now, but to comply.
If this is sinful, if I'm wrong to do it,
So much the worse for him who drove me
  to it.
The fault can surely not be charged to me.

Tartuffe. Madam, the fault is mine, if fault
  there be,
And . . .

Elmire. Open the door a little, and peek
  out;
I wouldn't want my husband poking
  about.

Tartuffe. Why worry about the man? Each
  day he grows
More gullible; one can lead him by the
  nose.
To find us here would fill him with
  delight,
And if he saw the worst, he'd doubt his
  sight.

Elmire. Nevertheless, do step out for a
  minute
Into the hall, and see that no one's
  in it.

SCENE 6

ORGON, ELMIRE.

Orgon (*coming out from under the table*).
That man's a perfect monster, I must
  admit!
I'm simply stunned. I can't get over it.

Elmire. What, coming out so soon? How
  premature!
Get back in hiding, and wait until you're
  sure.
Stay till the end, and be convinced completely;
We mustn't stop till things are proved
  concretely.

Orgon. Hell never harbored anything so
  vicious!

Elmire. Tut, don't be hasty. Try to be judi-
  cious.
Wait, and be certain that there's no mistake.
No jumping to conclusions, for Heaven's
  sake!

(*She places* Orgon *behind her, as* Tartuffe
  reenters.)

SCENE 7

TARTUFFE, ELMIRE, ORGON.

Tartuffe (*not seeing* Orgon). Madam, all
  things have worked out to perfection;
I've given the neighboring rooms a full
  inspection;
No one's about; and now I may at last . . .

Orgon (*intercepting him*). Hold on, my
  passionate fellow, not so fast!
I should advise a little more restraint.
Well, so you thought you'd fool me, my
  dear saint!

How soon you wearied of the saintly life—
Wedding my daughter, and coveting my
  wife!
I've long suspected you, and had a feeling
That soon I'd catch you at your double-
  dealing.
Just now, you've given me evidence galore;
It's quite enough; I have no wish for more.

Elmire (*to* Tartuffe). I'm sorry to have
  treated you so slyly,
But circumstances forced me to be wily.

Tartuffe. Brother, you can't think . . .

Orgon.   No
  more talk from you;
Just leave this household, without more ado.

Tartuffe. What I intended . . .

Orgon.   That seems
  fairly clear.
Spare me your falsehoods and get out of
  here.

Tartuffe. No, I'm the master, and you're
  the one to go!
This house belongs to me, I'll have you
  know,
And I shall show you that you can't hurt
  me
By this contemptible conspiracy,
That those who cross me know not what

they do,
And that I've means to expose and punish
  you,
Avenge offended Heaven, and make you
  grieve
That ever you dared order me to leave.

SCENE 8

ELMIRE, ORGON.

Elmire. What was the point of all that
  angry chatter?

Orgon. Dear God, I'm worried. This is no
  laughing matter.

Elmire. How so?

Orgon.   I fear I understood his drift.
  I'm much disturbed about that deed of gift.

Elmire. You gave him . . .?

Orgon.   Yes, it's all been
  drawn and signed.
But one thing more is weighing on my
  mind.

Elmire. What's that?

Orgon.   I'll tell you; but first
  let's see if there's
A certain strongbox in his room upstairs.

ACT FIVE

SCENE 1

ORGON, CLÉANTE.

Cléante. Where are you going so fast?

Orgon.   God knows!

Cléante.   Then wait;

Let's have a conference, and deliberate
On how this situation's to be met.

Orgon. That strongbox has me utterly upset;
This is the worst of many, many shocks.

Cléante. Is there some fearful mystery in
  that box?

Orgon. My poor friend Argas brought that
  box to me
With his own hands, in utmost secrecy;

'Twas on the very morning of his flight.
It's full of papers which, if they came to light,
Would ruin him—or such is my impression.

Cléante. Then why did you let it out of your possession?

Orgon. Those papers vexed my conscience, and it seemed best
To ask the counsel of my pious guest.
The cunning scoundrel got me to agree
To leave the strongbox in his custody,
So that, in case of an investigation,
I could employ a slight equivocation
And swear I didn't have it, and thereby,
At no expense to conscience, tell a lie.

Cléante. It looks to me as if you're out on a limb.
Trusting him with that box, and offering him
That deed of gift, were actions of a kind
Which scarcely indicate a prudent mind.
With two such weapons, he has the upper hand,
And since you're vulnerable, as matters stand,
You erred once more in bringing him to bay.
You should have acted in some subtler way.

Orgon. Just think of it: behind that fervent face,
A heart so wicked, and a soul so base!
I took him in, a hungry beggar, and then . . .
Enough, by God! I'm through with pious men:
Henceforth I'll hate the whole false brotherhood,
And persecute them worse than Satan could.

Cléante. Ah, there you go—extravagant as ever!
Why can you not be rational? You never
Manage to take the middle course, it seems,
But jump, instead, between absurd extremes.
You've recognized your recent grave mistake
In falling victim to a pious fake;
Now, to correct that error, must you embrace
An even greater error in its place,
And judge our worthy neighbors as a whole
By what you've learned of one corrupted soul?
Come, just because one rascal made you swallow
A show of zeal which turned out to be hollow,
Shall you conclude that all men are deceivers,
And that, today, there are no true believers?
Let atheists make that foolish inference;
Learn to distinguish virtue from pretense,
Be cautious in bestowing admiration,
And cultivate a sober moderation.
Don't humor fraud, but also don't asperse
True piety; the latter fault is worse,
And it is best to err, if err one must,
As you have done, upon the side of trust.

SCENE 2

DAMIS, ORGON, CLÉANTE.

Damis. Father, I hear that scoundrel's uttered threats
Against you; that he pridefully forgets
How, in his need, he was befriended by you,
And means to use your gifts to crucify you.

Orgon. It's true, my boy, I'm too distressed for tears.

Damis. Leave it to me, Sir; let me trim his ears.

Faced with such insolence, we must not
  waver.
I shall rejoice in doing you the favor
Of cutting short his life, and your distress.

Cléante. What a display of young hot-
  headedness!
Do learn to moderate your fits of rage.
In this just kingdom, this enlightened age,
One does not settle things by violence.

SCENE 3

MADAME PERNELLE, MARIANE, ELMIRE, DORINE,
DAMIS, ORGON, CLÉANTE.

Madame Pernelle. I hear strange tales of
  very strange events.

Orgon. Yes, strange events which these
  two eyes beheld.
The man's ingratitude is unparalleled.
I save a wretched pauper from starvation,
House him, and treat him like a blood
  relation,
Shower him every day with my largesse,
Give him my daughter, and all that I
  possess;
And meanwhile the unconscionable[1]
  knave
Tries to induce my wife to misbehave;
And not content with such extreme
  rascality,
Now threatens me with my own liberality,
And aims, by taking base advantage of
The gifts I gave him out of Christian love,
To drive me from my house, a ruined man,
And make me end a pauper, as he began.

Dorine. Poor fellow!

Madame Pernelle. No, my son, I'll never
  bring
Myself to think him guilty of such a thing.

Orgon. How's that?

Madame Pernelle. The righteous always
  were maligned.

Orgon. Speak clearly, Mother. Say what's
  on your mind.

Madame Pernelle. I mean that I can smell
  a rat, my dear.
You know how everybody hates him, here.

Orgon. That has no bearing on the case at
  all.

Madame Pernelle. I told you a hundred
  times, when you were small,
That virtue in this world is hated ever;
Malicious men may die, but malice never.

Orgon. No doubt that's true, but how does
  it apply?

Madame Pernelle. They've turned you
  against him by a clever lie.

Orgon. I've told you, I was there and saw it
  done.

Madame Pernelle. Ah, slanderers will
  stop at nothing, Son.

Orgon. Mother, I'll lose my temper . . . For
  the last time,
I tell you I was witness to the crime.

Madame Pernelle. The tongues of spite
  are busy night and noon,
And to their venom no man is immune.

Orgon. You're talking nonsense. Can't you
  realize
I saw it; saw it; saw it with my eyes?
Saw, do you understand me? Must I shout
  it
Into your ears before you'll cease to doubt it?

Madame Pernelle. Appearances can
  deceive, my son. Dear me,

---

1. **unconscionable** (un kän' shən ə bəl): not guided
or held back by conscience.

We cannot always judge by what we see.

Orgon. Drat! Drat!

Madame Pernelle. One often interprets
things awry;
Good can seem evil to a suspicious eye.

Orgon. Was I to see his pawing at Elmire
As an act of charity?

Madame Pernelle. Till his guilt is clear,
A man deserves the benefit of the doubt.
You should have waited, to see how things
turned out.

Orgon. Great God in Heaven, what more
proof did I need?
Was I to sit there, watching, until he'd . . .
You drive me to the brink of impropriety.

Madame Pernelle. No, no, a man of such
surpassing piety
Could not do such a thing. You cannot
shake me.
I don't believe it, and you shall not make me.

Orgon. You vex me so that, if you weren't
my mother,
I'd say to you . . . some dreadful thing or
other.

Dorine. It's your turn now, Sir, not to be
listened to;
You'd not trust us, and now she won't trust
you.

Cléante. My friends, we're wasting time
which should be spent
In facing up to our predicament.
I fear that scoundrel's threats weren't
made in sport.

Damis. Do you think he'd have the nerve
to go to court?

Elmire. I'm sure he won't: they'd find it all
too crude
A case of swindling and ingratitude.

Cléante. Don't be too sure. He won't be at

a loss
To give his claims a high and righteous
gloss;
And clever rogues with far less valid cause
Have trapped their victims in a web of
laws.
I say again that to antagonize
A man so strongly armed was most unwise.

Orgon. I know it; but the man's appalling
cheek
Outraged me so, I couldn't control my
pique.

Cléante. I wish to Heaven that we could
devise
Some truce between you, or some compromise.

Elmire. If I had known what cards he held,
I'd not
Have roused his anger by my little plot.

Orgon (*to Dorine, as Monsieur Loyal enters*).
What is that fellow looking for? Who is he?
Go talk to him—and tell him that I'm busy.

SCENE 4

MONSIEUR LOYAL, MADAME PERNELLE, ORGON,
DAMIS, MARIANE, DORINE, ELMIRE, CLÉANTE.

Monsieur Loyal. Good day, dear sister.
Kindly let me see
Your master.

Dorine.   He's involved with company,
And cannot be disturbed just now, I fear.

Monsieur Loyal. I hate to intrude; but
what has brought me here
Will not disturb your master, in any
event.
Indeed, my news will make him most
content.

Dorine. Your name?

Monsieur Loyal. Just say that I bring
greetings from

Monsieur Tartuffe, on whose behalf I've
    come.

Dorine (*to* Orgon). Sir, he's a very gracious
    man, and bears
  A message from Tartuffe, which he declares
  Will make you most content.

Cléante. Upon my word.
  I think this man had best be seen, and
    heard.

Orgon. Perhaps he has some settlement to
    suggest.
  How shall I treat him? What manner
    would be best?

Cléante. Control your anger, and if he
    should mention
  Some fair adjustment, give him your full
    attention.

Monsieur Loyal. Good health to you,
    good Sir. May Heaven confound
  Your enemies, and may your joys abound.

Orgon (*aside, to* Cléante). A gentle saluta-
    tion: it confirms
  My guess that he is here to offer terms.

Monsieur Loyal. I've always held your
    family most dear;
  I served your father, Sir, for many a year.

Orgon. Sir, I must ask your pardon; to my
    shame,
  I cannot now recall your face or name.

Monsieur Loyal. Loyal's my name; I come
    from Normandy,
  And I'm a bailiff, in all modesty.
  For forty years, praise God, it's been my
    boast
  To serve with honor in that vital post,
  And I am here, Sir, if you will permit
  The liberty, to serve you with this writ . . .

Orgon. To—*what?*

Monsieur Loyal. Now, please, Sir, let us

have no friction:
  It's nothing but an order of eviction.
  You are to move your goods and family out
  And make way for new occupants, with
    out
  Deferment or delay, and give the keys . . .

Orgon. I? Leave this house?

Monsieur Loyal.   Why yes, Sir, if
    you please.
  This house, Sir, from the cellar to the
    roof,
  Belongs now to the good Monsieur
    Tartuffe,
  And he is lord and master of your estate
  By virtue of a deed of present date,
  Drawn in due form, with clearest legal
    phrasing . . .

Damis. Your insolence is utterly amazing!

Monsieur Loyal. Young man, my business
    here is not with you,
  But with your wise and temperate father,
    who,
  Like every worthy citizen, stands in awe
  Of justice, and would never obstruct the
    law.

Orgon. But . . .

Monsieur Loyal. Not for a million, Sir,
    would you rebel
  Against authority; I know that well.
  You'll not make trouble, Sir, or interfere
  With the execution of my duties here.

Damis. Someone may execute a smart tattoo
  On that black jacket of yours, before
    you're through.

Monsieur Loyal. Sir, bid your son be
    silent. I'd much regret
  Having to mention such a nasty threat
  Of violence, in writing my report.

Dorine (*aside*). This man Loyal's a most
    disloyal sort!

Monsieur Loyal. I love all men of upright
   character,
And when I agreed to serve these papers,
   Sir,
It was your feelings that I had in mind.
I couldn't bear to see the case assigned
To someone else, who might esteem you
   less
And so subject you to unpleasantness.

Orgon. What's more unpleasant than
   telling a man to leave
His house and home?

Monsieur Loyal. You'd like a short
   reprieve?
If you desire it, Sir, I shall not press you,
But wait until tomorrow to dispossess you.
Splendid. I'll come and spend the night
   here, then,
Most quietly, with half a score of men.
For form's sake, you might bring me, just
   before
You go to bed, the keys to the front door.
My men, I promise, will be on their best
Behavior, and will not disturb your rest.
But bright and early, Sir, you must be
   quick
And move out all your furniture, every
   stick:
The men I've chosen are both young and
   strong,
And with their help it shouldn't take you
   long.
In short, I'll make things pleasant and
   convenient,
And since I'm being so extremely lenient,
Please show me, Sir, a like consideration,
And give me your entire cooperation.

Orgon (*aside*). I may be all but bankrupt,
   but I vow
I'd give a hundred louis,[2] here and now,
Just for the pleasure of landing one good
   clout
Right on the end of that complacent snout.

Cléante. Careful; don't make things worse.

Damis.   My bootsole itches
To give that beggar a good kick in the
   breeches.

Dorine. Monsieur Loyal, I'd love to hear
   the whack
Of a stout stick across your fine broad
   back.

Monsieur Loyal. Take care: a woman too
   may go to jail if
She uses threatening language to a bailiff.

Cléante. Enough, enough, Sir. This must
   not go on.
Give me that paper, please, and then
   begone.

Monsieur Loyal. Well, *au revoir*. God give
   you all good cheer!

Orgon. May God confound you, and him
   who sent you here!

SCENE 5

ORGON, CLÉANTE, MARIANE, ELMIRE, MADAME
PERNELLE, DORINE, DAMIS.

Orgon. Now, Mother, was I right or not?
   This writ
Should change your notion of Tartuffe a
   bit.
Do you perceive his villainy at last?

Madame Pernelle. I'm thunderstruck. I'm
   utterly aghast.

Dorine. Oh, come, be fair. You mustn't
   take offense
At this new proof of his benevolence.
He's acting out of selfless love, I know.
Material things enslave the soul, and so
He kindly has arranged your liberation

---

2. **louis** (lo͞o′ ē): French gold coins.

From all that might endanger your
   salvation.

Orgon. Will you not ever hold your
   tongue, you dunce?

Cléante. Come, you must take some
   action, and at once.

Elmire. Go tell the world of the low trick
   he's tried.
   The deed of gift is surely nullified
   By such behavior, and public rage will not
   Permit the wretch to carry out his plot.

SCENE 6

VALÈRE, ORGON, CLÉANTE, ELMIRE, MARIANE,
MADAME PERNELLE, DAMIS, DORINE.

Valère. Sir, though I hate to bring you
   more bad news,
   Such is the danger that I cannot choose.
   A friend who is extremely close to me
   And knows my interest in your family
   Has, for my sake, presumed to violate
   The secrecy that's due to things of state,
   And sends me word that you are in a
   plight
   From which your one salvation lies in
   flight.
   That scoundrel who's imposed upon you
   so
   Denounced you to the King an hour ago
   And, as supporting evidence, displayed
   The strongbox of a certain renegade
   Whose secret papers, so he testified,
   You had disloyally agreed to hide.
   I don't know just what charges may be
   pressed,
   But there's a warrant out for your arrest;
   Tartuffe has been instructed, furthermore,
   To guide the arresting officer to your door.

Cléante. He's clearly done this to facilitate
   His seizure of your house and your estate.

Orgon. That man, I must say, is a vicious
   beast!

Valère. Quick, Sir; you mustn't tarry in the
   least.
   My carriage is outside, to take you hence;
   This thousand louis should cover all
   expense.
   Let's lose no time, or you shall be undone;
   The sole defense, in this case, is to run.
   I shall go with you all the way, and place
   you
   In a safe refuge to which they'll never
   trace you.

Orgon. Alas, dear boy, I wish that I could
   show you
   My gratitude for everything I owe you.
   But now is not the time; I pray the Lord
   That I may live to give you your reward.
   Farewell, my dears; be careful . . .

Cléante.   Brother,
   hurry.
   We shall take care of things; you needn't
   worry.

SCENE 7

THE OFFICER, TARTUFFE, ORGON, VALÈRE, MADAME
   PERNELLE, ELMIRE, MARIANE, CLÉANTE, DORINE,
   DAMIS.

Tartuffe. Gently, Sir, gently; stay right
   where you are.
   No need for haste; your lodging isn't far.
   You're off to prison, by order of the
   Prince.

Orgon. This is the crowning blow, you
   wretch; and since
   It means my total ruin and defeat,
   Your villainy is now at last complete.

Tartuffe. You needn't try to provoke me;
   it's no use.
   Those who serve Heaven must expect
   abuse.

Cléante. You are indeed most patient,
sweet, and blameless.

Dorine. How he exploits the name of
Heaven! It's shameless.

Tartuffe. Your taunts and mockeries are all
for naught;
To do my duty is my only thought.

Mariane. Your love of duty is most
meritorious,
And what you've done is little short of
glorious.

Tartuffe. All deeds are glorious, Madam,
which obey
The sovereign prince who sent me here
today.

Orgon. I rescued you when you were destitute;
Have you forgotten that, you thankless
brute?

Tartuffe. No, no, I well remember every-
thing;
But my first duty is to serve my King.
That obligation is so paramount
That other claims, beside it, do not count;
And for it I would sacrifice my wife,
My family, my friend, or my own life.

Elmire. Hypocrite!

Dorine. All that we most revere,
he uses
To cloak his plots and camouflage his ruses.

Cléante. If it is true that you are animated
By pure and loyal zeal, as you have stated,
Why was this zeal not roused until you'd
sought
To make Orgon a cuckold, and been
caught?
Why weren't you moved to give your
evidence
Until your outraged host had driven you
hence?

I shan't say that the gift of all his treasure
Ought to have damped your zeal in any
measure;
But if he is a traitor, as you declare,
How could you condescend to be his heir?

Tartuffe (*to the* Officer). Sir, spare me all
this clamor; it's growing shrill.
Please carry out your orders, if you will.

Officer. Yes, I've delayed too long, Sir.
Thank you kindly.
You're just the proper person to remind
me.
Come, you are off to join the other
boarders
In the King's prison, according to his
orders.

Tartuffe. Who? I, Sir?

Officer. Yes.

Tartuffe. To prison? This
can't be true!

Officer. I owe an explanation, but not to
you.

(*to* Orgon)

Sir, all is well; rest easy, and be grateful.
We serve a Prince to whom all sham is
hateful,
A Prince who sees into our inmost hearts,
And can't be fooled by any trickster's arts.
His royal soul, though generous and
human,
Views all things with discernment and
acumen;
His sovereign reason is not lightly swayed,
And all his judgments are discreetly
weighed.
He honors righteous men of every kind,
And yet his zeal for virtue is not blind.
Nor does his love of piety numb his wits
And make him tolerant of hypocrites.
'Twas hardly likely that this man could
cozen

A King who's foiled such liars by the
   dozen.
With one keen glance, the King perceived
   the whole
Perverseness and corruption of his soul,
And thus high Heaven's justice was dis-
   played:
Betraying you, the rogue stood self-
   betrayed.
The King soon recognized Tartuffe as one
Notorious by another name, who'd done
So many vicious crimes that one could fill
Ten volumes with them, and be writing
   still.
But to be brief: our sovereign was appalled
By this man's treachery toward you, which
   he called
The last, worst villainy of a vile career,
And bade me follow the impostor here
To see how gross his impudence could be,
And force him to restore your property.
Your private papers, by the King's command,
I hereby seize and give into your hand.
The King, by royal order, invalidates
The deed which gave this rascal your
   estates,
And pardons, furthermore, your grave
   offense
In harboring an exile's documents.
By these decrees, our Prince rewards you
   for
Your loyal deeds in the late civil war,
And shows how heartfelt is his satisfaction
In recompensing any worthy action.
How much he prizes merit, and how he
   makes
More of men's virtues than of their
   mistakes.

Dorine. Heaven be praised!

Madame Pernelle. I breathe again, at last.

Elmire. We're safe.

Mariane.   I can't believe the
   danger's past.

Orgon (*to* Tartuffe). Well, traitor, now you
   see . . .

Cléante. Ah, Brother, please,
   Let's not descend to such indignities.
   Leave the poor wretch to his unhappy
      fate,
   And don't say anything to aggravate
   His present woes; but rather hope that he
   Will soon embrace an honest piety,
   And mend his ways, and by a true repen-
      tance
   Move our just King to moderate his
      sentence.
   Meanwhile, go kneel before your
      sovereign's throne
   And thank him for the mercies he has
      shown.

Orgon. Well said: let's go at once and,
      gladly kneeling,
   Express the gratitude which all are feeling.
   Then, when that first great duty has been
      done,
   We'll turn with pleasure to a second one,
   And give Valère, whose love has proven
      so true,
   The wedded happiness which is his due.

Thinking About the Play

A PERSONAL RESPONSE

sharing impressions

1. What are your feelings about the characters in this play? Jot down your ideas in your journal.

constructing interpretations

2. Were you satisfied by the ending of the play?
Think about
- whether the ending feels natural
- whether the ending was predictable or surprising
- other ways the play might have ended

3. Why do you think Orgon is so influenced by Tartuffe?
Think about
- the kind of person Orgon is
- the kind of person Tartuffe is
- why other characters are not fooled by Tartuffe
- why other characters have trouble convincing Orgon of Tartuffe's hypocrisy

4. Which character in the play do you think is the most admirable? Support your opinion with examples from the play.

5. What values do you think Molière is promoting in this play?
Think about
- the qualities displayed by Tartuffe
- the lesson Orgon learns
- which characters might come closest to Molière's ideals

A CREATIVE RESPONSE

6. Do you think any of the characters in the play will change because of this experience? Use details from the play to support your opinion.

A CRITICAL RESPONSE

7. Which aspects of the play seem the most humorous to you?
Think about
- the kinds of characters portrayed
- the relationships between the characters
- the use of dramatic and verbal irony in the play
- diction, or word choice

8. When *Tartuffe* was first performed, it was considered by many to be offensive. Based on your understanding of the play, who do you think might have been offended? Explain your answer.

Analyzing the Writer's Craft

CHARACTERIZATION IN DRAMA

In this play how does the audience or reader learn what Tartuffe is really like?

Building a Literary Vocabulary. Characterization refers to the techniques that a writer uses to develop characters. The techniques used in fiction and in drama are different in some ways and alike in others. In a short story or novel, a writer can describe a character's physical appearance and behavior. In the script of a play, the writer provides some of the same information through stage directions, so that when the play is performed, the audience learns about the characters by observing them onstage. The writer of fiction can also show what a character is like by describing the character's inner thoughts. In a play, characters' thoughts are made known only when characters talk to themselves in monologues or to the audience in asides. In both fiction and drama, characters are revealed through their own actions and words as well as through the actions and words of other characters. In the first two acts of this play, Tartuffe does not appear on the stage at all, yet from the very first scene the audience learns about him through the speeches of the other characters. This technique serves to build up interest in his character. Then when he does appear in Act Three, what he says and does confirms and deepens the characterization of him already begun.

Application: Analyzing Characterization. Working with several other students choose three favorite characters. Go through the play to identify passages that develop the traits of the characters. For each passage indicate whether characterization comes from a character's conversation, from asides, from stage directions, or from the speeches of other characters. Then try to sum up each character in a phrase; for example, Tartuffe might be summed up as "a lecherous fraud and a hypocrite." Compare your work with that of other groups.

Connecting Reading and Writing

1. Write **director's notes** that outline the physical characteristics you would want to see portrayed by the actor who plays Tartuffe. Make sure to comment on such characteristics as posture, mannerisms, facial expressions, and gestures.

Option: Write a **memo** to the director of a movie based on *Tartuffe* advising who you think would be the best actor to play Tartuffe.

2. Write a **dramatic script** for an updated version of the play that reflects modern-day values and relationships.

Option: Create a **comic strip** based on a modern adaptation of *Tartuffe*.

3. You are Orgon. Write a new **will** to reflect your changed values after the episode with Tartuffe.

Option: Create a **letter** that Orgon might write to his brother describing the change he has undergone.

A Piece of String

GUY DE MAUPASSANT   1850–1893   FRANCE

A biography of Maupassant appears on page 747.

Approaching the Story

Guy de Maupassant (gē də mō på san′), considered one of the world's greatest short story writers, is known for his realistic portrayal of French peasant life in the late nineteenth century and for his critical attitude toward human nature and society. "A Piece of String" is set in the French province of Normandy, where Maupassant was born. The arduous nature of country life in Normandy is reflected in the peasants' dress, manners, and way of life, which have remained the same for hundreds of years.

Building Vocabulary

These essential words are footnoted within the story.

interminable (in tʉr′ mi nə bəl): He was soon lost in the . . . crowd, which was busy with **interminable** bargainings. (page 589)

credence (krēd′ 'ns): "You will not make me believe . . . that . . . a man worthy of **credence** mistook this cord for a pocketbook." (page 591)

attest (ə test′): The peasant, furious, lifted his hand . . . to **attest** his honor. (page 591)

incredulity (in′ krə do͞o′ lə tē): He only met with **incredulity**. It made him ill at night. (page 591)

Connecting Writing and Reading

Recall an experience in which you were falsely accused of wrongdoing, or imagine how it would feel to go through such an experience. In your journal describe your feelings. As you read, see if the main character experiences some of the same feelings when he is falsely accused.

*A*LONG ALL THE roads around Goderville the peasants and their wives were coming toward the burgh because it was market day. The men were proceeding with slow steps, the whole body bent forward at each movement of their long twisted legs, deformed by their hard work, by the weight on the plow which, at the same time, raised the left shoulder and swerved the figure, by the reaping of the wheat which made the knees spread to make a firm "purchase,"[1] by all the slow and painful labors of the country. Their blouses, blue, "stiff-starched," shining as if varnished, ornamented with a little design in white at the neck and wrists, puffed about their bony bodies, seemed like balloons ready to carry them off. From each of them a head, two arms, and two feet protruded.

Some led a cow or a calf by a cord, and their wives, walking behind the animal, whipped its haunches with a leafy branch to hasten its progress. They carried large baskets on their arms from which, in some cases, chickens and, in others, ducks thrust out their heads. And they walked with a quicker, livelier step than their husbands. Their spare straight figures were wrapped in a scanty little shawl, pinned over their flat bosoms, and their heads were enveloped in a white cloth glued to the hair and surmounted by a cap.

Then a wagon passed at the jerky trot of a nag, shaking strangely, two men seated side by side and a woman in the bottom of the vehicle, the latter holding on to the sides to lessen the hard jolts.

In the public square of Goderville there was a crowd, a throng of human beings and animals mixed together. The horns of the cattle, the tall hats with long nap of the rich peasant, and the headgear of the peasant women rose above the surface of the assembly. And the clamorous, shrill, screaming voices made a continuous and savage din which sometimes was dominated by the robust lungs of some countryman's laugh, or the long lowing of a cow tied to the wall of a house.

All that smacked of the stable, the dairy and the dirt heap, hay and sweat, giving forth that unpleasant odor, human and animal, peculiar to the people of the field.

Maître Hauchecome, of Breaute,[2] had just arrived at Goderville, and he was directing his steps toward the public square, when he perceived upon the ground a little piece of string. Maître Hauchecome, economical like a true Norman, thought that everything useful ought to be picked up, and he bent painfully, for he suffered from rheumatism. He took the bit of thin cord from the ground and began to roll it carefully when he noticed Maître Malandain,[3] the harness maker, on the threshold of his door, looking at him. They had heretofore had business together on the subject of a halter, and they were on bad terms, being both good haters. Maître Hauchecome was seized with a sort of shame to be seen thus by his enemy, picking a bit of string out of the dirt. He concealed his "find" quickly under his blouse, then in his trousers' pocket; then he pretended to be still looking on the ground for something which he did not find, and he went toward the market, his head forward, bent double by his pains.

He was soon lost in the noisy and slowly moving crowd, which was busy with <u>interminable</u>[4] bargainings. The peasants milked, went and came, perplexed, always in fear of being cheated, not daring to decide, watching

---

1. purchase: position of the body necessary in order to move a large weight.

2. Maître Hauchecome, of Breaute (me′ trə ōsh kôm′, bre ōt′): *maître* is French for *master.*

3. Malandain (mà län dan′).

4. interminable (in tʉr′ mi nə bəl): lasting, or seeming to last, forever; endless.

the vendor's eye, ever trying to find the trick in the man and the flaw in the beast.

The women, having placed their great baskets at their feet, had taken out the poultry which lay upon the ground, tied together by the feet, with terrified eyes and scarlet crests.

They heard offers, stated their prices with a dry air and impassive face, or perhaps, suddenly deciding on some proposed reduction, shouted to the customer who was slowly going away: "All right, Maître Authirne,[5] I'll give it to you for that."

Then little by little the square was deserted, and the Angelus[6] ringing at noon, those who had stayed too long, scattered to their shops.

At Jourdain's[7] the great room was full of people eating, as the big court was full of vehicles of all kinds, carts, gigs, wagons, dump carts, yellow with dirt, mended and patched, raising their shafts to the sky like two arms, or perhaps with their shafts in the ground and their backs in the air.

Just opposite the diners seated at the table, the immense fireplace, filled with bright flames, cast a lively heat on the backs of the row on the right. Three spits were turning on which were chickens, pigeons, and legs of mutton; and an appetizing odor of roast beef and gravy dripping over the nicely browned skin rose from the hearth, increased the jovialness, and made everybody's mouth water.

All the aristocracy of the plow ate there, at Maître Jourdain's, tavern keeper and horse dealer, a rascal who had money.

The dishes were passed and emptied, as were the jugs of yellow cider. Everyone told his affairs, his purchases, and sales. They discussed the crops. The weather was favorable for the green things but not for the wheat.

Suddenly the drum beat in the court, before the house. Everybody rose except a few indifferent persons, and ran to the door, or to the windows, their mouths still full and napkins in their hands.

After the public crier had ceased his drumbeating, he called out in a jerky voice, speaking his phrases irregularly:

"It is hereby made known to the inhabitants of Goderville, and in general to all persons present at the market, that there was lost this morning, on the road to Benzeville, between nine and ten o'clock, a black leather pocketbook containing five hundred francs[8] and some business papers. The finder is requested to return same with all haste to the mayor's office or to Maître Fortune Houlbreque[9] of Manneville, there will be twenty francs reward."

Then the man went away. The heavy roll of the drum and the crier's voice were again heard at a distance.

Then they began to talk of this event, discussing the chances that Maître Houlbreque had of finding or not finding his pocketbook.

And the meal concluded. They were finishing their coffee when a chief of the gendarmes[10] appeared upon the threshold.

He inquired:

"Is Maître Hauchecome, of Breaute, here?"

Maître Hauchecome, seated at the other end of the table, replied:

"Here I am."

And the officer resumed:

"Maître Hauchecome, will you have the goodness to accompany me to the mayor's office? The mayor would like to talk to you."

The peasant, surprised and disturbed, swal-

---

5. Authirne (ō tērn').

6. Angelus (an' jə ləs): the church bells that ring to announce the Angelus prayer, which is recited at morning, noon, and night.

7. Jourdain (zhōōr dan').

8. five hundred francs: French currency worth about one hundred dollars when the story was written.

9. Fortune Houlbreque (fôr tün' ōōl' brek').

10. gendarmes (zhän dàrm'): armed police.

lowed at a draught his tiny glass of brandy, rose, and, even more bent than in the morning, for the first steps after each rest were specially difficult, set out, repeating: "Here I am, here I am."

The mayor was awaiting him, seated on an armchair. He was the notary of the vicinity, a stout, serious man, with pompous phrases.

"Maître Hauchecome," said he, "you were seen this morning to pick up, on the road to Benzeville, the pocketbook lost by Maître Houlbreque, of Manneville."

The countryman, astounded, looked at the mayor, already terrified, by this suspicion resting on him without his knowing why.

"Me? Me? Me pick up the pocketbook?"

"Yes, you, yourself."

"Word of honor, I never heard of it."

"But you were seen."

"I was seen, me? Who says he saw me?"

"Monsieur Malandain, the harness maker."

The old man remembered, understood, and flushed with anger.

"Ah, he saw me, the clodhopper, he saw me pick up this string, here, M'sieu',[11] the Mayor." And rummaging in his pocket he drew out the little piece of string.

But the mayor, incredulous, shook his head.

"You will not make me believe, Maître Hauchecome, that Monsieur Malandain, who is a man worthy of credence,[12] mistook this cord for a pocketbook."

The peasant, furious, lifted his hand, spat at one side to attest[13] his honor, repeating:

"It is nevertheless the truth of the good God, the sacred truth, M'sieu' the Mayor. I repeat it on my soul and my salvation."

The mayor resumed:

"After picking up the object, you stood like a stilt, looking a long while in the mud to see if any piece of money had fallen out."

The good, old man choked with indignation and fear.

"How anyone can tell—how anyone can tell—such lies to take away an honest man's reputation! How can anyone—"

There was no use in his protesting, nobody believed him. He was confronted with Monsieur Malandain, who repeated and maintained his affirmation. They abused each other for an hour. At his own request, Maître Hauchecome was searched, nothing was found on him.

Finally the mayor, very much perplexed, discharged him with the warning that he would consult the public prosecutor and ask for further orders.

The news had spread. As he left the mayor's office, the old man was surrounded and questioned with a serious or bantering curiosity, in which there was no indignation. He began to tell the story of the string. No one believed him. They laughed at him.

He went along, stopping his friends, beginning endlessly his statement and his protestations, showing his pockets turned inside out, to prove that he had nothing.

They said:

"Old rascal, get out!"

And he grew angry, becoming exasperated, hot, and distressed at not being believed, not knowing what to do and always repeating himself.

Night came. He must depart. He started on his way with three neighbors to whom he pointed out the place where he had picked up the bit of string; and all along the road he spoke of his adventure.

In the evening he took a turn in the village of Breaute, in order to tell it to everybody. He only met with incredulity.[14]

---

11. M'sieu' (mə syör'): shortened form of *monsieur*, French word for *mister* or *sir*.

12. credence (krēd' 'ns): belief; trust.

13. attest (ə test'): to testify to; to be proof of.

14. incredulity (in' krə doo' lə tē): unwillingness or inability to believe; doubt.

It made him ill at night.

The next day about one o'clock in the afternoon, Marius Paumelle, a hired man in the employ of Maître Breton, husbandman at Ymanville,[15] returned the pocketbook and its contents to Maître Houlbreque of Manneville.

This man claimed to have found the object in the road; but not knowing how to read, he had carried it to the house and given it to his employer.

The news spread through the neighborhood. Maître Hauchecome was informed of it. He immediately went the circuit and began to recount his story completed by the happy climax. He was in triumph.

"What grieved me so much was not the thing itself, as the lying. There is nothing so shameful as to be placed under a cloud on account of a lie."

He talked of his adventure all day long, he told it on the highway to people who were passing by, in the wineshop to people who were drinking there, and to persons coming out of church the following Sunday. He stopped strangers to tell them about it. He was calm now, and yet something disturbed him without his knowing exactly what it was. People had the air of joking while they listened. They did not seem convinced. He seemed to feel that remarks were being made behind his back.

On Tuesday of the next week he went to the market at Goderville, urged solely by the necessity he felt of discussing the case.

Malandain, standing at his door, began to laugh on seeing him pass. Why?

He approached a farmer from Crequetot,[16] who did not let him finish, and giving him a thump in the stomach said to his face:

"You big rascal."

Then he turned his back on him.

Maître Hauchecome was confused, why was he called a big rascal?

When he was seated at the table in Jourdain's tavern he commenced to explain "the affair."

A horse dealer from Monvilliers[17] called to him:

"Come, come, old sharper, that's an old trick; I know all about your piece of string!"

Hauchecome stammered:

"But since the pocketbook was found."

But the other man replied:

"Shut up, papa, there is one that finds, and there is one that reports. At any rate you are mixed with it."

The peasant stood choking. He understood. They accused him of having had the pocketbook returned by a confederate, by an accomplice.

He tried to protest. All the table began to laugh.

He could not finish his dinner and went away, in the midst of jeers.

He went home ashamed and indignant, choking with anger and confusion, the more dejected that he was capable with his Norman cunning of doing what they had accused him of, and ever boasting of it as of a good turn. His innocence to him, in a confused way, was impossible to prove, as his sharpness was known. And he was stricken to the heart by the injustice of the suspicion.

Then he began to recount the adventures again, prolonging his history every day, adding each time new reasons, more energetic protestations, more solemn oaths which he imagined and prepared in his hours of solitude, his whole mind given up to the story of the string. He was believed so much the less as his defense

---

15. **Marius Paumelle, . . . Breton, husbandman at Ymanville** (màr yüs' pō mel', brǝ tōn', ē män vēl'): *husbandman* is an archaic word meaning "farmer."
16. **Crequetot** (krek tō').
17. **Monvilliers** (mōn vēl yer').

was more complicated and his arguing more subtle.

"Those are lying excuses," they said behind his back.

He felt it, consumed his heart over it, and wore himself out with useless efforts. He wasted away before their very eyes.

The wags now made him tell about the string to amuse them, as they make a soldier who has been on a campaign tell about his battles. His mind, touched to the depth, began to weaken.

Toward the end of December he took to his bed.

He died in the first days of January, and in the delirium of his death struggles he kept claiming his innocence, reiterating:

"A piece of string, a piece of string—look—here it is, M'sieu' the Mayor."

*T*hinking About the Story

A PERSONAL RESPONSE

sharing impressions

1. How did you feel about Maître Hauchecome at the end of the story? Describe your feelings in your journal.

constructing interpretations

2. What part, if any, do you think Maître Hauchecome plays in bringing about his own downfall?

Think about
- his reputation before the false accusation
- the nature of his relationship with Maître Malandain
- his behavior when no one believes him innocent

3. Why do the peasants of Goderville refuse to believe Maître Hauchecome?

Think about
- the characteristics of the peasants revealed at the opening of the story
- the way the peasants behave at the market
- your response to question 2

4. Why do you think Maître Hauchecome tries so hard to persuade others of his innocence?

5. If Maître Hauchecome had not so insistently protested his innocence, how might the story be different?

6. What ironies do you see in this story?
Think about
- irony as a contrast between what is expected and what actually exists
- how Maître Hauchecome's reputation before the incident contributes to his problems after the incident
- the characters and events in the story

7. In your opinion, what idea does Maupassant seem to be conveying about the relationship between the individual and the community? Use examples from the story to support your response.

8. Guy de Maupassant wrote that "life is merciless . . . full of inexplicable, illogical, and contradictory catastrophes." How might this story be different if Maupassant had not believed this to be true?

Analyzing the Writer's Craft

CHARACTERIZATION IN FICTION

After the pocketbook is returned, Maître Hauchecome becomes obsessed with telling his story: "Then he began to recount the adventures again, prolonging his history every day, adding each time new reasons, more energetic protestations, more solemn oaths which he imagined and prepared in his hours of solitude. . . ." What does this description of his actions reveal about Maître Hauchecome's character?

Building a Literary Vocabulary. Characterization refers to the techniques that a writer uses to develop characters. Recall the four basic methods of characterization in fiction: (1) through description of a character's physical appearance; (2) through a character's speech, thoughts, feelings, or actions; (3) through the speech, feelings, thoughts, or actions of other characters; (4) through direct comments about a character's nature. In this passage describing Maître Hauchecome's actions, Maupassant reveals Hauchecome's need to have people think well of him and to have his actions judged fairly and accurately.

Application: Analyzing Characterization. Working in a small group, go back through the story and identify three details that reveal Maître Hauchecome's character. For each detail identify the characterization method Maupassant uses. Then as a group decide which method of characterization most contributes to understanding the character. Share your observations with another group of students.

Connecting Reading and Writing

1. Imagine that you are a provincial official assigned to defend Maître Hauchecome at his trial for the theft. Write your opening **speech** for the trial in which you explain how Maître Hauchecome himself is the victim in this situation.

Option: Make **notes** for your questioning of Maître Malandain when he is called to the witness stand.

2. Imagine that "A Piece of String" is being turned into a made-for-television movie. Write the television **script** for the scene between Maître Hauchecome and the mayor.

Option: Reread the description of the market and write **instructions** for filming that scene. Be sure to explain what scenery and props should be used.

3. Read another story by Guy de Maupassant, noting details of plot, character, setting, and theme. Create a **chart** comparing that story with "A Piece of String" for a book club deciding which story to read.

Option: Write an **expository essay** for a literary magazine in which you compare the two stories.

4. Review your prereading journal entry in which you described your feelings about a false accusation. Write a **letter** to the person(s) who accused you, explaining how you felt at the time and whether your feelings have changed.

Option: Make a list of five **guidelines** that a person falsely accused might follow to try to establish his or her innocence.

5. Research the French region of Normandy in the late nineteenth century. Write a **summary** of your findings for a classmate who wants to learn more about the setting of the story.

Option: Create **captions** for a travel brochure about the region showing such things as types of clothing worn, nature of the topography, and building styles.

The Pearl

YUKIO MISHIMA   1925–1970   JAPAN

A biography of Mishima appears on page 747.

Approaching the Story

The controversial author of "The Pearl," Yukio Mishima (yōō′ kē ō′ mish′ i mä′), is best known for his commentary on the complex social mores, or accepted ways of behaving, that govern a society's behavior. In Japanese society, for example, the need to "save face" by maintaining dignity in an awkward situation often motivates an individual's actions. This story is set in contemporary Japan and portrays an episode in the lives of five friends from middle-class society.

Building Vocabulary

These essential words are footnoted within the story.

implicitly (im plis′ it lē): [They] could be trusted **implicitly** not to divulge . . . the number of candles on today's cake. (page 597)

incensed (in sensd′): She was **incensed** at a hostess who could create such an impossible situation. (page 598)

loquacious (lō kwā′ shəs): Though normally relaxed and **loquacious** in each other's company, they now lapsed into a long silence. (page 601)

modicum (mäd′ i kəm): There might be a **modicum** of truth even in the assertions of Mrs. Yamamoto. (page 603)

castigation (kas′ ti gā′ shən): There had been times in her **castigation** of that lady when she had allowed herself to be blinded by emotion. (page 603)

Connecting Writing and Reading

Picture yourself in the following situations: (1) You are giving an assigned speech to your class when you realize that your shirt is on inside out. What do you do or say? (2) You are invited to a party that you do not want to attend. How do you get out of going without offending anyone? (3) You attend a social event with the family of a friend. You discover that they expect you to pay your own way, but you have brought no money. What do you do?

What you do in an awkward situation depends in part on the social mores of your society. In this story, too, social expectations influence the actions of characters. As you read, notice the degree to which mores determine behavior.

DECEMBER 10 WAS Mrs. Sasaki's[1] birthday, but since it was Mrs. Sasaki's wish to celebrate the occasion with the minimum of fuss, she had invited to her house for afternoon tea only her closest friends. Assembled were Mesdames Yamamoto, Matsumura, Azuma, and Kasuga[2] —all four being forty-three years of age, exact contemporaries of their hostess.

These ladies were thus members, as it were, of a Keep-Our-Ages-Secret Society and could be trusted <u>implicitly</u>[3] not to divulge to outsiders the number of candles on today's cake. In inviting to her birthday party only guests of this nature, Mrs. Sasaki was showing her customary prudence.

On this occasion Mrs. Sasaki wore a pearl ring. Diamonds at an all-female gathering had not seemed in the best of taste. Furthermore, pearls better matched the color of the dress she was wearing on this particular day.

Shortly after the party had begun, Mrs. Sasaki was moving across for one last inspection of the cake when the pearl in her ring, already a little loose, finally fell from its socket. It seemed a most inauspicious event for this happy occasion, but it would have been no less embarrassing to have everyone aware of the misfortune, so Mrs. Sasaki simply left the pearl close by the rim of the large cake dish and resolved to do something about it later. Around the cake were set out the plates, forks, and paper napkins for herself and the four guests. It now occurred to Mrs. Sasaki that she had no wish to be seen wearing a ring with no stone while cutting this cake, and accordingly she removed the ring from her finger and very deftly, without turning around, slipped it into a recess in the wall behind her back.

Amid the general excitement of the exchange of gossip, and Mrs. Sasaki's surprise and pleasure at the thoughtful presents brought by her guests, the matter of the pearl was very quickly forgotten. Before long it was time for the customary ceremony of lighting and extinguishing the candles on the cake. Everyone crowded excitedly about the table, lending a hand in the not untroublesome task of lighting forty-three candles.

Mrs. Sasaki, with her limited lung capacity, could hardly be expected to blow out all that number at one puff, and her appearance of utter helplessness gave rise to a great deal of hilarious comment.

The procedure followed in serving the cake was that, after the first bold cut, Mrs. Sasaki carved for each guest individually a slice of whatever thickness was requested and transferred this to a small plate, which the guest then carried back with her to her own seat. With everyone stretching out hands at the same time, the crush and confusion around the table was considerable.

On top of the cake was a floral design executed in pink icing and liberally interspersed with small silver balls. These were silver-painted crystals of sugar—a common enough decoration on birthday cakes. In the struggle to secure helpings, moreover, flakes of icing, crumbs of cake, and a number of these silver balls came to be scattered all over the white tablecloth. Some of the guests gathered these stray particles between their fingers and put them on their plates. Others popped them straight into their mouths.

In time all returned to their seats and ate their portions of cake at their leisure, laughing. It was not a homemade cake, having been

---

1. **Sasaki** (sä sä′ kē).
2. **Mesdames Yamamoto, Matsumura, Azuma, and Kasuga** (mā däm′, yä mä mō̂′ tô, mät so͞o mo͞o′ rä, ä′ zo͞o mä, kä′ so͞o gä): *Mesdames* is the plural form of the French title for a married woman, *Madame,* equivalent to *Mrs.*
3. **implicitly** (im plis′ it lē): absolutely; unquestioningly.

ordered by Mrs. Sasaki from a certain high-class confectioner's, but the guests were unanimous in praising its excellence.

Mrs. Sasaki was bathed in happiness. But suddenly, with a tinge of anxiety, she recalled the pearl she had abandoned on the table, and rising from her chair as casually as she could, she moved across to look for it. At the spot where she was sure she had left it, the pearl was no longer to be seen.

Mrs. Sasaki abhorred losing things. At once and without thinking, right in the middle of the party, she became wholly engrossed in her search, and the tension in her manner was so obvious that it attracted everyone's attention.

"Is there something the matter?" someone asked.

"No, not at all, just a moment. . . ."

Mrs. Sasaki's reply was ambiguous, but before she had time to decide to return to her chair, first one, then another, and finally every one of her guests had risen and was turning back the tablecloth or groping about on the floor.

Mrs. Azuma, seeing this commotion, felt that the whole thing was just too deplorable for words. She was incensed[4] at a hostess who could create such an impossible situation over the loss of a solitary pearl.

Mrs. Azuma resolved to offer herself as a sacrifice and to save the day. With a heroic smile she declared: "That's it then! It must have been a pearl I ate just now! A silver ball dropped on the tablecloth when I was given my cake, and I just picked it up and swallowed it without thinking. It *did* seem to stick in my throat a little. Had it been a diamond, now, I would naturally return it—by an operation, if necessary—but as it's a pearl, I must simply beg your forgiveness."

This announcement at once resolved the company's anxieties, and it was felt, above all, that it had saved the hostess from an embarrassing predicament. No one made any

attempt to investigate the truth or falsity of Mrs. Azuma's confession. Mrs. Sasaki took one of the remaining silver balls and put it in her mouth.

"Mm," she said. "Certainly tastes like a pearl, this one!"

Thus, this small incident, too, was cast into the crucible of good-humored teasing, and there—amid general laughter—it melted away.

When the party was over, Mrs. Azuma drove off in her two-seater sportscar, taking with her in the other seat her close friend and neighbor Mrs. Kasuga. Before two minutes had passed, Mrs. Azuma said, "Own up! It was you who swallowed the pearl, wasn't it? I covered up for you and took the blame on myself."

This unceremonious manner of speaking concealed deep affection, but however friendly the intention may have been, to Mrs. Kasuga a wrongful accusation was a wrongful accusation. She had no recollection whatsoever of having swallowed a pearl in mistake for a sugar ball. She was—as Mrs. Azuma too must surely know—fastidious in her eating habits, and if she so much as detected a single hair in her food, whatever she happened to be eating at the time immediately stuck in her gullet.

"Oh, really now!" protested the timid Mrs. Kasuga in a small voice, her eyes studying Mrs. Azuma's face in some puzzlement. "I just couldn't do a thing like that!"

"It's no good pretending. The moment I saw that green look on your face, I knew."

The little disturbance at the party had seemed closed by Mrs. Azuma's frank confession, but even now it had left behind it this strange awkwardness. Mrs. Kasuga, wondering how best to demonstrate her innocence, was at the same time seized by the fantasy that a solitary pearl was lodged somewhere in her

---

4. **incensed** (in sensd'): extremely angered.

intestines. It was unlikely, of course, that she should mistakenly swallow a pearl for a sugar ball, but in all that confusion of talk and laughter, one had to admit that it was at least a possibility. Though she thought back over the events of the party again and again, no moment in which she might have inserted a pearl into her mouth came to mind—but after all, if it was an unconscious act, one would not expect to remember it.

Mrs. Kasuga blushed deeply as her imagination chanced upon one further aspect of the matter. It had occurred to her that when one accepted a pearl into one's system, it almost certainly—its luster a trifle dimmed, perhaps, by gastric juices—reemerged intact within a day or two.

And with this thought the design of Mrs. Azuma, too, seemed to have become transparently clear. Undoubtedly Mrs. Azuma had viewed this same prospect with embarrassment and shame and had therefore cast her responsibility onto another, making it appear that she had considerately taken the blame to protect a friend.

Meanwhile, Mrs. Yamamoto and Mrs. Matsumura, whose homes lay in a similar direction, were returning together in a taxi. Soon after the taxi had started, Mrs. Matsumura opened her handbag to make a few adjustments to her make-up. She remembered that she had done nothing to her face since all that commotion at the party.

As she was removing the powder compact, her attention was caught by a sudden dull gleam as something tumbled to the bottom of the bag. Groping about with the tips of her fingers, Mrs. Matsumura retrieved the object and saw to her amazement that it was a pearl.

Mrs. Matsumura stifled an exclamation of surprise. Recently her relationship with Mrs. Yamamoto had been far from cordial, and she had no wish to share with that lady a discovery with such awkward implications for herself.

Fortunately, Mrs. Yamamoto was gazing out the window and did not appear to have noticed her companion's momentary start of surprise.

Caught off balance by this sudden turn of events, Mrs. Matsumura did not pause to consider how the pearl had found its way into her bag but immediately became a prisoner of her own private brand of school-captain morality. It was unlikely—she thought—that she would do a thing like this, even in a moment of abstraction. But since, by some chance, the object had found its way into her handbag, the proper course was to return it at once. If she failed to do so, it would weigh heavily upon her conscience. The fact that it was a pearl, too—an article you could call neither all that expensive nor yet all that cheap—only made her position more ambiguous.

At any rate, she was determined that her companion, Mrs. Yamamoto, should know nothing of this incomprehensible development—especially when the affair had been so nicely rounded off, thanks to the selflessness of Mrs. Azuma. Mrs. Matsumura felt she could remain in the taxi not a moment longer, and on the pretext of remembering a promise to visit a sick relative on her way back, she made the driver set her down at once, in the middle of a quiet residential district.

Mrs. Yamamoto, left alone in the taxi, was a little surprised that her practical joke should have moved Mrs. Matsumura to such abrupt action. Having watched Mrs. Matsumura's reflection in the window just now, she had clearly seen her draw the pearl from her bag.

At the party Mrs. Yamamoto had been the very first to receive a slice of cake. Adding to her plate a silver ball which had spilled onto the table, she had returned to her seat—again before any of the others—and there had noticed that the silver ball was a pearl. At this discovery she had at once conceived a malicious plan. While all the others were preoccupied with the cake, she had quickly slipped the pearl into the handbag left on the next chair by that insufferable hypocrite Mrs. Matsumura.

Stranded in the middle of a residential district where there was little prospect of a taxi, Mrs. Matsumura fretfully gave her mind to a number of reflections on her position.

First, no matter how necessary it might be for the relief of her own conscience, it would be a shame, indeed, when people had gone to such lengths to settle the affair satisfactorily, to go and stir up things all over again; and it would be even worse if in the process—because of the inexplicable nature of the circumstances—she were to direct unjust suspicions upon herself.

Secondly—notwithstanding these considerations—if she did not make haste to return the pearl now, she would forfeit her opportunity forever. Left till tomorrow (at the thought Mrs. Matsumura blushed), the returned pearl would be an object of rather disgusting speculation and doubt. Concerning this possibility, Mrs. Azuma herself had dropped a hint.

It was at this point that there occurred to Mrs. Matsumura, greatly to her joy, a master scheme which would both salve her conscience and at the same time involve no risk of exposing her character to any unjust suspicion. Quickening her step, she emerged at length onto a comparatively busy thoroughfare, where she hailed a taxi and told the driver to take her quickly to a certain celebrated pearl shop on the Ginza. There she took the pearl from her bag and showed it to the attendant, asking to see a pearl of slightly larger size and clearly superior quality. Having made her purchase, she proceeded once more, by taxi, to Mrs. Sasaki's house.

Mrs. Matsumura's plan was to present this newly purchased pearl to Mrs. Sasaki, saying she had found it in her jacket pocket. Mrs. Sasaki would accept it and later attempt to fit it into the ring. However, being a pearl of a different size, it would not fit into the ring, and Mrs. Sasaki—puzzled—would try to return it to Mrs. Matsumura, but Mrs. Matsumura would refuse to have it returned. Thereupon Mrs. Sasaki would have no choice but to reflect as follows: The woman has behaved in this way in order to protect someone else. Such being the case, it is perhaps safest simply to accept the pearl and forget the matter. Mrs. Matsumura has doubtless observed one of the three ladies in the act of stealing the pearl. But at least, of my four guests, I can now be sure that Mrs. Matsumura, if no one else, is completely without guilt. Whoever heard of a thief stealing something and then replacing it with a similar article of greater value?

By this device Mrs. Matsumura proposed to escape forever the infamy of suspicion and equally—by a small outlay of cash—the pricks of an uneasy conscience.

To return to the other ladies. After reaching home, Mrs. Kasuga continued to feel painfully upset by Mrs. Azuma's cruel teasing. To clear herself of even a ridiculous charge like this—she knew—she must act before tomorrow or it would be too late. That is to say, in order to offer positive proof that she had not eaten the pearl, it was above all necessary for the pearl itself to be somehow produced. And, briefly, if she could show the pearl to Mrs. Azuma immediately, her innocence on the gastronomic count (if not on any other) would be firmly established. But if she waited until tomorrow, even though she managed to produce the pearl, the shameful and hardly mentionable suspicion would inevitably have intervened.

The normally timid Mrs. Kasuga, inspired with the courage of impetuous action, burst from the house to which she had so recently returned, sped to a pearl shop in the Ginza, and selected and bought a pearl which, to her eye, seemed of roughly the same size as those silver balls on the cake. She then telephoned Mrs. Azuma. On returning home, she explained, she had discovered in the folds of the bow of her sash the pearl which Mrs. Sasaki had lost, but since she felt too ashamed to return it by herself, she wondered if Mrs. Azuma would be so kind as to go with her, as soon as possible. Inwardly Mrs. Azuma considered the story a little unlikely, but since it was the request of a good friend, she agreed to go.

Mrs. Sasaki accepted the pearl brought to her by Mrs. Matsumura and, puzzled at its failure to fit the ring, fell obligingly into that very train of thought for which Mrs. Matsumura had prayed; but it was a surprise to her when Mrs. Kasuga arrived about an hour later, accompanied by Mrs. Azuma, and returned another pearl.

Mrs. Sasaki hovered perilously on the brink of discussing Mrs. Matsumura's prior visit but checked herself at the last moment and accepted the second pearl as unconcernedly as she could. She felt sure that this one at any rate would fit, and as soon as the two visitors had taken their leave, she hurried to try it in the ring. But it was too small and wobbled loosely in the socket. At this discovery Mrs. Sasaki was not so much surprised as dumbfounded.

On the way back in the car, both ladies found it impossible to guess what the other might be thinking, and though normally relaxed and <u>loquacious</u>[5] in each other's company, they now lapsed into a long silence.

Mrs. Azuma, who believed she could do nothing without her own full knowledge, knew for certain that she had not swallowed the pearl herself. It was simply to save everyone from embarrassment that she had cast shame aside and made that declaration at the party—more particularly, it was to save the situation for her friend, who had been fidgeting about and looking conspicuously guilty. But what was she to think now? Beneath the peculiarity of Mrs. Kasuga's whole attitude, and beneath this elaborate procedure of having herself accompany her as she returned the pearl, she sensed that there lay something much deeper. Could it be that Mrs. Azuma's intuition had touched upon a weakness in her friend's make-up which it was forbidden to touch upon and that by thus driving her friend into a corner, she had transformed an unconscious, impulsive kleptomania into a deep mental derangement beyond all cure?

Mrs. Kasuga, for her part, still retained the suspicion that Mrs. Azuma had genuinely swallowed the pearl and that her confession at the party had been the truth. If that was so, it had been unforgivable of Mrs. Azuma, when everything was smoothly settled, to tease her so cruelly on the way back from the party, shifting the guilt onto herself. As a result, timid creature that she was, she had been panic-striken and, besides spending good money, had felt obliged to act out that little play—and was it not exceedingly ill-natured of Mrs. Azuma that even after all this, she still refused to confess it was she who had eaten the pearl? And if Mrs. Azuma's innocence was all pretense, she herself—acting her part so painstakingly—must appear in Mrs. Azuma's eyes as the most ridiculous of third-rate comedians.

To return to Mrs. Matsumura: That lady, on her way back from obliging Mrs. Sasaki to accept the pearl, was feeling now more at ease in her mind and had the notion to make a leisurely reinvestigation, detail by detail, of the events of the recent incident. When going to collect her portion of the cake, she had most certainly left her handbag on the chair. Then,

---

5. loquacious (lō kwā′ shəs): talkative, especially in a fluently expressive way.

while eating the cake, she had made liberal use of the paper napkin—so there could have been no necessity to take a handkerchief from her bag. The more she thought about it, the less she could remember having opened her bag until she touched up her face in the taxi on the way home. How was it, then, that a pearl had rolled into a handbag which was always shut?

She realized now how stupid she had been not to have remarked this simple fact before, instead of flying into a panic at the mere sight of the pearl. Having progressed this far, Mrs. Matsumura was struck by an amazing thought. Someone must purposely have placed the pearl in her bag in order to incriminate her. And of the four guests at the party, the only one who would do such a thing was, without doubt, the detestable Mrs. Yamamoto. Her eyes glinting with rage, Mrs. Matsumura hurried toward the house of Mrs. Yamamoto.

From her first glimpse of Mrs. Matsumura standing in the doorway, Mrs. Yamamoto knew at once what had brought her. She had already prepared her line of defense.

However, Mrs. Matsumura's cross-examination was unexpectedly severe, and from the start it was clear that she would accept no evasions.

"It was you, I know. No one but you could do such a thing," began Mrs. Matsumura, deductively.

"Why choose me? What proof have you? If you can say a thing like that to my face, I suppose you've come with pretty conclusive proof, have you?" Mrs. Yamamoto was at first icily composed.

To this Mrs. Matsumura replied that Mrs. Azuma, having so nobly taken the blame on herself, clearly stood in an incompatible relationship with mean and despicable behavior of this nature; and as for Mrs. Kasuga, she was much too weak-kneed for such dangerous work; and that left only one person—herself.

Mrs. Yamamoto kept silent, her mouth shut tight like a clamshell. On the table before her gleamed the pearl which Mrs. Matsumura had set there. In the excitement she had not even had time to raise a teaspoon, and the Ceylon tea she had so thoughtfully provided was beginning to get cold.

"I had no idea that you hated me so." As she said this, Mrs. Yamamoto dabbed at the corners of her eyes, but it was plain that Mrs. Matsumura's resolve not to be deceived by tears was as firm as ever.

"Well, then," Mrs. Yamamoto continued, "I shall say what I had thought I must never say. I shall mention no names, but one of the guests . . . "

"By that, I suppose, you can only mean Mrs. Azuma or Mrs. Kasuga?"

"Please, I beg at least that you allow me to omit the name. As I say, one of the guests had just opened your bag and was dropping something inside when I happened to glance in her direction. You can imagine my amazement! Even if I had felt *able* to warn you, there would have been no chance. My heart just throbbed and throbbed, and on the way back in the taxi—oh, how awful not to be able to speak even then! If we had been good friends, of course, I could have told you quite frankly, but since I knew of your apparent dislike for me . . ."

"I see. You have been very considerate, I'm sure. Which means, doesn't it, that you have now cleverly shifted the blame onto Mrs. Azuma and Mrs. Kasuga?"

"Shifted the blame! Oh, how can I get you to understand my feelings? I only wanted to avoid hurting anyone."

"Quite. But you didn't mind hurting me, did you? You might at least have mentioned this in the taxi."

"And if you had been frank with me when you found the pearl in your bag, I would probably have told you, at that moment, everything I had seen—but no, you chose to leave the taxi at once, without saying a word!"

For the first time, as she listened to this, Mrs. Matsumura was at a loss for a reply.

"Well, then. Can I get you to understand? I wanted no one to be hurt."

Mrs. Matsumura was filled with an even more intense rage.

"If you are going to tell a string of lies like that," she said, "I must ask you to repeat them, tonight if you wish, in my presence, before Mrs. Azuma and Mrs. Kasuga."

At this Mrs. Yamamoto started to weep.

"And thanks to you," she sobbed reprovingly, "all my efforts to avoid hurting anyone will have come to nothing."

It was a new experience for Mrs. Matsumura to see Mrs. Yamamoto crying, and though she kept reminding herself not to be taken in by tears, she could not altogether dismiss the feeling that perhaps somewhere, since nothing in this affair could be proved, there might be a modicum[6] of truth even in the assertions of Mrs. Yamamoto.

In the first place—to be a little more objective—if one accepted Mrs. Yamamoto's story as true, then her reluctance to disclose the name of the guilty party, whom she had observed in the very act, argued some refinement of character. And just as one could not say for sure that the gentle and seemingly timid Mrs. Kasuga would never be moved to an act of malice, so even the undoubtedly bad feeling between Mrs. Yamamoto and herself could, by one way of looking at things, be taken as actually lessening the likelihood of Mrs. Yamamoto's guilt. For if she was to do a thing like this, with their relationship as it was, Mrs. Yamamoto would be the first to come under suspicion.

"We have differences in our natures," Mrs. Yamamoto continued tearfully, "and I cannot deny that there are things about yourself which I dislike. But for all that, it is really too bad that you should suspect me of such a petty trick to get the better of you. . . . Still, on thinking it over, to submit quietly to your accusations might well be the course most consistent with what I have felt in this matter all along. In this way I alone shall bear the guilt, and no other will be hurt."

After this pathetic pronouncement, Mrs. Yamamoto lowered her face to the table and abandoned herself to uncontrolled weeping.

Watching her, Mrs. Matsumura came, by degrees, to reflect upon the impulsiveness of her own behavior. Detesting Mrs. Yamamoto as she had, there had been times in her castigation[7] of that lady when she had allowed herself to be blinded by emotion.

When Mrs. Yamamoto raised her head again after this prolonged bout of weeping, the look of resolution on her face, somehow remote and pure, was apparent even to her visitor. Mrs. Matsumura, a little frightened, drew herself upright in her chair.

"This thing should never have been. When it is gone, everything will be as before." Speaking in riddles, Mrs. Yamamoto pushed back her disheveled hair and fixed a terrible, yet hauntingly beautiful, gaze upon the top of the table. In an instant she had snatched up the pearl from before her and, with a gesture of no ordinary resolve, tossed it into her mouth. Raising her cup by the handle, her little finger elegantly extended, she washed the pearl down her throat with one gulp of cold Ceylon tea.

Mrs. Matsumura watched in horrified fascination. The affair was over before she had time to protest. This was the first time in her life she had seen a person swallow a pearl, and there was in Mrs. Yamamoto's manner some-

---

6. **modicum** (mäd′ i kəm): a small amount.
7. **castigation** (kas′ ti ga′ shən): the act of punishing or scolding severely, especially by criticizing publicly.

thing of that desperate finality one might expect to see in a person who had just drunk poison.

However, heroic though the action was, it was above all a touching incident, and not only did Mrs. Matsumura find her anger vanished into thin air, but so impressed was she by Mrs. Yamamoto's simplicity and purity that she could only think of that lady as a saint. And now Mrs. Matsumura's eyes too began to fill with tears, and she took Mrs. Yamamoto by the hand.

"Please forgive me, please forgive me," she said. "It was wrong of me."

For a while they wept together, holding each other's hands and vowing to each other that henceforth they would be the firmest of friends.

When Mrs. Sasaki heard rumors that the relationship between Mrs. Yamamoto and Mrs. Matsumura, which had been so strained, had suddenly improved, and that Mrs. Azuma and Mrs. Kasuga, who had been such good friends, had suddenly fallen out, she was at a loss to understand the reasons and contented herself with the reflection that nothing was impossible in this world.

However, being a woman of no strong scruples, Mrs. Sasaki requested a jeweler to refashion her ring and to produce a design into which two new pearls could be set, one large and one small, and this she wore quite openly, without further mishap.

Soon she had completely forgotten the small commotion on her birthday, and when anyone asked her age, she would give the same untruthful answers as ever.

Thinking About the Story

A PERSONAL RESPONSE

*sharing
impressions*

1. What do you think about the behavior of the four women? In your journal briefly describe your impressions.

*constructing
interpretations*

2. Why do you think these women behave as they do?
   Think about
   • personal characteristics attributed to each of them
   • how they interact with each other
   • the position they are placed in when it appears that the pearl is missing
   • ways in which they try to save face
   • the social mores that can be inferred from this story

3. Explain whether you think Mrs. Yamamoto's swallowing of the pearl is a good resolution to the situation.

4. Which of the characters do you think is most responsible for the confusion resulting from the loss of the pearl? Why?

A CREATIVE RESPONSE

5. If Mrs. Azuma had not claimed to have swallowed the pearl, how might the outcome of the story be different?

A CRITICAL RESPONSE

6. What message do you think Mishima conveys about the society in which the characters live? Use examples from the story to support your opinion.

7. Do you think the incidents described in the story could happen in contemporary American society? Why or why not?

Analyzing the Writer's Craft

SATIRE AND TONE

How do you think Mishima wants readers to feel about the characters and their problems?

Building a Literary Vocabulary. Satire is a literary technique in which ideas or customs are ridiculed for the purpose of improving society. The tone, or writer's attitude, that comes through in a satire may be gently witty, mildly abrasive, or bitterly critical. In "The Pearl" the rather trivial misplacing of a pearl drives four friends into a complicated and ridiculous series of maneuvers. The characters end up looking foolish because of the lengths to which they go to avoid having anyone think unsuitable thoughts about them. Mishima's satire depends on the mildly ironic or sarcastic tone with which he describes the reactions of the characters to the loss of the pearl. For example, when the narrator says "Mrs. Azuma resolved to offer herself as a sacrifice and to save the day," he does not expect the reader to take the statement literally.

Application: Understanding Satire and Tone. Working with a partner, list phrases or lines from the story that reveal Mishima's tone in the story. After identifying these examples, explain in writing what you think is being satirized. Be prepared to share your opinion with the class.

Connecting Reading and Writing

1. Read another story from Mishima's *Death in Midsummer and Other Stories*, from which "The Pearl" was taken. Based on these two stories, write a **review** of Mishima's work for a school literary magazine. Make sure to comment on elements such as character, theme, and tone in both stories.

Option: Write a **letter** to the head of the English department at your school, comparing the two works and recommending one of them for inclusion in next year's curriculum.

2. Create a **poster** announcing auditions for the stage version of "The Pearl." Be sure your poster includes specific details about the cast of characters.

Option: Write **stage directions** for one scene from the story, for example the scene in which the pearl first disappears or the final scene between Mrs.

Matsumura and Mrs. Yamamoto.

3. Write a brief **satirical sketch** for the school newspaper, exposing a social situation in your school that you believe needs improvement.

Option: Write an **editorial** stating your opinion about that same situation for your school newspaper.

4. Create an **annotated map** to share with a classmate who is confused about events in "The Pearl." Show the various locations—for example, the women's homes and the jewelry stores—and what event(s) happen in each.

Option: Write a **time line** of events to help a classmate organize information from the story. Indicate the characters that are involved in each event.

Santa's Children

ITALO CALVINO   1923–1985   ITALY

A biography of Calvino appears on page 739.

Approaching the Story

Italo Calvino's (ē′ tä lô̄ käl vē′ nô̄) clever use of irony and whimsy have made him one of the most popular Italian fiction writers of the twentieth century. "Santa's Children" is from *Marcovaldo, or The Seasons in the City*, a collection of short stories about Marcovaldo, an unskilled worker who lives in an industrial city of northern Italy. The earliest stories in this book are set during a time of poverty after World War II. The later stories, including "Santa's Children," are set in the mid-1960's when, according to Calvino, "the illusions of an economic boom flourished." Calvino attacks such illusions, writing in a satirical tone that is evident as the story begins.

Building Vocabulary

These essential words are footnoted within the story.

placated (plā′ kāt′ id): The heavy conflicts of interest are **placated** and give way to a new rivalry. (page 608)

jaded: After a while they were **jaded** and paid no further attention. (page 610)

Connecting Writing and Reading

What qualities do you think characterize Christmas in the present-day United States? In your journal, make a cluster diagram of words and phrases that you associate with Christmas. Then, as you read "Santa's Children," jot down words and phrases that describe the writer's view of Christmas.

Santa's Children

N O PERIOD OF the year is more gentle and good, for the world of industry and commerce, than Christmas and the weeks preceding it. From the streets rises the tremulous sound of the mountaineers' bagpipes; and the big companies, till yesterday coldly concerned with calculating gross product and dividends, open their hearts to human affections and to smiles. The sole thought of Boards of Directors now is to give joy to their fellow man, sending gifts accompanied by messages of goodwill both to other companies and to private individuals; every firm feels obliged to buy a great stock of products from a second firm to serve as presents to third firms; and those firms, for their part, buy from yet another firm further stocks of presents for the others; the office windows remain aglow till late, specially those of the shipping department, where the personnel work overtime wrapping packages and boxes; beyond the misted panes, on the sidewalks covered by a crust of ice, the pipers advance. Having descended from the dark mysterious mountains, they stand at the downtown intersections, a bit dazzled by the excessive lights, by the excessively rich shop windows; and heads bowed, they blow into their instruments; at that sound, among the businessmen the heavy conflicts of interest are placated[1] and give way to a new rivalry: to see who can present the most conspicuous and original gift in the most attractive way.

---

1. **placated** (plā′ kāt′ id): pacified; calmed.

At Sbav and Co. that year the Public Relations Office suggested that the Christmas presents for the most important persons should be delivered at home by a man dressed as Santa Claus.

The idea won the unanimous approval of the top executives. A complete Santa Claus outfit was bought: white beard, red cap and tunic edged in white fur, big boots. They had the various delivery men try it on to see whom it fitted best, but one man was too short and the beard touched the ground; another was too stout and couldn't get into the tunic; another was too young; yet another was too old and it wasn't worth wasting make-up on him.

While the head of the Personnel Office was sending for other possible Santas from the various departments, the assembled executives sought to develop the idea: the Human Relations Office wanted the employees' Christmas packages also to be distributed by Santa Claus, at a collective ceremony; the Sales Office wanted Santa to make a round of the shops as well; the Advertising Office was worried about the prominence of the firm's name, suggesting that perhaps they should tie four balloons to a string with the letters S.B.A.V.

All were caught up in the lively and cordial atmosphere spreading through the festive, productive city; nothing is more beautiful than the sensation of material goods flowing on all sides and, with it, the goodwill each feels toward the others; for this, this above all, as the skirling sound of the pipes reminds us, is what really counts.

In the shipping department, goods—material and spiritual—passed through Marcovaldo's hands, since it represented merchandise to load and unload. And it was not only through loading and unloading that he shared in the general festivity but also by thinking that at the end of that labyrinth of hundreds of thousands of packages there waited a package belonging to him alone, prepared by the Human Relations Office—and even more, by figuring how much was due him at the end of the month, counting the Christmas bonus and his overtime hours. With that money, he too would be able to rush to the shops and buy, buy, buy, to give presents, presents, presents, as his most sincere feelings and the general interests of industry and commerce decreed.

The head of the Personnel Office came into the shipping department with a fake beard in his hand. "Hey, you!" he said to Marcovaldo. "See how this beard looks on you. Perfect! You're Santa then. Come upstairs. Get moving. You'll be given a special bonus if you make fifty home deliveries per day."

Got up as Santa Claus, Marcovaldo rode through the city on the saddle of the motorbike-truck laden with packages wrapped in varicolored paper, tied with pretty ribbons, and decorated with twigs of mistletoe and holly. The white cotton beard tickled him a little, but it protected his throat from the cold air.

His first trip was to his own home, because he couldn't resist the temptation of giving his children a surprise. At first, he thought, they won't recognize me. Then I bet they'll laugh!

The children were playing on the stairs. They barely looked up. "Hi, Papà."

Marcovaldo was let down. "Hmph . . . Don't you see how I'm dressed?"

"How are you supposed to be dressed?" Pietruccio[2] said. "Like Santa Claus, right?"

"And you recognized me first thing?"

"Easy! We recognized Signor Sigismondo,[3] too; and he was disguised better than you!"

"And the janitor's brother-in-law!"

"And the father of the twins across the street!"

---

2. Pietruccio (pē e trōōch′ chē ō).

3. Signor Sigismondo (sē nyôr′ sē gēz mōn′ dō): *Signor* is the Italian equivalent of *Mr.*

"And the uncle of Ernestina—the girl with the braids!"

"All dressed like Santa Claus?" Marcovaldo asked, and the disappointment in his voice wasn't due only to the failure of the family surprise but also because he felt that the company's prestige had somehow been impaired.

"Of course. Just like you," the children answered. "Like Santa Claus. With a fake beard, as usual." And turning their backs on him, the children became absorbed again in their games.

It so happened that the Public Relations Offices of many firms had had the same idea at the same time; and they had recruited a great number of people, jobless for the most part, pensioners, street vendors, and had dressed them in the red tunic with the cotton-wool beard. The children, the first few times, had been amused, recognizing acquaintances under that disguise, neighborhood figures, but after a while they were jaded[4] and paid no further attention.

The game they were involved in seemed to absorb them entirely. They had gathered on a landing and were seated in a circle. "May I ask what you're plotting?" Marcovaldo inquired.

"Leave us alone, Papà; we have to fix our presents."

"Presents for whom?"

"For a poor child. We have to find a poor child and give him presents."

"Who said so?"

"It's in our school reader."

Marcovaldo was about to say: "You're poor children yourselves!" But during this past week he had become so convinced that he was an inhabitant of the Land of Plenty, where all purchased and enjoyed themselves and exchanged presents, that it seemed bad manners to mention poverty; and he preferred to declare: "Poor children don't exist any more!"

Michelino[5] stood up and asked: "Is that why you don't bring us presents, Papà?"

Marcovaldo felt a pang at his heart. "I have to earn some overtime now," he said hastily, "and then I'll bring you some."

"How do you earn it?"

"Delivering presents," Marcovaldo said.

"To us?"

"No, to other people."

"Why not to us? It'd be quicker."

Marcovaldo tried to explain. "Because I'm not the Human Relations Santa Claus, after all; I'm the Public Relations Santa Claus. You understand?"

"No."

"Never mind." But since he wanted somehow to apologize for coming home empty-handed, he thought he might take Michelino with him on his round of deliveries. "If you're good, you can come and watch your Papà taking presents to people," he said, straddling the seat of the little delivery wagon.

"Let's go. Maybe I'll find a poor child," Michelino said and jumped on, clinging to his father's shoulders.

In the streets of the city Marcovaldo encountered only other red-and-white Santas, absolutely identical with him, who were driving panel trucks or delivery carts or opening the doors of shops for customers laden with packages or helping carry their purchases to the car. And all these Santas seemed concentrated, busy, as if they were responsible for the operation of the enormous machine of the Holiday Season.

And exactly like them, Marcovaldo ran from one address to another, following his list, dismounted from his seat, sorted the packages in the wagon, selected one, presented it to the person opening the door, pronouncing the words: "Sbav and Company wish a Merry Christmas and a Happy New Year," and pocketed the tip.

---

4. **jaded:** dulled by excesses.
5. **Michelino** (mē kä lē′ nô).

This tip could be substantial and Marcovaldo might have been considered content, but something was missing. Every time, before ringing at a door, followed by Michelino, he anticipated the wonder of the person who, on opening the door, would see Santa Claus himself standing there before him; he expected some fuss, curiosity, gratitude. And every time he was received like the postman, who brings the newspaper day after day.

He rang at the door of a luxurious house. A governess answered the door. "Oh, another package. Who's this one from?"

"Sbav and Company wish a . . ."

"Well, bring it in," and she led Santa Claus down a corridor filled with tapestries, carpets, and majolica[6] vases. Michelino, all eyes, followed his father.

The governess opened a glass door. They entered a room with a high ceiling, so high that a great fir tree could fit beneath it. It was a Christmas tree lighted by glass bubbles of every color, and from its branches hung presents and sweets of every description. From the ceiling hung heavy crystal chandeliers, and the highest branches of the fir caught some of the glistening drops. Over a large table were arrayed glass, silver, boxes of candied fruit and cases of bottles. The toys, scattered over a great rug, were as numerous as in a toyshop, mostly complicated electronic devices and model spaceships. On that rug, in an empty corner, there was a little boy about nine years old, lying prone, with a bored, sullen look. He was leafing through an illustrated volume, as if everything around him were no concern of his.

"Gianfranco,[7] look. Gianfranco," the governess said. "You see? Santa Claus has come back with another present."

"Three hundred twelve," the child sighed, without looking up from his book. "Put it over there."

"It's the three hundred and twelfth present that's arrived," the governess said. "Gianfranco

is so clever. He keeps count; he doesn't miss one. Counting is his great passion."

On tiptoe Marcovaldo and Michelino left the house.

"Papà, is that little boy a poor child?" Michelino asked.

Marcovaldo was busy rearranging the contents of the truck and didn't answer immediately. But after a moment, he hastened to protest: "Poor? What are you talking about? You know who his father is? He's the president of the Society for the Implementation of Christmas Consumption/Commendatore—"[8]

He broke off, because he didn't see Michelino anywhere. "Michelino! Michelino! Where are you?" He had vanished.

I bet he saw another Santa Claus go by, took him for me, and has gone off after him . . . Marcovaldo continued his rounds, but he was a bit concerned and couldn't wait to get home again.

At home, he found Michelino with his brothers, good as gold.

"Say, where did you go?"

"I came home to collect our presents . . . the presents for that poor child . . ."

"What? Who?"

"The one that was so sad . . . the one in the villa, with the Christmas tree . . ."

"Him? What kind of a present could you give him?"

"Oh, we fixed them up very nice . . . three presents, all wrapped in silver paper."

The younger boys spoke up: "We all went together to take them to him! You should have seen how happy he was!"

---

6. **majolica** (mə jäl′ i kə): a variety of richly decorated Italian pottery.

7. **Gianfranco** (jē än fraŋ′ kô).

8. **Commendatore** (kôm men′ dä tō′ rā): a title, used to address or refer to a member of the aristocratic class, that nostalgically recollects the time of knights and chivalry.

"I'll bet!" Marcovaldo said. "That was just what he needed to make him happy: your presents!"

"Yes, ours! . . . He ran over right away to tear off the paper and see what they were . . ."

"And what were they?"

"The first was a hammer: that big round hammer, the wooden kind . . ."

"What did he do then?"

"He was jumping with joy! He grabbed it and began to use it!"

"How?"

"He broke all the toys! And all the glass-ware! Then he took the second present . . ."

"What was that?"

"A slingshot. You should have seen him. He was so happy! He hit all the glass balls on the Christmas tree. Then he started on the chandeliers . . ."

"That's enough. I don't want to hear any more! And the . . . third present?"

"We didn't have anything left to give, so we took some silver paper and wrapped up a box of kitchen matches. That was the present that made him happiest of all. He said: They never let me touch matches! He began to strike them, and . . ."

"And?"

". . . and he set fire to everything!"

Marcovaldo was tearing his hair. "I'm ruined!"

The next day, turning up at work, he felt the storm brewing. He dressed again as Santa Claus, in great haste, loaded the presents to be delivered onto the truck, already amazed that no one had said anything to him, and then he saw, coming toward him, the three section chiefs: the one from Public Relations, the one from Advertising, and the one from Sales.

"Stop!" they said to him. "Unload everything. At once!"

This is it, Marcovaldo said to himself, and could already picture himself fired.

"Hurry up! We have to change all the pack-ages!" the three section chiefs said. "The Society for the Implementation of Christmas Consumption has launched a campaign to push the Destructive Gift!"

"On the spur of the moment like this," one of the men remarked. "They might have thought of it sooner . . ."

"It was a sudden inspiration the President had," another chief explained. "It seems his little boy was given some ultramodern gift articles, Japanese, I believe, and for the first time the child was obviously enjoying himself . . ."

"The important thing," the third added, "is that the Destructive Gift serves to destroy articles of every sort: just what's needed to speed up the pace of consumption and give the market a boost . . . All in minimum time and within a child's capacities . . . The President of the Society sees a whole new horizon opening out. He's in seventh heaven, he's so enthusiastic . . ."

"But this child . . ." Marcovaldo asked, in a faint voice: "did he really destroy much stuff?"

"It's hard to make an estimate, even a hazy one, because the house was burned down . . ."

Marcovaldo went back to the street, illuminated as if it were night, crowded with mamas and children and uncles and grannies and packages and balloons and rocking horses and Christmas trees and Santa Clauses and chickens and turkeys and fruit cakes and bottles and bagpipers and chimney sweeps and chestnut vendors shaking pans of chestnuts over round, glowing black stoves.

And the city seemed smaller, collected in a luminous vessel, buried in the dark heart of a forest among the age-old trunks of the chestnut trees and an endless cloak of snow. Somewhere in the darkness the howl of the wolf was heard; the hares had a hole buried in the snow, in the warm red earth under a layer of chestnut burrs.

A jack-hare came out, white, onto the snow; he twitched his ears, ran beneath the moon, but he was white and couldn't be seen, as if he weren't there. Only his little paws left a light print on the snow, like little clover leaves. Nor could the wolf be seen, for he was black and stayed in the black darkness of the forest. Only if he opened his mouth, his teeth were visible, white and sharp.

There was a line where the forest, all black, ended and the snow began, all white. The hare ran on this side, and the wolf on that.

The wolf saw the hare's prints on the snow and followed them, always keeping in the black, so as not to be seen. At the point where the prints ended there should be the hare, and the wolf came out of the black, opened wide his red maw and his sharp teeth, and bit the wind.

The hare was a bit farther on, invisible; he scratched one ear with his paw and escaped, hopping away.

Is he here? There? Is he a bit farther on?

Only the expanse of snow could be seen, white as this page.

A PERSONAL RESPONSE

sharing impressions

1. In your journal record any thoughts, feelings, and questions you have about this story.

constructing interpretations

2. How do you think the episode of the hare and the wolf relates to the rest of the story?

Think about
- why the hare is associated with white and the wolf associated with black
- how the hare disappears into the snow, leaving the wolf to bite the wind.
- what the two animals might represent
- what the writer might be saying about Christmas

3. Based on the writer's view of Christmas, what do you think is the most serious fault of the society portrayed in this story?

Think about
- why there are so many Santas around town
- why Gianfranco loves the gifts from Marcovaldo's children more than the other 312 he received
- why The Society for the Implementation of Christmas Consumption exists
- the Destructive Gift campaign

4. To what degree does Marcovaldo share the values of the rest of his society?

A CREATIVE RESPONSE

5. If this story were set in the present-day United States, would it be different? Refer to your prereading cluster diagram to help you formulate a response.

A CRITICAL RESPONSE

6. Based on your interpretation of the story, who do you think are the "Santa's Children" referred to in the title? Explain your answer.

Analyzing the Writer's Craft

SATIRE AND POINT OF VIEW

Reread the opening sentence and explain what view of Christmas the writer expresses.

Building a Literary Vocabulary. Satire is a literary technique in which ideas or customs are ridiculed for the purpose of improving society. "Santa's Children" is satiric from the very first sentence. The phrase "No period of the year is more gentle and good" leads the reader to expect a traditional holiday sentiment of peace and goodwill. Instead, the next phrase "for the world of industry and commerce" ironically undercuts the holiday sentiment by referring to the commercial exploitation of Christmas.

Point of view enhances the satire of this story. Point of view refers to the kind of narrator used in a literary work. Because "Santa's Children" is told from a third-person point of view, the narrator is not a direct participant in the action and is free to comment on it. In the opening paragraphs, the narrator sets the satiric tone by parroting the corporate jargon that praises Christmas for promoting business success. Then the narrator enters Marcovaldo's mind to reveal a well-intentioned but confused man sincerely trying to make his family happy yet influenced by the commercial values around him. By showing Marcovaldo's befuddled attempts to fit into the business world and his inability to explain that world to his children, the narrator implies criticism of a society that seduces yet shuts out the ordinary citizen.

Application: Analyzing Satire. In a group analyze the following paragraphs to determine what ideas or behaviors Calvino is criticizing.

On page 609, beginning "All were caught up in the lively and cordial atmosphere . . ."

On page 610, beginning "Marcovaldo was about to say . . ."

On page 611, beginning "This tip could be substantial . . ."

On page 612, beginning "'The important thing,' the third added . . ."

Share your interpretations with the class.

Connecting Reading and Writing

1. Design **Christmas cards** to be sent by each of the following characters: Marcovaldo, Michelino, Gianfranco, and Gianfranco's father.

Option: Have each character make a **list** of Christmas gifts he would like to give or receive.

2. Imagine that you work for the Society for the Implementation of Christmas Consumption. Write a **press release** announcing, explaining, and praising the Destructive Gift.

Option: Advertise the Destructive Gift in a **catalog** of holiday gifts.

3. Write a **proposal** to the publisher of this story that explains how you would illustrate the story with photos. Be sure to specify which scenes you have in mind.

Option: Write a **character sketch** of Marcovaldo to be used by an artist hired to illustrate the story. Be sure to include a physical description.

Tale of the Computer That Fought a Dragon

STANISLAW ŁEM   born 1921   POLAND

A biography of Łem appears on page 745.

Approaching the Story

Stanislaw Łem is a well-known writer who often uses science fiction as a vehicle for social commentary. This story is about an imaginary king in an imaginary country, but it concerns a very real and controversial science: cybernetics, the development of computers with artificial intelligence. The unfamiliar names of creatures and objects in the story as well as the incredible events described lure readers into the fantasy world of Cyberia, where cyberbeetles and cyberflies abound and where cybernetic weapons and cyberfoes pose a daily threat.

Building Vocabulary

These essential words are footnoted within the story.

bellicose (bel′ i kōs′): There were twice as many military [devices], for the King was most **bellicose**. (page 617)

mettle (met′ ′l): He had a strategic computer, a machine of uncommon **mettle**. (page 617)

sallies: Now it was cosmic wars and **sallies** that he dreamed of. (page 617)

verisimilitude (ver′ ə si mil′ ə tōōd): The electrodragon wasn't . . . pretending, but battled with the utmost **verisimilitude**. (page 618)

Connecting Writing and Reading

Think of various tasks that you would gladly hand over to a "smart" computer, one with near-human intelligence. In your journal describe how such a computer might perform those tasks for you. As you read, compare your use of an intelligent computer with the ways intelligent computers are used in Cyberia.

KING POLEANDER Partobon, ruler of Cyberia, was a great warrior, and being an advocate of the methods of modern strategy, above all else he prized cybernetics as a military art. His kingdom swarmed with thinking machines, for Poleander put them everywhere he could; not merely in the astronomical observatories or the schools, but he ordered electric brains mounted in the rocks upon the roads, which with loud voices cautioned pedestrians against tripping; also in posts, in walls, in trees, so that one could ask directions anywhere when lost; he stuck them onto clouds, so they could announce the rain in advance, he added them to the hills and valleys—in short, it was impossible to walk on Cyberia without bumping into an intelligent machine. The planet was beautiful, since the King not only gave decrees for the cybernetic perfecting of that which had long been in existence, but he introduced by law entirely new orders of things. Thus for example in his kingdom were manufactured cyberbeetles and buzzing cyberbees, and even cyberflies—these would be seized by mechanical spiders when they grew too numerous. On the planet cyberbosks of cybergorse[1] rustled in the wind, cybercalliopes and cyberviols sang—but besides these civilian devices there were twice as many military, for the King was most bellicose.[2] In his palace vaults he had a strategic computer, a machine of uncommon mettle;[3] he had smaller ones also, and divisions of cybersaries, enormous cybermatics and a whole arsenal of every other kind of weapon, including powder. There was only this one problem, and it troubled him greatly, namely, that he had not a single adversary or enemy and no one in any way wished to invade his land and thereby provide him with the opportunity to demonstrate his kingly and terrifying courage, his tactical genius, not to mention the simply extraordinary effectiveness of his cybernetic weaponry. In the absence of genuine enemies and aggressors, the King had his engineers build artificial ones, and against these he did battle and always won. However, inasmuch as the battles and campaigns were genuinely dreadful, the populace suffered no little injury from them. The subjects murmured when all too many cyberfoes had destroyed their settlements and towns, when the synthetic enemy poured liquid fire upon them; they even dared voice their discontent when the King himself, issuing forth as their deliverer and vanquishing the artificial foe, in the course of the victorious attacks laid waste to everything that stood in his path. They grumbled even then, the ingrates, though the thing was done on their behalf.

Until the King wearied of the war games on the planet and decided to raise his sights. Now it was cosmic wars and sallies[4] that he dreamed of. His planet had a large Moon, entirely desolate and wild; the King laid heavy taxes upon his subjects to obtain the funds needed to build whole armies on that Moon and have there a new theater of war. And the subjects were more than happy to pay, figuring that King Poleander would now no longer deliver them with his cybermatics nor test the strength of his arms upon their homes and heads. And so the royal engineers built on the Moon a splendid computer, which in turn was to create all manner of troops and self-firing gunnery. The King lost no time in testing the machine's prowess this way and that; at one point he ordered it—by telegraph—to execute

---

1. **cyberbosks of cybergorse:** *Bosk* means "a small wooded place"; *gorse* is a kind of prickly evergreen shrub. Combined with the prefix *cyber*, they become one of Łem's invented phrases, meaning "computerized forests of computerized trees."
2. **bellicose** (bel′ i kōs′): eager to fight; warlike.
3. **mettle** (met′ 'l): stamina.
4. **sallies:** sudden attacks.

a volt-vault electrosault: for he wanted to see if it was true, what his engineers had told him, that that machine could do anything. If it can do anything, he thought, then let it do a flip. However, the text of the telegram underwent a slight distortion and the machine received the order that it was to execute not an electrosault, but an electrosaur—and this it carried out as best it could.

Meanwhile the King conducted one more campaign, liberating some provinces of his realm seized by cyberknechts; he completely forgot about the order given the computer on the Moon—then suddenly giant boulders came hurtling down from there; the King was astounded, for one even fell on the wing of the palace and destroyed his prize collection of cyberads, which are dryads[5] with feedback. Fuming, he telegraphed the Moon computer at once, demanding an explanation. It didn't reply, however, for it no longer was: the electrosaur had swallowed it and made it into its own tail.

Immediately the King dispatched an entire armed expedition to the Moon, placing at its head another computer, also very valiant, to slay the dragon, but there was only some flashing, some rumbling, and then no more computer nor expedition; for the electrodragon wasn't pretend and wasn't pretending, but battled with the utmost verisimilitude,[6] and had moreover the worst of intentions regarding the kingdom and the King. The King sent to the Moon his cybernants, cyberneers, cyberines and lieutenant cybernets; at the very end he even sent one cyberalissimo, but it too accomplished nothing; the hurly-burly lasted a little longer, that was all. The King watched through a telescope set up on the palace balcony.

The dragon grew; the Moon became smaller and smaller, since the monster was devouring it piecemeal and incorporating it into its own body. The King saw then, and his subjects did

also, that things were serious, for when the ground beneath the feet of the electrosaur was gone, it would for certain hurl itself upon the planet and upon them. The King thought and thought, but he saw no remedy and knew not what to do. To send machines was no good, for they would be lost, and to go himself was no better, for he was afraid. Suddenly the King heard, in the stillness of the night, the telegraph chattering from his royal bedchamber. It was the King's personal receiver, solid gold with a diamond needle, linked to the Moon; the King jumped up and ran to it; the apparatus meanwhile went *tap-tap*, *tap-tap*, and tapped out this telegram: THE DRAGON SAYS POLEANDER PARTOBON BETTER CLEAR OUT BECAUSE HE THE DRAGON INTENDS TO OCCUPY THE THRONE!

The King took fright, quaked from head to toe, and ran, just as he was, in his ermine nightshirt and slippers, down to the palace vaults, where stood the strategy machine, old and very wise. He had not as yet consulted it, since prior to the rise and uprise of the electrodragon they had argued on the subject of a certain military operation; but now was not the time to think of that—his throne, his life was at stake!

He plugged it in, and as soon as it warmed up he cried:

"My old computer! My good computer! It's this way and that, the dragon wishes to deprive me of my throne, to cast me out, help, speak, how can I defeat it?!"

"Uh-uh," said the computer. "First you must admit I was right in that previous business, and secondly, I would have you address me only as Digital Grand Vizier,[7] though you

---

5. **dryads:** wood nymphs.
6. **verisimilitude** (ver′ ə si mil′ ə to͞od): the appearance of being true or real.
7. **vizier** (vi zir′): originally a Turkish word referring to a high officer in the government.

may also say to me: 'Your Ferromagneticity!' "[8]

"Good, good, I'll name you Grand Vizier, I'll agree to anything you like, only save me!"

The machine whirred, chirred, hummed, hemmed, then said:

"It is a simple matter. We build an electrosaur more powerful than the one located on the Moon. It will defeat the lunar one, settle its circuitry once and for all and thereby attain the goal!"

"Perfect!" replied the King. "And can you make a blueprint of this dragon?"

"It will be an ultradragon," said the computer. "And I can make you not only a blueprint, but the thing itself, which I shall now do; it won't take a minute, King!" And true to its word, it hissed, it chugged, it whistled and buzzed, assembling something down within itself, and already an object like a giant claw, sparking, arcing, was emerging from its side, when the King shouted:

"Old computer! Stop!"

"Is this how you address me? I am the Digital Grand Vizier!"

"Ah, of course," said the King. "Your Ferromagneticity, the electrodragon you are making will defeat the other dragon, granted, but it will surely remain in the other's place. How then are we to get rid of it in turn?!"

"By making yet another, still more powerful," explained the computer.

"No, no! In that case don't do anything, I beg you. What good will it be to have more and more terrible dragons on the Moon when I don't want any there at all?"

"Ah, now that's a different matter," the computer replied. "Why didn't you say so in the first place? You see how illogically you express yourself? One moment . . . I must think."

And it churred and hummed, and chuffed and chuckled, and finally said:

"We make an antimoon with an antidragon, place it in the Moon's orbit (here some-

thing went snap inside), sit around the fire and sing: *Oh, I'm a robot full of fun, water doesn't scare me none, I dives right in, I gives a grin, tra la the livelong day!!*"

"You speak strangely," said the King. "What does the antimoon have to do with that song about the funny robot?"

"What funny robot?" asked the computer. "Ah, no, no, I made a mistake, something feels wrong inside, I must have blown a tube." The King began to look for the trouble, finally found the burnt out tube, put in a new one, then asked the computer about the antimoon.

"What antimoon?" asked the computer, which meanwhile had forgotten what it said before. "I don't know anything about an antimoon . . . one moment, I have to give this thought."

It hummed, it huffed, and it said:

"We create a general theory of the slaying of electrodragons, of which the lunar dragon will be a special case, its solution trivial."

"Well, create such a theory!" said the King.

"To do this I must first create various experimental dragons."

"Certainly not! No thank you!" exclaimed the King. "A dragon wants to deprive me of my throne. Just think what might happen if you produced a swarm of them!"

"Oh? Well then, in that case we must resort to other means. We will use a strategic variant of the method of successive approximations. Go and telegraph the dragon that you will give it the throne on the condition that it perform three mathematical operations, really quite simple . . ."

The King went and telegraphed, and the dragon agreed. The King returned to the computer.

"Now," it said, "here is the first operation: tell it to divide itself by itself!"

---

8. Ferromagneticity: an invented title meaning "Highly Magnetic One."

The King did this. The electrosaur divided itself by itself, but since one electrosaur over one electrosaur is one, it remained on the Moon and nothing changed.

"Is this the best you can do?!" cried the King, running into the vault with such haste that his slippers fell off. "The dragon divided itself by itself, but since one goes into one once, nothing changed!"

"That's all right. I did that on purpose— the operation was to divert attention," said the computer. "And now tell it to extract its root!" The King telegraphed to the Moon, and the dragon began to pull, push, pull, push, until it crackled from the strain, panted, trembled all over, but suddenly something gave—and it extracted its own root!

The King went back to the computer.

"The dragon crackled, trembled, even ground its teeth, but extracted the root and threatens me still!" he shouted from the doorway. "What now, my old . . . I mean, Your Ferromagneticity?!"

"Be of stout heart," it said. "Now go tell it to subtract itself from itself!"

The King hurried to his royal bedchamber, sent the telegram, and the dragon began to subtract itself from itself, taking away its tail first, then legs, then trunk, and finally, when it saw that something wasn't right, it hesitated, but from its own momentum the subtracting continued, it took away its head and became zero, in other words, nothing: the electrosaur was no more!

"The electrosaur is no more," cried the joyful King, bursting into the vault. "Thank you, old computer . . . many thanks . . . you have worked hard . . . you have earned a rest, so now I will disconnect you."

"Not so fast, my dear," the computer replied. "I do the job and you want to disconnect me, and you no longer call me Your Ferromagneticity?! That's not nice, not nice at all! Now I myself will change into an electrosaur, yes, and drive you from the kingdom, and most certainly rule better than you, for you always consulted me in all the more important matters; therefore, it was really I who ruled all along, and not you . . ."

And huffing, puffing, it began to change into an electrosaur; flaming electroclaws were already protruding from its sides when the King, breathless with fright, tore the slippers off his feet, rushed up to it and with the slippers began beating blindly at its tubes! The computer chugged, choked, and got muddled in its program—instead of the word "electrosaur" it read "electrosauce," and before the King's very eyes the computer, wheezing more and more softly, turned into an enormous, gleaming-golden heap of electrosauce, which, still sizzling, emitted all its charge in deep blue sparks, leaving Poleander to stare dumbstruck at only a great, steaming pool of gravy . . .

With a sigh the King put on his slippers and returned to the royal bedchamber. However, from that time on he was an altogether different king: the events he had undergone made his nature less bellicose, and to the end of his days he engaged exclusively in civilian cybernetics and left the military kind strictly alone.

Thinking About the Story

A PERSONAL RESPONSE

sharing impressions

1. How do you feel about intelligent computers after reading the story? Briefly describe your feelings in your journal.

constructing interpretations

2. What do you think Łem is satirizing most in this story?

3. Do you think the problems of Cyberia are caused more by humans—the king and his subjects—or by intelligent computers?

Think about
- the description of the king and his subjects
- the advice of the strategy machine
- the malfunctions of the computers in the story

A CREATIVE RESPONSE

4. If King Poleander had not been bellicose, how might this story be different?

A CRITICAL RESPONSE

5. How would you describe Łem's tone in the story? Go back through the story and find examples of sentences that reveal his attitude.

Analyzing the Writer's Craft

THEME AND SCIENCE FICTION

Recall your answer to question 2 regarding what Łem is satirizing most in this story. How might his ideas apply to society today?

Building a Literary Vocabulary. Theme is the central idea or message in a work of literature. Generally, short stories present several themes, one of which usually predominates. Most science fiction comments on present-day society through the writer's conception of a past or future society. Some science fiction writers create believable worlds while others, like Łem, create fantasy worlds that have familiar elements. In "Tale of the Computer That Fought a Dragon," Łem uses the character of King Poleander, who almost destroys his kingdom by fighting foes of his own creation, to raise the issue of what qualities make a good leader, a question that continues to be crucial in today's society. Łem further raises serious questions about the appropriate use of powerful technology, especially as it promotes the production of weapons and the continued existence of war.

Application: Exploring Theme. Two important themes presented in the story are: (1) misuse of power by people poses a threat to humanity, and (2) machines pose a threat to humanity. Get together with several classmates and form two small debate groups, one group taking the position that human beings are the greater threat and the other side taking the position that machines pose a greater threat. Present your ideas to the rest of the class. Then ask your classmates to assess the supporting evidence from the story given for each position and then decide which theme predominates in the story.

*C*onnecting Reading and Writing

1. Read another science fiction story by Łem—for example, "The Electronic Bard"— or a story by another science fiction writer such as Isaac Asimov or Ray Bradbury. Create a **chart** in which you compare the story to "Tale of the Computer That Fought a Dragon" in terms of plot, character, setting, and theme. Provide copies of your chart for classmates interested in science fiction.

Option: Write a **letter** to a friend explaining which story you liked more, and why.

2. Design a **poster** advertising a movie based on this story. Be sure your poster includes inventions from the story, such as the electrosaur and other cybercreatures.

Option: Write **guidelines** for creating the special effects that would be needed in a film version of the story.

3. Write an **outline** for a science fiction story based on a terrific new cybernetic machine of your own invention.

Option: Create the first two pages of an **instruction manual** for your invention. Illustrate and describe the capabilities of your new cybernetic machine.

Vocational Counselling

CHRISTA REINIG   born 1926   GERMANY

A biography of Reinig appears on page 750.

*A*pproaching *the Story*

"Vocational Counselling" breaks from the traditional short story form in both structure and appearance. The story is Christa Reinig's (rī′ niH) unconventional response to the question "Why do you write?" In the story Reinig describes an encounter with a computer that is programmed to choose appropriate careers, or vocations, for people. The selection appears to be a reminiscence, but it is actually a work of fiction in which the writer herself is a character. The computer in the story has capabilities far beyond anything that has been developed even today. However, the rest of the story accurately reflects German life during her youth in the 1930's and 1940's. Reinig grew up under the regimes of Nazi Germany and communist East Germany, two states that exercised rigid control over people's private lives. In her story, the computer represents the totalitarian state.

*B*uilding *Vocabulary*

These essential words are footnoted within the story.

guttural (gut′ ər əl): The computer talked in its **guttural**, electronic voice. (page 624)

atrophied (a′ trə fēd): Their eyes have **atrophied** because they have been living in darkness for so long. (page 625)

*C*onnecting *Writing and Reading*

Of the factors listed below, which do you think should be most important in determining your career choice? Which should be least important?

skills and abilities	family traditions or expectations
scores on a job aptitude test	interests and hobbies
advice from a career counsellor	chance
the needs of your country, community, or ethnic group	
the types of jobs available in a certain location	

Explain your answers in your journal. As you read this selection, keep in mind your views about what should determine career choice.

Vocational Counselling

I was still a child, "talked like a child, was bright like a child and had childlike notions." But as far as the state was concerned, I was finishing school and next year I would go out into the real world, into the state. We formed lines in front of the white doors, the boys and girls separately. We read the flyers which they had handed to us at the door:

> In the testing booth absolute silence must prevail. Concentrate! If you do not understand the question, press the blue button. You have one minute to formulate your answer. At the sound of the bell, get up and leave the room.

The fact that someone suddenly addressed me by the polite form[1] was no comfort to me. It increased my fears. As I finally confronted "it," alone in a humming room, I was trembling and I pressed the red button—the red button on my left. But I did not get it at all that I had given myself away as being left-handed. I could not sit down properly. My child's behind was wiggling on the stool. I had to go to the bathroom. A minute later I had forgotten about it.

The computer talked in its guttural,[2] electronic voice:

> Comrade[3] Reinig! Do you remember when you consciously heard the word *work* for the first time and what emotions it evoked in you?

Reinig: I consciously heard the word for the first time in the expression "without work" and it evoked pleasant emotions in me.

Computer: What images can you remember?

Reinig: It was in Humboldt Park. The men were sitting close together on benches, folding chairs or on the borders of the lawn. In front of them, on their knees they had cigar boxes and shoe cartons full of little pictures from their cigarette packages. They visited each other and exchanged the pictures back and forth. One

---

1. **polite form:** German, like many other languages, has two forms for the second-person pronoun *you*. One is used for close friends, family, and children. The other, the polite form, is more formal. Use of this form implies that the computer is treating Reinig like an adult.
2. **guttural** (gut′ ər əl): produced in the throat; harsh; rasping.
3. **Comrade:** a form of address used in many communist countries.

Greta Garbo for one Emil Jannings.[4] One French fighter plane for one Focke-Wulf,[5] one Chinese Mandarin for one Huron Warrior in ceremonial garb. The whole of Humboldt Park was one big market swarming with these men exchanging little pictures. Later they said that the nightmarish time of unemployment was over and we could all look to the future with joy. I said to myself these adults are nuts, and secretly I decided to be unemployed one day.

Computer: What are the dominating feelings when early in the morning the sound of an alarm clock tears you from your sleep?

Reinig: I feel a great sorrow in my heart.

Computer: During the course of the day, do you repeatedly feel a great sorrow in your heart?

Reinig: No, once I have managed to get out of bed, the worst part of the day is behind me.

Computer: What is your favorite occupation?

Reinig: Reading.

Computer: What do you like to read best?

Reinig: Karl May, John Kling, Billy Jenkins, Rolf Torring, Jorn Farrow, Tom Mix.

Computer: What is your favorite book?

Reinig: Olaf K. Abelsen,[6] *At the Fires of Eternity*. I must have read it a dozen times and I can recite it from memory.

Computer: Give a short summary of the contents.

Reinig: Well, the group of travelers is being followed by gangsters. One does not know why, because it is a story in installments. The gangsters blow up the island. Because of that, the group of travelers gets under the earth into a dark volcanic landscape, weakly lighted by a distant fire. There are animals there, too—crocodiles, bats. These animals are blind, their eyes have atrophied[7] because they have been living in darkness for so long. Then the travelers discover the remains of an ancient Mayan

---

4. **Greta Garbo . . . Emil Jannings:** Greta Garbo (1905–1990) was a famous American film actress; Emil Jannings (1884–1950) was a famous German film actor.
5. **Focke-Wulf** (fô′ kə vo͝olf): a kind of German war plane.
6. **Karl May . . . Tom Mix . . . Olaf K. Abelsen:** Tom Mix was an American actor who played cowboy roles. The other names are of writers of popular adventure stories in the mid-twentieth century.
7. **atrophied** (a′ trə fēd): wasted away from lack of use.

culture. As they are about to recover the treasures, someone shoots poisoned arrows at them. It is not the Indians, however, but the gangsters who are pursuing them. The fire of eternity changes, and there is a volcanic eruption. The travelers are blown up from the depths and thrown into the sea. There they find each other again while fighting the waves. That is the end. The next volume is missing, but I believe they are rescued.

Computer: Did you ever try to read a classical work by Schiller or Goethe?[8]

Reinig: Yes, I once tried to read a sea adventure play by Goethe or Schiller.

The familiar humming sound stopped. Suddenly there was complete silence. Then there was a soft, hoarse little cough that did not stop. In a sense it had been quite pleasant until now. But then I realized that I had bared the lining of my heart, not to a sympathetic soul, but to a machine which must have cost at least many millions of dollarrubles. And I had wrecked it. Worse, at any moment it would explode and tear me to pieces. That might be better; at least I would not have to pay for it. How many years would it take to pay for it by working it off? I would rather prepare myself for death. Then there was that humming again. Our Father—thank God.

Computer: Did you ever try to read a classical work by Goethe or Schiller?

Reinig: Torquato Tasso.[9]

The crazier these exotic names are the better one can remember them. Schimborassotschomolungmakiliman-dscharo! Why doesn't he ask me something like that?

Computer: Describe the artistic impressions which you have received.

Reinig: The book got in with our furniture and junk in some way. It got lost there and surfaced now and then. Finally I felt sorry. I always read the last page first. They mentioned a ship's sinking. The hero, battling the waves, was trying to hold onto a cliff. Then, again, the sequel was also missing. Possibly he was rescued, for if

---

8. Schiller or Goethe (gö′ tə): considered the greatest German writers. They hold a position similar to that of Shakespeare in English.

9. Torquato Tasso (tôr kwä′ tô täs′ ô): a play by Goethe based on the life of Tasso, the medieval Italian writer of an epic poem filled with romantic fantasy and adventure. The play dramatizes the conflict between the poet's inner nature and the demands of the outer world.

the shipwrecked man gets too close to the cliffs, he is finished. He would simply be dashed to pieces. Then I read the beginning, too. It was about some people or other who were walking around in a museum and looking at figures. I quickly had enough of this, and how the shipwreck happened, I never did find out.

Computer: Your good marks in school are incompatible with your unreasonable reading. How do you explain this contradiction?

Reinig: My mother gave me a high school textbook for Christmas. But since I go to elementary school, the book was completely useless. It did not fit our course of studies at all and I never did use it. And therefore I read it anyway.

Computer: Do you have any special vocational plans?

Reinig: Originally I wanted to go to the Trojan War. But then I learned that it was already over and people thought there would be no more war. So then I switched over to the Odyssey. I got my facts confused and prepared myself mentally to discover America. With time I got smarter and realized that there are things which cannot happen because they have already happened. I concentrated on the Antarctic in case something would turn up for me there, since I am first in tobogganing. In travel descriptions I read that modern seafaring consists only of removing rust and painting with red lead. So I got myself into an identity crisis, which was strengthened because I slowly had to realize that I was indeed a girl, and with that all of my previous vocational plans were thwarted in any case. Luckily, a little later on I got a prescription for glasses. This solved all of my problems, including the problems of sex. For the boys really had me run the gauntlet[10] and shouted with sadistic pleasure: "My last will for lasses, one with glasses!" Wherever I appeared, they started up. Then, however, winter came and the boys as usual pummeled all the girls with snowballs. Only I was spared. Wherever I appeared, they warned each other: "Watch out, not her, she has glasses." This gave me new courage and I decided to become a professor and to excavate Mayan[11] pyramids. And to that thought I have actually stuck until today.

Computer: You will be a writer. Within two minutes you can register a protest, and, for this, press the green button.

---

10. **run the gauntlet:** to be put through a series of obstacles or difficulties.

11. **Mayan** (mä′ yən): pertaining to the tribe of Indians who inhabited the Yucatan, British Honduras, and North Guatemala, known for their highly developed civilization.

Within two seconds I pressed the button.

Computer: Counterproposal?

Reinig: Oh, please, may I not at least become a politician? I could work my way up to becoming chancellor and become the highest servant of my people. I have always been able to speak well.

Computer: Laziness in combination with ambition would allow for both possibilities. On them a political as well as a literary career can be based. In your case only the second possibility can be considered because your intelligence is not sufficient for politics.

And then it seemed to me as if I were suddenly hearing a human voice, loving, concerned and personal. But that cannot be true. It was and remained a machine. It must only be my grateful memory that falsified something.

Computer: And, moreover, I am responsible for your further well-being. If something unpleasant should happen to you, one would reproach me and maintain that I was programmed incorrectly.—Objection refused.

Thirty years later I had another encounter with a computer. I stepped into the testing booth and with cocky indifference pressed the red button on the—right side and sat down.

Computer: Comrade Reinig, why do you write?

Reinig: I write because Comrade Computer prescribed it for me.

The bell rang and I left the room.

Thinking About the Story

A PERSONAL RESPONSE

sharing impressions

1. What are your feelings toward young Reinig? Describe your reaction to her in your journal.

constructing interpretations

2. What do you learn about the young Reinig's personality from her responses to the computer?

3. What is your reaction to the way Reinig is counselled by the computer about a career choice?

Think about
- the rules associated with the counselling process
- the attitude the computer displays toward her
- whether the computer is right to decide that she become a writer
- your own views, which you explored in your journal, about what should determine career choice

A CREATIVE RESPONSE

4. What would be lost from the story if the second encounter with the computer were not included?

A CRITICAL RESPONSE

5. What aspects of society are satirized in this story?

Think about
- the computer as representing the totalitarian state
- the young Reinig's comments about work and unemployment
- her fear that she has wrecked the computer or that it will attack her
- the computer's comparison of careers in writing and politics
- other statements that seem to criticize social conditions

6. Consider Christa Reinig not as a character but as the writer of this story. What answer do you think she gives to the question "Why do you write?"

7. Do Reinig and Stanislaw Łem, the author of the preceding story, share the same view of computers? Compare the writers' attitudes.

8. To what extent is this story relevant to present-day life in the United States?

Think about
- the career counselling offered to students in this country
- ways in which computers affect our daily lives
- how nonconformity is viewed by our society

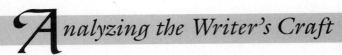
Analyzing the Writer's Craft

EXPERIMENTAL FICTION

Does this work meet your expectations of what a story should be?

Building a Literary Vocabulary. Experimental fiction breaks with the conventions, or accepted rules, of traditional fiction. For example, an experimental work might have a beginning and an end but no middle. It might be a set of incomplete notes instead of a sustained narrative. It might be narrated by a self-conscious writer who feels free to comment on what he or she has written and to begin again if dissatisfied. "Vocational Counselling" could be classified as experimental fiction. For instance, its insertion of a futuristic element—a vocational counselling computer—into the Germany of the past challenges the reader's expectations about setting.

Application: Analyzing Experimental Fiction. Divide into groups of four or five students. List ways in which this story overturns conventions regarding characters, plot, form (the physical appearance of the text on the page), and point of view (the perspective from which the story is narrated). Discuss how the unconventional organization of the story is related to its message, or theme.

Six Feet of the Country

NADINE GORDIMER   born 1923   SOUTH AFRICA

A biography of Gordimer appears on page 743.

Approaching the Story

The novels and short stories of Nadine Gordimer, a white South African, show the effects of apartheid upon personal relationships. Apartheid, as you may recall from the excerpt from *Kaffir Boy* in Unit 4, is the system of racial discrimination supported by the government of South Africa. In "Six Feet of the Country," Gordimer examines the experiences and attitudes of a British couple—a businessman and a former actress—who have moved to the South African countryside.

Building Vocabulary

These essential words are footnoted within the story.

imbued (im byo͞od′): Lerice . . . has sunk into the business of running the farm with all the serious intensity with which she once **imbued** the shadows in a playwright's mind. (page 632)

histrionical (his′ trē än′ i kul): I find Lerice's earthy enthusiasms just as irritating as I once found her **histrionical** ones. (page 632)

expostulated (eks päs′ chə lāt′ id): Now Petrus **expostulated** with him. (page 637)

laconic (lə kän′ ik): They were shocked, in a **laconic** fashion, by their own mistake. (page 638)

Connecting Writing and Reading

Based on the title, "Six Feet of the Country," and on the information provided in Approaching the Story, what do you predict about this story? In your journal jot down your ideas. As you read, compare your prediction to what actually happens.

Six Feet of the Country

MY WIFE AND I are not real farmers—not even Lerice, really. We bought our place, ten miles out of Johannesburg on one of the main roads, to change something in ourselves, I suppose; you seem to rattle about so much within a marriage like ours. You long to hear nothing but a deep, satisfying silence when you sound a marriage. The farm hasn't managed that for us, of course, but it has done other things, unexpected, illogical. Lerice, who I thought would retire there in Chekhovian sadness for a month or two and then leave the place to the servants while she tried yet again to get a part she wanted and become the actress she would like to be, has sunk into the business of running the farm with all the serious intensity with which she once imbued[1] the shadows in a playwright's mind. I should have given it up long ago if it had not been for her. Her hands, once small and plain and well kept—she was not the sort of actress who wears red paint and diamond rings—are hard as a dog's pads.

I, of course, am there only in the evenings and at weekends. I am a partner in a travel agency, which is flourishing—needs to be, as I tell Lerice, in order to carry the farm. Still, though I know we can't afford it, and though the sweetish smell of the fowls Lerice breeds sickens me, so that I avoid going past their runs, the farm is beautiful in a way I had almost forgotten—especially on a Sunday morning when I get up and go out into the paddock and see not the palm trees and fishpond and imitation-stone birdbath of the suburbs but white ducks on the dam, the lucerne[2] field brilliant as window-dresser's grass, and the little, stocky, mean-eyed bull, lustful but bored, having his face tenderly licked by one of his ladies. Lerice comes out with her hair uncombed, in her hand a stick dripping with cattle dip. She will stand and look dreamily for a moment, the way she would pretend to look sometimes in those plays. "They'll mate tomorrow," she will say. "This is their second day. Look how she loves him, my little Napoleon." So that when people come to see us on Sunday afternoon, I am likely to hear myself saying as I pour out the drinks, "When I drive back home from the city every day past those rows of suburban houses, I wonder how the devil we ever did stand it . . . Would you care to look around?" And there I am, taking some pretty girl and her husband stumbling down to our riverbank, the girl catching her stockings on the mealie-stooks and stepping over cow turds humming with jewel-green flies while she says, ". . .the *tensions* of the damned city. And you're near enough to get into town to a show, too! I think it's wonderful. Why, you've got it both ways!"

And for a moment I accept the triumph as if I *had* managed it—the impossibility that I've been trying for all my life: just as if the truth was that you could get it "both ways," instead of finding yourself with not even one way or the other but a third, one you had not provided for at all.

But even in our saner moments, when I find Lerice's earthy enthusiasms just as irritating as I once found her histrionical[3] ones and she finds what she calls my "jealousy" of her capac-

---

1. **imbued** (im byood′): filled completely; saturated.
2. **lucerne** (loo surn′): a chiefly British term for alfalfa.
3. **histrionical** (his′ trē än′ i kul): theatrical; dramatic.

ity for enthusiasm as big a proof of my inadequacy for her as a mate as ever it was, we do believe that we have at least honestly escaped those tensions peculiar to the city about which our visitors speak. When Johannesburg people speak of "tension," they don't mean hurrying people in crowded streets, the struggle for money, or the general competitive character of city life. They mean the guns under the white men's pillows and the burglar bars on the white men's windows. They mean those strange moments on city pavements when a black man won't stand aside for a white man.

Out in the country, even ten miles out, life is better than that. In the country, there is a lingering remnant of the pretransitional stage; our relationship with the blacks is almost feudal. Wrong, I suppose, obsolete, but more comfortable all around. We have no burglar bars, no guns. Lerice's farm boys have their wives and their piccanins[4] living with them on the land. They brew their sour beer without the fear of police raids. In fact, we've always rather prided ourselves that the poor devils have nothing much to fear, being with us; Lerice even keeps an eye on their children, with all the competence of a woman who has never had a child of her own, and she certainly doctors them all—children and adults—like babies whenever they happen to be sick.

It was because of this that we were not particularly startled one night last winter when the boy Albert came knocking at our window long after we had gone to bed. I wasn't in our bed but sleeping in the little dressing room-cum-linen room next door because Lerice had annoyed me and I didn't want to find myself softening toward her simply because of the sweet smell of the talcum powder on her flesh after her bath. She came and woke me up. "Albert says one of the boys is very sick," she said. "I think you'd better go down and see. He wouldn't get us up at this hour for nothing."

"What time is it?"

"What does it matter?" Lerice is maddeningly logical.

I got up awkwardly as she watched me—how is it I always feel a fool when I have deserted her bed? After all, I know from the way she never looks at me when she talks to me at breakfast next day that she is hurt and humiliated at my not wanting her—and I went out, clumsy with sleep.

"Which of the boys is it?" I asked Albert as we followed the dance of my torch.

"He's too sick. Very sick," he said.

"But who? Franz?" I remembered Franz had had a bad cough for the past week.

Albert did not answer; he had given me the path and was walking along beside me in the tall, dead grass. When the light of the torch caught his face, I saw that he looked acutely embarrassed. "What's this all about?" I said.

He lowered his head under the glance of the light. "It's not me, baas.[5] I don't know. Petrus he send me."

Irritated, I hurried him along to the huts. And there, on Petrus's iron bedstead, with its brick stilts, was a young man, dead. On his forehead there was still a light, cold sweat; his body was warm. The boys stood around as they do in the kitchen when it is discovered that someone has broken a dish—uncooperative, silent. Somebody's wife hung about in the shadows, her hands wrung together under her apron.

I had not seen a dead man since the war. This was very different. I felt like the others—extraneous, useless. "What was the matter?" I asked.

The woman patted at her chest and shook her head to indicate the painful impossibility of breathing.

---

4. **piccanins** (pik′ ə ninz): a derogatory term for native African children.

5. **baas** (bäs): a term of address used in South Africa for a white man.

He must have died of pneumonia.

I turned to Petrus. "Who was this boy? What was he doing here?" The light of a candle on the floor showed that Petrus was weeping. He followed me out the door.

When we were outside, in the dark, I waited for him to speak. But he didn't. "Now, come on, Petrus, you must tell me who this boy was. Was he a friend of yours?"

"He's my brother, baas. He came from Rhodesia to look for work."

Guide for Interpretation

Think about the narrator's attitude toward Petrus and the other farmhands. As you read on, consider how his attitude makes you feel about him as a character.

The story startled Lerice and me a little. The young boy had walked down from Rhodesia to look for work in Johannesburg, had caught a chill from sleeping out along the way, and had lain ill in his brother Petrus's hut since his arrival three days before. Our boys had been frightened to ask us for help for him because we had never been intended ever to know of his presence. Rhodesian natives are barred from entering the Union unless they have a permit; the young man was an illegal immigrant. No doubt our boys had managed the whole thing successfully several times before; a number of relatives must have walked the seven or eight hundred miles from poverty to the paradise of zoot suits,[6] police raids, and black slum townships that is their Egoli,[7] City of Gold—the African name for Johannesburg. It was merely a matter of getting such a man to lie low on our farm until a job could be found with someone who would be glad to take the risk of prosecution for employing an illegal immigrant in exchange for the services of someone as yet untainted by the city.

Well, this was one who would never get up again.

"You would think they would have felt they could tell *us*," said Lerice next morning. "Once

the man was ill. You would have thought at least—" When she is getting intense over something, she has a way of standing in the middle of a room as people do when they are shortly to leave on a journey, looking searchingly about her at the most familiar objects as if she had never seen them before. I had noticed that in Petrus's presence in the kitchen, earlier, she had had the air of being almost offended with him, almost hurt.

In any case, I really haven't the time or inclination any more to go into everything in our life that I know Lerice, from those alarmed and pressing eyes of hers, would like us to go into. She is the kind of woman who doesn't mind if she looks plain, or odd; I don't suppose she would even care if she knew how strange she looks when her whole face is out of proportion with urgent uncertainty. I said, "Now I'm the one who'll have to do all the dirty work, I suppose."

She was still staring at me, trying me out with those eyes—wasting her time, if she only knew.

"I'll have to notify the health authorities," I said calmly. "They can't just cart him off and bury him. After all, we don't really know what he died of."

She simply stood there, as if she had given up—simply ceased to see me at all.

I don't know when I've been so irritated. "It might have been something contagious," I said. "God knows." There was no answer.

I am not enamored of holding conversations with myself. I went out to shout to one of the boys to open the garage and get the car ready for my morning drive to town.

As I had expected, it turned out to be quite a business. I had to notify the police as well as

---

6. zoot suits: men's flashy suits of a once-popular style, with broadly padded shoulders and baggy trousers.

7. Egoli (ē gô′ lē).

Guide for Interpretation

Consider the different responses of the narrator and Lerice to the death of Petrus's brother. Ask yourself what their responses might suggest about the strength of their relationship and about the differences between them.

the health authorities and answer a lot of tedious questions: How was it I was ignorant of the boy's presence? If I did not supervise my native quarters, how did I know that that sort of thing didn't go on all the time? And when I flared up and told them that so long as my natives did their work, I didn't think it my right or concern to poke my nose into their private lives, I got from the coarse, dull-witted police sergeant one of those looks that come not from any thinking process going on in the brain but from that faculty common to all who are possessed by the master-race theory—a look of insanely inane certainty. He grinned at me with a mixture of scorn and delight at my stupidity.

Then I had to explain to Petrus why the health authorities had to take away the body for a post-mortem—and, in fact, what a post-mortem was. When I telephoned the health department some days later to find out the result, I was told that the cause of death was, as we had thought, pneumonia and that the body had been suitably disposed of. I went out to where Petrus was mixing a mash for the fowls and told him that it was all right, there would be no trouble; his brother had died from that pain in his chest. Petrus put down the paraffin tin and said, "When can we go to fetch him, baas?"

"To fetch him?"

"Will the baas please ask them when we must come?"

I went back inside and called Lerice, all over the house. She came down the stairs from the spare bedrooms, and I said, "*Now* what am I going to do? When I told Petrus, he just asked calmly when they could go and fetch the body. They think they're going to bury him themselves."

"Well, go back and tell him," said Lerice. "You must tell him. Why didn't you tell him then?"

When I found Petrus again, he looked up politely. "Look, Petrus," I said. "You can't go to fetch your brother. They've done it already—they've *buried* him, you understand?"

"Where?" he said slowly, dully, as if he thought that perhaps he was getting this wrong.

"You see, he was a stranger. They knew he wasn't from here, and they didn't know he had some of his people here, so they thought they must bury him." It was difficult to make a pauper's grave sound like a privilege.

"Please, baas, the baas must ask them." But he did not mean that he wanted to know the burial place. He simply ignored the incomprehensible machinery I told him had set to work on his dead brother; he wanted the brother back.

"But, Petrus," I said, "how can I? Your brother is buried already. I can't ask them now."

"Oh, baas!" he said. He stood with his bran-smeared hands uncurled at his sides, one corner of his mouth twitching.

"Good God, Petrus, they won't listen to me! They can't, anyway. I'm sorry, but I can't do it. You understand?"

He just kept on looking at me, out of his knowledge that white men have everything, can do anything; if they don't, it is because they won't.

And then, at dinner, Lerice started. "You could at least phone," she said.

"Christ, what d'you think I am? Am I supposed to bring the dead back to life?"

But I could not exaggerate my way out of this ridiculous responsibility that had been thrust on me. "Phone them up," she went on. "And at least you'll be able to tell him you've done it and they've explained that it's impossible."

She disappeared somewhere into the kitchen quarters after coffee. A little later she came back to tell me, "The old father's coming down from Rhodesia to be at the funeral. He's got a permit and he's already on his way."

Unfortunately, it was not impossible to get the body back. The authorities said that it was somewhat irregular but that since the hygiene conditions had been fulfilled, they could not refuse permission for exhumation. I found out that, with the undertaker's charges, it would cost twenty pounds. Ah, I thought, that settles it. On five pounds a month, Petrus won't have twenty pounds—and just as well, since it couldn't do the dead any good. Certainly I should not offer it to him myself. Twenty pounds—or anything else within reason, for that matter—I would have spent without grudging it on doctors or medicines that might have helped the boy when he was alive. Once he was dead, I had no intention of encouraging Petrus to throw away, on a gesture, more than he spent to clothe his whole family in a year.

When I told him, in the kitchen that night, he said, "Twenty pounds?"

I said, "Yes, that's right, twenty pounds."

For a moment, I had the feeling, from the look on his face, that he was calculating. But when he spoke again I thought I must have imagined it. "We must pay twenty pounds!" he said in the faraway voice in which a person speaks of something so unattainable it does not bear thinking about.

"All right, Petrus," I said and went back to the living room.

The next morning before I went to town, Petrus asked to see me. "Please, baas," he said, awkwardly, handing me a bundle of notes. They're so seldom on the giving rather than the receiving side, poor devils, they don't really know how to hand money to a white man. There it was, the twenty pounds, in ones and halves, some creased and folded until they were soft as dirty rags, others smooth and fairly new—Franz's money, I suppose, and Albert's, and Dora the cook's, and Jacob the gardener's, and God knows who else's besides, from all the farms and small holdings round about. I took it in irritation more than in astonishment, really—irritation at the waste, the uselessness of this sacrifice by people so poor. Just like the poor everywhere, I thought, who stint themselves the decencies of life in order to ensure themselves the decencies of death. So incomprehensible to people like Lerice and me, who regard life as something to be spent extravagantly and, if we think about death at all, regard it as the final bankruptcy.

Guide for Interpretation

Notice the way the narrator contrasts his own values with those of the farmhands. As you continue reading this story, consider other ways in which their values differ.

The farmhands don't work on Saturday afternoon anyway, so it was a good day for the funeral. Petrus and his father had borrowed our donkey cart to fetch the coffin from the city, where, Petrus told Lerice on their return, everything was "nice"—the coffin waiting for them, already sealed up to save them from what must have been a rather unpleasant sight after two weeks' interment. (It had taken all that time for the authorities and the undertaker to make the final arrangements for moving the body.) All morning, the coffin lay in Petrus's hut, awaiting the trip to the little old burial ground, just outside the eastern boundary of our farm, that was a relic of the days when this was a real farming district rather than a fashionable rural estate. It was pure chance that I happened to be down there near the fence when the procession came past; once again Lerice had forgotten her promise to me and had made the house uninhabitable on a Saturday afternoon. I had come home and been infuriated to find her in a pair of filthy old slacks and with her hair uncombed since the night before, having all the varnish scraped from the living-room floor, if you please. So I had taken my No. 8 iron and gone off to practice my approach shots. In my annoyance, I had forgotten about the funeral, and was reminded only when I saw the procession coming up the path along the outside of the fence toward me; from where I was standing, you can see the graves quite clearly, and that day the sun glinted on bits of broken pottery, a lopsided homemade cross, and jam jars brown with rainwater and dead flowers.

I felt a little awkward and did not know whether to go on hitting my golf ball or stop at least until the whole gathering was decently past. The donkey cart creaks and screeches with every revolution of the wheels, and it came along in a slow, halting fashion somehow peculiarly suited to the two donkeys who drew it, their little potbellies rubbed and rough, their heads sunk between the shafts, and their ears flattened back with an air submissive and downcast; peculiarly suited, too, to the group of men and women who came along slowly behind. The patient ass. Watching, I thought, you can see now why the creature became a Biblical symbol. Then the procession drew level with me and stopped, so I had to put down my club. The coffin was taken down off the cart—it was a shiny, yellow-varnished wood, like cheap furniture—and the donkeys twitched their ears against the flies. Petrus, Franz, Albert, and the old father from Rhodesia hoisted it on their shoulders, and the procession moved on, on foot. It was really a very awkward moment. I stood there rather foolishly at the fence, quite still, and slowly they filed past, not looking up, the four men bent beneath the shiny wooden box, and the straggling troop of mourners. All of them were servants or neighbors' servants whom I knew as casual, easygoing gossipers about our lands or kitchen. I heard the old man's breathing.

I had just bent to pick up my club again when there was a sort of jar in the flowing solemnity of their processional mood; I felt it at once, like a wave of heat along the air or one of those sudden currents of cold catching at your legs in a placid stream. The old man's voice was muttering something; the people had stopped, confused, and they bumped into one another, some pressing to go on, others hissing them to be still. I could see that they were embarrassed, but they could not ignore the voice; it was much the way that the mumblings of a prophet, though not clear at first, arrest the mind. The corner of the coffin the old man carried was sagging at an angle; he seemed to be trying to get out from under the weight of it. Now Petrus expostulated[8] with him.

The little boy who had been left to watch the donkeys dropped the reins and ran to see. I don't know why—unless it was for the same reason people crowd around someone who has fainted in a cinema—but I parted the wires of the fence and went through, after him.

Petrus lifted his eyes to me—to anybody—with distress and horror. The old man from Rhodesia had let go of the coffin entirely, and the three others, unable to support it on their own, had laid it on the ground, in the pathway. Already there was a film of dust lightly wavering up its shiny sides. I did not understand what the old man was saying; I hesitated to interfere. But now the whole seething group turned on my silence. The old man himself came over to me, with his hands outspread and shaking, and spoke directly to me, saying something that I could tell from the tone, without understanding the words, was shocking and extraordinary.

"What is it, Petrus? What's wrong?" I appealed.

Petrus threw up his hands, bowed his head

---

8. expostulated (eks päs′ chə lāt′ id): reasoned earnestly about improper conduct; protested.

in a series of hysterical shakes, then thrust his face up at me suddenly. "He says, 'My son was not so heavy.'"

Silence. I could hear the old man breathing; he kept his mouth a little open, as old people do.

"My son was young and thin," he said at last, in English.

Again silence. Then babble broke out. The old man thundered against everybody; his teeth were yellowed and few, and he had one of those fine, grizzled, sweeping mustaches one doesn't often see nowadays, which must have been grown in emulation of early Empire builders. It seemed to frame all his utterances with a special validity. He shocked the assembly; they thought he was mad, but they had to listen to him. With his own hands he began to prize the lid off the coffin, and three of the men came forward to help him. Then he sat down on the ground; very old, very weak, and unable to speak, he merely lifted a trembling hand toward what was there. He abdicated, he handed it over to them; he was no good anymore.

They crowded round to look (and so did I), and now they forgot the nature of this surprise and the occasion of grief to which it belonged and for a few minutes were carried up in the astonishment of the surprise itself. They gasped and flared noisily with excitement. I even noticed the little boy who had held the donkeys jumping up and down, almost weeping with rage because the backs of the grownups crowded him out of his view.

In the coffin was someone no one had ever seen before: a heavily built, rather light-skinned native with a neatly stitched scar on his forehead—perhaps from a blow in a brawl that had also dealt him some other, slower-working injury that had killed him.

I wrangled with the authorities for a week over that body. I had the feeling that they were shocked, in a laconic[9] fashion, by their own mistake but that in the confusion of their anonymous dead they were helpless to put it right. They said to me, "We are trying to find out" and "We are still making inquiries." It was as if at any moment they might conduct me into their mortuary and say, "There! Lift up the sheets; look for him—your poultry boy's brother. There are so many black faces—surely one will do?"

And every evening when I got home, Petrus was waiting in the kitchen. "Well, they're trying. They're still looking. The baas is seeing to it for you, Petrus," I would tell him. "God, half the time I should be in the office I'm driving around the back end of town chasing after this affair," I added aside, to Lerice, one night.

She and Petrus both kept their eyes turned on me as I spoke, and, oddly, for those moments they looked exactly alike, though it sounds impossible: my wife, with her high, white forehead and her attenuated Englishwoman's body, and the poultry boy, with his horny bare feet below khaki trousers tied at the knee with string and the peculiar rankness of his nervous sweat coming from his skin.

"What makes you so indignant, so determined about this now?" said Lerice suddenly.

I stared at her. "It's a matter of principle. Why should they get away with a swindle? It's time these officials had a jolt from someone who'll bother to take the trouble."

She said, "Oh." And as Petrus slowly opened the kitchen door to leave, sensing that the talk had gone beyond him, she turned away, too.

I continued to pass on assurances to Petrus every evening, but although what I said was the same and the voice in which I said it was the same, every evening it sounded weaker. At last, it became clear that we would never get

---

9. laconic (lə kän′ ik): sparing of words; terse.

Petrus's brother back, because nobody really knew where he was. Somewhere in a graveyard as uniform as a housing scheme, somewhere under a number that didn't belong to him, or in the medical school, perhaps, laboriously reduced to layers of muscle and strings of nerve? Goodness knows. He had no identity in this world anyway.

It was only then, and in a voice of shame, that Petrus asked me to try and get the money back.

"From the way he asks, you'd think he was robbing his dead brother," I said to Lerice later. But as I've said, Lerice had got so intense about this business that she couldn't even appreciate a little ironic smile.

I tried to get the money; Lerice tried. We both telephoned and wrote and argued, but nothing came of it. It appeared that the main expense had been the undertaker, and after all he had done his job. So the whole thing was a complete waste, even more of a waste for the poor devils than I had thought it would be.

The old man from Rhodesia was about Lerice's father's size, so she gave him one of her father's old suits, and he went back home rather better off, for the winter, than he had come.

Thinking About the Story

A PERSONAL RESPONSE

sharing impressions

1. How do you feel about the ending of this story? Jot down your impressions in your journal.

constructing interpretations

2. What do you think of the narrator's comment at the end of the story that the old man "went back home rather better off . . . than he had come"?

3. Whose values appeal to you the most in this story? Support your response with examples from the story.

4. Analyze the relationship between the narrator and Lerice.
   Think about
   • how the narrator describes their marriage
   • each person's values
   • the effect of the incident on their relationship

5. How do your prereading predictions compare with the actual story? Use examples to explain your response.

A CREATIVE RESPONSE

6. Could the narrator have done anything differently about the mix-up of the corpses? Explain.

7. What do you consider the strongest conflict in this story, and why?

8. How would you explain the main message about South African society communicated in this story?

> ***Think about***
> - the picture of the black people that you formed from reading this story
> - the narrator's final remarks about Petrus's dead brother
> - the significance of the title of this story
> - which character is portrayed most sympathetically

Analyzing the Writer's Craft

POINT OF VIEW

Think about the voice in which the writer relates the events of this story.

Building a Literary Vocabulary. Point of view refers to the narrative method, or the kind of narrator, used in a literary work. In the first-person point of view, the narrator is a character in the work who tells everything in his or her own words. In "Six Feet of the Country," Nadine Gordimer uses the first-person point of view. All the events are recounted by Lerice's husband, a narrator who participates in the action of the story.

Application: Analyzing Point of View. Go back through the story and identify the passages that have a strong effect on you. Rewrite one passage from the third-person point of view. Then in a small group discuss the two versions and their effects. Speculate about why Nadine Gordimer might have chosen the first-person point of view.

Connecting Reading and Writing

1. How do you think Petrus feels about the mistakes that happen in this story? Write a **journal entry** in which he expresses his feelings.

Option: Have Petrus reveal his feelings in a **poem** to be published along with this story.

2. Write a **memo** to a social studies teacher recommending that Gordimer's story and the excerpt from *Kaffir Boy* be required reading for a unit on South Africa.

Option: Write a **letter** to the parents of the students, explaining your recommendation.

3. If you were a marriage counselor, what would you tell the narrator and Lerice about their relationship? In a **case study,** analyze their relationship and suggest improvements.

Option: Explore their relationship in an **advice column** for a popular magazine.

The Prisoner Who Wore Glasses

BESSIE HEAD   1937–1986   SOUTH AFRICA / BOTSWANA

A biography of Head appears on page 743.

Approaching the Story

In the 1960's Bessie Head fled from South Africa to neighboring Botswana to escape the discrimination she suffered because her parents were of different races. In South Africa the official policy of apartheid decrees that the races must be kept strictly separate. The white minority controls the government and uses its power to enforce apartheid and maintain dominance over the black majority. Those who resist apartheid are jailed. The two main characters of "The Prisoner Who Wore Glasses," which is set on a South African prison farm, are a black political prisoner and a prison guard, or warder. The warder is an Afrikaner, a white South African of Dutch descent, and speaks English with a heavy accent.

Building Vocabulary

These essential words are footnoted within the story.

bedlam (bed′ ləm): His mind travelled back . . . through the . . . **bedlam** in which he had lived. (page 643)

ruefully (rōō′ fəl ē): "Let's face it," he thought **ruefully**. "I'm only learning right now what it means to be a politician." (page 643)

tirade (tī′ rād′): All throughout the **tirade** from his chief, Warder Hannetjie failed to defend himself. (page 645)

Connecting Writing and Reading

In your journal define what you think it means to be assertive. On a scale of 1 to 10, rate how important it is to be assertive in order to get what you want at home and at school. As you read the story, compare your ideas about assertiveness to the assertiveness displayed by the two main characters.

The Prisoner Who Wore Glasses

SCARCELY A BREATH of wind disturbed the stillness of the day, and the long rows of cabbages were bright green in the sunlight. Large white clouds drifted slowly across the deep blue sky. Now and then they obscured the sun and caused a chill on the backs of the prisoners who had to work all day long in the cabbage field. This trick the clouds were playing with the sun eventually caused one of the prisoners who wore glasses to stop work, straighten up and peer shortsightedly at them. He was a thin little fellow with a hollowed-out chest and comic knobbly knees. He also had a lot of fanciful ideas, because he smiled at the clouds.

"Perhaps they want me to send a message to the children," he thought tenderly, noting that the clouds were drifting in the direction of his home some hundred miles away. But before he could frame the message, the warder in charge of his work span[1] shouted:

"Hey, what you tink you're doing, Brille?"

The prisoner swung round, blinking rapidly, yet at the same time sizing up the enemy. He was a new warder, named Jacobus Stephanus Hannetjie.[2] His eyes were the color of the sky, but they were frightening. A simple, primitive, brutal soul gazed out of them. The prisoner bent down quickly, and a message was quietly passed down the line:

"We're in for trouble this time, comrades."

"Why?" rippled back up the line.

"Because he's not human," the reply rippled down, and yet only the crunching of the spades as they turned over the earth disturbed the stillness.

This particular work span was known as Span One. It was composed of ten men, and they were all political prisoners. They were grouped together for convenience, as it was one of the prison regulations that no black warder should be in charge of a political prisoner lest this prisoner convert him to his views. It never seemed to occur to the authorities that this very reasoning was the strength of Span One and a clue to the strange terror they aroused in the warders. As political prisoners they were unlike the other prisoners in the sense that they felt no guilt, nor were they outcasts of society. All guilty men instinctively cower, which was why it was the kind of prison where men got knocked out cold with a blow at the back of the head from an iron bar. Up until the arrival of Warder Hannetjie, no warder had dared beat any member of Span One and no warder had lasted more than a week with them. The battle was entirely psychological. Span One was assertive, and it was beyond the scope of white warders to handle assertive black men. Thus, Span One had got out of control. They were the best thieves and liars in the camp. They lived all day on raw cabbages. They chatted and smoked tobacco. And since they moved, thought and acted as one, they had perfected every technique of group concealment.

Trouble began that very day between Span One and Warder Hannetjie. It was because of the shortsightedness of Brille. That was the nickname he was given in prison and is the Afrikaans[3] word for someone who wears glass-

---

1. **work span:** work brigade or work group.
2. **Jacobus Stephanus Hannetjie** (yä′ kô̄ bo͝os ste′ fä no͝os hä′ net ye).
3. **Afrikaans** (af′ ri käns′): the dialect of Dutch spoken by South Africans of Dutch descent.

es. Brille could never judge the approach of the prison gates, and on several previous occasions he had munched on cabbages and dropped them almost at the feet of the warder, and all previous warders had overlooked this. Not so Warder Hannetjie.

"Who dropped that cabbage?" he thundered.

Brille stepped out of line.

"I did," he said meekly.

"All right," said Hannetjie. "The whole Span goes three meals off."

"But I told you I did it," Brille protested.

The blood rushed to Warder Hannetjie's face.

"Look 'ere," he said. "I don't take orders from a kaffir. I don't know what kind of kaffir you tink you are. Why don't you say baas. I'm your baas. Why don't you say baas, hey?"

Brille blinked his eyes rapidly, but by contrast his voice was strangely calm.

"I'm twenty years older than you," he said. It was the first thing that came to mind, but the comrades seemed to think it a huge joke. A titter swept up the line. The next thing, Warder Hannetjie whipped out a knobkerrie[4] and gave Brille several blows about the head. What surprised his comrades was the speed with which Brille had removed his glasses, or else they would have been smashed to pieces on the ground.

That evening in the cell Brille was very apologetic.

"I'm sorry, comrades," he said. "I've put you into a hell of a mess."

"Never mind, brother, they said. What happens to one of us, happens to all."

"I'll try to make up for it, comrades," he said. "I'll steal something so that you don't go hungry."

Privately, Brille was very philosophical about his head wounds. It was the first time an act of violence had been perpetrated against him, but he had long been a witness of extreme, almost unbelievable human brutality. He had twelve children, and his mind travelled back that evening through the sixteen years of bedlam[5] in which he had lived. It had all happened in a small, drab little three-bedroom house in a small, drab little street in the Eastern Cape and the children kept coming year after year because neither he nor Martha managed the contraceptives the right way and a teacher's salary never allowed moving to a bigger house and he was always taking exams to improve this salary only to have it all eaten up by hungry mouths. Everything was pretty horrible, especially the way the children fought. They'd get hold of each other's heads and give them a good bashing against the wall. Martha gave up somewhere along the line, so they worked out a thing between them. The bashings, biting and blood were to operate in full swing until he came home. He was to be the bogeyman, and when it worked, he never failed to have a sense of godhead at the way in which his presence could change savages into fairly reasonable human beings.

Yet somehow it was this chaos and mismanagement at the center of his life that drove him into politics. It was really an ordered, beautiful world with just a few basic slogans to learn along with the rights of mankind. At one stage, before things became very bad, there were conferences to attend, all very far away from home.

"Let's face it," he thought ruefully.[6] "I'm only learning right now what it means to be a politician. All this while I've been running away from Martha and the kids."

And the pain in his head brought a hard lump to his throat. That was what the children did to each other daily and Martha wasn't

---

4. **knobkerrie:** a short club with a knobbed end.
5. **bedlam** (bed′ ləm): a condition of noise and confusion.
6. **ruefully** (rōō′ fəl ē): regretfully.

managing and if Warder Hannetjie had not interrupted him that morning he would have sent the following message:

"Be good comrades, my children. Cooperate, then life will run smoothly."

The next day Warder Hannetjie caught this old man with twelve children stealing grapes from the farm shed. They were an enormous quantity of grapes in a ten-gallon tin, and for this misdeed the old man spent a week in the isolation cell. In fact, Span One as a whole was in constant trouble. Warder Hannetjie seemed to have eyes at the back of his head. He uncovered the trick about the cabbages, how they were split in two with the spade and immediately covered with earth and then unearthed again and eaten with split-second timing. He found out how tobacco smoke was beaten into the ground, and he found out how conversations were whispered down the wind.

For about two weeks Span One lived in acute misery. The cabbages, tobacco and conversations had been the pivot of jail life to them. Then one evening they noticed that their good old comrade who wore the glasses was looking rather pleased with himself. He pulled out a four-ounce packet of tobacco by way of explanation and the comrades fell upon it with great greed. Brille merely smiled. After all, he was the father of many children. But when the last shred had disappeared, it occurred to the comrades that they ought to be puzzled. Someone said:

"I say, brother. We're watched like hawks these days. Where did you get the tobacco?"

"Hannetjie gave it to me," said Brille.

There was a long silence. Into it dropped a quiet bombshell.

"I saw Hannetjie in the shed today," and the failing eyesight blinked rapidly. "I caught him in the act of stealing five bags of fertilizer, and he bribed me to keep my mouth shut."

There was another long silence.

"Prison is an evil life," Brille continued, apparently discussing some irrelevant matter. "It makes a man contemplate all kinds of evil deeds."

He held out his hand and closed it.

"You know, comrades," he said. "I've got Hannetjie. I'll betray him tomorrow."

Everyone began talking at once.

"Forget it, brother. You'll get shot."

Brille laughed.

"I won't," he said. "That is what I mean about evil. I am a father of children and I saw today that Hannetjie is just a child and stupidly truthful. I'm going to punish him severely because we need a good warder."

The following day, with Brille as witness, Hannetjie confessed to the theft of the fertilizer and was fined a large sum of money. From then on Span One did very much as they pleased while Warder Hannetjie stood by and said nothing. But it was Brille who carried this to extremes. One day, at the close of work Warder Hannetjie said:

"Brille, pick up my jacket and carry it back to the camp."

"But nothing in the regulations says I'm your servant, Hannetjie," Brille replied coolly.

"I've told you not to call me Hannetjie. You must say, baas," but Warder Hannetjie's voice lacked conviction. In turn, Brille squinted up at him.

"I'll tell you something about this baas business, Hannetjie," he said. "One of these days we are going to run the country. You are going to clean my car. Now, I have a fifteen-year-old son and I'd die of shame if you had to tell him that I ever called you baas."

Warder Hannetjie went red in the face and picked up his coat.

On another occasion Brille was seen to be walking about the prison yard, openly smoking tobacco. On being taken before the prison commander, he claimed to have received the tobacco from Warder Hannetjie. All throughout the tirade[7] from his chief, Warder Hannetjie failed to defend himself, but his nerve broke completely. He called Brille to one side.

"Brille," he said. "This thing between you and me must end. You may not know it, but I have a wife and children and you're driving me to suicide."

"Why don't you like your own medicine, Hannetjie?" Brille asked quietly.

"I can give you anything you want," Warder Hannetjie said in desperation.

"It's not only me but the whole of Span One," said Brille cunningly. "The whole of Span One wants something from you."

Warder Hannetjie brightened with relief.

"I tink I can manage if it's tobacco you want," he said.

Brille looked at him, for the first time struck with pity and guilt. He wondered if he had carried the whole business too far. The man was really a child.

"It's not tobacco we want, but you," he said. "We want you on our side. We want a good warder because without a good warder we won't be able to manage the long stretch ahead."

Warder Hannetjie interpreted this request in his own fashion, and his interpretation of what was good and human often left the prisoners of Span One speechless with surprise. He had a way of slipping off his revolver and picking up a spade and digging alongside Span One. He had a way of producing unheard-of luxuries like boiled eggs from his farm nearby and things like cigarettes, and Span One responded nobly and got the reputation of being the best work span in the camp. And it wasn't only take from their side. They were awfully good at stealing certain commodities like fertilizer which were needed on the farm of Warder Hannetjie.

---

7. **tirade** (ti′ rād′): a long angry or scolding speech.

Thinking About the Story

A PERSONAL RESPONSE

sharing impressions

1. How do you feel about the relationship between Brille and Hannetjie? Describe your feelings in your journal.

constructing interpretations

2. Why do you think Hannetjie becomes such a "good warder" at the end of the story?

3. In your opinion, what is this story saying about assertiveness and cooperation?
Think about
- why each man thinks he has the right to be assertive
- how effective each man's assertiveness is
- how the men cooperate at the end of the story

4. What connections do you see between Brille's relationship with his children and his relationship with Hannetjie? Use details from the story to support your answer.

A CREATIVE RESPONSE

5. If Brille had not caught Hannetjie stealing fertilizer, how might the relationship between the two have been different?

A CRITICAL RESPONSE

6. Do you think the descriptions of the two characters make them seem like real people or more like the stereotypes of cruel oppressor and noble victim? Go back through the story to find specific details to support your answer.

7. In your opinion, which story sends a stronger message—"Six Feet of the Country" or "The Prisoner Who Wore Glasses"?

8. Of all the issues raised in these works of social criticism and political protest, which issues do you think are most relevant to the situation in which you live? Explain.

Analyzing the Writer's Craft

CONFLICT AND THEME

Why do you think Brille gets in trouble with Hannetjie so often at the beginning of the story?

Building a Literary Vocabulary. The struggle between opposing forces that is the basis for the plot of a story is called the conflict. An external conflict can occur between characters, between a character and society, or between a character and nature. In "The Prisoner Who Wore Glasses," a series of minor conflicts occurs between Brille and Hannetjie that expresses the more fundamental conflicts between the two men. On one level their conflict is personal—Brille fights Hannetjie because the warder tries to take away the prisoner's self-respect. On another level their conflict might be seen as representing a clash of social forces: Hannetjie represents the white political structure in South Africa, trying to hang onto its power, while Brille represents the black political movement, demanding equality and humane treatment. Each

man is motivated by deeply ingrained social and political beliefs. By examining their motives and determining which beliefs the writer portrays sympathetically, the reader can determine the theme of the story.

Application: Analyzing Conflict and Theme. In a group of three or four, go back through the story and identify the different instances of conflict between Brille and Hannetjie. Create a chart in which you list each incident and identify the nature of the conflict, the beliefs that motivate Brille and Hannetjie, which character is in control when the incident ends, and what the incident might represent in terms of the larger conflict between whites and blacks. Then as a group decide on the main theme, or perception about life, that Bessie Head wants to share with her readers. Discuss your conclusions with the class.

Connecting Reading and Writing

1. Imagine that you are Hannetjie at the end of the story. Write a **report** analyzing Brille's character for a parole hearing.

Option: Create a **petition** for parole that Brille might write on his own behalf.

2. Write a **letter** from Brille to his children in which he gives them fatherly advice about assertiveness and cooperation in politics and in daily relationships.

Option: Write the outline for a **lecture** on

assertiveness and cooperation that Brille might deliver to a group of young black students.

3. On a **book jacket** for an anthology that contains the Nadine Gordimer and Bessie Head stories you have just read, compare and contrast the way the stories portray apartheid and race relations.

Option: In an **expository essay**, compare and contrast the relationship between Petrus and the narrator in "Six Feet of the Country" with the relationship between Brille and Hannetjie.

The Censors

LUISA VALENZUELA born 1938 ARGENTINA

A biography of Valenzuela appears on page 753.

Approaching the Story

Have you ever become so engrossed in a challenge, such as surpassing your best score on a video game, that nothing else seemed important? If so, you might identify with Juan, the main character in Luisa Valenzuela's (lōō ē′ sä vä len zwe′ lä) "The Censors." In this story, set in a fictitious Latin American country, censorship has reached new bureaucratic heights.

Note as you read that the names Juan and Juancito, the diminutive form of Juan, refer to the same person.

OOR JUAN! ONE day they caught him with his guard down before he could even realize that what he had taken as a stroke of luck was really one of fate's dirty tricks. These things happen the minute you're careless and you let down your guard, as one often does. Juancito let happiness—a feeling you can't trust—get the better of him when he received from a confidential source Mariana's new address in Paris and he knew that she hadn't forgotten him. Without thinking twice, he sat down at his table and wrote her a letter. *The* letter that keeps his mind off his job during the day and won't let him sleep at night (what had he scrawled, what had he put on that sheet of paper he sent to Mariana?).

Juan knows there won't be a problem with the letter's contents, that it's irreproachable, harmless. But what about the rest? He knows that they examine, sniff, feel, and read between the lines of each and every letter, and check its tiniest comma and most accidental stain. He knows that all letters pass from hand to hand and go through all sorts of tests in the huge censorship offices and that, in the end, very few continue on their way. Usually it takes months, even years, if there aren't any snags; all this time the freedom, maybe even the life, of both sender and receiver is in jeopardy. And that's why Juan's so down in the dumps: thinking that something might happen to Mariana because of his letters. Of all people, Mariana, who must finally feel safe there where she always dreamed she'd live. But he knows that the Censor's Secret Command operates all over the world and cashes in on the discount in air rates; there's nothing to stop them from going as far as that hidden Paris neighborhood, kidnapping Mariana, and returning to their cozy homes, certain of having fulfilled their noble mission.

Well, you've got to beat them to the punch, do what everyone tries to do: sabotage the machinery, throw sand in its gears, get to the bottom of the problem so as to stop it.

This was Juan's sound plan when he, like many others, applied for a censor's job—not because he had a calling or needed a job: no, he applied simply to intercept his own letter, a consoling but unoriginal idea. He was hired immediately, for each day more and more censors are needed and no one would bother to check on his references.

Ulterior motives couldn't be overlooked by the Censorship Division, but they needn't be too strict with those who applied. They knew how hard it would be for those poor guys to find the letter they wanted and even if they did, what's a letter or two when the new censor would snap up so many others? That's how Juan managed to join the Post Office's Censorship Division, with a certain goal in mind.

The building had a festive air on the outside which contrasted with its inner staidness. Little by little, Juan was absorbed by his job and he felt at peace since he was doing everything he could to get his letter for Mariana. He didn't even worry when, in his first month, he was sent to Section K where envelopes are very carefully screened for explosives.

It's true that on the third day, a fellow worker had his right hand blown off by a letter, but the division chief claimed it was sheer negligence on the victim's part. Juan and the other employees were allowed to go back to their work, albeit feeling less secure. After work, one of them tried to organize a strike to demand higher wages for unhealthy work, but Juan didn't join in; after thinking it over, he reported him to his superiors and thus got promoted.

You don't form a habit by doing something once, he told himself as he left his boss's office. And when he was transferred to Section J, where letters are carefully checked for poison dust, he felt he had climbed a rung in the ladder.

By working hard, he quickly reached Section E where the work was more interesting, for he could now read and analyze the letters' contents. Here he could even hope to get hold of his letter which, judging by the time that had elapsed, had gone through the other sections and was probably floating around in this one.

Soon his work became so absorbing that his noble mission blurred in his mind. Day after day he crossed out whole paragraphs in red ink, pitilessly chucking many letters into the censored basket. These were horrible days when he was shocked by the subtle and conniving ways employed by people to pass on subversive messages; his instincts were so sharp that he found behind a simple "the weather's unsettled" or "prices continue to soar" the wavering hand of someone secretly scheming to overthrow the Government.

His zeal brought him swift promotion. We don't know if this made him happy. Very few letters reached him in Section B—only a handful passed the other hurdles—so he read them over and over again, passed them under a magnifying glass, searched for microprint with an electronic microscope, and tuned his sense of smell so that he was beat by the time he made it home. He'd barely manage to warm up his soup, eat some fruit, and fall into bed, satisfied with having done his duty. Only his darling mother worried, but she couldn't get him back on the right road. She'd say, though it wasn't always true: Lola called, she's at the bar with the girls, they miss you, they're waiting for you. Or else she'd leave a bottle of red wine on the table. But Juan wouldn't overdo it: any distraction could make him lose his edge and the perfect censor had to be alert, keen, attentive, and sharp to nab cheats. He had a truly patriotic task, both self-denying and uplifting.

His basket for censored letters became the best fed as well as the most cunning basket in the whole Censorship Division. He was about to congratulate himself for having finally discovered his true mission, when his letter to Mariana reached his hands. Naturally, he censored it without regret. And just as naturally, he couldn't stop them from executing him the following morning, another victim of his devotion to his work.

LITERATURE
OF INSIGHT

Reviewing Concepts

CHARACTER AND CONFLICT: KEYS TO UNDERSTANDING ——————————

*making
connections*

The selections in this unit provide thought-provoking and often profound insights into human life. Typically the writers accomplish this by focusing on characters who face various kinds of conflict. A character may struggle against another person, the pressures of society, or the forces of nature. Two elements within a character may be in conflict. Depending on how the conflict is resolved, the character—or at least the reader—gains some new understanding of the world and human existence. In *The Inferno,* for example, the main character, who is Dante himself, faces three wild animals, representing worldliness and sin, who block the true path of his journey through life. He can only resolve this conflict by embarking on a longer and more difficult journey through Hell and Purgatory. He learns that human beings, under the guidance of reason, need to understand the nature and consequence of sin.

Choose at least ten characters from the selections you have read in this unit. For each, identify the conflict that he or she faces and the insight or understanding that results. Record your findings on a chart similar to the one below. Note: in some cases an insight may be clear to the reader but not to the character involved.

Character	Conflict	Insight
Dante in *The Inferno*	With three wild beasts representing sin.	Human beings, under the guidance of reason, need to understand the nature and consequence of sin.

*describing
connections*

Review your chart and decide which insights seem most relevant to your life. Based on your choices, write a **letter** to a publisher recommending that certain selections be included in an anthology on conflict.

Flower Vendor, EMILIO AMERO.
Galeria Sin Fronteras, Austin, Texas.

Creative Diversions:

Literature to Entertain

*"The good writer is first of all
an enchanter."*

VLADIMIR NABOKOV

Telling a Good Story

All good stories give pleasure as well as communicate insights about human life. Some stories, however, primarily entertain. The writers of such works tease, amuse, surprise, and thrill. Readers typically respond by saying, "That was a good story."

In the works in this section, the act of storytelling is visible. The storytellers, whether they are narrators addressing readers or characters speaking to other characters, announce that they are about to tell a tale. Sometimes they stop and ask for a response to events.

Who can help but respond to a good story? A good story holds the reader spellbound. The characters, who may be queens, peasants, soldiers, or grocers, have glorious passions or comical flaws. They are well drawn enough to seem real and worth caring about.

A good story presents a provocative situation, which may be as familiar as thwarted love or as exotic as abandonment in the desert. Suspense keeps the reader engaged in the unfolding plot. Questions arise, and persist, until they are resolved at the end. Often the resolution seems unexpected, yet inevitable. Like the punch line of a good joke, the final event or revelation in a good story may be a surprise, yet it will seem upon reflection to be the only one that really fits.

Through a good story you explore the twists and turns of life and the human character. Relax and let the story carry you along. These stories may not leave you greatly enlightened; they may not even leave you happy. They should, however, leave you satisfied that you have been entertained.

Literary Vocabulary

INTRODUCED IN THIS SECTION

Foreshadowing. Foreshadowing is a writer's use of hints or clues to indicate events that will occur later in a narrative. This technique creates suspense while preparing the reader for what is to come. At the beginning of "The Heir," for example, Sŏgun, reading to his cousin Sŏkhŭi, is asked by her, "Why did the man leave his home?" Sŏgun does not answer; instead he blushes and tries to discontinue their reading. The cousin's question and Sŏgun's apparent discomfort foreshadow his own eventual departure from the house of his relatives.

REVIEWED IN THIS SECTION

Suspense

Woodcut, 1919, FRANS MASEREEL.
From *Passionate Journey* byFrans Masereel.
© Europa Verlag, Zurich, Switzerland.

Chevrefoil

MARIE DE FRANCE   c. 1200   FRANCE

A biography of Marie de France appears on page 746.

*A*pproaching the Poem

Marie de France, the earliest known French woman poet, excelled at writing the *lai*, which is a short narrative poem. "Chevrefoil" (shev' rə fwål) recounts an episode in the tragic love story of Tristan and Isolt. According to the story, Tristan travels from England to Ireland to ask Princess Isolt to marry his uncle, King Mark of Cornwall. On their return journey, Tristan and Isolt accidentally drink a love potion intended for Isolt and King Mark on their wedding night. The potion causes Tristan and Isolt to fall in love, but it does not destroy their loyalty to the king, whom Isolt eventually marries. In time, King Mark suspects the love between his wife and nephew and banishes Tristan from the kingdom. "Chevrefoil" relates an incident that occurs after Tristan and Isolt have been separated for a year.

Throughout the poem, Isolt is referred to as "the queen."

*C*onnecting Writing and Reading

Based on your own observations and experiences, which of the following sayings seems more true to life?

Out of sight, out of mind.

Absence makes the heart grow fonder.

In your journal, explain your opinion. As you read "Chevrefoil," compare your view of love with the view illustrated by the story of Tristan and Isolt.

I should like very much
to tell you the truth
about the *lai* men call *Chevrefoil*—
why it was composed and where it came from.
5   Many have told and recited it to me
and I have found it in writing,
about Tristan and the queen
and their love that was so true,
that brought them much suffering
10 and caused them to die the same day.
King Mark was annoyed,
angry at his nephew Tristan;
he exiled Tristan from his land
because of the queen whom he loved.
15 Tristan returned to his own country,
South Wales, where he was born,
he stayed a whole year;
he couldn't come back.
Afterward he began to expose himself
20 to death and destruction.
Don't be surprised at this:
for one who loves very faithfully
is sad and troubled
when he cannot satisfy his desires.
25 Tristan was sad and worried,
so he set out from his land.
He traveled straight to Cornwall,
where the queen lived,
and entered the forest all alone—
30 he didn't want anyone to see him;
he came out only in the evening
when it was time to find shelter.
He took lodging that night,
with peasants, poor people.
35 He asked them for news
of the king—what he was doing.
They told him they had heard
that the barons had been summoned by ban.[1]
They were to come to Tintagel[2]
40 where the king wanted to hold his court;
at Pentecost[3] they would all be there,
there'd be much joy and pleasure,
and the queen would be there too.
Tristan heard and was very happy;

1. **summoned by ban:** officially called together by the king.

2. **Tintagel:** a castle in Cornwall, the county at the southwest tip of England.

3. **Pentecost:** a day in late May or early June that is the fiftieth day after Easter.

45   she would not be able to go there
    without his seeing her pass.
    The day the king set out,
    Tristan also came to the woods
    by the road he knew
50   their assembly must take.
    He cut a hazel tree in half,
    then he squared it.
    When he had prepared the wood,
    he wrote his name on it with his knife.
55   If the queen noticed it—
    and she should be on the watch for it,
    for it had happened before
    and she had noticed it then—
    she'd know when she saw it,
60   that the piece of wood had come from her love.
    This was the message of the writing
    that he had sent to her:
    he had been there a long time,
    had waited and remained
65   to find out and to discover
    how he could see her,
    for he could not live without her.
    With the two of them it was just
    as it is with the honeysuckle
70   that attaches itself to the hazel tree:
    when it has wound and attached
    and worked itself around the trunk,
    the two can survive together;
    but if someone tries to separate them,
75   the hazel dies quickly
    and the honeysuckle with it.
    "Sweet love, so it is with us:
    You cannot live without me, nor I without you."
    The queen rode along:
80   she looked at the hillside
    and saw the piece of wood; she knew what it was,
    she recognized all the letters.
    The knights who were accompanying her,
    who were riding with her,
85   she ordered to stop:
    she wanted to dismount and rest.
    They obeyed her command.
    She went far away from her people

and called her girl
90 Brenguein, who was loyal to her.
She went a short distance from the road;
and in the woods she found him
whom she loved more than any living thing.
They took great joy in each other.
95 He spoke to her as much as he desired,
she told him whatever she liked.
Then she assured him
that he would be reconciled with the king—
for it weighed on him
100 that he had sent Tristan away;
he'd done it because of the accusation.
Then she departed, she left her love,
but when it came to the separation,
they began to weep.
105 Tristan went to Wales,
to wait until his uncle sent for him.
For the joy that he'd felt
from his love when he saw her,
by means of the stick he inscribed
110 as the queen had instructed,
and in order to remember the words,
Tristan, who played the harp well,
composed a new *lai* about it.
I shall name it briefly:
115 in English they call it *Goat's Leaf*,
the French call it *Chevrefoil*.
I have given you the truth
about the *lai* that I have told here.

Thinking About the Poem

A PERSONAL RESPONSE

sharing
impressions

1. What are your feelings about the reunion between Tristan and Isolt? Describe your feelings in your journal.

constructing
interpretations

2. Based on your prereading notes, decide how the view of love presented in this poem compares with your own view of love.

3. What seems to be the most outstanding quality of Tristan's love for Isolt?
   Think about
   • how Tristan acts when they are apart
   • why he returns to Cornwall despite his banishment
   • how the lovers feel when they are together

4. Why do you think the speaker ends this *lai* by referring to the *lai* that Tristan composed?

A CREATIVE RESPONSE

5. If this poem had actually been the *lai* that Tristan composed, how do you think it might have been different?

A CRITICAL RESPONSE

6. In your opinion, why has the love story of Tristan and Isolt remained famous for hundreds of years?
   Think about
   • the view of love it presents
   • your own experiences with love

7. Compare "Chevrefoil" with Shakespeare's sonnet that begins "No longer mourn for me when I am dead" (page 299). Which portrayal of romantic love do you prefer? Use examples from the poems to explain your choice.

from # The Decameron

GIOVANNI BOCCACCIO   1313?–1375   ITALY

A biography of Boccaccio appears on page 739.

*A*pproaching the Story

Giovanni Boccaccio (jô vän′ nē bô kä′ chō) is best known for his masterpiece, *The Decameron*, the title of which means "Ten Days' Work." The piece is a frame story, that is, it contains stories within a story. In the frame, or outer story, three lords and seven ladies have fled to the countryside to escape the plague ravaging Florence, Italy, in 1348. For ten days they tell stories, each day selecting a person to be king or queen and to preside over the storytelling. *The Decameron* contains one hundred stories told within this frame. As the following story begins, a lord named Filostrato (fē lôs strä′ tô) has just finished telling a story, and the appointed queen orders one of the ladies, Filomena (fē lô mā′ nä), to begin hers. Her story is about a simpleton named Calandrino (kä län drē′ nô), who appears in several other stories in *The Decameron* prior to this one. Also in the story are his two friends, Bruno and Buffalmacco (bōō fäl mäk′ kô), who usually outwit him.

*C*onnecting Writing and Reading

In your journal create a chart similar to the one that follows. In one column list the qualities you associate with a person who plays tricks. In the other column list the qualities you associate with a person who has tricks played on him or her.

Trickster	Victim

As you read, see how the characters in the story compare with your impressions of tricksters and their victims.

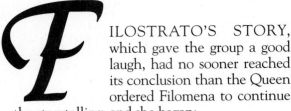

ILOSTRATO'S STORY, which gave the group a good laugh, had no sooner reached its conclusion than the Queen ordered Filomena to continue the storytelling; and she began:

Gracious ladies, just as Filostrato was moved by the mention of Maso's name to tell the story you have just heard, in like manner, I am inspired by the mention of the names of Calandrino and his companions to tell you another tale about them which, I believe, will amuse you.

There is no need for me to explain to you who Calandrino, Bruno, and Buffalmacco were, for you have already heard a great deal about them in an earlier tale; and so getting on with my story, let me say that Calandrino owned a little farm not far from Florence, which he had acquired by way of his wife's dowry, and from it, along with the other produce which he collected there, every year he received a pig; and it was his regular custom to go to the country around December with his wife to slaughter the pig, and to have it salted there.

Now it happened once, at a time when his wife was not feeling very well, that Calandrino went by himself to slaughter the pig; when Bruno and Buffalmacco heard about this and learned that his wife was not going to be there with him, they went to stay for a few days with a priest who was a great friend of theirs and who lived near Calandrino. On the very morning of their arrival, Calandrino had slaughtered the pig; seeing them with the priest, he called them over and said: "I bid you welcome. I would like you to see what a good farmer I am," and he took them into the house and showed them this pig.

When they saw what a fine pig it was and learned from Calandrino that he intended to salt it for his family, Bruno said to him:

"Hey! You must be crazy! Sell it and let's enjoy the money and tell your wife it was stolen from you."

Calandrino replied:

"No, she won't believe me, and she'll run me out of the house. Stay out of this. I'd never do anything like that."

They tried to convince him with all sorts of arguments, but it was no use. Then Calandrino invited them to supper, but so begrudgingly that they refused to eat with him, and off they went, leaving him there.

Bruno said to Buffalmacco: "What would you say to stealing that pig of his tonight?"

Buffalmacco replied: "And how could we do that?"

Bruno replied: "I've already figured out how to do it, provided he doesn't move it from where it was just now."

"Well," concluded Buffalmacco, "let's do it; why shouldn't we do it? And then we can all enjoy it here together, you, me, and the priest."

The priest declared that this plan was very much to his liking; then Bruno said:

"Now this calls for a bit of skill. Buffalmacco, you know how greedy Calandrino is and how happy he is to have a drink when somebody else pays the bill; let's go and take him to the tavern; let the priest pretend to be our host and pay for all the drinks; we won't let him pay for anything, and Calandrino will drink himself silly, and then the rest will be easy, since there is no one else in the house."

And so they did just as Bruno suggested. Calandrino, seeing that the priest would not allow him to pay, began to drink in earnest, and while usually it never took much to get him drunk, this time he drank a great deal. It was already late in the evening when he left the tavern, and, not wishing to eat supper, he went home, and thinking that he had locked the door, he left it open and went to bed.

Buffalmacco and Bruno went to eat supper with the priest; after they had eaten, they collected the tools they needed to get into Calandrino's house the way Bruno had planned, and they quietly made their way there; but when they found the door open, they went straight in and carried the pig off to the priest's home, where they stowed it away and then went off to bed.

In the morning, after the wine had cleared from his brain, Calandrino got up, and when he went downstairs, he looked around and saw that his pig was gone and the door wide open; and so he asked a number of people if they knew who had taken his pig, but unable to find it, he began making a racket, crying, "Ah, poor me, my pig has been stolen." When Bruno and Buffalmacco got out of bed they went straight over to Calandrino's to hear what he would have to say about his pig. When Calandrino saw them, he called them over and on the verge of tears he said: "Oh, my friends, my pig has been stolen from me!"

Bruno drew close to him and whispered: "I'm amazed; so you finally got smart for once in your life."

"Oh, no," said Calandrino, "I'm really telling the truth."

"That-a-boy, that's the way," Bruno said, "tell it loud and clear so it looks the way it should."

Then Calandrino started shouting louder and saying:

"God's body, I'm speaking the truth, it has been stolen from me!"

And Bruno replied:

"Well put, that's perfect, just right, scream louder, make yourself heard, it'll seem truer that way!"

Calandrino insisted:

"You'll drive my soul to the devil: I'm telling the truth and you don't believe me, but I swear, may I be hanged by the neck, if my pig hasn't been stolen!"

Then Bruno said:

"Ah, how can this be? I saw it here just yesterday; do you think you can make me believe it just flew out of here?"

Calandrino answered: "It's just like I'm telling you."

"Ah," remarked Bruno, "how can that be?"

"That's it, yes sirree," declared Calandrino, "and now that's the end of me, and I don't know how I can go home now. My wife will never believe me, and even if she does, I'll have no peace from her for a year."

Then Bruno said:

"God help me, if it's true, this is a serious matter; but you know, Calandrino, this is exactly what I told you to say yesterday. You wouldn't be trying to fool your wife and us at the same time, would you?"

Calandrino began to scream and say:

"Ah, why are you driving me crazy and making me curse God, His saints, and everything else? I'm telling you that the pig was stolen from me last night."

Then Buffalmacco said:

"If that's the case, we must try to find some way to get it back again if possible."

"And what way," asked Calandrino, "is there?"

Then Buffalmacco replied:

"Well, for sure, nobody came all the way from India to steal this pig from you; one of these neighbors of yours must have done it, and so, if you can bring them all together, I can perform the bread-and-cheese test, and then we'll see at once who has the pig."

"Just great," said Bruno, "you'll do splendidly with your bread-and-cheese test, especially with the fine people that live around here! It's clear that one of them stole it, and they would catch on to what we're doing and refuse to come."

"What can we do, then?" asked Buffalmacco.

Bruno replied:

"We could do it with some nice ginger cookies, and some good Vernaccia[1] wine, and invite them all for a drink. They won't think anything of it and will come, and then we can bless the ginger cookies just as if they were bread and cheese."

Buffalmacco said:

"Yep, that's it for sure! And you, Calandrino, what do you say? Are we going to do it?"

Calandrino replied:

"By all means, I beg you, for the love of God, go ahead and do it; I wouldn't feel half so bad, if only I knew who took my pig."

"Well, that's it," Bruno said, "I'm prepared to go all the way into Florence for the things you need, if you give me the money."

Calandrino had around forty copper pennies, which he gave to Bruno. And Bruno went to Florence to a friend of his who was an apothecary and bought a pound of excellent ginger cookies, having him prepare two of them from cheaper ginger, which he had mixed into a confection of fresh hepatic aloes.[2] Then he had them sprinkled with sugar just like the other cookies and in order not to lose them or mix them up with the others, he had them marked with a certain sign, by which he could easily recognize them; and after purchasing a flask of good Vernaccia wine, he returned to the country and said to Calandrino:

"You must invite all those you suspect to come and have a drink with you tomorrow morning: it's a holiday, and everyone will be happy to come, and this evening, along with Buffalmacco, I'll cast the spell on the ginger cookies and bring them to your house tomorrow morning, and for your sake, I, myself, will give them out and do and say what must be done and said."

Calandrino did just that. And the next morning, after he gathered together around the elm in front of the church a considerable group of farm laborers and whatever young Florentines happened to be staying in the country at the time, Bruno and Buffalmacco came around with the box of cookies and the flask of wine; and getting them all to stand in a circle, Bruno announced:

"Gentlemen, I must tell you the reason why you are here, so that if anything happens to cause you displeasure, you will not blame it on me. Last night, Calandrino, who is right here, was robbed of one of his fine pigs, and he has not been able to discover who took it; and since it could have been stolen only by someone here, in order to find out who has taken it, he is going to give each of you in turn one of these cookies to eat and something to drink. I warn you in advance that the one who stole the pig will be unable to swallow the cookie. On the contrary, it will taste more bitter than poison to him, and he will spit it out; and so, in order not to disgrace himself in the presence of so many people, perhaps it would be better for the person who stole the pig to confess now to the priest, and I can forget the entire affair."

Everyone there said they would gladly eat one of the cookies, and so Bruno lined them up, placing Calandrino among them, and beginning at one end of the line, he started giving a ginger cookie to each of them; and when he reached Calandrino, he took one of the special cookies and put it in his hand. Calandrino, without hesitating, popped it into his mouth and began to chew, but his tongue had no sooner tasted the bitter aloes than Calandrino, unable to stand the bitter taste, spit it out. Everyone was looking at everyone else to see who was going to spit his out; Bruno, who had not yet finished handing them out, pretended not to notice anything, when he heard a voice behind him say: "Hey, Calandrino, what's the meaning of this?" He quickly turned around and, seeing that

---

1. **Vernaccia** (ver näch′ chē ä).
2. **hepatic aloes:** mixture containing bitter herbs.

Calandrino had spit his out, he declared: "Wait a minute, perhaps something else caused him to spit; try another one." Picking out the second one, he stuck it into Calandrino's mouth and then went on to finish handing out the rest of them. If the first one had seemed bitter to Calandrino, this second one seemed even more bitter; but since he was ashamed to spit it out, he chewed it a bit and kept it in his mouth, until his eyes began to produce tears the size of hazelnuts; and finally, when he could bear it no longer, he spit it out as he had done with the first one. Buffalmacco was pouring out drinks for the group, as was Bruno, and when they and all the others saw what happened, everyone said that it had to be Calandrino himself who had stolen the pig; and there were even some in the group who reproached him harshly.

But when the crowd had broken up, leaving Bruno and Buffalmacco behind with Calandrino, Buffalmacco began to say:

"I was certain right from the start that it was you who stole it yourself, and that you were trying to make us believe that it had been stolen from you just so you wouldn't have to stand us to a round of drinks with the money you received from the profits."

Calandrino, who had still not spat out the bitterness of the aloes, began swearing he had not taken it.

But Buffalmacco said, "Come on now, buddy, tell us how much you got out of it. Did it fetch six florins?"[3]

When Calandrino heard this, he was at the point of despair, but then Bruno said to him:

"Listen to this, Calandrino. There was a fellow in the group we were eating and drinking with today who told me you had a young girl up here you were keeping for your amusement and that you gave her whatever you could scrape together, and he was convinced you had sent her this pig. You've really become quite a trickster! There was that time you led us along the Mugnone River to pick up those black stones, and after leading us on a wild-goose chase, you took off for home and then tried to make us believe you had really made the discovery! And now, once again, you think with your oaths you can make us believe that this pig, which you either gave away or sold, was actually stolen from you. We've caught on to your tricks by now; you can't fool us anymore! And to tell you the truth, that's why we took so much trouble to cast the spell, and now, unless you give us two brace of capons[4] we mean to tell Monna Tessa[5] everything."

Seeing that they would not believe him, and feeling that he had enough trouble as it was without letting himself in for a battle with his wife's temper, Calandrino gave them the two brace of capons; and after they had salted the pig they took back everything with them to Florence, leaving Calandrino behind with a loss and the expense of their laughter.

---

3. **florins** (flôr′ inz): gold coins of medieval Florence.
4. **two brace of capons:** two pairs of roosters fattened for eating.
5. **Monna Tessa:** Calandrino's wife.

Thinking About the Story

A PERSONAL RESPONSE

sharing impressions

1. How do you feel about what happens to Calandrino? Jot down your impressions in your journal.

constructing interpretations

2. What might you say to Bruno and Buffalmacco if you met them after their return to Florence?

3. What do you think is the main reason that the trick played on Calandrino works?

Think about
- Bruno and Buffalmacco's skills as tricksters
- Calandrino's qualities of character
- what you wrote in your journal about tricksters and their victims

A CREATIVE RESPONSE

4. How do you think you would have responded to this story if Calandrino had outsmarted Bruno and Buffalmacco?

A CRITICAL RESPONSE

5. What do you find ironic about this story? Cite examples from the story to support your answer.

Think about
- verbal irony, when a character says one thing and means another
- situational irony, when there is a contrast between what a character expects and what actually happens
- dramatic irony, when there is a contrast between what a character knows and what the reader knows

6. What do you think is the most important message about human nature conveyed by this story?

Connecting Reading and Writing

1. Rewrite Filomena's **story** in a modern setting. Then, together with several classmates, tape-record the stories to create a collection of variations on *The Decameron*.

Option: Write the story in the form of a comic **monologue** that a modern entertainer might deliver to an audience.

2. Read a few other stories from Boccaccio's *The Decameron*. Then write a **memo** to your teacher, recommending that one of these stories be read and studied along with Filomena's.

Option: Imagine that a friend plans to read the stories that you have previewed. Write a **note** to your friend recommending one in particular.

A Passion in the Desert

HONORÉ DE BALZAC   1799–1850   FRANCE

A biography of Balzac appears on page 738.

Approaching the Story

"A Passion in the Desert" by Honoré de Balzac (ô nô *re'* də bȧl zȧk') is another example of a frame story, or a story within a story. The narrator meets an old soldier who recounts the story of a young man who served in Egypt as part of the army of the French emperor Napoleon Bonaparte. The setting of the story told by the old soldier is the Egyptian desert, where intense waves of heat and light distort perception.

Building Vocabulary

These essential words are footnoted within the story.

verdure (vʉr' jər): It was their **verdure** seen from afar which had brought hope. (page 669)

clemency (klem' ən sē): The poor Provençal ate his dates, . . . casting his eyes . . . on his terrible companion to watch her uncertain **clemency**. (page 672)

pacific (pə sif' ik): He noticed what a **pacific** attitude his companion remained in. (page 673)

languor (laŋ' gər): Her eyes, full of **languor**, turned still more gently . . . toward the Provençal. (page 674)

predatory (pred' ə tôr' ē): She found abundant food in her **predatory** excursions. (page 675)

coquette (kō ket'): The **coquette** quivered when she felt her friend stroke her head. (page 675)

Connecting Writing and Reading

Think about what the word *passion* means to you. In your journal create a cluster diagram of words that you associate with passion. As you read, compare your ideas with what this story conveys about the concept of passion.

A Passion in the Desert

I WAS AT the menagerie.[1]

The first time I saw Monsieur Martin enter the cages I uttered an exclamation of surprise. I found myself next to an old soldier with the right leg amputated, who had come in with me. His face had attracted my attention. He had one of those intrepid heads, stamped with the seal of warfare, and on which the battles of Napoleon are written. Besides, he had that frank good-humored expression that always impresses me favorably. He was without doubt one of those troopers who are surprised at nothing, who find matter for laughter in the contortions of a dying comrade, who bury or plunder him quite lightheartedly, who stand intrepidly in the way of bullets;—in fact, one of those men who waste no time in deliberation, and would not hesitate to make friends with the devil himself. After looking very attentively at the proprietor of the menagerie getting out of his box, my companion pursed up his lips with an air of mockery and contempt, with that peculiar and expressive twist which superior people assume to show they are not taken in. Then, when I was expatiating on the courage of Monsieur Martin, he smiled, shook his head knowingly, and said, "Easy enough!"

"How 'easy enough'?" I said. "If you would only explain me the mystery I should be obliged."

After a few minutes, during which we made acquaintance, we went to dine at the first *restaurateur's*[2] whose shop caught our eye. At dessert a bottle of champagne completely refreshed and brightened up the memories of this odd old soldier. He told me his story as follows:

During the expedition in Upper Egypt under General Desaix,[3] a Provençal[4] soldier fell into the hands of the Mangrabins,[5] and was taken by these Arabs into the deserts beyond the falls of the Nile.

Guide for Interpretation

Think about your impression of the old soldier so far. As you continue your reading, notice whether your impression of him changes or stays the same.

In order to place a sufficient distance between themselves and the French army, the Mangrabins made forced marches and only rested during the night. They camped round a well overshadowed by palm trees under which they had previously concealed a store of provisions. Not surmising that the notion of flight would occur to their prisoner, they contented themselves with binding his hands, and after eating a few dates, and giving provender to their horses, went to sleep.

When the brave Provençal saw that his enemies were no longer watching him, he made use of his teeth to steal a scimitar,[6] fixed the blade between his knees, and cut the cords which prevented him using his hands; in a moment he was free. He at once seized a rifle and a dagger, then taking the precaution to provide himself with a sack of dried dates, oats,

---

1. **menagerie** (mə naj′ ər ē): a collection of animals on exhibit, such as a zoo or circus.
2. *restaurateur* (res′ tər ə tʉr′): a person who owns and operates a restaurant.
3. **Desaix** (de zā′).
4. *Provençal* (prô vän sàl′): from the province of Provence in southern France.
5. **Mangrabins** (män grà ban′).
6. **scimitar** (sim′ ə tər): a short curved sword.

and powder and shot, and to fasten a scimitar to his waist, he leaped on to a horse and spurred on vigorously in the direction where he thought to find the French army. So impatient was he to see a bivouac[7] again that he pressed on the already tired courser at such speed that its flanks were lacerated with his spurs, and at last the poor animal died, leaving the Frenchman alone in the desert.

After walking some time in the sand with all the courage of an escaped convict, the soldier was obliged to stop, as the day had already ended. In spite of the beauty of an oriental sky at night, he felt he had not strength enough to go on. Fortunately he had been able to find a small hill, on the summit of which a few palm trees shot up into the air; it was their verdure[8] seen from afar which had brought hope and consolation to his heart. His fatigue was so great that he lay down upon a rock of granite, capriciously cut out like a camp bed; there he fell asleep without taking any precaution to defend himself while he slept. He had made the sacrifice of his life. His last thought was one of regret. He repented having left the Mangrabins, whose nomad life seemed to smile on him now that he was far from them and without help. He was awakened by the sun, whose pitiless rays fell with all their force on the granite and produced an intolerable heat—for he had had the stupidity to place himself inversely to the shadow thrown by the verdant majestic heads of the palm trees. He looked at the solitary trees and shuddered—they reminded him of the graceful shafts crowned with foliage which characterize the Saracen columns in the cathedral of Arles.[9]

But when, after counting the palm trees, he cast his eyes around him, the most horrible despair was infused into his soul. Before him stretched an ocean without limit. The dark sand of the desert spread further than sight could reach in every direction, and glittered like steel struck with bright light. It might have been a sea of looking glass, or lakes melted together in a mirror. A fiery vapor carried up in streaks made a perpetual whirlwind over the quivering land. The sky was lit with an oriental splendor of insupportable purity, leaving naught for the imagination to desire. Heaven and earth were on fire.

The silence was awful in its wild and terrible majesty. Infinity, immensity, closed in upon the soul from every side. Not a cloud in the sky, not a breath in the air, not a flaw on the bosom of the sand, ever moving in diminutive waves; the horizon ended as at sea on a clear day, with one line of light, definite as the cut of a sword.

The Provençal threw his arms round the trunk of one of the palm trees, as though it were the body of a friend, and then in the shelter of the thin straight shadow that the palm cast upon the granite, he wept. Then sitting down he remained as he was, contemplating with profound sadness the implacable scene, which was all he had to look upon. He cried aloud, to measure the solitude. His voice, lost in the hollows of the hill, sounded faintly and aroused no echo—the echo was in his heart. The Provençal was twenty-two years old:—he loaded his carbine.

"There'll be time enough," he said to himself, laying on the ground the weapon which alone could bring him deliverance.

Looking by turns at the black expanse and the blue expanse, the soldier dreamed of France—he smelled with delight the gutters of Paris—he remembered the towns through which he had passed, the faces of his fellow

7. **bivouac** (biv′ wak′): a temporary camp of soldiers.
8. **verdure** (vur′ jər): the fresh green color of growing things.
9. **Saracen** (sar′ ə sən) **columns . . . Arles** (àrl): Saracen architecture is brilliantly colored and heavily decorated, sometimes with patterns derived from foliage. Arles is a city in Provence.

soldiers, the most minute details of his life. His southern fancy soon showed him the stones of his beloved Provence, in the play of the heat which waved over the spread sheet of the desert. Fearing the danger of this cruel mirage, he went down the opposite side of the hill to that by which he had come up the day before. The remains of a rug showed that this place of refuge had at one time been inhabited; at a short distance he saw some palm trees full of dates. Then the instinct which binds us to life awoke again in his heart. He hoped to live long enough to await the passing of some Arabs, or perhaps he might hear the sound of cannon; for at this time Bonaparte was traversing Egypt.

This thought gave him new life. The palm tree seemed to bend with the weight of the ripe fruit. He shook some of it down. When he tasted this unhoped-for manna,[10] he felt sure that the palms had been cultivated by a former inhabitant—the savory, fresh meat of the dates was proof of the care of his predecessor. He passed suddenly from dark despair to an almost insane joy. He went up again to the top of the hill, and spent the rest of the day in cutting down one of the sterile palm trees, which the night before had served him for shelter. A vague memory made him think of the animals of the desert; and in case they might come to drink at the spring, visible from the base of the rocks but lost further down, he resolved to guard himself from their visits by placing a barrier at the entrance of his hermitage.

In spite of his diligence, and the strength which the fear of being devoured asleep gave him, he was unable to cut the palm in pieces, though he succeeded in cutting it down. At eventide the king of the desert fell; the sound of its fall resounded far and wide, like a sigh in the solitude; the soldier shuddered as though he had heard some voice predicting woe.

But like an heir who does not long bewail a deceased parent, he tore off from this beautiful tree the tall broad green leaves which are its poetic adornment, and used them to mend the mat on which he was to sleep.

Fatigued by the heat and his work, he fell asleep under the red curtains of his wet cave.

In the middle of the night his sleep was troubled by an extraordinary noise; he sat up, and the deep silence around allowed him to distinguish the alternative accents of a respiration whose savage energy could not belong to a human creature.

A profound terror, increased still further by the darkness, the silence, and his waking images, froze his heart within him. He almost felt his hair stand on end, when by straining his eyes to their utmost he perceived through the shadow two faint yellow lights. At first he attributed these lights to the reflection of his own pupils, but soon the vivid brilliance of the night aided him gradually to distinguish the objects around him in the cave, and he beheld a huge animal lying but two steps from him. Was it a lion, a tiger, or a crocodile?

The Provençal was not educated enough to know under what species his enemy ought to be classed; but his fright was all the greater, as his ignorance led him to imagine all terrors at once; he endured a cruel torture, noting every variation of the breathing close to him without daring to make the slightest movement. An odor, pungent like that of a fox, but more penetrating, profounder—so to speak—filled the cave, and when the Provençal became sensible of this, his terror reached its height, for he could no longer doubt the proximity of a terrible companion, whose royal dwelling served him for a shelter.

Presently the reflection of the moon descending on the horizon, lit up the den, rendering gradually visible and resplendent the spotted skin of a panther.

---

10. manna: spiritual sustenance; anything badly needed that comes unexpectedly.

This lion of Egypt slept, curled up like a big dog, the peaceful possessor of a sumptuous niche at the gate of a *hôtel*;[11] its eyes opened for a moment and closed again; its face was turned toward the man. A thousand confused thoughts passed through the Frenchman's mind; first he thought of killing it with a bullet from his gun, but he saw there was not enough distance between them for him to take proper aim—the shot would miss the mark. And if it were to wake!—the thought made his limbs rigid. He listened to his own heart beating in the midst of the silence, and cursed the too violent pulsations which the flow of blood brought on, fearing to disturb that sleep which allowed him time to think of some means of escape.

Twice he placed his hand on his scimitar, intending to cut off the head of his enemy; but the difficulty of cutting the stiff short hair compelled him to abandon this daring project. To miss would be to die for *certain*, he thought; he preferred the chances of fair fight, and made up his mind to wait till morning; the morning did not leave him long to wait.

He could now examine the panther at ease; its muzzle was smeared with blood.

"She had a good dinner," he thought, without troubling himself as to whether her feast might have been on human flesh. "She won't be hungry when she gets up."

It was a female. The fur on her belly and flanks was glistening white; many small marks like velvet formed beautiful bracelets round her feet; her sinuous tail was also white, ending with black rings; the overpart of her dress, yellow like unburnished gold, very lissom and soft, had the characteristic blotches in the form of rosettes, which distinguish the panther from every other feline species.

This tranquil and formidable hostess snored in an attitude as graceful as that of a cat lying on a cushion. Her blood-stained paws, nervous and well armed, were stretched out before her face, which rested upon them, and from which radiated her straight slender whiskers, like threads of silver.

If she had been like that in a cage, the Provençal would doubtless have admired the grace of the animal, and the vigorous contrasts of vivid color which gave her robe an imperial splendor; but just then his sight was troubled by her sinister appearance.

The presence of the panther, even asleep, could not fail to produce the effect which the magnetic eyes of the serpent are said to have on the nightingale.

For a moment the courage of the soldier began to fail before this danger, though no doubt it would have risen at the mouth of a cannon charged with shell. Nevertheless, a bold thought brought daylight to his soul and sealed up the source of the cold sweat which sprang forth on his brow. Like men driven to bay, who defy death and offer their bodies to the smiter, so he, seeing in this merely a tragic episode, resolved to play his part with honor to the last.

"The day before yesterday the Arabs would have killed me perhaps," he said; so considering himself as good as dead already, he waited bravely, with excited curiosity, his enemy's awakening.

When the sun appeared, the panther suddenly opened her eyes; then she put out her paws with energy, as if to stretch them and get rid of cramp. At last she yawned, showing the formidable apparatus of her teeth and pointed tongue, rough as a file.

She licked off the blood which stained her paws and muzzle, and scratched her head with reiterated gestures full of prettiness.

---

11. hôtel (ō′ tel): a mansion.

"All right, make a little toilet,"[12] the Frenchman said to himself, beginning to recover his gaiety with his courage; "we'll say good-morning to each other presently," and he seized the small short dagger which he had taken from the Mangrabins. At this moment the panther turned her head toward the man and looked at him fixedly without moving.

The rigidity of her metallic eyes and their insupportable luster made him shudder, especially when the animal walked toward him. But he looked at her caressingly, staring into her eyes in order to magnetize her, and let her come quite close to him; then with a movement both gentle and affectionate, as though he were caressing the most beautiful of women, he passed his hand over her whole body, from the head to the tail, scratching the flexible vertebrae which divided the panther's yellow back. The animal waved her tail, and her eyes grew gentle; and when for the third time the Frenchman accomplished this interested flattery, she gave forth one of those purrings by which our cats express their pleasure; but this murmur issued from a throat so powerful and so deep, that it resounded through the cave like the last vibrations of an organ in a church. The man, understanding the importance of his caresses, redoubled them. When he felt sure of having extinguished the ferocity of his capricious companion, whose hunger had so fortunately been satisfied the day before, he got up to go out of the cave; the panther let him go out, but when he had reached the summit of the hill she sprang with the lightness of a sparrow hopping from twig to twig, and rubbed herself against his legs, putting up her back after the manner of all the race of cats. Then regarding her guest with eyes whose glare had softened a little, she gave vent to that wild cry which naturalists compare to the grating of a saw.

"She is exacting," said the Frenchman, smiling.

He was bold enough to play with her ears; he scratched her head as hard as he could. When he saw he was successful he tickled her skull with the point of his dagger, watching for the moment to kill her, but the hardness of her bones made him tremble for his success.

The sultana of the desert showed herself gracious to her slave; she lifted her head, stretched out her neck, and manifested her delight by the tranquillity of her attitude. It suddenly occurred to the soldier that to kill this savage princess with one blow he must poniard her in the throat.

He raised the blade, when the panther, satisfied, no doubt, laid herself gracefully at his feet, and cast up at him glances in which, in spite of their natural fierceness, was mingled confusedly a kind of goodwill. The poor Provençal ate his dates, leaning against one of the palm trees, and casting his eyes alternately on the desert in quest of some liberator and on his terrible companion to watch her uncertain clemency.[13]

The panther looked at the place where the date stones fell, and every time that he threw one down, her eyes expressed an incredible mistrust.

She examined the man with an almost commercial prudence. However, this examination was favorable to him, for when he had finished his meager meal she licked his boots with her powerful rough tongue, brushing off with marvelous skill the dust gathered in the creases.

"Ah, but when she's really hungry!" thought the Frenchman.

In spite of the shudder this thought caused him, the soldier began to measure curiously the proportions of the panther, certainly one of the most splendid specimens of its race. She

---

12. make a little toilet: wash and freshen up.

13. clemency (klem′ ən sē): a merciful quality in one who has power or authority.

was three feet high and four feet long without counting her tail; this powerful weapon, rounded like a cudgel, was nearly three feet long. The head, large as that of a lioness, was distinguished by a rare expression of refinement. The cold cruelty of a tiger was dominant, it was true, but there was also a vague resemblance to the face of a sensual woman.

Indeed, the face of this solitary queen had something of the gaiety of a drunken Nero: she had satiated herself with blood, and she wanted to play.

The soldier tried if he might walk up and down, and the panther left him free, contenting herself with following him with her eyes, less like a faithful dog than a big Angora cat, observing everything, and every movement of her master.

When he looked round, he saw, by the spring, the remains of his horse; the panther had dragged the carcass all that way; about two-thirds of it had been devoured already. The sight reassured him.

It was easy to explain the panther's absence, and the respect she had had for him while he slept. The first piece of good luck emboldened him to tempt the future, and he conceived the wild hope of continuing on good terms with the panther during the entire day, neglecting no means of taming her and remaining in her good graces.

He returned to her, and had the unspeakable joy of seeing her wag her tail with an almost imperceptible movement at his approach. He sat down then, without fear, by her side, and they began to play together; he took her paws and muzzle, pulled her ears, rolled her over on her back, stroked her warm, delicate flanks. She let him do whatever he liked, and when he began to stroke the hair on her feet she drew her claws in carefully.

The man, keeping the dagger in one hand, thought to plunge it into the belly of the too confiding panther, but he was afraid that he would be immediately strangled in her last convulsive struggle; besides, he felt in his heart a sort of remorse which bid him respect a creature that had done him no harm. He seemed to have found a friend, in a boundless desert; half unconsciously he thought of his first sweetheart, whom he had nicknamed "Mignonne"[14] by way of contrast, because she was so atrociously jealous, that all the time of their love he was in fear of the knife with which she had always threatened him.

The memory of his early days suggested to him the idea of making the young panther answer to this name, now that he began to admire with less terror her swiftness, suppleness, and softness. Toward the end of the day he had familiarized himself with his perilous position; he now almost liked the painfulness of it. At last his companion had got into the habit of looking up at him whenever he cried in a falsetto voice, "Mignonne."

At the setting of the sun Mignonne gave, several times running, a profound melancholy cry.

"She's been well brought up," said the light-hearted soldier; "she says her prayers." But this mental joke only occurred to him when he noticed what a pacific[15] attitude his companion remained in. "Come, _ma petite blonde_,[16] I'll let you go to bed first," he said to her, counting on the activity of his own legs to run away as quickly as possible, directly she was asleep, and seek another shelter for the night.

The soldier awaited with impatience the hour of his flight, and when it had arrived he walked vigorously in the direction of the Nile; but hardly had he made a quarter of a league in the sand when he heard the panther bounding after him, crying with that saw-like cry,

14. **Mignonne** (mē nyôn′) _French:_ darling.
15. **pacific** (pə sif′ ik): peaceful; calm; tranquil.
16. **_ma petite blonde_** (mà pə tēt′ blônd) _French:_ my little blonde.

more dreadful even than the sound of her leaping.

"Ah!" he said, "then she's taken a fancy to me; she has never met anyone before, and it is really quite flattering to have her first love."

That instant the man fell into one of those movable quicksands so terrible to travelers and from which it is impossible to save one's self. Feeling himself caught, he gave a shriek of alarm; the panther seized him with her teeth by the collar and, springing vigorously backward, drew him, as if by magic, out of the whirling sand.

"Ah, Mignonne!" cried the soldier, caressing her enthusiastically; "we're bound together for life and death—but no jokes, mind!" and he retraced his steps.

From that time the desert seemed inhabited. It contained a being to whom the man could talk, and whose ferocity was rendered gentle by him, though he could not explain to himself the reason for their strange friendship. Great as was the soldier's desire to stay up on guard, he slept.

On awakening he could not find Mignonne; he mounted the hill, and in the distance saw her springing toward him after the habit of these animals, who cannot run on account of the extreme flexibility of the vertebral column. Mignonne arrived, her jaws covered with blood; she received the wonted caress of her companion, showing with much purring how happy it made her. Her eyes, full of languor,[17] turned still more gently than the day before toward the Provençal, who talked to her as one would to a tame animal.

"Ah! mademoiselle, you are a nice girl, aren't you? Just look at that! so we like to be made much of, don't we? Aren't you ashamed of yourself? So you have been eating some Arab or other, have you? that doesn't matter. They're animals just the same as you are; but don't you take to eating Frenchmen, or I shan't like you any longer."

She played like a dog with its master, letting herself be rolled over, knocked about, and stroked, alternately; sometimes she herself would provoke the soldier, putting up her paw with a soliciting gesture.

Some days passed in this manner. This companionship permitted the Provençal to appreciate the sublime beauty of the desert; now that he had a living thing to think about, alternations of fear and quiet, and plenty to eat, his mind became filled with contrasts, and his life began to be diversified.

Solitude revealed to him all her secrets, and enveloped him in her delights. He discovered in the rising and setting of the sun sights unknown to the world. He knew what it was to tremble when he heard over his head the hiss of a bird's wings, so rarely did they pass, or when he saw the clouds, changing and many-colored travelers, melt into one another. He studied in the night-time the effects of the moon upon the ocean of sand, where the simoom[18] made waves swift of movement and rapid in their change. He lived the life of the Eastern day, marveling at its wonderful pomp; then, after having reveled in the sight of a hurricane over the plain where the whirling sands made red, dry mists and death-bearing clouds, he would welcome the night with joy, for then fell the healthful freshness of the stars, and he listened to imaginary music in the skies. Then solitude taught him to unroll the treasures of dreams. He passed whole hours in remembering mere nothings, and comparing his present life with his past.

At last he grew passionately fond of the tigress; for some sort of affection was a necessity.

Whether it was that his will powerfully projected had modified the character of his companion, or whether, because she found abun-

---

17. **languor** (laŋ' gər): laziness; lethargy.
18. **simoom** (si mōōm'): a hot, violent, sand-laden wind of the African or Asian deserts.

dant food in her predatory[19] excursions in the deserts, she respected the man's life, he began to fear for it no longer, seeing her so well tamed.

He devoted the greater part of his time to sleep, but he was obliged to watch like a spider in its web that the moment of his deliverance might not escape him, if anyone should pass the line marked by the horizon. He had sacrificed his shirt to make a flag with, which he hung at the top of a palm tree, whose foliage he had torn off. Taught by necessity, he found the means of keeping it spread out, by fastening it with little sticks; for the wind might not be blowing at the moment when the passing traveler was looking through the desert.

It was during the long hours, when he had abandoned hope, that he amused himself with the panther. He had come to learn the different inflections of her voice, the expressions of her eyes; he had studied the capricious patterns of all the rosettes which marked the gold of her robe. Mignonne was not even angry when he took hold of the tuft at the end of her tail to count the rings, those graceful ornaments which glittered in the sun like jewelry. It gave him pleasure to contemplate the supple, fine outlines of her form, the graceful pose of her head. But it was especially when she was playing that he felt most pleasure in looking at her; the agility and youthful lightness of her movements were a continual surprise to him; he wondered at the supple way in which she jumped and climbed, washed herself and arranged her fur, crouched down and prepared to spring. However rapid her spring might be, however slippery the stone she was on, she would always stop short at the word "Mignonne."

One day, in a bright midday sun, an enormous bird coursed through the air. The man left his panther to look at this new guest; but after waiting a moment the deserted sultana growled deeply.

"My goodness! I do believe she's jealous," he cried, seeing her eyes become hard again; "the soul of Virginie has passed into her body, that's certain."

The eagle disappeared into the air, while the soldier admired the curved contour of the panther.

But there was such youth and grace in her form! she was beautiful as a woman! the blond fur of her robe mingled well with the delicate tints of faint white which marked her flanks.

The profuse light cast down by the sun made this living gold, these russet markings, to burn in a way to give them an indefinable attraction.

The man and the panther looked at one another with a look full of meaning; the coquette[20] quivered when she felt her friend stroke her head; her eyes flashed like lightning—then she shut them tightly.

"She has a soul," he said, looking at the stillness of this queen of the sands, golden like them, solitary and burning like them.

Ah! how did it all end?

Alas; as all great passions do end—in a misunderstanding. From some reason *one* suspects the other of treason; they don't come to an explanation through pride, and quarrel and part from sheer obstinacy. Yet sometimes at the best moments a single word or a look are enough.

"Well," the old fellow continued, "with her sharp teeth she one day caught hold of my leg—gently, I dare say; but I, thinking she would devour me, plunged my dagger into her throat. She rolled over, giving a cry that froze my heart; and I saw her dying, still looking at me without anger. I would have given all the

---

19. **predatory** (pred′ ə tôr′ ē): hunting.
20. **coquette** (kō ket′): a flirt.

world—my cross even, which I had not got then—to have brought her to life again. It was as though I had murdered a real person; and the soldiers who had seen my flag, and were come to my assistance, found me in tears.

"Well, sir," he said, after a moment of silence, "since then I have been in war in Germany, in Spain, in Russia, in France; I've certainly carried my carcass about a good deal, but never have I seen anything like the desert.

Ah! yes, it is very beautiful!"

"What did you feel there?" I asked him.

"Oh! that can't be described, young man! Besides, I am not always regretting my palm trees and my panther. I should have to be very melancholy for that. In the desert, you see, there is everything, and nothing."

"Yes, but explain—"

"Well," he said, with an impatient gesture, "it is God without mankind."

Thinking About the Story

A PERSONAL RESPONSE

sharing impressions

1. How do you feel about the soldier's experience in the desert? Describe your feelings in your journal.

constructing interpretations

2. What does the last line of the story suggest about the soldier's perceptions of the desert?

3. How would you judge the character of the soldier?

Think about
- whether he is justified in killing the panther
- how the narrator describes him at the beginning of the story
- how he handles the dangers of the desert
- how the word *passion* might be applied to his experiences

4. What connections can you find between the soldier's relationship with the panther and romantic relationships between men and women?

Think about
- the way the soldier describes the panther's physical appearance
- the companionship each finds with the other
- the amount of trust and mistrust the soldier feels
- the reason the soldier names the panther Mignonne
- why the story is called "A Passion in the Desert"

5. If the soldier's experience with the panther had taken place in a setting other than the desert, how might the story have been different?

A CRITICAL RESPONSE

6. What do you think is gained by having the soldier's story about the panther framed by the story of the first-person narrator's encounter with the soldier?

7. According to many critics, Balzac was largely responsible for establishing the short story as a respected literary form. How would you rank Balzac as a storyteller? Use examples from the story to support your opinion.

8. Compare Balzac's portrayal of the panther in this story with Isak Dinesen's portrayal of Lulu in the excerpt from *Out of Africa*.

Think about
- the techniques used by each writer to portray the animal
- the relationships depicted between humans and animals

Analyzing the Writer's Craft

SUSPENSE

Why do you think Balzac does not reveal the identity of the soldier until the end of the story?

Building a Literary Vocabulary. Suspense is the excitement or tension that readers feel as they become involved in a story and eager to know the outcome of events. Much of the suspense in Balzac's story comes from the fact that the reader does not know what will happen to the panther and the soldier until the end. This uncertainty keeps the reader wondering whether the panther will attack the soldier and whether the soldier will be rescued.

Application: Measuring Suspense. Working with a partner, make a line graph to show how suspenseful you found each part of the story. On the horizontal line list the important events. On the vertical line write the numbers 1 through 10. Then using a scale of 1 (least suspenseful) to 10 (most suspenseful), place a dot on the graph above each event and across from the number that indicates the intensity of suspense you felt. When you have finished, connect the dots. Compare your line graph with that of another pair of students.

Connecting Reading and Writing

1. Write a **character sketch** of the old soldier for a veterans' magazine. Include details about his character directly provided by the narrator and characteristics revealed about the soldier in the story he tells.

Option: Use the details stated and revealed about the character of the old soldier to write a **casting call** for his role in the stage version of the story.

2. Put yourself in the role of one of the soldiers who arrives to rescue the solitary soldier in the desert. Write a **report** to your superior officers describing the physical and psychological condition in which you find the soldier.

Option: Write a **letter** to the soldier's family explaining—as tactfully as you can—what has happened to him.

3. Write a **poem** that the soldier might have written for a nature magazine, in which he appreciates the mystery and beauty that the panther represents to him.

Option: Write a **diary entry** that the soldier might have written in which he expresses wonderment about his experience with the panther.

4. Imagine that you are planning a film version of "A Passion in the Desert." Write **instructions** for the special effects needed to create the setting for the movie.

Option: Create a **poster** advertising the movie, being sure to depict the setting and to include an enticing description of the action.

5. Research the topic of desert survival. **Outline** your findings in preparation for an oral presentation to your class.

Option: Write a **research report** on the information you gather to share with a classmate who knows nothing about desert survival.

Metonymy, or The Husband's Revenge

RACHEL DE QUEIROZ   born 1910   BRAZIL

A biography of de Queiroz appears on page 750.

Approaching the Story

In her novels, plays, and short stories, Rachel de Queiroz (rä chel' de ke' ē rôs) has written richly of the Latin American world. The situation she describes in this short story, however, could happen anywhere. The narrator of "Metonymy" begins by discussing a figure of speech and from there launches into a compelling tale with an unexpected twist.

Building Vocabulary

These essential words are footnoted within the story.

rebuke (ri byook'): I accepted his **rebuke** with humility. (page 680)

rhetoric (ret' ər ik): Ever since, I have been using metonymy—my only bond with classical **rhetoric**. (page 680)

illicit (il lis' it): Fate . . . does not like **illicit** love. (page 682)

Connecting Writing and Reading

Imagine that you have been cheated, have had something valuable stolen from you, have had a friend break an important promise, or have become very, very jealous. Which of these things would you feel like doing?

smashing dishes	plotting to get back at the person
picking a fight with the person	trying to forget the incident
crying	writing a hate letter
attempting a reconciliation	lashing out at anybody who got in your way

Describe briefly in your journal how you might express your anger or seek revenge. Then compare your reactions with the reaction of the main character.

Metonymy, or The Husband's Revenge

METONYMY. I LEARNED the word in 1930 and shall never forget it. I had just published my first novel. A literary critic had scolded me because my hero went out into the night "chest unbuttoned."

"What deplorable nonsense!" wrote this eminently sensible gentleman. "Why does she not say what she means? Obviously, it was his shirt that was unbuttoned, not his chest."

I accepted his rebuke[1] with humility, indeed with shame. But my illustrious Latin professor, Dr. Matos Peixoto,[2] came to my rescue. He said that what I had written was perfectly correct; that I had used a respectable figure of speech known as metonymy; and that this figure consisted in the use of one word for another word associated with it—for example, a word representing a cause instead of the effect, or representing the container when the content is intended. The classic instance, he told me, is "the sparkling cup"; in reality, not the cup but the wine in it is sparkling.

The professor and I wrote a letter, which was published in the newspaper where the review had appeared. It put my unjust critic in his place. I hope he learned a lesson. I know I did. Ever since, I have been using metonymy—my only bond with classical rhetoric.[3]

Moreover, I have devoted some thought to it, and I have concluded that metonymy may be more than a figure of speech. There is, I believe, such a thing as practical or applied metonymy. Let me give a crude example, drawn from my own experience. A certain lady of my acquaintance suddenly moved out of the boardinghouse where she had been living for years and became a mortal enemy of the woman who owned it. I asked her why. We both knew that the woman was a kindly soul; she had given my friend injections when she needed them, had often loaned her a hot water bottle, and had always waited on her when she had her little heart attacks. My friend replied: "It's the telephone in the hall. I hate her for it. Half the time when I answered it, the call was a hoax or joke of some sort."

"But the owner of the boardinghouse didn't perpetrate these hoaxes. She wasn't responsible for them."

"No. But whose telephone was it?"

I know another case of applied metonymy, a more disastrous one, for it involved a crime. It happened in a city of the interior, which I shall not name for fear that someone may recognize the parties and revive the scandal. I shall narrate the crime but conceal the criminal.

Well, in this city of the interior there lived a man. He was not old, but he was spent, which is worse than being old. In his youth he had suffered from beriberi.[4] His legs were weak, his chest was tired and asthmatic, his skin was yellowish, and his eyes were rheumy. He was, however, a man of property; he owned the house in which he lived and the one next to it, in which he had set up a grocery store. Therefore, although so unattractive personally, he was able to find himself a wife. In all justice

---

1. **rebuke** (ri byo͞ok′): sharp scolding or reprimand.
2. **Matos Peixoto** (mä′ tôs pā zhô′ tô).
3. **rhetoric** (ret′ ər ik): the art of using words effectively in speaking or writing.
4. **beriberi** (ber′ ē ber′ ē): a disease caused by poor diet that results in nerve disorders and sometimes swelling of the body.

to him, he did not tempt fate by marrying a beauty. Instead, he married a poor, emaciated girl who worked in a men's clothing factory. By her face one would have thought that she had consumption.[5] So our friend felt safe. He did not foresee the effects of good nutrition and a healthful life on a woman's appearance. The girl no longer spent eight hours a day at a sewing table. She was the mistress of her house. She ate well: fresh meat, cucumber salad, pork fat with beans and manioc[6] mush, all kinds of sweets, and oranges, which her husband bought by the gross for his customers. The effects were like magic. Her body filled out, especially in the best places. She even seemed to grow taller. And her face—what a change! I may have forgotten to mention that her features, in themselves, were good to begin with. Moreover, money enabled her to embellish her natural advantages with art; she began to wear make-up, to wave her hair, and to dress well.

Lovely, attractive, she now found her sickly, prematurely old husband a burden and a bore. Each evening, as soon as the store was closed, he dined, mostly on milk (he could not stomach meat), took his newspaper, and rested on his chaise longue[7] until time to go to bed. He did not care for movies or for soccer or for radio. He did not even show much interest in love. Just a sort of tepid, tasteless cohabitation.

And then Fate intervened: it produced a sergeant.

Granted, it was unjust for a young wife, after being reconditioned at her husband's expense, to employ her charms against the aforesaid husband. Unjust; but, then, this world thrives on injustice, doesn't it? The sergeant—I shall not say whether he was in the army, the air force, the marines, or the fusiliers,[8] for I still mean to conceal the identities of the parties—the sergeant was muscular, young, ingratiating, with a manly, commanding voice and

a healthy spring in his walk. He looked gloriously martial in his high-buttoned uniform.

One day, when the lady was in charge of the counter (while her husband lunched), the sergeant came in. Exactly what happened and what did not happen is hard to say. It seems that the sergeant asked for a pack of cigarettes. Then he wanted a little vermouth. Finally he asked permission to listen to the sports broadcast on the radio next to the counter. Maybe it was just an excuse to remain there awhile. In any case, the girl said it would be all right. It is hard to refuse a favor to a sergeant, especially a sergeant like this one. It appears that the sergeant asked nothing more that day. At most, he and the girl exchanged expressive glances and a few agreeable words, murmured so softly that the customers, always alert for something to gossip about, could not hear them.

Three times more the husband lunched while his wife chatted with the sergeant in the store. The flirtation progressed. Then the husband fell ill with a grippe,[9] and the two others went far beyond flirtation. How and where they met, no one was able to discover. The important thing is that they were lovers and that they loved with a forbidden love, like Tristan and Isolde or Paolo and Francesca.[10]

---

5. **consumption** (kən sump′ shən): tuberculosis.

6. **manioc** (man′ ē äk′): a tropical plant with edible roots.

7. **chaise longue** (shāz′ lôŋ′): a couchlike chair with support for the back and a seat long enough to support a person's outstretched legs.

8. **fusiliers** (fyoo′ zi lirz′): special regiment of soldiers.

9. **grippe** (grip): the flu.

10. **Tristan and Isolde or Paolo and Francesca** (tris′ tən, i sōl′ də, pä′ ô lô, frän ches′ kä): two legendary pairs of lovers. (See "Chevrefoil," page 656, and *The Inferno*, page 468.)

Then Fate, which does not like illicit[11] love and generally punishes those who engage in it, transferred the sergeant to another part of the country.

It is said that only those who love can really know the pain of separation. The girl cried so much that her eyes grew red and swollen. She lost her appetite. Beneath her rouge could be seen the consumptive complexion of earlier times. And these symptoms aroused her husband's suspicion, although, curiously, he had never suspected anything when the love affair was flourishing and everything was wine and roses.

He began to observe her carefully. He scrutinized her in her periods of silence. He listened to her sighs and to the things she murmured in her sleep. He snooped around and found a postcard and a book, both with a man's name in the same handwriting. He found the insignia of the sergeant's regiment and concluded that the object of his wife's murmurs, sighs, and silences was not only a man but a soldier. Finally he made the supreme discovery: that they had indeed betrayed him. For he discovered the love letters, bearing airmail stamps, a distant postmark, and the sergeant's name. They left no reasonable doubt.

For five months the poor fellow twisted the poisoned dagger of jealousy inside his own thin, sickly chest. Like a boy who discovers a bird's nest and, hiding nearby, watches the eggs increasing in number every day, so the husband, using a duplicate key to the wood chest where his wife put her valuables, watched the increase in the number of letters concealed there. He had given her the chest during their honeymoon, saying, "Keep your secrets here." And the ungrateful girl had obeyed him.

Every day at the fateful hour of lunch, she replaced her husband at the counter. But he was not interested in eating. He ran to her room, pulled out a drawer in her bureau, removed the chest from under a lot of panties, slips, and such, took the little key out of his pocket, opened the chest, and anxiously read the new letter. If there was no new letter, he reread the one dated August 21; it was so full of realism that it sounded like dialogue from a French movie. Then he put everything away and hurried to the kitchen, where he swallowed a few spoonfuls of broth and gnawed at a piece of bread. It was almost impossible to swallow with the passion of those two thieves sticking in his throat.

When the poor man's heart had become utterly saturated with jealousy and hatred, he took a revolver and a box of bullets from the counter drawer; they had been left, years before, by a customer as security for a debt which had never been paid. He loaded the revolver.

One bright morning at exactly ten o'clock, when the store was full of customers, he excused himself and went through the doorway that connected the store with his home. In a few seconds the customers heard the noise of a row, a woman's scream, and three shots. On the sidewalk in front of the shopkeeper's house they saw his wife on her knees, still screaming, and him, with the revolver in his trembling hand, trying to raise her. The front door of the house was open. Through it, they saw a man's legs, wearing khaki trousers and boots. He was lying face down, with his head and torso in the parlor, not visible from the street.

The husband was the first to speak. Raising his eyes from his wife, he looked at the terror-stricken people and spotted among them his favorite customer. He took a few steps, stood in the doorway, and said:

---

11. illicit (il lis' it): not allowed by law or custom; improper.

"You may call the police."

At the police station he explained that he was a deceived husband. The police chief remarked, "Isn't this a little unusual? Ordinarily you kill your wives. They're weaker than their lovers."

The man was deeply offended.

"No," he protested. "I would be utterly incapable of killing my wife. She is all that I have in the world. She is refined, pretty, and hardworking. She helps me in the store, she understands bookkeeping, she writes the letters to the wholesalers. She is the only person who knows how to prepare my food. Why should I want to kill my wife?"

"I see," said the chief of police. "So you killed her lover."

The man shook his head.

"Wrong again. The sergeant—her lover—was transferred to a place far from here. I discovered the affair only after he had gone. By reading his letters. They tell the whole story. I know one of them by heart, the worst of them. . . ."

The police chief did not understand. He said nothing and waited for the husband to continue, which he presently did:

"Those letters! If they were alive, I would kill them, one by one. They were shameful to read—almost like a book. I thought of taking an airplane trip. I thought of killing some other sergeant here, so that they would all learn a lesson not to fool around with another man's wife. But I was afraid of the rest of the regiment; you know how these military men stick together. Still, I had to do something. Otherwise I would have gone crazy. I couldn't get those letters out of my head. Even on days when none arrived, I felt terrible, worse than my wife. I had to put an end to it, didn't I? So today, at last, I did it. I waited till the regular time and, when I saw the wretch appear on the other side of the street, I went into the house, hid behind a door, and lay there waiting for him."

"The lover?" asked the police chief stupidly.

"No, of course not. I told you I didn't kill her lover. It was those letters. The sergeant sent them—but *he* delivered them. Almost every day, there he was at the door, smiling, with the vile envelope in his hand. I pointed the revolver and fired three times. He didn't say a word; he just fell. No, Chief, it wasn't her lover. It was the mailman."

Thinking About the Story

A PERSONAL RESPONSE

*sharing
impressions*

1. How do you feel about the husband's action at the end of the story? Express your feelings briefly in your journal.

*constructing
interpretations*

2. Which character do you sympathize with most, and why?

A CREATIVE RESPONSE

3. How might the story be different if the sergeant had not been transferred?

A CRITICAL RESPONSE

4. How would you describe the tone of this story?
   Think about
   • the definition of tone as the attitude a writer takes toward a subject
   • the narrator's introductory anecdote about the word *metonymy*
   • the narrator's commentary interspersed throughout the story
   • who, if anyone, is treated as a sympathetic character
   • the outcome of the story

5. Do you think this story has a message? Explain your view.

6. In your opinion, which of the first four authors in this part of the book—Marie de France, Boccaccio, Balzac, or de Queiroz—is most successful in "telling a good story"? Explain why you think so.

Analyzing the Writer's Craft

FORESHADOWING

Did the ending of this story surprise you? What clues in the story could have helped prepare you for the way it ended?

Building a Literary Vocabulary. Foreshadowing is a writer's use of hints or clues to indicate events that will occur later in a narrative. This technique creates suspense and at the same time prepares the reader for what is to come. In "Metonymy, or The Husband's Revenge," for instance, the second part of the title provides a clue that the husband will seek some kind of revenge. Readers may easily overlook this clue, however, and the actual ending may still come as a surprise, especially since it is contrary to what readers would ordinarily expect.

Application: Recognizing Foreshadowing. Working with a partner, read the story again and identify passages that foreshadow an unfortunate or violent outcome of some kind. Then look for clues that lay the groundwork for the ending that takes place. Compare your findings with those of other groups in the class.

Connecting Reading and Writing

1. Consider what the wife's reflections might be concerning this event and express them in the form of a **first-person account** that she writes for herself.

Option: Imagine the exchange that might take place between the police officer and the wife following the murder. Write down what they say in a set of **questions and answers.** Make a recording of the exchange and play it for your class.

2. Write a **letter** that you think the wife might send to the sergeant, telling him what has happened and what she has decided to do.

Option: Write a brief **summary** of what might happen next in the story if it were continued.

3. Think back to the "chest unbuttoned" and "the sparkling cup," the examples of metonymy provided at the beginning of the story. List additional examples of this **figure of speech**. Some examples may be ones you have heard or read; others can be your creation. Share your list with the class.

Option: Create several **cartoons** for your classmates that illustrate literally your examples of metonymy.

The Form of the Sword

JORGE LUIS BORGES (1899–1986) ARGENTINA

A biography of Borges appears on page 739.

Approaching the Story

Jorge Luis Borges (hôr′ hə lo͞o ēs′ bôr′ hes) is an Argentine writer whose stories often portray high-action adventure in dreamlike settings. The story you are about to read is a frame story. In the "frame" the narrator describes his encounter with an English landowner who has been the subject of curious speculation on the part of his South American neighbors. The Englishman, whose own story forms the central part of "The Form of the Sword," recalls an incident that occurred in Ireland during the civil war some years before.

HIS FACE WAS crossed with a rancorous scar: a nearly perfect ashen arc which sank into his temple on one side and his cheek on the other. His real name is of no importance: in Tacuarembo[1] everyone knew him as the Englishman of La Colorada.[2] The great landowner of these parts, Cardoso,[3] had not been interested in selling; I have heard that the Englishman had recourse to an unexpected argument: he told him the secret history of the scar. The Englishman had come from the frontier, from Rio Grande del Sur;[4] there were those who said he had been a smuggler in Brazil. His fields were overgrown with underbrush; the wells were bitter; to remedy these faults, the Englishman worked alongside his *peones*.[5] They say he was strict to the point of cruelty but scrupulously fair. They also say he was a drinking man: a couple of times a year he would lock himself up in a room in the tower, and two or three days later he would emerge as if from a bout of insanity or from the battlefield, pale, tremulous, abashed—and as authoritarian as ever. I remember his glacial eyes, his energetic thinness, his gray mustache. He had scant dealings with anyone; true, his Spanish was rudimentary, contaminated with Brazilian. Apart from an occasional commercial letter or pamphlet, he received no correspondence.

The last time I made a trip through the northern provinces, a flash flood in the Caraguatá arroyo[6] forced me to spend the night at La Colorada. I was only there a few minutes when I felt that my presence was inopportune. I tried getting into the good

---

1. **Tacuarembo** (tä kwä *rem′* bô).
2. **La Colorada** (lä kô lô *rä′* dä).
3. **Cardoso** (kär dô′ sô).
4. **Rio Grande del Sur** (*rē′* ô grän′ dä del so͞o*r*).
5. **peones** (pē ô′ nes) *Spanish*: peasants.
6. **Caraguatá arroyo** (kä *rä* gwä tä′ ə r*o*ĭ′ ō): an arroyo is a narrow ravine.

graces of the Englishman; I resorted to the least acute of all the passions: patriotism. I said that a country with the spirit of England was invincible. My interlocutor[7] agreed, but he added with a smile that he was not English. He was Irish, from Dungarvan. Having said this, he stopped himself, as if he had revealed a secret.

After supper, we went out to look at the sky. It had cleared, but behind the ridge of the mountains, the south, fissured and shot through with lightning flashes, was brewing up another storm. Back in the deserted dining room, the waiter who had served us supper brought out a bottle of rum. We drank steadily, in silence.

I do not know what hour of the night it might have been when I realized that I was drunk; I do not know what inspiration or exultation or tedium made me mention the scar. The Englishman's face changed color. For a few seconds, I thought he was going to ask me to leave. Finally he said, in a normal voice, "I'll tell you the story of my wound on one condition: that you do not minimize the opprobrium[8] it calls forth, that you not belittle a single infamous circumstance."

I agreed. And this, then, is the story he recounted, in a mixture of English, Spanish, and Portuguese:

About 1922, in a city in Connaught,[9] I was one of many men conspiring for Irish independence. Of my comrades, some survived to engage in peaceful pursuits; others, paradoxically, fight in the desert and at sea under the English colors; another, the man of greatest worth, died in the courtyard of a barracks, at dawn, before a firing squad of soldiers drowsy with sleep; still others (not the most unfortunate ones) met their fate in the anonymous and nearly secret battles of the civil war. We were Republicans, Catholics; we were, I suspect, romantics. For us, Ireland was not only the utopian[10] future and the intolerable present; it was a bitter and loving mythology, it was the circular towers and red bogs, it was the repudiation of Parnell[11] and the enormous epics which sing of the theft of bulls who in a former incarnation were heroes and in others were fish and mountains. . . . On one evening I shall never forget, we were joined by a comrade from Munster: a certain John Vincent Moon.

He was scarcely twenty years old. He was thin and soft at the same time. He gave one the uncomfortable impression of being invertebrate. He had studied, with fervor and vanity, every page of some communist manual or other; dialectic materialism[12] served him as a means to end any and all discussion. The reasons that one man may have to abominate another, or love him, are infinite: Moon reduced universal history to a sordid economic conflict. He asserted that the revolution is predestined to triumph. I told him that only lost causes can interest a gentleman. . . . By then it was nighttime. We continued our disagreements along the corridor, down the stairs, into the vague streets. The judgments emitted by Moon impressed me less than their unattractive and apodictic[13] tone. The new comrade did not argue: he passed judgment with obvious disdain and a certain fury.

As we came to the outlying houses, a sud-

---

7. interlocutor (in' tər läk' yo͞o tər): one who takes part in a conversation; talker; interpreter.

8. opprobrium (ə prō' brē əm): scorn or contempt, especially involving condemnation.

9. Connaught (kä' nôt).

10. utopian (yo͞o tō' pē ən): based on ideas of perfection in social and political organization.

11. Parnell: Charles Stewart Parnell, advocate of home rule for Ireland.

12. dialectic materialism (dī ə lek' tik): philosophy developed by Karl Marx.

13. apodictic (ap' ə dik' tik): involving or expressing necessary truth; absolutely certain.

den exchange of gunfire caught us by surprise. (Just before or after, we skirted the blank wall of a factory or barracks.) We took refuge along a dirt road; a soldier, looming gigantic in the glare, rushed out of a burning cabin. He shrieked at us and ordered us to halt. I pressed on; my comrade did not follow me. I turned back; John Vincent Moon was frozen in his tracks, fascinated and eternalized, as it were, by terror. I rushed to his side, brought down the soldier with a single blow, shook and pounded Vincent Moon, berated him, and ordered him to follow me. I was forced to yank him by his arm; a passionate fear paralyzed him. We fled through a night suddenly shot through with blazes. A burst of rifle fire sought us out; a bullet grazed Moon's right shoulder; while we ran among the pines, he broke into feeble sobbing.

During that autumn of 1922, I had taken refuge in a country house belonging to General Berkeley. This officer (whom I had never seen) was carrying out some administrative assignment in Bengal. His house, though it was less than a hundred years old, was dark and deteriorated and abounded in perplexing corridors and vain antechambers. A museum and an enormous library usurped the ground floor: controversial and incompatible books which, somehow, make up the history of the nineteenth century; scimitars from Nishapur,[14] in whose arrested circular arcs the wind and violence of battle seem to last. We entered (I seem to remember) through the back part of the house. Moon, his lips dry and quivering, muttered that the events of the evening had been very interesting. I dressed his wound and brought him a cup of tea. (His "wound," I saw, was superficial.) Suddenly he stammered perplexedly, "But you took a considerable chance."

I told him not to worry. (The routine of the civil war had impelled me to act as I had acted. Besides, the capture of a single one of our men could have compromised our cause.)

The following day Moon had recovered his aplomb.[15] He accepted a cigarette and severely cross-questioned me concerning "the economic resources of our revolutionary party." His questions were quite lucid. I told him (in all truth) that the situation was serious. Shattering volleys of rifle fire reverberated in the south. I told Moon that our comrades expected us. My trench coat and revolver were in my room; when I returned, I found Moon stretched on the sofa, his eyes shut. He thought he had fever; he spoke of a painful shoulder spasm.

I realized then that his cowardice was irreparable. I awkwardly urged him to take care of himself and took my leave. I blushed for this fearful man, as if I, and not Vincent Moon, were the coward. What one man does is something done, in some measure, by all men. For that reason, a disobedience committed in a garden contaminates the human race; for that reason, it is not unjust that the crucifixion of a single Jew suffices to save it. Perhaps Schopenhauer is right: I am all others, any man is all men, Shakespeare is in some way the wretched John Vincent Moon.

We spent nine days in the enormous house of the general. Of the agony and splendor of the battle I shall say nothing: my intention is to tell the story of this scar which affronts me. In my memory, those nine days form a single day; except for the next to the last, when our men rushed a barracks and we were able to avenge, man for man, the sixteen comrades who had been machine-gunned at Elphin. I would slip out of the house toward dawn, in the confusion of the morning twilight. I was back by dusk. My companion would be waiting for me upstairs: his wound did not allow him to come down to meet me. I can see him

---

14. **Nishapur** (ni′ shə po͞or).
15. **aplomb** (ə pläm′): poise; composure.

with some book of strategy in his hand: F. N. Maude or Clausewitz.[16] "The artillery is my preferred arm," he conceded one night. He would inquire into our plans; he liked to censure or revamp them. He was also in the habit of denouncing our "deplorable economic base." Dogmatic and somber, he would prophesy a ruinous end. *C'est une affaire flambee*,[17] he would murmur. In order to show that his being a physical coward made no difference to him, he increased his intellectual arrogance. Thus, for better or for worse, passed nine days.

On the tenth, the city definitively fell into the hands of the Black and Tans. Tall, silent horsemen patrolled the streets. The wind was filled with ashes and smoke. At an intersection in the middle of a square, I saw a corpse—less tenacious in my memory than a manikin—upon which some soldiers interminably practiced their marksmanship. . . . I had left my quarters as the sunrise hung in the sky. I returned before midday. In the library, Moon was talking to someone; by his tone of voice I realized that he was using the telephone. Then I heard my name; then that I would return at seven; then the suggestion that I be arrested as I crossed the garden. My reasonable friend was selling me reasonably. I heard him requesting certain guarantees of personal security.

At this point my story becomes confused, its thread is lost. I know I pursued the informer down the dark corridors of nightmare and the deep stairs of vertigo.[18] Moon had come to know the house very well, much better than I. Once or twice I lost him. I cornered him before the soldiers arrested me. From one of the general's mounted sets of arms I snatched down a cutlass; with the steel half-moon I sealed his face, forever, with a half-moon of blood. Borges, I have confessed this to you, a stranger. *Your* contempt will not wound me as much.

Here the narrator stopped. I noticed that his hands were trembling.

"And Moon?" I asked him.

"He was paid the Judas-money and fled to Brazil. And that afternoon, he watched some drunks in an impromptu firing squad in the town square shoot down a manikin."

I waited in vain for him to go on with his story. At length I asked him to continue.

A sob shook his body. And then, with feeble sweetness, he pointed to the white arced scar.

"You don't believe me?" he stammered. "Don't you see the mark of infamy[19] written on my face? I told you the story the way I did so that you would hear it to the end. I informed on the man who took me in: I am Vincent Moon. Despise me."

---

16. Clausewitz (klɑu′ zə wits).

17. *C'est une affaire flambée* (set ün à fer′ flän be′) *French*: idiom meaning "It is a lost cause."

18. vertigo (vʉr′ ti gō′): a condition in which one has the feeling of whirling, causing imbalance; a dizzy, confused state of mind.

19. infamy (in′ fə mē): disgrace, especially when it is widely known and involves well-deserved and extreme contempt; notoriety.

Sparking
the Imagination

A flight of the imagination." This phrase is as familiar as "a flock of geese" or "a bouquet of flowers." Ordinary life may be a matter of walking, running, or crawling, but the life of the imagination allows people to soar over and beyond the world they know. Through imagination, they push back the limits of experience, exploring what might be or what might have been. They go not only faster but farther than they could on the feet of realism.

The imaginative works in this section of the book can be classified as fantasy, literature that consciously disregards the restraints of reality. Some works of fantasy create fabulous dream worlds; others introduce unbelievable elements into a mostly realistic world. Fantasy presents a challenge to readers, who are asked to accept, without question, impossible occurrences. In a fantasy, narration is often ambiguous, leaving readers unsure of what happens at the end of a story or even what is happening throughout. But when the imagination is engaged, readers readily take up the challenge.

What good fantasy literature does is sidestep questions about accuracy and clarity to explore more tantalizing questions: What is reality? What are our hidden desires and capabilities? What does a pair of socks mean? What if . . . ? Let these works spark your imagination. And once it is sparked, let it fly.

Literary Vocabulary

INTRODUCED IN THIS SECTION

Style: Magical Realism. Style is the particular way that a piece of literature is written. Style refers not so much to what is said but to how it is said. Magical realism is a style of writing that often includes exaggeration, unusual humor, magical and bizarre events, dreams that come true, and superstitions that prove warranted. Magical realism differs from pure fantasy in combining fantastic elements with realistic elements such as recognizable characters, believable dialogue, a true-to-life setting, a matter-of-fact tone, and a plot that sometimes contains historic events.

Style: Diction. A significant component of style is diction, or a writer's choice of words. Diction encompasses both vocabulary (individual words) and syntax (the order or arrangement of words). Diction can be described in terms such as formal or informal, technical or common, abstract or concrete. In "Six Feet of the Country," for example, Nadine Gordimer uses informal diction to help portray the attitude of the narrator.

REVIEWED IN THIS SECTION

Plot Structure

Mood

Dialogue

The Night Face Up

JULIO CORTÁZAR   1914–1984   ARGENTINA

A biography of Cortázar appears on page 741.

Approaching the Story

Julio Cortázar (hōō′ lē ō kôr tä′ zər) is known for writing fantastic literature—fantastic in the sense of supernatural, uncanny, or weird. "Fantastic literature," he said, "is the most fictional of all literatures, given that by its own definition it consists of turning one's back on a reality universally accepted as normal." If "The Night Face Up" does not turn its back on reality, it certainly views reality with suspicion. Expect to feel unsure of your bearings as you read this story.

Building Vocabulary

These essential words are footnoted within the story.

solace (säl′ is): His single **solace** was to hear someone else confirm that the lights indeed had been in his favor. (page 693)

lucid (lōō′ sid): Completely **lucid,** . . . he gave his information to the officer. (page 693)

oblivion (ə bliv′ ē ən): He panted, looking for . . . **oblivion** for those images still glued to his eyelids. (page 697)

Connecting Writing and Reading

In your journal describe an experience of waking up from a vivid nightmare. What was frightening you in your dream? What made you realize that it was a dream and not reality? What were your feelings afterward? As you read this story, see whether the same sensations are felt by the main character as he moves between dream and reality.

**H**ALFWAY DOWN THE long hotel vestibule, he thought that probably he was going to be late, and hurried on into the street to get out his motorcycle from the corner where the next-door superintendent let him keep it. On the jewelry store at the corner, he read that it was ten to nine; he had time to spare. The sun filtered through the tall downtown buildings, and he—because for himself, for just going along thinking, he did not have a name—he swung onto the machine, savoring the idea of the ride. The motor whirred between his legs, and a cool wind whipped his pants legs.

He let the ministries[1] zip past (the pink, the white), and a series of stores on the main street, their windows flashing. Now he was beginning the most pleasant part of the run, the real ride: a long street bordered with trees, very little traffic, with spacious villas whose gardens rambled all the way down to the sidewalks, which were barely indicated by low hedges. A bit inattentive perhaps, but tooling along on the right side of the street, he allowed himself to be carried away by the freshness, by the weightless contraction of this hardly begun day. This involuntary relaxation, possibly, kept him from preventing the accident. When he saw that the woman standing on the corner had rushed into the crosswalk while he still had the green light, it was already somewhat too late for a simple solution. He braked hard with foot and hand, wrenching himself to the left; he heard the woman scream, and at the collision his vision went. It was like falling asleep all at once.

He came to abruptly. Four or five young men were getting him out from under the cycle. He felt the taste of salt and blood; one knee hurt, and when they hoisted him up, he yelped; he couldn't bear the pressure on his right arm. Voices which did not seem to belong to the faces hanging above him encouraged him cheerfully with jokes and assurances. His single solace[2] was to hear someone else confirm that the lights indeed had been in his favor. He asked about the woman, trying to keep down the nausea which was edging up into his throat. While they carried him face up to a nearby pharmacy, he learned that the cause of the accident had gotten only a few scrapes on the legs. "Nah, you barely got her at all, but when ya hit, the impact made the machine jump and flop on its side. . . ." Opinions, recollections of other smashups, take it easy, work him in shoulders first, there, that's fine, and someone in a dustcoat giving him a swallow of something soothing in the shadowy interior of the small local pharmacy.

Within five minutes the police ambulance arrived, and they lifted him onto a cushioned stretcher. It was a relief for him to be able to lie out flat. Completely lucid[3] but realizing that he was suffering the effects of a terrible shock, he gave his information to the officer riding in the ambulance with him. The arm almost didn't hurt; blood dripped down from a cut over the eyebrow all over his face. He licked his lips once or twice to drink it. He felt pretty good; it had been an accident, tough luck; stay quiet a few weeks, nothing worse. The guard said that the motorcycle didn't seem badly racked up. "Why should it," he replied. "It all landed on top of me." They both laughed, and when they got to the hospital, the guard shook his hand and wished him luck. Now the nausea was coming back little by little; meanwhile they were pushing him on a wheeled stretcher toward a pavilion farther back; rolling along under trees full of birds, he shut his eyes and

---

1. ministries (min′ is trēz): the headquarters for various government departments.
2. solace (säl′ is): something that comforts or relieves.
3. lucid (lōō′ sid): clearheaded; rational.

wished he were asleep or chloroformed. But they kept him for a good while in a room with that hospital smell, filling out a form, getting his clothes off, and dressing him in a stiff, grayish smock. They moved his arm carefully; it didn't hurt him. The nurses were constantly making wisecracks, and if it hadn't been for the stomach contractions, he would have felt fine, almost happy.

They got him over to X-ray, and twenty minutes later, with the still-damp negative lying on his chest like a black tombstone, they pushed him into surgery. Someone tall and thin in white came over and began to look at the X-rays. A woman's hands were arranging his head; he felt that they were moving him from one stretcher to another. The man in white came over to him again, smiling; something gleamed in his right hand. He patted his cheek and made a sign to someone stationed behind.

It was unusual as a dream because it was full of smells, and he never dreamt smells. First a marshy smell, there to the left of the trail the swamps began already, the quaking bogs[4] from which no one ever returned. But the reek lifted, and instead there came a dark, fresh composite fragrance, like the night under which he moved, in flight from the Aztecs. And it was all so natural, he had to run from the Aztecs who had set out on their manhunt, and his sole chance was to find a place to hide in the deepest part of the forest, taking care not to lose the narrow trail which only they, the Motecas,[5] knew.

What tormented him the most was the odor, as though, notwithstanding the absolute acceptance of the dream, there was something which resisted that which was not habitual, which until that point had not participated in the game. "It smells of war," he thought, his hand going instinctively to the stone knife which was tucked at an angle into his girdle of woven wool. An unexpected sound made him crouch suddenly stock-still and shaking. To be afraid was nothing strange, there was plenty of fear in his dreams. He waited, covered by the branches of a shrub and the starless night. Far off, probably on the other side of the big lake, they'd be lighting the bivouac fires; that part of the sky had a reddish glare. The sound was not repeated. It had been like a broken limb. Maybe an animal that, like himself, was escaping from the smell of war. He stood erect slowly, sniffing the air. Not a sound could be heard, but the fear was still following, as was the smell, that cloying incense of the war of the blossom.[6] He had to press forward, to stay out of the bogs and get to the heart of the forest. Groping uncertainly through the dark, stooping every other moment to touch the packed earth of the trail, he took a few steps. He would have liked to have broken into a run, but the gurgling fens[7] lapped on either side of him. On the path and in darkness, he took his bearings. Then he caught a horrible blast of that foul smell he was most afraid of, and leaped forward desperately.

"You're going to fall off the bed," said the patient next to him. "Stop bouncing around, old buddy."

He opened his eyes and it was afternoon, the sun already low in the oversized windows of the long ward. While trying to smile at his neighbor, he detached himself almost physically from the final scene of the nightmare. His arm, in a plaster cast, hung suspended from an apparatus with weights and pulleys. He felt thirsty, as though he'd been running for miles, but they didn't want to give him much water,

---

4. quaking bogs: areas of wet, spongy ground, probably containing quicksand.

5. Motecas (mō te′ käs).

6. war of the blossom: the name the Aztecs gave to a ritual war in which they took prisoners for sacrifice.

7. fens: low, flat, marshy lands.

barely enough to moisten his lips and make a mouthful. The fever was winning slowly and he would have been able to sleep again, but he was enjoying the pleasure of keeping awake, eyes half-closed, listening to the other patients' conversation, answering a question from time to time. He saw a little white push-cart come up beside the bed; a blond nurse rubbed the front of his thigh with alcohol and stuck him with a fat needle connected to a tube which ran up to a bottle filled with milky, opalescent liquid. A young intern arrived with some metal and leather apparatus which he adjusted to fit onto the good arm to check something or other. Night fell, and the fever went along dragging him down softly to a state in which things seemed embossed as through opera glasses;[8] they were real and soft and, at the same time, vaguely distasteful; like sitting in a boring movie and thinking that, well, still, it'd be worse out in the street, and staying.

A cup of marvelous golden broth came, smelling of leeks, celery, and parsley. A small hunk of bread, more precious than a whole banquet, found itself crumbling little by little. His arm hardly hurt him at all, and only in the eyebrow where they'd taken stitches a quick, hot pain sizzled occasionally. When the big windows across the way turned to smudges of dark blue, he thought it would not be difficult for him to sleep. Still on his back so a little uncomfortable, running his tongue out over his hot, too-dry lips, he tasted the broth still, and with a sigh of bliss, he let himself drift off.

First there was a confusion, as of one drawing all his sensations, for that moment blunted or muddled, into himself. He realized that he was running in pitch darkness, although, above, the sky crisscrossed with treetops was less black than the rest. "The trail," he thought. "I've gotten off the trail." His feet sank into a bed of leaves and mud, and then he couldn't take a step that the branches of shrubs did not whiplash against his ribs and legs. Out of breath, knowing despite the darkness and silence that he was surrounded, he crouched down to listen. Maybe the trail was very near, with the first daylight he would be able to see it again. Nothing now could help him to find it. The hand that unconsciously gripped the haft of the dagger climbed like a fen scorpion up to his neck, where the protecting amulet hung. Barely moving his lips, he mumbled the supplication of the corn which brings about the beneficent moons, and the prayer to Her Very Highness, to the distributor of all Motecan possessions. At the same time he felt his ankles sinking deeper into the mud, and the waiting in the darkness of the obscure grove of live oak grew intolerable to him. The war of the blossom had started at the beginning of the moon and had been going on for three days and three nights now. If he managed to hide in the depths of the forest, getting off the trail farther up past the marsh country, perhaps the warriors wouldn't follow his track. He thought of the many prisoners they'd already taken. But the number didn't count, only the consecrated period. The hunt would continue until the priests gave the sign to return. Everything had its number and its limit, and it was within the sacred period, and he on the other side from the hunters.

He heard the cries and leaped up, knife in hand. As if the sky were aflame on the horizon, he saw torches moving among the branches, very near him. The smell of war was unbearable, and when the first enemy jumped him, leaped at his throat, he felt an almost-pleasure in sinking the stone blade flat to the haft[9] into his chest. The lights were already around him, the happy cries. He managed to cut the air once or twice, then a rope snared him from behind.

---

8. opera glasses: small binoculars.
9. haft: the hilt, or handle, of a knife.

"It's the fever," the man in the next bed said. "The same thing happened to me when they operated on my duodenum. Take some water; you'll see, you'll sleep all right."

Laid next to the night from which he came back, the tepid shadow of the ward seemed delicious to him. A violet lamp kept watch high on the far wall like a guardian eye. You could hear coughing, deep breathing, once in a while a conversation in whispers. Everything was pleasant and secure, without the chase, no . . . But he didn't want to go on thinking about the nightmare. There were lots of things to amuse himself with. He began to look at the cast on his arm, and the pulleys that held it so comfortably in the air. They'd left a bottle of mineral water on the night table beside him. He put the neck of the bottle to his mouth and drank it like a precious liqueur. He could now make out the different shapes in the ward, the thirty beds, the closets with glass doors. He guessed that his fever was down, his face felt cool. The cut over the eyebrow barely hurt at all, like a recollection. He saw himself leaving the hotel again, wheeling out the cycle. Who'd have thought that it would end like this? He tried to fix the moment of the accident exactly, and it got him very angry to notice that there was a void there, an emptiness he could not manage to fill. Between the impact and the moment that they picked him up off the pavement, the passing out or what went on, there was nothing he could see. And at the same time he had the feeling that this void, this nothingness, had lasted an eternity. No, not even time, more as if, in this void, he had passed across something, or had run back immense distances. The shock, the brutal dashing against the pavement. Anyway, he had felt an immense relief in coming out of the black pit while the people were lifting him off the ground. With pain in the broken arm, blood from the split eyebrow, contusion on the knee; with all that, a relief in returning to daylight, to the day, and to feel sustained and attended. That was weird. Someday he'd ask the doctor at the office about that. Now sleep began to take over again, to pull him slowly down. The pillow was so soft, and the coolness of the mineral water soothed his fevered throat. The violet light of the lamp up there was beginning to get dimmer and dimmer.

As he was sleeping on his back, the position in which he came to did not surprise him, but on the other hand the damp smell, the smell of oozing rock, blocked his throat and forced him to understand. Open the eyes and look in all directions, hopeless. He was surrounded by an absolute darkness. Tried to get up and felt ropes pinning his wrists and ankles. He was staked to the ground on a floor of dank, icy stone slabs. The cold bit into his naked back, his legs. Dully, he tried to touch the amulet with his chin and found they had stripped him of it. Now he was lost; no prayer could save him from the final . . . From afar off, as though filtering through the rock of the dungeon, he heard the great kettledrums of the feast. They had carried him to the temple, he was in the underground cells of Teocalli[10] itself, awaiting his turn.

He heard a yell, a hoarse yell that rocked off the walls. Another yell, ending in a moan. It was he who was screaming in the darkness; he was screaming because he was alive, his whole body with that cry fended off what was coming, the inevitable end. He thought of his friends filling up the other dungeons and of those already walking up the stairs of the sacrifice. He uttered another choked cry; he could barely open his mouth, his jaws were twisted back as if with a rope and a stick, and once in a while they would open slowly with an endless exertion, as if they were made of rubber. The creaking of the wooden latches jolted him

---

10. Teocalli (tā ô kä′ yē): the great temple of the Aztecs.

like a whip. Rent, writhing, he fought to rid himself of the cords sinking into his flesh. His right arm, the strongest, strained until the pain became unbearable, and he had to give up. He watched the double door open, and the smell of the torches reached him before the light did. Barely girdled by the ceremonial loincloths, the priests' acolytes[11] moved in his direction, looking at him with contempt. Lights reflected off the sweaty torsos and off the black hair dressed with feathers. The cords went slack, and in their place the grappling of hot hands, hard as bronze; he felt himself lifted, still face up, and jerked along by the four acolytes who carried him down the passageway. The torchbearers went ahead, indistinctly lighting up the corridor with its dripping walls and a ceiling so low that the acolytes had to duck their heads. Now they were taking him out, taking him out, it was the end. Face up under a mile of living rock which, for a succession of moments, was lit up by a glimmer of torchlight. When the stars came out up there instead of the roof and the great terraced steps rose before him, on fire with cries and dances, it would be the end. The passage was never going to end, but now it was beginning to end, he would see suddenly the open sky full of stars, but not yet, they trundled him along endlessly in the reddish shadow, hauling him roughly along and he did not want that, but how to stop it if they had torn off the amulet, his real heart, the life center.

In a single jump he came out into the hospital night, to the high, gentle, bare ceiling, to the soft shadow wrapping him round. He thought he must have cried out, but his neighbors were peacefully snoring. The water in the bottle on the night table was somewhat bubbly, a translucent shape against the dark azure shadow of the windows. He panted, looking for some relief for his lungs, oblivion[12] for those images still glued to his eyelids. Each time he shut his eyes he saw them take shape instantly, and he sat up, completely wrung out but savoring at the same time the surety that now he was awake, that the night nurse would answer if he rang, that soon it would be daybreak, with the good, deep sleep he usually had at that hour, no images, no nothing . . . It was difficult to keep his eyes open; the drowsiness was more powerful than he. He made one last effort; he sketched a gesture toward the bottle of water with his good hand and did not manage to reach it; his fingers closed again on a black emptiness, and the passageway went on endlessly, rock after rock, with momentary ruddy flares, and face up he choked out a dull moan because the roof was about to end, it rose, was opening like a mouth of shadow, and the acolytes straightened up, and from on high a waning moon fell on a face whose eyes wanted not to see it, were closing and opening desperately, trying to pass to the other side, to find again the bare, protecting ceiling of the ward. And every time they opened, it was night and the moon, while they climbed the great terraced steps, his head hanging down backward now, and up at the top were the bonfires, red columns of perfumed smoke, and suddenly he saw the red stone, shiny with the blood dripping off it, and the spinning arcs cut by the feet of the victim whom they pulled off to throw him rolling down the north steps. With a last hope he shut his lids tightly, moaning to wake up. For a second he thought he had gotten there, because once more he was immobile in the bed, except that his head was hanging down off it, swinging. But he smelled death, and when he opened his eyes he saw the blood-soaked figure of the executioner-priest coming toward him with the stone knife in his hand. He managed to close his eyelids again, although he knew now he was not going to

---

11. acolytes (ak′ ə līts): attendants.
12. oblivion (ə bliv′ ē ən): the condition of being forgotten.

wake up, that he was awake, that the marvelous dream had been the other, absurd as all dreams are—a dream in which he was going through the strange avenues of an astonishing city, with green and red lights that burned without fire or smoke, on an enormous metal insect that whirred away between his legs. In the infinite lie of the dream, they had also picked him up off the ground, someone had approached him also with a knife in his hand, approached him who was lying face up, face up with his eyes closed between the bonfires on the steps.

Thinking About the Story

A PERSONAL RESPONSE

sharing impressions

1. What one word best describes the ending of this story? Record this word in your journal.

constructing interpretations

2. How do you explain the ending of this story? State what you think is reality.

Think about
- the possible effects of shock, fever, and pain-killing drugs on the main character's perceptions
- the main character's feeling that "he had passed across something, or had run back immense distances"
- his sensation of being again in his hospital bed but with his head hanging down, swinging
- his belief that he is not going to wake up and that his life in the city had been a dream

3. Recall what you wrote about waking from a nightmare. Compare your sensations to the sensations of the main character as he moves between dream and reality.

4. What parallels do you see between the main character's experiences in the modern world and the Aztec world?

A CREATIVE RESPONSE

5. If the main character's nightmares had begun when he was healthy, before his accident, how would your interpretation of the story have been affected?

6. Evaluate the writer's use of imagery in this story.

Think about
- imagery as words and phrases that appeal to the five senses
- how the imagery affects your perception of the main character
- how the imagery affects your view of the reality of the two worlds

7. Critic Alberto Manguel describes fantastic literature in the following way: "It makes use of our everyday world as a facade through which the undefinable appears. . . . Fantastic literature deals with what can be best defined as the impossible seeping into the possible. . . . Fantastic literature never really explains anything. . . . Fantastic literature thrives on surprise, on the unexpected logic that is born from its own rules." How does "The Night Face Up" illustrate these qualities?

Analyzing the Writer's Craft

PLOT STRUCTURE

Are the events in this story presented in a way that you are accustomed to?

Building a Literary Vocabulary. As you know, plot refers to the actions and events in a literary work. The plot moves forward because of a conflict, or struggle between opposing forces. In a traditional narrative, plot structure consists of the exposition, the rising action, the climax, and the falling action. The exposition lays the groundwork for the narrative and provides necessary background information. During the rising action, complications of the conflict build to a climax, or turning point. Interest and intensity reach their peak at this point. Following the climax is the falling action, which shows the results of the major events and resolves outstanding questions.

Application: Analyzing Plot Structure. As a class, discuss whether this story has a traditional plot structure. Consider the following questions in your discussion: What is the conflict? What do you learn in the exposition? Where does the rising action begin? What is the climax, and where does it occur? Is there falling action that shows how the conflict has been resolved?

Connecting Reading and Writing

1. Rewrite a section of this story as a **screenplay** for an episode of *The Twilight Zone.*

Option: Create a set of **comic-book panels** to retell part of this story.

2. Do research on the Aztec practice of ritual human sacrifice. In a **letter** to Cortázar, discuss how accurately you think he depicts this practice.

Option: Imagine that you are an archaeologist who specializes in ancient Aztec culture. Write a **note** to a fellow archaeologist commenting on the accuracy of Cortázar's portrayal of this culture.

3. Compare this story with another story in which time and reality are distorted—for example Daphne du Maurier's "Split Second," Ray Bradbury's "The Dragon," or Ambrose Bierce's "An Occurrence at Owl Creek Bridge." Evaluate the two stories on a **rating form** with categories for character development, vividness of setting, plot coherence, and thematic richness. Be prepared to support your ratings with specific comments on the two stories.

Option: Compare the stories in a **review** for a magazine devoted to literature of the fantastic.

4. Write a **narrative sketch** based on the experience of dreaming and waking that you wrote about in prereading. You might borrow techniques used in "The Night Face Up." Share your sketch with a friend.

Option: As an assignment for a film class, write a **synopsis** of a film based on your experience.

The Handsomest Drowned Man in the World

GABRIEL GARCÍA MÁRQUEZ born 1928 COLOMBIA

A biography of García Márquez appears on page 743.

Approaching the Story

Winner of the 1982 Nobel Prize in literature, Gabriel García Márquez (gä' vrē el' gär *s*ē' ä mär' kes) is known throughout the world for a style called magical realism, which blends elements of fantasy with facts of everyday life. In his novels and short stories, anything can happen—angels fall from the sky, pious young women ascend into heaven, dictators live for two hundred years. Yet the works themselves are set in a gritty, realistic world of poverty and violence, salt air and rust. "The Handsomest Drowned Man in the World" starts with an apparently straightforward event: a drowned man washes ashore on the beach of a barren Colombian fishing village. It then moves into a reality that challenges the imagination.

Building Vocabulary

These essential words are footnoted within the story.

destitute (des' tə tōōt'): They wept so much, for he was the most **destitute,** most peaceful, and most obliging man on earth. (page 705)

promontory (präm' ən tôr' ē): Pointing to the **promontory** of roses on the horizon, he would say, . . . *look there.* (page 706)

Connecting Writing and Reading

Think of someone whom you admire but do not know. The person might be someone at school, a historical figure, or a celebrity such as a rock star, a movie star, or a political leader. In your journal list words and phrases that describe what you imagine this person to be like. As you read the story, compare the imagined qualities you identified with the qualities attributed to the drowned man.

The Handsomest Drowned Man in the World

THE FIRST CHILDREN who saw the dark and slinky bulge approaching through the sea let themselves think it was an enemy ship. Then they saw it had no flags or masts and they thought it was a whale. But when it washed up on the beach, they removed the clumps of seaweed, the jellyfish tentacles, and the remains of fish and flotsam, and only then did they see that it was a drowned man.

They had been playing with him all afternoon, burying him in the sand and digging him up again, when someone chanced to see them and spread the alarm in the village. The men who carried him to the nearest house noticed that he weighed more than any dead man they had ever known, almost as much as a horse, and they said to each other that maybe he'd been floating too long and the water had got into his bones. When they laid him on the floor, they said he'd been taller than all other men because there was barely enough room for him in the house, but they thought that maybe the ability to keep on growing after death was part of the nature of certain drowned men. He had the smell of the sea about him, and only his shape gave one to suppose that it was the corpse of a human being, because the skin was covered with a crust of mud and scales.

They did not even have to clean off his face to know that the dead man was a stranger. The village was made up of only twenty-odd wooden houses that had stone courtyards with no flowers and which were spread about on the end of a desertlike cape. There was so little land that mothers always went about with the fear that the wind would carry off their children, and the few dead that the years had caused among them had to be thrown off the cliffs. But the sea was calm and bountiful, and all the men fit into seven boats. So when they found the drowned man they simply had to look at one another to see that they were all there.

That night they did not go out to work at sea. While the men went to find out if anyone was missing in neighboring villages, the women stayed behind to care for the drowned man. They took the mud off with grass swabs, they removed the underwater stones entangled in his hair, and they scraped the crust off with tools used for scaling fish. As they were doing that, they noticed that the vegetation on him came from faraway oceans and deep water and that his clothes were in tatters, as if he had sailed through labyrinths of coral. They noticed too that he bore his death with pride, for he did not have the lonely look of other drowned men who came out of the sea or that haggard, needy look of men who drowned in rivers. But only when they finished cleaning him off did they become aware of the kind of man he was, and it left them breathless. Not only was he the tallest, strongest, most virile, and best-built man they had ever seen, but even though they were looking at him there was no room for him in their imagination.

They could not find a bed in the village large enough to lay him on, nor was there a table solid enough to use for his wake. The tallest men's holiday pants would not fit him, nor the fattest ones' Sunday shirts, nor the shoes of the one with the biggest feet. Fascinated by his huge size and his beauty, the women then decided to make some pants from a large piece of sail and a shirt from some bridal Brabant[1] linen so that he could continue through his death with dignity. As they sewed, sitting in a circle and gazing at the corpse between stitches, it seemed to them that the wind had never been so steady nor the sea so restless as on that night, and they supposed that the change had something to do with the dead man. They thought that if that magnificent man had lived in the village, his house would have had the widest doors, the highest ceiling, and the strongest floor; his bedstead would have been made from a midship frame held together by iron bolts, and his wife would have been the happiest woman. They thought that he would have had so much authority that he could have drawn fish out of the sea simply by calling their names and that he would have put so much work into his land that springs would have burst forth from among the rocks so that he would have been able to plant flowers on the cliffs. They secretly compared him to their own men, thinking that for all their lives theirs were incapable of doing what he could do in one night, and they ended up dismissing them deep in their hearts as the weakest, meanest, and most useless creatures on earth. They were wandering through that maze of fantasy when the oldest woman, who as the oldest had looked upon the drowned man with more compassion than passion, sighed:

"He has the face of someone called Esteban."[2]

It was true. Most of them had only to take another look at him to see that he could not have any other name. The more stubborn among them, who were the youngest, still lived for a few hours with the illusion that when they put his clothes on and he lay among the flowers in patent leather shoes his name might be Lautaro.[3] But it was a vain illusion. There had not been enough canvas, the poorly cut and worse-sewn pants were too tight, and the hidden strength of his heart popped the buttons on his shirt. After midnight the whistling of the wind died down, and the sea fell into its Wednesday drowsiness.[4] The silence put an end to any last doubts: he was Esteban. The women who had dressed him, who had combed his hair, had cut his nails and shaved him were unable to hold back a shudder of pity when they had to resign themselves to his being dragged along the ground. It was then that they understood how unhappy he must have been with that huge body, since it bothered him even after death. They could see him in life, condemned to going through doors sideways, cracking his head on crossbeams, remaining on his feet during visits, not knowing what to do with his soft, pink, sea lion hands while the lady of the house looked for her most resistant chair and begged him, frightened to death, *sit here, Esteban, please*, and he, leaning against the wall, smiling, *don't bother, ma'am, I'm fine where I am*, his heels raw and his back roasted from having done the same thing so many times whenever he paid a visit, *don't bother, ma'am, I'm fine where I am*, just to avoid the embarrassment of breaking up the chair, and

---

1. Brabant (brä′ bänt).

2. Esteban (es te′ bän).

3. Lautaro (lou tä′ rô̄): the name of a Chilean Indian who became a national hero for leading an uprising against the Spanish in the sixteenth century.

4. Wednesday drowsiness (and later **Wednesday meat** and **Wednesday dead body**): an idiom peculiar to this type of fishing community. *Wednesday* can be considered to mean roughly "tiresome." The fishermen regularly returned from the sea on Thursday; therefore, by Wednesday people were running out of food, and the day offered little in the way of excitement or interest.

Dead Peasant, 1939, JOSE CHAVEZ MORADO.
The Art Institute of Chicago; William McCallin McKee Memorial Collection.

never knowing perhaps that the ones who said *don't go, Esteban, at least wait till the coffee's ready*, were the ones who later on would whisper *the big boob finally left, how nice, the handsome fool has gone*. That was what the women were thinking beside the body a little before dawn. Later, when they covered his face with a handkerchief so that the light would not bother him, he looked so forever dead, so defenseless, so much like their men that the first furrows of tears opened in their hearts. It was one of the younger ones who began the weeping. The others, coming to, went from sighs to wails, and the more they sobbed, the more they felt like weeping, because the drowned man was becoming all the more Esteban for them, and so they wept so much, for he was the most <u>destitute</u>,[5] most peaceful, and most obliging man on earth, poor Esteban. So when the men returned with the news that the drowned man was not from the neighboring villages either, the women felt an opening of jubilation in the midst of their tears.

"Praise the Lord," they sighed, "he's ours!"

The men thought the fuss was only womanish frivolity. Fatigued because of the difficult nighttime inquiries, all they wanted was to get rid of the bother of the newcomer once and for all before the sun grew strong on that arid, windless day. They improvised a litter with the remains of foremasts and gaffs, tying it together with rigging so that it would bear the weight of the body until they reached the cliffs. They wanted to tie the anchor from a cargo ship to him so that he would sink easily into the deepest waves, where fish are blind and divers die of nostalgia and bad currents would not bring him back to shore, as had happened with other bodies. But the more they hurried, the more the women thought of ways to waste time. They walked about like startled hens, pecking with the sea charms on their breasts, some interfering on one side to put a scapular[6] of the good wind on the drowned man, some on the

other side to put a wrist compass on him, and after a great deal of *get away from there, woman, stay out of the way, look, you almost made me fall on top of the dead man*, the men began to feel mistrust in their livers and started grumbling about why so many main-altar decorations for a stranger, because no matter how many nails and holy-water jars he had on him, the sharks would chew him all the same, but the women kept on piling on their junk relics, running back and forth, stumbling, while they released in sighs what they did not in tears, so that the men finally exploded with *since when has there ever been such a fuss over a drifting corpse, a drowned nobody, a piece of cold Wednesday meat*. One of the women, mortified by so much lack of care, then removed the handkerchief from the dead man's face, and the men were left breathless too.

He was Esteban. It was not necessary to repeat it for them to recognize him. If they had been told Sir Walter Raleigh, even they might have been impressed with his gringo[7] accent, the macaw on his shoulder, his cannibal-killing blunderbuss, but there could be only one Esteban in the world, and there he was, stretched out like a sperm whale, shoeless, wearing the pants of an undersized child, and with those stony nails that had to be cut with a knife. They had only to take the handkerchief off his face to see that he was ashamed, that it was not his fault that he was so big or so heavy or so handsome, and if he had known that this was going to happen, he would have

---

5. destitute (des′ tə tōōt′): living in complete poverty.
6. scapular (skap′ yə lər): two pieces of cloth joined together by strings, worn on the chest and back by some Roman Catholics as a token of religious devotion.
7. gringo (griŋ′ gō): in Latin America, that of a foreigner, especially a person from the United States or England.

looked for a more discreet place to drown in; seriously, I even would have tied the anchor off a galleon around my neck and staggered off a cliff like someone who doesn't like things in order not to be upsetting people now with this Wednesday dead body, as you people say, in order not to be bothering anyone with this filthy piece of cold meat that doesn't have anything to do with me. There was so much truth in his manner that even the most mistrustful men, the ones who felt the bitterness of endless nights at sea fearing that their women would tire of dreaming about them and begin to dream of drowned men, even they and others who were harder still shuddered in the marrow of their bones at Esteban's sincerity.

That was how they came to hold the most splendid funeral they could conceive of for an abandoned drowned man. Some women who had gone to get flowers in the neighboring villages returned with other women who could not believe what they had been told, and those women went back for more flowers when they saw the dead man, and they brought more and more until there were so many flowers and so many people that it was hard to walk about. At the final moment it pained them to return him to the waters as an orphan, and they chose a father and mother from among the best people, and aunts and uncles and cousins, so that through him all the inhabitants of the village became kinsmen. Some sailors who heard the weeping from a distance went off course, and people heard of one who had himself tied to the mainmast, remembering ancient fables about sirens.[8]

While they fought for the privilege of carrying him on their shoulders along the steep escarpment by the cliffs, men and women became aware for the first time of the desolation of their streets, the dryness of their courtyards, the narrowness of their dreams as they faced the splendor and beauty of their drowned man. They let him go without an anchor so that he could come back if he wished and whenever he wished, and they all held their breath for the fraction of centuries the body took to fall into the abyss. They did not need to look at one another to realize that they were no longer all present, that they would never be. But they also knew that everything would be different from then on, that their houses would have wider doors, higher ceilings, and stronger floors so that Esteban's memory could go everywhere without bumping into beams and so that no one in the future would dare whisper *the big boob finally died, too bad, the handsome fool has finally died*, because they were going to paint their house fronts gay colors to make Esteban's memory eternal, and they were going to break their backs digging for springs among the stones and planting flowers on the cliffs so that in future years at dawn the passengers on great liners would awaken, suffocated by the smell of gardens on the high seas, and the captain would have to come down from the bridge in his dress uniform, with his astrolabe,[9] his pole star, and his row of war medals and, pointing to the promontory[10] of roses on the horizon, he would say in fourteen languages, *look there, where the wind is so peaceful now that it's gone to sleep beneath the beds, over there, where the sun's so bright that the sunflowers don't know which way to turn, yes, over there, that's Esteban's village.*

---

8. ancient fables about sirens: a reference to Odysseus' having himself tied to the mast to resist the lure of the sweet songs of the sirens, or sea nymphs.

9. astrolabe (as′ trō lāb′): an old-fashioned navigational instrument for finding the altitude of a star.

10. promontory (präm′ ən tôr′ ē): a peak of high land that juts out into a body of water.

Thinking About the Story

A PERSONAL RESPONSE

sharing impressions

1. In your journal list words and phrases that describe your feelings about the villagers.

constructing interpretations

2. In your opinion, why does the village become known as Esteban's village?

3. Why do you think the villagers are changed by their experience with the drowned man?

Think about
- what is so unusual about his physical appearance
- why they give him a splendid funeral and choose a family for him
- how their perception of their own lives changes when they face "the splendor and beauty of their drowned man"
- how they plan to change the physical appearance of their village

4. What do you think the drowned man represents to the villagers?

Think about
- why they think the sea and the wind respond to his presence
- why both the women and the men are left breathless at the sight of his face
- the imagined qualities that both the women and the men attribute to him

A CREATIVE RESPONSE

5. How might the story have been different if the villagers had discovered who the drowned man was and where he came from?

A CRITICAL RESPONSE

6. Novelist and critic Mario Vargas Llosa writes, "Aracataca [García Márquez's birthplace]—like so many Latin American towns—lived on remembrances, myths, solitude, and nostalgia. García Márquez's entire literary work is built with this material which fed him throughout childhood." How is the village in this story similar to or different from García Márquez's birthplace as described by Vargas Llosa?

7. The name Esteban is the Spanish form of Stephen, the name of the first Christian martyr. Lautaro was a South American Indian who led an uprising against the Spanish conquerors. Why do you think the women choose to name the drowned man Esteban instead of Lautaro? Use specific details from the story to support your explanation.

Analyzing the Writer's Craft

STYLE: MAGICAL REALISM

What kind of story did the title lead you to expect?

Building a Literary Vocabulary. Style is the particular way that a piece of literature is written. Style refers not so much to what is said but to how it is said. García Márquez writes in a style called magical realism, which often includes exaggeration, unusual humor, magical and bizarre events, dreams that come true, and superstitions that prove warranted. Magical realism differs from pure fantasy in combining fantastic elements with realistic elements such as recognizable characters, believable dialogue, a true-to-life setting, a matter-of-fact tone, and a plot that sometimes contains historic events.

The first clue that this story exemplifies magical realism comes from the title. Realistically, a drowned person is a gruesome sight. García Márquez nevertheless indicates that although the body spent a long time in the water, the stranger remains extraordinarily handsome. His unexpected handsomeness is the catalyst that awakens the imaginations of the villagers. The fantastic elements of the story enhance and support the theme that imagination can transform otherwise barren lives.

Application: Analyzing Style. As a class divide into four teams to compete in a style-analysis contest. Each team should reread the story up to the sentence "'He has the face of someone called Esteban'" (page 703) and then make a chart with two columns. In the first column list magical elements, such as the villagers' belief that the drowned man continued to grow after death. In the second column list realistic elements, such as the description of the seaweed and jellyfish tentacles that coated the body. Then have a spokesperson from each team read the items on the team's chart to the class. Any examples that are listed by more than one team must be crossed off every team's list. Each team is allowed to keep only the examples that no other team has. The team with the most examples remaining is the winner.

Connecting Reading and Writing

1. Write a **description** of "Esteban's village" that could appear in a tourist guidebook many years after the funeral of the drowned man. Include the name and history of the village in your entry.

Option: For a magazine on home and landscape improvement, write an **article** describing how the village was transformed.

2. To continue the game started in the Writer's Craft exercise, reread the story from "'He has the face of someone called Esteban'" to the end. Make a **chart** listing the magical and realistic elements in the last part of the story. Share your chart.

Option: Define magical realism, using examples in this story, in an **essay** to be printed in a textbook.

3. Write a **fairy tale** for children, using elements of magical realism to enhance the plot.

Option: Prepare a **dramatic script** for your fairy tale and choose classmates to help you perform it.

The Youngest Doll

ROSARIO FERRÉ   born 1942   PUERTO RICO/U.S.

A biography of Ferré appears on page 742.

Approaching the Story

"The Youngest Doll" by Rosario Ferré (rō̂ sä′ rē ô̂ fer rā′) is set in Puerto Rico at the beginning of the twentieth century, a period of great change. The island had been controlled by powerful families who owned the sugar cane, coffee, and tobacco plantations on which the economy was based. The wealth and influence of these families declined after the Spanish-American War in 1898, when the island was surrendered to the United States. The economy, dominated by foreign investors, became more industrialized, and a class of newly rich businessmen and professionals arose.

This short story portrays members of the old aristocracy and the rising wealthy classes. Like the previous two stories, this story challenges the reader's expectations with strange turns of events.

Building Vocabulary

These essential words are footnoted within the story.

furtively (fʉr′ tiv lē): They would sit around her and **furtively** lift the starched ruffle of her skirt. (page 710)

ostentatious (äs′ tən tā′ shəs): He would always show up wearing . . . an **ostentatious** tiepin of extravagantly poor taste. (page 712)

exorbitant (eg zor′ bi tənt): The whole town . . . didn't mind paying **exorbitant** fees. (page 713)

Connecting Writing and Reading

In your journal jot down what comes to mind when you hear the term "living doll." What would be the gender, appearance, and personality of someone described by this label? Would you want to be described this way? As you read, be aware of how the term "living doll" changes and takes on new meanings in your mind.

The Youngest Doll

ARLY IN THE morning the maiden aunt took her rocking chair out onto the porch facing the cane fields, as she always did whenever she woke up with the urge to make a doll. As a young woman, she had often bathed in the river, but one day when the heavy rains had fed the dragontail current, she had a soft feeling of melting snow in the marrow of her bones. With her head nestled among the black rocks' reverberations, she could hear the slamming of salty foam on the beach rolled up with the sound of waves, and she suddenly thought that her hair had poured out to sea at last. At that very moment, she felt a sharp bite in her calf. Screaming, she was pulled out of the water and, writhing in pain, was taken home on a stretcher.

The doctor who examined her assured her it was nothing, that she had probably been bitten by an angry river prawn.[1] But days passed and the scab wouldn't heal. A month later the doctor concluded that the prawn had worked its way into the soft flesh of her calf and had nestled there to grow. He prescribed a mustard plaster so that the heat would force it out. The aunt spent a whole week with her leg covered with mustard from thigh to ankle, but when the treatment was over, they found that the ulcer had grown even larger and that it was covered with a slimy, stonelike substance that couldn't be removed without endangering the whole leg. She then resigned herself to living with the prawn permanently curled up in her calf.

She had been very beautiful, but the prawn hidden under the long, gauzy folds of her skirt stripped her of all vanity. She locked herself up in her house, refusing to see any suitors. At first she devoted herself entirely to bringing up her sister's children, dragging her enormous leg around the house quite nimbly. In those days, the family was nearly ruined; they lived surrounded by a past that was breaking up around them with the same impassive musicality with which the dining room chandelier crumbled on the frayed linen cloth of the dining room table. Her nieces adored her. She would comb their hair, bathe and feed them, and when she read them stories, they would sit around her and furtively[2] lift the starched ruffle of her skirt so as to sniff the aroma of ripe sweetsop[3] that oozed from her leg when it was at rest.

As the girls grew up, the aunt devoted herself to making dolls for them to play with. At first they were just plain dolls, with cotton stuffing from the gourd tree and stray buttons sewn on for eyes. As time passed, though, she began to refine her craft, gaining the respect and admiration of the whole family. The birth of a doll was always cause for a ritual celebration, which explains why it never occurred to the aunt to sell them for profit, even when the girls had grown up and the family was beginning to fall into need. The aunt had continued to increase the size of the dolls so that their height and other measurements conformed to those of each of the girls. There were nine of them, and the aunt made one doll for each per year, so it became necessary to set aside a room for the dolls alone. When the eldest turned eighteen, there were one hundred and twenty-

---

1. **prawn** (prôn): a shellfish similar to a large shrimp.
2. **furtively** (fur′ tiv lē): sneakily; not openly.
3. **sweetsop:** a sweet, pungent-smelling, quickly ripening tropical fruit common in Puerto Rico.

six dolls of all ages in the room. Opening the door gave the impression of entering a dovecote or the ballroom in the Czarina's[4] palace or a warehouse in which someone had spread out a row of tobacco leaves to dry. But the aunt did not enter the room for any of these pleasures. Instead, she would unlatch the door and gently pick up each doll, murmuring a lullaby as she rocked it: "This is how you were when you were a year old, this is you at two, and like this at three," measuring out each year of their lives against the hollow they left in her arms.

The day the eldest had turned ten, the aunt sat down in her rocking chair facing the cane fields and never got up again. She would rock away entire days on the porch, watching the patterns of rain shift in the cane fields, coming out of her stupor only when the doctor paid a visit or whenever she awoke with the desire to make a doll. Then she would call out so that everyone in the house would come and help her. On that day, one could see the hired help making repeated trips to town like cheerful Inca messengers, bringing wax, porcelain clay, lace, needles, spools of thread of every color. While these preparations were taking place, the aunt would call the niece she had dreamt about the night before into her room and take her measurements. Then she would make a wax mask of the child's face, covering it with plaster on both sides, like a living face wrapped in two dead ones. She would draw out an endless flaxen thread of melted wax through a pinpoint on its chin. The porcelain of the hands and face was always translucent; it had an ivory tint to it that formed a great contrast with the curdled whiteness of the bisque faces. For the body, the aunt would send out to the garden for twenty glossy gourds. She would hold them in one hand, and with an expert twist of her knife, would slice them up against the railing of the balcony, so that the sun and breeze would dry out the cottony guano[5] brains. After a few days, she would scrape off

the dried fluff with a teaspoon and, with infinite patience, feed it into the doll's mouth.

The only items the aunt would agree to use that were not made by her were the glass eyeballs. They were mailed to her from Europe in all colors, but the aunt considered them useless until she had left them submerged at the bottom of the stream for a few days, so that they could learn to recognize the slightest stirring of the prawns' antennae. Only then would she carefully rinse them in ammonia water and place them, glossy as gems and nestled in a bed of cotton, at the bottom of one of her Dutch cookie tins. The dolls were always dressed in the same way, even though the girls were growing up. She would dress the younger ones in Swiss embroidery and the older ones in silk guipure,[6] and on each of their heads she would tie the same bow, wide and white and trembling like the breast of a dove.

The girls began to marry and leave home. On their wedding day, the aunt would give each of them their last doll, kissing them on the forehead and telling them with a smile, "Here is your Easter Sunday." She would reassure the grooms by explaining to them that the doll was merely a sentimental ornament, of the kind that people used to place on the lid of grand pianos in the old days. From the porch, the aunt would watch the girls walk down the staircase for the last time. They would carry a modest checkered cardboard suitcase in one hand, the other hand slipped around the waist of the exuberant doll made in their image and likeness, still wearing the same old-fashioned kid slippers and gloves, and with Valenciennes[7] bloomers barely showing under

---

4. Czarina (zä rē′ nə): the wife of a czar, the emperor of Russia.

5. guano (gwä′ nō): relating to a type of palm tree.

6. guipure (gē pyo͝or′): a kind of lace.

7. Valenciennes (və len′ sē enz′): a kind of lace originating in the French city of Valenciennes.

their snowy, embroidered skirts. But the hands and faces of these new dolls looked less transparent than those of the old: they had the consistency of skim milk. This difference concealed a more subtle one: the wedding doll was never stuffed with cotton but filled with honey.

All the older girls had married and only the youngest was left at home when the doctor paid his monthly visit to the aunt, bringing along his son, who had just returned from studying medicine up north. The young man lifted the starched ruffle of the aunt's skirt and looked intently at the huge, swollen ulcer which oozed a perfumed sperm from the tip of its greenish scales. He pulled out his stethoscope and listened to her carefully. The aunt thought he was listening for the breathing of the prawn to see if it was still alive, and she fondly lifted his hand and placed it on the spot where he could feel the constant movement of the creature's antennae. The young man released the ruffle and looked fixedly at his father. "You could have cured this from the start," he told him. "That's true," his father answered, "but I just wanted you to come and see the prawn that has been paying for your education these twenty years."

From then on it was the young doctor who visited the old aunt every month. His interest in the youngest was evident from the start, so the aunt was able to begin her last doll in plenty of time. He would always show up wearing a pair of brightly polished shoes, a starched collar, and an ostentatious[8] tiepin of extravagantly poor taste. After examining the aunt, he would sit in the parlor, lean his paper silhouette against the oval frame of the chair and, each time, hand the youngest an identical bouquet of purple forget-me-nots. She would offer him ginger cookies, taking the bouquet squeamishly with the tips of her fingers, as if

she were handling a sea urchin turned inside out. She made up her mind to marry him because she was intrigued by his sleepy profile and also because she was deathly curious to see what the dolphin flesh was like.

On her wedding day, as she was about to leave the house, the youngest was surprised to find that the doll her aunt had given her as a wedding present was warm. As she slipped her arm around its waist, she looked at it curiously, but she quickly forgot about it, so amazed was she at the excellence of its craft. The doll's face and hands were made of the most delicate Mikado porcelain. In the doll's half-open and slightly sad smile she recognized her full set of baby teeth. There was also another notable detail: the aunt had embedded her diamond eardrops inside the doll's pupils.

The young doctor took her off to live in town, in a square house that made one think of a cement block. Each day he made her sit out on the balcony, so that passersby would be sure to see that he had married into high society. Motionless inside her cubicle of heat, the youngest began to suspect that it wasn't only her husband's silhouette that was made of paper, but his soul as well. Her suspicions were soon confirmed. One day, he pried out the doll's eyes with the tip of his scalpel and pawned them for a fancy gold pocket watch with a long embossed chain. From then on the doll remained seated on the lid of the grand piano, but with her gaze modestly lowered.

A few months later, the doctor noticed the doll was missing from her usual place and asked the youngest what she'd done with it. A sisterhood of pious ladies had offered him a healthy sum for the porcelain hands and face, which they thought would be perfect for the image of

---

8. ostentatious (äs′ tən tā′ shəs): showy; flashy.

the Veronica in the next Lenten procession.[9]

The youngest answered that the ants had at last discovered the doll was filled with honey and, streaming over the piano, had devoured it in a single night. "Since its hands and face were of Mikado porcelain," she said, "they must have thought they were made of sugar and at this very moment they are most likely wearing down their teeth, gnawing furiously at its fingers and eyelids in some underground burrow." That night the doctor dug up all the ground around the house, to no avail.

As the years passed, the doctor became a millionaire. He had slowly acquired the whole town as his clientele, people who didn't mind paying exorbitant[10] fees in order to see a genuine member of the extinct sugar cane aristocracy up close. The youngest went on sitting in her rocking chair on the balcony, motionless in her muslin and lace, and always with lowered eyelids. Whenever her husband's patients, draped with necklaces and feathers and carrying elaborate canes, would seat themselves beside her, shaking their self-satisfied rolls of flesh with a jingling of coins, they would notice a strange scent that would involuntarily remind them of a slowly oozing sweetsop. They would then feel an uncomfortable urge to rub their hands together as though they were paws.

There was only one thing missing from the doctor's otherwise perfect happiness. He noticed that although he was aging, the youngest still kept that same firm, porcelained skin she had had when he would call on her at the big house on the plantation. One night he decided to go into her bedroom to watch her as she slept. He noticed that her chest wasn't moving. He gently placed his stethoscope over her heart and heard a distant swish of water. Then the doll lifted her eyelids, and out of the empty sockets of her eyes came the frenzied antennae of all those prawns.

---

9. The Veronica in the next Lenten procession: The Veronica is the image of Jesus' face said in legend to have appeared on the veil or handkerchief used by Saint Veronica to wipe the bleeding face of Jesus. A Lenten procession is a ceremony held during Lent, the period of forty weekdays from Ash Wednesday to Easter held holy by Christian churches.
10. exorbitant (eg zor′ bi tənt): going beyond what is usual; excessive.

Thinking About the Story

A PERSONAL RESPONSE

sharing impressions

1. What questions do you have after reading this story? Note them in your journal.

constructing interpretations

2. How do you explain what the young doctor observes when he enters his wife's bedroom?

3. Does the term "living doll" have different associations for you now that you have read this story?

Think about
- how the term describes the dolls that the maiden aunt makes
- how the term describes the women in the story, particularly the youngest niece
- how positively or negatively you now view the term

4. Speculate about what the aunt hopes to accomplish by making dolls.

Think about
- what she does when she is not making dolls
- how closely the dolls resemble her nieces
- why she submerges the dolls' eyeballs in the stream
- what she means by telling her nieces, "Here is your Easter Sunday" as she gives them their wedding dolls

5. Which character is most evil and which is most victimized?

Think about
- the admission the old doctor makes to his son
- the reasons why the young doctor and the youngest niece marry
- the young doctor's treatment of his wife and the doll
- the degree of control the aunt has over her own fate and her youngest niece's fate

A CREATIVE RESPONSE

6. If the aunt had not belonged to an aristocratic family, would the prawn bite have affected her life in the same way?

A CRITICAL RESPONSE

7. How do you think the writer views Puerto Rican society at the turn of the century?

Think about
- the values of the old doctor, the young doctor, and the young doctor's clientele
- the values and position of the sugar cane aristocracy
- the lives led by the women in the story
- the possible symbolism of the prawn, the hidden ulcer, and the scent of oozing sweetsop

8. What common stylistic elements do you see in "The Youngest Doll," "The Handsomest Drowned Man in the World," and "The Night Face Up"?

Analyzing the Writer's Craft

MOOD

Think about the feeling you get as you read: "the aroma of ripe sweetsop that oozed from her leg."

Building a Literary Vocabulary. Mood is the feeling, or atmosphere, that the writer creates for the reader. One element that contributes strongly to mood is imagery, words and phrases that re-create experiences by appealing to any of the five senses. A literary work may evoke more than one mood, as the descriptions "bittersweet love story" and "tragicomedy" would suggest. In "The Youngest Doll" the image of ripe, oozing sweetsop creates a mood of both richness and decay.

Application: Defining Mood. At the top of a sheet of paper, write two words that describe two different moods you find in "The Youngest Doll." Below these labels list images from the story that help create these two moods. The images may be in different passages or in the same passage. Compare your findings with those of your classmates to see how many moods are evoked by the story and to reinforce your understanding of the relationship between mood and imagery.

Connecting Reading and Writing

1. Suppose a friend turns to you after reading this story and says, "I just don't get it." In an **informal note** to him or her, explain what you think happens in the story.

Option: Write your own **story** relating events from the viewpoint of the aunt, the youngest niece, or the doll itself.

2. Imagine that the doll has been acquired by a prestigious auction house and is being offered for sale. Write **catalog copy** describing the doll.

Option: Advertise the doll in a **TV commercial** for a home shopping network.

3. In an **essay** for your literature class, analyze the writer's comparison of women to dolls in this story

and comment on whether such a comparison is still valid among high school students today.

Option: Present your ideas in a **pamphlet** for distribution at a political rally.

4. Compare "The Youngest Doll" to another story by Rosario Ferré, such as "The Gift" in her collection *Sweet Diamond Dust* or "The Poisoned Tale" in *Short Stories by Latin American Women: The Magic and The Real.* Make some generalizations about Ferré's style and major themes and prepare a **list of questions** to ask her in a radio interview about her writing.

Option: Describe Ferré's style and themes in a brief **profile** intended for a reference book on Latin American writers.

Rhinoceros

EUGÈNE IONESCO   born 1912   ROMANIA / FRANCE

A biography of Ionesco appears on page 744.

*A*pproaching the Story

Audiences attending the plays of Eugène Ionesco (yo͞o zhen′ yə nes′ kō), one of the founders of the theater of the absurd, have learned to expect the unexpected. In Ionesco's short stories, too, he often describes bizarre incidents that are comic and yet disturbing. In "Rhinoceros," for example, he presents a series of puzzling transformations while exploring the choice between conformity and individuality.

*B*uilding Vocabulary

These essential words are footnoted within the story.

itinerant (ī tin′ ər ənt): The council has forbidden **itinerant** entertainers to stop on municipal territory. (page 717)

paradoxes (par′ ə däks′ əz): "How tiresome you are with your **paradoxes.**" (page 717)

pedant (ped′ 'nt): "You're a **pedant,** who isn't even sure of his own knowledge." (page 718)

mutations (myo͞o tā′ shənz): Were these **mutations** reversible? (page 725)

*C*onnecting Writing and Reading

Are you a conformist? Do you feel pressured to conform to the behavior and attitudes of your fellow students? In your journal create a bar graph that shows the degree to which you conform in areas such as clothing, extracurricular activities, taste in music, and attitude toward school. As you read, think about the issue of conformity in your own life and in the lives of the characters.

E WERE sitting outside the café, my friend Jean and I, peacefully talking about one thing and another, when we caught sight of it on the opposite pavement, huge and powerful, panting noisily, charging straight ahead and brushing against market stalls—a rhinoceros. People in the street stepped hurriedly aside to let it pass. A housewife uttered a cry of terror, her basket dropped from her hands, the wine from a broken bottle spread over the pavement, and some pedestrians, one of them an elderly man, rushed into the shops. It was all over like a flash of lightning. People emerged from their hiding places and gathered in groups which watched the rhinoceros disappear into the distance, made some comments on the incident and then dispersed.

My own reactions are slowish. I absent-mindedly took in the image of the rushing beast, without ascribing any very great importance to it. That morning, moreover, I was feeling tired and my mouth was sour, as a result of the previous night's excesses; we had been celebrating a friend's birthday. Jean had not been at the party; and when the first moment of surprise was over, he exclaimed: "A rhinoceros at large in town! Doesn't that surprise you? It ought not to be allowed."

"True," I said, "I hadn't thought of that. It's dangerous."

"We ought to protest to the Town Council."

"Perhaps it's escaped from the zoo," I said.

"You're dreaming," he replied. "There hasn't been a zoo in our town since the animals were decimated by the plague in the seventeenth century."

"Perhaps it belongs to the circus?"

"What circus? The council has forbidden <u>itinerant</u>[1] entertainers to stop on municipal territory. None have come here since we were children."

"Perhaps it has lived here ever since, hidden in the marshy woods round about," I answered with a yawn.

"You're completely lost in a dense alcoholic haze. . . ."

"Which rises from the stomach . . ."

"Yes. And has pervaded your brain. What marshy woods can you think of round about here? Our province is so arid they call it Little Castile."[2]

"Perhaps it sheltered under a pebble? Perhaps it made its nest on a dry branch?"

"How tiresome you are with your <u>paradoxes</u>.[3] You're quite incapable of talking seriously."

"Today, particularly."

"Today and every other day."

"Don't lose your temper, my dear Jean. We're not going to quarrel about that creature. . . ."

We changed the subject of our conversation and began to talk about the weather again, about the rain which fell so rarely in our region, about the need to provide our sky with artificial clouds, and other banal and insoluble questions.

We parted. It was Sunday. I went to bed and slept all day: another wasted Sunday. On Monday morning I went to the office, making a solemn promise to myself never to get drunk again, and particularly not on Saturdays, so as not to spoil the following Sundays. For I had one single free day a week and three weeks' holiday in the summer. Instead of drinking and

---

1. **itinerant** (ī tin′ ər ənt): traveling from place to place, as on a circuit.
2. **Castile** (kas tēl′): the dry central region of Spain.
3. **paradoxes** (par′ ə däks′ əz): statements that seem contradictory or absurd but may in fact be true.

making myself ill, wouldn't it be better to keep fit and healthy, to spend my precious moments of freedom in a more intelligent fashion: visiting museums, reading literary magazines and listening to lectures? And instead of spending all my available money on drink, wouldn't it be preferable to buy tickets for interesting plays? I was still unfamiliar with the avant-garde theater, of which I had heard so much talk; I had never seen a play by Ionesco. Now or never was the time to bring myself up-to-date.

The following Sunday I met Jean once again at the same café.

"I've kept my promise," I said, shaking hands with him.

"What promise have you kept?" he asked.

"My promise to myself. I've vowed to give up drinking. Instead of drinking I've decided to cultivate my mind. Today I am clearheaded. This afternoon I'm going to the Municipal Museum, and this evening I've a ticket for the theater. Won't you come with me?"

"Let's hope your good intentions will last," replied Jean. "But I can't go with you. I'm meeting some friends at the brasserie."[4]

"Oh, my dear fellow, now it's you who are setting a bad example. You'll get drunk!"

"Once in a while doesn't imply a habit," replied Jean irritably. "Whereas you . . ."

The discussion was about to take a disagreeable turn, when we heard a mighty trumpeting, the hurried clatter of some perissodactyl's[5] hoofs, cries, a cat's mewing; almost simultaneously we saw a rhinoceros appear, then disappear, on the opposite pavement, panting noisily and charging straight ahead.

Immediately afterwards a woman appeared holding in her arms a shapeless, bloodstained little object:

"It's run over my cat," she wailed, "it's run over my cat!"

The poor dishevelled woman, who seemed the very embodiment of grief, was soon surrounded by people offering sympathy.

Jean and I got up. We rushed across the street to the side of the unfortunate woman.

"All cats are mortal," I said stupidly, not knowing how to console her.

"It came past my shop last week!" the grocer recalled.

"It wasn't the same one," Jean declared. "It wasn't the same one: last week's had two horns on its nose—it was an Asian rhinoceros; this one had only one—it's an African rhinoceros."

"You're talking nonsense," I said irritably. "How could you distinguish its horns? The animal rushed past so fast that we could hardly see it; you hadn't time to count them. . . ."

"I don't live in a haze," Jean retorted sharply. "I'm clearheaded, I'm quick at figures."

"He was charging with his head down."

"That made it all the easier to see."

"You're a pretentious fellow, Jean. You're a pedant,[6] who isn't even sure of his own knowledge. For in the first place, it's the Asian rhinoceros that has one horn on its nose and the African rhinoceros that has two!"

"You're quite wrong; it's the other way about."

"Would you like to bet on it?"

"I won't bet against you. You're the one who has two horns," he cried, red with fury, "you Asiatic, you!" (He stuck to his guns.)

"I haven't any horns. I shall never wear them. And I'm not an Asiatic, either. In any case, Asiatics are just like other people."

Jean turned his back on me and strode off, cursing.

---

4. **brasserie** (bräs rē') *French:* a beer shop or saloon that sells food.

5. **perissodactyl** (pə ris' ō dak' til): an order of hoofed mammals having an uneven number of toes on each foot and including the horse, tapir, and rhinoceros.

6. **pedant** (ped' 'nt): a person who shows off his or her learning in a boring way.

I felt a fool. I ought to have been more conciliatory and not contradicted him: for I knew he could not bear it. The slightest objection made him foam at the mouth. This was his only fault, for he had a heart of gold and had done me countless good turns. The few people who were there and who had been listening to us had, as a result, quite forgotten about the poor woman's squashed cat. They crowded round me, arguing: some maintained that the Asian rhinoceros was indeed one-horned, and that I was right; others maintained that on the contrary the African rhinoceros was one-horned, and that therefore the previous speaker had been right.

"That is not the question," interposed a gentleman (straw boater,[7] small moustache, eyeglass, a typical logician's head) who had hitherto stood silent. "The discussion turned on a problem from which you have wandered. You began by asking yourselves whether today's rhinoceros is the same as last Sunday's or whether it is a different one. That is what must be decided. You may have seen one and the same one-horned rhinoceros on two occasions, or you may have seen one and the same two-horned rhinoceros on two occasions. Or again, you may have seen first one one-horned rhinoceros and then a second one-horned rhinoceros. Or else, first one two-horned rhinoceros and then a second two-horned rhinoceros. If on the first occasion you had seen a two-horned rhinoceros, and on the second a one-horned rhinoceros, that would not be conclusive either. It might be that since last week the rhinoceros had lost one of his horns and that the one you saw today was the same. Or it might be that two two-horned rhinceroses had each lost one of their horns. If you could prove that on the first occasion you had seen a one-horned rhinoceros, whether it was Asian or African, and today a two-horned rhinoceros, whether it was African or Asian—that doesn't matter—then we might

conclude that two different rhinoceroses were involved, for it is most unlikely that a second horn could grow in a few days, to any visible extent, on a rhinoceros's nose; this would mean that an Asian, or African, rhinoceros had become an African, or Asian, rhinoceros, which is logically impossible, since the same creature cannot be born in two places at once or even successively."

"That seems clear to me," I said. "But it doesn't settle the question."

"Of course," retorted the gentleman, smiling with a knowledgeable air, "only the problem has now been stated correctly."

"That's not the problem either," interrupted the grocer, who being no doubt of an emotional nature cared little about logic. "Can we allow our cats to be run over under our eyes by two-horned or one-horned rhinoceroses, be they Asian or African?"

"He's right, he's right," everybody exclaimed. "We can't allow our cats to be run over, by rhinoceroses or anything else!"

The grocer pointed with a theatrical gesture to the poor weeping woman, who still held and rocked in her arms the shapeless, bleeding remains of what had once been her cat.

Next day in the paper, under the heading Road Casualties Among Cats, there were two lines describing the death of the poor creature: "crushed underfoot by a pachyderm" it was said, without further details.

On Sunday afternoon I hadn't visited a museum; in the evening I hadn't gone to the theater. I had moped at home by myself, overwhelmed by remorse at having quarrelled with Jean.

"He's so susceptible, I ought to have spared his feelings," I told myself. "It's absurd to lose one's temper about something like

---

7. **straw boater:** a stiff hat of braided straw, with a flat crown and brim.

that . . . about the horns of a rhinoceros that one had never seen before . . . a native of Africa or of India, such faraway countries, what could it matter to me? Whereas Jean had always been my friend, a friend who . . . to whom I owed so much . . . and who . . ."

In short, while promising myself to go and see Jean as soon as possible and to make it up with him, I had drunk an entire bottle of brandy without noticing. But I did indeed notice it the next day: a sore head, a foul mouth, an uneasy conscience; I was really most uncomfortable. But duty before everything: I got to the office on time, or almost. I was able to sign the register just before it was taken away.

"Well, so you've seen rhinoceroses too?" asked the chief clerk, who, to my great surprise, was already there.

"Sure I've seen him," I said, taking off my town jacket and putting on my old jacket with the frayed sleeves, good enough for work.

"Oh, now you see, I'm not crazy!" exclaimed the typist Daisy excitedly. (How pretty she was, with her pink cheeks and fair hair! I found her terribly attractive. If I could fall in love with anybody, it would be with her. . . .) "A one-horned rhinoceros!"

"Two-horned!" corrected my colleague Emile Dudard,[8] Bachelor of Law, eminent jurist, who looked forward to a brilliant future with the firm and, possibly, in Daisy's affections.

"I've not seen it! And I don't believe in it!" declared Botard,[9] an ex-schoolmaster who acted as archivist. "And nobody's ever seen one in this part of the world, except in the illustrations to school textbooks. These rhinoceroses have blossomed only in the imagination of ignorant women. The thing's a myth, like flying saucers."

I was about to point out to Botard that the expression "blossomed" applied to a rhinoceros, or to a number of them, seemed to me inappropriate, when the jurist exclaimed: "All the same, a cat was crushed, and before witnesses!"

"Collective psychosis," retorted Botard, who was a freethinker, "just like religion, the opium of the people!"

"I believe in flying saucers myself," remarked Daisy.

The chief clerk cut short our argument:

"That'll do! Enough chatter! Rhinoceros or no rhinoceros, flying saucers or no flying saucers, work's got to be done."

The typist started typing. I sat down at my desk and became engrossed in my documents. Emile Dudard began correcting the proofs of a commentary on the Law for the Repression of Alcoholism, while the chief clerk, slamming the door, retired into his study.

"It's a hoax!" Botard grumbled once more, aiming his remarks at Dudard. "It's your propaganda that spreads these rumors!"

"It's not propaganda," I interposed.

"I saw it myself . . . ," Daisy confirmed simultaneously.

"You make me laugh," said Dudard to Botard. "Propaganda? For what?"

"You know that better than I do! Don't act the simpleton!"

"In any case, *I'm* not paid by the Pontenegrins!"[10]

"That's an insult!" cried Botard, thumping the table with his fist. The door of the chief clerk's room opened suddenly and his head appeared.

"Monsieur Boeuf[11] hasn't come in today."

"Quite true, he's not here," I said.

"Just when I needed him. Did he tell anyone he was ill? If this goes on I shall give him the sack . . . ."

---

8. **Emile Dudard** (ā mēl′ dü där′).

9. **Botard** (bô tär′).

10. **Pontenegrins** (pôn′ ne gran′).

11. **Boeuf** (bëf).

It was not the first time that the chief clerk had threatened our colleague in this way.

"Has one of you got the key to his desk?" he went on.

Just then Madame Boeuf made her appearance. She seemed terrified.

"I must ask you to excuse my husband. He went to spend the weekend with relations. He's had a slight attack of 'flu. Look, that's what he says in his telegram. He hopes to be back on Wednesday. Give me a glass of water . . . and a chair!" she gasped, collapsing onto the chair we offered her.

"It's very tiresome! But it's no reason to get so alarmed!" remarked the chief clerk.

"I was pursued by a rhinoceros all the way from home," she stammered.

"With one horn or two?" I asked.

"You make me laugh!" exclaimed Botard.

"Why don't you let her speak!" protested Dudard.

Madame Boeuf had to make a great effort to be explicit:

"It's downstairs, in the doorway. It seems to be trying to come upstairs."

At that very moment a tremendous noise was heard: the stairs were undoubtedly giving way under a considerable weight. We rushed out onto the landing. And there, in fact, amidst the debris, was a rhinoceros, its head lowered, trumpeting in an agonized and agonizing voice and turning vainly round and round. I was able to make out two horns.

"It's an African rhinoceros . . . ," I said, "or rather an Asian one."

My mind was so confused that I was no longer sure whether two horns were characteristic of the Asian or of the African rhinoceros, whether a single horn was characteristic of the African or of the Asian rhinoceros, or whether on the contrary two horns . . . In short, I was floundering mentally, while Botard glared furiously at Dudard.

"It's an infamous plot!" and, with an orator's gesture, he pointed at the jurist: "It's your fault!"

"It's yours!" the other retorted.

"Keep calm, this is no time to quarrel!" declared Daisy, trying in vain to pacify them.

"For years now I've been asking the board to let us have concrete steps instead of that rickety old staircase," said the chief clerk. "Something like this was bound to happen. It was predictable. I was quite right!"

"As usual," Daisy added ironically. "But how shall we get down?"

"I'll carry you in my arms," the chief clerk joked flirtatiously, stroking the typist's cheek, "and we'll jump together!"

"Don't put your horny hand on my face, you pachydermous creature!"

The chief clerk had not time to react. Madame Boeuf, who had got up and come to join us, and who had for some minutes been staring attentively at the rhinoceros, which was turning round and round below us, suddenly uttered a terrible cry:

"It's my husband! Boeuf, my poor dear Boeuf, what has happened to you?"

The rhinoceros, or rather Boeuf, responded with a violent and yet tender trumpeting, while Madame Boeuf fainted into my arms and Botard, raising his to heaven, stormed: "It's sheer lunacy! What a society!"

When we had recovered from our initial astonishment, we telephoned to the fire brigade, who drove up with their ladders and fetched us down. Madame Boeuf, although we advised her against it, rode off on her spouse's back toward their home. She had ample grounds for divorce (but who was the guilty party?), yet she chose rather not to desert her husband in his present state.

At the little bistro where we all went for lunch (all except the Boeufs, of course) we learnt that several rhinoceroses had been seen in various parts of the town: some people said seven, others seventeen, others again said thirty-two. In the face of this accumulated evidence, Botard could no longer deny the rhinoceric facts. But he knew, he declared, what to think about it. He would explain it to us some day. He knew the "why" of things, the "underside" of the story, the names of those responsible, the aim and significance of the outrage. Going back to the office that afternoon, business or no business, was out of the question. We had to wait for the staircase to be repaired.

I took advantage of this to pay a call on Jean, with the intention of making it up with him. He was in bed.

Guide for Interpretation

Notice that Boeuf's having become a rhinoceros and the reactions of the other characters to the incident are comical and absurd. As you continue to read, be alert to the cumulative effect of the various bizarre events in the story.

"I don't feel very well!" he said.

"You know, Jean, we were both right. There are two-horned rhinoceroses in the town as well as one-horned ones. It really doesn't matter where either sort comes from. The only significant thing, in my opinion, is the existence of the rhinoceros in itself."

"I don't feel very well," my friend kept on saying without listening to me, "I don't feel very well!"

"What's the matter with you? I'm so sorry!"

"I'm rather feverish, and my head aches."

More precisely, it was his forehead which was aching. He must have had a knock, he said. And in fact a lump was swelling up there, just above his nose. He had gone a greenish color, and his voice was hoarse.

"Have you got a sore throat? It may be tonsillitis."

I took his pulse. It was beating quite regularly.

"It can't be very serious. A few days' rest and you'll be all right. Have you sent for the doctor?"

As I was about to let go of his wrist, I noticed that his veins were swollen and bulging out. Looking closely, I observed that not only were the veins enlarged but the skin all round them was visibly changing color and growing hard.

"It may be more serious than I imagined," I thought. "We must send for the doctor," I said aloud.

"I felt uncomfortable in my clothes, and now my pajamas are too tight," he said in a hoarse voice.

"What's the matter with your skin? It's like leather. . . ." Then, staring at him: "Do you know what happened to Boeuf? He's turned into a rhinoceros."

"Well, what about it? That's not such a bad thing! After all, rhinoceroses are creatures like ourselves, with just as much right to live. . . ."

"Provided they don't imperil our own lives. Aren't you aware of the difference in mentality?"

"Do you think ours is preferable?"

"All the same, we have our own moral code, which I consider incompatible with that of these animals. We have our philosophy, our irreplaceable system of values . . . ."

"Humanism[12] is out of date! You're a ridiculous old sentimentalist. You're talking nonsense."

"I'm surprised to hear you say that, my dear Jean! Have you taken leave of your senses?"

It really looked like it. Blind fury had disfigured his face and altered his voice to such an extent that I could scarcely understand the words that issued from his lips.

"Such assertions, coming from you . . . ," I tried to resume.

He did not give me a chance to do so. He flung back his blankets, tore off his pajamas,

---

12. humanism: a philosophical movement that holds that humans can be moral and find meaning in life through reason.

and stood up in bed, entirely naked (he who was usually the most modest of men!), green with rage from head to foot.

The lump on his forehead had grown longer; he was staring fixedly at me, apparently without seeing me. Or, rather, he must have seen me quite clearly, for he charged at me with his head lowered. I barely had time to leap to one side; if I hadn't, he would have pinned me to the wall.

"You are a rhinoceros!" I cried.

"I'll trample on you! I'll trample on you!" I made out these words as I dashed toward the door.

I went downstairs four steps at a time, while the walls shook as he butted them with his horn, and I heard him utter fearful angry trumpetings.

"Call the police! Call the police! You've got a rhinoceros in the house!" I called out to the tenants who, in great surprise, looked out of their flats as I passed each landing.

On the ground floor I had great difficulty in dodging the rhinoceros, which emerged from the concierge's lodge and tried to charge me. At last I found myself out in the street, sweating, my legs limp, at the end of my tether.

Fortunately there was a bench by the edge of the pavement, and I sat down on it. Scarcely had I more or less got back my breath when I saw a herd of rhinoceroses hurrying down the avenue and nearing, at full speed, the place where I was. If only they had been content to stay in the middle of the street! But they were so many that there was not room for them all there, and they overflowed onto the pavement. I leapt off my bench and flattened myself against the wall: snorting, trumpeting, with a smell of leather and of wild animals in heat, they brushed past me and covered me with a cloud of dust. When they had disappeared, I could not go back to sit on the bench; the animals had demolished it, and it lay in fragments on the pavement.

I did not find it easy to recover from such emotions. I had to stay at home for several days. Daisy came to see me and kept me informed as to the changes that were taking place.

The chief clerk had been the first to turn into a rhinoceros, to the great disgust of Botard, who, nevertheless, became one himself twenty-four hours later.

"One must keep up with one's times!" were his last words as a man.

The case of Botard did not surprise me, in spite of his apparent strength of mind. I found it less easy to understand the chief clerk's transformation. Of course it might have been involuntary, but one would have expected him to put up more resistance.

Daisy recalled that she had commented on the roughness of his palms the very day that Boeuf had appeared in rhinoceros shape. This must have made a deep impression on him; he had not shown it, but he had certainly been cut to the quick.

"If I hadn't been so outspoken, if I had pointed it out to him more tactfully, perhaps this would never have happened."

"I blame myself, too, for not having been gentler with Jean. I ought to have been friendlier, shown more understanding," I said in my turn.

Daisy informed me that Dudard, too, had been transformed, as had also a cousin of hers, whom I did not know. And there were others, mutual friends, strangers.

"There are a great many of them," she said, "about a quarter of the inhabitants of our town."

"They're still in the minority, however."

"The way things are going, that won't last long!" she sighed.

"Alas! And they're so much more efficient."

Herds of rhinoceroses rushing at top speed through the streets became a sight that no longer surprised anybody. People would stand aside to let them pass and then resume their stroll, or attend to their business, as if nothing had happened.

"How can anybody be a rhinoceros! It's unthinkable!" I protested in vain.

More of them kept emerging from courtyards and houses, even from windows, and went to join the rest.

There came a point when the authorities proposed to enclose them in huge parks. For humanitarian reasons, the Society for the Protection of Animals opposed this. Besides, everyone had some close relative or friend among the rhinoceroses, which, for obvious reasons, made the project well-nigh impracticable. It was abandoned.

The situation grew worse, which was only to be expected. One day a whole regiment of rhinoceroses, having knocked down the walls of the barracks, came out with drums at their head and poured onto the boulevards.

At the Ministry of Statistics, statisticians produced their statistics: census of animals, approximate reckoning of their daily increase, percentage of those with one horn, percentage of those with two. . . . What an opportunity for learned controversies! Soon there were defections among the statisticians themselves. The few who remained were paid fantastic sums.

One day from my balcony I caught sight of a rhinoceros charging forward with loud trumpetings, presumably to join his fellows; he wore a straw boater impaled on his horn.

"The logician!" I cried. "He's one too? Is it possible?" Just at that moment Daisy opened the door.

"The logician is a rhinoceros!" I told her.

She knew. She had just seen him in the street. She was bringing me a basket of provisions.

"Shall we have lunch together?" she suggested. "You know, it was difficult to find anything to eat. The shops have been ransacked; they devour everything. A number of shops are closed 'on account of transformations,' the notices say."

"I love you, Daisy, please never leave me."

"Close the window, darling. They make too much noise. And the dust comes in."

"So long as we're together, I'm afraid of nothing, I don't mind about anything." Then, when I had closed the window: "I thought I should never be able to fall in love with a woman again."

I clasped her tightly in my arms. She responded to my embrace.

"How I'd like to make you happy! Could you be happy with me?"

"Why not? You declare you're afraid of nothing and yet you're scared of everything! What can happen to us?"

"My love, my joy!" I stammered, kissing her lips with a passion such as I had forgotten, intense and agonizing.

The ringing of the telephone interrupted us.

She broke from my arms, went to pick up the receiver, then uttered a cry: "Listen. . . ."

I put the receiver to my ear. I heard ferocious trumpetings.

"They're playing tricks on us now!"

"Whatever can be happening?" she inquired in alarm.

We turned on the radio to hear the news; we heard more trumpetings. She was shaking with fear.

"Keep calm," I said, "keep calm!"

She cried out in terror, "They've taken over the broadcasting station!"

"Keep calm, keep calm!" I repeated, increasingly agitated myself.

Next day in the street they were running about in all directions. You could watch for hours without catching sight of a single human being. Our house was shaking under the weight of our perissodactylic neighbors' hoofs.

"What must be must be," said Daisy. "What can we do about it?"

"They've all gone mad. The world is sick."

"It's not you and I who'll cure it."

"We shan't be able to communicate with anybody. Can you understand them?"

"We ought to try to interpret their psychology, to learn their language."

"They have no language."

"What do you know about it?"

"Listen to me, Daisy. We shall have children, and then they will have children. It'll take time, but between us we can regenerate humanity. With a little courage . . ."

"I don't want to have children."

"How do you hope to save the world, then?"

"Perhaps after all it's we who need saving. Perhaps we are the abnormal ones. Do you see anyone else like us?"

"Daisy, I can't have you talking like that!"

I looked at her in despair.

"It's we who are in the right, Daisy, I assure you."

"What arrogance! There's no absolute right. It's the whole world that is right—not you or me."

"Yes, Daisy, I *am* right. The proof is that you understand me and that I love you as much as a man can love a woman."

"I'm rather ashamed of what you call love, that morbid thing. . . . It cannot compare with the extraordinary energy displayed by all these beings we see around us."

"Energy? Here's energy for you!" I cried, my powers of argument exhausted, giving her a slap.

Then, as she burst into tears: "I won't give in, no, I won't give in."

She rose, weeping, and flung her sweet-smelling arms round my neck.

"I'll stand fast, with you, to the end."

She was unable to keep her word. She grew melancholy and visibly pined away. One morning when I woke up, I saw that her place in the bed was empty. She had gone away without leaving any message.

The situation became literally unbearable for me. It was my fault if Daisy had gone. Who knows what had become of her? Another burden on my conscience. There was nobody who could help me to find her again. I imagined the worst and felt myself responsible.

And on every side there were trumpetings and frenzied chargings and clouds of dust. In vain did I shut myself up in my own room, putting cotton wool in my ears: at night I saw them in my dreams.

"The only way out is to convince them." But of what? Were these mutations[13] reversible? And in order to convince them, one would have to talk to them. In order for them to relearn my language (which moreover I was beginning to forget), I should first have to learn theirs. I could not distinguish one trumpeting from another, one rhinoceros from another rhinoceros.

One day, looking at myself in the glass, I took a dislike to my long face: I needed a horn, or even two, to give dignity to my flabby features.

And what if, as Daisy had said, it was they who were in the right? I was out of date; I had missed the boat, that was clear.

I discovered that their trumpetings had after all a certain charm, if a somewhat harsh one. I should have noticed that while there was still time. I tried to trumpet: how feeble the sound was, how lacking in vigor! When I made greater efforts, I only succeeded in howling. Howlings are not trumpetings.

It is obvious that one must not always drift blindly behind events and that it's a good thing to maintain one's individuality. However, one must also make allowances for things; asserting one's own difference, to be sure, but yet . . . remaining akin to one's fellows. I no longer bore any likeness to anyone or to anything, except to ancient, old-

---

13. mutations (myo͞o tā′ shənz): changes, as in form, nature, and so on.

fashioned photographs which had no con- nection with living beings.

Each morning I looked at my hands, hoping that the palms would have hardened during my sleep. The skin remained flabby. I gazed at my too-white body, my hairy legs: oh for a hard skin and that magnificent green color, a decent, hairless nudity, like theirs!

My conscience was increasingly uneasy, unhappy. I felt I was a monster. Alas, I would never become a rhinoceros. I could never change.

I dared no longer look at myself. I was ashamed. And yet I couldn't, no, I couldn't.

*T*hinking About the Story

A PERSONAL RESPONSE

sharing impressions

1. How do you feel about what happens in this story? Jot down your impressions in your journal.

constructing interpretations

2. What do you predict will happen to the narrator?
   Think about
   • the role of conformity in the lives of the characters
   • what the narrator says about maintaining individuality
   • the narrator's feeling like a monster at the end of the story

3. How would you describe the transformations that take place in this story?
   Think about
   • physical changes and what they might mean
   • changes in the relationships between characters
   • changes in society

A CREATIVE RESPONSE

4. If you were a character in this story, do you think you would turn into a rhinoceros? Explain your answer.

A CRITICAL RESPONSE

5. What do you think the rhinoceroses in this story symbolize?
   Think about
   • details about their appearance and behavior
   • the narrator's comments about them
   • what the writer seems to be saying about the issue of conformity

6. The tone of "Rhinoceros" has been described as both serious and absurdly comical. Explain how both descriptions apply to the story.

7. How might the theme of the story be applied to your own life?
Think about
- what you wrote in your journal about conformity
- what Ionesco is saying about society

Analyzing the Writer's Craft

DIALOGUE

Think about what the conversations in this story suggest about the characters.

Building a Literary Vocabulary. Dialogue is written conversation between two or more characters. The use of dialogue brings characters to life and gives the reader insights into their qualities. For example, in "The Prisoner Who Wore Glasses," Brille's concern for his fellow prisoners and their compassion for him is revealed in the following

dialogue: "I'm sorry, comrades," he said. . . . "Never mind, brother," they said. "What happens to one of us, happens to all."

Application: Examining Dialogue. In a small group, read aloud the dialogue from an episode in this story. Identify what qualities of the characters are suggested through the dialogue. Then prepare an oral interpretation for the entire class in which you highlight those qualities.

Connecting Reading and Writing

1. Imagine that you are planning to direct a film version of this short story. Write a **letter** to the actor of your choice to persuade him to perform the part of the narrator.

Option: Write a **memo** to the producer explaining why you want a certain actor for the part.

2. Many critics have interpreted "Rhinoceros" as an allegory about Nazism in World War II. Do research on the nature of Nazism and its effects during World War II. Then write an **expository essay** for your classmates on this interpretation.

Option: Write a **lesson plan** outline that a teacher might use to teach "Rhinoceros."

3. Imagine that a school board member has objected to this story on the grounds that it is preposterous and a waste of time. Prepare **notes** for a speech before the school board supporting or challenging this objection.

Option: Express your views on this objection in an **editorial** for a classroom newspaper.

What I Have Been Doing Lately

JAMAICA KINCAID   born 1949   ANTIGUA / U. S.

A biography of Kincaid appears on page 745.

Approaching the Story

Jamaica Kincaid is a Caribbean-born writer now living in the United States. This story is an experimental work similar to some of the preceding stories: the characters are not named, events are left unexplained, and reality is uncertain.

Connecting Writing and Reading

Recall some of the more unusual aspects of the stories you have read in this section of the book. In your journal jot down words and phrases that come to mind. As you read, compare your impressions of the other stories with the bizarre and surprising aspects of this story.

**HAT I HAVE** been doing lately: I was lying in bed and the doorbell rang. I ran downstairs. Quick. I opened the door. There was no one there. I stepped outside. Either it was drizzling or there was a lot of dust in the air and the dust was damp. I stuck out my tongue and the drizzle or the damp dust tasted like government school ink. I looked north. I looked south. I decided to start walking north. While walking north, I noticed that I was barefoot. While walking north, I looked up and saw the planet Venus. I said, "It must be almost morning." I saw a monkey in a tree. The tree had no leaves. I said, "Ah, a monkey. Just look at that. A monkey." I walked for I don't know how long before I came up to a big body of water. I wanted to get across it but I couldn't swim. I wanted to get across it but it would take me years to build a boat. I wanted to get across it but it would take me I didn't know how long to build a bridge. Years passed and then one day, feeling like it, I got into my boat and rowed across. When I got to the other side, it was noon and my shadow was small and fell beneath me. I set out on a path that stretched out straight ahead. I passed a house, and a dog was sitting on the verandah, but it looked the other way when it saw me coming. I passed a boy tossing a ball in the air but the boy looked the other way when he saw me coming. I walked and I walked but I couldn't tell if I walked a long time because my feet didn't feel as if they would drop off. I turned around to see what I had left behind me but nothing was familiar. Instead of the straight path, I saw hills. Instead of the boy with his ball, I saw tall flowering trees. I looked up and the sky was without clouds and seemed near, as if it were the ceiling in my house and, if I stood on a chair, I could touch it with the tips of my fingers. I turned around and looked ahead of me

again. A deep hole had opened up before me. I looked in. The hole was deep and dark and I couldn't see the bottom. I thought, What's down there? so on purpose I fell in. I fell and I fell, over and over, as if I were an old suitcase. On the sides of the deep hole I could see things written, but perhaps it was in a foreign language because I couldn't read them. Still I fell, for I don't know how long. As I fell I began to see that I didn't like the way falling made me feel. Falling made me feel sick and I missed all the people I had loved. I said, "I don't want to fall anymore," and I reversed myself. I was standing again on the edge of the deep hole. I looked at the deep hole and I said, "You can close up now," and it did. I walked some more without knowing distance. I only knew that I passed through days and nights, I only knew that I passed through rain and shine, light and darkness. I was never thirsty and I felt no pain. Looking at the horizon, I made a joke for myself: I said, "The earth has thin lips," and I laughed.

Looking at the horizon again, I saw a lone figure coming toward me, but I wasn't frightened because I was sure it was my mother. As I got closer to the figure, I could see that it wasn't my mother, but still I wasn't frightened because I could see that it was a woman.

When this woman got closer to me, she looked at me hard and then she threw up her hands. She must have seen me somewhere before because she said, "It's you. Just look at that. It's you. And just what have you been doing lately?"

I could have said, "I have been praying not to grow any taller."

I could have said, "I have been listening carefully to my mother's words, so as to make a good imitation of a dutiful daughter."

I could have said, "A pack of dogs, tired from chasing each other all over town, slept in the moonlight."

Instead, I said, "What I have been doing

lately: I was lying in bed on my back, my hands drawn up, my fingers interlaced lightly at the nape of my neck. Someone rang the doorbell. I went downstairs and opened the door but there was no one there. I stepped outside. Either it was drizzling or there was a lot of dust in the air and the dust was damp. I stuck out my tongue and the drizzle or the damp dust tasted like government school ink. I looked north and I looked south. I started walking north. While walking north, I wanted to move fast, so I removed the shoes from my feet. While walking north, I looked up and saw the planet Venus, and I said, 'If the sun went out, it would be eight minutes before I would know it.' I saw a monkey sitting in a tree that had no leaves and I said, 'A monkey. Just look at that. A monkey. I picked up a stone and I threw it at the monkey.' The monkey, seeing the stone, quickly moved out of its way. Three times I threw a stone at the monkey and three times it moved away. The fourth time I threw the stone, the monkey caught it and threw it back at me. The stone struck me on my forehead over my right eye, making a deep gash. The gash healed immediately but now the skin on my forehead felt false to me. I walked for I don't know how long before I came to a big body of water. I wanted to get across, so when the boat came I paid my fare. When I got to the other side, I saw a lot of people sitting on the beach and they were having a picnic. They were the most beautiful people I had ever seen.

Everything about them was black and shiny. Their skin was black and shiny. Their shoes were black and shiny. Their hair was black and shiny. The clothes they wore were black and shiny. I could hear them laughing and chatting and I said, 'I would like to be with these people,' so I started to walk toward them; but when I got up close to them I saw that they weren't at a picnic and they weren't beautiful and they weren't chatting and laughing. All around me was black mud and the people all looked as if they had been made up out of the black mud. I looked up and saw that the sky seemed far away and nothing I could stand on would make me able to touch it with my fingertips. I thought, If only I could get out of this, so I started to walk. I must have walked for a long time because my feet hurt and felt as if they would drop off. I thought, If only just around the bend I would see my house and inside my house I would find my bed, freshly made at that, and in the kitchen I would find my mother or anyone else that I loved making me a custard. I thought, If only it was a Sunday and I was sitting in a church and I had just heard someone sing a psalm. I felt very sad so I sat down. I felt so sad that I rested my head on my own knees and smoothed my own head. I felt so sad I couldn't imagine feeling any other way again. I said, 'I don't like this. I don't want to do this anymore.' And I went back to lying in bed, just before the doorbell rang."

Thinking About the Story

A PERSONAL RESPONSE

sharing impressions

1. What are you left wondering about at the end of this story? Record your thoughts in your journal.

constructing interpretations

2. What is your understanding of the story's ending?
   Think about
   • what the narrator does not want to do anymore
   • how she is able to return to bed
   • who rings the doorbell

3. Speculate about the narrator of this story.
   Think about
   • her bizarre and surprising depiction of events
   • her age, personality, and past experiences
   • her relationship with her mother

4. How do you explain the differences in the narrator's two accounts of what she has been doing lately?
   Think about
   • whom she is speaking to as she gives each account
   • the three answers she says she could have given, but did not give, to the question "And just what have you been doing lately?"
   • whether she is describing the same journey in each account

A CREATIVE RESPONSE

5. How might the story continue?

A CRITICAL RESPONSE

6. What is the overall mood of the story? Explain.

7. Based on this story and others you have read in this section, create a new definition of plot.
   Think about
   • the traditional definition of plot as a series of interrelated events that progress because of a conflict, or struggle between opposing forces
   • the traditional structure of a plot, consisting of the exposition, rising action, climax, and falling action

8. Jamaica Kincaid immigrated to the United States from a tiny Caribbean island when she was seventeen. In what ways might her story reflect the experience of a new immigrant?

9. Do you find this story as inventive as others in **Sparking the Imagination?** Decide which story is based on the most intriguing idea.

Analyzing the Writer's Craft

STYLE: DICTION

What seems unusual about the narrator's manner of speaking?

Building a Literary Vocabulary. As you may remember, style refers to the particular way that a piece of literature is written. A significant component of style is diction, or a writer's choice of words. Diction encompasses both vocabulary (individual words) and syntax (the order or arrangement of words). Diction can be described in terms such as formal or informal, technical or common, abstract or concrete. In "What I Have Been Doing Lately" the narrator's diction is simple, even childish: "I ran downstairs. Quick. I opened the door. There was no one there." She uses short words and repeats certain constructions—"I looked," "I saw," "I walked." Contrast her diction with the more complex, formal diction of the narrator in "The Youngest Doll": "they lived surrounded by a past that was breaking up around them with the same impassive musicality with which the dining room chandelier crumbled on the frayed linen cloth of the dining room table."

Application: Analyzing Diction. Divide into groups of three or four. Write a short paragraph using diction characteristic of the narrator in "What I Have Been Doing Lately." Then write another paragraph using vocabulary and syntax that are uncharacteristic of the narrator. Exchange your paragraphs with those of another group and identify which paragraphs could have come from Kincaid's narrator. Defend your choice, pointing out specific qualities of the narrator's diction.

Connecting Reading and Writing

1. Drawing on your answer to question 5, write another **episode** in the same style and read it to classmates.

Option: Make your episode a **monologue** to be performed with appropriate props and gestures.

2. The structure of a work of literature is the way in which its parts are put together. Make a **graphic representation** of the structure of this story. The representation could be a diagram, a geometric shape, or some other figure. Explain how the story corresponds to your drawing.

Option: Analyze the story's structure in an **expository essay** for another student.

Fable

OCTAVIO PAZ   born 1914   MEXICO

Ode to My Socks

PABLO NERUDA   1904–1973   CHILE

Translated by Robert Bly

Biographies of Paz and Neruda appear on pages 749 and 748.

Approaching the Poems

Like the other selections in this section, the two poems you are about to read are written by modern authors who experiment with unexpected meanings.

The poetry of Nobel Prize winner Octavio Paz (ôk tä′ vyô päz) often contains elements of surrealism, in which dreamlike images from the unconscious mind are captured in writing. Paz calls the poem featured here a fable, a brief story that attempts to account for certain conditions existing in the natural world.

Nobel Prize winner Pablo Neruda (pä′ blō nə rōō′ də) designated his poem an ode, a kind of poem written—usually in a dignified style—to commemorate a person, event, or thing—in this case, a pair of socks.

Fable

The age of fire and the age of air
The youth of water springing
From green to yellow
                Yellow to red
5   From dream to vigil
                From desire to act
You needed only a step and that taken without effort
The insects then were jewels who were alive
The heat lay down to rest at the edge of the pool

10 Rain was the light hair of a willow-tree
  There was a tree growing within your hand
  And as it grew it sang laughed prophesied
  It cast the spells that cover space with wings
  There were the simple miracles called birds
15 Everything belonged to everyone
                   Everyone was everything
  Only one word existed immense without opposite
  A word like a sun
  One day exploded into smallest fragments
20 They were the words of the language that we speak
  They are the splintered mirrors where the world
                   can see itself   slaughtered

Ode to My Socks

         Moru Mori brought me
         a pair
         of socks
         which she knitted herself
5   with her sheepherder's hands,
         two socks as soft
         as rabbits.
         I slipped my feet
         into them
10   as though into
         two
         cases
         knitted
         with threads of
15   twilight
         and goatskin.
         Violent socks,
         my feet were
         two fish made
20   of wool,
         two long sharks,

sea-blue, shot
through
by one golden thread,
25 two immense blackbirds,
two cannons:
my feet
were honored
in this way
30 by
these
heavenly
socks.
They were
35 so handsome,
for the first time
my feet seemed to me
unacceptable
like two decrepit
40 firemen, firemen
unworthy
of that woven
fire,
of those glowing
45 socks.
Nevertheless,
I resisted
the sharp temptation
to save them somewhere
50 as schoolboys
keep
fireflies,
as learned men
collect
55 sacred texts,
I resisted
the mad impulse
to put them
into a golden
60 cage
and each day give them
birdseed
and pieces of pink melon.
Like explorers

65 in the jungle who hand
over the very rare
green deer
to the spit
and eat it
70 with remorse,
I stretched out
my feet
and pulled on
the magnificent
75 socks
and then my shoes.
The moral
of my ode is this:
beauty is twice
80 beauty
and what is good is doubly
good
when it is a matter of two socks
made of wool
85 in winter.

Reviewing Concepts

REALISM AND FANTASY: A DELICATE BALANCE

*making
connections*

In most of the selections in this unit, the writer has combined elements of both realism and fantasy to create a work that engages the reader's interest. In "A Passion in the Desert," for example, Balzac combines a fairly realistic setting and realistic characters with a plot that is, to some extent, beyond the realm of real world experience. This relationship between realism and fantasy might be illustrated in the following way:

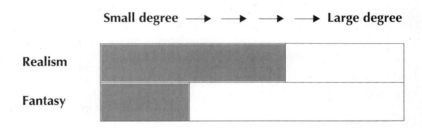

"A Passion in the Desert"

Small degree ⟶ ⟶ ⟶ ⟶ **Large degree**

| **Realism** |
| **Fantasy** |

Think through the unit and identify those selections that employ both realism and fantasy. Create a graph for each of these selections.

*describing
connections*

With several classmates discuss your graphs, using specific examples to explain your representations of the relationships between realism and fantasy. Then choose three selections that best illustrate the blending of realism and fantasy. For a teacher's guide write an **essay** in which you recommend the three selections to a teacher who wants to present this type of literature but has limited time.

Biographies of Authors

Ivo Andrić (1892–1975), Yugoslav novelist, short story writer, and poet, was born in Docu, Bosnia. The people and history of this area provided much of the substance of his works. Andrić's involvement in a political group led to his imprisonment during World War I, and it was during this internment that he wrote *Ex Ponto,* the work that first brought him acclaim. Andrić served in his country's diplomatic corps and was stationed in Berlin when the Nazis invaded Yugoslavia during World War II. He took refuge in his apartment in Belgrade, where he remained throughout the occupation virtually under house arrest. Devoting himself to his writing, Andrić produced the Bosnian Trilogy, which included *The Bridge on the Drina.* In 1961 Andrić received the Nobel Prize in literature "for the epic force with which he has depicted the themes and human destinies from the history of this country."

Honoré de Balzac (1799–1850) was a highly accomplished French novelist and short story writer. As a person, Balzac was thought to be awkward and unattractive and primarily interested in money, fame, and women. After studying law at the Sorbonne, he began writing sensational novels, using a pseudonym, and participating in get-rich-quick schemes that failed. Finally, Balzac gained respect as an author with the novels *The Chouans* and *The Physiology of Marriage.* His fame came just in time to save him from total financial destruction. Balzac wrote up to sixteeen hours a day to pay off his debts. Throughout his lifetime, he arranged his novels and short stories under one title, *The Human Comedy.* Although Balzac was not greatly appreciated in his own time, his innovative use of realism and naturalism greatly influenced today's literature.

Matsuo Bashō (1644–1694) is known as the greatest haiku poet of Japan. Early in his life he went to work for a noble family and became a companion to their son. When the son died, Bashō was greatly upset and left the family's service to become a wandering poet. He taught haiku to make a living. One day, according to legend, one of his students announced that he had thought of a poem: "Pluck off the wings of a bright red dragonfly and there a pepper pod will be." Bashō informed the student that he would never be a poet. A poet, according to Bashō, would have created this image: "Add but the wings to a bright red pepper pod and there a dragonfly will be." Whether the story is true or not, it reflects the deep compassion for all living things that, along with his superb technical skills as a poet, made Bashō a major figure in world literature.

Charles Baudelaire (1821–1867), founder of the French Symbolist movement and a major contributor to French literature and the development of modern poetry, received little recognition for his work during his lifetime. *Flowers of Evil* (1857), his greatest poetry collection, was pronounced immoral by the French courts and banned from publication. Though his pride and finances were greatly hurt, Baudelaire continued to write poetry and criticism and to indulge himself in an excessive lifestyle that wore away at his health and dwindling resources. In 1864, almost destitute, he attempted to support himself by lecturing. After two fruitless years he became seriously ill and died unrecognized at the age of forty-six. At his funeral, however, and already calling themselves his followers, were the writers who were to become the leaders of the Symbolist movement.

Giovanni Boccaccio (1313?–1375) and his close friend Petrarch (Unit 3) led very similar and equally impressive lives. Like Petrarch, Boccaccio was one of the first humanists. His father forced him to go to Naples to study law and business, but while there he continued to write stories about chivalry and romance. In 1340 he went to Florence, where he was finally able to devote full time to writing and studying. According to some accounts, he wrote many of his early works to Maria d'Aquino, after seeing her in church and falling in love with her. Ironically, the plague that infected Europe in those years both devastated and inspired him. The disease claimed Maria's life around 1348, the same time at which Boccaccio began writing *The Decameron,* his prose masterpiece in which the characters attempt to escape the black death.

Jorge Luis Borges (1899–1986) was an Argentine poet, short story writer, and essayist who learned to speak and read English before he learned Spanish. One of the first books he read was Mark Twain's *Huckleberry Finn.* In 1914 his family took him to Geneva, Switzerland, where he learned French and German and earned his bachelor's degree from the College of Geneva. Next the family lived in Majorca and Spain before returning to Buenos Aires in 1921. Borges now wrote poems about the history and beauty of his native city and began trying his hand at fiction as well. In 1938 he suffered a severe head wound, resulting in blood poisoning that almost cost him his life. After this experience he began to create his best poetry and the fantastic stories for which he is known. In 1955 Borges became director of the national library and a professor of English and American literature at the University of Buenos Aires. By this time, because of a hereditary affliction, he had become totally blind. In 1961 Borges and Samuel Beckett shared the prestigious Formentor Prize. Since then his poems and tales have been recognized as classics of twentieth-century world literature.

Yosa Buson (1716–1784) was a well-known Japanese painter as well as a great haiku poet. Born into a wealthy family in Kema, Japan, Buson left home at an early age to study with the masters of haiku. He traveled around Japan, staying with one teacher and then another, learning the many skills of this demanding poetic form. At age thirty-five, Buson settled in Kyoto to make his living as a painter and to continue working on his poetic technique. By the time he was in his sixties, he had gained a reputation as a highly respected poet. He wrote in the tradition of the great Bashō, but most critics agree he did not have Bashō's profound understanding of and compassion for all living beings. Buson's greatest contribution to the haiku tradition is probably his richly visual language that reflects the painter's love of detail and ornamentation.

Italo Calvino (1923–1985), Italian journalist, short story writer, and novelist, considered himself a fabulist, or writer of fables. "The mold of the most ancient fables," he said, "remains the irreplaceable scheme of all human stories." After the realism of his early work, Calvino experimented more and more with myth, allegory, and fable. In his trilogy *The Baron in the Trees, The Nonexistent Knight,* and *The Cloven Viscount* (1959–1962), he used allegorical fantasy to satirize contemporary social issues. The first of these novels is about a nineteenth-century nobleman who rejects the world in order to live a full and comfortable life aloft in the branches. Calvino's *Italian Folktales* (1959) was praised as a remarkable and extensive collection. Through his work Calvino wished to re-create a world where "people can still dream and yet understand." Also a translator and essayist, he was awarded the Premio Feltrinelli, Italy's equivalent of the Pulitzer Prize, in 1975.

Albert Camus (1913–1960), Algerian-born French writer, is considered one of the most important literary figures of the twentieth century. In his writing, which included novels, plays, essays, and stories, Camus expounded his view that through purposeful action, the individual can create meaning in an otherwise meaningless, absurd universe. Camus studied philosophy at the University of Algiers, but his academic career was aborted by attacks of tuberculosis. In 1942 he moved to Paris where, with Jean-Paul Sartre, he became an intellectual leader. Camus's essay *The Myth of Sisyphus* and his novel *The Stranger* (both 1942), are significant expressions of his philosophy. Other major works include *The Plague* (1947), *The Rebel* (1951), and *The Fall* (1956). Camus received the Nobel Prize in literature in 1957.

Rosario Castellanos (1925–1974) was a Mexican novelist, essayist, short story writer, dramatist, and poet who was concerned with promoting the status of women in society. She wrote her works at the same time that she was pursuing careers in teaching and politics. Castellanos earned a master's degree in philosophy in 1950 and received a grant to study at the University of Madrid. She also served as Mexico's ambassador to Israel, married and raised a son, and taught in Mexico and at the Universities of Colorado and Wisconsin. She received several writing awards, including the Sor Juana Inés de la Cruz award for her novel *Oficio de Tinieblas (Office of Shadows)*.

Rosalía de Castro (1837–1885) was a Spanish poet and novelist. More accurately, she has been called the outstanding modern writer in the Galician language, a dialect closely related to Portuguese. Castro was born in Galicia, a province in northwestern Spain. She wrote a number of novels but is best known for her poetry, in which she expressed her love for the Galician people and culture. Although she had little formal education, Castro could read French, draw, and play the piano and guitar. At the age of nineteen, she married the historian Manuel Murguía, with whom she had six children. When she was about thirty, Castro began to write more personally, expressing themes of anguish, lost love, and spiritual isolation. She died of cancer, leaving behind works in both Galician and Castilian Spanish, including her masterpiece, *Beside the River Sar.*

Colette (Sidonie-Gabrielle Colette) (1873–1954) was a French novelist whose work is characterized by an intense emphasis on immediate sensory experiences. Colette's first husband, Henri Gauthier-Villars, was a hack writer who discovered Colette's talent and encouraged her to publish her Claudine novels under his pen name, Willy, in the years 1900–1903. After their divorce in 1906, Colette pursued an independent career for several years both as a writer and a music hall performer. She wrote about this period of her life in *The Vagabond* (1910) and *Recaptured* (1913). She produced her finest work in the 1920's, including *Chéri* (1920) and *The Last of Chéri* (1926). By then a legendary figure, Colette spent her final years confined to her Paris apartment, crippled by arthritis and surrounded by her beloved cats. When she died in 1954, she had produced an impressive variety of literature and had received a number of distinguished literary honors.

Julio Cortázar (1914–1984), an Argentine novelist and short story writer, was born in Belgium and lived the last half of his life in France. He was known for his imagination and literary experimentation. As was common in his generation of Latin-American writers, Cortázar drew much inspiration from French and English literature, which he read voraciously. Cortázar began writing when he was a child, but for many years he felt his efforts were unworthy of publication. Finally in 1951, his *Bestiario* was published. The eight short stories in this work are marked by Cortázar's wit and his way of making ordinary events silently slip into the bizarre and the threatening. Perhaps Cortázar's best-known work is the short story "Las Babas del Diablo," on which Michaelangelo Antonioni's film *Blow-Up* was based. It is generally agreed that Cortázar's masterpiece is *Rayuela* (1963; translated as *Hopscotch*, 1966), a boldly experimental novel.

Sor Juana Inés de la Cruz (1648?–1695) was a well known charismatic scholar, essayist, and poet in Mexico. She showed her intellectual ability by learning to read at age three, writing poetry at age eight, and mastering Latin at age nine. Knowing she would never be able to study formally because she was female, Cruz joined a convent in 1669 to facilitate her academic pursuits. In reply to a written attack on her, Cruz composed her famous "Reply to Sor Philothea," defending the right of women to pursue academic interests. Sor Philothea, she later discovered, was actually the pen name of the bishop, who surprisingly praised her essay's brilliance of argument. In 1693, Cruz gave up her possessions and devoted herself to God. She died of the plague.

Léon Damas (1912–1978) left his native French Guiana in South America in order to study in Paris in the early 1930's. There he met other young black French-speaking poets from the French colonies, and together they formed the literary movement known as Négritude, promoting African identity, culture, and values. Damas's first book of poetry, *Pigments* (1937), announced that movement to the world. The work has been called "a cry of pain, an anguished inventory of the personal loss of Africa." Through their writings, the poets of Négritude attempted to strengthen African consciousness and to promote traditional African values. For many years Damas represented French Guiana in the French National Assembly. He spent his last years teaching college literature in Washington, D.C.

Dante Alighieri (1265–1321) wrote his greatest work during nineteen years of political exile. His masterpiece is *The Divine Comedy,* one of the most skillfully crafted and influential verse compositions in literary history. In the years leading up to his exile, his life was fairly happy. He was primarily self-educated and was a prominent citizen of Florence. He married Gemma Donati around 1285 and had at least three children, but he always secretly loved a woman named Beatrice, whom he had first seen when he was nine years old. In many of his writings, including *The Divine Comedy,* he idealized Beatrice as his spiritual guide and inspiration. Dante's political activity and influence in Florence brought about his exile in 1302. When the opposing faction came to power, he was banished from the city on a bogus charge of graft. After that he was a wanderer, sheltered in various Italian cities. He died still in exile.

Anita Desai (born 1937) examines in her writing the social problems of modern India, revealing the psychic pain and daily sorrows of an India that very few foreigners know. According to writer and critic Anne Tyler, Desai's readers are drawn into her dense, intricate world "so deeply . . . that we almost fear we won't be able to climb out again." Considered one of the most gifted of contemporary Indian writers, she is the author of several novels, including *Cry, The Peacock, Fire on the Mountain,* and *Clear Light of Day.* "Games at Twilight" (page 497) is the title story of her first volume of short stories.

Nafissatou Diallo (1941–1982) played a number of roles as mother, midwife, and child welfare nurse, but she always wanted to write about her father's life and her own. She composed her autobiography, *A Dakar Childhood,* in spare moments. In this work she comes across not as a heroine but as a character whose life experiences illustrate and explain the amazing changes that have taken place in Senegal in just one generation. The sorrows and joys portrayed in her work emphasize her belief that it is the simple people, not the famous, who support and carry the weight of the world.

Isak Dinesen (pen name of Karen Christenz Dinesen, Baroness Blixen-Finecke) (1885–1962) was born in Denmark in 1885. In 1914 she married her cousin, Baron Bror Blixen-Finecke, and they moved to Kenya to manage a coffee plantation. After her divorce in 1921, Dinesen managed the plantation herself. When falling coffee prices forced her return to Denmark in 1931, she began her second career as a writer. *Out of Africa* (1938) is an engrossing account of her years in Kenya, which she considered the best period of her life. Dinesen said she saw herself as "a storyteller, not a writer," and indeed her stories, included in the collections *Seven Gothic Tales* (1934) and *Winter's Tales* (1942), reveal her considerable gift for narrative.

Odysseus Elytis (born 1911) is a Greek poet and winner of the 1979 Nobel Prize in literature. Profoundly influenced by the surrealism of the French poet Paul Eluard, Elytis began to publish his own verse in the 1930's. It was characterized by imaginative explorations of the unconscious. In 1959, after a silence of more than a decade during which he struggled to find his creative voice, Elytis published an intricately composed masterpiece, *The Axion Esti.* In awarding him the Nobel Prize, the Swedish Academy said that his poetry "depicts with sensuous strength and intellectual clearsightedness modern man's struggle for freedom and creativity."

Rosario Ferré (born 1942) comes from a traditional upper-class family in Ponce, Puerto Rico. The author of poetry, novels, and stories for children and adults, Ferré began writing in 1970 when her short story "The Youngest Doll" was published. Her first book, a collection of short stories and verse called *Pandora's Papers* (1976), was an immediate success. One critic called it "a constant tearing apart of memory, imagination, and word—impossible to read with indifference." A painstaking writer, Ferré has said that she usually revises a story at least eighteen times before she considers it finished. Subjects common in Ferré's works include feminist concerns, ancient myths, and the life and people of her beloved Puerto Rico.

Gabriel García Márquez (born 1928), a writer of novels and short stories, is one of the central figures in the so-called magical realism movement in Latin American literature. Born into poverty in Colombia, García Márquez began his career as a journalist. While acknowledging the influence on his work of Faulkner, Hemingway, and other American and English authors, he says that it was journalism that taught him that "the key is to tell it straight." García Márquez's work is characterized by magical realism, a combination of realism and fantasy. His best-known work is *One Hundred Years of Solitude* (1967), an epic work that one critic said "should be required reading for the entire human race." In 1982 García Márquez was awarded the Nobel Prize in literature.

Nadine Gordimer (born 1923), a novelist and short story writer, was born into a middle-class white family in the Transvaal, South Africa. Gordimer is known for her beautifully crafted work on themes of exile, alienation, and life's missed opportunities. Originally she concentrated on the short story, but as her subject matter grew increasingly complex she turned to the novel. Much of her writing is set in South Africa, and her characters are inevitably shaped by the political situation there. Gordimer uses her talents and influence to oppose the apartheid system that she hates, but she refuses to let her writing become propaganda. Gordimer lives in Johannesburg, South Africa, and has lectured and taught in the United States. Her novel *The Conservationist* (1974) won the Booker McConnell Prize. Her later works include *Burger's Daughter* (1979), *July's People* (1981), and *A Sport of Nature* (1987).

Le Ly Hayslip (born 1949) was the youngest of six children in a traditional Buddhist farming family in Vietnam. She was twelve when the Vietnam war turned her life into a nightmare of imprisonments, torture, and threats of execution. Her autobiographical work *When Heaven and Earth Changed Places* (1989) recounts how she survived the experience, both emotionally and physically. Hayslip now lives in Los Angeles and works for the East Meets West Foundation, a relief and world peace organization that she founded.

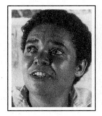

Bessie Head (1937–1986) was an African novelist and short story writer whose life and work reflected her deep concern for the people and politics of her continent. Head, who herself suffered from alienation and rejection at an early age, was especially sympathetic to the plight of women, children, and the rural poor. A native of South Africa, she eventually sought asylum in Botswana, where she lived until her death. Her first novel, *When Rain Clouds Gather,* was published in 1968. It was followed by two other novels, two works of historical nonfiction, and various short stories. For Head, the primary role of literature was to reflect the daily lives of common people.

Heinrich Heine (1797–1856) half-heartedly pursued careers in business and law before finding his niche in poetry. His fame was established in 1827 with a collection of poems entitled *Book of Songs;* many of them have been set to music. Heine moved to Paris in 1831 and took a ten-year leave from poetry to write critical essays about the governments of France and Germany. He also wrote social commentaries and essays on the history of literature before re-entering the world of poetry with *New Poems* in 1844. Heine's health deteriorated rapidly due to spinal tuberculosis. He became paralyzed and confined to his bed—as he termed it, his "mattress grave." His poems during his last eight years are rather somber, but many of them are now regarded as among his finest.

Eugène Ionesco (born 1912) is a Romanian-born French dramatist and literary critic and one of the founders of the Theater of the Absurd. His plays were among the first to contain "antilogical" elements and did much to bring about a revolution in dramatic techniques. After attending the University of Bucharest, Ionesco worked for a Doctorate in Paris and published his first drama, *The Bald Soprano,* in 1949. Other well-known works include *Exit the King, Thirst and Hunger,* and *Killing Game.* In his works he addresses basic human concerns such as the struggle for identity, the search for meaning in life, and the fear of death. He was admitted into the French Academy, a prestigious group of French scholars and writers, in 1970.

Kobayashi Issa (1763–1828) was a Japanese poet who dealt with adversity all his life. Forced to leave his home at fourteen because of his stepmother, Issa moved to the city of Edo. There he studied with the poet Chikua Nirokuan, eventually becoming a master of haiku. Some of his poems celebrate the joys one can find in a life filled with sorrow. Works like *Travel Gleanings* (1795) and *Diary of My Father's Days* (1803) endeared Issa to the Japanese people. Marrying in 1814, he lost four infants, then his wife. He died before his third wife delivered a healthy daughter.

Carolina Maria de Jesus (1913–1977) was different from others who lived in the *favelas,* or slums, of São Paulo, Brazil, because she could read and write. To keep herself from feeling the full weight of her situation—caring for her three small children and living where "the smells came in through the rotting walls"—de Jesus began to write fantasy stories. She also kept a diary which, in its clear, simple prose, became her lifeline out of the slum. It was discovered by a journalist who happened to be visiting the *favela.* The diary was published, becoming a literary sensation and selling more copies than any other Brazilian book in history. De Jesus became a celebrity. However, she felt her goals were still not reached because the suffering of her neighbors had not been alleviated.

Ruth Prawer Jhabvala (born 1927) comes from a Polish family, was born in Germany, and was raised and educated in England. In 1951 she married C.S.H. Jhabvala, an Indian architect, and moved with him to India. There she began to write novels, short stories, and screenplays, and raised three children. Jhabvala's unique position as an outsider intimate with India has provided much material for her stories. From her first novel, *Amrita,* she has been well received. Her work combines biting satire with compassionate sensitivity, and she is frequently compared to Jane Austen. One critic wrote of them both that "by focusing the brilliance of their absolute attention on one small piece of human frailty, glory, or folly, they convince us . . . that in fact they understand everything."

Jomo Kenyatta (1890?–1978) was born in Kenya when it was a colony under British rule. "Once upon a time an elephant made a friendship with a man," begins Jomo Kenyatta's tale of his tribe's relations with its colonial rulers. The man let the elephant put his trunk into the hut, but then "slowly he pushed his head inside, and finally flung the man out in the rain." Kenyatta's life was devoted to restoring his country to its people. His horizons broadened as he acquired a European education in Kenya, followed by seventeen years working and studying in England. He returned to Kenya but was imprisoned for his supposed role in the violent uprising known as Mau Mau. After nine years of detention he emerged as a strong and popular leader to head the newly independent Kenya as its first president.

Takarai Kikaku (1661–1707) was the pen name of Takemoto Yasoka. At the age of sixteen he became a pupil of the famous Japanese haiku master Bashō. In the years between 1600 and the mid-nineteenth century, known as the *kinsei* period, haiku masters supported themselves by asking a fee for each poem submitted by students for correction. When Bashō died in 1694, Kikaku and nine other students of Bashō became haiku masters themselves, making their living the same way and often asserting that they alone possessed certain writing secrets that Bashō had left behind. Kikaku, because of the originality of his work, was recognized as probably the best of Bashō's disciples.

Jamaica Kincaid (born 1949) was born and raised in St. John's, Antigua, in the West Indies. She emigrated to the United States at age seventeen and became a staff writer for the *New Yorker* in 1976. Antigua, however, stayed with her. Two books, *At the Bottom of the River* and *Annie John,* celebrate in poetic, tactile language the realities of life on the island and reveal Kincaid's bittersweet relationship with her homeland. In the nonfiction work *A Small Place,* feelings of anger rise to the surface as Kincaid protests the racism, government corruption, and poverty in Antigua. Reviewer Peggy Ellsberg called it "rage laced with lyricism." Kincaid's novel *Lucy* appeared in 1990 to considerable acclaim. She received the Morton Dauwen Zabel Award in 1983.

Selma Lagerlöf (1858–1940) loved her grandmother's stories when she was a child. Of her grandmother's death, she later wrote, "It was as if the door to a wonderful magic world . . . had been locked." Lagerlöf then used her skills to unlock that door, writing many stories for children, including *The Wonderful Adventure of Nils.* In her works Lagerlöf incorporated the myths and folklore of her native Sweden. In doing this she shunned the movement of realism in the late nineteenth century and helped to start a romantic revival. Her work was so successful that in 1909 she became the first woman to receive the Nobel Prize in literature, and in 1914 she was the first woman to become a member of the Swedish Academy.

Élisabeth Vigée Lebrun (1755–1842) was a French portrait painter who enjoyed a very long and successful career. In 1779 she was summoned to Versailles to paint the Queen of France, Marie Antoinette. In the process she became the friend of the Queen, and her portraits of her are among her most famous. Married to an art dealer, Vigée-Lebrun managed to support her mother, her daughter, and her husband by means of her painting, despite her husband's frequent gambling losses. At the outbreak of the French Revolution she escaped to Italy and thereafter traveled widely, doing portraits of prominent people and mingling with them socially. As a painter she was a careful observer of human features and personalities, and she recorded her observations in her memoirs, published in 1835.

Stanislaw Łem (born 1921) has been called one of the world's greatest science fiction writers. Born in Lvov, Poland, Łem was trained in medicine but soon turned to writing as a career. Łem writes in his native Polish, and his nearly fifty books have been translated into more than thirty languages. Extraordinarily inventive and witty, Łem's stories examine such themes as the purpose of life and the relationship between humans and their technology. His sharp humor frequently targets bureaucrats, pompous academics, and other examples of human arrogance and folly. Among his best-known works are *The Cyberiad, The Star Diaries,* and *A Perfect Vacuum.*

Li Po (701–762) was one of China's greatest poets. When he was nineteen, he left his family in order to wander in the Yangtze River Valley. Around the age of thirty he married and began to write poetry. Later, after another period of wandering he arrived at the capital. When he did not receive an official position there, he joined a group of royal poets who wrote verse to celebrate events of the court. His poetry was now beginning to be recognized, but he was uncomfortable with court intrigues, and resumed his wanderings. Soon he had acquired considerable fame and became an unofficial poet laureate for Prince Lin, a son of the emperor. When the prince was executed for treason, Li Po was imprisoned for a time until his reputation made possible his release. Li Po had a romantic view of life, and his verse celebrated the joys of wine and friendship, nature and solitude.

Naguib Mahfouz (also spelled Najib Mahfuz) (born 1911) has written nearly forty novels and short story collections, more than thirty screenplays, and several stage plays. Practically a household name in the Middle East, Mahfouz was little known in the West until 1988 when he became the first Arabic writer to win the Nobel Prize in literature. His writing often deals with social injustice and the political history of Egypt and is sometimes compared with the works of such social realists as Dickens and Balzac. His major work, *Al-Thulathiyya,* is a 1,500-page trilogy that spans three generations of Cairo families. Other works include *Children of Gebelawi,* which was banned in Egypt because of its controversial treatment of religion, and *God's World,* a collection of short stories from which "The Happy Man" is taken.

Marie de France (c. 1200) is the earliest known French female poet. Her life is mysterious; among the few facts known about her are her name and her authorship of the *Lais,* a collection of romances in verse narrative form. Through these stories about the problems of relationships, Marie de France reintroduced love as a subject in literature. The extensive literary references in her works suggest that she was well educated, possibly a member of the nobility. However obscure the facts of her life, her revival of the love theme left an indelible mark upon literature.

José Martí (1853–1895) has been called the apostle and martyr of the Cuban revolution. As early as his teen years, Martí was urging independence from Spanish rule. Deported to Spain in 1871, he studied Spanish literature and wrote poetry. Eventually he settled in New York where he became the driving force of the Cuban revolutionary movement. He supported himself as a journalist, writing articles about the United States for Latin American newspapers and critical essays for the New York *Sun. On Art and Literature* and *Inside the Monster* are compilations of these. Martí was killed by Spanish soldiers as he and other revolutionaries attempted to invade Cuba. Martí's poems, not surprisingly, express themes of love and freedom. Critic Luis A. Barait states that his work gives a spiritual and moral message to all men.

Mark Mathabane (born 1960) experienced overwhelming poverty, incessant hunger, inadequate education, and terrifying violence in his homeland of Alexandra, South Africa. Mathabane's determination to escape his situation is the subject of his autobiography, *Kaffir Boy: The True Story of a Black Youth's Coming of Age in Apartheid South Africa* (1986). He received an education because his mother, a washerwoman, stood in lines for a year to get the necessary papers. Helped by white tennis professionals, he got to the United States by winning a tennis scholarship. He now lives in the United States, where he works as a freelance writer and lectures on South Africa.

Guy de Maupassant (1850–1893) was born in France, the son of a stockbroker. From an early age, Maupassant was interested in writing. However, he spent many years as a soldier and then as a government employee before he met with literary success. Maupassant is known as one of the creators and early masters of the short story form. "A Piece of String," "The Necklace," and "The Umbrella" are among his most famous works.

Aharon Megged (born 1920) is an Israeli novelist, playwright, journalist, and short story writer. Born in Poland, Megged lived in a small village there before moving to Israel, where he joined a kibbutz when he was eighteen. Though his books often deal with subjects close to his own life, such as the kibbutz and the values of Israeli society, Megged states that his work has also been influenced by European writers such as Kafka, Svevo, Gogol, and Chekhov. Megged's writings include *Mikreh ha-kssil* (1960; published in English as *Fortunes of a Fool,* 1963) and *ha-Hai 'al ha-met* (1965; published in English as *Living On the Dead,* 1970).

Czeslaw Milosz (born 1911) was awarded the Nobel Prize in literature in 1980. His poetry and political writings reflect a diverse life experience. His first poems, written in law school in the 1930's, criticized totalitarian politics. During World War II, his writings aided the Polish underground resistance to the Nazis. After the war, Milosz became a diplomat representing the Communist Polish government, but in 1951 he broke with the government and reluctantly emigrated to France. In 1953 he published a prose work, *The Captive Mind,* which examined the effects of Communism on creativity. Since 1960, Milosz has been a professor of Slavic languages at the University of California, Berkeley. His poetry now probes aspects of American culture.

Yukio Mishima (pen name of Hiraoka Kimitake) (1925–1970) had a career that began and ended spectacularly. At the age of 19, his first publication brought him instant acclaim. At the age of forty-five, he committed *seppuku,* a ritual form of suicide. His fascination with the Japanese past led him to adapt traditional *No* plays to the modern stage; his dramatic abilities showed up in film writing, acting, and directing. His novels, focusing on intricate character development, were popular and critical successes. Mishima became an author of world stature, often called the literary genius of his postwar generation. Of his decision to take his own life, he wrote shortly before his death: "I came to wish to sacrifice myself for the old, beautiful tradition of Japan, which is disappearing very quickly day by day."

Gabriela Mistral (pen name of Lucila Godoy Alcayaga) (1889–1957), a Chilean poet and educator, was awarded the Nobel Prize in literature in 1945. She was the first woman poet and the first Latin American to receive this honor. Upon hearing that she had been chosen, she commented, "Perhaps it was because I was the candidate of women and children." Mistral's poetry, inspired by her personal tragedies, is rich in themes of sorrow and frustrated motherhood. Mistral was denied motherhood when the suicide of her fiancé left her devastated and discouraged from ever marrying. This incident led to three of her poetry collections: *Desolation, Tenderness,* and *Destruction.* Later, Mistral's life was again plagued by suicide when two close friends killed themselves in 1942 and her nephew, whom she had helped to raise, drank arsenic a year later. Mistral taught widely in Chile and in the United States.

Molière (stage name of Jean-Baptiste Poquelin) (1622–1673) is considered the greatest French playwright of all time. Molière rejected a career in his father's business and founded a theatrical group that had some success in the competitive world of Paris theater for three years before failing. From 1646 to 1658, the company eked out a living touring the provinces; during this time Molière began to write comic farce. From 1659 until his death in 1673, he wrote at least one major play a year. His most famous works include *The School for Wives* (1662), *Tartuffe* (1664), and *The Misanthrope* (1666).

Baron de Montesquieu (born Charles Louis de Secondat) (1689–1755) was a French political philosopher. Montesquieu inherited his title and large estate from his uncle. Although he enjoyed high society life, he was also a great scholar and shrewd critic of his times. He satirized French institutions and values in *The Persian Letters,* a series of 160 fictional letters between two Persian travelers. His most important work, a political treatise titled *The Spirit of Laws,* inspired the Declaration of the Rights of Man (the French equivalent of the American colonies' Declaration of Independence) and the Constitution of the United States.

Pablo Neruda (pen name of Ricardo Neftalí Reyes) (1904–1973) was a Chilean poet and senator. He neglected his university studies to write, and the two poetry collections that resulted were published in the early 1920's. These early poems were primarily lyrical and festive. Between 1927 and 1938, Neruda traveled to Europe and Asia as a diplomat representing the Chilean government. In 1934 he lived in Madrid, where he befriended the Spanish poet Federico García Lorca. Neruda's poetry became more surrealistic during his time abroad. After the Spanish Civil War and the subsequent murder of García Lorca, Neruda joined the Communist Party and shifted the focus of his poetry to political and social criticism. Neruda was awarded the Lenin Prize for Peace in 1953 and the Nobel Prize in literature in 1971.

Abioseh Nicol (pen name of Dr. Davidson Nicol) (born 1924) has had a distinguished career as a writer, physician, medical researcher, and diplomat. He is from Sierra Leone in West Africa, and he has said that he started writing because most of those who wrote about blacks "seldom gave any nobility to their African characters." Married and the father of five children, Nicol writes of middle-class Africans and their complicated cultural heritage. His poems and short stories appear in such volumes as *The Truly Married Woman* (1965) and *West African Verse* (1967). Nicol was the first African elected a fellow at Cambridge University in England. As a medical researcher, he played an important role in discovering the structure of human insulin. He also served as his country's ambassador to the United Nations.

Omar Khayyám (1050?–1123?) was a poet in Persia, the land that is now Iran and Iraq. He was also a scientist and mathematician and the author of important works on astronomy and geometry. His astronomical calculations made possible the reform of the calendar that was then in use. An unusually brilliant man, Omar also mastered the subjects of philosophy, history, medicine, and jurisprudence. Omar is best known in the West for the collection of quatrains attributed to him and popularly known through Edward FitzGerald's inventive paraphrasing in *The Rubáiyát of Omar Khayyám.* Omar's original verses were somewhat disconnected, but FitzGerald combined them into the continuous and well-known poem that celebrates the joys of sensual pleasures.

Ovid (born Publius Ovidius Naso) (43 B.C.–A.D. 17) has been described as the greatest Roman poet of his generation. Against the wishes of his father, who urged him toward a career in law, Ovid devoted himself to writing witty and elegant poems about love. Works such as *Amores* and *The Art of Love* established his success. His masterpiece, though, was *The Metamorphoses,* a verse narrative in fifteen books. This collection of 200 stories involving transformations is regarded as a model of craft and a treasured store of ancient legends and myths. In A.D. 8 the emperor Augustus, for reasons unknown, banished Ovid to an isolated village on the coast of the Black Sea. Ovid died there in exile.

Octavio Paz (born 1914) is a Mexican poet, essayist, and diplomat who was the recipient of the Nobel Prize in literature in 1990. Paz attended the University of Mexico and published his first book, *Forest Moon,* at age nineteen. He joined the diplomatic service in 1943 and served in many countries including France, Switzerland, and Japan. After World War II, he became a major literary figure with the publication of *The Labyrinth of Solitude,* an exploration of Mexican culture and thought. He published the poetry collection *Liberty Under Oath* in 1960 and served as the Mexican ambassador to India from 1962 to 1968. Paz has taught at a number of universities, among them Cambridge and Harvard.

Petrarch (Italian name Francesco Petrarca) (1304–1374) was forced to study law by his father. Upon his father's death, Petrarch abandoned law to study Greek and Latin literature and write poetry. In 1327, he reportedly saw a woman named Laura in church on Good Friday and instantly fell in love with her, even though she was married. Most of the 366 poems in Petrarch's *Canzoniere* (*Book of Songs*) are written about Laura, and she also appears in his *Trionfi* (*Triumphs*). Petrarch perfected the love sonnet in these works. A devoted humanist, he was also responsible for the rediscoveries of Cicero and Livy as great classical writers. He was considered the literary and cultural leader of his time, and in 1341 he was crowned poet laureate of Rome, the first since ancient days.

Plato (c. 427– c. 347 B.C.) was born to a wealthy family in Athens. His father died when he was young, and his mother remarried a politically and culturally active Athenian. Plato planned to become a politician but was discouraged by his relatives' unethical practices in that field and by the execution of his friend, the philospher Socrates, on the wrongful charge of corrupting Athenian youth. Plato presented the views and teaching methods of Socrates in a number of dialogues which have greatly influenced modern Western thought. Returning to Athens after many years of travel, Plato founded the Academy, considered by some scholars to be the first university.

Alexander Pushkin (1799–1837) succeeded in becoming Russia's national poet despite a personal life that often hindered his career. After excelling in languages at the Czar's school and entering civil service, Pushkin was exiled to southern Russia for writing insurrectionist poetry. Gambling and loose living alienated him from his family and caused his expulsion from civil service in 1824. Forced to live at his father's estate for two years, Pushkin associated with peasants and absorbed Russian folklore, experiences which influenced his writing. During this time he wrote *Boris Godunov* and began *Eugene Onegin,* a novel in verse. Maturity helped him produce his best work from 1826 to 1831. Pushkin was fatally wounded when he challenged an admirer of his wife to a duel.

Aisin-Gioro P'u Yi (also known as Henry P'u Yi) (1906–1967) was the last emperor of China, crowned at the age of three. Forced to leave the Imperial Palace by the Chinese Nationalist army, he took refuge in the Japanese colony at Tientsin. During World War II the Japanese, at war with China, made him head of their puppet state in Manchuria. After being captured by Russians at the end of the war, P'u Yi was returned to China for trial as a war criminal. Under the Communist government he was re-educated and trained as a laborer. During this time he wrote the autobiography *From Emperor to Citizen,* assisted by a government editor. He was pardoned in 1959 and worked as a mechanic in a botanical garden until his death.

Rachel de Queiroz (born 1910), a Brazilian writer best known for her realistic novels, is also an award-winning dramatist and highly regarded translator. At the age of nineteen, de Queiroz made a sensational literary debut with the publication of her first novel, *The Year '15.* Both this work and *The Three Marias* (1939) challenge the traditionally submissive role played by women in Brazilian society. In the 1940's de Queiroz began writing newspaper columns on subjects of general interest; these gained her a wide following. Many of her essays appear in collections. Plays by de Queiroz include *Lampião* (1953), which recounts the antics of a famous rural outlaw. In recognition of her life's work, the Brazilian Academy of Letters awarded her the Machado de Assis Prize.

Jean-Joseph Rabéarivelo (1901–1937) was the first major French-language poet in Africa. He was born on the island of Madagascar during the time when it was colonized by France. His startling, surrealistic poems are influenced both by Malagasy tradition and the French Symbolist movement of the late nineteenth century. *Presque-songes* (*Nearly Dreams,* 1934) and *Traduit de la Nuit* (*Translation of the Night,* 1935) are said to be the most important collections of his work. Affected by drug addiction and hurt by being denied permission to visit France, Rabéarivelo took his own life.

Dahlia Ravikovitch (also spelled Dalia Rabikovitz) (born 1936) is a leading Israeli poet. She was born in Ramat Gan, Palestine (now Israel). She is a former high school teacher and a writer of short stories as well as poetry. English translations of her work are *A Dress of Fire* (1976) and *The Window: New and Selected Poems* (1989).

Christa Reinig (born 1926) grew up poor, without a father, in Berlin. During World War II she worked as an apprentice florist and a factory worker. Later she studied art history and archaeology at Humboldt University in East Germany. In 1964 she went to West Germany to receive a literary prize and decided to remain there. Reinig's early works are poems portraying the horror of war. Her later prose works include *The Three Ships* (1965) and *Orion: New Signs of the Zodiac* (1968), a collection of short sketches reflecting on modern life. *Heavenly and Earthly Geometry* (1975) is an autobiographical novel that displays Reinig's irreverent sense of humor and reveals her philosophical conflicts with the East German state.

Oscar Ribas (1909–1961) was an ethnologist, folklorist, and novelist from Angola. He moved frequently during his childhood because of his father's position as Angola's Director of Plantations. When Ribas was sixteen, he wrote his first novel, *Passing Clouds,* and two years later wrote his second, *Expiation of an Error.* His promising writing career was interrupted when he became blind at twenty-one. He returned to writing nineteen years later, publishing two short story collections and a three-volume study of traditional Angolan oral literature. Ribas received a literary prize from the Institute of Angola for his book *Ilundo: Angolan Divinations and Rites.*

Ru Zhijuan (born 1925) is a Chinese short story writer, dramatist, and novelist. Because of her family's financial hardships, she was unable to attend school until the age of eleven. Following her education, she taught briefly at a primary school. Later she joined the army and became an actress in the Modern Drama Troupe of the Battle Front. She won two awards for literary and artistic creativity from her military district. After leaving the army, she worked as an editor and published the novel *Story Before Dawn* and collections of short stories about the lives of women. She is a member of the editorial committee for Shanghai Literature.

Juan Rulfo (1918–1986) was a Mexican writer who contributed greatly to Latin American literature despite having written only two major works in his lifetime. After studying law and impounding ships during World War II, Rulfo held positions as an editor and a scriptwriter but always pursued his main interest—the writing of fiction. He helped create the magical realism movement by fusing in his work the bitter realities of Mexican life with the primitive and magical beliefs of the common people. His short story collection *The Burning Plain* and his novel *Pedro Paramo* transcend mere social themes, analyzing the philosophical aspects of life and death. In 1970 Rulfo received Mexico's National Prize of Letters.

Nelly Sachs (1891–1970) was a German-born Jewish poet and playwright. Her long life was divided sharply in two by the rise of the Nazis and their systematic genocide of the Jewish people in the Holocaust. Born in Berlin, Nelly was the only child in a family that loved art and literature. She began writing at seventeen. Her early work explored the common roots of Judaism and Christianity; it often resembled fairy tales. In the 1930's Sachs saw friends and relatives carried off to Nazi concentration camps. In 1940, she and her mother fled from Germany to Sweden, aided by the writer Selma Lagerlöf. There Sachs resumed writing, her new subject being the destruction and resurrection of the Jewish people. She shared the 1966 Nobel Prize in literature with the Hebrew writer Shmuel Yosef Agnon.

Sappho (610–580 B.C.) is considered one of the greatest lyric poets of all time, although only fragments of her poems survive. She was born on Lesbos, an island in the Aegean Sea. During her childhood she lived in Sicily because of her father's political exile. Sappho was an aristocrat and probably wrote much of her poetry for recitation at social gatherings. She was the leader of a group of women who studied music and poetry and perhaps worshipped Aphrodite. Many of her poems are addressed to these women or to her daughter Cleis. Sappho's very passionate and carefully crafted poetry inspired Plato to call her the Tenth Muse.

Léopold Sédar Senghor (born 1906) is a Senegalese poet and statesman. He graduated from the University of Paris in 1931 and later earned master's and doctorate degrees. With fellow students Aimé Césaire and Léon Damas he founded the Négritude literary movement, which affirmed blackness and African culture. Upon returning to Senegal, Senghor entered politics and fought for an end to French rule of his country. In 1960 he became the first president of an independent Senegal, serving until 1981. Senghor was awarded honorary doctorates from universities in four countries. In 1984 he became the first African elected to the French Academy, a group of French scholars and writers.

William Shakespeare (1564–1616) is often considered the greatest writer who ever lived. He contributed brilliant drama and poetry to the body of English literature. As a child in Stratford, he studied Latin and literature six days a week. In 1582 he married Anne Hathaway, and they subsequently had three children. Few other details of Shakespeare's private life are known. By 1592 he was living and acting in London, his early plays already successful productions. His flesh-and-blood characters, vivid imagery, and clever puns kept audiences enthralled. Though his Globe Theater was sometimes closed by plague or fire, Shakespeare never stopped writing. The tragedies *Julius Caesar, Hamlet, Othello,* and *Macbeth,* written toward the end of his career, are probably his greatest works.

Sŏ Kiwŏn (born 1930) was a Korean student in the early 1950's before he left the university to fight in the Korean War. He wrote about a war that "failed to provide an inspiration for self-dedication" and a postwar society "fraught with contradictions and absurdity." His personal experience lends authenticity to his work, which has been praised for its psychological depth. According to one reviewer, Sŏ Kiwŏn writes of "life devoid of dreams and hopes and the landscape of the mind's wilderness."

Sophocles (496–406 B.C.) was a Greek author of more than one hundred plays, only seven of which remain today. When he was young, Sophocles was an excellent wrestler, dancer, and player of the lyre. In 468 B.C. he defeated his teacher Aeschylus to take first prize in an annual playwrighting competition. That first place award was followed by twenty-four others. Sophocles was an innovator in drama: he was the first dramatist to have more than three actors on stage simultaneously, to utilize a large chorus, and to use painted scenery. He wrote plays throughout his life, completing *Oedipus at Colonus* when he was almost ninety years old.

Tacitus (A.D. C. 56–C. 120) was a Roman orator, politician, historian, and writer of prose. He worked in various areas of army administration before working his way up to consul in A.D. 97. The following year he published two of his works: *Agricola,* an account of his father-in-law's army career, and *Germania,* a history of the Germanic groups that lived on the Rhine. Later Tacitus published the *Annals,* a critical history of Roman politics from the reigns of Augustus to Nero. Tacitus was a strong proponent of republican government and criticized the imperial Roman system in his writing.

Rabindranath Tagore (1861–1941) stands beside Gandhi as an embodiment of Indian culture in the early twentieth century. He was an artist and musician as well as the creator of poems, novels, short stories, plays, songs, and essays. He founded schools and took an active role in numerous cultural institutions. Tagore was a pioneer of Bengali literature in all its forms. He also wrote in English, reaching out toward Western culture. The 1913 Nobel Prize in literature was one of the many honors awarded him. Raised in a prosperous family who valued culture, he was educated in India and England. He married, had five children, and wrote prodigiously until his death at the age of eighty.

T'ao Ch'ien (365–427) was considered one of the greatest poets of the "fields and gardens," a major subject of third-century Chinese poetry. He was born to a poor family and supported his aged parents by working for the government in his twenties and thirties. Eventually becoming disgusted by government corruption and the formalities required of him, T'ao Ch'ien resigned his post and moved with his wife and children to a farm south of the Yangtze River. Here he wrote poetry and lived a quiet life. Despite frequent periods of food shortage and other problems, he remained on the farm, cultivating chrysanthemums, praising the virtues of wine, and writing poetry. He preferred to live in this way, he said, rather than "cringe for five pecks of rice" working for the government.

Leo Tolstoy (1828–1910), Russian novelist, short story writer, dramatist, and critic, is best known for his two masterpieces *War and Peace* and *Anna Karenina*. Orphaned at age nine, Tolstoy was raised by a socialite aunt in Kazan, East Russia. He married Sophia Behrs in 1862, and although he had a happy home life at first, Tolstoy felt torn between his responsibilities as a wealthy landowner and his desire to live a moral life through asceticism. The latter proved more attractive; many of his works contain themes of love, humility, self-denial, and nonviolence. Though these ascetic tendencies were important in his writing, they also led to the alienation of his wife and thirteen children. In 1910 he left the family estate following a family argument and died a few days later.

Luisa Valenzuela (born 1938) is one of the best-known writers of short stories and novels in Latin America. She was born in Argentina, and became a journalist in her teens, working for the magazine *Quince Abriles* and the Buenos Aires newspaper *La Mación*. In 1967 she published a book of thirteen short stories and a novel under the title *Los Heréticos*. Other fiction includes *The Lizard's Tail* (1983) and *Crime of the Other* (1989). Valenzuela's writing often contains humor and irony. An important theme in her work is the search for freedom, both political and personal. She once said that she writes to shake people up.

Virgil (70–19 B.C.) is known today as the greatest Roman poet and the author of the epic, *The Aeneid*. He turned to writing poems after discovering his lack of talent as a lawyer and orator. This shy, peace-loving man, the son of farmers, lived and studied throughout Italy before settling in Rome. His fame as a poet began when Maecenas, an influential patron of the arts, read Virgil's *Eclogues* and the *Georgics*, instructional poems on farming. Maecenas asked him to write patriotic poems, and the result was *The Aeneid*. Virgil himself was dissatisfied with the twelve books of his epic that he had completed, and before leaving for travel in Greece he asked that it be destroyed in the event of his death. In Greece he caught a fever and died, but Augustus, emperor at the time, ignored Virgil's wishes and published the unfinished work, which is Virgil's masterpiece.

William Wordsworth (1770–1850) is universally recognized as one of the great English poets. With his powerful imagination, fed by the beauty of nature, and his talent for writing poetic lines that speak basic truths, he became a leader of the romantic movement in England. He was born in the beautiful Lake District of northern England and spent much of his youth walking the countryside there. During these solitary rambles he stored up images and emotions that found their way into his writing. Wordsworth took a degree at Cambridge and spent some time in Europe, getting caught up in the spirit of the French Revolution. In 1795 he settled in Dorsetshire with his sister Dorothy, not far from where the poet Samuel Taylor Coleridge was living. The remarkable friendship of the three of them had much to do with the birth of a new school of poetry. Romanticism was introduced to England with the publication of *Lyrical Ballads* (1798), written by Wordsworth and Coleridge together. Wordsworth and his sister moved to the Lake District in 1799, and in 1802 he married an old school friend, Mary Hutchinson. In those years he produced much of his best work. Wordsworth was proclaimed poet laureate in 1843.

Index of Essential Vocabulary

J

jaded, 607, 610

K

keening, 484, 489

L

laconic, 631, 638
lamentation, 204, 231, 468, 472
langour, 667, 674
languishing, 302, 303
lapidary, 270, 274
legitimacy, 324, 326
libation, 42, 53
loquacious, 596, 601
lucid, 692, 693
lucidity, 392, 395
lugubrious, 497, 502
luminous, 270, 274
lute, 182

M

magnanimity, 315, 319
malevolence, 505, 506
malice, 364, 367
mettle, 616, 617
mien, 354, 355
modicum, 596, 603
morality, 83, 88
mores, 421, 428
mortify, 540, 567
motley, 375
mutations, 716, 725
myriads, 310, 311

O

oblivion, 692, 697
omen, 163, 169
opprobrium, 687
ostentatious, 709, 712

P

pacific, 667, 673
paradoxes, 716, 717
parody, 382, 385
parrying, 129, 135
pedant, 716, 718
perverse, 204, 227
piety, 266, 268
pious, 540, 542
placated, 607, 608
placatingly, 449, 451
plundered, 163, 165
poaching, 270, 274
predatory, 667, 675
predestined, 60, 69
prefiguring, 297, 299
premonition, 102, 105
prerogative, 378
pretext, 102, 106
primordial, 129, 136
prodigious, 346, 348, 379
promontory, 701, 706
propitiate, 346, 349
propitiatory, 442, 445
prostrate, 120
protocol, 442, 446
protracted, 505, 507
psalm, 278
punctilious, 484, 494

R

ramparts, 129, 131
rancor, 143, 146, 200, 201
rebuke, 679, 680
recompense, 42, 45
reconciliation, 442, 446
recondite, 404
recourse, 442, 446
renounce, 534
renounced, 91, 99

repentance, 310, 311
reproach, 249, 251
reprobation, 442, 444
repulse, 204, 205
resound, 324, 326
retinue, 375
rhetoric, 679, 680
ruefully, 641, 643

S

sack, 163, 167
sallies, 616, 617
savored, 532
sententiously, 204, 214
solace, 692, 693
sporadic, 259
stentorian, 505, 508
stratagem, 163, 168
stupor, 42, 51
succor, 26, 29
suffused, 270, 274
suppliant, 26, 29, 143, 156
supplication, 315, 316
surfeit, 143, 153
surreptitiously, 484, 489

T

taciturn, 91, 99

tardive, 411
temerity, 497, 500
tirade, 641, 645
transcending, 534

U

unbiased, 315, 320
unconscionable, 540, 579
untrammeled, 382, 389
utopian, 687

V

vacillate, 255
vengeance, 194, 195
verdure, 667, 669
verisimilitude, 616, 618
vertigo, 689
vied, 259
vindictive, 392, 394
virtue, 83, 85
votive, 278
vouchsafed, 354, 357
vulgar, 266, 267

W

wont, 449, 456

Index of Literary Terms

Index of Writing Modes and Formats

Index of Authors and Titles

Art Credits

Cover

Cross Stratification (detail), 1984, Sally Bachman. Twining Weavers, Arroyo Seco, New Mexico.

Author Photographs

AP/Wide World Photos, Inc., New York: Ivo Andrić 738, Mark Mathabane 746, Yukio Mishima 747, Gabriela Mistral 747, Juan Rulfo 751, Rabindranath Tagore 753; Jerry Bauer, Rome, Italy: Ruth Prawer Jhabvala 744; The Bettmann Archive, New York: Odysseus Elytis 742, Gabriel García Márquez 743, Guy de Maupassant 747, Aisin-Gioro P'u Yi 750, Nelly Sachs 751; Jane Boun/Camera Press, London: Anita Desai 742; Rene Burri/Magnum Photos, Inc., New York: Julio Cortazar 741; Camera Press/Globe Photos, New York: Naguib Mahfouz 746, Léopold Senghor 752; Henri Cartier-Bresson/Magnum Photos, Inc., New York: Eugène Ionesco 744; Culver Pictures, New York: Omar Khayyám 748, Sophocles 752; Bertil Dahlgren/Camera Press/Globe Photos, New York: Pablo Neruda 748; German Information Center, New York: Christa Reinig 750; Burt Glinn/Magnum Photos, Inc., New York: Dahlia Ravikovitch 750; T. Goldblatt/Camera Press/Globe Photos, New York: Bessie Head 743; The Granger Collection, New York: Honoré de Balzac 738, Charles Baudelaire 738, Giovanni Boccaccio 739, Albert Camus 740, Colette 740, Sor Juana Inés de la Cruz 741,

Dante Alighieri 741, Isak Dinesen 742, Selma Lagerlöf 745, Élisabeth Vigée Lebrun 745, Molière 748, Baron de Montesquieu 748, Octavio Paz 749, Petrarch 749, Plato 749, Virgil 753, William Wordsworth 766; Harris and Ewing/Globe Photos, New York: José Martí 746; Heibonsha Limited, Publishers: Yosa Buson 739, Issa 744; Historical Pictures Service, Chicago: Ovid 749, Sappho 751, Tacitus 752, Leo Tolstoy 753; Kakimori-Bunko: Takarai Kikaku 745; Nan Kené-Arthur/U.S. Photo Graphics, El Cajon, California: LeLy Hayslip 743; Jan Kopec/Camera Press/Globe Photos, Inc., New York: Czeslaw Milosz 747; Korean Cultural Service, New York: Sŏ Kiwŏn 752; Tadeusz Matkovski/Camera Press/Globe Photos, New York: Stanislaw Łem 745; Susan Meiselas/Magnum Photos, Inc., New York: Jorge Louis Borges 739; Collection of the National Palace Museum, Taiwan, Republic of China: T'ao Ch'ien 753; New Orleans Museum of Art: Bashō 738; North Wind Archives, Alfred, Maine: William Shakespeare 752; Novosti/Camera Press/Globe Photos, New York: Alexander Pushkin 749; P.I.P./Globe Photos, New York: Jomo Kenyatta 744; Friedrich Rauch/Camera Press/Globe Photos, New York: Henrich Heine 743; Salgado/Magnum Photos, Inc., New York: Italo Calvino 739; Schomburg Center for Research in Black Culture, The New York Public Library, Astor, Lenox & Tilden Foundations, New York: Léon Damas 741, Jamaica Kincaid 745, Jean-Joseph Rabeárivelo 750; Francis Stoppelman, Mexico City, Mexico: Rosario Castellanos 740, Rosalía de Castro 740, Rachel de Queiroz 750; Horst Tappe/Camera Press/Globe Photos, London: Nadine Gordimer 743; Tokyo National Museum, Li Po 746, pen and ink portrait by Liang K'ai, 13th Century; George Torok: Carolina Maria de Jesus 744; United Nations, New York: Abioseh Nicol 748.